"Cornelis Bennema, well known for his treatment of imitation (mimesis) in the Fourth Gospel, offers in this volume a comprehensive study of its relative presence, form, and function across the writings of the New Testament and the apostolic fathers, informed by its origins in Greco-Roman antiquity. This is an impressive analysis, a rich resource, and a major contribution which both furthers historical research and offers wisdom for contemporary application."

—**William Loader**
Murdoch University

"'Imitation' is a crucial yet under-researched concept in early Christian thinking. In this excellent study—that magnificently covers the texts of the New Testament and beyond—Bennema restores it to its central place as an instrument for moral transformation, enabling the believer to become more like Christ in character and conduct. Essential reading for anyone with an interest in early Christian ethics and philosophy."

—**Helen K. Bond**
University of Edinburgh

"In this rich study Cornelis Bennema makes a major contribution to the study of Christian mimesis, exploring its theological and ethical aspects both historically and theologically. Situating Christian ideas in their Jewish, Greek, and Roman contexts, he examines how mimesis operates as a sensory, cognitive, and volitional process and reveals how Christians develop it in new ways. All students of early Christian theology, ethics, and education will want to engage with his illuminating and thought-provoking argument."

—**Teresa Morgan**
Yale Divinity School

"How should Christians imitate Christ? Through poverty? Love of neighbor? Martyrdom? This matter of mimesis—the imitation of Christ—is tough to navigate, which is what makes this book so significant! With the deft hand of a veteran scholar, Cornelis Bennema tackles this topic by chaperoning us judiciously through ancient texts, from Plato to Paul to Polycarp. If you wonder how to imitate Christ in our twenty-first-century world, you'd do well to devote yourself to this exemplary book."

—**Jack Levison**
Southern Methodist University

"From Greco-Roman philosophy to contemporary work in science and philosophy, imitation plays a central role in the formation of communal and personal identity. In this groundbreaking book, Bennema offers the first wide-ranging study of imitation in the New Testament and early Christian texts in the context of the Roman Empire, and draws out its implications for religious-ethical formation today. *Imitation in Early Christianity* will become the authoritative guide for anyone seeking to understand the intersection of Christian faith with ethics and transformation."

—**Susan Eastman**
Duke Divinity School

"Cornelis Bennema carefully traces the use of ethical mimesis, the practice of achieving a meaningful, moral life by imitating appropriate models. A fundamental element of many Greco-Roman thinkers, mimetic theory influenced post-biblical Jewish literature and played a significant role in some early Christian texts, particularly the Fourth Gospel and Pauline Epistles, where the model is no ordinary human being. Bennema explores this topic with careful attention to the complexity of mimetic theory and practice and to the nuances of individual texts. In cordial but critical dialogue with an impressive array of scholars, he offers a valuable resource for understanding a vital part of early Christian thinking coupled with helpful reflections on practical implications for contemporary Christians."

—**Harold Attridge**
Yale Divinity School

"Surprisingly, the concept of imitation in early Christianity has been underexamined in recent scholarship even though it has been a staple of Christian piety across the ecclesial traditions. In this fine study, Bennema more than makes up for this lack. Via a rigorous and extensive examination of the ancient literature, Bennema shows that imitation is a dynamic and creative concept central to the ethical vision of the first generations of Christians. *Imitation in Early Christianity* is a perceptive and engaging study of a neglected concept that contemporary disciples need to revisit."

—**Michael P. Jensen**
Sydney College of Divinity

Imitation in Early Christianity

Mimesis and Religious-Ethical Formation

Cornelis Bennema

William B. Eerdmans Publishing Company
Grand Rapids, Michigan

Wm. B. Eerdmans Publishing Co.
2006 44th Street SE, Grand Rapids, MI 49508
www.eerdmans.com

© 2025 Cornelis Bennema
All rights reserved
Published 2025

Book design by Lydia Hall

Printed in the United States of America

31 30 29 28 27 26 25   1 2 3 4 5 6 7

ISBN 978-0-8028-7992-9

Library of Congress Cataloging-in-Publication Data

A catalog record for this book is available from the Library of Congress.

Contents

Foreword by Michael J. Gorman		xi
Preface		xiii
List of Abbreviations		xv
1.	**Mimesis in Early Christianity**	1
	1.1. A Peek into Early Christian Literature	5
	1.2. A Peek into Scholarship	7
	1.3. A Statement of the Problem	11
	1.4. The Validity of Our Study	14
	1.5. The Language and Concept of Early Christian Mimesis	16
	1.6. An Explanation of Our Study	23

Part 1: Mimesis in Antiquity

2.	**Mimesis in Greco-Roman Antiquity**	29
	2.1. Mimesis in Greek Antiquity	32
	2.1.1. Theatrical Mimesis and Civic Education	34
	2.1.2. Plato and Aristotle	36
	2.1.3. The Isocratean Tradition	41
	2.2. Mimesis in Roman Antiquity	46
	2.2.1. Cicero	47

CONTENTS

	2.2.2. Seneca (the Younger)	51
	2.2.3. Quintilian	56
	2.2.4. Plutarch	59
	2.3. A Model of Greco-Roman Mimesis	64
	Excursus: Further Support for Our Model from Greco-Roman Literature	69
	2.4. Conclusion	72
3.	**Mimesis in Jewish Antiquity**	75
	3.1. Mimesis in the Hebrew Bible	76
	3.1.1. The Case for Mimesis in the Hebrew Bible	76
	3.1.2. Possible Mimetic Texts in the Hebrew Bible	78
	3.1.3. A More Nuanced Concept of Mimesis in the Hebrew Bible	82
	3.1.4. Conclusion	84
	3.2. Mimesis in Second Temple Judaism	85
	3.2.1. Hellenistic Judaism—the LXX and Pseudepigrapha	86
	3.2.2. Josephus	87
	3.2.3. Philo	89
	3.2.4. The Rabbinic Traditions	93
	3.3. Conclusion	97

PART 2: MIMESIS IN EARLY CHRISTIANITY

4.	**Mimesis in the Synoptics and Acts**	103
	4.1. Following Jesus as Mimesis?	105
	4.2. Mimesis in the Gospel of Mark	109
	4.2.1. Conceptual Traces of Mimesis in Following Jesus	111
	4.2.2. The Markan Mimetic Language	114
	4.2.3. Further Concepts of Mimesis—Gethsemane	116
	4.2.4. Mimetic Characters	118
	4.2.5. Conclusion	122

	4.3. Mimesis in the Gospel of Matthew	123
	4.3.1. Conceptual Traces of Mimesis in Following Jesus	125
	4.3.2. Mimesis in the Sermon on the Mount	126
	4.3.3. Mimetic Language in the Rest of Matthew	134
	4.3.4. Further Concepts of Mimesis	136
	4.3.5. Conclusion	137
	4.4. Mimesis in Luke–Acts	138
	4.4.1. Conceptual Traces of Mimesis in Following Jesus	139
	4.4.2. The Lukan Mimetic Language	141
	4.4.3. Further Concepts of Mimesis—the Lord's Supper and Gethsemane	144
	4.4.4. Mimetic Characters	146
	4.4.5. Conclusion	150
	4.5. Conclusion	151
5.	**Mimesis in John's Gospel and Letters**	156
	5.1. Mimesis in Johannine Scholarship	157
	5.2. The Johannine Mimetic Language	161
	5.3. Divine Mimesis	174
	5.3.1. The Son–Father Mimesis	175
	5.3.2. The Spirit–Jesus Mimesis	182
	5.3.3. Conclusion	183
	5.4. The Believer–Jesus/God Mimesis	185
	5.4.1. Discipleship and Mimesis	185
	5.4.2. The Footwashing	187
	5.4.3. Actualizing the Love Command through Mimesis	193
	5.4.4. Existential Mimesis	200
	5.4.5. Conclusion	205
	5.5. The Place of Mimesis in Johannine Ethics	207
	5.6. A Model of Johannine Mimesis	213

	5.7. The Practice of Mimesis in Johannine Christianity	218
	5.7.1. The Mimesis of an "Absent" Jesus	219
	5.7.2. The Content of Mimesis	220
	5.7.3. Applied Hermeneutics	222
	5.7.4. Conclusion	223
	5.8. Conclusion	225
6.	**Mimesis in the Pauline Letters**	228
	6.1. Mimesis in Pauline Scholarship	229
	6.1.1. A Survey of Pauline Studies	229
	6.1.2. A Statement of the Problem	238
	6.2. 1–2 Thessalonians	240
	6.2.1. Being Imitators and Being Imitated (1 Thess 1:5–8)	241
	6.2.2. Imitating the Unseen Judean Churches (1 Thess 2:13–16)	246
	6.2.3. A Neglected Aspect of Imitation (2 Thess 3:6–13)	250
	6.2.4. The Place of Mimesis in Paul's Ethics for the Thessalonians	252
	6.2.5. Conclusion	254
	6.3. 1–2 Corinthians	255
	6.3.1. The Imitation of Paul Mediated through Timothy (1 Cor 4:16)	255
	6.3.2. The Imitation of Christ Mediated through Paul (1 Cor 11:1)	259
	6.3.3. Traces of Imitation in 1 Corinthians	262
	6.3.4. Imitating Other Churches (1 Cor 16; 2 Cor 8)	264
	6.3.5. Conclusion	266
	6.4. Philippians	267
	6.4.1. Christ as the Supreme Example for Imitation	268
	6.4.2. Paul as an Imitator of Christ	274
	6.4.3. Timothy and Epaphroditus as Imitators of Christ	280
	6.4.4. Other Believers as Examples for Imitation	282
	6.4.5. Conclusion	284

	6.5. Ephesians	286
	6.6. The Pastoral Epistles	288
	6.7. Other Pauline Letters	292
	6.7.1. Galatians	292
	6.7.2. Romans	294
	6.7.3. Colossians	297
	6.7.4. Philemon	298
	6.8. A Model of Pauline Mimesis	299
	6.9. Conclusion	303
	6.9.1. The Scope of Pauline Mimesis	303
	6.9.2. The Nature and Content of Pauline Mimesis	306
	6.9.3. Modes of Pauline Mimesis	310
	6.9.4. The Place of Mimesis in Pauline Ethics	313
	6.9.5. Conclusion	313
7.	**Mimesis in the Rest of the New Testament**	315
	7.1. Hebrews	316
	7.2. 1 Peter	319
	7.3. Conclusion	321
8.	**Mimesis in the Apostolic Fathers**	323
	8.1. Clement of Rome	324
	8.2. Ignatius of Antioch	327
	8.3. Polycarp of Smyrna	332
	8.4. The Letter of Barnabas	335
	8.5. The Letter to Diognetus	336
	8.6. The Didache	337
	8.7. The Shepherd of Hermas	338
	8.8. Conclusion	338

CONTENTS

Part 3: Synthesis

9. **Summary—the Research Findings**   345

    9.1. Summary of Our Findings   345

    9.2. Answering Our Primary Research Questions   350

        Question 1: Where do the historical origins of the early Christian concept of mimesis lie?   350

        Question 2: What language did early Christian authors use to articulate the concept of mimesis?   353

        Question 3: Is the early Christian concept of mimesis consistent, varying, or developing—and what is its place in early Christian ethics?   355

        Question 4: How could early Christians imitate an absent Jesus or Paul—and what should they imitate about them?   361

10. **Conclusion—the Hermeneutics of Mimesis**   364

    10.1. Early Christian Mimesis as a Complex Hermeneutical Process   364

    10.2. Early Christian Mimesis and Applied Hermeneutics   369

    10.3. The Book's Takeaways   372

Appendix: The Mimetic Language of Early Christianity   377

Bibliography   381

Index of Authors   413

Index of Subjects   420

Index of Scripture and Other Ancient Sources   425

Foreword

This book is the work of someone who is likely the world's leading expert on its topic: imitation, or mimesis, in the ancient world and in the New Testament. Cor Bennema has previously published a monograph, *Mimesis in the Johannine Literature*, as well as several articles, on the topic.[1] He has also presented papers on the subject at various academic conferences. This volume continues and advances that scholarly interest.

But this is not just another book from an expert on the subject. It is a thorough and comprehensive study on mimesis in Greco-Roman, Hebrew Bible, Second Temple Jewish, and early Christian texts. For its primary focus, early Christianity, Cor moves beyond his earlier work on the Johannine and Pauline writings to include the rest of the New Testament and the Apostolic Fathers. The range of primary and secondary sources engaged, including works from several very different fields of study, is impressive even for a seasoned scholar.

The word "mimesis" can mean different things to different people, and the term is therefore used quite loosely at times, even by scholars. Bennema insists that we can acknowledge a concept of mimesis only if there is mimetic language to support the claim. This methodological move will be controversial in some circles, as will the book's sliding scale that assigns a weak, medium, or strong presence of mimesis to various texts. But the advantage of this approach is to make our understanding of imitation more precise, more nuanced.

---

1. *Mimesis in the Johannine Literature: A Study in Johannine Ethics*, LNTS 498 (New York: Bloomsbury T&T Clark, 2017); "Mimesis in John 13: Cloning or Creative Articulation?," *NovT* 56 (2014): 261–74; "Mimetic Ethics in the Gospel of John," in *Metapher–Narratio–Mimesis–Doxologie: Begründungsformen frühchristlicher und antiker Ethik*, ed. Ulrich Volp, Friedrich W. Horn, and Ruben Zimmermann, WUNT 356 (Tübingen: Mohr Siebeck, 2016), 205–17; "Moral Transformation through Mimesis in the Johannine Tradition," *TynBul* 69 (2018): 183–203; and "A Shared (Graeco-Roman) Model of Mimesis in John and Paul?," *JSNT* 43 (2020): 173–93.

FOREWORD

Cor Bennema's book should be received not as a project devoted to a narrow ethical topic, but as part of his larger concerns, both academic and pastoral, about Christian ethics. In addition to imitation, Cor has explored New Testament ethics more broadly, focusing at times on the work of the Spirit and at other times on characterization and character formation (especially virtue ethics), both in texts and in real life. These are ultimately not three discrete subjects but a unified triad: character, Spirit, imitation.

As a scholar whose own work has focused on participation, especially in the Pauline and Johannine literature, I welcome this contribution. Focusing on mimesis helps to put feet on the experience of participating in Christ or abiding in Jesus. The book also makes it clear that mimesis is a volitional and hermeneutical undertaking: an individual or community must discern which people to imitate, and which character traits and actions to emulate in concrete times and places.

Cor Bennema has made his mark primarily in British, European, and South Asian contexts. His influence in those places will certainly continue, but it is a gift to scholars, students, and pastors that his contributions will now be better known also in North America, building on earlier work published in the United States. More importantly, this comprehensive treatment of mimesis will, I hope, help elevate the place of imitation in biblical studies, Christian ethics, and Christian life no matter where those endeavors are pursued.

MICHAEL J. GORMAN
St. Mary's Seminary & University

Preface

My research on the ethical concept of mimesis (or imitation) in early Christianity began in 2012 and took place in two phases. In phase 1, I examined the Johannine writings, resulting in the first monograph on the subject, *Mimesis in the Johannine Literature: A Study in Johannine Ethics*, LNTS 498 (London: T&T Clark 2017). In phase 2, I broadened the scope of my research in two ways. First, I explored both Jewish and Greco-Roman antiquity to locate the origins of the early Christian concept of mimesis. Second, I examined the early Christian writings, both the New Testament and the Apostolic Fathers, in order to understand the nature and workings of mimesis and the place it occupies in early Christian ethics. The result is this first organized study on mimesis as a religious-ethical concept in early Christianity.

Certain materials in this book have appeared elsewhere. Some Greco-Roman material in chapter 2 appeared in the article "A Shared (Graeco-Roman) Model of Mimesis in John and Paul?," *JSNT* 43 (2020): 173–93. This article also developed my model of early Christian mimesis, which is largely based on the Johannine and Pauline writings (see sections 5.6, 6.8, and 10.1). Chapter 5 is largely based on my 2017 monograph on Johannine mimesis and subsequent articles in *TynBul* (2018) and *ExpTim* (2020) that extended my 2017 work. Section 6.2 on mimesis in the Thessalonian correspondence relies on my article "Paul's Paraenetic Strategy of Example and Imitation in 1–2 Thessalonians," *ETL* 98 (2022): 219–38.

I must thank various people who have been instrumental in this project. I thank Bloomsbury T&T Clark for allowing me to reuse the material from the 2017 monograph mentioned above. I thank the people at Eerdmans, especially Trevor Thompson (senior acquisitions editor), James Ernest (executive vice president and editor-in-chief), and Jennifer Hoffman (senior project editor) for their support in publishing this study. I am grateful to Grace Andrews for preparing the index of Scripture and other ancient sources. I thank Professors Michael Gorman and

PREFACE

Jan van der Watt for reviewing the manuscript and their constructive comments. I am especially grateful to Mike Gorman for introducing me to Trevor Thompson at Eerdmans, and to Mark Cartledge, principal of London School of Theology, for encouraging me in my research. Both have also stood by me during difficult times a few years ago. Once again, I profoundly thank my wife, Susan, for her competent and vigorous copy editing (I discovered that even quotations are not safe from her corrections). Above all, I give thanks to the Father and Son, whom I seek to follow and imitate.

COR BENNEMA
*London School of Theology, UK,
and Faculty of Theology and Religion,
University of the Free State, South Africa*

Abbreviations

AB	Anchor Bible
ABRL	Anchor Bible Reference Library
AELKZ	*Allgemeine evangelisch-lutherische Kirchenzeitung*
AnBib	Analecta Biblica
ASNU	Acta Seminarii Neotestamentici Upsaliensis
ATANT	Abhandlungen zur Theologie des Alten und Neuen Testaments
AYB	Anchor Yale Bible
BBR	*Bulletin for Biblical Research*
BBRSup	Bulletin for Biblical Research Supplement Series
BDAG	Bauer, Walter, Frederick W. Danker, William F. Arndt, and F. Wilbur Gingrich, eds. *A Greek-English Lexicon of the New Testament and Other Early Christian Literature*. 3rd ed. Chicago: University of Chicago Press, 2000
BECNT	Baker Exegetical Commentary on the New Testament
BETL	Bibliotheca Ephemeridum Theologicarum Lovaniensium
BHT	Beiträge zur historischen Theologie
Bib	*Biblica*
BibInt	*Biblical Interpretation*
BINS	Biblical Interpretation Series
BLE	*Bulletin de littérature ecclésiastique*
BNTC	Black's New Testament Commentaries
BThSt	Biblisch-Theologische Studien
BWANT	Beiträge zur Wissenschaft vom Alten und Neuen Testament
BZNW	Beihefte zur Zeitschrift für die neutestamentliche Wissenschaft
CBQ	*Catholic Biblical Quarterly*
CJAS	Christianity and Judaism in Antiquity
ClAnt	*Classical Antiquity*

ABBREVIATIONS

CNNTE	Contexts and Norms of New Testament Ethics
ConBNT	Coniectanea Biblica: New Testament Series
CP	*Classical Philology*
CurBR	*Currents in Biblical Research*
DSD	*Dead Sea Discoveries*
ETL	*Ephemerides Theologicae Lovanienses*
ExpTim	*Expository Times*
HBT	*Horizons in Biblical Theology*
HKNT	Handkommentar zum Neuen Testament
HNT	Handbuch zum Neuen Testament
HTR	*Harvard Theological Review*
Int	*Interpretation*
IVP	InterVarsity Press
JAC	*Jahrbuch für Antike und Christentum*
JCPS	Jewish and Christian Perspectives Series
JECH	*Journal of Early Christian History*
JECS	*Journal of Early Christian Studies*
JETS	*Journal of the Evangelical Theological Society*
JJS	*Journal of Jewish Studies*
JPT	*Journal of Pentecostal Theology*
JRAI	*Journal of the Royal Anthropological Institute*
JRH	*Journal of Religious History*
JSJ	*Journal for the Study of Judaism*
JSNT	*Journal for the Study of the New Testament*
JSNTSup	Journal for the Study of the New Testament Supplement Series
JSOT	*Journal for the Study of the Old Testament*
JSOTSup	Journal for the Study of the Old Testament Supplement Series
JSPL	*Journal for the Study of Paul and His Letters*
JTI	*Journal of Theological Interpretation*
JTS	*Journal of Theological Studies*
LCL	Loeb Classical Library
LNTS	Library of New Testament Studies
MJT	Marburger Jahrbuch Theologie
MThSt	Marburger Theologische Studien
MTZ	*Münchener theologische Zeitschrift*
NCBC	New Cambridge Bible Commentary
Neot	*Neotestamentica*
NIBC	New International Biblical Commentary
NICNT	New International Commentary on the New Testament

NICOT	New International Commentary on the Old Testament
NIGTC	New International Greek Testament Commentary
NovT	*Novum Testamentum*
NovTSup	Supplements to Novum Testamentum
NTC	New Testament Commentary
NTL	New Testament Library
NTS	*New Testament Studies*
OTE	Old Testament Essays
ÖTK	Ökumenischer Taschenbuch-Kommentar
PBMS	Paternoster Biblical Monograph Series
Presb	*Presbyterion*
PTM	Paternoster Theological Monographs
RB	*Revue biblique*
RKK	Religionspädagogische Kontexte und Konzepte
RS	*Religious Studies*
RTP	*Revue de théologie et de philosophie*
SA	Studia Anselmiana
SANT	Studien zum Alten und Neuen Testaments
SBB	Stuttgarter biblische Beiträge
SBEC	Studies in the Bible and Early Christianity
SBFA	Studium Biblicum Franciscanum Analecta
SBL	Society of Biblical Literature
SBLAB	Society of Biblical Literature Academia Biblica
SBLDS	Society of Biblical Literature Dissertation Series
SBLECL	Society of Biblical Literature Early Christianity and Its Literature
SBS	Stuttgarter Bibelstudien
SCE	*Studies in Christian Ethics*
SIJD	Schriften des Institutum Judaicum Delitzschianum
SNTSMS	Society for New Testament Studies Monograph Series
SPCK	Society for Promoting Christian Knowledge
SR	*Studies in Religion*
STAC	Studies and Texts in Antiquity and Christianity
SwJT	*Southwestern Journal of Theology*
TDNT	*Theological Dictionary of the New Testament*. Edited by Gerhard Kittel and Gerhard Friedrich. Translated by Geoffrey W. Bromiley. 10 vols. Grand Rapids: Eerdmans, 1964–1976
TENTS	Text and Editions for New Testament Study
ThHK	Theologischer Handkommentar zum Neuen Testament (Leipzig)
THKNT	Theologischer Handkommentar zum Neuen Testament (Stuttgart)

ABBREVIATIONS

TLG	Thesaurus Linguae Graecae
TNTC	Tyndale New Testament Commentaries
TS	*Theological Studies*
TTZ	*Trierer theologische Zeitschrift*
TynBul	*Tyndale Bulletin*
VC	*Vigiliae Christianae*
VF	*Verkündigung und Forschung*
VTSup	Supplements to Vetus Testamentum
WBC	Word Biblical Commentary
WRGW	Writings from the Greco-Roman World
WUNT	Wissenschaftliche Untersuchungen zum Neuen Testament
ZAC	*Zeitschrift für Missionswissenschaft und Religionswissenschaft*
ZECNT	Zondervan Exegetical Commentary on the New Testament
ZMR	*Zeitschrift für Missionswissenschaft und Religionswissenschaft*
ZNW	*Zeitschrift für die neutestamentliche Wissenschaft und die Kunde der älteren Kirche*

Mimesis in Early Christianity

This book is a study of mimesis as a religious-ethical concept in early Christianity. Mimesis or imitation is central to human life. We are social beings innately wired to imitate. Humans grow and develop by imitating others: babies learn to talk by imitating their parents; children grow up imitating their parents, teachers, and other role models; adults develop their thinking, behavior, and skills by imitating others.[1] In fourth-century classical Athens, Aristotle had already observed that "from childhood, it is innate for humans to imitate (μιμεῖσθαι), and in this humans are different from other living beings that they are most capable of imitation (μιμητικός) and learn their first lessons through imitation (μίμησις)" (*Poetics* 1448b5–9 [own translation]).

As Matthew Potolsky states, "Mimesis is among the oldest terms in literary and artistic theory, and it is certainly among the most fundamental. It so defines our way of thinking about art, literature and representation more generally that we rely on the concept even if we have never heard of it or do not know its history."[2] Additionally, Michael Jensen asserts that "imitation of others . . . is basic to the formation of the human subject. It is really not a matter of choosing whether we will imitate someone, but who it is we will imitate."[3] Hence, mimesis is more pervasive than people realize. While mimesis, strictly speaking, is broader than

---

1. See Christoph Wulf, "Mimetic Learning," *Designs for Learning* 1 (2008): 56–67; Ray Archee, "Æmulatio, Imitatio and Mimesis in Tertiary Education," *Procedia—Social and Behavioral Sciences* 174 (2015): 2418–24. Imitation also has negative connotations, and we tend to reject forms of imitation such as counterfeit goods, forged documents, or plagiarized research. See further Daniel Becker, Annalisa Fischer, and Yola Schmitz, eds., *Faking, Forging, Counterfeiting: Discredited Practices at the Margins of Mimesis* (Bielefeld: Transcript Verlag, 2018).

2. Matthew Potolsky, *Mimesis* (New York: Routledge, 2006), 1.

3. Michael Jensen, "Imitating Paul, Imitating Christ: How Does Imitation Work as a Moral Concept?," *Churchman* 124 (2010): 17–36, at 17.

or arguably different from imitation, I use imitation as synonymous with mimesis but not in the narrow sense of copying, simplistic replication, or counterfeiting.[4] In the words of Scott Garrels, "Far from being the simple and mindless act that we typically associate it with ('monkey see, monkey do'), imitation is now understood as a complex, generative, and multidimensional phenomenon at the heart of what makes us human."[5]

In Christianity, the idea of mimesis or imitation (especially *imitatio Christi*) has been studied by theologians more than biblical scholars and is more fashionable in pietist than in academic circles. The fifteenth-century book *The Imitation of Christ* by Thomas à Kempis is probably the most popular devotional work apart from the Bible.[6] Christian philosopher Søren Kierkegaard even asserted that "only the imitator is the true Christian."[7] During the 1990s and early 2000s, the acronym WWJD (What Would Jesus Do) became popular among evangelical Christians, a statement of their desire to behave like Jesus, that is, to imitate him. A fast-growing trend among evangelical Christians in North America strives for mimesis at two levels—the mimesis of Jews and mimetic discipleship of Jesus-the-Jew among gentile adherents to Messianic Judaism.[8] Other sections of the church, however, such as the Reformed tradition, are critical of the concept of imitating Jesus because they perceive moral endeavor to be at odds with their doctrine of salvation by grace; they consider such striving an affront to the uniqueness of Christ.[9]

---

4. See also Stephen Halliwell, *The Aesthetics of Mimesis: Ancient Texts and Modern Problems* (Princeton: Princeton University Press, 2002), 152; Joachim Duyndam, "Hermeneutics of Imitation: A Philosophical Approach to Sainthood and Exemplariness," in *Saints and Role Models in Judaism and Christianity*, ed. Marcel Poorthuis and Joshua Schwartz, JCPS 7 (Leiden: Brill, 2004), 7–21, at 11; Archee, "Æmulatio," 2419.

5. Scott R. Garrels, "Human Imitation: Historical, Philosophical, and Scientific Perspectives," in *Mimesis and Science: Empirical Research on Imitation and the Mimetic Theory of Culture and Religion*, ed. Scott R. Garrels (East Lansing, MI: Michigan State University Press, 2011), 1–38, at 1.

6. Kempis's book, however, is not overtly about imitation, and his monastic imitation of Christ has been criticized (see the discussion in Soon-Gu Kwon, *Christ as Example: The Imitatio Christi Motive in Biblical and Christian Ethics*, Uppsala Studies in Social Ethics 21 [Uppsala: Uppsala University Press, 1998], 86–98).

7. Søren Kierkegaard, *Practice in Christianity*, Kierkegaard's Writings 20, trans. Howard V. Hong and Edna H. Hong (Princeton: Princeton University Press, 1991), 256. See also Martin Buber, "Nachahmung Gottes," in *Martin Buber Werkausgabe*, vol. 20, *Schriften zum Judentum*, ed. Michael Fishbane and Paul Mendes-Flohr (Gütersloh: Gütersloher Verlagshaus, 2018), 35–44; Dietrich Bonhoeffer, *Nachfolge* (Munich: Kaiser, 1958) (the allusion to imitation in the word *Nachfolge* is lost in the English title *The Cost of Discipleship*).

8. Hillary Kaell, "Under the Law of God: Mimesis and Mimetic Discipleship among Jewish-Affinity Christians," *JRAI* 22 (2016): 496–515.

9. See, for example, the various articles in the journal *Modern Reformation* 18, no. 2 (2009)

1. Mimesis in Early Christianity

Candida Moss claims, "New Testament scholars have exhibited an astonishing and often unjustified reluctance to speak of the imitation of Christ as a theme in the earliest Christian literature."[10] She explains how this *"imitatio* anxiety" among scholars is grounded in (1) the dominance of *imitatio Christi* in Roman Catholicism, (2) the perceived threat of *imitatio Christi* to soteriology and Christology, and (3) the repulsive idea that martyrdom may be central to the Christian experience.[11] This shows that the study of mimesis in Christianity is not straightforward. Jason Hood, in fact, identifies three contemporary approaches to the concept of imitating Christ: (1) a liberal imitation of a social Christ (e.g., the work of Burridge in section 1.2), (2) a shallow, undiscerning, individualistic imitation of a moral Christ (e.g., the WWJD movement), and (3) a reluctance or resistance to imitating Christ (e.g., the Reformed tradition).[12]

There is another challenge to the study of mimesis. Although mimesis is central to nearly all areas of human thought and action, there is no uniform definition or criteria to distinguish it from related concepts. In their seminal account of the history of mimesis, Gunter Gebauer and Christoph Wulf go so far as to conclude that posing the question "What is mimesis?" leads to error because it is not a homogeneous concept in history.[13] Instead, their historical reconstruction of important phases in the development of mimesis shows that "a spectrum of meanings

---

(an issue dedicated to the imitation of Christ); Alister McGrath, "In What Way Can Jesus Be a Moral Example for Christians?," *JETS* 34 (1991): 289–98; Ernst Käsemann, "Kritische Analyse von Phil 2,5–11," in *Exegetische Versuche und Beginnungen I* (Göttingen: Vandenhoeck & Ruprecht, 1960), 51–95. In my view, McGrath misrepresents the concept of mimesis as mere human achievement of imitating an external example. In 1960, E. J. Tinsley had already noted that the concept of imitating Christ has not always been perceived well (*The Imitation of God in Christ: An Essay on the Biblical Basis of Christian Spirituality* [London: SCM, 1960], 23). For more nuanced discussions of Protestant ethics and imitation, see John B. Webster, "The Imitation of Christ," *TynBul* 37 (1986): 95–120 (he argues that imitating Christ connects the indicative and imperative aspects of Christian ethics); Jimmy Agan, "Departing from—and Recovering—Tradition: John Calvin and the Imitation of Christ," *JETS* 56 (2013): 801–14 (he recovers Calvin's teaching on the imitation of Christ).

10. Candida R. Moss, *The Other Christs: Imitating Jesus in Ancient Christian Ideologies of Martyrdom* (Oxford: Oxford University Press, 2010), 21.

11. Moss, *Other Christs*, 21–23.

12. Jason B. Hood, *Imitating God in Christ: Recapturing a Biblical Pattern* (Downers Grove, IL: IVP Academic, 2013), 14–15, 183–89.

13. Gunter Gebauer and Christoph Wulf, *Mimesis: Culture, Art, Society* (Berkeley: University of California Press, 1995), 309. Others also point out the difficulty of encapsulating the meaning of mimesis (Halliwell, *Aesthetics of Mimesis*, 13–16; Potolsky, *Mimesis*, 1). Göran Sörbom remarks that the theory of mimesis was not a well-articulated theory in antiquity but more a "fundamental outlook shared by most authors, philosophers and educated audiences" ("The Classical

of mimesis has unfolded over the course of its historical development, including the act of resembling, of presenting the self, and expression as well as mimicry, *imitatio*, representation, and nonsensuous similarity."[14] However, despite mimesis being a vague, ambivalent, and fluid concept, it "moves with history, coming to expression in forms appropriate to respective historical periods."[15] One redeeming feature is that underlying the various instances of mimesis in each historical period is an Aristotelian understanding of the concept.[16] In fact, Potolsky asserts that "the theory of mimesis remains so tied to its origins in the works of Plato and Aristotle that few thinkers before the twentieth century sought to redefine or rethink it in any substantial way," while also acknowledging that mimesis took on different meanings and forms in different contexts.[17]

This observation has implications for our study. For example, we can study the past (how early Christians understood and practiced mimesis) for the sake of the present (how early Christian mimesis can inform contemporary practice). If the concept of mimesis represents a relatively stable trajectory from Plato and Aristotle to today, and assuming that early Christian mimesis can be situated on this trajectory, we can legitimately extrapolate the early Christian concept of mimesis to today. The academic task is often perceived as merely providing a historical or descriptive analysis of a particular concept or theme in ancient writings. However, the analysis of early Christian writings should also uncover a theological and prescriptive dimension because the early Christian authors were active theologians and practitioners in (service of) the church. This view is corroborated by the fact that early Christian traditions have been preserved and handed down through generations not simply to inform the theological beliefs of the church but also to guide its practices in each era. I write as a "critical insider" in that I am both an academic and a practicing Christian. Accordingly, I will examine the writings of early Christian authors on how they understood mimesis and instructed their audiences to practice it. Standing in the Christian tradition, I will

---

Concept of Mimesis," in *A Companion to Art Theory*, ed. Paul Smith and Carolyn Wilde [Oxford: Blackwell, 2002], 19–28, at 19).

14. Gebauer and Wulf, *Mimesis*, 1. Elsewhere, they note, "There was already great complexity to the concept of mimesis in classical Greece. . . . Plato did not manage to elaborate a unified concept of mimesis but applied and evaluated it variously depending on context" (*Mimesis*, 25). For the concept of mimesis as representation in Greco-Roman antiquity, see Verity Platt, *Facing the Gods: Epiphany and Representation in Graeco-Roman Art, Literature and Religion* (Cambridge: Cambridge University Press, 2011).

15. Gebauer and Wulf, *Mimesis*, 2–5 (quotation from p. 5).
16. Gebauer and Wulf, *Mimesis*, 309.
17. Potolsky, *Mimesis*, 5.

1. Mimesis in Early Christianity

also seek to understand how contemporary Christians can continue the practice of early Christian mimesis.

Let me briefly explain how this chapter will prepare for the rest of the book. Glances at early Christian literature (section 1.1) and scholarship (section 1.2) will provide a foretaste of the detailed study to follow, inform us about the current state of affairs, and help in formulating our key questions (section 1.3). Section 1.4 is an *apologia* for the book to avoid alienating potential readers. Section 1.5 will clarify our understanding of mimesis vis-à-vis related concepts such as analogy and reciprocity, and section 1.6 will explain our study.

1.1. A Peek into Early Christian Literature

Most of our study will be a detailed analysis of the early Christian writings, but a quick glance may arouse interest and reveal the challenges that lie ahead. The lexeme μιμεῖσθαι ("to imitate") occurs eleven times in the New Testament (mainly in Paul) and eighteen times in the Apostolic Fathers.[18] In the Pauline tradition, we notice that Paul often issues the directive to imitate him (1 Cor 4:16; 11:1; Phil 3:17; 2 Thess 3:7, 9; but see also 1 Thess 1:6). Even though Paul clarifies in 1 Cor 11:1 that the call to imitate him is rooted in his imitation of Christ, Paul's call to imitate him is nevertheless audacious. Besides, these texts do not seem to indicate what Paul's audience should imitate about him. Furthermore, Paul obviously wrote letters to churches when he was unable to be with them, so how could Pauline Christians imitate an absent Paul whom they could not observe? This seems to imply that imitation can be conveyed through other means than direct observation.

In the Johannine tradition, the lexeme μιμεῖσθαι occurs only once—in 3 John 11, as a general command to imitate what is good, and it is not immediately clear what this refers to. John, however, seems to prefer other language than the lexeme μιμεῖσθαι to express the concept of imitation. Imitation supposes a resemblance between the person who sets an example and the one who emulates it, so we could consider so-called comparative language—words such as "like(wise)," "(just) as," and "similarly." In the Johannine literature, we find the recurrent expression, "Just as Jesus did, so also the disciples should do." The episode that illustrates this best is the footwashing in John 13, where Jesus exhorts his disciples to imitate him in

---

18. In the New Testament, see 1 Cor 4:16; 11:1; Eph 5:1; Phil 3:17; 1 Thess 1:6; 2:14; 2 Thess 3:7, 9; Heb 6:12; 13:7; 3 John 11. In the Apostolic Fathers, see 1 Clem. 17:1; Diogn. 10:4–6 (4 times); Ign. *Eph.* 1:1; 10:2, 3; Ign. *Magn.* 10:1; Ign. *Trall.* 1:2; Ign. *Rom.* 6:3; Ign. *Phld.* 7:2; Ign. *Smyrn.* 12:1; Pol. *Phil.* 1:1; 8:2; Mart. Pol. 1:2; 17:3; 19:1.

serving one another in loving humility: "For I gave you an example (ὑπόδειγμα), that *just as* (καθώς) I have done to you, you *also* (καί) should do" (13:15).[19] Further on in John 13, Jesus provides another example for his disciples to imitate: "I give you a new commandment, that you love one another. *Just as* (καθώς) I have loved you, you *also* (καί) should love one another" (13:34; see also 15:12). This mimetic καθώς language occurs elsewhere in John's Gospel with reference to obedience (15:10), unity (17:11, 21–22), existence (17:14, 16), and mission (17:18; 20:21), and in his first letter in relation to behavior (1 John 2:6), purity (1 John 3:3), and being righteous (1 John 3:7). The Johannine tradition reveals a pattern where Jesus regularly sets the example that the disciples should imitate, and John often uses the comparative conjunction καθώς to communicate this concept of mimesis.

It is far more difficult to find a concept of mimesis in the Synoptic Gospels. The lexeme μιμεῖσθαι does not occur in the Synoptics, but the prominent concept of following Jesus could imply mimesis. After all, should the disciples, besides taking in Jesus's teachings, not also learn by observing and imitating him? For example, in Mark's Gospel, when the disciples are sent out during their internship with Jesus (6:7–13), they seem to be doing the same things Jesus did (1:34, 38–39). Even so, we can hardly expect that the disciples should imitate everything about Jesus, so this requires investigation. Elsewhere, Matt 5:48 ("Be perfect, just as your heavenly Father is perfect") and Luke 6:36 ("Be merciful, just as your Father is merciful") seem to indicate mimesis, but the imitation of God is unusual and needs unpacking.

Beyond the New Testament, the writings of the apostolic fathers from the first half of the second century are relevant for two reasons: (1) they contain eighteen occurrences of the lexeme μιμεῖσθαι (see n. 18), and (2) they present the idea of martyrdom as the ideal *imitatio Christi*. For example, Martyrdom of Polycarp narrates the death of Polycarp, bishop of Smyrna, around AD 155, stating that "[Polycarp] was not merely an illustrious teacher, but also a pre-eminent martyr, whose martyrdom all desire to imitate, as having been altogether consistent with the Gospel of Christ" (Mart. Pol. 19:1). In fact, the author depicts all martyrs as imitators of Christ: "The martyrs, as disciples and imitators of the Lord, we worthily love on account of their extraordinary affection towards their own King and Master, of whom may we also be made companions and fellow-disciples" (Mart. Pol. 17:3). We should examine how the New Testament prepares for this extreme form of imitation.

The authoritative source document for early Christians was the Hebrew Bible or Old Testament, so we should include this document in our quest for mimesis. Initially, we can think of texts such as Gen 1:26, where humankind is created in the image of God (but does this refer to imitation or representation?), and Deut

---

19. Unless otherwise noted, translations of the Bible are the author's.

10:18–19, which says that God looks after the stranger and that the Israelites should also love the stranger because they were once strangers in Egypt. A more common text for a possible idea of mimesis is Lev 19:2, where God commands the Israelites to be holy because he is holy. However, the connection is causal (כִּי in the MT; ὅτι in the LXX) rather than comparative. Interestingly, tracing the reception of this holiness command in the New Testament, we find that Matt 5:48 and Luke 6:36 use comparative conjunctions (ὡς and καθώς, respectively), whereas 1 Pet 1:15–16 preserves the causal connection ὅτι. More generally, Israel is often urged "to walk in the way of the Lord" and "to follow after God," but does this refer to imitation or just obedience? Hence, it is not clear whether the Old Testament speaks of imitating God. This raises the question of where early Christians got the concept of mimesis.

1.2. A Peek into Scholarship

When we mine the early Christian literature for the concept of mimesis, we do so in conversation with scholarship. A quick sketch of the scholarly landscape will inform us about the current state of affairs and ongoing debates. The 1960s is an appropriate starting point for our inquiry for two reasons. First, this decade saw several wide-ranging studies on the subject of mimesis in early Christianity.[20] The most significant studies are those by Ernest Tinsley, Willis Peter de Boer, and Anselm Schulz.[21]

---

20. There were, of course, studies on mimesis before then (e.g., Albrecht Oepke, "Nachfolge und Nachahmung Christi im Neuen Testament," *AELKZ* 71 [1938]: 853–69; David M. Stanley, "Become Imitators of Me: The Pauline Conception of Apostolic Tradition," *Bib* 40 [1959]: 859–77), but these did not have the same impact as those in the 1960s.

21. Tinsley, *Imitation* (see n. 9 for details); Willis Peter de Boer, *The Imitation of Paul: An Exegetical Study* (Kampen: Kok, 1962); Anselm Schulz, *Nachfolgen und Nachahmen: Studien über das Verhältnis der neutestamentlichen Jüngerschaft zur urchristlichen Vorbildethik*, SANT 6 (Munich: Kösel, 1962). Less significant studies are Raymond Thysman's extensive overview article on the imitation of Christ in the New Testament ("L'Éthique de l'Imitation du Christ dans le Nouveau Testament: Situation, Notations et Variations du Thème," *ETL* 42 [1966]: 138–75) and that of C. Merrill Proudfoot, who argues that the Pauline concept of "suffering with Christ" has more to do with participation in Christ than the imitation of Christ ("Imitation or Realistic Participation? A Study of Paul's Concept of 'Suffering with Christ,'" *Int* 17 [1963]: 140–60). For a more detailed overview of studies in the 1960s, see Otto Merk, "Nachahmung Christi: Zu ethischen Perspektiven in der paulinischen Theologie," in *Wissenschaftsgeschichte und Exegese: Gesammelte Aufsätze zum 65. Geburtstag*, ed. Roland Gebauer, Martin Karrer, and Martin Meiser, BZNW 95 (Berlin: de Gruyter, 1998), 302–36, at 305–10.

Tinsley develops a biblical theology of mimesis that has five characteristics. First, "the way" is the dominant imagery that holds together the concept of mimesis in the Old and New Testaments, where God and Jesus are the way, and Israel and Christians imitate God/Jesus by walking in the way. Second, mimesis is rooted in real historical events (especially the Exodus and Jesus's ministry), thus providing visible, concrete exemplars for imitation. Third, in the New Testament, the imitation of God has taken the form of the imitation of Christ, either directly or through exemplary Christians. Fourth, mimesis occurs mainly in the contexts of liturgy/worship (the festivals and sacraments) and the ethical life of Christians. Fifth, mimesis is not a slavish, literal imitation or copying but a dynamic, creative process of conformity to Christ/God.[22] We will see, however, that Tinsley sometimes uses the idea of mimesis rather loosely (see, e.g., chapter 3, n. 10, and chapter 4, nn. 7–8).

For his study on the imitation of Paul, de Boer lays a broad foundation by examining the usage of the terms μιμεῖσθαι and τύπος ("example") (and their cognates), as well as the concepts of imitation and personal example in Greek, Jewish, and Christian literature. He argues that imitation in Greek antiquity is not so much about copying or exact reproduction but refers to the idea of bringing to expression, representation, and portrayal in the areas of the fine arts, cosmology, education, and ethics.[23] Contra Tinsley, de Boer argues that the Old Testament has no clear teachings on the imitation of God, but when Greek culture came into contact with Jewish culture (the process of Hellenization), the New Testament uses the concept of imitation primarily in the area of ethics where it refers to the moral development of a person's character and conduct.[24] According to de Boer, the goal of imitation is transformation (Christians becoming like Christ), and the common pattern of what needs imitation across the New Testament writings involves self-giving, self-denial, and humility.[25]

Like de Boer, Schulz contends that the concept of imitation is extremely limited in the Old Testament and only becomes more noticeable in Hellenistic and Rabbinic Judaism through the spread of Greek thinking (Hellenization), where the concept originated.[26] In the New Testament, imitation is solely an ethical concept, with God, Jesus, and people as examples of moral Christian behavior.[27] So, Tinsley,

---

22. Tinsley, *Imitation*. Stephen Smalley is influenced by Tinsley's work but does not go beyond him ("The Imitation of Christ in the New Testament," *Themelios* 3 [1965]: 13–22; see also "The Imitation of Christ in 1 Peter," *Churchman* 75 [1961]: 172–78).

23. De Boer, *Imitation of Paul*, 1–8.

24. De Boer, *Imitation of Paul*, 13–16, 29–41, 89–91.

25. De Boer, *Imitation of Paul*, 69–70, 90–91, 207.

26. Schulz, *Nachfolgen und Nachahmen*, 202–4, 213–25.

27. Schulz, *Nachfolgen und Nachahmen*, 201, 205. Schulz explains the imitation of God, Christ, and people in chapters 8–10, respectively.

1. Mimesis in Early Christianity

de Boer, and Schulz all agree that mimesis is more about creative expression than literal replication, but they disagree on the origins of early Christian mimesis. While Tinsley sees a trajectory of imitation from "walking in God's ways" in the Old Testament to "following Jesus" in the New Testament, de Boer and Schulz contend that early Christian mimesis is the result of cross-pollination with Greek thought.

The second reason for starting with the 1960s is that several studies specifically examine the relationship between the concept of "following Jesus" (in the Gospels) and "imitating Christ" (in the Pauline Corpus), but with different results. For example, Edvin Larsson argues that although *die Nachfolge Jesu* ("the following of Jesus") and *die Nachahmung Christi* ("the imitation of Christ") are distinct ideas, imitation becomes part of following and hence should be subsumed under discipleship.[28] Conversely, de Boer argues that the language of "following Jesus" in the Gospels belongs to the concept of imitation.[29] Schulz and Hans Dieter Betz argue that, linguistically and conceptually, the concepts of following Jesus in the Gospels and imitating Christ in Paul are distinct; only at a theological-hermeneutical level do they denote a single concept of discipleship. They also argue that the "following" language of the Gospels stems from a Palestinian-Jewish origin, while the notion of mimesis is Hellenistic in origin. According to them, *die Nachahmung Christi* results from the Hellenistic interpretation of *die Nachfolge Jesu*. That is, early Christians took the theological-hermeneutical step of continuing or converting the Palestinian-Jewish concept of following Jesus into the Hellenistic concept of imitating Christ.[30]

From the 1970s onwards, many specialized studies on the concept of imitation in the New Testament (especially in Paul) started to appear, which we will engage in subsequent chapters, but we have to jump forward to the twenty-first century to find further comprehensive studies on mimesis.[31] David Capes first shows that

---

28. Edvin Larsson, *Christus als Vorbild: Eine Untersuchung zu den paulinischen Tauf- und Eikontexten*, ASNU 23 (Lund-Uppsala: Gleerup, 1962), 17, 29–47.

29. De Boer, *Imitation of Paul*, 51–57.

30. Schulz, *Nachfolgen und Nachahmen*, 202–4, 213–25, 332–35; Hans Dieter Betz, *Nachfolge und Nachahmung Jesu Christi im Neuen Testament*, BHT 37 (Tübingen: Mohr [Siebeck], 1967), 3, 40–43, 186–89. More specifically, Betz contends that mimesis originated in the Hellenistic mystery cults (*Nachfolge und Nachahmung*, 48–101). The debate on following Jesus versus imitating Christ has not ceased. See, for example, Walter J. Ong, "Mimesis and the Following of Christ," *Religion and Literature* 26, no. 2 (1994): 73–77; Hans Jürgen Milchner, *Nachfolge Jesu und Imitatio Christi: die theologische Entfaltung der Nachfolgethematik seit den Anfängen der Christenheit bis in die Zeit der devotio moderna—unter besonderer Berücksichtigung religionspädagogischer Ansätze*, RKK 11 (Münster: LIT, 2004), 7–20; Victor A. Copan, "Μαθητής and Μιμητής: Exploring an Entangled Relationship," *BBR* 17 (2007): 313–23.

31. Exceptions are the following wide-ranging studies during 1970–2000: Barnabas Lindars, "Imitation of God and Imitation of Christ," *Theology* 76 (1973): 394–402 (for him, biblical ethics is primarily about the human response in obedience to the covenant God, and the imitation of

there was a literary ethos in Greco-Roman and Jewish Hellenistic cultures where the virtuous lives of notable people were upheld as models for imitation. He then argues that although the concept of imitating Christ was prevalent in early Christianity even before the composition of the Gospels (especially in Paul), the Gospels, as ancient biographies of Jesus, provided Christians with the necessary script for imitation.[32] Like Capes, Richard Burridge approaches imitation in the New Testament via genre. Based on his seminal work that the Gospels are ancient Greco-Roman biographies,[33] Burridge extends his findings to the area of New Testament ethics, arguing that ancient biographies often present the subject's moral character as an example for imitation.[34] He advocates a broad understanding of imitating Jesus along the lines of an open and accepting attitude toward others, especially in acts of humility and self-giving.[35] However, Burridge arguably uses the lens of "imitation" to explore New Testament ethics too broadly or imprecisely. Hood thus classifies Burridge's approach as representative of "a liberal imitation of a social Christ."[36]

Andrew Kille raises the issue of how Paul's audience could imitate Paul and Jesus when they are absent. He argues that readers can reconstruct "symbolic models" of Jesus and Paul from the text and that the issue is not what they should imitate from the accounts of Jesus's life but what values they can learn from Jesus's way of living.[37] In a significant study on the imitation of Christ's suffering and death in the acts of the martyrs of the first four centuries, Candida Moss contends that this concept of martyrological mimesis goes back to the New Testament and Apostolic Fathers.[38] She asserts that early Christian literature presents Jesus as a

---

Christ is limited to producing such response); Henri Crouzel, "L'Imitation et la 'Suite' de Dieu et du Christ dans les Premiers Siècles Chrétiens ainsi que leurs Sources Gréco-Romaines et Hébraïques," *JAC* 21 (1978): 7–41; Michael Griffiths, *The Example of Jesus* (London: Hodder and Stoughton, 1985); Kwon, *Christ as Example*, 55–84 (Kwon engages specifically with Larsson and Betz about the relationship between following Jesus in the Gospels and imitating Christ in Paul).

32. David B. Capes, "*Imitatio Christi* and the Gospel Genre," *BBR* 13 (2003): 1–19.

33. Richard A. Burridge, *What Are the Gospels? A Comparison with Graeco-Roman Biography*, 2nd ed. (Grand Rapids: Eerdmans, 2004 [orig. 1992]).

34. Richard A. Burridge, *Imitating Jesus: An Inclusive Approach to New Testament Ethics* (Grand Rapids: Eerdmans, 2007), 28–29, 73. While Capes builds, *inter alia*, on Burridge's 1992 work (see n. 33), Burridge himself develops the mimetic aspect of the Gospel genre only in 2007.

35. Burridge, *Imitating Jesus*, 77, 144–48, 183–84, 222–24, 280–83, 343–45. Burridge sees this pattern of imitating Jesus's open acceptance of others in each of the Gospels as well as Paul.

36. Hood, *Imitating God*, 14n7. See n. 12 above for his classifications.

37. D. Andrew Kille, "Imitating Christ: Jesus as Model in Cognitive Learning Theory," in *Text and Community: Essays in Memory of Bruce M. Metzger*, ed. J. Harold Ellens, NTM 19 (Sheffield: Sheffield Phoenix Press, 2007), 251–63.

38. Moss, *Other Christs*, 19–20.

model for imitation, where "in the absence of a codified ethical system, the person and teachings of Jesus became the guiding principle for Christian behavior."[39]

In the first full-length treatment on mimesis since the 1960s, Jason Hood develops a biblical theology of imitation, arguing that imitation is an essential aspect of Christianity, even of being human.[40] In contrast to most scholars, Hood argues that the New Testament concept of imitating Jesus is firmly rooted in the Old Testament concept of imitating God rather than a Greco-Roman concept of mimesis.[41] It is problematic that Hood defines imitation somewhat loosely and hastily early on in the book—it is primarily about adopting a mindset—rather than deriving it from specific terms in the text.[42] Finally, Joshua Cockayne has given us a brief but significant study on the hermeneutics of imitation. In light of cognitive psychology, he explains the concept of imitating Christ as a radical transformative process that is rooted in the *contemporary* experience of Christ.[43]

This preview of scholarship shows that the 1960s and the last two decades were the most fruitful in the study of mimesis in early Christianity. The 1960s is an appropriate starting point for our inquiry because studies in this period raised issues that are still discussed in contemporary scholarship.

1.3. A Statement of the Problem

These previews of primary and secondary literature raise several issues, from which we can identify four key areas of debate, fronted by questions, that will shape our inquiry.[44]

1. *Where do the historical origins of the early Christian concept of mimesis lie?* Scholars differ on whether the origins of early Christian mimesis lie in Hebraic or

---

39. Moss, *Other Christs*, 20.

40. Hood, *Imitating God*, 14, 16 (see n. 12 above for details).

41. Tinsley had already made a case for the New Testament concept of mimesis being rooted in the Old Testament, but Hood seems unaware of his work. Hood has also not interacted with the work of de Boer, Schulz, and Betz, thus missing the significance of the 1960s as a fruitful decade of mimesis studies.

42. Hood, *Imitating God*, 12 (see also 74, 132). At the end of his book, Hood sharpens his definition: "Biblical imitation is a matter of aligning character, belief, mindset or action with a pattern or template so that the copy reflects the original" (*Imitating God*, 210). Nevertheless, while his "broad, flexible approach to imitation" (*Imitating God*, 12) that is not limited to passages where imitation is mentioned explicitly may be correct, he does not outline which literal terms feed into the concept of imitation, nor does he develop criteria to distinguish among imitation, analogy, and reciprocity.

43. Joshua Cockayne, "The Imitation Game: Becoming Imitators of Christ," *RS* 53 (2017): 3–24.

44. We will answer these four big questions in section 9.2.

IMITATION IN EARLY CHRISTIANITY

Greek thought. While some scholars (Tinsley, Griffiths,[45] Hood) contend that the New Testament concept of mimesis is rooted in the Old Testament, the majority (e.g., de Boer, Schulz, Betz) have argued that it results from the cross-pollination of Greek thinking in the time leading up to the Common Era. Tinsley and Hood essentially construct a biblical theology of mimesis without considering the Greco-Roman environment in which early Christianity was embedded.[46] Nevertheless, if mimesis is fundamental to human life, it would have featured in ancient Semitic cultures. So, even if most scholars are right in claiming that discourse on mimesis started in Greek antiquity and found its way into early Christian thinking (and Second Temple Judaism) through the process of Hellenization, we must still examine whether the Old Testament paved the way for the assimilation of the Hellenistic concept of mimesis in Second Temple Jewish and early Christian literature. We will, therefore, seek to determine what religious or philosophical influences gave rise to the early Christian concept of mimesis.

2. *What language did early Christian authors use to articulate the concept of mimesis?* The lexeme μιμεῖσθαι ("to imitate") occurs mainly in Paul and the Apostolic Fathers, but John seems to have developed his own mimetic language, while the Synoptics and the Old Testament have no explicit mimetic language. Yet, many scholars agree that the *concept* of mimesis in early Christianity is broader than this lexeme. De Boer, for example, also sees mimetic connotations in the terms for "example" (τύπος, ὑπόδειγμα, ὑπογραμμός).[47] Others use the concept loosely or imprecisely (Tinsley, Griffiths,[48] Burridge, Hood). This raises the question of how many terms and ideas we can include in the concept of mimesis.[49] While it is common to work with concepts or ideas at a more abstract level to make sense of the text, we must ensure that such conceptualization is grounded in the text.

---

45. Griffiths, *Example of Jesus*, 27–28 (see n. 31 for details).
46. Tinsley's chapter 2, "'Mimesis' in the Ancient World," for example, is a mere four pages.
47. De Boer, *Imitation of Paul*, 17, 23, 83–84.
48. Griffiths's concept of imitating Jesus is derived mainly from related concepts such as "disciples," "followers," "apprentices," "witnesses," and "the way," and is insufficiently anchored in the text (*Example of Jesus*, 43–53).
49. Friedrich W. Horn probably puts too many ideas into the concept in viewing mimesis as a collective concept (*Sammelbegriff*) that is present in *all* the New Testament writings and includes notions of imitation, example, correspondence, and following ("Mimetische Ethik im Neuen Testament," in *Metapher–Narratio–Mimesis–Doxologie: Begründungsformen frühchristlicher und antiker Ethik*, ed. Ulrich Volp, Friedrich W. Horn, and Ruben Zimmermann, CNNTE 7, WUNT 356 [Tübingen: Mohr Siebeck, 2016], 195–204, at 200). In contrast, de Boer seeks to determine the scope of imitation, that is, whether "every parallelism, likeness, similarity, resemblance, and conformity between Christ and the believer come under the heading 'imitation of Christ'" (*Imitation of Paul*, 65).

1. Mimesis in Early Christianity

Our understanding of the early Christian concept of mimesis must be rooted in "real" words of early Christian literature. Hence, this study will outline the *mimetic language* of early Christian authors to determine the semantic domain of mimesis and clarify what we are looking for. In defining the concept of mimesis, we must also explain how it relates to concepts such as analogy, correspondence, reciprocity, participation, representation, and exemplification.

3. *Is the early Christian concept of mimesis consistent, varying, or developing—and what is its place in early Christian ethics?* On the surface, early Christian literature seems to distinguish between "following Jesus" in the Gospels, "imitating Christ" in Paul, and martyrdom as the ideal *imitatio Christi* in the Apostolic Fathers. We noted earlier that John mentions the imitation of Jesus, while Paul stresses the imitation of himself (although based on Jesus's example). We must also explore whether the second-century idea of martyrdom as the ideal *imitatio Christi* is rooted in the New Testament or an entirely new development. Hence, we must establish the scope, nature, and workings of mimesis in each major section of early Christian literature. We will also seek to situate mimesis within the larger field of early Christian ethics and ascertain whether mimesis is central or peripheral to it.

4. *How could early Christians imitate an absent Jesus or Paul—and what should they imitate about them?* Mimesis flows from a sensory process where the imitator usually observes what needs imitating. The concept of early Christian mimesis seems at odds with this because how could early Christians imitate Jesus or Paul who were absent? When early Christianity expanded in the first century after Jesus had ascended to the Father, Jesus's examples and instructions were preserved in the Gospels, but how could Christians imitate Jesus whom they could not observe?[50] When Paul instructs Christians to imitate him, he is not present with the church he is writing to. Has the blueprint for mimesis mutated from firsthand observation to second-hand instruction for what to imitate? Regarding the imitation of Jesus, the issue is more complex because the Jesus from the past is also the resurrected and exalted Jesus of the present. Consequently, *which* Jesus should Christians (then and now) imitate: (1) the historical Jesus preserved in the Gospel texts (Capes), (2) a "symbolic" Jesus constructed from the text (Kille), or (3) the "contemporary" Jesus experienced today (Cockayne)?[51] Moreover, what

---

50. Richard Bauckham has made a compelling case that the Gospels were either written by eyewitnesses (Matthew and John) or based on eyewitness accounts (Mark and Luke) (*Jesus and the Eyewitnesses: The Gospels as Eyewitness Testimony*, 2nd ed. [Grand Rapids: Eerdmans, 2017]). Hence, the Gospels are (based on) accounts from those who had first-hand observed Jesus's example and teaching (see, e.g., John's claim "we have seen" in John 1:14 and 1 John 1:1–3).

51. Like Capes and Kille, Jensen also notes that since imitation involves observation of the

exactly should early Christians imitate about Jesus or Paul: (1) specific actions, (2) their underlying intentions or attitudes (Burridge, Cockayne),[52] or (3) a general mindset of moral discernment (Jensen [see section 1.4 below], Kille, Hood)?

These key areas of contention, combined with the notion that there is no comprehensive study on the concept of mimesis in early Christianity, are probably sufficient reasons to warrant a fresh study. Nevertheless, some readers may still be skeptical about imitation as an acceptable Christian concept (see also n. 9), so I will provide an additional *apologia* for our book.

1.4. THE VALIDITY OF OUR STUDY

Is it appropriate or even possible to imitate Jesus? Such a question raises issues that are potentially problematic for the legitimacy of the study of mimesis.[53] We noted earlier that the tension between the imitation and uniqueness of Christ troubles the Protestant Reformed tradition and causes "*imitatio* anxiety," to use Moss's words (see n. 11). Michael Jensen addresses the dilemma of how it is possible to imitate Jesus, who is also considered to be unique (and in a sense inimitable).[54] Examining the concept of imitation in Paul, Jensen argues that it is possible to imitate Christ and uphold his uniqueness at the same time because believers are to imitate the mindset (φρόνησις) of Christ and then deliberate what actions result from this rather than imitate his actions mindlessly.[55] Hence, the imitation of Christ is an intellectual activity, "a phronesis of analogy and imagi-

---

exemplar, the absence of Christ (and Paul) necessitates the mediation of the original exemplar in some way ("Imitating Paul," 28).

52. See also Thysman, who contends that imitating Christ refers primarily to moral conformity to Christ, to imitating Christ's fundamental attitudes, such as love, humility, service, mutual aid, renunciation, obedience, and faithful patience ("L'Éthique de l'Imitation du Christ," 170–72). Similarly, John Howard Yoder argues that believers should not seek to imitate Jesus in every aspect of his lifestyle (e.g., being celibate, a carpenter, a rural itinerant preacher) but in servanthood and forgiveness (*The Politics of Jesus*, 2nd ed. [Grand Rapids: Eerdmans, 1994], 130–31). While most scholars do not declare their position, they seem to support a combination of (1) and (2).

53. Linda Trinkaus Zagzebski also addresses several objections to the imitation of exemplars (*Exemplarist Moral Theory* [Oxford: Oxford University Press, 2017], 23–28). For a popular treatment of arguments against and for the imitation of Christ, see C. D. "Jimmy" Agan, *The Imitation of Christ in the Gospel of Luke: Growing in Christlike Love for God and Neighbor* (Phillipsburg, NJ: P&R, 2014), 1–20.

54. Jensen, "Imitating Paul," 17–36.

55. Jensen, "Imitating Paul," 21, 31.

1. Mimesis in Early Christianity

native performance," where believers are at liberty to consider Christ's mindset and attitudes and then enact them faithfully for the edification of the church.[56] In addition, I contend that the imitation and uniqueness of Christ are not conflicting ideas because the call to imitate Christ is for those who are "in Christ" to use a Pauline phrase. In other words, people should not imitate Christ in order to become Christian; rather, those who already belong to Christ are called to imitate him in order to become Christlike.[57] Hence, imitation is a subset of participation in Christ and discipleship/sanctification.[58]

In other circles, there are reservations about the authenticity of mimesis in relation to ethics, that is, whether imitating someone constitutes a genuine moral act. Birger Gerhardsson observes that since Immanuel Kant's stress on autonomous acts versus heteronomous ethics, acts of imitation have never carried the same weight as the original: "A blameless ethical action must have its start within the acting subject itself; it must be autonomous. To imitate somebody else, even if it is the Christ, is to take on a borrowed dress; it is not genuine moral action."[59] However, in referring to the imitation of Christ's love, Gerhardsson contends that mimesis *can* be an autonomous act:

> Imitation means to try on a role, exemplified in an actual life of an actual person. But the concrete model does not confront us as something *which is not us* (heteronomous); it has its resonance in the agape which is part of all human existence. Thus if we interpret the imitation as an imitation of Christ's agape, then it cannot be characterized as a foreign pattern pressed from without upon the imitator, a heteronomous norm. It is a total attitude, which must be internalized in a person so that it is governed from within: it becomes one's "I-ideal." In that way the imitation comes to maturity and becomes an independent, creative attitude, in which thinking and decisions of one's own are necessary.[60]

---

56. Jensen, "Imitating Paul," 31–33 (quotation from p. 31).

57. Likewise, Jensen stresses that imitating Christ is not about acquiring an identity but enacting it ("Imitating Paul," 30, 33).

58. Grant Macaskill even asserts, "Imitation of Christ is an inadequate account of Christian ethics unless it is embedded within this broader participatory and transformative account" ("of dynamic *koinonia* with God") (*Union with Christ in the New Testament* [Oxford: Oxford University Press, 2013], 307–8).

59. Birger Gerhardsson, "Agape and Imitation of Christ," in *Jesus, the Gospels, and the Church: Essays in Honor of William R. Farmer*, ed. E. P. Sanders (Macon, GA: Mercer University Press, 1987), 163–76, at 173.

60. Gerhardsson, "Agape," 175 (original emphasis).

Similarly, since Christ is the model for imitation, but believers are free to discern how they imitate him, Jensen claims that "Paul teaches an imitative practice which is neither restrictively heteronomous nor completely autonomous."[61] Rebecca Langlands also notes that "imitation has been especially deprecated in the light of the strong value attached in later, post-Enlightenment Western tradition to autonomy, independence and individuality, with which it is seen to be at odds."[62] Her study, however, shows that ethical imitation in Roman antiquity was not at odds with autonomy but incorporated innovation and creativity while retaining a sense of one's own individual nature.[63] As we study the concept of mimesis in antiquity, we will see that the views of Gerhardsson, Jensen, and Langlands endorse our own; namely that mimesis consists of creative, cognitive, and volitional actions for which a person is responsible rather than a mindless cloning for which one might not be held accountable.

A final aspect regarding the possibility of mimesis is more hermeneutical and practical. Mimesis, as far as it relates to people, usually requires that a person be observed in order to be imitated. This creates a problem for the concept of mimesis because how could early Christians—and, by extension, contemporary Christians—imitate a person who is absent, whether Jesus or Paul? Section 1.3 shows this is a relevant concern among scholars and one of the key issues that we will address in this book (see also section 9.2). Having addressed several objections to the imitation of Christ, if we can accept that mimesis is a legitimate subject of study, the next step is to clarify our understanding of mimesis.

1.5. The Language and Concept of Early Christian Mimesis

When we explore early Christian literature to understand what constitutes mimesis, we will use a twofold hermeneutical strategy. *Linguistically*, we will outline the mimetic language early Christian authors used to determine the semantic domain of the concept of mimesis. *Conceptually*, we will be attentive to whether a particular text refers to the concept of mimesis or related concepts such as analogy and reciprocity. First, however, we will provisionally clarify our understanding of the concept of early Christian mimesis.

Defining Mimesis. We noted earlier that although mimesis is central to nearly all areas of human thought and action, there is no uniform definition and no

---

61. Jensen, "Imitating Paul," 18.
62. Rebecca Langlands, *Exemplary Ethics in Ancient Rome* (Cambridge: Cambridge University Press, 2018), 8–9.
63. Langlands, *Exemplary Ethics*, 9.

agreed criteria to distinguish it from related concepts. In early Christianity, mimesis is a religious-ethical concept because it relates to the behavior of Christians in relation to their God and fellow Christians. We can call this "mimetic ethics" or "ethical mimesis" as far as it relates to people's moral behavior and character shaped by mimesis.[64] I use the term "ethics" to refer to the moral values and principles that govern the conduct and character of a particular group of Christians or "believers" in relation to their God and fellow human beings, as envisaged by the early Christian writings.[65] While ethics is usually limited to the realm of human interaction, I broaden early Christian ethics to the divine realm because the early Christian writings (1) present God as a moral being who extends various divine goods to people and operates at the human level through the incarnation, and (2) use the human category of "family" to explain the divine–human relationship.

Mimesis, as an ethical concept, aims at moral development in that a person imitates someone in order to become a better person and improve their character.[66] In early Christianity, the moral goal of mimesis was Christlikeness or conformity to Christ, where Christians imitated Jesus (or God) in order to become like Christ (or God), a process also known as theosis or deification. As a result, my working definition of mimesis as an ethical concept is that "person B represents or emulates person A in activity or state X in order to become like person A."[67] With regard to the most common form of early Christian mimesis, this means that

---

64. For the importance of mimesis for human morality from the perspectives of divergent disciplines (e.g., philosophy, scholasticism, and neuroscience), see Sally K. Severino and Nancy K. Morrison, "Three Voices / One Message: The Importance of Mimesis for Human Morality," *Contagion: Journal of Violence, Mimesis, and Culture* 19 (2012): 139–66.

65. I use the term "believers" to refer to people who have devoted themselves to Jesus, and synonymous terms are "disciples" or "Jesus followers."

66. István Czachesz explains, "We imitate individuals of high status (called the *prestige bias*), because some of that behavior might help us achieve status, too. Turning to early Christianity, this means that imitating Paul, Jesus, the apostles, martyrs, and other holy persons, who were highly esteemed by the early Church, is a normal and expectable phenomenon" ("From Mirror Neurons to Morality: Cognitive and Evolutionary Foundations of Early Christian Ethics," in *Metapher–Narratio–Mimesis–Doxologie: Begründungsformen frühchristlicher und antiker Ethik*, ed. Ulrich Volp, Friedrich W. Horn, and Ruben Zimmermann, CNNTE 7, WUNT 356 [Tübingen: Mohr Siebeck, 2016], 271–87, at 279–80 [original emphasis]).

67. For a similar understanding, see Zagzebski, *Exemplarist Moral Theory*, 24. Likewise, Ruben Zimmermann defines mimetic ethics as "the imitation of a person as a role model with a view toward his or her conduct or character. Mimetic ethics in this sense could therefore also be described as *role model ethics*" (*The Logic of Love: Discovering Paul's "Implicit Ethics" through 1 Corinthians*, trans. Dieter T. Roth [Lanham, MD: Fortress Academic, 2018], 70 [original emphasis]). Some people distinguish between imitation and emulation, claiming that the latter refers to imitating someone with the intention or desire to surpass or improve on the exemplar. If,

believers (person B) imitate Jesus (person A) in order to become like him. To put it differently, Jesus (person A) functions as a virtuous role model who sets the example (activity or state X) for the believer (person B) to imitate in order to become like him (person A). Some early Christian writings present two kinds or types of mimesis: (1) *"performative mimesis,"* which is most common and can be defined as "person B imitates person A in activity X," and (2) *"existential mimesis,"* which is less common (mostly in John, rarely in Paul and Ignatius, once in Matthew) and can be defined as "person B imitates person A in a particular state of being." We will now consider the linguistic expressions that could potentially convey mimesis to indicate what we should be looking for in the early Christian literature.

Mimetic Language. Our philological quest for the semantic domain of early Christian mimesis should not be limited to explicit mimetic language, the lexeme μιμεῖσθαι, but include terms such as τύπος, ὑπόδειγμα, and ὑπογραμμός because mimesis involves the imitation of examples.[68] Also, if mimesis is a subset of analogy (see below), we should go further and extend our linguistic analysis to include comparative particles or connectives such as καθώς, ὥσπερ, οὕτως, ὡς, ὅμοιος, and ὁμοίως in exploring potential mimesis in these texts. We must bear in mind that a comparative particle itself does not necessarily indicate mimesis; only a literary context can do that. For example, both mimesis and analogy are often articulated by the comparative conjunction καθώς (see n. 73). So, the presence of this term is inconclusive, and we need further contextual indicators to decide which concept is in view.

In addition, not every passage in early Christian literature will indicate mimesis "beyond reasonable doubt." For this reason, I will introduce a heuristic device to gauge the mimetic strength of a particular passage. While it can be straightforward to identify mimesis in a text, there are times that mimesis is implied or tentative. But instead of an either/or scenario where we must decide if a passage contains mimesis or not, I will use a sliding scale to assess the "mimetic strength" of a passage. In other words, we will employ a "mimetic continuum" that indicates the relative mimetic strength of specific passages in the early Christian literature. The instrument of mimetic strength and its indicators "weak," "medium," and "strong" are used heuristically to convey our certainty of the presence of mimesis in a passage.[69]

---

however, mimesis is more about creative and dynamic imitation rather than simplistic replication, the alleged distinction between imitation and emulation is superfluous.

68. Interestingly, we will see that παράδειγμα does *not* denote mimesis in the New Testament whereas it does in Greco-Roman writings.

69. I avoid spelling out the terms "weak," "medium," and "strong." While some may question such an "intuitive" or "subjective" approach and prefer more precise definitions or "objective" cri-

Mimesis and Exemplification. Benjamin Fiore and Thomas Blanton explain that exemplification and imitation are associated but not synonymous terms. Exemplification is a comprehensive process that involves (1) the selection of a particular action to guide behavior, (2) the depiction of that action in discourse, and (3) the imitation (i.e., copying or repeating) of that action by people. Hence, imitation is just one element of the broader process of exemplification.[70] This notion of exemplification is similar to our definition of mimesis and our understanding of mimesis as a comprehensive process (see section 2.3). Although our model of mimesis is broader than the models of exemplification proposed by others (see section 2.3), we do not need to differentiate between them. In contrast, I must clarify how mimesis differs from related concepts such as analogy and reciprocity.

Mimesis and Analogy. Analogy refers to a correspondence, resemblance, or parallel between persons, actions, or objects that are otherwise different. For example, "the kingdom of God is like a mustard seed" is an analogy that associates a particular aspect of the kingdom of God (its spectacular growth despite its small beginnings) with that of a mustard seed (Mark 4:30–32). Likewise, the work of the Spirit is likened to the blowing of the wind (John 3:8). The Spirit does not imitate the wind; rather, the work of the Spirit is explained by means of a comparison to the workings of the wind. Mimesis is a subset or narrower form of analogy in that (ethical) mimesis refers to the close resemblance between two persons in a specific activity or condition of existence.[71]

Without claiming to be exhaustive or applicable to mimesis in general, I suggest four criteria or guidelines for distinguishing mimesis from analogy in the early Christian writings.

---

teria for what constitutes "weak," "medium," and "strong" mimesis, I do not think this is achievable. Besides, we noted earlier that there is no uniform definition of mimesis or precise criteria to determine what constitutes it (see nn. 13–14). Hence, I simply use the terms "weak," "medium," and "strong" to express my level of confidence about the presence of mimesis in a particular text.

70. Benjamin Fiore and Thomas R. Blanton, "Paul, Exemplification, and Imitation," in *Paul in the Greco-Roman World: A Handbook*, ed. J. Paul Sampley, 2nd ed. (London: Bloomsbury T&T Clark, 2016), 169–95, at 169. Other scholars who focus on exemplification or exemplarity, include Zagzebski, *Exemplarist Moral Theory*; Matthew B. Roller, *Models from the Past in Roman Culture: A World of Exempla* (Cambridge: Cambridge University Press, 2018); Langlands, *Exemplary Ethics*; Katie Marcar, "Following in the Footsteps: Exemplarity, Ethnicity and Ethics in 1 Peter," *NTS* 68 (2022): 253–73.

71. According to the Oxford English Dictionary, imitation is "the adoption, whether conscious or not, during a learning process, of the behavior or attitudes of some specific person or model," while analogy refers to "a comparison between one thing and another, typically for the purpose of explanation or clarification."

IMITATION IN EARLY CHRISTIANITY

1. Mimesis is *intentional* on the part of the imitator (person B knowingly seeks to imitate person A in something), whereas analogy is often observed or created by an external person (person C notes a correspondence between entities A and B). The intentionality or creation of the analogy does not lie with the comparable entities but with the outsider. Using our earlier example, to state that the Spirit imitates the wind in its workings would overstretch the expression and assume intentionality. Instead, it is Jesus who intentionally makes this comparison to clarify the Spirit's working.[72]

2. Mimesis, as it relates to people (which is the case in early Christianity), requires that one person perform an action that serves as an *example* for another person to emulate. In contrast, with analogy, a person can behave like others without being emulated. For example, Luke 11:1, John 5:23, Acts 15:8, Rom 1:13, and 1 Cor 15:49 are instances of analogy, indicated by the comparative conjunction καθώς ("just as") rather than mimesis.[73]

3. Mimesis requires *tangible* or *perceptible acts*—both the original and mimetic acts. Mimesis is a sensory process where the imitator observes a concrete example (rather than an abstract idea) and produces a corresponding mimetic act that is likewise tangible. Authentic mimesis requires a close resemblance between the

---

[72]. According to Halliwell, Aristotle also views intentionality as that which distinguishes between mimesis and analogy: "Mimetic likenesses entail an intentionality that is ultimately natural in origin but becomes embodied in culturally evolved and institutionalized forms. This is one reason why not all likenesses are mimetic: not all likeness has the intentional grounding that is a necessary condition of artistic mimesis" (*Aesthetics of Mimesis*, 156). While the lexeme μιμεῖσθαι was used in a variety of ways in antiquity (see chapters 2–3 in the present volume), in early Christianity it is only used in an ethical sense and has a volitional aspect. Hence, when Philo uses μιμεῖσθαι to state that the shape of a theater "imitates" that of the ear (*Post.* 104), this denotes analogy between two objects rather than (ethical) mimesis—the theater does not seek to imitate the ear. Rather, Philo observes that the theater's shape resembles that of the ear. Victor A. Copan mentions a few more examples where μιμεῖσθαι denotes analogy between objects (*Saint Paul as Spiritual Director: An Analysis of the Imitation of Paul with Implications and Applications to the Practice of Spiritual Direction* [Colorado Springs, CO: Paternoster, 2007], 46).

[73]. In Luke 11:1, the disciples request Jesus to teach them to pray "just as" (καθώς) John the Baptist also taught his disciples. The idea is not that Jesus observed and imitated how John taught his disciples to pray but that Jesus, like John, would teach his disciples to pray. In John 5:23, people are expected to honor Jesus "just as" (καθώς) they honor God, that is, they are to act analogously towards both Jesus and God. In Acts 15:8, Peter declares that God has acted in a similar manner (καθώς is used) to both gentiles and Jews in granting them the Holy Spirit. Rom 1:13 is another example of analogy when Paul states the desire that his ministry among the Romans may be "just as" (καθώς) fruitful as it has been among the gentiles. In 1 Cor 15:49, Paul's statement, "just as (καθώς) we have borne the image of the man of dust, we will also bear the image of the man of heaven," denotes again analogy rather than imitation.

original act and the mimetic act but not always a one-to-one correspondence. In contrast, an analogy can correspond with ideas without any perceptible presence of the two things that are compared (e.g., "the kingdom of God is like a mustard seed").[74] In the previous section, we noted that early Christianity could talk about the imitation of Jesus or Paul when they were absent—an indicator that the exemplar could be accessible through means other than direct observation, something our study must confirm and explain.[75]

4. The aim of ethical mimesis is *moral transformation*, where the imitator seeks to become like the other person (wholly or in a particular aspect), whereas the aim of analogy is to explain. For example, Jesus uses various analogies in the Synoptics to explain to his audiences what the kingdom of God is like, while in John's Gospel, Jesus encourages his followers to imitate him so that they may become like him, for example, in humility (13:14–16), love (13:34), and unity (17:11).[76]

Mimesis and Reciprocity. In ancient societies, as many scholars have shown, social relations were characterized by benefaction and reciprocity. The practice of one party bestowing a benefit (basic goods, services, or other favors) and the other party returning a benefit (reciprocity) established and maintained most social relations in first-century Mediterranean cultures. The most common relationship in which reciprocity occurred was the patron–client relationship, an asymmetrical relationship between people who were not social equals, but reciprocity also occurred in private or ideal friendship, a symmetrical relationship between social equals.[77]

---

74. Hence, an example does not necessarily lead to mimesis. An example can remain in the abstract realm to explain a concept by way of analogy, like Jesus's example of a mustard seed to explain the growth of the kingdom of God.

75. This correlates to the criterion of accessibility in literary mimesis, related to the likelihood that the author of a later text had access to an earlier text for imitation (Dennis Ronald MacDonald, "Imitation," in *Oxford Encyclopedia of Bible and Ethics*, ed. Robert L. Brawley [Oxford: Oxford University Press, 2014], 407–10, at 408).

76. Gebauer and Wulf mention characteristics of mimesis that overlap with ours: (1) mimesis involves an *identification* of one person with another; (2) mimesis includes both an *active* and a *cognitive* component; (3) mimesis denotes a *physical action*; (4) mimesis has a *performative* aspect (*Mimesis*, 5). I will bring out the cognitive aspect of mimesis in later chapters.

77. Bruce J. Malina and Richard L. Rohrbaugh, *Social-Science Commentary on the Gospel of John* (Minneapolis: Fortress, 1998), 117–19; Bruce J. Malina, *The New Testament World: Insights from Cultural Anthropology*, 3rd ed. (Louisville: Westminster John Knox, 2001), 94–96; Eric C. Stewart, "Social Stratification and Patronage in Ancient Mediterranean Societies," in *Understanding the Social World of the New Testament*, ed. Dietmar Neufeld and Richard E. DeMaris (London: Routledge, 2010), 156–66, at 156–58; Martin M. Culy, *Echoes of Friendship in the Gospel of John*, NTM 30 (Sheffield: Sheffield Phoenix Press, 2010), 42–62.

Taking the Johannine writings as a case in point, reciprocity differs from mimesis in three ways:

1. With mimesis, the exemplar upholds an *example* to follow or emulate, whereas, with reciprocity, a person bestows a *benefit* on another person by returning the favor in the form of other goods or services. Regarding John's Gospel, for example, 13:15 indicates mimesis (Jesus washes the disciples' feet as an example for them to follow), while instances of reciprocity are found in 3:16 (God's gift of his Son to the world is to be reciprocated by belief) and 15:13–14 (Jesus's gift of friendship, shown in laying down his life, should be reciprocated by keeping his commandments).[78]

2. With mimesis, the movement is *unidirectional* or *linear* (person C imitates person B, who imitates person A), whereas, with reciprocity, the movement is *bidirectional* or *circular* (person A confers a gift to person B, who returns the favor to person A, or a gift can go from person A to person B to person C, back to person A).[79] The Johannine writings show, for example, a linear mimetic chain of love: just as the Father loves Jesus, so Jesus loves the disciples (15:9), and just as Jesus loved the disciples, so they must love one another (13:34; 15:12).

3. The aim of ethical mimesis is *moral transformation* (the imitator seeks to become like the exemplar), whereas the aim of reciprocity is to maintain social relations and, in the case of patronage, maintain dependency and social hierarchy. In the Johannine writings, mimesis is an ethical concept relating primarily to the transformation of the believers' conduct and character, whereas reciprocity is a social concept relating to the exchange of goods and services between patrons and clients or between friends.[80]

Since mimesis has resisted a precise definition throughout history, I will, at times, hold my criteria loosely (and explain why) to distinguish between different concepts. When I appeal to the above criteria, I will use, for example, the notation "M&A criterion 1" to refer to the first criterion to distinguish between mimesis and

---

78. The concept of reciprocity is also expressed by John's so-called "indwelling" or "abiding" language, μένειν ἐν or (εἶναι) ἐν (e.g., John 6:56; 10:38; 14:10–11, 20; 15:4–5; 17:21, 23; 1 John 3:24; 4:13, 16).

79. See also Richard Seaford, "Introduction," in *Reciprocity in Ancient Greece*, ed. Christopher Gill, Norman Postlethwaite, and Richard Seaford (Oxford: Oxford University Press, 1998), 1–12, at 2n2.

80. Regarding Johannine ethics, while Jan G. van der Watt puts reciprocity and mimesis at the same level (*A Grammar of the Ethics of John: Reading John from an Ethical Perspective*, 2 vols., WUNT 431, 502 [Tübingen: Mohr Siebeck, 2019, 2023], 1:257–62, 525; 2:84–100, 393–94, 417), I contend that mimesis goes deeper to the heart of Johannine ethics than reciprocity (Cornelis Bennema, "The Centre of Johannine Ethics," in *The Ethics of John: Retrospect and Prospects*, ed. Jan G. van der Watt and Matthijs den Dulk, BINS 227 [Leiden: Brill, 2025], 142–62).

analogy, and "M&R criterion 2" to refer to the second criterion in the section on mimesis and reciprocity. Having done the preliminary work, I will now outline the nature of the study, its main thesis, and the plan and approach.

1.6. An Explanation of Our Study

Nature, Scope, Limitations. This book is a literary, historical, and theological study of mimesis as a religious-ethical concept in early Christianity. A *literary* study is essential because we rely on literary sources to inform us about the nature and practice of mimesis in antiquity. The scope of our inquiry includes the relevant literature in ancient Jewish, Greco-Roman, and Christian traditions. A literary study is also required because scholars sometimes use the concept of mimesis or imitation imprecisely without showing a sound textual basis. Besides, there is no explicit mimetic language in the Hebrew Bible, and the lexeme μιμεῖσθαι only occurs eleven times in the New Testament and eighteen times in the writings of the apostolic fathers. Hence, if the early Christian concept of mimesis is broader than this lexeme, we must establish the mimetic language of early Christian authors through a close reading of the text.

The study is *historical* in that we will seek to trace the historic origins of the early Christian concept of mimesis in the Jewish and Greco-Roman traditions. Besides examining the New Testament as the source text of early Christians, we will also consider the works of the apostolic fathers as significant sources to understand early Christianity because they cover the period from the passing of the earliest Christian leaders such as James, Peter, Paul, and John to the middle of the second century.

Finally, the study is *theological* because the early Christian authors were theologians who related the concept of mimesis to the religious-ethical life of believers with their God. Early Christian mimesis pertains both to God's behavior towards his people and to people's behavior towards God and as such, it belongs to the realm of Christian ethics or moral theology. This mimetic ethics (or ethical mimesis), referring to people's behavior and character shaped by mimesis, aims at moral development where believers seek to imitate Jesus (or exemplary believers) in order to become more Christlike and corresponding to the ethos (i.e., beliefs, values, and norms) of God's world as the early Christian writings present it.

In terms of limitations, our study focuses on mimetic ethics and hence will not deal with the aesthetic aspect of mimesis (e.g., in art, music, and literature)[81]

---

81. For this, see the seminal work of Eric Auerbach, *Mimesis: The Representation of Reality in*

or with literary mimesis (where an author imitates a literary form or style from another author).[82]

Thesis. Our study will show that mimesis is a sensory, cognitive, and volitional process where the imitator observes an exemplary person, discerns what needs imitation, and interprets how to articulate and perform the mimetic act. Any approach that views mimesis as a mindless or superficial replication or cloning misses the point. Our thesis is that *early Christian mimesis was a dynamic, participatory, creative, and cognitive process within the context of divine family education with the goal for Christians to represent and resemble Christ in character and conduct.* Within the context of God's household or church, early Christian mimesis is a didactic instrument for moral transformation, shaping the behavior and character of Christians in order for them to become like him. We will discover that the physical absence of the main exemplar, whether Jesus or Paul, was not an obstacle to imitation because early Christians could use means other than direct observation. This will provide a template for how the imitation of Christ can be mediated and practiced today.

Plan and Approach. Our study consists of three parts. Part 1 will explore the concept of mimesis in Greco-Roman antiquity (chapter 2) and Jewish antiquity (chapter 3) to determine the origins of early Christian mimesis. Part 2 examines each major section of early Christian literature—the Synoptics and Acts (chapter 4), the Johannine literature (chapter 5), the Pauline literature (chapter 6), the rest of the New Testament (Hebrews, the Catholic Epistles, and Revelation in chapter 7), and the Apostolic Fathers (chapter 8). For each early Christian seg-

---

Western Literature (Princeton: Princeton University Press, 1953), but also Halliwell, *Aesthetics of Mimesis*. For the concept of mimetic hermeneutics in narrative theory, see Paul Ricoeur, *Time and Narrative*, vol. 1 (Chicago: University of Chicago Press, 1984), 52–90.

82. For the concept of literary mimesis in biblical scholarship, see Stefan Lücking, *Mimesis der Verachteten: Eine Studie zur Erzählweise von Mk 14,1–11*, SBS 152 (Stuttgart: Katholisches Bibelwerk, 1992); Gert J. Steyn, "Luke's Use of *ΜΙΜΗΣΙΣ*? Re-opening the Debate," in *The Scriptures in the Gospels*, ed. C. M. Tuckett, BETL 131 (Leuven: Peeters, 1997), 551–57; Dennis Ronald MacDonald, ed., *Mimesis and Intertextuality in Antiquity and Christianity* (Harrisburg, PA: Trinity Press International, 2001); MacDonald, "Imitations of Greek Epic in the Gospels," in *The Historical Jesus in Context*, ed. Amy-Jill Levine, Dale C. Allison, and John Dominic Crossan (Princeton: Princeton University Press, 2006), 372–84; Matthew Ryan Hauge, "The Creation of Person in Ancient Narrative and the Gospel of Mark," in *Character Studies and the Gospel of Mark*, ed. Christopher W. Skinner and Matthew Ryan Hauge, LNTS 483 (London: Bloomsbury T&T Clark, 2014), 63–72; Brad McAdon, *Rhetorical Mimesis and the Mitigation of Early Christian Conflicts: Examining the Influence That Greco-Roman Mimesis May Have in the Composition of Matthew, Luke, and Acts* (Eugene, OR: Wipf and Stock, 2018); Eric Eve, *Relating the Gospels: Memory, Imitation and the Farrer Hypothesis*, LNTS 592 (London: T&T Clark, 2021).

ment, we will (1) provide a peek into relevant scholarship, (2) pay close attention to the mimetic language being used, (3) perform a close reading of relevant texts in order to determine the scope, nature, and workings of mimesis, and (4) seek to determine whether mimesis is central or peripheral to its ethics. Part 3 will pull together our findings and theorize further about the concept of early Christian mimesis. We will summarize our findings and answer the four "big" questions that have framed our inquiry (chapter 9). Drawing on these findings more broadly, we will seek to explain the complexities of early Christian mimesis as a hermeneutical process, explore the ongoing relevance of early Christian mimesis, and state the key takeaways of the book (chapter 10). Indexes of authors, sources, and subjects at the end of the book (together with a Table of Contents at the start) will provide the reader quick access to relevant portions of our study.

PART 1

Mimesis in Antiquity

2

Mimesis in Greco-Roman Antiquity

The discourse on mimesis originated in Greek antiquity (with Plato and Aristotle) and carried on in the Roman era.¹ Etymologically, the lexeme μιμεῖσθαι refers to the innovative and organized representation of nature through the fine arts, but in due course, it spread to the realms of religion, family, and education to express the imitation of God, parent, and teacher.² With few exceptions, scholars agree that, due to extended contact with the Greco-Roman traditions, Hellenistic Judaism and early Christianity adopted the concept of mimesis into the overlapping spheres of religion, education, and family. In Judeo-Christian traditions, it has become almost exclusively an ethical concept, conveying the idea of imitating an exemplary person to become virtuous.³ Greco-Roman antiquity, therefore, is the appropriate methodological starting point for our study.

Another reason to start with Greco-Roman antiquity to understand mimesis is that the Greeks and Romans describe and discuss the workings of mimesis, whereas early Christian authors simply refer to the concept. This makes it easier to construct a model of mimesis from the Greco-Roman traditions. Compared to the early Christian writings, the lexeme μιμεῖσθαι and the concept of "example" (e.g., τύπος, παράδειγμα) are abundantly present in Greco-Roman literature.⁴ To

1. For informed discussions on mimesis in antiquity, see Gebauer and Wulf, *Mimesis*, 25–59; Halliwell, *Aesthetics of Mimesis*; Potolsky, *Mimesis*, 15–70; Gabriel Zoran, "Between Appropriation and Representation: Aristotle and the Concept of Imitation in Greek Thought," *Philosophy and Literature* 39 (2015): 468–86; Alexander H. Zistakis, "Mimēsis—Imitation as Representation in Plato and His Modern Successors," in *The Many Faces of Mimesis*, ed. Heather L. Reid and Jeremy C. DeLong (Sioux City, IA: Parnassos, 2018), 159–71.

2. See, for example, de Boer, *Imitation of Paul*, 1–8.

3. We noted in section 1.3 that while most scholars accept that the origins of Judeo-Christian mimesis lie in the Greco-Roman traditions, Tinsley and Hood contend that the New Testament concept of mimesis is rooted in the Old Testament. We will examine their case in chapter 3.

4. The Thesaurus Linguae Graecae (TLG) database shows that the concept of mimesis is widespread in Greco-Roman literature: the verb μιμεῖσθαι has about 1,850 occurrences, and the

PART 1   MIMESIS IN ANTIQUITY

make our study feasible, I will focus on select Greco-Roman authors who provide the most helpful and systematic discussion on the topic.[5]

The main aim of this chapter is to discover the mechanics or workings of human mimesis or ethical mimesis in the Greco-Roman traditions, where the imitator seeks to emulate an exemplary person in order to become virtuous. We can then, in subsequent chapters, assess to what extent the Greco-Roman mimetic traditions prepare the way for the concept of mimesis in the Hellenistic Jewish and early Christian traditions. In other words, we will seek to develop a model of mimesis in Greco-Roman antiquity and use it heuristically to examine the extent to which the Judeo-Christian traditions adhere to it. Any model will involve a level of abstraction, conceptualization, and systematization. While some scholars are averse to models, I contend that, in our case, they are useful for finding commonalities between different early Christian traditions. While early Christianity was variegated, there was nevertheless a common set of beliefs and practices (rooted in the person and teachings of Jesus) that made it a recognizable system—one in which I seek to situate the concept and practice of mimesis.

I will now outline the logic and structure of this chapter. Discourse on mimesis started in Plato's *Republic* (written between 380–360 BCE) and Aristotle's *Poetics* (c. 350–335 BCE). Plato (428/427–348/347 BCE) and his student Aristotle (384–322 BCE) disagreed on the nature and function of mimesis, and their theories have framed the debate on mimesis till today.[6] While their opposing ideas are foundational for our understanding of mimesis, the concept was already familiar in the Athenian theater, so we will start there. The remainder of the chapter will deal with prominent Greco-Roman orators/educators. As Wayne Meeks explains, in ancient society, especially in the context of the *polis*, disputes were settled by argument, so the Greeks and Romans valued and cultivated the skills of oratory and rhetoric.[7] As this chapter will show, mimesis plays a prominent role in rhe-

---

μιμη* group about 1,000 occurrences in the Abridged TLG. Likewise, the Perseus Digital Library Project (http://www.perseus.tufts.edu) indicates that the lexemes μιμεῖσθαι and *imitatio* occur in over 600 Greco-Roman documents. James Petitfils notes that in Greek antiquity, the moral use of παράδειγμα occurs in poetry and the *encomium* rather than the rhetorical traditions (where it functions as a form of proof in argumentation). In Roman antiquity, however, the role of *exemplum* for moral formation gains more significance (*Mos Christianorum: The Roman Discourse of Exemplarity and the Jewish and Christian Language of Leadership*, STAC 99 [Tübingen: Mohr Siebeck, 2016], 19–32).

5. The English translations of Greco-Roman writings are taken from the Loeb Classical Library unless indicated otherwise.

6. Gebauer and Wulf, *Mimesis*, 309; Halliwell, *Aesthetics of Mimesis*, 5; Potolsky, *Mimesis*, 5.

7. Wayne A. Meeks, *The Moral World of the First Christians*, Library of Early Christianity 6 (Philadelphia: Westminster, 1986), 20, 40–41. Jacqueline de Romilly also notes that while Athe-

30

2. Mimesis in Greco-Roman Antiquity

torical education, so I will select specific ancient orators/educators and examine their moral discourses in order to articulate a model of the workings of mimesis in Greco-Roman antiquity. While we admittedly focus on the intellectual elite and their written discourses on mimesis, Meeks asserts that common people had ready access to professional orators and their moral discourses as they often spoke in public spaces.[8] In addition, others have noted a much broader mimetic ethos in Greco-Roman antiquity.[9] We will start with Isocrates, a prominent orator/educator in classical Athens (436–338 BCE), because he was the first to promulgate imitation as an educational method for acquiring oratorical skills.[10] Isocrates was

---

nian theater in the fifth century was tied to Athenian politics, from the fourth century on, politics became more the interest of Attic oratory (*A Short History of Greek Literature* [Chicago: University of Chicago Press, 1985], 89).

8. Meeks, *Moral World*, 63. He explains that although literacy in the Greco-Roman empire was very low (less than 10 percent on average), people of all classes had access to moral discourse and the art of persuasion (rhetoric) by listening to professional orators on the street corners, theater, open forums, and legal courts (*Moral World*, 62–63). Abraham J. Malherbe also outlines how philosophical ethics and moral discourse were popularized and penetrated many levels of society (*Moral Exhortation: A Greco-Roman Sourcebook*, Library of Early Christianity 4 [Philadelphia: Westminster, 1986], 13).

9. Rubén R. Dupertois detects a mimetic ethos across a broad range of texts—from the writings of elite educationalists (e.g., Plato, Aristotle, Cicero, Quintilian) and the *progymnasmata* (rhetorical exercise handbooks) to educational papyri ("Writing and Imitation: Greek Education in the Greco-Roman World," *Forum* 1 [2007]: 3–29, at 4–7). Likewise, Benjamin Fiore shows the ubiquity of the use of examples and calls to imitation in Greco-Roman antiquity: (1) *rhetorical handbooks* aimed at moral education by imitating great examples (e.g., Plutarch's *Lives*, Valerius Maximus's *Memorable Deeds and Sayings*); (2) in *apprenticeship*, a young aristocrat learned to imitate his mentor; (3) in the *classroom*, a teacher (as a proxy parent) exemplifies a virtuous lifestyle for students to imitate; and (4) *hortatory letters*, where epistolary presence may be more effective than physical presence, allow the audience to conceptualize virtue from historical examples (e.g., Seneca's *Epistles*) ("Paul, Exemplification, and Imitation," in *Paul in the Greco-Roman World: A Handbook*, ed. J. Paul Sampley [New York: Trinity Press International, 2003], 228–57, at 228–37). See also Benjamin Fiore, *The Function of Personal Example in the Socratic and Pastoral Epistles*, AnBib 105 (Rome: Biblical Institute Press, 1986), 26–44. Based on an extensive survey of eulogistic inscriptions, statues, and literary evidence, James R. Harrison demonstrates the prevalence of a mimetic ethos or culture of imitation in Greco-Roman civic life, where "great men" were held up as models for posterity—especially the emperor in the early imperial period ("The Imitation of the 'Great Man' in Antiquity: Paul's Inversion of a Cultural Icon," in *Christian Origins and Greco-Roman Culture: Social and Literary Contexts for the New Testament*. Vol. 1 of *Early Christianity in Its Hellenistic Context*, ed. Stanley E. Porter and Andrew W. Pitts, TENTS 9 [Leiden: Brill, 2013], 213–54, at 222–45).

10. Edward P. J. Corbett, "The Theory and Practice of Imitation in Classical Rhetoric," *College Composition and Communication* 22 (1971): 243–50, at 243; Andrew W. Pitts, "The Origins of Greek Mimesis and the Gospel of Mark: Genre as a Potential Restraint in Assessing Markan Imitation,"

an exemplar for Cicero (106–43 BCE), who in turn influenced Seneca (4 BCE–65 CE) and Quintilian (35–100 CE), so we can expect a degree of continuity in their understanding of mimesis.[11]

2.1. Mimesis in Greek Antiquity

De Boer explains that, originally, the lexeme μιμεῖσθαι had to do with the creative and orderly expression of the harmony, rhythm, potentiality, and forces of nature in the fine arts (painting, dance, sculpture, poetry). The essence of mimesis was "not so much in terms of sameness, complete likeness, exact reproduction, but rather in terms of bringing to expression, representation, portrayal."[12] Over time, however, the concept of mimesis extended to other areas of life. In *metaphysics*, mimesis became an important cosmological concept in Plato to explain the ontological relationship between the lower world of reality and the higher world of ideas.[13]

For our study of mimesis in early Christianity, however, the following spheres of mimesis will be important. In *religion*, people's goal was to imitate or assimilate to God or the gods. Plato writes, for example, "We ought to try to escape from earth to the dwelling of the gods as quickly as we can; and to escape is to become like God, so far as this is possible; and to become like God is to become righteous and holy and wise" (*Theaet.* 176b; see also *Tim.* 29e, 44–47; *Phaedr.* 248a, 253a–b; Aristotle, *Eth. nic.* 1177b31–33, 1178b27).[14] Subsequently, George van Kooten shows that the idea of someone imitating God "so far as he is able" in Plato's *Phaedr.* 252c–d is an outworking of assimilation to God "so far as this is possible" in *Theaet.*

---

in *Ancient Education and Early Christianity*, ed. Matthew Ryan Hauge and Andrew W. Pitts, LNTS 533 (New York: Bloomsbury T&T Clark, 2016), 107–36, at 107.

11. See also Elaine Fantham, "Imitation and Decline: Rhetorical Theory and Practice in the First Century after Christ," *CP* 73 (1978): 102–16, at 102–3.

12. De Boer, *Imitation of Paul*, 1–2 (quotation from p. 2). See also, Halliwell, *Aesthetics of Mimesis*, 15–16. For the cultic origins of mimesis, see Betz, *Nachfolge und Nachahmung*, 48–61 (he then explores the spread of this cultic phenomenon of mimesis on pp. 61–84).

13. Wilhelm Michaelis, "μιμέομαι, μιμητής, συμμιμητής," in *TDNT* 4:659–74, at 661–62; Betz, *Nachfolge und Nachahmung*, 113–16.

14. "To become like God" means to become as rational as possible (Christopher Rowe, "Plato," in *The Cambridge Companion to Greek and Roman Philosophy*, ed. David Sedley [Cambridge: Cambridge University Press, 2003], 98–124, at 110). Differently, George H. van Kooten asserts that "to become like God" is *ethical* in orientation because it is defined as "to become righteous" (*Paul's Anthropology in Context: The Image of God, Assimilation to God, and Tripartite Man in Ancient Judaism, Ancient Philosophy and Early Christianity*, WUNT 232 [Tübingen: Mohr Siebeck, 2008], 130).

176b.[15] While assimilation to God does not necessarily imply mimesis, the idea of gods as role models for human imitation is present in Greek antiquity.[16]

In the *family* and in *education*, children were expected to imitate their parents and teachers in order to become like these role models.[17] For example, Euripides, a Greek playwright in the fifth century BCE, records the passionate appeal of a father to his daughter: "I beg of you, grant me this favor and imitate the ways of your righteous father. For children the fairest renown is this, to be born of a noble father and to take after him in character" (*Helen* 939–943). In connection with education, the lexeme μιμεῖσθαι extended to the realm of ethics, and pupils were expected to imitate their teacher.[18] Dupertois shows that imitation is central to every stage of Greco-Roman education, and there was general agreement on a small group of classical authors who served as good models.[19]

Notably, the spheres of family and education overlapped so that the family functioned as a microcosm of the *polis* and the teacher as an extended parent.[20] We shall see that these Greek concepts of imitation continued in Roman culture.[21] So, the

---

15. Van Kooten, *Paul's Anthropology*, 132. He also claims that the Stoic notion of the imitation of God is the equivalent of the Platonic notion of assimilation to God (*Paul's Anthropology*, 105–6, 159–60).

16. See de Boer, *Imitation of Paul*, 26–28; Schulz, *Nachfolgen und Nachahmen*, 206–13; Betz, *Nachfolge und Nachahmung*, 120–30 (he looks at both Greek and Roman literature); Elizabeth A. Castelli, *Imitating Paul: A Discourse of Power* (Louisville: Westminster John Knox, 1991), 71–78; van Kooten, *Paul's Anthropology*, 124–60 (he sees instances where assimilation to God refers to becoming like God through imitation); Christoph Jedan, "Metaphors of Closeness: Reflections on *Homoiōsis Theōi* in Ancient Philosophy and Beyond," *Numen* 60 (2013): 54–70; Suzan J. M. Sierksma-Agteres, "Imitation in Faith: Enacting Paul's Ambiguous *Pistis Christou* Formulations on a Greco-Roman Stage," *International Journal of Philosophy and Theology* 77 (2016): 119–53, at 127–34; David Sedley, "Becoming Godlike," in *The Cambridge Companion to Ancient Ethics*, ed. Christopher Bobonich (Cambridge: Cambridge University Press, 2017), 319–37. Sedley explains that for Plato and Aristotle the contemplative, intellectual life is superior to the moral and civic life because even though the virtuous civic life leads to human happiness (εὐδαιμονία), the intellectual life (and the mind as the divine component in humans), resembles the divine and is the preferred route to εὐδαιμονία ("Godlike," 323, 325, 327, 335–36).

17. See, for example, Copan, *Saint Paul*, 54–58 (although he mentions a range of seemingly random examples from both Greek and Jewish texts across five centuries); Sierksma-Agteres, "Imitation in Faith," 122. For the use of personal example in Greco-Roman society, see Fiore, *Personal Example*, 33–35; Castelli, *Imitating Paul*, 82–85; Teresa Morgan, *Popular Morality in the Early Roman Empire* (Cambridge: Cambridge University Press, 2007), 122–59.

18. De Boer, *Imitation of Paul*, 2, 6–7, 25–26.

19. Dupertois, "Writing and Imitation," 4–8. For a general treatment of the role of mimesis in ancient education, see Pitts, "Origins of Greek Mimesis," 109–29.

20. Meeks, *Moral World*, 21; Fiore, "Paul," 234; Fiore, *Personal Example*, 34–35.

21. For a broader discussion of the reception of Aristotelian ethics in the Roman era, see

ancient Greco-Roman world knew about imitating others—whether god, parent, or teacher. Important for our study is that, as de Boer points out, "the process of imitation need not be a dull uncreative repetition of something or someone else. Imitation may also include the creative activity of bringing things, ideas, and persons to expression."[22] Before we examine the writings of Plato, Aristotle, and prominent orators, we will briefly look at mimesis in fifth-century BCE Athenian drama.

2.1.1. Theatrical Mimesis and Civic Education

In Greek antiquity, philosophy, theater, poetry, music, and the other arts related inextricably to daily life with all its religious, political, and ethical dimensions.[23] Regarding the dynamics of classic Attic tragedy in the fifth century BCE, Martha Nussbaum explains that at religious festivals (especially in honor of Dionysus), the entire city gathered to watch and rate the performance of several dramas. The plot of tragic dramas revolved around the reversal in the fortunes of a hero(ine), who was typically a good person endowed by fortunes such as good birth and status. The reversal caused or threatened to cause extreme misery and suffering, but such catastrophe may be averted at the last minute. Dramas in ancient Greek theater were assessed on their ethical and political content, and the spectators were actively involved in deliberation through strong emotional responses.[24] Ancient drama exemplified the moral religious-political dilemmas facing the citizens of the *polis* and hence could be considered part of the people's civic education.[25]

Ferenc Hörcher expands on the link between Athenian drama and civic education, stating, "Dramas, and in particular tragedies helped to articulate the city's political expectations from the citizens.... Theatre was regarded by the Athenian

---

Christopher Gill, "The Transformation of Aristotle's Ethics in Roman Philosophy," in *The Reception of Aristotle's Ethics*, ed. Jon Miller (Cambridge: Cambridge University Press, 2012), 31–52. He concludes that while Aristotle was not adopted wholesale but reinterpreted in light of Roman intellectual debate (especially in Stoic ethics), Aristotelian ethical ideas remained important throughout the Roman era ("Transformation," 51–52).

22. De Boer, *Imitation of Paul*, 8. Examining Theon's *Progymnasmata*, Pitts stresses that even in the early stages of education, students did not simply duplicate the oratory of great writers from the past but *reworked* their models through mimetic paraphrase ("Origins of Greek Mimesis," 111–13).

23. Martha C. Nussbaum, "Philosophy and Literature," in *The Cambridge Companion to Greek and Roman Philosophy*, ed. David Sedley (Cambridge: Cambridge University Press, 2003), 211–41, at 212.

24. Nussbaum, "Philosophy," 216–17.

25. See also Meeks, *Moral World*, 21–23.

2. Mimesis in Greco-Roman Antiquity

elite as a complex educational kit, which secured an emotional-intellectual experience through which the members of the audience learnt to reflect properly on the political challenges of their city."[26] Drawing on Aristotle's *Poetics* 1449b, Hörcher explains that Greek drama imitated or represented contemporaneous events with actors personifying protagonists as they played out the story in front of an audience that responded emotionally and intellectually.[27] Through mimetic drama, Athenian citizens learned about civic life and discerned how to behave as virtuous citizens and what mistakes to avoid.[28]

In classical Athenian drama, characters in a play reveal moral choices, and the actor imitates a character (impersonation) in order to draw the audience into an emotional response. As George Kennedy puts it, "Often the crucial factor is the ethical and emotional quality of the action or person imitated."[29] Potolsky calls this dynamic of interaction between spectator and spectacle "theatrical mimesis."[30] Classical Athenian drama, therefore, was not only about entertainment but aimed at instructing the audience about life in the *polis*, so mimesis was used in service of civic education. While Plato was apprehensive about the influence of mimetic tragedy on its audience, Aristotle was not. In tragedy, for Aristotle, there is "no divorce between understanding and emotion, thought and feeling, because to feel in the right way toward the right things just *is*, on an Aristotelian psychology, one integral part of understanding their human sense and meaning."[31] We will now examine Plato and Aristotle in greater depth as they laid the foundation for the concept of mimesis in antiquity (and even today).[32]

---

26. Ferenc Hörcher, "Dramatic Mimesis and Civic Education in Aristotle, Cicero and Renaissance Humanism," *Aisthesis* 10 (2017): 87–96, at 88.

27. Hörcher, "Dramatic Mimesis," 88–89. Aristotle, *Poetics* 1449b24–27 states: "Tragedy, then, is mimesis (μίμησις) of an action which is elevated, complete, and of magnitude; in language embellished by distinct forms in its sections; employing the mode of enactment, not narrative; and through pity and fear accomplishing the catharsis of such emotion."

28. Hörcher, "Dramatic Mimesis," 91.

29. George A. Kennedy, *Classical Rhetoric and Its Christian and Secular Tradition from Ancient to Modern Times* (London: Croom Helm, 1980), 117. Likewise, Halliwell states, "Audiences of tragedy . . . are thus conceived of as engaged observers" (*Aesthetics of Mimesis*, 81).

30. Potolsky, *Mimesis*, 73. For a popular treatment of mimesis in theater, see Paul Woodruff, *The Necessity of Theatre: The Art of Watching and Being Watched* (Oxford: Oxford University Press, 2008), 123–40.

31. Halliwell, *Aesthetics of Mimesis*, 203 (original emphasis).

32. For a brief introduction to Plato and Aristotle's views on mimesis, see Andrea Nightingale, "Mimesis: Ancient Greek Literary Theory," in *Literary Theory and Criticism: An Oxford Guide*, ed. Patricia Waugh (Oxford: Oxford University Press, 2006), 37–47.

2.1.2. Plato and Aristotle

The background and origins of the pre-Platonic concept of mimesis are not clear and the concept related to a range of meanings, such as "imitation," "representation," and "portrayal."[33] Halliwell even issues a warning that "the etymology of Greek *mim-* terms is irrecoverable with any confidence . . . and we know very little about the early history of the word group to which the noun *mimēsis*, itself not attested before the fifth century, belongs."[34] Also, in Plato, mimesis is a heterogeneous concept where meanings fluctuate and contradict each other.[35] As Gebauer and Wulf explain, there is no unified concept of mimesis in Plato. Prior to his critique of mimesis in the *Republic*, Plato could refer to mimesis positively, for example, stating that "all our polity (πολιτεία) is framed as a representation (μίμησις) of the fairest and best life" (*Leg.* 817b), or that the earthly world is a representation/imitation (μίμησις) of the heavenly world (*Tim.* 39d–e).[36] Aristotle develops Plato's concept of mimesis and restricts it to aesthetics (poetry, art, music).[37] Even so, our interest is in human mimesis or mimetic ethics—the imitation of role models in order to become like the models—because mimesis is almost exclusively an ethical concept in early Christianity.

This takes us to Plato's critique of mimesis in books 3 and 10 of the *Republic*, where he examines the role of mimesis in education in the context of civic life. Plato is concerned with the education of the guardian class so that they can fulfill the duties assigned to them by the state. Young people essentially learn through imitation, striving to become like the model, so the selection of appropriate models is crucial. Poetry plays a major role in education because it is a primary source for providing young people with examples and models. Since negative models hamper the ability of young people to fulfill their state-assigned duties as guardians later, Plato seeks to curate poetry and the models contained in it.[38] This needs elaboration.

In book 3 of the *Republic*, Plato (through the persona of Socrates) examines the relation between mimesis and education, stressing that poetry is an important source of a youth's experience with examples and models. In order to realize

---

33. Gebauer and Wulf, *Mimesis*, 27–30; Halliwell, *Aesthetics of Mimesis*, 14–22. See also Zoran, "Appropriation," 472–75.

34. Halliwell, *Aesthetics of Mimesis*, 17.

35. Stephen Halliwell detects no less than ten uses of mimetic terminology in Plato (*Aristotle's Poetics* [London: Bloomsbury Academic, 1986], 121).

36. Gebauer and Wulf, *Mimesis*, 31–33.

37. Gebauer and Wulf, *Mimesis*, 6, 25. See also Halliwell, *Aesthetics of Mimesis*, 25, 38.

38. Gebauer and Wulf, *Mimesis*, 25, 33.

2. Mimesis in Greco-Roman Antiquity

poetry's potential to influence the youth's education, mimesis is brought into play, with the aim that the youth becomes like the models.[39] Hence, mimesis has a transformative capacity: "Implied in the mimesis of specific behavior is a change on the part of the imitator; the intention is to emulate a model and appropriate its abilities."[40] As Halliwell explains, "(poetic) narratives induce and shape belief in their audiences, a premise reinforced by the consideration that gods and heroes, the central characters in so many myths, have a paradigmatic standing in the value systems of the culture."[41]

Plato is deeply suspicious of poetry because (1) it can contain negative representations of gods and heroes, which, if imitated, will have a detrimental effect on the youth's education, and (2) it is excessive in that it contains more than is needed for someone to fulfill their assigned tasks as guardians.[42] Potolsky explains that Plato is not opposed to poetry in itself (he supports educational stories that ethically shape their audiences) but to the so-called "mimetic poets" who imitate the character (as in a theatrical performance) over against poets who simply narrate a story in their own voice without taking on a character role. According to Plato, these mimetic poets should be exiled from the republic. Plato argues that the guardians of the city must not be mimetic narrators; rather, they should supervise or control these stories and only promote imitations of good behavior in young people.[43] As Halliwell clarifies, "Where poetry uses the dramatic mode, the reciter is drawn intensely into, and thereby takes on, the mental and ethical cast of each speaker. So mimesis functions here as a process whereby the world of

---

39. Gebauer and Wulf, *Mimesis*, 33–34. According to Halliwell "poetry was one of the most influential forms of discourse in the traditional life of the polis" (*Aesthetics of Mimesis*, 49).

40. Gebauer and Wulf, *Mimesis*, 36. Elsewhere, Plato also acknowledges the educational role of mimesis: "The children, when they have learnt their letters and are getting to understand the written word as before they did only the spoken, are furnished with works of good poets to read as they sit in class, and are made to learn them off by heart: here they meet with many admonitions, many descriptions and praises and eulogies of good men in times past, that the boy in envy may imitate them and yearn to become even as they" (*Prot.* 325e–326a).

41. Halliwell, *Aesthetics of Mimesis*, 52. Elsewhere he calls this "psychological assimilation" in that "repeated indulgence in imaginative enactment of behavior (i.e., in mimetic role playing) shapes the disposition of the agent" (*Aesthetics of Mimesis*, 75).

42. Gebauer and Wulf, *Mimesis*, 33–35. Halliwell contends that Homeric epic and Attic tragedy are the underlying concern in the *Republic*'s critique of poetry because mimetic tragedy has a significant capacity to shape the ways in which people view and judge the world (*Aesthetics of Mimesis*, 26–27). It is unsurprising that Plato is especially critical of Homer since, as Dupertois explains, "The preeminence of Homer as a literary model in education and literature in the Greco-Roman world is unparalleled" ("Writing and Imitation," 7).

43. Potolsky, *Mimesis*, 18–21.

the poem *becomes* the world of the mind imaginatively (re)en-acting it.... These practices, inculcated through education, invite the reciter to step with imaginatively rich feeling into the roles of the poetic agents, much more so than with the habits of silent reading."[44]

The following extract from book 3 of the *Republic* illustrates Plato's reasoning:

> "So don't [poets] achieve this either by a simple narrative, or by means of imitation, or a combination of both?" ... "But whenever [the mimetic poet] makes a speech as if he were another person, are we going to say that he will then model his speech as far as possible on that of the individual himself who he announces is about to speak?" ... "Then in such circumstances, it seems that both he and the rest of the poets are making their narrative by imitation." ... "I think I can now make clear to you what I couldn't before, the fact that of poetry and storytelling: the one is done entirely by means of imitation, i.e., tragedy and comedy exactly as you say, and the other is the recital of the poet himself, and you would find it in particular, I suppose, in the dithyramb." ... "Or have you not observed that if imitations continue from childhood on, they become natural habits, physically, vocally and mentally?" ... "So we shall not allow those we claim to care about and who must become good men themselves, to impersonate, as they are men, a woman, either a young or an old one." ... "Then these are the two forms of expression [pure narration and narration effected through imitation] I was talking about" ... "Shall we allow into our state all these models?" ... "Then it would seem that if a man who is able because of his skills to become versatile and impersonate everything were to arrive in our state wishing to show off himself and his poems, ... we would send him away to another city ... while we ourselves would employ a more austere and less pleasing poet and story teller on account of his usefulness, who could reproduce for us the diction of a decent man and who would express his words in those forms which we laid down from the beginning [i.e., pure narration]." (*Resp.* 392d–398b)

In sum, Plato considers the mimetic narration of a story to be unnatural and have negative effects on young people, who become what they imitate. In seeking to regulate the ethical influence of mimesis, he proposes a ban on the mimetic poets from the city and that the guardians only tell appropriate stories (without mimetic narration) that promote the imitation of good people.

In book 10, as Potolsky explains, Plato extends the banning of mimetic poets to *all poetry* from the city. Plato argues that the best republic is governed by reason,

---

44. Halliwell, *Aesthetics of Mimesis*, 52–53 (original emphasis).

2. Mimesis in Greco-Roman Antiquity

whereas mimesis is contrary to reason. Mimesis is not a representation of reality but merely a reflection or semblance of reality. Imitators merely mirror or copy others' work and have no knowledge of what they represent. Mimesis does not involve knowledge but merely plays on emotion. Hence, in Plato's view, mimesis is opposed to both reality (it only reflects or gives an appearance of reality) and reason (it does not involve genuine knowledge).[45] Since the mimetic effects of tragedy go beyond the theater, and Plato seeks to avoid being ruled by emotion rather than reason, he resolves that all poetry should be banned from his republic.[46] For Plato, in art, both painting and poetry imitate reality (material objects in painting, human action and emotion in poetry); in education, children imitate the stories they hear, and this imitation shapes them; and in the theater, the audience identifies with, and imitates, the actor. Since mimesis affects individual and collective responses from birth to adulthood, it is no longer a matter of stories but a microcosm of political life and a danger to the health of the republic.[47] Consequently, the broad context of mimesis is the political-ethical life of the Greek *polis*. Since poetry, with its inherent promotion of mimesis, had a detrimental effect on education and civic life, Plato wanted to censor poetry and even banish it from the republic.[48]

Aristotle also recognizes the prominent role of mimesis in education: "From childhood, it is innate for humans to imitate (μιμεῖσθαι), and in this humans are different from other living beings, that they are most capable of imitation (μιμητικός) and learn their first lessons through imitation (μίμησις)" (*Poetics* 1448b5–9 [own translation]). Like Plato, Aristotle is concerned with controlling and limiting the role models that are available to youth because one becomes what one sees and hears (*Pol.* 1336a–b).[49] However, Aristotle does not share Plato's skepticism. For Aristotle, mimesis (in poetry and art) is not merely imitation but has creative and rational aspects.[50] The following extract from his *Poetics* shows that for Aristotle, pleasure and cognition are part of mimesis:[51]

45. Potolsky, *Mimesis*, 22–25.
46. Potolsky, *Mimesis*, 27.
47. Potolsky, *Mimesis*, 27–29.
48. For a more comprehensive account of Plato's attitudes towards mimesis, see Arne Melberg, *Theories of Mimesis*, Literature, Culture, Theory 12 (Cambridge: Cambridge University Press, 1995), 10–43.
49. Hallvard Fossheim, "Mimesis in Aristotle's Ethics," in *Making Sense of Aristotle: Essays in Poetics*, ed. Øivind Andersen and Jon Haarberg (London: Bloomsbury Academic, 2001), 73–86, at 82.
50. Potolsky, *Mimesis*, 33–37. See also de Boer, *Imitation of Paul*, 5–6; Melberg, *Theories of Mimesis*, 45–47; Halliwell, *Aesthetics of Mimesis*, 177–91; Nightingale, "Mimesis," 37–47.
51. As Halliwell puts it, Aristotle's concept of mimesis in the *Poetics* "entails the interlocking

It can be seen that poetry was broadly engendered by a pair of causes, both natural. For it is an instinct of human beings, from childhood, to engage in mimesis (μιμεῖσθαι) (indeed, this distinguishes them from other animals: man is the most mimetic (μιμητικός) of all, and it is through mimesis (μίμησις) that he develops his earliest understanding); and equally natural that everyone enjoys mimetic objects (μιμήμασι). A common occurrence indicates this: we enjoy contemplating the most precise images of things whose actual sight is painful to us, such as the forms of the vilest animals and of corpses. The explanation of this too is that understanding (μανθάνειν) gives great pleasure not only to philosophers but likewise to others too, though the latter have a smaller share in it. This is why people enjoy looking at images, because through contemplating them it comes about that they understand and infer (μανθάνειν καὶ συλλογίζεσθαι) what each element means, for instance that "this person is so-and-so." For, if one happens not to have seen the subject before, the image will not give pleasure *qua* mimesis but because of its execution or colour, or for some other such reason. Because mimesis comes naturally to us, as do melody and rhythm (that metres are categories of rhythms is obvious), in the earliest times those with special natural talents for these things gradually progressed and brought poetry into being from improvisations. (*Poetics* 1448b5–23)

Admittedly, Plato's concept of mimesis is not entirely void of reason. Blossom Stefaniw notes that for Plato, mimesis was a cognitive process: "Since Plato is so confident that there is no gap between knowing what is right and doing what is right, pedagogy and epistemology take on key ethical roles. Given his belief that better imitation results from better knowledge, competent mimesis naturally requires good pedagogy."[52] Nevertheless, it is Aristotle who develops the creative and cognitive aspects of mimesis. As Halliwell sums up, "The cognition of mimetic works entails, in essence, the perception and understanding of their representational content and structure."[53] Consequently, Aristotle is critical of indiscriminate mimesis: "The fact is that [the proud] try to imitate (μιμοῦνται) the great-souled man without being really like him, and only copy him in what they

---

functioning of three elements—pleasure, understanding, and emotion" (*Aesthetics of Mimesis*, 177). Elsewhere, he captures the gist of *Poetics* 1448b10–12 as "the cognitively grounded pleasure taken in mimesis" (*Aesthetics of Mimesis*, 184).

52. Blossom Stefaniw, "A Disciplined Mind in an Orderly World: Mimesis in Late Antique Ethical Regimes," in *Metapher–Narratio–Mimesis–Doxologie: Begründungsformen frühchristlicher und antiker Ethik*, ed. Ulrich Volp, Friedrich W. Horn, and Ruben Zimmermann, CNNTE 7, WUNT 356 (Tübingen: Mohr Siebeck, 2016), 235–55, at 239.

53. Halliwell, *Aesthetics of Mimesis*, 199.

2. Mimesis in Greco-Roman Antiquity

can, reproducing his contempt for others but not his virtuous conduct" (*Eth. nic.* 1124b). Hence, mimesis must include a cognitive dimension to avoid reducing it to a mechanical process of mindless cloning.

While the concept of mimesis rarely features in his *Nicomachean Ethics*, Aristotle seems to imply that good role models facilitate practicing the virtues and thus achieving the good life. For him, a person achieves the supreme moral good, εὐδαιμονία ("happiness," "well-being," "flourishing"), through practicing the virtues—a process he calls "habituation" (*Eth. nic.* 1103a–1104a). However, just as learning to play the harp can produce both good and bad harpists, and hence, one needs a (good) teacher, by implication, one must have good role models to perform the right activities or correct habituation (*Eth. nic.* 1103b). Elaborating on *Eth. nic.* 1176a, Hallvard Fossheim contends that students "should turn to the good man and the good man's actions as the source of insight into the human good . . . not in order to know, but in order to become more of what [the good man] already is."[54]

Friends can also be good role models. In his discussion on friends, Aristotle states that "it is clear that in everything we must imitate (μιμεῖσθαι) the better person" (*Eth. nic.* 1171b12 [own translation]). Andreas Vakirtzis explains that virtuous people can continue to cultivate their *eudaimonic* state through "character friendship" (*Eth. nic.* 1156b), where they select certain patterns in a friend's conduct and "copy" (ἀπομάττονται) these to their own life to enhance their moral development (*Eth. nic.* 1172a11–14).[55] This "copying" is not slavish imitation but a process of "interpretative mimesis" where a person observes, interprets, and imitates a virtuous action in keeping with one's own personality and abilities.[56] Hence, for Aristotle, mimesis plays a role in moral development and a person achieving εὐδαιμονία. Moreover, mimesis has creative and cognitive aspects and should not be reduced to replication.

We now turn to ancient rhetorical education to examine the role of mimesis in the moral discourses of prominent orators. I will seek to show how Greco-Roman orators understood mimetic ethics to be crucial for moral education.

2.1.3. The Isocratean Tradition

Isocrates (436–338 BCE) was a prominent Attic orator in the classical era (the fifth to fourth centuries BCE) and a contemporary of Plato. Isocrates could recommend

---

54. Fossheim, "Mimesis in Aristotle's Ethics," 81.
55. Andreas Vakirtzis, "Mimesis, Friendship, and Moral Development in Aristotle's Ethics," *Rhizomata* 3 (2015): 125–42, at 126–31.
56. Vakirtzis, "Mimesis," 136–37.

the imitation of both present and past examples: "Be not satisfied with praising good men, but imitate (μιμεῖσθε) them as well" (*Nicocles or the Cyprians* 61); "Make it your practice to talk of things that are good and honourable, that your thoughts may through habit come to be like your words. Whatever seems to you upon careful thought to be the best course, put this into effect. If there are men whose reputations you envy, imitate (μιμοῦ) their deeds" (*To Nicocles* 38); "Now I have come before you and spoken this discourse, believing that if we will only imitate (μιμησώμεθα) our ancestors we shall both deliver ourselves from our present ills and become the saviours, not of Athens alone, but of all the Hellenes" (*Areop.* 84).[57] However, the best examples for imitation, according to Isocrates, are to be found among one's family (e.g., *To Philip* 113). Two discourses in particular, *Evagoras* and *Ad Demonicum*, yield valuable insights into the workings of mimesis.

In the discourse *Evagoras*, Isocrates presents the late Evagoras, king of Salamis in Cyprus (c. 411–374 BCE), as a model ruler to Evagoras's son Nicocles. When Isocrates learns that Nicocles is honoring his father with various celebrations such as dance, music, and athletic contests, he suggests that it would be a greater honor if Evagoras's virtuous life is remembered for posterity *in words* (*Evag.* 1–4). Isocrates realizes that to praise the virtues of Evagoras in prose is far more difficult than in poetry which uses embellishment, meter, and harmony (*Evag.* 5–11). Nevertheless, Isocrates accepts the challenge and begins his account of the deeds and character of Evagoras (*Evag.* 12–72). He then explains to Nicocles why commemorating great men from the past in *written* discourse rather than statues is superior: (1) statues present bodily beauty, but deeds and character can only be observed in discourse, (2) written portrayals published throughout Greece have a far greater reach than statues which are limited to the cities where they stand, and (3) it is easier for those who desire virtue to imitate great men whose character and lives are embodied in discourse (*Evag.* 73–75). Isocrates thus submits his written account of Evagoras to Nicocles for contemplation, study, and imitation in order for him to achieve moral progress and transformation:

> For these reasons especially I have undertaken to write this discourse because I believed that for you, for your children, and for all the other descendants of Evagoras, it would be by far the best incentive, if someone should assemble his achievements, give them verbal adornment, and submit them to you for your contemplation and study. For we exhort young men to the study of philosophy by praising others in order that they, emulating (ζηλοῦντες) those who are eulogized, may desire to adopt the same pursuits, but I appeal to you and

---

57. See further Isocrates, *Archid.* 82–84; *On the Peace* 36–37, 142.

yours, using as examples (παραδείγμασι) not aliens, but members of your own family, and I counsel you to devote your attention to this, that you may not be surpassed in either word or deed by any of the Hellenes.... It is my task, therefore, and that of your other friends, to speak and to write in such fashion as may be likely to incite you to strive eagerly after those things which even now you do in fact desire; and you it behooves not to be negligent, but as at present so in the future to pay heed to yourself and to discipline your mind that you may be worthy of your father and of all your ancestors.... It is in your power not to fail in this; for if you persevere in the study of philosophy and make as great progress as heretofore, you will soon become the man it is fitting you should be. (*Evag.* 76–77, 80–81)

It follows that Isocrates did not have a simplistic or reductionist approach to mimesis. Elsewhere, Isocrates stresses that Nicocles should also seek to be an example for others: "Do not think that while all other people should live with sobriety, kings may live with license; on the contrary, let your own self-control stand as an example to the rest, realizing that the manners of the whole state are copied (ὁμοιοῦται) from its rulers" (*To Nicocles* 31).

In the discourse *Ad Demonicum*, Pseudo-Isocrates instructs Demonicus, the son of his friend Hipponicus, in moral conduct.[58] According to Pseudo-Isocrates, the learning process involves associating oneself with exemplary people to observe their lives and imitate them in order to become virtuous, and while he can point Demonicus to the exemplary lives of people like Heracles and Theseus, the most accessible example is, in fact, Demonicus's own father, Hipponicus:

Therefore, I have not invented a hortatory exercise, but have written a moral treatise; and I am going to counsel you on the objects to which young men should aspire and from what actions they should abstain, and with what sort of men they should associate and how they should regulate their own lives. For only those who have traveled this road in life have been able in the true sense to attain to virtue—that possession which is the grandest and the most enduring in the world.... This [virtue] is easy to learn from the labours of Heracles and the exploits of Theseus, whose excellence of character has impressed upon their exploits so clear a stamp of glory that not even endless time can cast oblivion upon their achievements. Nay, if you will but recall also your father's

---

58. While most scholars contend that a student of Isocrates rather than Isocrates wrote this speech, the ideas are not dissimilar to Isocrates's views (Yun Lee Too, *The Rhetoric of Identity in Isocrates: Text, Power, Pedagogy* [Cambridge: Cambridge University Press, 1995], 58n53).

principles, you will have from your own house a noble illustration (παράδειγμα) of what I am telling you. . . . I have produced a sample of the nature of Hipponicus, after whom you should pattern your life as after an ensample (πρὸς ὃν δεῖ ζῆν σε ὥσπερ πρὸς παράδειγμα), regarding his conduct as your law, and striving to imitate and emulate (μιμητὴν δὲ καὶ ζηλωτήν) your father's virtue; for it were a shame, when painters represent the beautiful among animals, for children not to imitate (μὴ μιμεῖσθαι) the noble among their ancestors. . . . for, as it is the nature of the body to be developed by appropriate exercises, it is the nature of the soul to be developed by moral precepts. Wherefore I shall endeavour to set before you concisely by what practices I think you can make the most progress toward virtue and win the highest repute in the eyes of all other men. (*Demon.* 5–12)

In the remainder of the discourse, Pseudo-Isocrates lists various moral precepts and practices that produce virtue, often stressing the need to observe and discern what to imitate. Towards the end of the discourse, Pseudo-Isocrates urges Demonicus to select the best examples of people for imitation:

With these examples (παραδείγμασι) before you, you should aspire to nobility of character, and not only abide by what I have said, but acquaint yourself with the best things in the poets as well, and learn from the other wise men also any useful lessons they have taught. For just as we see the bee settling on all the flowers, and sipping the best from each, so also those who aspire to culture ought not to leave anything untasted, but should gather useful knowledge from every source. (*Demon.* 51–52)[59]

It is evident from these examples that mimesis in the Isocratean tradition has a cognitive dimension and is more than replication. We can say more, however, about the creative and cognitive aspects of the Isocratean mimetic process. In stressing that mimesis for Isocrates is not about slavish copying or repetition of

---

59. Isocrates states elsewhere that moral progress is achieved when a person "will select from all the actions of men which bear upon his subject those examples which are the most illustrious and the most edifying; and, habituating himself to contemplate and appraise such examples, he will feel their influence not only in the preparation of a given discourse but in all the actions of his life" (*Antid.* 277). On this text, Robert Hariman concludes that the mimetic process takes time: "Character cannot be developed quickly, but it can be developed over time through reflective, critical study of models of wise action" ("Civic Education, Classical Imitation, and Democratic Polity," in *Isocrates and Civic Education*, ed. Takis Poulakos and David Depew [Austin: University of Texas Press, 2004], 217–34, at 224).

the model, Yun Lee Too explains that students should revise and adapt the model to their particular needs.[60] Robert Hariman highlights that Isocrates, in his speech *Against the Sophists*, contrasts the Sophists' educational program of literal imitation with his school's program of creative imitation. According to Isocrates, civic education as literal imitation is not useful; successful imitation requires the student to differ from the teacher's example enough to show judgment of what to use of the teacher's example to suit a specific situation.[61] Outlining his pedagogical principles, Isocrates states that to become a good orator requires, besides the necessary aptitude, much study, practice, and a creative mind. In the educational process, the teacher must not only explain the principles of oratory with great precision but also present himself as an example of oratory for his students to imitate:

> For I hold that to obtain a knowledge of the elements out of which we make and compose all discourses is not so very difficult if anyone entrusts himself, not to those who make rash promises, but to those who have some knowledge of these things. But to choose from these elements those which should be employed for each subject, to join them together, to arrange them properly, and also, not to miss what the occasion demands but appropriately to adorn the whole speech with striking thoughts and to clothe it in flowing and melodious phrase—these things, I hold, require much study and are the task of a vigorous and imaginative mind: for this, the student must not only have the requisite aptitude but he must learn the different kinds of discourse and practise himself in their use; and the teacher, for his part, must so expound the principles of the art with the utmost possible exactness as to leave out nothing that can be taught, and, for the rest, he must in himself set such an example of oratory that the students who have taken form under his instruction and are able to pattern after him (ὥστε τοὺς ἐκτυπωθέντας καὶ μιμήσασθαι δυναμένους) will, from the outset, show in their speaking a degree of grace and charm which is not found in others. When all of these requisites are found together, then the devotees of philosophy will achieve complete success. (*Against the Sophists* 16–18)

From our examination of the Isocratean tradition, we see the contours of a model of mimesis emerging: would-be imitators are presented with (1) worthy examples from past and present (especially from one's family) for (2) observation, (3) study, and (4) imitation in order to achieve (5) moral progress and become

---

60. Too, *Rhetoric of Identity*, 191.
61. Hariman, "Civic Education," 218–23.

PART 1   MIMESIS IN ANTIQUITY

virtuous. Isocrates could even present himself, albeit implicitly, as an example for others.[62] In his polemical speech *Against the Sophists*, for example, Isocrates recommends his philosophy of creative imitation over the Sophists' practice of literal imitation (see above). Elsewhere, Isocrates states that some of his (envious) peers imitate him and even use his discourses as models for their students (*Panath.* 16; see also *To Philip* 11–12, 27). It is clear that Isocrates situates mimetic education in the context of the *polis*; that is, mimesis is instrumental in civic education.[63] Hariman, for example, argues that by locating the process of imitation within the context of the Athenian city, Isocrates could redefine political discourse as a creative process in which many speakers and audiences collaborated and developed a comprehensive "voice of the city."[64] We now turn to the Roman era to explore the extent to which Roman authors continued or developed the Greek mimetic tradition.

2.2. Mimesis in Roman Antiquity

We noted earlier that the Greco-Roman world was characterized by a mimetic ethos or culture of imitation, as evidenced by a broad range of literature, inscriptions, statues, and educational practices (see n. 9). Sam Wilkinson adds that in Roman antiquity, the *mos maiorum* was an unwritten shared code of morality that demanded imitation, and if the emperor reinterpreted the *mos maiorum*, he became the new moral example to follow. Since the morality of the emperor largely determined the Roman ethical system, the imperial moral code was malleable.[65] One source of ethical material that informs us about this culture of imitation is the genre of *exempla*, where "an exemplary story (*chreia* in Greek, *exemplum* in Latin) is the short, pithy account of a saying or action of a famous man (or less often, woman)."[66] In her ground-breaking work on popular morality in the Roman Empire, Teresa Morgan shows that by the beginning of the Roman era exemplary

---

62. Too, *Rhetoric of Identity*, 186–92; Malcolm Heath, "Rhetoric and Pedagogy," in *The Oxford Handbook of Rhetorical Studies*, ed. Michael J. MacDonald (Oxford: Oxford University Press, 2017), 73–83, at 77–78.

63. For comprehensive treatments of Isocrates's program of mimetic education in the context of the *polis*, see Too, *Rhetoric of Identity*, 184–99; Hariman, "Civic Education," 217–34; Chelsea Mina Bowden, "Isocrates' Mimetic Philosophy" (MA diss., Ohio State University, 2012).

64. Hariman, "Civic Education," 225.

65. Sam Wilkinson, *Republicanism during the Early Roman Empire* (London: Continuum, 2012), 113–33.

66. Morgan, *Popular Morality*, 5.

2. Mimesis in Greco-Roman Antiquity

stories were prevalent in both Greek and Latin, and embedded in a range of literature, such as epic poetry, encomium, biography, oratory, and educational theory.[67] Similarly, Roland Mayer notes that "the imitation of examples was a practice central to Roman social life, moral behaviour, and literary production."[68]

The most comprehensive study on Roman *exempla* is by Rebecca Langlands, in which she develops an account of Roman "exemplary ethics," which she defines as "an ethics based on a body of exemplary stories which are used as a medium for communicating not only moral values (such as 'courage' and 'justice') but also ethical issues and debates, as well as a complex of meta-exemplary principles that guide learners in handling exempla and implementing their lessons."[69] Her study shows that creative imitation and critical thinking are key features of Roman exemplary ethics.[70] She explains that Roman exemplary ethics advanced Aristotelian virtue ethics by making Aristotle's philosophical and theoretical virtue ethics practical to everyday Roman life through specific examples and ethical stories that were easily disseminated and applied.[71] Nevertheless, she notes that ethics based on *exempla* are not explicitly theorized in Roman literature, whereas ethical imitation is discussed in the rhetorical literature.[72] Since our focus is on the Roman rhetorical traditions, our study will supplement that of Langlands. Hence, we will now turn to select moral discourses of Cicero, Seneca, Quintilian, and Plutarch to examine what these yield regarding the workings of mimesis.

2.2.1. Cicero

Marcus Tullius Cicero (106–43 BCE) was a statesman, orator, lawyer, and philosopher whose concept of rhetorical learning through imitation was primarily in service of civic education.[73] The theme of imitation occurs frequently in Cicero's

---

67. Morgan, *Popular Morality*, 123. For the widespread use of *exampla* in the Roman era, see Morgan, *Popular Morality*, 122–59.

68. Roland G. Mayer, "Roman Historical *Exempla* in Seneca," in *Seneca: Oxford Readings in Classical Studies*, ed. John G. Fitch (Oxford: Oxford University Press, 2008), 299–315, at 300.

69. Langlands, *Exemplary Ethics*, 3–4. Others who have explored the widespread use of Greco-Roman *exempla* include William Turpin, "Tacitus, Stoic *Exempla*, and the *praecipuum munus annalium*," *ClAnt* 27 (2008): 359–404; Peter-Ben Smit, *Paradigms of Being in Christ: A Study of the Epistle to the Philippians*, LNTS 476 (New York: Bloomsbury T&T Clark, 2013), 16–30; Petitfils, *Mos Christianorum*, 17–46.

70. Langlands, *Exemplary Ethics*, 8, 336–37.

71. Langlands, *Exemplary Ethics*, 126–27.

72. Langlands, *Exemplary Ethics*, 86, 95–96.

73. For Cicero's program of civic education through imitation, see Hörcher, "Dramatic Mimesis," 91–93; Harrison, "Imitation," 225–27.

De officiis, a three-volume treatise to instruct his son Marcus. Cicero's advice to young people who aspire to greatness in public life is to select suitable examples for imitation and to associate with them (presumably to observe them) in order to become like them:

> As, then, in everything else brain-work is far more important than mere handwork, so those objects which we strive to attain through intellect and reason gain for us a higher degree of gratitude than those which we strive to gain by physical strength. The best recommendation, then, that a young man can have to popular esteem proceeds from self-restraint, filial affection, and devotion to kinsfolk. Next to that, young men win recognition most easily and most favourably, if they attach themselves to men who are at once wise and renowned as well as patriotic counsellors in public affairs. And if they associate constantly with such men, they inspire in the public the expectation that they will be like them, seeing that they have themselves selected them for imitation (*ad imitandum*). (*Off.* 2.46)

He recommends certain figures of the past as models for oratory and conversational speech (*Off.* 1.132–134) but can also present himself as an example for his son to follow: "For I may boast to you, my son Marcus; for to you belong the inheritance of that glory of mine and the duty of imitating my deeds" (*Off.* 1.78; see also 3.6). At the same time, Cicero indicates that discernment is essential to the process of imitation. He warns against blindly imitating everything about one's ancestors; one should not imitate their faults or the virtues beyond one's abilities (*Off.* 1.121).[74]

De oratore describes a dialogue between Lucius Crassus and Marcus Antonius, in which Cicero draws on great historical examples such as Isocrates, although preferring Roman examples, to describe the true or ideal orator (see, e.g., *De or.* 1.6–23; 2.92–95). As Elaine Fantham explains, Cicero knows of two (competing) forms of imitation—the imitation of past Athenian orators and that of contemporary Roman orators—and *De oratore* focuses on the latter.[75] For our purposes, *De or.* 2.85–98 is instructive since we learn how Antonius draws on practical experience to argue for what makes a good orator. Those who have a natural

---

74. Cicero critiques, for example, those who readily imitate Lucius Lucullus's magnificent villas but not his virtues (*Off.* 1.140).

75. Elaine Fantham, "Imitation and Evolution: The Discussion of Rhetorical Imitation in Cicero *De oratore* 2.87–97 and Some Related Problems of Ciceronian Theory," *CP* 73 (1978): 1–16, at 2.

2. Mimesis in Greco-Roman Antiquity

ability for oratory should first select a suitable model to imitate and then imitate only the best features of the model through constant practice:[76]

> Let this then be my first counsel, that we show the student whom to copy (*imitetur*), and to copy in such a way as to strive with all possible care to attain the most excellent qualities of his model. Next let practice be added, whereby in copying he may reproduce the pattern of his choice and not portray him as time and again I have known many copyists do, who in copying hunt after such characteristics as are easily copied or even abnormal and possibly faulty.... Let him then, who hopes by imitation (*imitatione*) to attain this likeness, carry out his purpose by frequent and large practice. (*De or.* 2.90, 96)

Cicero stresses that discernment is needed in both the selection of a model and what to imitate from the model: "[The student] who is to proceed aright must first be watchful in making his choice [of a model for imitation], and afterwards extremely careful in striving to attain the most excellent qualities of the model he has approved" (*De or.* 2.92). To support his claims, Antonius refers to Sulpicius as a positive and Fusius as a negative example. Antonius had observed that many students imitate what is easy (e.g., someone's dress, attitude, or posture) or even what is imperfect (e.g., something offensive in one's character), and mentions Fusius as someone who did not know how to choose an appropriate model and who preferred to copy the blemishes in the model that he did choose (*De or.* 2.91). Conversely, when Antonius notes young Sulpicius's potential for oratory, he advises him to pursue the profession and choose Crassus as an example for imitation. Sulpicius eagerly follows Antonius's advice but also selects Antonius as his master. After just one year, Antonius notes that the combination of study and imitation has resulted in a remarkable transformation of Sulpicius's oratory skills:[77]

> I [M. Antonius] instantly perceived [Sulpicius's] quality and did not miss the opportunity, but urged him to regard the law-courts as his school of instruction, choosing what master he pleased, but Lucius Crassus if he would take my advice; he caught at this suggestion and assured me that he would follow it, adding, out of politeness of course, that I too should be his teacher. Scarcely a year had elapsed, after this advisory talk with me, when our friend prosecuted Gaius Norbanus, whom I was defending. Incredible was the difference I saw

---

76. See also Fantham, "Imitation and Evolution," 4–5; Langlands, *Exemplary Ethics*, 113–14.
77. Elsewhere, Antonius acknowledges that there are also people whose achievements result from their own natural abilities rather than imitating others (*De or.* 2.98).

> between the Sulpicius of that day and of a year earlier. Assuredly Nature herself was leading him into the grand and glorious style of Crassus, but could never have made him proficient enough, had he not pressed forward on that same way by careful imitation (*imitatione*), and formed the habit of speaking with every thought and all his soul fixed in contemplation of Crassus. (*De or.* 2.89)

The main reason for Sulpicius's success, Elaine Fantham explains, was that his temperament or nature suited the oratory style of Crassus rather than that of Antonius.[78] Elsewhere, Cicero points to Isocrates's use of contrasting methods in training two different students (*De or.* 3.26–37) to show that a good teacher will "direct the pupil where his natural bent leads him."[79] Thus, the realization of an aspiring orator's potential requires a fusion of natural abilities with the right model for imitation, which implies that the best rhetorical traditions do not demand the exact cloning of one oratory style but can have "controlled divergence" within a generation.[80] Based on a brief history of Greek oratory in *De or.* 2.92–95, Cicero shows that mimesis allows for continuity and development, effecting an "oratory evolution" across generations where each generation of orators retained a style similar to yet distinct from that of the previous generation. Hence, imitation is reproduction because imitator-pupils go on to become models for imitation.[81] For Cicero, mimesis thus involves both nature and nurture, similarity and difference—good imitation involves selecting the best models (those that correspond to one's own nature and talents) and seeking to improve on those models (combining the best of the models with one's own talents).[82]

Cicero's other writings show similar aspects of mimesis. Regarding the selection and observation of people worthy of imitation, he exhorts young people (especially those of noble birth) to imitate the example of honorable statesmen who have gone before in order to attain honor, dignity, and praise (*Sest.* 47–48, 65, 68), but he also recommends "living examples" (*Div. Caec.* 25; see also *Verr.* 2.3.41). Cicero suggests

---

78. Fantham, "Imitation and Evolution," 4, 14.
79. Fantham, "Imitation and Evolution," 13.
80. Fantham, "Imitation and Evolution," 13–14.
81. Fantham, "Imitation and Evolution," 5–11. At the same time, Cicero also notes that oratory tends to decline when memory of past examples is fading: "As long as the imitation of these [past models] persisted, so long did their kind of oratory and course of training endure. Afterwards, when these men were dead and all remembrance of them gradually grew dim and then vanished away, certain other less spirited and lazier styles of speaking flourished" (*De or.* 2.95). Fantham thus rightly remarks that Cicero conceived imitation as a memory-based process ("Imitation and Evolution, 12n34).
82. See also Fantham, "Imitation and Evolution," 14.

that imitating a living example in one's family would be most effective (*Mur.* 66), but he could also present himself as an example for imitation: "Follow my example; you have always commended me" (*Phil.* 11.23). Giuseppe La Bua argues that Cicero consciously sets himself up as a model for imitation: "He advertised himself as a follower of specific moral and political models of behavior and promoted himself, at the same time, as an *exemplum* worthy of imitation. By replicating ancient role models and expressing pride in his own political achievements he created an image of himself as a credible statesman and an exemplary advocate."[83]

Essential to the process of imitation is discernment or analysis of what is observed. Thus, Cicero writes, "But I believe that the immortal gods implanted souls in human bodies so as to have beings who would care for the earth and who, while contemplating the celestial order, would imitate (*imitarentur*) it in the moderation and consistency of their lives" (*Sen.* [*Cato the Elder: On Old Age*] 77). Elsewhere, he recommends the "observation" and study of past examples: "How many pictures of high endeavour the great authors of Greece and Rome have drawn for our use, and bequeathed to us, not only for our contemplation, but for our emulation (*imitandum*)! These I have held ever before my vision throughout my public career, and have guided the workings of my brain and my soul by meditating upon patterns of excellence" (*Arch.* 14). Cicero's influence on Seneca and Quintilian is evidenced in their writings, to which we now turn.

2.2.2. Seneca (*the Younger*)

Seneca (4 BCE–65 CE) was a Roman Stoic philosopher and statesman. For our study, we will look at the *Epistulae Morales ad Lucilium*, a collection of 124 letters dealing with moral issues written to Lucilius, the procurator of Sicily during the reign of Nero. From these letters, we learn that Cicero serves as a significant example for Seneca. On an issue of language, Seneca writes, "I have Cicero as authority for the use of this word, and I regard him as a powerful authority" (*Ep.* 58.6). In *Ep.* 100.7, Seneca recommends Cicero's writing style over that of others: "Read Cicero: his style has unity; it moves with a modulated pace, and is gentle without being degenerate. The style of Asinius Pollio, on the other hand, is 'bumpy,' jerky, leaving off when you least expect it. And finally, Cicero always stops gradually; while Pollio breaks off." On the topic of aligning oneself with the order of the universe, Seneca writes, "Let us address Jupiter, the pilot of this world-mass, as did our great

---

83. Giuseppe La Bua, *Cicero and Roman Education: The Reception of the Speeches and Ancient Scholarship* (Cambridge: Cambridge University Press, 2019), 302. Indeed, Cicero became an influential example for Quintilian (*Inst.* 10.1.108, 112).

Cleanthes in those most eloquent lines—lines which I shall allow myself to render in Latin, after the example of the eloquent Cicero. If you like them, make the most of them; if they displease you, you will understand that I have simply been following the practice of Cicero (*secutum Ciceronis exemplum*)" (*Ep.* 107.10).

In this large collection, some letters provide insight into Seneca's understanding of the workings and relevance of mimesis.[84] In *Ep.* 6, Seneca states that he is keen to share with Lucilius the knowledge that has transformed him. However, while he will send Lucilius the relevant books (and mark up the relevant passages), Seneca points out that living examples are more beneficial:

> I shall therefore send to you the actual books; and in order that you may not waste time in searching here and there for profitable topics, I shall mark certain passages, so that you can turn at once to those which I approve and admire. Of course, however, the living voice and the intimacy of a common life will help you more than the written word. You must go to the scene of action, first, because men put more faith in their eyes than in their ears, and second, because the way is long if one follows precepts, but short and helpful, if one follows patterns (*exempla*). Cleanthes could not have been the express image of Zeno, if he had merely heard his lectures; he shared in his life, saw into his hidden purposes, and watched him to see whether he lived according to his own rules. Plato, Aristotle, and the whole throng of sages who were destined to go each his different way, derived more benefit from the character than from the words of Socrates. It was not the class-room of Epicurus, but living together under the same roof, that made great men of Metrodorus, Hermarchus, and Polyaenus. (*Ep.* 6.5–6)

In his advice to Lucilius, Seneca advocates associating with appropriate role models, where students can observe and study the lives of great men, because (1) learning through observing and imitating exemplars is superior to reading books, and (2) it is faster than following precepts. This letter near the start of the collection seems foundational because Seneca elaborates on these mimetic dynamics in subsequent letters.

In *Ep.* 7, Seneca stresses that choosing the right models requires discernment because one should select exemplars that lead to moral improvement: "You should

---

84. In his overview of the widespread use of example and call to imitation in Greco-Roman antiquity, Fiore draws specific attention to Seneca's moral epistles, where Seneca presents himself as a friend who advises and instructs, suggesting that epistolary presence (personal presence achieved through a letter) may be more effective and purer than physical presence ("Paul," 235–36; *Personal Example*, 88).

2. Mimesis in Greco-Roman Antiquity

not copy the bad simply because they are many, nor should you hate the many because they are unlike you. Withdraw into yourself, as far as you can. Associate with those who will make a better man of you. Welcome those whom you yourself can improve" (*Ep.* 7.8). So, in *Ep.* 104, Seneca urges Lucilius to "live with" (i.e., study and cultivate) great men from the past, such as Socrates, Zeno, Chrysippus, and Cato (*Ep.* 104.16–33). Nevertheless, while Seneca promotes both past and living examples, he prefers the latter. In *Ep.* 52, for example, Seneca's advice on selecting appropriate role models is that although he acknowledges that one can learn from past examples, he recommends appropriate living examples—those who practice what they teach—because their lives can be observed:

> "Whom," you say, "shall I call upon? Shall it be this man or that?" There is another choice also open to you; you may go to the ancients; for they have the time to help you. We can get assistance not only from the living, but from those of the past. Let us choose, however, from among the living, not men who pour forth their words with the greatest glibness, turning out commonplaces and holding, as it were, their own little private exhibitions,—not these, I say, but men who teach us by their lives, men who tell us what we ought to do and then prove it by practice, who show us what we should avoid, and then are never caught doing that which they have ordered us to avoid. Choose as a guide one whom you will admire more when you see him act than when you hear him speak. (*Ep.* 52.7–9)

William Turpin shows that the Stoics considered *exempla* to be useful for moral reflection because people often lacked the insight to make the right choices, and reflecting on the actions of others could help in this.[85] Similarly, in her study of Seneca's family ethics, Liz Gloyn notes, "*Exempla* are good to think with; they do not offer their readers simple, easy lessons, but require reflection to be understood."[86] She argues that for Seneca, those close to us are particularly effective educational models, and hence, the family (as a microcosm of the state) offers a better source of *exempla* for moral behavior than historical figures.[87] For Seneca, the ultimate aim of a virtuous life is to become an example oneself: "Let us be included among the ideal types of history (*simus inter exempla*)" (*Ep.* 98.14).[88] As Turpin notes, the Stoics were aware of "the connection between exempla from the

---

85. Turpin, "Tacitus," 369–73, 395.
86. Liz Gloyn, *The Ethics of the Family in Seneca* (Cambridge: Cambridge University Press, 2017), 130.
87. Gloyn, *Ethics of the Family*, 10, 203.
88. Fiore, "Paul," 235; Mayer, "*Exempla* in Seneca," 299.

past and their own potential as role models in the present, and for the future."[89] For Seneca, *exempla* played a vital role in the moral life of society because they "perpetually represent to succeeding generations the sort of actions which lead us to conceptualize 'moral excellence.'"[90]

Discernment is not only needed in one's choice of models but also in what to imitate. In *Ep.* 33, Seneca critiques the concept of slavish imitation of others or mere replication of precepts, suggesting that one should seek to improve on their models:

> For a man, however, whose progress is definite, to chase after choice extracts and to prop his weakness by the best known and the briefest sayings and to depend upon his memory, is disgraceful; it is time for him to lean on himself. He should make such maxims and not memorize them. For it is disgraceful even for an old man, or one who has sighted old age, to have a note-book knowledge. "This is what Zeno said." But what have you yourself said? "This is the opinion of Cleanthes." But what is your own opinion? How long shall you march under another man's orders? Take command, and utter some word which posterity will remember. Put forth something from your own stock. For this reason I hold that there is nothing of eminence in all such men as these, who never create anything themselves, but always lurk in the shadow of others, playing the role of interpreters, never daring to put once into practice what they have been so long in learning. They have exercised their memories on other men's material. But it is one thing to remember, another to know. Remembering is merely safeguarding something entrusted to the memory; knowing, however, means making everything your own; it means not depending upon the copy and not all the time glancing back at the master. "Thus said Zeno, thus said Cleanthes, indeed!" Let there be a difference between yourself and your book! How long shall you be a learner? From now on be a teacher as well! "But why," one asks, "should I have to continue hearing lectures on what I can read?" "The living voice," one replies, "is a great help." Perhaps, but not the voice which merely makes itself the mouthpiece of another's words, and only performs the duty of a reporter. Consider this fact also. Those who have never attained their mental independence begin, in the first place, by following the leader in cases where everyone has deserted the leader; then, in the second place, they follow him in matters where the truth is still being investigated. However, the truth will never be discovered if we rest contented with discoveries already made. Besides, he who follows another not only discovers nothing, but is not

89. Turpin, "Tacitus," 373.
90. Mayer, "*Exempla* in Seneca," 312.

even investigating. What then? Shall I not follow in the footsteps of my predecessors? I shall indeed use the old road, but if I find one that makes a shorter cut and is smoother to travel, I shall open the new road. Men who have made these discoveries before us are not our masters, but our guides. Truth lies open for all; it has not yet been monopolized. And there is plenty of it left even for posterity to discover. (*Ep.* 33.7–11)

In *Ep.* 84, Seneca stresses that mimesis is a creative and cognitive activity rather than mere replication. He arrives at this insight from observing how bees make a new substance (honey) from the juices collected from various flowers (*Ep.* 84.3–4; see also Isocrates, *Demon.* 52). Hence, like Cicero, Seneca recommends an eclectic approach to choosing what to imitate from multiple models, in keeping with one's natural abilities, in order to create something new:

We also, I say, ought to copy these bees, and sift whatever we have gathered from a varied course of reading, for such things are better preserved if they are kept separate; then, by applying the supervising care with which our nature has endowed us,—in other words, our natural gifts,—we should so blend those several flavours into one delicious compound that, even though it betrays its origin, yet it nevertheless is clearly a different thing from that whence it came. This is what we see nature doing in our own bodies without any labour on our part; the food we have eaten, as long as it retains its original quality and floats in our stomachs as an undiluted mass, is a burden; but it passes into tissue and blood only when it has been changed from its original form. So it is with the food which nourishes our higher nature,—we should see to it that whatever we have absorbed should not be allowed to remain unchanged, or it will be no part of us. We must digest it; otherwise it will merely enter the memory and not the reasoning power.... Even if there shall appear in you a likeness to him who, by reason of your admiration, has left a deep impress upon you, I would have you resemble him as a child resembles his father, and not as a picture resembles its original; for a picture is a lifeless thing. "What," you say, "will it not be seen whose style you are imitating (*imiteris*), whose method of reasoning, whose pungent sayings?" I think that sometimes it is impossible for it to be seen who is being imitated, if the copy is a true one; for a true copy stamps its own form upon all the features which it has drawn from what we may call the original, in such a way that they are combined into a unity. (*Ep.* 84.5–9)

The use of the cognitive terms "sift," "digest," and "reasoning" indicates that for Seneca, the selection of models and what to imitate about them, as well as the

PART 1   MIMESIS IN ANTIQUITY

mental processing of what is being imitated, should lead to transformation. Although the original influences can be detected, the end result is something new rather than a mere copy. For Seneca, the selection of an appropriate model leads to moral progress or character transformation:[91]

> "Cherish some man of high character, and keep him ever before your eyes, living as if he were watching you, and ordering all your actions as if he beheld them." Such, my dear Lucilius, is the counsel of Epicurus; he has quite properly given us a guardian and an attendant. We can get rid of most sins, if we have a witness who stands near us when we are likely to go wrong. The soul should have someone whom it can respect,—one by whose authority it may make even its inner shrine more hallowed. Happy is the man who can make others better, not merely when he is in their company, but even when he is in their thoughts! And happy also is he who can so revere a man as to calm and regulate himself by calling him to mind! One who can so revere another, will soon be himself worthy of reverence. Choose therefore a Cato; or, if Cato seems too severe a model, choose some Laelius, a gentler spirit. Choose a master whose life, conversation, and soul-expressing face have satisfied you; picture him always to yourself as your protector or your pattern (*exemplum*). For we must indeed have someone according to whom we may regulate our characters. (*Ep.* 11.8–10)

The contours of the mimetic model that emerged from the Isocratean tradition become clearer in Cicero and Seneca: (1) to select and associate with appropriate exemplars; (2) to observe them; (3) to discern what needs emulation; (4) to emulate (aspects of) the exemplar; and (5) moral progression/transformation. Our examination of Quintilian and Plutarch will reveal whether their writings support this model.

2.2.3. *Quintilian*

Marcus Fabius Quintilian (35–100 CE) was a Roman educator and rhetorician. Around 95 CE, he published the *Institutio Oratoria*, a twelve-volume textbook on the theory and practice of rhetoric, and book 10 is important for our study.[92] Cice-

---

91. Sierksma-Agteres, "Imitation in Faith," 125. Reinhard Feldmeier notes that, in *Ep.* 31.11, Seneca exhorts the drawing closer to God and assimilating to him ("'As Your Heavenly Father Is Perfect': The God of the Bible and Commandments in the Gospel," *Int* 70 [2016]: 431–44, at 433).

92. For the role of imitation in Quintilian's pedagogy, see Robert E. Terrill, "Reproducing Virtue: Quintilian, Imitation, and Rhetorical Education," *Advances in the History of Rhetoric* 19

2. Mimesis in Greco-Roman Antiquity

ro's influence on Quintilian is evident from the following excerpt where Quintilian endorses Cicero as the prime example for imitation:

> It seems to me, in fact, that Cicero, having devoted himself entirely to the imitation (*ad imitationem*) of the Greeks, succeeded in reproducing the forcefulness of Demosthenes, the abundance of Plato, and the elegance of Isocrates.... It was not without reason that his contemporaries said he was "king" of the courts, and that for posterity Cicero has become not so much the name of a man as a synonym for eloquence itself. Let us fix our eyes on him, let him be the model (*exemplum*) we set before ourselves; if a student comes to love Cicero, let him assure himself that he has made progress. (*Inst.* 10.1.108–109, 112)

Quintilian notes that instruction accompanied by personal example is crucial in the mimetic process of learning and much more powerful than mere instruction:

> However, while a stock of words may be acquired in this way, we should not read or listen solely for the sake of the words. For in the same sources are to be found examples (*exempla*) of everything we teach, examples which are in fact more powerful than those found in the textbooks (at least when the learner has reached the stage of being able to understand without a teacher and follow on his own) because the orator demonstrates what the teacher only prescribed. (*Inst.* 10.1.15)

Quintilian continues, asserting that the object for imitation must be studied and interpreted:

> Reading is independent; it does not pass over us with the speed of a performance, and you can go back over it again and again if you have any doubts or if you want to fix it firmly in your memory. Let us go over the text again and work on it. We chew our food and almost liquefy it before we swallow, so as to digest it more easily; similarly, let our reading be made available for memory and imitation (*memoriae imitationique*), not in an undigested form, but, as it were, softened and reduced to pap by frequent repetition. (*Inst.* 10.1.19)

Section 2 of book 10 opens by emphasizing that imitation is innate and vital in every branch of learning:

(2016): 157–71; Adriana Maria Schippers, "Dionysius and Quintilian: Imitation and Emulation in Greek and Latin Literary Criticism" (PhD diss., Leiden University, 2019), 125–85, esp. 132–38.

> It is from these and other authors worth reading that we must draw our stock of words, the variety of our Figures, and our system of Composition, and also guide our minds by the patterns (*exemplum*) they provide of all the virtues. It cannot be doubted that a large part of art consists of imitation (*imitatione*). Invention of course came first and is the main thing, but good inventions are profitable to follow. Moreover, it is a principle of life in general that we want to do for ourselves what we approve in others. Children follow the outlines of letters so as to become accustomed to writing; singers find their model in their teacher's voice, painters in the works of their predecessors, and farmers in methods of cultivation which have been tested by experience. In a word, we see the rudiments of every branch of learning shaped by standards prescribed for it. (*Inst.* 10.2.1–2)

While mimesis is a sensory process in which the student observes what needs imitating, Quintilian notes that this could easily become reductionist and repetitious without any effect. He stresses that mimesis must not be limited to mere replication but should be creative and innovative, aimed at improvement or moral progress:[93]

> That [mindless imitation] would make us like certain painters, who study only to learn how to copy pictures by means of measurements and lines. It is a disgrace too to be content merely to attain the effect you are imitating. Once again, what would have happened if no one had achieved more than the man he was following? . . . [W]e should still be going to sea on rafts, and the only painting would consist in drawing outlines round the shadows cast by objects in the sun. Take a comprehensive view: no art has remained as it was when it was discovered, or come to a stop in its early stages. Or are we to condemn our own age to the unique misery of being the first period in which nothing grows? And nothing does grow by imitation (*imitatione*) alone. But if we are not allowed to add to previous achievements, how can we hope for our ideal orator? (*Inst.* 10.2.6–9)

It is this need for innovation, improvement, and excellence that leads Quintilian to stress the need for discernment in the mimetic process:

Everything in this field of study [i.e., oratory] therefore needs to be subjected to the most careful judgement. First, whom should we imitate (*quos imitemur*)?

---

93. See also Fantham, "Imitation and Decline," 104; Pitts, "Origins of Greek Mimesis," 112–14.

2. Mimesis in Greco-Roman Antiquity

Many people have developed a longing to be like the worst and most decadent speakers. Secondly, what is it in our chosen authors that we should prepare ourselves to reproduce? Even great authorities have some blemishes, which are criticized both by the learned and by the authors themselves in their mutual recriminations. If only the imitators of good qualities improved on them as much as the imitators of bad qualities exaggerate these! And even those who have judgement enough to avoid faults should not be satisfied with producing an image of excellence, a mere outer skin, as it were, or rather a "shape" like those which Epicurus says are given off by the surfaces of bodies. But this is what happens to those who adapt themselves to the superficial impression made by a speech without considering its excellences in depth. (*Inst.* 10.2.14–16)

Like Cicero and Seneca, Quintilian's advice is that imitation should be in keeping with the student's natural abilities (*Inst.* 10.2.19–21). He also recommends an eclectic approach to choosing models because different court cases require different approaches or styles (*Inst.* 10.2.23–26).[94] Quintilian concludes by stressing the need for close observance and study of the chosen models—not merely in terms of their speech but also their style and skill—in order to imitate the models accurately and even improve on them by blending the best of the models and one's own qualities (*Inst.* 10.2.27–28).[95] Recognizing Quintilian's advocacy of imitation aimed at progress, Fantham argues that the developing orator cannot simply rely on the teacher's lectures on various oratory models but must be able to undertake his *own* analysis to understand true imitation.[96]

2.2.4. Plutarch

Plutarch (46–119 CE) was a Middle Platonist philosopher and biographer. Plutarch's *Lives* are biographies of famous Greek men and their Roman counterparts to show their moral virtues or failings.[97] Tyler Smith points out that "Plutarch regularly

---

94. Fantham argues that Quintilian's eclectic approach contrasts Cicero's singular approach in *De oratore* ("Imitation and Decline," 107). Be that as it may, elsewhere, Cicero does not appear to limit attachment to a single model (see section 2.2.1). Models for imitation are not only those from the past but also the teacher as a "living example" (*Inst.* 2.2.8; see also Cicero, *Off.* 1.78) (Pitts, "Origins of Greek Mimesis," 113).

95. See also Fantham, "Imitation and Decline," 108–9; Kathleen M. Vandenberg, "Revisiting Imitation Pedagogies in Composition Studies from a Girardian Perspective," *Contagion: Journal of Violence, Mimesis, and Culture* 18 (2011): 111–34, at 115; Pitts, "Origins of Greek Mimesis," 114.

96. Fantham, "Imitation and Decline," 109. We also saw this in Seneca, *Ep.* 84.

97. While Sookgoo Shin also looks at Plutarch's *Lives*, he starts with Plutarch's *Progress in*

PART 1   MIMESIS IN ANTIQUITY

reminds readers that his chief concern is not to record the events of the past but to explore the moral character (ἦθος) of famous men as models for imitation."[98] Likewise, Alexei Zadorojnyi states, "Plutarch markets his biographical work as a resource for ethical mimesis."[99] While there is regular mention of a hero imitating a great person or a god in a particular activity (see, e.g., *Thes.* 11.1; *Rom.* 29.2; *Lyc.* 27.3; *Sol.* 29.3; *Pel.* 26.5; *Mar.* 35.1; *Cim.* 14.3; *Cat. Min.* 65.4; *Brut.* 2.1), only a few *Lives* show insights into Plutarch's understanding of the workings of mimesis.

In *Per.* 1.2–3, Plutarch describes the process of sensory perception where a person can choose to look at and be edified by a worthy object in order to make a connection with one's intellectual vision. He thus states that the admiration of virtuous deeds may likewise stimulate imitation, stressing that the one who performs the admirable deed must also be worthy of imitation. Moreover, discernment must be exercised in the mimetic process in order to achieve moral formation:

> Such objects are to be found in virtuous deeds; these implant in those who search them out a great and zealous eagerness which leads to imitation (μίμησιν). In other cases, admiration of the deed is not immediately accompanied by an impulse to do it. Nay, many times, on the contrary, while we delight in the work, we despise the workman, as, for instance, in the case of perfumes and dyes; we take a delight in them, but dyers and perfumers we regard as illiberal and vulgar folk.... For it does not of necessity follow that, if the work delights you with its grace, the one who wrought it is worthy of your esteem. Wherefore the spectator is not advantaged by those things at sight of which no ardour for imitation arises in the breast, nor any uplift of the soul arousing zealous impulses to do the like. But virtuous action straightway so disposes a man that he no sooner admires the works of virtue than he strives to emulate those who wrought them.... The Good creates a stir of activity towards itself, and implants at once in the spectator an active impulse; it does not form his

---

Virtue (*Virt. prof.*) to argue that "conversion" (the transfer of allegiance and membership to a particular group) starts the journey of moral progress and involves two stages: (1) the study of philosophy to ground the person in the convictions and beliefs of the group and (2) the imitation of virtuous deeds (*Ethics in the Gospel of John: Discipleship as Moral Progress*, BINS 168 [Leiden: Brill, 2019], 42–47).

98. Tyler Smith, *The Fourth Gospel and the Manufacture of Minds in Ancient Historiography, Biography, Romance, and Drama*, BINS 173 (Leiden: Brill, 2019), 80.

99. Alexei V. Zadorojnyi, "Mimesis and the (Plu)past in Plutarch's Lives," in *Time and Narrative in Ancient Historiography: The "Plupast" from Herodotus to Appian*, ed. Christopher B. Krebs and Jonas Grethlein (Cambridge: Cambridge University Press, 2012), 175–98, at 177.

2. Mimesis in Greco-Roman Antiquity

character by ideal representation (μιμήσει) alone, but through the investigation of its work it furnishes him with a dominant purpose. (*Per.* 1.4; 2.2–3)

Elsewhere, Plutarch also stresses that discernment is required in what to imitate about the exemplar: "But although Demosthenes, as it would appear, did not regard the other characteristics of Pericles as suitable for himself, he admired and sought to imitate the formality of his speech and bearing" (*Dem.* 9.3). As Tim Duff explains, most protagonists are not stock examples of virtue or vice, so moral judgments are left implicit and readers must discern where an action is to be praised or blamed.[100]

The following excerpts show that the mimetic process contains aspects of association with a worthy exemplar in order to observe and discern what to imitate. In *Demetrius*, Plutarch states that "the arts . . . proceed by the use of reason to the selection and adoption of what is appropriate, and to the avoidance and rejection of what is alien to themselves" (*Demetr.* 1.2). He then uses another analogy to make the point that exposure to good and bad examples leads to a greater appreciation of imitating the good:

> Ismenias the Theban used to exhibit both good and bad players to his pupils on the flute and say, "you must play like this one," or again, "you must not play like this one"; and Antigenidas used to think that young men would listen with more pleasure to good flute-players if they were given an experience of bad ones also. So, I think, we also shall be more eager to observe and imitate (θεαταὶ καὶ μιμηταί) the better lives if we are not left without narratives of the blameworthy and the bad. (*Demetr.* 1.6)

In *Tiberius et Caius Gracchus*, Plutarch speaks of how Tiberius became virtuous and worthy of praise already at a young age. He recounts an incident where young Tiberius served in Africa to show that the association with, and study of, a role model stimulates imitation:

> The younger Tiberius, accordingly, serving in Africa under the younger Scipio, who had married his sister, and sharing his commander's tent, soon learned to

---

100. Tim Duff, *Plutarch's Lives: Exploring Virtue and Vice* (Oxford: Clarendon Press, 1999), 54–56. In my work on characterization in Greco-Roman antiquity, I have extensively argued that many protagonists in Greco-Roman literature are more complex and varied than previously assumed (Cornelis Bennema, *A Theory of Character in New Testament Narrative* [Minneapolis: Fortress, 2014], 35–44).

understand that commander's nature (which produced many great incentives towards the emulation of virtue and its imitation in action [ζῆλον ἀρετῆς καὶ μίμησιν ἐπὶ τῶν πράξεων]), and soon led all the young men in discipline and bravery. (*Ti. C. Gracch.* 4.4)

Plutarch's other writings present similar aspects of the mimetic process, one example being that moral progress through imitation starts with admiration. Just as words leading to actions constitute progress, so admiration for successful men should lead to imitating them in order to make moral progress (*Virt. prof.* 84b–c). In *Adol. poet. aud.* 8, Plutarch stresses that young people should not simply accept all they read in poetry about the heroes; rather, they should exercise discernment to determine what to imitate:

> Let the young man, then, not get into the habit of commending anything like this, nor let him be plausible and adroit in making excuses or in contriving some specious quibbles to explain base actions, but rather let him cherish the belief that poetry is an imitation (μίμησιν) of character and lives, and of men who are not perfect or spotless or unassailable in all respects, but pervaded by emotions, false opinions, and sundry forms of ignorance, who yet through inborn goodness frequently change their ways for the better. For if the young man is so trained, and his understanding so framed, that he feels elation and a sympathetic enthusiasm over noble words and deeds, and an aversion and repugnance for the mean, such training will render his perusal of poetry harmless. But the man who admires everything, and accommodates himself to everything, whose judgement, because of his preconceived opinion, is enthralled by the heroic names, will, like those who copy (οἱ . . . ἀπομιμούμενοι) Plato's stoop or Aristotle's lisp, unwittingly become inclined to conform to much that is base. (*Adol. poet. aud.* 8 [26a–b])

At the same time, Plutarch exhorts imitators not to be blind to the faults in exemplars:

> But since "love is blind regarding the loved one," as Plato says, and it is rather our enemies who by their unseemly conduct afford us an opportunity to view our own, neither our joy at their failures nor our sorrow at their successes ought to go without being employed to some purpose, but we should take into account both their failures and successes in studying how by guarding against the former we may be better than they, and by imitating (μιμούμενοι) the latter no worse. (*Inim. util.* 11 [92f])

2. Mimesis in Greco-Roman Antiquity

Elsewhere too, Plutarch stresses the need for discernment in the mimetic process (*Rect. rat. aud.* 6; *Curios.* 11). As Zadorojnyi explains, since "historical examples are not directly transferable into our mimetic present... refraction, calibration and discrimination appear to be a priori settings for negotiating mimesis," so mimesis always includes a cognitive element.[101] Likewise, Duff notes that the subjects of Plutarch's *Lives* (statesmen and soldiers) are very different from Plutarch's readers, which makes the imitation of the models difficult. Nevertheless, the *Lives* contain material for moral reflection—"timeless" moral virtues that readers can gather and imitate in their own lives.[102] Shin contends that Plutarch wanted his readers to develop their moral reasoning first through the study of philosophy before discerning what to imitate when they read his *Lives* and thus being able to make moral progress.[103]

In *Adul. am.*, Plutarch warns against superficial imitation: "But just as false and counterfeit imitations of gold imitate only its brilliancy and lustre, so apparently the flatterer, imitating the pleasant and attractive characteristics of the friend, always presents himself in a cheerful and blithe mood, with never a whit of crossing or opposition" (*Adul. am.* 2 [50a–b]). A little further, Plutarch warns against imitating everything uncritically:

> I have no use for a friend that shifts about just as I do and nods assent just as I do (for my shadow better performs that function), but I want one that tells the truth as I do, and decides for himself as I do. This is one method, then, of detecting the flatterer; but here follows a second point of difference which ought to be observed, in his habits of imitation. The true friend is neither an imitator (μιμητής) of everything nor ready to commend everything, but only the best things. (*Adul. am.* 8–9 [53b–c])

Plutarch follows Plato in stating that the imitation of God is most virtuous: "Consider first that God, as Plato says, offers himself to all as a pattern (παράδειγμα) of every excellence, thus rendering human virtue, which is in some sort an assimilation to himself, accessible to all who can 'follow God'" (*Sera* 5 [550d]).[104] When it comes to human exemplars, Plutarch recommends examples from one's

---

101. Zadorojnyi, "Mimesis," 180–81 (quotation from p. 181).
102. Duff, *Plutarch's Lives*, 66–69.
103. Shin, *Ethics in the Gospel of John*, 46.
104. "To follow God" (ἕπεσθαι θεῷ) is to imitate him. For Plutarch's notion of assimilation to God, see van Kooten, *Paul's Anthropology*, 148–54.

family—he praises the man who "patterns his life after the fairest examples in his family line" (*Arat.* 1.2)—or from the past, handed down through history (*Cons. Apoll.* 33).

Plutarch's contribution to our understanding of mimesis is summed up well by Zadorojnyi:

> Mimesis holds out a sort of magic key to unlock the Plutarchan discoursal programme, given that it brings together history, ethics, aesthetics and the ontological world-order. Yet at all times it is necessary to validate mimesis against the normative priorities. Even the most creditable models (Lycurgus, Cato, the divine) must be contextualized and approached with level-headed calibration. The *Parallel Lives* showcase the complexities of mimetic deployment of the plupast, for better or worse, by the characters and, importantly, by the internal audiences. Plutarch's primary concern, however, is to induce positive ethical response in the external readers.[105]

We are now in a position to articulate a model of mimesis across the Greco-Roman traditions.

2.3. A Model of Greco-Roman Mimesis

Our examination of the Greco-Roman traditions has shown that although mimesis as a didactic strategy for moral and civic education has its origins in the Athenian theater and the work of Plato and Aristotle, the concept is developed and discussed in greater detail in the works of Isocrates, Cicero, Seneca, Quintilian, and Plutarch.[106] Based on their moral discourses, I infer a common model of the workings of mimesis in Greco-Roman antiquity comprising five aspects:

1. *Selection and Association.* The aspiring student chooses or is presented with an exemplary model for imitation and associates himself with that person. The selection of models worthy of imitation requires discernment. Good imitation

---

105. Zadorojnyi, "Mimesis," 190.
106. While there is discussion on a possible decline of Roman oratory and *exempla* between Cicero and Quintilian, Fantham concludes that "eloquence declined from Cicero's time to Quintilian's, yet thanks to Roman study of Greek theory, imitation was advocated for the student as vigorously in *De oratore* as in the *Institutio*" ("Imitation and Decline," 115). Likewise, Langlands shows that "exemplary ethics was alive and well at the end of the first century" (*Exemplary Ethics*, 234–55 [quotation from p. 255]).

2. *Mimesis in Greco-Roman Antiquity*

should involve selecting the best models that keep with one's own character and natural gifts (see especially Cicero and Seneca).
2. *Observation.* Mimesis is, by nature, a sensory process in which one must closely observe exemplary people in order to imitate them.
3. *Discernment/Interpretation.* The exemplar must be studied in order to discern what is worthy of imitation. Hence, mimesis includes a cognitive, interpretative dimension to avoid reducing it to a mechanical process of simplistic repetition. One should discern and imitate only the best features of the model/exemplar.
4. *Imitation/Emulation.* Having observed and understood the model, the imitator articulates this in a concrete mimetic act. In Greco-Roman antiquity, acceptable imitation had less to do with cloning or simple replication and more with creative and innovative emulation.[107] Langlands even mentions examples where, due to the different circumstances between the imitator and the model, the mimetic act is different from the original act. Hence, imitation is "a process of creative transformation of the original exemplum into a new exemplum that befits the new circumstances."[108]
5. *Transformation/Assimilation.* Insofar as mimesis relates to education or family, the aim is moral development, where one imitates the teacher or parent in order to become a virtuous or better person. Such moral progress is the result of making an eclectic choice of models to imitate, being creative rather than merely repetitive, and seeking to improve on the model(s).[109]

Regarding the selection and observance of an appropriate example for imitation (stages 1–2), Isocrates, Cicero, Seneca, Quintilian, and Plutarch all show that the object for imitation could be both contemporary, "living" examples and examples of great men from the past. I draw attention to a study by David Capes, who shows that in Greco-Roman culture, the virtuous lives of notable people were held up as models for imitation, and while living models were preferable, the lives of great men of the past could be "observed" from oral and published accounts and therefore imitated.[110]

---

107. Michelle Linda Fletcher explains that a sharp distinction between "imitation" (μίμησις/*imitatio*), as being associated with copying/repetition, and "emulation" (ζῆλος–ζήλωσις/*aemulatio*) with creativity is unwarranted (*Reading Revelation as Pastiche: Imitating the Past*, LNTS 571 [New York: Bloomsbury T&T Clark, 2017], 38–39). See also the discussion in Schippers, concluding that while the terms have different connotations, they are complementary within the concept of "imitation" ("Dionysius and Quintilian," 17–61).
108. Langlands, *Exemplary Ethics*, 118–20 (quotation from p. 120).
109. See also Fantham, "Imitation and Evolution," 13–14; Fletcher, *Reading Revelation*, 37–39.
110. Capes, "*Imitatio Christi*," 3–7. Copan also mentions the imitation of "living" and "past"

We have also seen that discernment or the use of one's cognitive faculties is crucial at virtually every stage of the mimetic process—from selecting appropriate models and studying them to discerning what needs imitation and deciding on the mimetic act. I will refer to this cognitive concept in service of mimesis as *"moral reasoning."* Langlands states that "this faculty of moral discrimination, to be refined over one's life and continually sharpened on the whetstone of Roman exempla, is the critical faculty with which Romans learned to engage with their exempla, and it is similar to the Aristotelian concept of *phronesis* or 'critical thinking.'"[111] Moral reasoning thus refers to the use of discernment and interpretation throughout the entire mimetic process.

We turn to other scholars, in chronological order, who have proposed similar models. While Gunter Gebauer and Christoph Wulf do not construct a model of the workings of mimesis, they delineate four aspects: (1) mimesis involves identification of one person with another; (2) mimesis includes both an active and a cognitive component; (3) mimesis denotes a physical action; and (4) mimesis has a performative aspect.[112] Victor Copan presents a five-stage model of imitation: (1) initial contact with the model; (2) attraction to the model; (3) desire to be like the model; (4) intentional scrutiny of and reflection on the model; and (5) "performing the model," i.e., seeking to replicate or adapt the model in one's own life to improve one's character.[113] While Copan's model largely coheres with ours, the basis of his model is too thin, relying mainly on Philo, *Praem.* 114–116.[114] Exploring the imitation of literary models in Greco-Roman education, Dupertois

---

examples (*Saint Paul*, 46–47). Likewise, Turpin notes that while the Stoics preferred living examples, historical examples were still valuable ("Tacitus," 366). Turpin notes several aspects of Stoic *exempla* that support our findings: e.g., (1) *exempla* could provide moral education as effectively as doctrinal arguments or moral precepts; (2) *exempla* are useful vehicles for moral reflection, helping people think through their own situation; and (3) Stoics believed they could become *exempla* for others ("Tacitus," 365–73). Mayer states that while the Greeks largely resorted to examples from the past, the Romans also valued contemporary examples ("*Exempla* in Seneca," 302–3). Similarly, Petitfils notes that Roman authors typically preferred familial Roman *exempla* rather than historical (Greek) *exempla* (*Mos Christianorum*, 24). See also nn. 75 and 87 above.

111. Langlands, *Exemplary Ethics*, 9. Elsewhere she states that "the process of imitating a model is not mindless, but requires the operation of critical faculties and the skills of creation and innovation" (*Exemplary Ethics*, 120). Jo-Ann A. Brant also notes that mimesis in Greek antiquity is an active, creative, and cognitive process with an ethical dimension ("The Place of Mimēsis in Paul's Thought," *SR* 22 [1993]: 285–300, at 286–88).

112. Gebauer and Wulf, *Mimesis*, 5. At the end of their study, they identify twelve aspects (*Mimesis*, 316–20).

113. Copan, *Saint Paul*, 63–64, 71.

114. Besides, contra Copan's claim (*Saint Paul*, 63–64), *Praem.* 114 does not mention the "gazing" upon good models.

detects a mimetic ethos that is characterized by five features: (1) close familiarity with the prominent models; (2) the imitation of multiple models and selecting the best aspects; (3) acknowledging or concealing the dependence on a literary model; (4) creativity; and (5) the literary models were both a standard to aim at and a target to surpass.[115]

Andreas Vakirtzis examines the idea of friendship in Aristotle and detects a mimetic model that comprises selection, interpretation, imitation, and moral development.[116] Matthew Roller articulates a model of Roman exemplarity consisting of four operations: (1) action (performed publicly before an audience); (2) evaluation (of the action's significance, either positively or negatively); (3) commemoration (of the action, performer, and evaluation through a monument such as an inscription, statue, or painting); and (4) norm-setting (the performed, evaluated, and commemorated action becomes part of the moral framework of the community or *mos maiorum* as a model to imitate or avoid).[117] Examining a broad range of Greek and Roman authors, Adriana Schippers identifies the following stages in the mimetic process: (1) the intensive and repeated study of a wide variety of literary models; (2) the acquisition of a sharp judgment; (3) the selection of what is best in the models chosen; and (4) the eclectic and original composition of a new work of literature.[118]

I draw special attention to Rebecca Langlands's study because she has provided the most comprehensive model of Greco-Roman "exemplary ethics," which has a close affinity with ours.[119] I developed my model in 2019 (published in 2020),[120] but I was unaware of Langlands's 2018 study at that time. While I examined various moral discourses in Greco-Roman rhetoric to gain insight into the workings of mimesis, Langlands focuses on the literary genre of *exempla* or concise ethical stories in order to outline "the various stages and aspects of moral learning that constitute exemplary ethics and the detailed moral framework within which members of the Roman community engaged with exemplary tales."[121] She identi-

---

115. Dupertois, "Writing and Imitation," 12–14. Except for the third feature, the other aspects are also found in our model.

116. Vakirtzis, "Mimesis," 125–42.

117. Roller, *Models from the Past*, 5–8.

118. Schippers, "Dionysius and Quintilian," 241. She stresses again that "the notions of μίμησις and ζῆλος and *imitatio* and *aemulatio* need not (always) be distinguished (see also n. 107 above).

119. Langlands, *Exemplary Ethics*, 86–111. For a broader moral philosophy of exemplary ethics, see Linda Zagzebski, "Exemplarist Virtue Theory," *Metaphilosophy* 41 (2010): 41–57; Zagzebski, *Exemplarist Moral Theory*.

120. Cornelis Bennema, "A Shared (Graeco-Roman) Model of Mimesis in John and Paul?," *JSNT* 43 (2020): 173–93.

121. Langlands, *Exemplary Ethics*, 7. She acknowledges that while ethical imitation is rarely discussed in ancient literature, it is theorized in rhetorical training (*Exemplary Ethics*, 95).

fies six stages or aspects of Roman exemplary ethics: (1) admiration and wonder (the exemplar evokes admiration and awe in the learner); (2) comparison (the *exemplum* provokes learners to compare themselves to the hero); (3) *aemulatio* (the *exemplum* ignites aspiration in the learner to develop the same moral qualities as the hero); (4) modeling (the *exemplum* offers a template for imitation); (5) cognition (besides observation and imitation, the learner should develop an understanding of what is imitated); and (6) discernment (the learner should grasp more advanced ethical issues and meta-exemplary principles).[122] Langlands's fifth and sixth aspects (cognition and discernment) correspond to our third aspect (discernment/interpretation), but our fifth aspect (transformation/assimilation) is missing from her model.[123] Although she takes a different approach (focusing on concise moral stories rather than moral discourses), Langlands's finding that "creative imitation" and "critical thinking" are key features in Roman exemplary ethics supports and consolidates our findings that Greco-Roman mimesis is a cognitive, creative process.

While our model of mimesis is largely derived from the Greco-Roman rhetorical traditions, Andrew Pitts shows that Greco-Roman historiography functions as a branch of rhetoric and thus continues the mimetic tradition.[124] Likewise, William Kurz reveals the use of narrative models for imitation across several genres in ancient Greco-Roman literature, such as historiography, biography, and novel.[125] Langlands also points to the correspondence between ancient Roman ethical imitation and literary imitation: "The ethical imitation (*imitatio* or *aemulatio*) that is a key element of this learning process therefore has much in common with the literary *imitatio* much practised and theorised in ancient literature."[126] Our inferred mimetic model is (of course) not found everywhere in its entirety, but many Greco-Roman authors reflect aspects of our model in their writings. This is not surprising, given the prevalent mimetic culture in Greco-Roman antiquity (see also n. 9). Schippers claims that a broad range of Greek and Roman authors "drew

---

122. Langlands, *Exemplary Ethics*, 86–88. She then elaborates on this schema on pp. 88–111. Elsewhere she argues that Roman *exempla* do not have a single, fixed meaning but have a capacity for moral complexity; they are multivalent in that they are open to more than one ethical interpretation (*Exemplary Ethics*, 59–62).

123. Admittedly, Langlands does state that the engagement with *exempla* in moral learning will modify behavior (*Exemplary Ethics*, 86).

124. Pitts, "Origins of Greek Mimesis," 119–29.

125. William Kurz, "Narrative Models for Imitation in Luke-Acts," in *Greeks, Romans, and Christians: Essays in Honor of Abraham J. Malherbe*, ed. David L. Balch, Everett Ferguson, and Wayne A. Meeks (Minneapolis: Augsburg Fortress, 1990), 171–89, at 176–84.

126. Langlands, *Exemplary Ethics*, 8.

from and contributed to a shared discourse of imitation."[127] Since it is impossible to be exhaustive, we just provide a few examples in the following excursus.

※※※

Excursus: Further Support for Our Model from Greco-Roman Literature

Xenophon (430–355 BCE), a contemporary of Plato, describes in his *Cyropaedia* various mimetic strategies that King Cyrus had put in place to cope with his vast empire. Cyrus stressed, for example, the importance of personal example: "[Cyrus] believed that he could in no way more effectively inspire a desire for the beautiful and the good than by endeavouring, as their sovereign, to set before his subjects a perfect model of virtue in his own person" (*Cyr.* 8.1.21). Elsewhere, Cyrus presents himself as an example to imitate of his organizational skills:

> And [Cyrus] gave orders to all the satraps he sent out to imitate him in everything that they saw him do: they were, in the first place, to organize companies of cavalry and charioteers from the Persians who went with them and from the allies; to require as many as received lands and palaces to attend at the satrap's court and exercising proper self-restraint to put themselves at his disposal in whatever he demanded; to have the boys that were born to them educated at the local court, just as was done at the royal court; and to take the retinue at his gates out hunting and to exercise himself and them in the arts of war. (*Cyr.* 8.6.10)

Realizing the importance of personal example, Cyrus can even initiate a chain of imitation:

> "Please observe also that among all the directions I am now giving you, I give no orders to slaves. I try to do myself everything that I say you ought to do. And even as I bid you follow my example, so do you also instruct those whom you appoint to office to follow yours." And as Cyrus then effected his organization, even so unto this day all the garrisons under the king are kept up, and

---

127. Schippers, "Dionysius and Quintilian," 190.

PART 1   MIMESIS IN ANTIQUITY

all the courts of the governors are attended with service in the same way; so all households, great and small, are managed; and by all men in authority the most deserving of their guests are given preference with seats of honour; all the official journeyings are conducted on the same plan and all the political business is centralized in a few heads of departments. (*Cyr.* 8.6.13–14)

In his collection of Socratic dialogues, Xenophon presents the importance of mimesis for Socrates. Socrates never professed to teach virtue, but by showing himself to be a virtuous man, he expected to inspire others to become virtuous by imitating his example: "By letting his own light shine, he led his disciples to hope that through imitation of him they would develop likewise" (*Mem.* 1.2.3). Hence, we find here the aspects of observation, imitation, and transformation.[128] When Pericles notes that the Athenians have become degenerate and wonders how they can recover the old virtue, Socrates points out that imitating good models leads to moral transformation: "I see no mystery about it. If they find out the practices of their ancestors and practice them as well as they did, they will come to be as good as they were; or failing that, they need but to imitate those who now hold preeminence and follow their practices, and if they are equally careful in observing them, they will be as good as they, and, if more careful, even better" (*Mem.* 3.5.14). In *Mem.* 3.10.1–8, Socrates points out at length to painters and sculptors that they can imitate, i.e., represent, the "activities of the soul" such as feelings and virtues in their art.

Demosthenes (384–322 BCE), a contemporary of Aristotle, often stresses that statues of great men from the past were erected not to be gazed at in wonder but to urge onlookers to imitate their virtues (*Syntax.* 13.26; *Rhod. lib.* 15.35; see also *Olynth.* 3.21). Concerned with the moral decline in Athens, Demosthenes exhorts contemporary Athenians to find examples to imitate among their forefathers regarding sound judgment and being incorruptible (*Fals. leg.* 19.268–273).

Greek historian Polybius (c. 200–118 BCE) is aware of the value of historical examples as paradigms of behavior: "All historians . . . have impressed on us that the soundest education and training for a life of active politics is the study of History, and that the surest and indeed the only method of learning how to bear bravely the vicissitudes of fortune, is to recall the calamities of others" (*Hist.* 1.1.2), and, "It will also be seen how many and how great advantages accrue to the student from

---

128. According to M. John-Patrick O'Connor, "the linchpin of imitation for Xenophon is one's proximity to Socrates," which is best illustrated in the example of Euthydemus, who resolves to spend extensive time with Socrates and adopt his practices (*Mem.* 4.2.40) (*The Moral Life according to Mark*, LNTS 667 [London: Bloomsbury T&T Clark, 2022], 25).

the systematic treatment of history" (*Hist.* 1.2.8).[129] Then, in his account of the life of Philopoemen of Megalopolis, Polybius admits that the history of exemplary people has greater educational value than the history of cities: "For inasmuch as it is more possible to emulate (ζηλῶσαι) and to imitate (μιμήσασθαι) living men than lifeless buildings, so much more important for the improvement of a reader is it to learn about the former" (*Hist.* 10.21.4).[130]

Regarding Dionysius of Halicarnassus (c. 60 BCE–7 CE), Schippers states that in *On Imitation,* "Dionysius insists on 'imitation' (μίμησις) as a perceptive and highly creative process, consisting of intensive study, the critical selection of the best features of a range of authors, and the eclectic and original composition of a new piece of art."[131] In his *Roman Antiquities*, Dionysius shows his awareness of the importance of historical examples for his contemporary audience: "For I look upon these matters [those of Larcius, Rome's first dictator] as being most useful to my readers, since they will afford a great abundance of noble and profitable examples, not only to lawgivers and leaders of the people, but also to all others who aspire to take part in public life and to govern the state" (*Ant. rom.* 5.75.1).[132]

Like Cicero and Seneca, Theon (mid to late first century CE) advocates being eclectic in the choice of exemplars:

> Do not imitate only one model but all the most famous of the ancients. Thus we shall have copious, numerous, and varied resources on which to draw. It is wrong to limit imitation to a single author; those who imitate only Demosthenes become stiff, tiresome, and obscure, and those who want to imitate only Lysias are thin, weak, and clumsy. "When someone admires what is good in all and understands how to conform his thought to that, so that there exists in him a kind of ideal model of style which each can mold in accordance with his own nature, he does not seem constrained to fix his eyes on a single style, but he acquires, spontaneously for his personal use, a part of all these excellences." (*Exercises* 13.105)[133]

Epictetus (50–135 CE), a Greek Stoic philosopher, is acutely aware that rulers should be good examples because subjects will observe and imitate their rulers.

---

129. Kurz, "Narrative Models," 177.
130. I noted this passage in O'Connor, *Moral Life*, 16.
131. Schippers, "Dionysius and Quintilian," 1. *On Imitation* contains a systematic discussion of imitation but has only survived in fragments.
132. Kurz, "Narrative Models," 178.
133. George A. Kennedy, trans., *Progymnasmata: Greek Textbooks of Prose Composition and Rhetoric*, WRGW 10 (Leiden: Brill, 2003), 68–69.

He recounts an incident when the governor of Epirus showed favoritism to an actor in the theater and then complained to Epictetus that he was publicly blamed for this. Epictetus then replied, "Why are you angry if they imitated you? For whom have the people to imitate but you, their superior? Whom do they look to but you, when they go to the theatres? . . . You ought to know, then, that when you enter the theatre, you enter as a standard of behaviour and as an example to the rest, showing them how they ought to act in the theatre" (*Diatr.* 3.4.3–5). When it comes to one's choice of profession, Epictetus recommends careful examination of several practices and whether they suit one's nature but cautions against simply imitating everything (like an ape) without discernment (*Diatr.* 3.15; *Ench.* 29). In his *Diatr.* 3.22.45–49, Epictetus presents himself as an example of the good life, free from all possessions. In *Diatr.* 2.14, Epictetus reflects on methods of instruction to learn certain professions. He then mentions several things that a philosopher must learn: (1) that there is a God who provides for everything, (2) what the Gods are like, and (3) to seek to become like them—to be an imitator of God (*Diatr.* 2.14.11–13).[134]

※※

2.4. Conclusion

The aim of this chapter was not to outline the concept of mimesis in all areas of Greco-Roman antiquity but to focus specifically on *ethical mimesis* related to human character and conduct and to articulate a model that shows the workings of mimesis. The benefit of examining Greco-Roman antiquity is that its various authors *describe and discuss* the concept and process of mimesis, whereas the Judeo-Christian traditions often simply mention the concept. In other words, the study of mimesis in Greco-Roman antiquity uniquely provided us a peek into its workings and the issues that were considered by those who advocated its use. We learned that in the Greek tradition, mimesis was a creative and cognitive process and could not be reduced to mere replication. The Roman tradition adopted the Greek notion of mimesis as a critical, creative practice of emulation and transformation rather than mechanical copying. Good mimesis both resembled and differed from the original.[135] Although mimesis resists a precise definition, it ap-

---

134. This passage came to my attention in Sierksma-Agteres, "Imitation in Faith," 132–33.
135. Potolsky, *Mimesis*, 54–57. See also Pitts, "Origins of Greek Mimesis," 116–19. A. K. M. Adam turns to postmodern theories to show that imitation is not about superficial cloning but involves

2. Mimesis in Greco-Roman Antiquity

pears that underlying all forms of mimesis in Greco-Roman antiquity is the idea of *corresponding representation*.[136]

Our study of select Greek and Roman authors shows that mimesis occurred in the overlapping spheres of religion, family, and education, featuring the imitation of god, parents, and teachers. In addition, the Greco-Roman traditions show the existence of a *shared discourse of imitation*, which allowed us to infer a common model of the mechanics of mimesis. This model of mimetic ethics consists of five aspects: (1) the selection of and association with an appropriate exemplar; (2) the careful observation of the exemplar; (3) discernment of what should be imitated; (4) the imitation of virtuous behavior discerned in the exemplar; (5) the transformation or moral progress that results from continually imitating virtuous people. Examining the various models that scholars have produced has been useful in that they largely endorse or validate our model and show broad agreement on how mimesis worked in Greco-Roman antiquity. Langlands's "exemplary ethics" is especially similar to our concept of mimetic ethics, which is an ethics driven by example and imitation. What these scholars have not done, however, due to the nature of their work, is examine the extent to which early Christianity reflects this model. Only Copan relates his model to the Pauline literature, whereas we will examine the entire New Testament and Apostolic Fathers.

We learned that the Greco-Roman mimetic traditions reveal different forms or modes of mimesis. The most common form is *direct observation*, where the imitator can observe or study the exemplar and determine what to imitate. However, there are also instances of *mediated mimesis*, where the example for imitation is facilitated by other means. One form of mediated mimesis is *textually mediated mimesis*, where an author presents in his writing an exemplary person from the past for his audience to study and emulate. Based on the information in the text, the audience can construct a mental picture of the exemplar to "observe" and imitate. Occasionally, an author presents himself as an exemplar (see, e.g., Isocrates, *Panath.* 16; Cicero, *Off.* 1.78; Seneca, *Ep.* 98.13).[137] It may also be that an imitator is reminded of and can visualize a past exemplar, for instance by seeing an inscription or statue, which we may call *mnemonic mimesis* (see also the mention of remembrance in Isocrates, *Evag.* 3; Seneca, *Ep.* 33.7–8).[138]

---

both "sameness" and "difference" ("Walk This Way: Repetition, Difference, and the Imitation of Christ," *Int* 55 [2001]: 19–33). However, we do not need to resort to postmodernism to make this point; the ancient Greeks had already understood mimesis to be dynamic and creative.

136. See also Halliwell, *Aesthetics of Mimesis*, 16–18; Gebauer and Wulf, *Mimesis*, 27–29; de Boer, *Imitation of Paul*, 15.

137. Fiore calls this "epistolary presence," personal presence achieved through a letter (see n. 84).

138. Harrison deftly demonstrates how inscriptions and statues facilitated mimesis in Greco-Roman antiquity ("Imitation," 223–38).

PART 1   MIMESIS IN ANTIQUITY

Most scholars agree that, owing to prolonged contact with Greco-Roman traditions, early Christianity adopted the concept of mimesis, so we will examine the extent to which the early Christian writings correspond to our Greco-Roman model of mimesis. First, however, we turn to the Jewish traditions—the pre-Greek, Semitic tradition preserved in the Hebrew Bible as well as Hellenistic Judaism and the rabbinic traditions of the Second Temple period—because some scholars (e.g., Tinsley, Hood) claim that early Christian mimesis is indebted to the Old Testament.

3

MIMESIS IN JEWISH ANTIQUITY

Jewish scholar Martin Buber famously remarked, "The imitation of God—not of a wishful image of God, but of the real God, and not of a human mediator, but of God himself—is the central paradox of Judaism. A paradox—for how can a person imitate the invisible, the incomprehensible, the amorphous and one who cannot be fashioned?"[1] In this chapter, we will examine the concept of mimesis in ancient Jewish traditions—both the Semitic tradition preserved in the Hebrew Bible (section 3.1) and Hellenistic Judaism and the rabbinic traditions of the Second Temple period (section 3.2).[2] In keeping with our focus on ethical mimesis, we will not explore the idea of literary mimesis, where one author imitates a literary form or style from another (see also section 1.6).[3] I am mainly interested in how mimesis leads to moral transformation (imitation in order to become a better or more godly person) than possible ontological transformation.[4] The aim

---

1. Buber, "Nachahmung Gottes," 39. Originally: "Die Nachahmung Gottes, nicht des Wunschgebilds, sondern des wirklichen Gottes, und nicht eines menschgestaltigen Mittlers, sondern Gottes selber, ist die zentrale Paradoxie des Judentums. Eine Paradoxie—denn wie vermöchte der Mensch den Unsichtbaren, Unfaßbaren, Gestaltlosen, nicht zu Gestaltenden nachzuahmen?" In contrast, Buber writes, "Mimesis in Greek antiquity is based on an image of God rather than the real God; the Greek can only imitate what he has made" ("Nachahmung Gottes," 36).

2. In section 3.1, I will also refer to the LXX, the Greek translation of the Hebrew Bible, if the Greek and Hebrew terms are synonymous.

3. Hence, the following works are excluded from our investigation: John Van Seters, "Creative Imitation in the Hebrew Bible," *SR* 29 (2000): 395–409; William A. Tooman, "Between Imitation and Interpretation: Reuse of Scripture and Composition in Hodayot (1QHa) 11:6–19," *DSD* 18 (2011): 54–73; Martin Friis, *Image and Imitation: Josephus' Antiquities 1–11 and Greco-Roman Historiography*, WUNT 2/472 (Tübingen: Mohr Siebeck, 2018).

4. For a comprehensive treatment of how early Jewish anthropology depicts an ontological transformation of the self when it encounters the divine, see Tyson L. Putthoff, *Ontological As-*

of this chapter is to test the claim of some scholars that the roots of early Christian mimesis lie in Jewish traditions rather than Greco-Roman ones.

3.1. Mimesis in the Hebrew Bible

3.1.1. The Case for Mimesis in the Hebrew Bible

Two scholars in particular, E. J. Tinsley and Jason Hood, have argued that the concept of mimesis in the New Testament is rooted in the Hebrew Bible or Christian Old Testament.[5] So, we will start by assessing their evidence before we explore potential mimetic texts in the Hebrew Bible.

Tinsley argues that the Old Testament imagery of "the way" is fundamental to the notion of mimesis in that Israel imitates God by following or walking in God's ways. In the historical event of the Exodus, God not only literally set out the way for the Israelites but was himself the way as their guide, example, and companion, and the historical event became metaphorically "the way of life" as taught by God.[6] Mimesis relates to the imagery of "the way" in that Israel's imitation of God is expressed by phrases such as "to walk in the way of the Lord" and "to follow after God."[7] Israel's imitation of God occurs mainly in the areas of liturgy and ethics. In liturgy, Israel corporately remembers and enacts the main redemptive-historical events through the great festivals of Passover, Weeks, and Tabernacles.

---

pects of Early Jewish Anthropology: The Malleable Self and the Presence of God, BRLJ 53 (Leiden: Brill, 2017). Most instances of transformation Putthoff examines (e.g., those described in Jos. Asen., Philo, *Opif.* 144, and b. Soṭah 49a) are not so much the result of mimesis (*imitatio Dei*) but of contemplation (*visio Dei*).

5. Others who contend that the New Testament concept of mimesis is rooted in the Old Testament include Griffiths, *Example of Jesus*, 27–28 (although he also recognizes the influence of Greek culture on Jewish thought on pp. 18–21); Kathy Ehrensperger, *Paul and the Dynamics of Power: Communication and Interaction in the Early Christ-Movement* (New York: T&T Clark, 2007), 139–42 (she also admits the presence of the Greek notion of mimesis in Paul's writings); Mavis M. Leung, "Ethics and *Imitatio Christi* in 1 John: A Jewish Perspective," *TynBul* 69 (2018): 111–31. The differences between the Hebrew Bible and the Christian Old Testament in terms of the names and order of the books have no consequences for our investigation of those texts that might allude to mimesis.

6. Tinsley, *Imitation of God*, 31–34.

7. Tinsley, *Imitation of God*, 35. Tinsley then unpacks the imitation of God as a "way of life," specifically as the way of Torah, the way of sonship, and the way of knowledge, relating to the offices of prophet, king, and priest (*Imitation of God*, 35–44).

3. Mimesis in Jewish Antiquity

In ethics, Israel is tasked with imitating God's behavior toward his people, both in their private and corporate lives.[8] I have two issues with his argument. First, the concepts "walking in the way of God" and "following after God" are not linked to any mimetic language but seem to indicate obedience rather than mimesis.[9] It seems that these concepts enable or facilitate mimesis rather than convey it. In other words, it is *as* the Israelites follow after God that they can observe and imitate him. Second, Tinsley sees mimesis too readily in instances where there seems only to be an analogy or correspondence of ideas.[10]

Hood also argues that the New Testament concept of imitating Jesus is firmly rooted in the Old Testament concept of imitating God rather than a Greco-Roman concept of mimesis.[11] For Hood, imitation is at the heart of human identity because, as God's image-bearers (Gen 1:26), humans represent God in this world by imitating his character and actions.[12] A few critical remarks are necessary. First, Hood defines imitation too quickly and loosely early on in the book—it is primarily about adopting a mindset—rather than deriving it from specific terms in the text.[13] As a result, he sees imitation where it seems, at times, closer to analogy. It

---

8. Tinsley, *Imitation of God*, 50–64. While Donald L. Williams does not use the terms "imitation" or "mimesis," his account of the Israelite cult where worshippers re-enact or re-present God's salvific-historical acts strengthens Tinsley's argument that there is a mimetic aspect in Israel's liturgical worship ("The Israelite Cult and Christian Worship" in *The Use of the Old Testament in the New and Other Essays*, ed. James M. Efird [Durham, NC: Duke University Press, 1972], 110–24, at 113–20).

9. See also de Boer, *Imitation of Paul*, 31–38 (including his critique of Tinsley on pp. 36–38). Christopher J. H. Wright presents a via media, suggesting that "walking in God's ways" refers to both obeying God's commands and imitating God (*Old Testament Ethics for the People of God* [Leicester: Inter-Varsity, 2004], 40).

10. For example, Tinsley states that in Jer 22:16 Josiah knew and imitated God's providential care for the poor and needy (*Imitation of God*, 43). However, this verse simply shows that Josiah's godlike behavior is based on his understanding of God. Or, with reference to 1 Sam 20:14 and 2 Sam 9:3, Tinsley states that Israel should imitate God's steadfast love (*Imitation of God*, 60), but the context does not contain mimetic language and the expectation is more likely to behave *like* God.

11. Hood seems unaware of Tinsley's work and has also not interacted with de Boer, Schulz, and Betz.

12. Hood, *Imitating God*, 20–26. He develops this idea in his chapter 2.

13. Hood, *Imitating God*, 12 (see also pp. 74, 132). At the end of his book, Hood sharpens his definition: "Biblical imitation is a matter of aligning character, belief, mindset or action with a pattern or template so that the copy reflects the original" (*Imitating God*, 210). Although his "broad, flexible approach to imitation" (*Imitating God*, 12) recognizes that imitation is not limited to passages where the term is mentioned explicitly, he often does not explain how imitation is inferred from the text.

is far from clear, for example, whether the creation of humanity in God's image implies imitation, correspondence, participation, representation, or reflection. Second, while the scope of his study is impressive, the semi-popular treatment of the subject lacks the necessary exegetical robustness and proper grounding in the ancient world. For example, to support his claim that the New Testament concept of imitation is rooted in the Old Testament, he asserts that both testaments have the phrase "be holy as I am holy" (presumably referring to Lev 19:2 and 1 Pet 1:16).[14] However, these texts contain a causal relation between God and humans ("be holy *because* [כִּי; ὅτι] I am holy") rather than a comparative one.

In sum, Tinsley and Hood do *not* make a robust case for the presence of mimesis in the Hebrew Bible, and we need to explore other texts to determine whether ancient Israelites could conceive of imitating God or other people. Both Tinsley and Hood delineate a biblical theology of mimesis while ignoring the Greco-Roman literature, where discourse on mimesis originated, and its possible influence on early Christian authors regarding mimesis.[15] In limiting their work to biblical texts, they create the impression that imitation is specifically a Christian concept.

3.1.2. Possible Mimetic Texts in the Hebrew Bible

We will first consider those texts in the Hebrew Bible that seem to express mimesis most clearly.

Humans as the Image of God (Gen 1:26–27). Most scholars understand the "image (צֶלֶם; εἰκών) of God" in Genesis (1:26–27; 5:1, 3; 9:6), often in conjunction with "likeness," in terms of representation, that is, the image is the place where God manifests himself and is present.[16] For Buber, the "image of God" is the basis for imitating God. People are destined to resemble God, that is, to complete the image in which they are created and which they carry within them in order to experience the perfection of being like God (but not in this life).[17] Van Kooten sees a connection between Gen 1:26–27 and Ezek 1:26–28, where, in contrast to pagan idolatry, humans (and not idols) are regarded as the likeness of God.[18] He then explores the reception history of man as God's image in Second Temple Judaism and concludes that there is a variety of understandings: (1) to present a contrast

---

14. Hood, *Imitating God*, 184.
15. Tinsley's chapter 2, "'Mimesis' in the Ancient World," is a mere four pages.
16. Van Kooten, *Paul's Anthropology*, 1–2.
17. Buber, "Nachahmung Gottes," 40. See also Griffiths, *Example of Jesus*, 27.
18. Van Kooten, *Paul's Anthropology*, 3–7.

between humanity as the only image of God and idolatrous images of pagan gods, (2) the image of God as a reference to human rationality—divine anthropology, and (3) a physical understanding of God's image.[19] In the New Testament, Christ is identified as the "image of God" (Col 1:15) and Christians are assimilated to this image (συμμόρφους τῆς εἰκόνος; Rom 8:29), being transformed into this image (τὴν αὐτὴν εἰκόνα μεταμορφούμεθα; 2 Cor 3:18), or being renewed according to this image (τὸν ἀνακαινούμενον εἰς ἐπίγνωσιν κατ' εἰκόνα; Col 3:10). While "image" does not necessarily indicate imitation, it has connotations of resemblance and representation.[20]

To Imitate God's Holiness (Lev 19:2). In Lev 19:2, the particle כִּי (and ὅτι in the LXX) is causal rather than comparative—"you will be holy *because* I am holy"—thus indicating that the reason for Israel's need to be holy is God's own holiness rather than a case of Israel being urged to imitate God's holiness.[21] Patrick Hartin states, "The Israelites are called to holiness, not in imitation of God, but as a *consequence* of their relationship with God."[22] Others, however, contend that mimesis is in view.[23] For example, Baruch Levine states that to achieve holiness, Israel is required to observe God's laws and commandments, that is, to emulate God's attributes.[24] While some might say that imitating God would require observing him (which was impossible to conceive for the Israelites) rather than observing his commandments, the counter-argument would be that the Hebrew Bible has recorded God's acts so that one can indirectly "observe" God by studying his laws and commandments. By this measure, Lev 19:2 (see also 11:44–45) could contain *implied* mimesis, though explicit mimetic language is absent. Jacob Milgrom thus contends that the imitation of God implied by Lev 19:2 could read, "Just as God

---

19. Van Kooten, *Paul's Anthropology*, 7–47.

20. Betz rejects the notion of imitation in relation to creation in Gen 1:26–27 (and Gen 5:1–3; Sir 17:1–3; Wis 2:23) (*Nachfolge und Nachahmung*, 87–89).

21. See also de Boer, *Imitation of Paul*, 39–40. Betz also interprets Lev 19:2 in terms of obedience rather than imitation (*Nachfolge und Nachahmung*, 90).

22. Patrick J. Hartin, "Ethics in the Letter of James, the Gospel of Matthew, and the Didache: Their Place in Early Christian Literature," in *Matthew, James, and Didache: Three Related Documents in Their Jewish and Christian Settings*, ed. Huub van de Sandt and Jürgen K. Zangenberg, SBL Symposium Series 45 (Atlanta: Society of Biblical Literature, 2008), 289–314, at 302 (emphasis added).

23. While Jan Joosten asserts that those who deny the idea of imitating God in Lev 19:2 are mistaken, he does not explain how the Israelites could imitate God's holiness (*People and Land in the Holiness Code: An Exegetical Study of the Ideational Framework of the Law in Leviticus 17–26*, VTSup 67 [Leiden: Brill, 1996], 131–32).

24. Baruch A. Levine, *The JPS Torah Commentary: Leviticus* (Philadelphia: Jewish Publication Society, 1989), 125, 256.

PART 1   MIMESIS IN ANTIQUITY

differs from human beings, so Israel should differ from the nations."[25] He suggests that the call to imitate God must not be taken literally (one cannot become like God) but refers to living a godly life; observance of God's commandments leads to God's attribute of holiness—not to God but to godliness.[26] Similarly, Alan Mittleman states, "Later Jewish tradition took the significance of 'be holy, for God is holy' to mean: be Godlike insofar as that is possible for human beings. Emulate the moral attributes of God such as compassion, forgiveness, patience, and truthfulness."[27] Hence, to imitate God in his holiness is not to assimilate to God but to godliness. While God is transcendent, invisible, and wholly other, he is not absent. The record of God's character and conduct in the Hebrew Bible enables his people to "observe" and "imitate" him in order to become godly. A quick glance ahead reveals an interesting development in the New Testament: Matt 5:48 and Luke 6:36, which allude to Lev 19:2, have changed the causal particle כִּי/ὅτι in Lev 19:2 into a comparative one—ὡς and καθώς, respectively (see further chapter 4).

To Imitate God's Justice and Love (Deut 10:17–19). Deut 10:17–18 presents God as impartial, especially in providing justice for the vulnerable and demonstrating love to the sojourner. Then, we read in 10:19, "You shall also love the sojourner, because (כִּי) you were sojourners in the land of Egypt" (see also Lev 19:34). As in Lev 19:2, the causal particle כִּי indicates that Israel's experiences are the grounds for treating well the sojourners in their midst. While the idea of imitating God's impartial behavior is implicit, there is no actual mimetic language to support this.[28]

Other texts. There are other texts in the Hebrew Bible that arguably contain a sense of imitation, albeit without explicit mimetic language and sometimes outside the realm of ethics. In Exod 20:8–11, the prohibition to work on the Sabbath is patterned on God's example of resting on the seventh day. In Exod 25:9, 40, Moses is instructed to make the tabernacle according to the example or model (תַּבְנִית; παράδειγμα/τύπος) God will show him. Similarly, in 1 Chr 28:11–12, David gives Solomon the template (תַּבְנִית; παράδειγμα) for the temple that Solomon is about to construct. While both texts imply imitation in that someone builds a physical construction according to a given design, this does not relate to ethical behavior.

25. Jacob Milgrom, *Leviticus 17–22*, AB 3a (Garden City, NY: Doubleday, 2000), 1604.
26. Milgrom, *Leviticus 17–22*, 1605–6.
27. Alan L. Mittleman, *A Short History of Jewish Ethics: Conduct and Character in the Context of Covenant* (Chichester: Wiley-Blackwell, 2012), 31–32. Nevertheless, Mittleman himself questions whether this is what emulative holiness means in Leviticus.
28. See also Milgrom, *Leviticus 17–22*, 1605. W. H. Paul Thompson, however, contends that some Deuteronomic texts (1:16–17; 10:17–19; 16:18–20) implicitly convey that Israel should mirror or imitate God's impartial ethos (*Pauline Slave Welfare in Historical Context: An Equality Analysis*, WUNT 2/570 [Tübingen: Mohr Siebeck, 2023], 169–71).

3. Mimesis in Jewish Antiquity

In Deut 12:30, Moses urges Israel not to follow or "imitate" the idolatrous practices of other nations. In Isa 51:1–2, the exhortation to those who pursue righteousness to look to Abraham arguably implies imitating him.[29] Then there are narratives where a leader functions as a role model for a successor, such as Moses for Joshua and Elijah for Elisha. However, the idea is conceptual rather than linguistically explicit. The book of Jonah arguably teaches that Jonah failed to "imitate" God's compassion and mercy. Stephen Chapman and Laceye Warner thus state that the lesson for Jonah (and hence Israel) is that "God wants Israel to strive to be more like God, not angry but gracious," and for Israel to imitate God's mission to rescue humankind and all creation.[30] However, again, this is at best implied.

Summary. In the Hebrew Bible, even if some texts seemingly indicate mimesis with regard to ethical behavior (e.g., Gen 1:26–27; Lev 19:2; Deut 10:18–19; 12:30), and this is contentious, the concept of mimesis does not seem integral to Hebrew thought.[31] While the Hebrew Bible presents the idea that Israel should reflect God's character and behavior, this is not explicitly linked to or expressed in mimetic language. Rather, when the Hebrew Bible speaks of Israel's behavior corresponding to or resembling that of God, the language is mainly causal rather than comparative. In passages where the idea of mimesis is arguably strongest, such as Lev 19:2 and Deut 10:18–19, the notion is that Israel should behave in a certain way *because* (כִּי/ὅτι) of who God is or what he does rather than behave *just as* God does, although that may be implied. We also argued that the figurative language of "walking in God's ways" does not in itself denote mimesis but can lead to it.[32] Hence, I consider the concept of mimesis in the Hebrew Bible to be implicit and "weak."[33] Nevertheless, Second Temple Jewish literature shows that the accounts of the virtuous lives of saints in the Hebrew Bible can serve as examples for imitation when such stories are read or heard in later times (see section 3.2).

---

29. H. H. Drake Williams, "Imitate Me as I Imitate Christ: Considering the Jewish Perspective in Paul's Use of Imitation in 1 Corinthians," in *The Crucified Apostle: Essays on Peter and Paul*, ed. Todd A. Wilson and Paul R. House, WUNT 2/450 (Tübingen: Mohr Siebeck, 2017), 209–24, at 213.

30. Stephen B. Chapman and Laceye C. Warner, "Jonah and the Imitation of God: Rethinking Evangelism and the Old Testament," *JTI* 2 (2008): 43–69, at 59.

31. Contra Yoder, who contends that the concept of imitating or following God was quite prevalent in the Old Testament (*Politics of Jesus*, 113–14).

32. See also Williams, "Imitate Me as I Imitate Christ," 214.

33. Likewise, de Boer concludes that "the imitation of God is neither one of the clear teachings of the Old Testament nor an integral part of the thinking of the Old Testament people" (*Imitation of Paul*, 41). According to Betz, Israel is given the possibility to live according to the Torah, but this should not be understood as the imitation of God (*Nachfolge und Nachahmung*, 89–90).

3.1.3. A More Nuanced Concept of Mimesis in the Hebrew Bible

Notwithstanding any reservations regarding mimesis in the Hebrew Bible, there has been a tradition for almost a century, from Buber in 1926 (see n. 1) to Barton in 2014 (see n. 39), that upholds the concept of *imitatio Dei* in the Hebrew Bible.[34] Gordon Wenham contends that the ethical ideal in the Old Testament is the imitation of God. Being created in God's image, human beings are God's representatives on earth, and their behavior should reflect and imitate God's character and actions, such as fidelity, love, generosity, and forgiveness.[35] While I agree in part, Wenham's claim that Lev 19:2 is "the key to biblical ethical theory" goes beyond what the text warrants.[36] Likewise, Eckart Otto overstates his case, claiming that the *imitatio Dei* is the core (*Zern*) or center (*Zentrum*) of Old Testament ethics.[37] More nuanced are a number of scholars who have argued that while the concept of imitating God is present in the Hebrew Bible, there are also instances where God cannot be imitated. Hence, the *imitatio Dei* is not the basis for or center of Old Testament ethics.

John Barton contends that besides explicit laws (divine commands) and "natural law" (conformity to the created moral order), the Old Testament also contains the idea of imitating God: "Good conduct for human beings consists in doing such things as one might suppose God would do, if God were human."[38] Elsewhere, he states that the creation of human beings in God's image implies that "God and humankind share a common ethical perception, so that God is not only the *commander* but also the *paradigm* of all moral conduct."[39] According to him, a number of passages in Deuteronomy, for example, encourage the Israelites to model their conduct on God's (e.g., Deut 5:15; 10:17–19; 15:15; 24:17–18).[40] While

---

[34]. For brief overviews of the contributions of Buber, Eichrodt, Hempel, Otto, Barton, Davies, and Houston, see Esias E. Meyer, "The Dark Side of the *Imitatio Dei*. Why Imitating the God of the Holiness Code Is Not Always a Good Thing," *OTE* 22 (2009): 373–83, at 374–77; Leung, "Ethics," 114–18.

[35]. Gordon J. Wenham, "The Gap between Law and Ethics in the Bible," *JJS* 48 (1997): 17–29, at 26–27.

[36]. Wenham, "Law and Ethics," 27. In his commentary, Gordon J. Wenham does not substantiate his assertion that the Israelites are to imitate God (*The Book of Leviticus*, NICOT 3 [Grand Rapids: Eerdmans, 1979], 264–65).

[37]. Eckart Otto, "Forschungsgeschichte der Entwürfe einer Ethik im Alten Testament," *VF* 36 (1991): 3–37, at 20.

[38]. John Barton, *Understanding Old Testament Ethics: Approaches and Explorations* (Louisville: Westminster John Knox, 2003), 29. See also Barton's exploratory study on the subject, "Understanding Old Testament Ethics," *JSOT* 9 (1978): 44–64.

[39]. John Barton, *Ethics in Ancient Israel* (Oxford: Oxford University Press, 2014), 267 (original emphasis).

[40]. Barton, *Old Testament Ethics*, 30; idem, *Ethics in Ancient Israel*, 265.

Barton sees an idea of imitating God in Lev 19:2, he admits that this text is "a narrow base on which to argue that imitation of God is the typical or central model for ethical conduct in the Old Testament."[41] Although uncertain of how many concrete examples of the imitation of God the Hebrew Bible contains, he bases the idea on the general assumption that "God acts according to moral standards that human beings also share."[42] For Barton, the Torah is not so much composed of divine commands but teachings on how to live a moral life and how to "walk with" God. Human life can run in parallel with the divine life and be connected through the idea of imitating God.[43]

Like Barton, Eryl Davies argues that Old Testament ethics cannot be limited to God as the lawgiver and the source of ethical commands but must include the idea of God as the pattern of ethical behavior to be imitated.[44] He, too, starts with Lev 19:2, arguing that the idea of imitating God's holiness is expressed in the rest of Lev 19 by specific moral behavior in Israel's daily life.[45] Davies then surveys Exodus, the Prophets, Psalms, and Old Testament narratives, arguing that the implied concept of imitating God is largely based on the assumption that "the character and actions of God were not presented as morally neutral observations; rather, they were designed to inculcate a sense of duty and moral responsibility in the people and to provide them with a model of the type of behaviour that should be mirrored in their own lives."[46] Davies is aware that the concept of imitating God holds potential dangers and needs a nuanced explanation; not all of God's attributes (e.g., his jealousy, majesty, or retribution) should be imitated.[47]

In a similar vein, Walter Houston argues that the Hebrew Bible refers both explicitly and implicitly to the imitation of God, but it is *not* the key to all Old Testament ethics.[48] He contends that Lev 19:2 (or, more generally, the Holiness Code in Lev 17–26) calls for Israel to imitate God's transcendence and separateness

---

41. Barton, *Ethics in Ancient Israel*, 264.

42. Barton, *Old Testament Ethics*, 51–52 (quotation from p. 52).

43. Barton, *Old Testament Ethics*, 52–53. Cyril S. Rodd sharply critiques Barton and Davies on the idea of imitating God in the Hebrew Bible (*Glimpses of a Strange Land: Studies in Old Testament Ethics* [Edinburgh: T&T Clark, 2001], 65–76), but see Barton's robust rebuttal (*Ethics in Ancient Israel*, 267–71).

44. Eryl W. Davies, "Walking in God's Ways: The Concept of *Imitatio Dei* in the Old Testament," in *In Search of True Wisdom: Essays in Old Testament Interpretation in Honour of Ronald E. Clements*, ed. Edward Ball, JSOTSup 300 (Sheffield: Sheffield Academic Press, 1999), 99–115.

45. Davies, "Walking in God's Ways," 101–2.

46. Davies, "Walking in God's Ways," 102–9 (quotation from p. 109).

47. Davies, "Walking in God's Ways," 112–13.

48. Walter J. Houston, "The Character of YHWH and the Ethics of the Old Testament: Is *Imitatio Dei* Appropriate?," *JTS* 58 (2007): 1–25.

from the profane and unclean.[49] Like Barton, he sees the idea of imitating God in a number of texts in Deuteronomy (5:15; 10:17–19; 15:15; 24:17–18).[50] More by implication, Houston considers God's deliverance of Israel from slavery in Egypt to be the model for the practice of social justice and God's compassionate and gracious character to be a model for the practice of retributive justice.[51] However, like Davies, Houston highlights the roles of God as the world ruler that should not be imitated, such as his treatment of Pharaoh and the Egyptians.[52]

Esias Meyer supports the views of Barton and Houston that the imitation of God cannot be a paradigm on which to build Old Testament ethics. Meyer supplements their case by arguing that the portrayals of God as a landowner and slave owner in Lev 25 should not and cannot be imitated. He concludes that the Old Testament encourages the imitation of *some* of God's acts, but the *imitatio Dei* does not lie at the heart of Old Testament ethics.[53]

3.1.4. Conclusion

Our examination of the Hebrew Bible regarding mimesis has produced mixed results. On the one hand, there is no explicit mimetic language in the Hebrew Bible; on the other hand, it is difficult to deny that it alludes to the concept of imitating God. While some scholars (Tinsley, Hood, Wenham, Otto) are too confident about the concept of the imitation of God in the Hebrew Bible, other scholars (Barton, Davies, Houston, Meyer) make a more convincing and nuanced case that the concept of imitating some aspects of God is present in the Hebrew Bible.[54] We found that the concept of imitating God is not present throughout the Hebrew Bible but occurs primarily in the Pentateuch, so we cannot justifiably speak of an Old Testament concept of imitating God as a distinct ethical model. Between deontological ethics (divine commands) and the ethical ideal (to be holy), the Hebrew Bible also contains *narrative ethics*, outlining the norms, values, and behavior expected from Israel, and it is here that we find the implied idea of imitating God. At the same time, while some acts of God can be imitated, others cannot, so discernment is

---

49. Houston, "Character of YHWH," 8–9.
50. Houston, "Character of YHWH," 10–11.
51. Houston, "Character of YHWH," 10–18.
52. Houston, "Character of YHWH," 20–25.
53. Meyer, "Dark Side," 377–82.
54. Leung also supports the views of Barton, Davies, and Houston ("Ethics," 119–20). Thompson concludes that Israel should imitate God's impartiality in the treatment of, for example, slave and free, rich and poor (*Pauline Slave Welfare*, 202).

required. The concept of imitating God is rooted in God's holiness, stressing his transcendence and separateness from the profane and unclean. In addition, the Hebrew Bible stresses the covenantal relationship that characterizes God and his people. To live in proximity to a holy God requires appropriate behavior from Israel, including the implied idea of imitating some attributes of God.

3.2. Mimesis in Second Temple Judaism

We learned that the concept of mimesis barely appears in the Hebrew Bible, and the specific idea of imitating God is virtually absent, which is unsurprising given its highly transcendental view of God. While there are instances where mimesis may be implied with regard to human conduct in the Hebrew Scriptures, the concept of mimesis is not prevalent.[55] Approaching the Common Era, however, the Greek concept of mimesis seems to have found its way into Jewish thinking because we find references to this concept in the LXX, Pseudepigrapha, Josephus, Philo, and rabbinic writings.[56]

Capes notes that Hellenistic Jewish authors, like their Greco-Roman counterparts, could present their audiences with the virtuous lives of people, both contemporary and past, as models to be imitated.[57] He shows that various Jewish authors in the Greco-Roman period, such as the author of Wisdom of Solomon, 4 Maccabees, and Philo, used the Hebrew Bible to point to virtuous people from Israel's past as examples for imitation. In other words, "Scripture . . . served as a way of keeping alive the memory of these outstanding persons."[58] This is an important observation. While the Hebrew Bible does not explicitly indicate mimesis, it can do so implicitly when later audiences hear or read the stories of great people from the past, such as Abraham, Moses, Joseph, and David. The zealous action of Phinehas in Num 25, for example, fueled the actions of Judas Maccabeus centuries later (1 Macc 2:23–26; Philo, *Mos.* 1.302–303) and arguably those of Paul the "zealous" Pharisee (Gal 1:13–14; Phil 3:4–6; Acts 8:1–3; 9:1–2; 22:3).

---

55. See also Michaelis, "μιμέομαι," in *TDNT*, 4:663; de Boer, *Imitation of Paul*, 29–41; Betz, *Nachfolge und Nachahmung*, 86–93.

56. See de Boer, *Imitation of Paul*, 24–91; Betz, *Nachfolge und Nachahmung*, 84–101; Castelli, *Imitating Paul*, 59–87.

57. Capes, "Imitatio Christi," 7–10.

58. Capes, "Imitatio Christi," 9. Likewise, Kurz notes how the Maccabean patriarch Mattathias in his farewell speech presents several biblical models to his sons for emulation (1 Macc 2:49–70) ("Narrative Models," 180–82).

3.2.1. Hellenistic Judaism—the LXX and Pseudepigrapha

The Septuagint, or LXX, contains some instances of mimesis but not always in relation to ethics, which is the focus of our study. For example, we noted earlier that God provided Moses with the blueprint (παράδειγμα/τύπος) of the tabernacle, and David did likewise with Solomon regarding the temple (Exod 25:9, 40; 1 Chr 28:11–12). We read elsewhere that the Jerusalem temple is an imitation (μίμημα) of the heavenly tabernacle (Wis 9:8). However, these instances are not in the ethical realm.

In the following cases, however, mimesis relates more clearly to ethics. In Deut 12:30, Moses exhorts Israel not to follow (ἐπακολουθεῖν) or "imitate" the idolatrous practices of other nations, which has ethical implications. Similarly, in Wis 15:9, potters imitate (μιμεῖται) metal workers in producing idols. Sometimes, a person's behavior becomes an example (ὑπόδειγμα) for others, such as Enoch in Sir 44:16 and Eleazar in 2 Macc 6:28, 31.[59] More generally, the author of Wisdom of Solomon observes that when virtue is present or available, people imitate (μιμοῦνται) it (Wis 4:2). The author of 2 Maccabees condemns those priests who, in support of Jason's Hellenization project, sought to imitate (ἐξομοιοῦσθαι) Greek practices and neglected their temple duties (2 Macc 4:16).

The book that contains the most mimetic language is the martyrological account of 4 Maccabees. In 4 Macc 6:18–19, Eleazar reasons that, having lived a virtuous life, one should not later in life become a negative example (παράδειγμα/τύπος) to young people. Elsewhere, the first of seven brothers to be tortured by Antiochus IV encourages the others to imitate him (μιμήσασθέ με, ἀδελφοί) in faithful endurance (4 Macc 9:23). The seven brothers also encourage each other to imitate (μιμεῖσθαι) Shadrach, Meshach, and Abednego (see Dan 3:12), who showed courage in the face of torture (4 Macc 13:9). Then, when Antiochus IV sees the courage and endurance of the seven brothers, he presents them as an example (ὑπόδειγμα) for his own soldiers (4 Macc 17:23).

Turning to the pseudepigrapha, most instances of mimesis occur in the Sibylline Oracles, the Testament of the Twelve Patriarchs, and the Letter of Aristeas, albeit not always in relation to ethics. In a few instances, τύπος is used to refer to the image, type, or pattern of humans, possibly rooted in Gen 1:26–27 (1 En.

---

59. While Kurz notes that Sirach only mentions Enoch as a ὑπόδειγμα, he contends that other figures in Sir 44:1–50:24 also function as examples of both virtue and vice ("Narrative Models," 183–84). Williams also notes that while there is no explicit mimetic language in 1 Macc 2:51–61, the exhortation to remember and consider the deeds of Israel's great people in every generation points to the idea of imitation ("Imitate Me," 217).

106:5, 10; Sib. Or. 1:99, 309; 3:27). In Sib. Or. 1:331–333, a Christian redaction mentions specifically that Christ is the exact τύπος of God (see also Sib. Or. 8:269–271). T. Levi 8:14 refers to a new priesthood according to the τύπος of other nations. Some instances, however, relate to ethics. In Sib. Or. 2:146, we find a proverbial saying, "Do not imitate evil" (μὴ μιμοῦ κακότητα), similar to what we find in 3 John 11 (see also Ps.-Phoc. 77; Ahiqar 26:15); and Sib. Or. 4:35–36 mentions that the wise or godly person will not imitate (μιμεῖσθαι) those who are insolent. The Testament of the Twelve Patriarchs contains a reference to the imitation of God (T. Ash. 4:3), as well as the imitation of exemplary people such as Joseph (T. Benj. 3:1), Abraham (T. Ab. 20:15) and, more generally, a good person (T. Benj. 4:1). In the Letter of Aristeas, there are direct injunctions to imitate God's goodness or gentleness (Let. Aris. 188, 210), or indirect, to imitate the righteous conduct of the king, who imitates God's goodness (Let. Aris. 280–281).[60] In 4 Ezra 15:48, we even find the idea of national imitation when the author states that Asia has imitated Babylon in its evil practices.

Both the LXX and pseudepigrapha deploy the standard Greek mimetic language, and some occurrences refer to mimetic ethics, although these do not reveal insight into the workings of mimesis. What this does show, however, is that Hellenistic Judaism seems to have adopted Greek mimetic thought.[61]

3.2.2. Josephus

Josephus uses a range of standard mimetic terms (e.g., μιμεῖσθαι, μίμησις, μιμητής, τύπος, ὑπόδειγμα, παράδειγμα), mostly in his *Antiquities*.[62] However, we will focus on those instances that relate to ethics. It is worth noting that Josephus introduces the concept of mimesis, especially in recounting biblical accounts about Israel's leaders.[63] In his preface, Josephus mentions the paradigmatic value of historical examples for his readers:

60. See also Capes, "*Imitatio Christi*," 9.
61. As can be expected, there was less assimilation of Greek thought in Palestinian Judaism. For example, the Dead Sea Scrolls contain no evidence of mimetic concepts (see de Boer, *Imitation of Paul*, 46n91; Schulz, *Nachfolgen und Nachahmen*, 222). Besides, as Lehel Lészai explains, in the Qumran community, "The teachers kept changing and for this reason a trustful, intimate relationship could not develop between the teacher and his disciples. The emphasis was on the doctrine not on the teacher" (*Discipleship in the Synoptics* [Cluj: Presa Universitară Clujeană, 2017], 108).
62. Across Josephus's writings, the lexeme μιμεῖσθαι occurs sixty-three times (fifty-four times in *Ant.*), τύπος nine times (eight times in *Ant.*), παράδειγμα twenty-two times (twenty times in *Ant.*), and ὑπόδειγμα six times (all in *Ant.*).
63. While this corroborates Capes's findings above, Capes himself does not refer to Josephus.

PART 1   MIMESIS IN ANTIQUITY

> The reader is therefore to know, that Moses deemed it exceedingly necessary, that he who would conduct his own life well, and give laws to others, in the first place should consider the Divine Nature, and upon the contemplation of God's operations, should thereby imitate the best of all patterns, so far as it is possible for human nature to do, and to endeavour to follow after it. (*Ant.* 1.19)[64]

A few examples will demonstrate this tendency. On the positive side, Seth is presented as a virtuous man whose children imitated his virtues (*Ant.* 1.68), Abraham was an example of goodness for Lot (*Ant.* 1.200),[65] the Israelites imitated their leader Moses in eating the manna (*Ant.* 3.28), young men who had a regard for virtue imitated Phinehas's courage and killed those who were guilty of the same crime as Zimri (*Ant.* 4.154), and the Israelite tribes imitated the behavior of the Benjamites (*Ant.* 5.129). Conversely, Josephus recounts the warning to Israelites not to imitate the idolatrous, lawless surrounding nations (*Ant.* 5.98), that Samson imitated the wrong customs of foreign nations (*Ant.* 5.306), and that David's army had failed to remember and imitate successful war tactics from the past (*Ant.* 7.142–143).

In *Ant.* 8–10, Josephus documents Israel's monarchy and distinguishes between good and wicked kings based on whom they imitated. Regarding Solomon, for example, Josephus notes that early in his career, Solomon imitated David in the things David excelled in (*Ant.* 8.24). But later, he started to imitate the practices of his foreign wives (*Ant.* 8.193). Josephus then sums up Solomon's life: "This [Solomon] did, notwithstanding that he had his father as a most excellent and domestic pattern of virtue, and knew what a glorious character he had left behind him, because of his piety toward God; nor did he imitate David, although God had twice appeared to him in his sleep, and exhorted him to imitate his father: so he died ingloriously" (*Ant.* 8.196). Josephus continues to categorize good and wicked kings by their mimetic behavior (e.g., *Ant.* 8.251, 315; 9.44, 99, 173, 243, 282;

O'Connor remarks that "Josephus integrates biographical discourse into his historiography for morally formative ends" (*Moral Life*, 35).

64. This text came to my notice in Kurz, "Narrative Models," 179. For a detailed account of Josephus's portrayal of Moses's exemplary leadership, see Petitfils, *Mos Christianorum*, 98–114.

65. While Josephus's lengthy account of Abraham contains no explicit mimetic language (*Ant.* 1.148–256), his introduction to Abraham betrays an exemplary dimension: "He was a person of great sagacity, both for understanding all things and persuading his hearers, and . . . he determined to renew and to change the opinion all men happened then to have concerning God, for he was the first that ventured to publish this notion, 'That there was but one God'" (*Ant.* 1.154–155). For Abraham as an example for imitation, see Annette Yoshiko Reed, "The Construction and Subversion of Patriarchal Perfection: Abraham and Exemplarity in Philo, Josephus, and the Testament of Abraham," *JSJ* 40 (2009): 185–212, at 195–203.

10.37, 47, 50). Closer to his own time, Josephus describes how Jason, the brother of Onias, promoted the Greek way of life and people started to imitate the practices of other nations (*Ant.* 12.239–241); how King Antipater imitated negative practices (*Ant.* 17.109–110); and how Archelaus sought to provide a virtuous example to his prospective subjects (*Ant.* 17.312–313). Josephus clearly understood that Israel's leaders were role models and that their sons and subjects would imitate them, whether in good or bad behavior.

In his *Antiquities*, Josephus employs the concept of mimesis primarily in service of role models in leadership, recounting great people from Israel's distant and recent past—some of whom modeled good behavior while others modeled bad behavior—and how others imitated their example. Josephus's use of the concept of ethical mimesis falls within the scope of the Greco-Roman mimetic traditions. Like the Greco-Roman counterparts, Josephus shows that mimesis is an important ethical dynamic in the overlapping areas of family and civic life. Josephus's novelty is that while the concept of mimesis is latent in the Hebrew Bible, he freely uses mimesis in recounting Israel's leadership traditions.

3.2.3. Philo

Philo deploys a rich variety of mimetic language, often in a Platonic cosmological and anthropological sense to express that something is a copy of something else.[66] A few examples will reveal the range of mimesis in Philo. Like the ancient Greeks, Philo affirms that art is an imitation (μίμημα) and representation (ἀπεικόνισμα) of nature (*Ebr.* 90). His assertion that the shape of the theater imitates or is modeled on (μιμεῖσθαι) that of the ear (*Post.* 104) denotes analogy between the two objects rather than ethical mimesis. Regarding the construction of the tabernacle, he notes that God showed Moses the model (παράδειγμα), and then Bezaleel made imitations (μιμήματα) of the archetypal models (ἀρχέτυπα) Moses had provided (*Leg.* 3.102; see also *Mos.* 2.74; *Somn.* 1.206).

Philo also uses mimetic language in an ethical sense to speak of human behavior and occasionally provides insight into the workings of ethical mimesis. In *Mos.* 1.3, he explains that the reason for providing a full account of the life of Moses is to preserve "a record of virtuous men and praiseworthy lives, so that honorable actions, whether ancient or modern, might not be buried in silence, and thus

---

66. For example, the lexeme μιμεῖσθαι occurs 139 times, τύπος eighty-three times, ὑπόδειγμα four times, παράδειγμα eighty-seven times, and the ζηλ* group 150 times. See also Michaelis, "μιμέομαι," in *TDNT*, 4:664–65; de Boer, *Imitation of Paul*, 10; Betz, *Nachfolge und Nachahmung*, 130–35.

have all recollection of them lost."[67] Philo echoes the Greco-Roman sentiment of mimesis in the areas of family and education. Generally, pupils are to imitate their teacher (*Sacr.* 65) and children their father (*Sacr.* 68). Philo endorses the imitation of close family members (*Ebr.* 95; *Mos.* 1.325), recognizing that the imitation of virtuous domestic examples can shape a person's life (*Spec.* 4.182).

Like Josephus, Philo uses mimetic language to refer to various exemplary people of Israel's past. Abraham is presented as a model of "zeal for piety" (*Abr.* 60).[68] In *Mos.* 1.302–303, Philo recounts how pious Israelites observed and imitated Phinehas's action and killed those who had defiled the nation. Following a general exhortation to practice (rather than simply listen to) what is good by observing and imitating (μιμεῖσθαι) the lives of virtuous people, Philo mentions Jacob as an example of one who did not only listen to his parents but imitated their virtuous actions (*Congr.* 69–70).[69] For Philo, Moses's fellowship with God and his access to the invisible world made him the ideal example for imitation (παράδειγμα ... μιμεῖσθαι) (*Mos.* 1.158–159).[70] Philo then extends Moses's example to general leadership, stating that subjects will generally follow the ruler's example, whether good or bad (*Mos.* 1.160–161). Thus, Moses becomes the archetypal model (ἀρχέτυπον παράδειγμα) for leadership (*Virt.* 70), with Joshua as an imitator (μιμητής) of Moses (*Virt.* 66).[71] Philo also points to virtuous people in general as examples of ethical living. In *Migr.* 133, Philo uses the imagery of athletics to exhort people to finish the course of life without stumbling by imitating (μιμεῖσθαι) good runners. In recounting Lot's negative behavior, Philo mentions how Lot ignored the principle that imitating a good person (in this case, Abraham) leads to moral progress (*Migr.* 149). In *Praem.* 114–115, Philo stresses that imitating good models can change and improve lives.[72]

Philo uses mimetic language to explain his doctrine of creation. Just as a good model facilitates good imitation, so God used the invisible world as a template or pattern (τύπος/παράδειγμα) for the creation of the visible world (*Opif.* 16–19).

67. I noted this text in O'Connor, *Moral Life*, 30.

68. Reed, "Construction," 193.

69. See also Copan, who states that Philo clearly distinguishes between the learning of theories/words through listening and the learning of life through imitation (*Saint Paul*, 68).

70. Copan notes in Philo's writings several insights into the workings of mimesis: Moses observed the invisible God; Moses's life reflects God's nature; Moses's life becomes a model for imitation; this model can become imprinted on the lives of others (*Saint Paul*, 69).

71. For a detailed account of Philo's portrayal of Moses's exemplary leadership, see Petitfils, *Mos Christianorum*, 115–32.

72. Contra Carlos Lévy, who contends that human role models seem superfluous in Philo's understanding of moral progress ("Philo's Ethics," in *The Cambridge Companion to Philo*, ed. Adam Kamesar [Cambridge: Cambridge University Press, 2009], 146–71, at 166).

3. Mimesis in Jewish Antiquity

Philo then describes the creation of humanity according to the image of God (κατ' εἰκόνα θεοῦ; *Opif.* 25). God is the model (παράδειγμα) of the divine image, which in turn is the model of humanity, so Philo keeps "the image of God" as the middle term between God and humanity (*Leg.* 3.96). Elsewhere, when Philo asserts that man is an imitation (μίμημα) and representation (ἀπεικόνισμα) of God (*Opif.* 139; *Det.* 83), he does not mean in totality or physical form but in mind, infused with rationality or divine πνεῦμα (*Opif.* 69, 134–135). Hence, while the Hebrew Bible is, at most, suggestive of the idea of imitation regarding humans as the "image of God," Philo clearly brings Gen 1:26–27 within the scope of imitation.[73]

In several instances, Philo subscribes to the Platonic notion that assimilation to God is achieved by practicing virtue and imitating God. Being related to God because of the divine πνεῦμα, man seeks to closely follow him (i.e., imitate him) in the way of virtue (ἑπόμενος κατ' ἴχνος αὐτῷ ταῖς ὁδοῖς, ἃς λεωφόρους ἀνατέμνουσιν ἀρεταί; *Opif.* 144).[74] In *Virt.* 205, Philo states that Adam, created in God's image and likeness, was expected to follow (i.e., imitate) God's virtues as much as possible. Elsewhere, he asserts that to imitate (μιμεῖσθαι) the works of God is to cultivate virtue (*Leg.* 1.47–48); hence, human virtue is an imitation (μίμημα) and representation (ἀπεικόνισμα) of heavenly virtue (*Leg.* 1.45). While the godly man *imitates* God in his works (μιμεῖσθαι θεοῦ τὰ ἔργα), the ungodly *assume* equality with God (οἴεσθαι ἴσος εἶναι θεῷ) (*Leg.* 1.48–49). Humans should imitate God to the best of their abilities, especially in being generous or forgiving (*Virt.* 168; *Spec.* 4.73). Elsewhere, Philo

---

73. Philo's creation account is complex in that he describes two types of man: the heavenly man of Gen 1:26 (incorporeal, invisible, incorruptible, immortal), who was created in the image and likeness of God, and the earthly man of Gen 2:7, called Adam, a composition of earthly substance (dust and clay) and divine πνεῦμα (*Leg.* 1.31–33; *Opif.* 25, 69, 134–135). The resemblance of the heavenly man to God in "image" and "likeness" was not in looks or form but in *mind*, the most important part of the soul (*Opif.* 69). The body of the earthly man was made of earthly substance and mortal, but his soul proceeded from God and was immortal (*Opif.* 135). The soul of the earthly man consisted of two parts: the rational soul or mind, made by and through God, into which God breathed the divine πνεῦμα, and the irrational soul, made by God through the mind (*Leg.* 1.36–42; *Her.* 55). The rational soul or mind of Adam was patterned after the Logos and participated in God's πνεῦμα (*QG* 2.62; *Leg.* 1.42); it received the imprint (τύπος) of divine power (πνεῦμα) (*Det.* 83). So, God is the archetypal Mind, whose essence is πνεῦμα (*Spec.* 4.123), and both the heavenly and the earthly man partake in this divine πνεῦμα but differently, in that the earthly man is an inferior expression of the divine πνεῦμα than the heavenly man is. See further Cornelis Bennema, *The Power of Saving Wisdom: An Investigation of Spirit and Wisdom in Relation to the Soteriology of the Fourth Gospel*, WUNT 2/148 (Tübingen: Mohr Siebeck, 2002), 72–73; van Kooten, *Pauline Anthropology*, 48–69.

74. While Putthoff provides a comprehensive treatment of assimilation to God in *Opif.* 144, he does not explicitly relate it to mimesis—he merely states that the mind can enter God's presence, mimic him, and partake in his ontological state (*Ontological Aspects*, 85–99, at 90–91).

states that humans should imitate God by living untroubled (*Opif.* 79), keeping the Sabbath (*Decal.* 100), and (for parents) procreating (*Spec.* 2.225; *Decal.* 120).[75] In *Mos.* 1.158, Philo describes Moses in divine terms (θεὸς καὶ βασιλεύς), how his fellowship (κοινωνία) with God and access to the divine realm resulted in his assimilation to God (θεοειδής). Kings/rulers are exhorted to imitate God if they aspire to assimilation to God: "Therefore it is right for good rulers of a nation to imitate [God] in these points, if they have any anxiety to attain to a similitude to God" (ταῦτα μιμεῖσθαι προσήκει τοὺς ἀγαθοὺς ἄρχοντας, εἴ γέ τις αὐτοῖς φροντίς ἐστιν ἐξομοιώσεως τῆς πρὸς θεόν; *Spec.* 4.188). Van Kooten logically connects Philo's doctrine of creation and mimetic ethics. He argues that having been created after the image of God, man should cultivate this likeness by imitating God and assimilating himself to God—the ultimate goal of ethics (e.g., *Opif.* 144; *Virt.* 166–168).[76] He notes that Philo is aware of the *locus classicus* of the Platonic doctrine of assimilation to God (*Fug.* 63 quotes Plato, *Theaet.* 176a–b), and assimilation to God through virtue can only occur through the Logos, who is a model for ethical imitation.[77]

In Philo, the widespread use of mimetic language is in keeping with the ordinary Greek usages. While he employs the concept of mimesis in the areas of family and education, he is most innovative in using mimesis in a theological-ethical sense. While his theological-ethical use of mimesis does not go beyond what is found in Greek antiquity, he is able to integrate his Jewish faith and the Greek concept of mimesis in a way that the Hebrew Bible does not. Although Philo rarely provides explicit information about the workings of ethical mimesis, it is possible to detect individual aspects of our model of Greco-Roman mimesis in his writings: (1) selection/association (implied in the exhortations to adhere to good models), (2) observation (θεαθῆναι in *Mos.* 1.303; κατανοεῖν in *Mos.* 1.158; several references to domestic examples for imitation imply that they could be observed), (3) discernment (*Migr.* 12; implied in the exhortations to cultivate virtue and assimilate to God), (4) imitation (see the many examples mentioned above), and (5) transformation/assimilation (*Migr.* 149; *Mos.* 1.158; *Spec.* 4.182, 188; *Praem.* 114–115).[78]

---

75. For further examples, see Schulz, *Nachfolgen und Nachahmen*, 216; Betz, *Nachfolge und Nachahmung*, 132–33.

76. Van Kooten, *Paul's Anthropology*, 181–99. See also Schulz, *Nachfolgen und Nachahmen*, 216–20; Betz, *Nachfolge und Nachahmung*, 131.

77. Van Kooten, *Paul's Anthropology*, 186–87, 192. See also Sierksma-Agteres, "Imitation in Faith," 129. Sierksma-Agteres contends that, for Philo, Abraham and Moses are the supreme examples of the virtue of *pistis* ("faithfulness," "trust"), leading to assimilation to God ("Imitation in Faith," 133–34).

78. While Copan detects similar mechanics of imitation in Philo, he infers these from *Praem.* 114–116 rather than the entire Philonic corpus (*Saint Paul*, 63–64), although elsewhere he infers

3. Mimesis in Jewish Antiquity

3.2.4. The Rabbinic Traditions

The rabbinic traditions contain a few instances of mimesis in relation to ethical behavior.[79] In m. Šabb. 6.9, we read that the sages object to Rabbi Meir's decision to permit certain practices on the Sabbath for fear that this would amount to imitating the behavior of the Amorites (see also b. B. Qam. 91b). In b. 'Erub. 62ab, there is a concern about Israelites living in a heathen's dwelling since this may lead to imitating his behavior. In b. Yoma 15a, Rabbi Judah imitates the movements of a whip in order to show the correct way of sprinkling various sacrifices (see also b. Zebaḥ 38a). Another text, b. Sanh. 52b, mentions that although Scripture authorizes the sword, Jews should not imitate the Roman method of decapitation by the sword. However, these instances of imitation refer merely to copying specific actions and offer no insight into the workings of mimesis or if mimesis can facilitate moral progress.

More profitable are rabbinic traditions that interpret a text from the Hebrew Bible in terms of mimesis. Milgrom notes a few instances where rabbinic traditions infer a general imitation of God from the Hebrew Bible. Sipra Shemini 12.3 (a halakhic midrash on Leviticus) interprets Lev 19:2 in comparative terms: "Just as I [God] am holy, so you are holy." Elsewhere, Abba Saul interprets the phrase "This is my God, and I will praise him" (Exod 15:2) in terms of imitating God: "This is my God, and I will be like him: *just as* he is gracious and compassionate, *so* you should be gracious and compassionate" (b. Šabb. 133b).[80]

In addition to this more general imitation of God, Arthur Marmorstein notes that the rabbis could speak of specific imitation of God, where people might imitate divine attributes such as mercy, piety, and justice (see, e.g., b. Soṭah 14a; Tg. Ps.-J. on Deut 34:6).[81] A few excerpts will help clarify this. Expounding on the phrase "after the Lord your God shall you walk" (Deut 13:4), Rabbi Ḥama ben R. Ḥanina says:

> The meaning is that one should follow the attributes of the Holy One.... Just as He clothes the naked, as it is written: "And the Lord God made for Adam and

---

insights into the workings of mimesis from *Mos.* 1.158 (p. 69). In addition, contra Copan's claim, *Praem.* 114 does not mention the "gazing" upon good models.

79. While most rabbinic literature is later than the second century CE, some ideas may go back to the first century.

80. Milgrom, *Leviticus 17–22*, 1603–4. For more examples of Abba Saul's teaching on the imitation of God, see Arthur Marmorstein, "The Imitation of God (*Imitatio Dei*) in the Haggadah," in A. Marmorstein, *Studies in Jewish Theology*, ed. J. Rabbinowitz and M. S. Lew (New York: Oxford University Press, 1950), 106–21, at 111–12.

81. Marmorstein, "Imitation of God," 113–14.

for his wife garments of skin, and clothed them" (Genesis 3:21), so too, should you clothe the naked. Just as the Holy One, Blessed be He, visits the sick, as it is written with regard to God's appearing to Abraham following his circumcision: "And the Lord appeared unto him by the terebinths of Mamre" (Genesis 18:1), so too, should you visit the sick. Just as the Holy One, Blessed be He, consoles mourners, as it is written: "And it came to pass after the death of Abraham, that God blessed Isaac his son" (Genesis 25:11), so too, should you console mourners. Just as the Holy One, Blessed be He, buried the dead, as it is written: "And he was buried in the valley in the land of Moab" (Deuteronomy 34:6), so too, should you bury the dead. (b. Soṭah 14a)

Targum Pseudo-Jonathan on Deut 34:6 records similar words:

Blessed be the Name of the Lord of the world, who hath taught us His righteous way. He hath taught us to clothe the naked, as He clothed Adam and Hava; He hath taught us to unite the bridegroom and the bride in marriage, as He united Hava to Adam. He hath taught us to visit the sick, as He revealed Himself to Abraham when he was ill, from being circumcised; He hath taught us to console the mourners, as He revealed Himself again to Jakob when returning from Padan, in the place where his mother had died. He hath taught us to feed the poor, as He sent Israel bread from heaven; He hath taught us to bury the dead by (what He did for) Mosheh.

Elsewhere, Targum Pseudo-Jonathan on Lev 22:28 adds the exhortation to imitate God in being merciful (see also Luke 6:36) as a rationale to the prohibition to kill an animal with its young on the same day: "Sons of Israel, my people, as our Father in heaven is merciful, so shall you be merciful on earth: neither cow, nor ewe, shall you sacrifice along with her young on the same day." Pirqe Rabbi Eliezer 16.3 (a haggadic-midrash on the Torah) mentions that people learn lovingkindness from God's acts of loving-kindness:[82]

Whence do we learn of the service of loving-kindness for bridegrooms? We learn (this) from the Holy One, blessed be He; for He Himself bestowed loving-kindness upon Adam and his help-mate. The Holy One, blessed be He, said to

---

82. Similarly, Pirqe R. El. 17.1 states, "Whence do we learn of the service of loving-kindness to mourners? From the Omnipresent, who alone showed loving-kindness to Moses, His servant, and buried him with His own hand" (Felix Böhl, "Das Rabbinische Verständnis des Handelns in der Nachahmung Gottes," *ZMR* 58 [1974]: 134–41, at 138).

3. Mimesis in Jewish Antiquity

the ministering angels: Come ye and let us show loving-kindness to Adam and his help-mate. The Holy One, blessed be He, descended with the ministering angels to show loving-kindness to Adam and his help-mate. The Holy One, blessed be He, said: More beloved unto Me is the service of loving-kindness than sacrifices and burnt-offering which Israel, in the future, will bring on the altar before Me, as it is said, "For I desired love, and not sacrifice" (Hos. 6:6).

Finally, commenting on Psalm 89:6 ("For who in the skies can be compared to the LORD?"), Midr. Tanḥ. Bechukotai 4 states, "The Holy One, blessed be He, said, 'Whoever performs deeds like Mine shall be [considered] like Me.'"[83]

There is no consensus on how widespread the idea of imitating God is in rabbinic literature. At one end, we have Betz, who contends that references to the imitation of God are only sporadic in the rabbinic literature and not developed.[84] De Boer is more generous.[85] So is Schulz, who contends that the Old Testament obligation to obey God's commandments is interpreted by the rabbis as an ethical imitation of divine behavior.[86] Similarly, Micheline Chaze finds several instances of the imitation of God in the Targums and Haggadah.[87] At the other end of the spectrum, we have Marmorstein's claim that "the Haggadah is permeated with the idea that God and Israel resemble each other in holiness."[88] It would be safe to take the middle ground that although the rabbinic literature contains some references to the imitation of God, this idea is not developed to the extent we have seen in the Greco-Roman traditions. This is unsurprising, but we must concede that the rabbis nevertheless developed the latent idea of imitating God in the Hebrew Bible and made it more explicit occasionally.[89]

At the same time, however, with the formation of rabbinic schools for Torah study, pupils were expected, as in Greco-Roman society, to imitate their rabbinic teachers.[90] Birger Gerhardsson explains that ancient historiography had a didactic

---

83. Böhl, "Rabbinische Verständnis," 139.
84. Betz, *Nachfolge und Nachahmung*, 95–101.
85. De Boer, *Imitation of Paul*, 42–43.
86. Schulz, *Nachfolgen und Nachahmen*, 222–23.
87. Micheline Chaze, *L'Imitatio Dei dans le Targum et la Aggada* (Leuven: Peeters, 2005).
88. Marmorstein, "Imitation of God," 120.
89. Schulz even considers that the Hellenistic understanding of following God as imitation in Philo may have influenced the reinterpretation of the Old Testament in the later rabbinic traditions (*Nachfolgen und Nachahmen*, 225).
90. De Boer, *Imitation of Paul*, 43–44; Griffiths, *Example of Jesus*, 21–24. While the existence of "formal" schools in the tannaitic period (10–200 CE) is debated, de Boer is undoubtedly correct that pupils sought to imitate their teacher. For a brief introduction to the rabbinic educational system, see Craig A. Evans, "Judaism, Post-A.D. 70," in *Dictionary of the Later New Testament &*

purpose in that the rabbinic traditions provided examples to be emulated. The pupil was to seek the tutelage of a rabbi, memorize his teaching, observe his actions, and imitate him.[91] The well-known anecdote of Rabbi Kahana, who hid underneath the bed of his teacher when he and his wife had sexual intercourse, shows how far the idea of observing the teacher could go: "R. Kahana once went in and hid under Rab's bed. He heard him chatting [with his wife] and joking and doing what he required. He said to him: One would think that R. Abba's mouth had never sipped the dish before! He said to him: Kahana, are you here? Go out, because it is rude. He replied: It is a matter of Torah, and I require to learn" (b. Ber. 62a).

Gerhardsson also tells us that the rabbis were conscious that their lives were visible examples or teaching for their pupils to imitate. To illustrate, he mentions that the school of Shammai is instructive in that the *Shema* must be read lying down, while the school of Hillel is not prescriptive.[92] So, in t. Ber. 1.1 we find the following conversation between the Shammite Rabbi Ishmael and the Hillelite Rabbi Eleazar regarding the reading of the *Shema*:

> It happened with R. Ishmael and R. Eleazar ben Azariah that they were resting in the same place and R. Ishmael was lying down and R. Eleazar ben Azariah was [standing up] straight. It came time to say Shema. R. Ishmael stood up straight and R. Eleazar lay down. Said to him R. Ishmael: "What is this Elaezar?" He said [back] to him: "Ishmael, my brother! . . . I who was straight, lay down, you that was lying down, stood up straight?" So R. Ishmael said to him: "You lay down to fulfil the words of the House of Shammai, I stood up straight to fulfil the words of the House of Hillel." [A different explanation] "[I arose] so that the students should not see [that you did like the House of Shammai] and make your words [a] permanent [law]."[93]

Its Developments, ed. Ralph P. Martin and Peter H. Davids (Downers Grove, IL: InterVarsity Press, 1997), 605–11, at 608–9. Ron Naiweld's treatment of mimesis in the disciple–rabbi relationship is too abstract and insufficiently grounded in rabbinic texts ("Mastering the Disciple: Mimesis in the Master–Disciples Relationships of Rabbinic Literature," in *Metapher–Narratio–Mimesis–Doxologie: Begründungsformen frühchristlicher und antiker Ethik*, ed. Ulrich Volp, Friedrich W. Horn, and Ruben Zimmermann, CNNTE 7, WUNT 356 [Tübingen: Mohr Siebeck, 2016], 257–70).

91. Birger Gerhardsson, *Memory and Manuscript: Oral Tradition and Written Transmission in Rabbinic Judaism and Early Christianity* (Grand Rapids: Eerdmans, 1998 [orig. 1961]), 182–83. See also Lészai, *Discipleship*, 119.

92. Gerhardsson, *Memory and Manuscript*, 185–86.

93. Text taken from http://www.sefaria.org.

3. Mimesis in Jewish Antiquity

Hence, the rabbinic teacher knew that his pupils would infer halakhic opinions from his conduct as a form of visual teaching and imitate him.[94]

3.3. Conclusion

Our study of mimesis as an ethical concept in ancient Jewish traditions has yielded interesting results. Since mimesis is an innate mechanism of human development, one would expect mimesis to be present in every culture and not exclusive to Greco-Roman culture. We did indeed find mimetic ideas in the Hebrew Bible, but they were surprisingly few and mainly implicit. In other words, while the Hebrew Bible contains traces or seeds of mimesis (mainly in the Pentateuch), the concept is certainly not developed. However, when Greek culture started to influence Jewish thought (a process called "Hellenization"), these seeds came to fruition in several Jewish writings of the Second Temple period.

Nevertheless, while the cross-pollination with Greek culture caused the Greek concept of mimesis to blossom in Second Temple Judaism, we cannot assume it did so everywhere to the same extent. Josephus and Philo used the Greek concept of mimesis most extensively but very differently. While Josephus uses the concept of mimesis primarily in a historical-ethical sense in the overlapping areas of family and civic life to show how Israel's leaders functioned as (good and bad) examples for imitation, Philo uses mimesis more broadly in a theological-ethical sense in the overlapping areas of religion, family, and education, from the creation of the world and humanity to the imitation of God through a virtuous life. Hence, just as Greek culture permeated all of Judaism to various extents, the concept of mimesis found its way into Jewish thinking in different degrees and ways, so we cannot speak of a homogeneous concept of mimesis in Second Temple Judaism.

Some scholars have also noted the scope of the Jewish concept of mimesis. Capes, for example, contends that the concept of mimesis in Second Temple Judaism particularly served to encourage faithful Jews during periods of persecution and suffering but also notes the idea of imitating God by keeping the commandments, doing justice, and showing generosity, goodness, and mercy.[95] Likewise, Drake Williams concludes, "Rather than urging obedience, a Jewish perspective on imitation reveals that the word is employed frequently in relation to godly virtues. These include following the Law, showing courage, displaying wisdom, embracing

---

94. Gerhardsson, *Memory and Manuscript*, 186–87. Besides t. Ber. 1.1, Gerhardsson mentions other examples, such as t. Demai 5.24; b. ʿErub. 93b–94a; b. Meg. 28b; b. Šabb. 21a; b. B. Bat. 130b.
95. Capes, *"Imitatio Christi,"* 9–10.

piety, and demonstrating righteous living."[96] While Felix Böhl acknowledges that the concept of mimesis in both Philo and the rabbinic traditions is indebted to Hellenistic thought, he notes a crucial difference. For Philo, the imitation of God is rooted in creation (Gen 1:26) and occurs primarily by means of the Logos as an intermediary divine being or demiurge. The rabbis, however, connect the imitation of God more with the holiness command and in keeping with the personal God of the Hebrew Bible.[97]

We also learned that the various Jewish mimetic expressions stay within the linguistic and conceptual confines of Greco-Roman usage and do not provide additional insights into the workings of mimesis. This means we can consider how the Jewish mimetic traditions resemble the Greco-Roman model of mimesis that we constructed in the previous chapter. While no single Second Temple Jewish writing fully presents the Greco-Roman mimetic model, we note that aspects of the mimetic model feature in Second Temple Jewish literature. A few examples might help. In 4 Macc 17:23, when Antiochus IV observes the courageous behavior of the seven brothers, he presents them as an example for his own soldiers. In T. Benj. 4:1, people are exhorted to observe the good person in order to imitate him. T. Ab. 20:15 contains an exhortation to imitate Abraham's hospitality in order to attain eternal life, which arguably amounts to transformation. In the rabbinic traditions, aspiring disciples would associate themselves with a rabbi in order to observe his behavior, absorb his teachings, and imitate him. Across Philo's writings, we find all aspects of the Greco-Roman mimetic model, which is unsurprising given that Philo had embraced the Greek cultural project (without compromising his Jewish ideals).

While the Jewish mimetic traditions contain instances where the imitator is able to observe the exemplar directly (e.g., 4 Macc 9:23; 17:23; Philo, *Sacr*. 65, 68; *Ebr*. 95; *Spec*. 4.182; the rabbinic pupil–rabbi relationship), there are also instances of *mediated mimesis*, that is, instances where the example for imitation cannot be observed by the imitator and mimesis is mediated by other means. One form is *textually mediated mimesis*, where an author presents in his writing an exemplary person to his audience as an example to be observed and emulated. We noted that Philo and especially Josephus use this form of mimesis by recording the past lives of exemplary people so that their hearers or readers could visualize and imitate them.[98] Another form is *mnemonic mimesis*, where a historical exemplar is mediated to the imitator in the present through remembrance. In 4 Macc 13:9,

---

96. Williams, "Imitate Me," 224.
97. Böhl, "Rabbinische Verständnis," 141.
98. See also Capes, *"Imitatio Christi,"* 7–10; Copan, *Saint Paul*, 47.

3. Mimesis in Jewish Antiquity

for example, the brothers who were martyred by Antiochus IV encouraged one another to recall the courage of Shadrach, Meshach, and Abednego as they once faced torture. The implication is that remembering past heroes could evoke a mental picture of exemplary behavior that can be imitated.

Another instance is found in *Ant.* 7.142–143, where Josephus refers to an episode from David's wars. When castigating his army for having used the wrong war tactic, David urges them to remember (μνημονεύειν) the past example (παράδειγμα) of Abimelech, who used a similar war tactic with disastrous consequences. Josephus portrays David describing the incident with Abimelech in detail so that his army could visualize it and avoid imitating it. Josephus then concludes, "The best method of making war with success was to remember (ἔχειν μνήμην) the mistakes of former wars, and what good or bad success had attended them in similar dangerous cases, so as to imitate (μιμεῖσθαι) the one, and avoid the other" (*Ant.* 7.143). The retelling of this incident may even have served as an example for the Jews who were struggling against their Roman overlords in Josephus's own time.

We can now evaluate the claim of some scholars that the New Testament concept of mimesis is rooted in the Old Testament. I conclude that the pre-Greek Hebraic tradition preserved in the Hebrew Bible (or Old Testament) cannot adequately explain the concept of mimesis in early Christianity. In the Hebrew Bible, the concept of mimesis is latent but not developed as a distinct ethical model. At most, we can see the seeds of mimetic ideas, which come to fruition when Second Temple Judaism comes into contact with Greek thought and culture. By the first century, the Greco-Roman concept of mimesis had also found its way into early Christianity. I thus suggest that the seeds for the New Testament concept of mimesis were latent in the Old Testament, and Greek thought germinated these for the New Testament authors. This development will be the subject of investigation in the next chapters.

PART 2

Mimesis in Early Christianity

4

MIMESIS IN THE SYNOPTICS AND ACTS

In the previous chapters, we investigated the concept of mimesis in Greco-Roman and Jewish antiquity. We learned that a latent concept of mimesis in the Hebrew Bible became more palpable in Second Temple Judaism when the latter came into contact with Greek thought and culture. In part 2, we will examine to what extent early Christianity adopted (and adapted) the concept of mimesis. We will start with the Synoptics and Acts (chapter 4), continue with John (chapter 5) and Paul (chapter 6), and finish with the rest of the New Testament (chapter 7) and the Apostolic Fathers (chapter 8). For each section of early Christian literature, we will delineate the mimetic language as the basis for examining the concept of mimesis to prevent operating merely at the level of ideas. We will also consider to what extent there is correspondence with the model of mimesis we found in the Greco-Roman traditions.

The focus of this chapter is the concept of mimesis in the Synoptics and Acts, particularly the disciples' or believers' imitation of Jesus or God.[1] While much has been written on discipleship in the Gospels, rarely do scholars touch on the subject of mimesis.[2] Those who do address the subject often do not develop it.

---

1. I will not consider those who look at mimesis as other than an ethical concept. For example, David P. Parris explores mimesis as a hermeneutical concept, drawing on Ricœur's threefold hermeneutical approach to mimesis ("Imitating the Parables: Allegory, Narrative and the Role of Mimesis," *JSNT* 25 [2002]: 33–53). Likewise, Graham Ward explores the hermeneutical nature of narrative and mimesis in Mark ("Mimesis: The Measure of Mark's Christology," *Journal of Literature & Theology* 8 [1994]: 1–29). Octavian Baban focuses on literary mimesis—how Luke's concept of journeys draws on the journey motif in Hellenistic novels (*On the Road Encounters in Luke–Acts: Hellenistic Mimesis and Luke's Theology of the Way* [Milton Keynes: Paternoster, 2006], ch. 2).

2. For the concept of discipleship in the Synoptics Gospels, see Ernest Best, *Following Jesus: Discipleship in the Gospel of Mark*, JSNTSup 4 (Sheffield: JSOT Press, 1981); Best, *Disciples and Discipleship: Studies in the Gospel according to Mark* (Edinburgh: T&T Clark, 1986); Stephen Barton,

PART 2   MIMESIS IN EARLY CHRISTIANITY

For example, while Sylvia Wilkey Collinson recognizes an element of imitation in the concept of discipleship, she establishes this link rather loosely from ancient education models where the learner observes and imitates the teacher.³ Or, based on Mark 8:33–9:1, Shiner simply states that "the narrative portrayal of Jesus provides a model for the listeners, who are to pick up their own crosses and follow."⁴ The question is whether discipleship or following Jesus involves imitation. Do the Synoptic Gospels present Jesus as a model to imitate, and is it the disciple's aim to become like Jesus? To answer this question, we will examine whether the verb ἀκολουθεῖν ("to follow") has connotations of imitation in the Synoptics (section 4.1). Beyond this, we will examine whether the Synoptics contain other expressions of mimesis. After all, the lexeme μιμεῖσθαι does not occur in the Synoptics.

We will turn to each of the Synoptic Gospels, outlining what scholarship has noticed about mimesis, examining the potential mimetic language in order to determine the nature of mimesis, and finally, determining the place of mimesis in the Evangelists' ethics.⁵ While such an approach can be tedious, it avoids the flaw in Burridge's *Imitating Jesus*. The strength of Burridge's work is his hypothesis that the genre of the Gospels as ancient biographies means they present Jesus as an example to imitate.⁶ The weakness is that he does not define imitation but applies it loosely (one should imitate Jesus's open acceptance of others) without linking it to specific words or phrases. Similarly, Tinsley's assertion that to follow Jesus implies following his way of life, that is, to imitate him, is too general.⁷ Even his specific examples of the disciples' imitation of God or Jesus—being perfect/merciful (Matt 5:48; Luke 6:36), renunciation (Mark 8:34; Luke 14:33), Torah-obedience

---

Discipleship and Family Ties in Mark and Matthew, SNTSMS 80 (Cambridge: Cambridge University Press, 1994); Michael J. Wilkins, *Discipleship in the Ancient World and Matthew's Gospel*, 2nd ed. (Grand Rapids: Baker, 1995); Whitney Taylor Shiner, *Follow Me! Disciples in Markan Rhetoric*, SBLDS 145 (Atlanta: Scholars Press, 1995); Richard N. Longenecker, ed., *Patterns of Discipleship in the New Testament* (Grand Rapids: Eerdmans, 1996), chs. 1–3; Sylvia Wilkey Collinson, *Making Disciples: The Significance of Jesus' Educational Methods for Today's Church*, PTM (Milton Keynes: Paternoster, 2004); Kathleen Elizabeth Mills, *The Kinship of Jesus: Christology and Discipleship in the Gospel of Mark* (Eugene, OR; Wipf and Stock, 2016); Lészai, *Discipleship*, 2017.

3. Collinson, *Making Disciples*, 12–14, 35–36, 41, 69.
4. Shiner, *Follow Me*, 272.
5. Without committing to a particular hypothesis of literary dependency, I support the majority view that Mark's Gospel was written first, which Matthew and Luke used as a source.
6. Burridge, *Imitating Jesus*, 28–31, 73–78. For the mimetic aspect of the ancient biography, see also section 1.2 (on Capes and Burridge), section 2.2.4 (on Plutarch's *Lives*), and section 9.2 (under question 2).
7. Tinsley, *Imitation of God*, 102. Kwon also sees, too readily, the imitation of Christ in the Gospels (*Christ as Example*, 62–64).

(Mark 3:35; Luke 6:46), humility (Mark 10:42–45), and suffering (Mark 10:39)—are more general characteristics of discipleship and do not always constitute mimesis.[8] Griffiths, too, often operates at a conceptual level—his concept of imitating Jesus is derived mainly from related concepts such as "disciples," "followers," "apprentices," "witnesses," and "the way," and is insufficiently anchored in the text.[9] Moreover, when he highlights aspects of Jesus's life that can be imitated—service, patience/endurance, suffering, gentleness/meekness, humility, obedience, and love—very few of his references come from the Synoptics.[10] Noting the idea in antiquity that a disciple was to follow a master/teacher and imitate him, Hood also sees, too readily at times, a concept of imitating Jesus in the Synoptics.[11] Mindful of these pitfalls, we will seek to carry out a close reading of the Synoptic accounts and develop a more text-based concept of mimesis.

4.1. Following Jesus as Mimesis?

Discipleship undoubtedly involves relationship (personal attachment to the teacher), loyalty (allegiance to the teacher), and learning (adherence to the teacher's instruction).[12] So, it would seem obvious that a disciple sought to imitate (aspects of) the teacher. However, the question is whether the verb ἀκολουθεῖν ("to follow"), which is central to the Synoptic understanding of discipleship, suggests imitation. Discipleship is a major theme in the Synoptics, where people commit to following Jesus and pledging allegiance to him. The act of "following Jesus," expressed mainly by the verb ἀκολουθεῖν (eighteen occurrences in Mark, twenty-five in Matthew, and twenty-one in Luke–Acts), is demonstrated by a variety of people: the (twelve) disciples (e.g., Mark 1:18; 6:1; Matt 4:20–22; 19:27; Luke 5:11; 18:28), the crowd (e.g., Mark 5:24; Matt 4:25; 8:1; Luke 9:11), and other potential disciples (e.g., Mark 8:34; Matt 8:19; 10:38; Luke 9:23; 18:22). The image of a person coming "after/behind" (ὀπίσω) Jesus is synonymous with the concept of following him (see, e.g., Mark 8:34). Important for our study is to determine whether the

---

8. Tinsley, *Imitation of God*, 114–16. We will see that only Matt 5:48/Luke 6:36 and Mark 10:42–45 qualify as mimesis. Tinsley is more accurate when it comes to mimesis in Acts (see section 4.4.4 below).

9. Griffiths, *Example of Jesus*, 43–53.

10. Griffiths, *Example of Jesus*, 86–103. Nevertheless, it must be noted that he regards the imitation of Jesus as a deliberate and purposeful copying of his lifestyle, which requires thinking and volition (*Example of Jesus*, 44, 80, 182).

11. Hood, *Imitating God*, 71–81.

12. Wilkins, *Discipleship*, 11–13, 93.

PART 2   MIMESIS IN EARLY CHRISTIANITY

Synoptic concept of discipleship includes the idea of imitating Jesus in order to become like him or whether discipleship goes no further than involvement in Jesus's life and mission.

I will not examine the term μαθητής ("disciple," "learner," "apprentice," "adherent") because although the term occurs frequently in the Synoptics (forty-six times in Mark; seventy-two in Matt; sixty-five in Luke–Acts), it is not explained. For example, μαθητής is only used six times in the singular and then only by Jesus in a generic sense (Matt 10:24, 25; Luke 6:40; 14:26, 27, 33). In contrast, the term almost always occurs in the plural to refer to the twelve disciples—Jesus's inner group that is chosen to be with him and to be trained for their apostolic mission. Besides, μαθητής is rarely linked with ἀκολουθεῖν and never with μανθάνειν ("to learn").[13] Instead, the Synoptics prefer to invest in the concept of ἀκολουθεῖν, linking it to a variety of people—the twelve disciples, the crowds, and would-be disciples—and explaining its various aspects.

Scholars differ significantly on the mimetic potential of "following Jesus" (see also section 1.2). Tinsley, for example, holds that "following Jesus" means imitating him. He argues that the Old Testament idea of Israel imitating God by following or walking in his ways takes a trajectory into the New Testament, first, in Jesus's walking in the way of Israel and thus becoming "the way," and second, in the discipleship language of following Jesus.[14] For Tinsley, to follow Jesus is to follow his way of life, hence to imitate him.[15] De Boer disagrees with Tinsley that "to walk in God's ways" suggests imitating God's actions and conduct. Rather, God's ways are the ways that God has prescribed for people, and walking in God's ways is akin to keeping his commandments.[16] Nevertheless, de Boer admits that the concept of "following Jesus" in the Gospels hints at, and is part of, imitation.[17] Schulz and Betz, who each examine the continuity between the notion of following Jesus in the Gospels and that of imitating Christ in Paul, argue that despite the strong philological and conceptual discontinuity, there is some theological-hermeneutical continuity in that both notions promote a single concept of discipleship. For ex-

---

13. In Mark 8:34, Jesus explains aspects of following him to both the disciples and the crowd (the parallel passage Matt 16:24 omits the crowd). None of the four occurrences of μανθάνειν (Matt 9:13; 11:29; 24:32; Mark 13:28) is explicitly linked with μαθητής, although the twelve disciples are Jesus's audience in Mark 13:28 and its parallel Matt 24:32. The related verb μαθητεύειν ("to be or make a disciple") only occurs in Matt 13:52; 27:57; 28:19 and provides no information about the content of discipleship.

14. Tinsley, *Imitation of God*, chs. 3–7. See also Smalley, "Imitation of Christ in the New Testament," 15–16.

15. Tinsley, *Imitation of God*, 102.

16. De Boer, *Imitation of Paul*, 33–38.

17. De Boer, *Imitation of Paul*, 50–57. Horn also includes following (besides other ideas) in the concept of mimesis ("Mimetische Ethik," 200).

4. Mimesis in the Synoptics and Acts

ample, they contend that although the verb ἀκολουθεῖν does not mean "to imitate," the meaning is sometimes implied.[18]

Larsson argues that imitation is part of following and, hence, should be subsumed under discipleship.[19] Noting that the Synoptics do not contain mimetic language, Moss also concludes that "the practice of following Christ effectively is embodied imitation."[20] Others contend that following Jesus does *not* mean imitating him.[21] Walter Ong, for example, asserts, "Despite all the talk over many centuries concerning the 'imitation of Christ', the fact is that in the Gospel accounts Jesus *never* says to anyone that they should 'imitate' him. He does say, over and over again, 'Follow me.'"[22] Ong goes so far as to claim that imitation and following are in *contrast* because he views imitation as mechanical replication, whereas following is a venturesome participation.[23]

This brief survey shows that for some scholars, "following Jesus" (in the Gospels) is synonymous (Tinsley) or continuous with "imitating Jesus" (in Paul) (Schulz and Betz, but only at a theological level). Others contend that "imitating Jesus" falls within the gamut of "following Jesus" (Larsson, Thysman, Kwon, Hawthorne, Copan, Milchner, Burridge, Moss) or vice versa, that the language of "following Jesus" is part of the concept of "imitating Jesus" (de Boer, Horn). Still others contend that following Jesus and imitating him are unrelated (Kittel, Rengstorf, Hengel) or even incompatible concepts (Ong).

I consider de Boer's analysis of ἀκολουθεῖν helpful in navigating the range of options. He argues that the language of "following Jesus" in the Gospels has connotations of imitation.[24] While we cannot assume that the verb ἀκολουθεῖν means "to imitate," in the Jewish educational system, for a pupil "to follow" meant "learning

---

18. Schulz, *Nachfolgen und Nachahmen*, 332–35; Betz, *Nachfolge und Nachahmung*, 3, 40–43, 186–89.

19. Larsson, *Christus als Vorbild*, 17. Others who concur that imitation is part of following Jesus or discipleship include Thysman, "L'Éthique de l'Imitation du Christ," 143–56; Kwon, *Christ as Example*, 60–61; Gerald F. Hawthorne, "The Imitation of Christ: Discipleship in Philippians," in *Patterns of Discipleship in the New Testament*, ed. Richard N. Longenecker (Grand Rapids: Eerdmans, 1996), 163–79, at 165–66; Copan, "Μαθητής and Μιμητής," 323; Milchner, *Nachfolge Jesu*, 12; Burridge, *Imitating Jesus*, 74. See also Hood, *Imitating God*, 66, 72–73.

20. Moss, *Other Christs*, 28.

21. For example, Gerhard Kittel views ἀκολουθεῖν as participation rather than imitation ("ἀκολουθέω, κτλ," in *TDNT* 1:210–16, at 214). Karl H. Rengstorf also concludes that imitation was not part of discipleship of Jesus ("μανθάνω, κτλ," in *TDNT* 4:390–461, at 441–55). Likewise, Martin Hengel states that "following after [Jesus] did *not* mean imitating individual actions of his" (*The Charismatic Leader and His Followers*, trans. James C. G. Greig [Edinburgh: T&T Clark, 1981], 53).

22. Ong, "Mimesis," 73 (original emphasis).

23. Ong, "Mimesis," 74–75.

24. De Boer, *Imitation of Paul*, 51–54.

the way of life of the master, and of making that way of life his own."²⁵ According to de Boer, when Jesus established a close fellowship with his disciples, he had in mind the rabbinic educational system of the time where pupils were to adopt a way of life and to be like their teachers.²⁶ When it comes to the expression "following Jesus," there is an additional aspect, namely participation in his life and fate, which would require a measure of imitation.²⁷ On the one hand, de Boer agrees with Kittel that "following Jesus" is in no way a case of imitating him; on the other, he contends that following Jesus "can upon occasion lead to situations and circumstances which most strikingly resemble those which Christ experienced.... The matter of imitation is not foreign to such a situation."²⁸ De Boer concludes that although "the idea of imitation is not to be found in the expression 'following Jesus' as such ... this expression portrays a situation in which imitation not only very likely will develop, but where it must develop."²⁹

In sum, our study of the Synoptics reveals that no explicit linguistic expression ties ἀκολουθεῖν to mimesis; instead, we will see that there are only conceptual traces of mimesis. Conversely, where there are more explicit occurrences of the disciples' imitating Jesus (e.g., Matt 5:48; 20:27–28; Luke 17:10), there is no mention of the verb ἀκολουθεῖν. In short, mimesis seems to be a possible, even likely, *effect* of following—in other words, following Jesus *facilitates* mimesis. Instead of arguing that following Jesus means imitating him, I suggest that believers follow Jesus *in order to* imitate him. It is *as* people follow Jesus that they can observe and imitate him. I, therefore, conclude that ἀκολουθεῖν does not equate to mimesis; rather, mimesis is the *goal* of following Jesus. We note that discipleship for the original disciples involved both a literal following (to travel with Jesus) and a fig-

---

25. De Boer, *Imitation of Paul*, 51. For the concept of imitation in ancient Jewish and Greco-Roman education (mimetic learning), see, besides our chapters 2–3, de Boer, *Imitation of Paul*, 25–26, 42–44; Wilkins, *Discipleship*, chs. 1–3; Jan G. van der Watt, *Family of the King: Dynamics of Metaphor in the Gospel according to John*, BINS 47 (Leiden: Brill, 2000), 273–79; Andrea Wilson Nightingale, "Liberal Education in Plato's *Republic* and Aristotle's *Politics*," in *Education in Greek and Roman Antiquity*, ed. Yun Lee Too (Leiden: Brill, 2001), 133–73, at 136–39; Collinson, *Making Disciples*, 12–23; Stephen E. Witmer, *Divine Instruction in Early Christianity*, WUNT 2/246 (Tübingen: Mohr Siebeck, 2008), 97–98.

26. De Boer, *Imitation of Paul*, 54. See also our section 3.2.4. In contrast, Hengel contends that Jesus was *not* a rabbi and the rabbinical teacher–pupil relationship does *not* explain Jesus's call to certain individuals to follow him. Hengel insists, "Following after [Jesus] did *not* mean imitating individual actions of his" (*Charismatic Leader*, 42–57 [quotation from p. 53, original emphasis]).

27. De Boer, *Imitation of Paul*, 52.

28. De Boer, *Imitation of Paul*, 53–54 (quotation from p. 54).

29. De Boer, *Imitation of Paul*, 54.

urative following (to show allegiance to Jesus and his teachings). While the literal following is no longer possible for later believers, the figurative following remains as valid as it was for the original disciples. In effect, ἀκολουθεῖν is conceptually linked to mimesis in so far as following Jesus as a disciple *facilitates* imitating him. Nevertheless, we will explore these conceptual traces of mimesis in "following Jesus" in each of the Synoptics.

4.2. Mimesis in the Gospel of Mark

While it would be untrue to say that scholarship has not noticed the idea of imitation in Mark, most just mention the concept in passing. Frank Matera, for example, contends that Jesus is a model for human behavior in being faithful, compassionate, and watchful in prayer.[30] Collinson states that Jesus sets an example for his disciples to imitate in humility (Mark 9:33–37), servanthood (9:36–37, 42; 10:13–16), and faithfulness through costly obedience (14:33–41).[31] However, Matera and Collinson do not show how the texts they refer to establish mimesis. Likewise, Burridge states that "the readers of this text [Mark] are not called just to follow Jesus, but to imitate him in his words and deeds, life and death."[32] However, he does not deal with specific texts, so the question is which of Jesus's words and deeds and which aspects of his life and death should Markan readers imitate.

Some scholars, however, have noted a more sustained concept of mimesis in Mark. Philip Davis states that, for Mark, the Christian life is literally modeled on Christ: the disciples imitate Jesus in preaching and performing exorcisms and healings (1:17; 3:14–15; 6:12–13), enduring suffering and death (8:34–38; 13:11), and rejection (6:11).[33] He contends that the entire Markan story of Jesus can function as a blueprint for the Christian life precisely because Mark has not recorded inimitable acts such as the virginal conception and the resurrection.[34] Larry Hurtado affirms Davis's observation that, compared to Matthew and Luke's accounts, Mark's omissions of unique events, such as the infancy narrative and the resurrec-

---

30. Frank J. Matera, *New Testament Ethics: The Legacies of Jesus and Paul* (Louisville: Westminster John Knox, 1996), 31–34.

31. Collinson, *Making Disciples*, 35–36, 41.

32. Burridge, *Imitating Jesus*, 183–84 (quotation from p. 184).

33. Philip G. Davis, "Christology, Discipleship, and Self-Understanding in the Gospel of Mark," in *Self-Definition and Self-Discovery in Early Christianity: A Study in Changing Horizons*, ed. David J. Hawkin and Tom Robinson, SBEC 26 (Lewiston: Edwin Mellen Press, 1990), 101–19, at 108–9.

34. Davis, "Christology," 109.

PART 2   MIMESIS IN EARLY CHRISTIANITY

tion (assuming 16:8 represents the original ending of Mark), make Mark's story of Jesus a blueprint for the Christian life.[35] Davis and Hurtado thus assert that Mark's story is not simply a story about discipleship but *imitable* discipleship. Hurtado mentions several aspects of imitable discipleship: a commitment that can lead to death (8:34–37 in light of 8:31), sacrificial service (10:43–45), having surrogate family relationships (10:29–30 in light of 3:31–35), and courageous behavior when interrogated (14:53–65 in light of 13:9–11).[36]

Affirming Davis and Hurtado's views, Capes mentions other ways in which the Markan Jesus serves as a model for disciples to follow, but these are merely suggestive (as Capes admits) rather than evident.[37] Similarly, Hood notes imitable aspects of Jesus's life, such as his preaching, miracles, self-denial, and cross-bearing, and concludes that "Mark's whole story of Jesus can be read as a blueprint for the Christian life."[38] Most recently, Helen Bond holds up the life of the Markan Jesus as a model for the Christian life. Conceding that the verb "to imitate" (μιμεῖσθαι) does not appear in Mark, she proposes that "to follow (Jesus)" is the equivalent. She then mentions several features of Jesus's life that find echoes in the lives of his followers, such as baptism and being persecuted when preaching publicly.[39] As to the issue of what Jesus's followers are to emulate, Bond suggests that they are not to replicate literally all the aspects of Jesus's life but to emulate its qualities and virtues.[40] Nevertheless, while the "taking up of one's cross" may, metaphorically, allude to regular instances of self-denial, Bond does not exclude a literal aspect, such as persecution or martyrdom.[41]

Insightful as these views may be, they are not always sufficiently grounded in the Markan text. Instead, I suggest that a careful examination of the Markan text regarding its potential mimetic language will inform us about what Mark thinks his readers should imitate about Jesus.

---

35. Larry W. Hurtado, "Following Jesus in the Gospel of Mark—and Beyond," in *Patterns of Discipleship in the New Testament*, ed. Richard N. Longenecker (Grand Rapids: Eerdmans, 1996), 9–29, at 26.

36. Hurtado, "Following Jesus," 11–14, 26.

37. Capes, "*Imitatio Christi*," 14–15. Sometimes, he suggests a Markan mimetic pattern by going outside Mark: e.g., Jesus's making disciples (Mark 3:13–19) is a model for making other disciples (Matt 28:18–20).

38. Hood, *Imitating God*, 73–76 (quotation from p. 76).

39. Helen Bond, *The First Biography of Jesus: Genre and Meaning in Mark's Gospel* (Grand Rapids: Eerdmans, 2020), 156–59.

40. Bond, *Biography of Jesus*, 159–60.

41. Bond, *Biography of Jesus*, 160–61.

4. Mimesis in the Synoptics and Acts

4.2.1. Conceptual Traces of Mimesis in Following Jesus

It has been well recognized that discipleship is a central theme in Mark's Gospel. This theme is most often articulated by the combination of the verb ἀκολουθεῖν and the noun ὁδός ("way"), resulting in the concept of following Jesus "on the way" as discipleship (8:27; 9:33–34; 10:32, 52). The concept of "following Jesus" (as a disciple) applies to a variety of people: the (twelve) disciples (1:18; 2:14; 6:1; 8:34; 10:28. 32; 14:54), tax collectors and sinners (2:15), the crowd (3:7; 5:24; 8:34), the rich young man (10:21, although he fails to act), Bartimaeus (10:52), and some women (15:41). The expression of a person coming "after" (ὀπίσω) Jesus is synonymous with the concept of following Jesus as 1:17–18 and 8:34 indicate (see also 1:20). Jesus sums up the reward for following him in 10:30: (1) a manifold return of what was given up in this life, (2) linked with persecution, and (3) everlasting life in the future. Often, people follow Jesus at his invitation (1:17, 20; 2:14; 8:34; 10:21), and we must ask whether Mark sees it as anything more than a literal following. For our purposes, we ask whether Mark's concept of following Jesus alludes to imitating Jesus in order to become like him—hence mimesis.

I contend that in three of the eighteen references to ἀκολουθεῖν, the intention is to emulate Jesus's behavior. First, there is the idea that the disciples "imitate" the nature of Jesus's ministry. In 1:17, Jesus clarifies to his first disciples that in following him, the intention is for them to become "fishers of people." Then, in 3:13–15, Jesus articulates their mission when he appoints twelve apostles (ἀπόστολοι) for a twofold purpose, indicated by the two ἵνα clauses: (1) to be with him and (2) to be sent out (ἀποστέλλειν) to proclaim (κηρύσσειν) (the good news) and have authority to cast out demons. In 6:7–13, we get a peek into the disciples' future mission: in keeping with 3:14–15, Jesus sends them out (ἀποστέλλειν) having given them authority over unclean spirits, and subsequently they proclaim (κηρύσσειν) repentance, cast out demons, and heal the sick. Clearly, the disciples' mission is patterned on that of Jesus.[42] In Mark's account, the early phase of Jesus's Galilean ministry is defined by proclaiming the good news, casting out demons, and healing the sick (1:34, 38–39).[43] We could even say that Jesus had come to "fish" for

---

42. See also Tinsley, *Imitation of God*, 103–5; Griffiths, *Example of Jesus*, 145; Hood, *Imitating God*, 73; Davis, "Christology," 108–9.

43. Although the verb κηρύσσειν is used intransitively in 1:38–39, in light of 1:14 τὸ εὐαγγέλιον is the likely object of the verb. See also 3:14 where a variant reading inserts τὸ εὐαγγέλιον after κηρύσσειν, and 3:15 where a variant reading adds καὶ περιάγοντας κηρύσσειν τὸ εὐαγγέλιον καί to the end of the verse. Even though these readings are suspect, they show the logical inference that the proclamation of the good news is in view.

PART 2   MIMESIS IN EARLY CHRISTIANITY

people (1:17, 20; 2:14, 17; 10:45).[44] Hence, the disciples are shown to imitate Jesus in proclaiming the good news, healing the sick, and casting out demons as a result of purposefully being with Jesus. Arguably, this is only a conceptual trace of mimesis as the disciples follow Jesus.

The second instance when following Jesus could indicate mimesis is 8:34, when Jesus extends a general invitation to the crowd and the disciples to become his followers. Jesus specifies two requisites for, or characteristics of, following him—self-denial and cross-bearing. Jesus himself practices these principles: he renounces the right to be served and chooses to serve others instead (10:45); he yields his own desires in favor of what his Father wants (14:36); and he goes to the cross in people's stead (10:45; 15:25). By implication, Jesus suggests that his would-be followers will imitate him.[45] Despite leaving it open to whether "to take up the cross" should be taken literally or figuratively, Moss stresses that in both cases, the disciple's experience is equated with the death of Jesus, and hence following Jesus involves imitating him.[46]

The third instance of potential mimesis is found in 10:28. After Jesus challenges the rich man to sell everything he owns before following him (10:21), Peter mentions that he and his fellow disciples have done what the rich man was unable to do (10:28; see also 1:18, 20). For Mark, following Jesus implies giving up or leav-

---

44. See also Shiner, *Follow Me*, 175–76. Shiner notes that, in antiquity, students' strong commitment to their teachers is tied to their teaching, while in the Gospels the disciples are called to attach themselves to the *person* of Jesus (*Follow Me*, 192). Similarly, Suzanne Watts Henderson argues that Jesus's calling of his disciples contrasts with the Jewish rabbi–talmid model where would-be students request a rabbi take them on as students (with Hengel) and with the Greco-Roman model of philosopher-teachers where the teacher's reputation is the basis for recruitment (*Christology and Discipleship in the Gospel of Mark*, SNTSMS 135 [Cambridge: Cambridge University Press, 2006], 54–56). Instead, she supports Hengel's concept of an Old Testament charismatic leader (*Christology*, 54–58).

45. See also Griffiths, *Example of Jesus*, 47. Best argues that while the concept of imitation was absent from the teaching of the historical Jesus, an element of imitation gradually entered into the concept of discipleship—for example, in self-denial and cross-bearing—in Mark's understanding of "following Jesus." Even so, such imitation is only partial because no disciple could do all that Jesus did (*Following Jesus*, 36–41; *Disciples and Discipleship*, 13–16). C. Clifton Black contends, however, that the boundary between following Jesus and imitating him is not as hard and fast as Best suggests (*The Disciples according to Mark: Markan Redaction in Current Debate*, JSNTSup 27 [Sheffield: Sheffield Academic Press, 1989], 121, 303n133). Davis also questions Best's skepticism about the Markan motif of imitation ("Christology," 109).

46. Moss, *Other Christs*, 30–31. She perceptively notes that the Lukan parallel of Mark 8:34 cannot be read martyrologically because the additional phrase "daily" (καθ' ἡμέραν) in Luke 9:23 demands a figurative reading of the injunction to take up the cross (*Other Christs*, 31). See also Bond, *Biography of Jesus*, 160–61.

4. Mimesis in the Synoptics and Acts

ing behind everything—imitating Jesus in forsaking, for example, his career as a carpenter (6:3) and his family (3:20–21, 31–35). Nevertheless, the lack of specific mimetic language makes this a "weak" case of mimesis.

Related to the term ἀκολουθεῖν is the typical Markan phrase ἐν τῇ ὁδῷ ("on the way"), which is shorthand for "on the way of discipleship." The phrase occurs five out of six times in 8:22–10:52, Mark's major section on discipleship (8:27; 9:33, 34; 10:32, 52), and four of these speak of the disciples accompanying Jesus on the road. Along the way, Jesus informs his disciples that he will soon face suffering, rejection, and death (8:31; 9:31; 10:33–34). The disciples are seemingly invited to follow Jesus in the way of the cross and (partially) share in his experience. Yet, while the disciples follow Jesus on the road of discipleship, does Mark actually indicate that they should observe and imitate Jesus? While Jesus mentions several features of discipleship, such as self-denial (8:34), cross-bearing (8:34), self-giving (8:35–37), and servanthood (9:35; 10:43–44), when it comes to himself, he only mentions sacrificial service and self-giving (10:45). Although καὶ γάρ ("for also") links 10:45 to 10:43–44, this connection is causal (Jesus's servanthood being the reason or basis for the disciples' servanthood) rather than comparative (Jesus being an example to imitate). Vitally, the disciples' servanthood and self-giving will not have the same effect as that of Jesus. Nowhere does Mark mention that Jesus carries his own cross (ironically, Simon of Cyrene does it for him in 15:21). Nevertheless, Jesus's crucifixion on behalf of humanity arguably expresses the self-denial and cross-bearing that 8:34 asks of would-be disciples.[47] Even so, in my view, some scholars assert too quickly that to follow Jesus on the way means to imitate him.[48]

Looking back at our criteria for mimesis (see "Mimesis and Analogy" in section 1.5), the first three criteria are arguably fulfilled because the Markan concept of following involves two different characters (Jesus and the one who follows), and some tangible acts (Jesus shows concrete examples of proclamation, exorcism, and self-giving) that his followers can intentionally observe and imitate. However, these connections are conceptual and implied rather than being expressed

---

47. Bond considers Jesus's death as an example to follow in that in the passion narrative Jesus illustrates the kind of behavior that he expects from his followers (*Biography of Jesus*, 236–37).

48. See, for example, Willard M. Swartley, *Covenant of Peace: The Missing Peace in New Testament Theology and Ethics* (Grand Rapids: Eerdmans, 2006), 368–70; Capes, "Imitatio Christi," 13–14; Hood, *Imitating God*, 74–75; Bond, *Biography of Jesus*, 157. Hood sees a further mimetic pattern when Christians preach and are arrested (3:14; 13:9–13) like Jesus (1:14; 9:31; 10:33) (*Imitating God*, 75). I would classify this as analogy rather than mimesis because the connection is not rooted in any specific mimetic language. On the other end of the spectrum is Thomas Söding, who does not detect any mimesis in the concept of following Jesus ("Die Nachfolgeforderung Jesu im Markusevangelium," *TTZ* 94 [1985]: 292–310).

in mimetic language. The fourth criterion of mimesis is even more difficult to establish because Mark never explicitly mentions that the purpose of imitating Jesus is to become like him. However, it can be argued that the purpose of the disciples' imitation of Jesus is to become like him in his ministry, i.e., to continue the ministry of proclaiming and demonstrating the kingdom of God (see 1:14–15, 34, 39; 3:14–15; 6:7–13; 13:10; 16:15, 20). Based on the available evidence, I conclude that the Markan concept of following Jesus contains a "weak" element of mimesis in that following Jesus can *facilitate* imitating him.

4.2.2. The Markan Mimetic Language

In this section, I will uncover potential mimetic language and show that although Mark's Gospel contains various comparative particles, virtually none denote mimesis. For example, the conjunction καθώς occurs eight times and always refers to something that has been said, heard, done, or written, as in "as it is written" or "just as he had told" (1:2; 4:33; 9:13; 11:6; 14:16, 21; 15:8; 16:7; see also the use of ὡς in 7:6; 9:21; 10:1; 14:72). The adverb οὕτως often refers to something that either has preceded or will follow in the narrative (2:7, 8, 12; 14:59; 15:39). On two occasions, οὕτως denotes analogy but not mimesis. In 4:26, the phrase οὕτως ... ὡς expresses that the kingdom of God is like a scattered seed that seemingly grows by itself, and in 13:29, οὕτως indicates that the occurrence of "these things" signaling the imminent coming of the Son of Man is analogous to the budding fig tree announcing the coming of the summer in 13:28.[49] In the account of Jesus's transfiguration, οὕτως is used to indicate that the radiance of Jesus's clothes was beyond "imitation" (9:3). There is no mimesis in view because (1) there is no mention of an agent who produced the original act (though μετεμορφώθη in 9:2 probably is a divine passive), and (2) the "mimesis" is hypothetical—no person could replicate what had happened to Jesus's clothes. Only in 10:43 does οὕτως possibly indicate mimesis (see the discussion below).

Mark frequently employs the comparative conjunction ὡς to denote analogy or similarity but not mimesis (barring 10:15, for which see below). For example, the use of ὡς in 1:10 probably indicates analogy rather than mimesis, where the idea is that the Spirit's descent on Jesus is like that of a dove rather than that the Spirit

---

49. Although Jesus's question to the disciples, "Are you thus also (οὕτως καί) without understanding?" (7:18), could indicate that the disciples have imitated the crowd in failing to understand Jesus, such mimesis would have been unintentional (the disciples did not seek to become like the crowd) and hence fails M&A criterion 1 ("M&A" refers to "Mimesis and Analogy" in section 1.5). Besides, the use of οὕτως here probably denotes that the disciples' behavior resembles that of the crowd (analogy).

4. Mimesis in the Synoptics and Acts

sought to imitate a dove in the way it flies. In 1:22, Jesus's teaching is unlike that of the scribes because it is characterized by authority, but there is no idea of imitation; if anything, Jesus avoids imitating the authorities. In 4:31, Jesus compares the kingdom of God to a mustard seed in terms of its potential for extraordinary growth rather than saying that it imitates a mustard seed. In 6:15, the assertion that Jesus is like (ὡς) an Old Testament prophet indicates resemblance rather than people suggesting that Jesus was imitating a prophet of old. In 6:34, the narrator describes Jesus's compassion for the crowd in terms of analogy (the crowd is likened to sheep without a shepherd) rather than mimesis, where the crowd itself would seek to imitate a flock of sheep (similar reasoning applies to 8:24). In 12:25, ὡς indicates that, in the resurrection, people will be like angels and life will no longer be dependent on procreation (in marriage); hence, people's existence in the realm of God is analogous to that of angels rather than that people seek to imitate angels. The command "to love your neighbor as (ὡς) yourself" (12:31) indicates analogy (love of others should resemble self-love) rather than mimesis because mimesis would require two different persons (M&A criterion 2).[50] In 13:34, the return of the Son of Man is likened to that of a master returning unexpectedly from a journey. Here, Jesus uses a parable to explain his return by analogy rather than suggesting that he consciously seeks to imitate this imaginary person. In 14:48, Jesus states that the arresting party was treating him as if he were a social bandit (λῃστής) but there is no idea of him imitating such a person.

In 12:21, ὡσαύτως simply describes that the fate of the third brother is like that of the first and second brothers (marriage without producing offspring). In this hypothetical situation (hence M&A criterion 2 is not met), the point is not that the third brother seeks to imitate the first two brothers but simply suffers a similar fate (hence M&A criterion 1 is not met). In 14:31, ὡσαύτως tells us that the disciples simply reiterate Peter's words, so it would be excessive to call this mimesis (M&A criteria 1 and 2 are not met). In 9:26, the boy's posture after a violent collapse caused by the unclean spirit's departure resembles (ὡσεί) the unresponsive state of a corpse; the boy did not set out to imitate a corpse (M&A criteria 1 and 2 are not met). The comparative verb ὁμοιοῦν is used only in 4:30 and indicates analogy by asking what the kingdom of God can be likened to. The subsequent brief parable of the mustard seed is an example of such an analogy (see also the use of ὡς in 4:31), revealing that the kingdom of God also shows spectacular growth despite its small beginnings (4:31–32). The cognate adverb ὁμοίως also occurs once, in 15:31, and again, the idea is one of analogy rather than imitation—the chief priests and scribes mock Jesus just like the bystanders.

50. "M&A criterion 2" refers to criterion 2 of "Mimesis and Analogy" in section 1.5.

PART 2   MIMESIS IN EARLY CHRISTIANITY

In fact, I can only find two instances of mimetic language in Mark. First, in 10:13, people bring their children to Jesus to be blessed (see also 10:16), but the disciples express strong disapproval. Jesus is outraged and tells them that the kingdom of God belongs to such people (10:14). So much so, Jesus continues, that in order to enter the kingdom of God, they must receive this precious gift like (ὡς) a child (10:15). Hence, Jesus presents children as a tangible example of receptivity to imitate.[51] Second, in 10:43, οὕτως arguably denotes mimesis, but with Jesus telling his disciples not to behave like, that is not to imitate, the gentile authorities who lord it over the people. Although the gentile authorities are not actually present on that occasion, Jesus's example is tangible enough for the disciples to visualize. Instead, the disciples are urged to become servants because even Jesus had come to serve (10:43–45). The syntax counts against the idea that the disciples are to imitate Jesus's servanthood because the phrase καὶ γάρ ("for also/even") that links 10:45 with 10:43–44 is causal (Jesus's servanthood is the reason or basis for the disciples' servanthood) rather than comparative (Jesus as an example to imitate).[52] Nevertheless, the idea that Jesus presents himself as a model of self-giving and servanthood is difficult to deny, so I consider this a "weak" case of mimesis.[53]

4.2.3. Further Concepts of Mimesis—Gethsemane

Sometimes, the concept of mimesis is present or implied even when no explicit mimetic language is used. In Section 4.2.1, for example, while the term ἀκολουθεῖν

---

51. Dan O. Via, however, argues that Mark does not allude to a childlike quality; rather, the idea is that the movement of the adult back to a child signifies a new beginning (of the process of salvation) (*The Ethics of Mark's Gospel—In the Middle of Time* [Philadelphia: Fortress, 1985], 128–33). In my view, however, the verb δέχεσθαι ("to receive") indicates the quality to be imitated.

52. Similarly, Söding contends that 10:45 is about participation rather than imitation ("Nachfolgeforderung," 305). For Morna D. Hooker, however, the causal conjunction does not negate the idea of imitation; rather, Jesus's death provides the disciples with the means to follow his example (*The Gospel according to Saint Mark*, BNTC 2 [London: A&C Black, 1991], 247–48). Hooker also notes parallels of the concept of giving one's life a ransom for others in 4 Macc 6:29; 17:21, indicating that the martyrs "die, not as substitutes, but as *representatives* of their nation" (*Mark*, 250 [original emphasis]). There is thus a sense that the whole of Mark 10:45 presents Jesus as an example to imitate.

53. See also de Boer, *Imitation of Paul*, 54; Francis J. Moloney, *The Gospel of Mark: A Commentary* (Peabody, MA: Hendrickson, 2002), 207–8. There is a stronger case for mimesis in the parallel verse in Matthew 20:28, which has replaced Mark's causal conjunction γάρ with the comparative conjunction ὥσπερ (see section 4.3.3). Although Schulz notes this, he still sees too much mimesis in Mark 10:41–45 and is, in my view, also mistaken in thinking that the imitation of Jesus goes back to the *kerygma* of the early Church rather than to Jesus himself (*Nachfolgen und Nachahmen*, 252–65). Luke 22:26–27 also indicates the disciple–Jesus mimesis in servanthood, while Matthew is less explicit.

4. Mimesis in the Synoptics and Acts

does not constitute mimesis, we found three instances where a concept of mimesis could be linked to ἀκολουθεῖν. Here, in 14:32–42, I suggest that Jesus's watchfulness and prayer in Gethsemane is also an example for his followers to imitate. While the event in Gethsemane could merely be biographical (describing Jesus's unique experience) rather than exemplary, it is more likely that Jesus had taken Peter, James, and John so that they could observe and imitate him in watchful prayer.[54] In 14:38, Jesus urges his disciples to stay awake in order to pray (taking καί epexegetically) so that they may not enter a time of testing. Hence, Jesus did not request the disciples to pray for him but for their own sake.

We should note that all the key terms in 14:32–42 also occur in Jesus's eschatological discourse in Mark 13: (1) Jesus warns his followers γρηγορεῖν ("to be alert"; 13:34, 35, 37) about the day of the Lord and not καθεύδειν ("to sleep"; 13:36), (2) Jesus urges his followers προσεύχεσθαι ("to pray"; 13:18) in future tribulation lest no σάρξ ("flesh") survives (13:20), and (3) in times of "πειρασμός" ("testing"; 13:9), Jesus promises that the divine πνεῦμα will aid their testimony in front of hostile authorities (13:11).[55] The significance is that the disciples' experience in 14:32–42 is proleptic of the future reality described in Mark 13—a reality that can only be overcome with the help of the divine πνεῦμα in speech and prayer.[56]

In 14:38, Jesus does not simply address the disciples' situation but also speaks of his own experience.[57] The nouns πειρασμός and πνεῦμα in 14:38 allude to Jesus's earlier experiences in 1:12–13 and 8:11–12, where the noun πνεῦμα and the verb πειράζειν also occur in contexts of testing/opposition.[58] Jesus's agitated state in 14:33–34 suggests

---

54. It is even possible that the disciples could have observed Jesus had they not fallen asleep, although Mark does not indicate the exact distance between Jesus and his disciples (προελθὼν μικρόν; 14:35).

55. Many scholars have recognized the parallels between Mark 13 and 14:32–34: e.g., Joel Marcus, *Mark 8–16*, ABY 27a (New Haven, CT: Yale University Press, 2009), 976, 987; Karl Olav Sandnes, *Early Christian Discourses on Jesus' Prayer at Gethsemane*, NovTSup 166 (Leiden: Brill, 2016), 124–26.

56. For the argument that the referent of πνεῦμα in 14:38 is the divine Spirit, see Cornelis Bennema, "Whose Spirit Is Eager? The Referent of Πνεῦμα in Mark 14:38 and the Intended Comparison," *ZNW* 110 (2019): 104–14.

57. See also Raymond E. Brown, *The Death of the Messiah: From Gethsemane to the Grave*, 2 vols., ABRL (London: Yale University Press, 1994), 1:199–200 (although he understands the "willing spirit" to be the person who is in holy alignment with God's plans); Arnd Herrmann, *Versuchung im Markusevangelium: Eine Biblisch-Hermeneutische Studie*, BWANT 197 (Stuttgart: Kohlhammer, 2011), 224–25.

58. I have argued elsewhere that the divine Spirit is a secondary reference of πνεῦμα in 8:12 (Cornelis Bennema, "The Referent of Πνεῦμα in Mark 2:8 and 8:12 in Light of Early Jewish Traditions: A Study in Markan Anthropology," *Neot* 52 [2018]: 195–213).

PART 2   MIMESIS IN EARLY CHRISTIANITY

that Gethsemane is, once again, a scene of testing and requires prayer (14:35–36). Considering his exhortation to the disciples in 14:38, it would be reasonable to assume that Jesus himself was assisted by the divine spirit in Gethsemane. In short, the disciples are urged to imitate Jesus's watchfulness in prayer to deal with testing situations, even though they will only be able to do so in the same way as Jesus in the post-Easter era with the coming of the Spirit.[59] I consider this a "medium" case of mimesis.

4.2.4. Mimetic Characters

So far, we have looked at instances of the disciple–Jesus mimesis in the narrative where Jesus sets the example. At another level, however, Mark also seeks to inspire mimesis amongst his audience, namely in the way he presents other characters. Most of Mark's "minor characters" (characters that only appear in a single episode) display traits or behavior for Mark's audience to emulate. This concept of characters as mimetic agents is implicit rather than explicit. Helen Bond, however, is skeptical about the mimetic value of the Markan minor characters because (1) for Mark, Jesus is the true model to be emulated, and (2) the minor characters do not function as a "group" showing discipleship in general—they merely exemplify specific traits of discipleship.[60] However, Jesus, as the primary exemplar for discipleship, does not rule out minor characters as secondary models of discipleship, especially if the minor characters exemplify a trait of Jesus. Moreover, I have argued elsewhere that while the Markan disciples often fail in their discipleship (even though they remain at Jesus's side), the minor characters function as a "narrative group" to instruct the Markan audience about the kind of discipleship envisaged by Mark.[61] Although not exhaustive, the following examples will illustrate how the minor characters can exemplify specific traits of discipleship.

---

59. Likewise, Susan R. Garrett states that Jesus exhorts his followers to do as he has done (*The Temptations of Jesus in Mark's Gospel* [Grand Rapids: Eerdmans, 1998], 93–94). Sandnes argues that 14:37–38 resembles a *chreia* where Jesus becomes an example for the disciples to imitate in times of temptation and trial (*Discourses*, 133–34). However, Sandnes also contends that 14:38 refers to the human spirit, thus attributing Jesus's ability to face his destiny unaided to his being "a man of faith, trusting in God's omnipotence" (*Discourses*, 135). Francis Watson partially agrees in that while he acknowledges an exemplary dimension in 14:37–38, he contends that the biographical tendency dominates (*The Fourfold Gospel: A Theological Reading of the New Testament Portraits of Jesus* [Grand Rapids: Baker Academic, 2016], 142–43). Watson thinks that the tension of viewing Gethsemane as biographical or exemplary is more visible in Luke (see section 4.4.3). Others who see an element of imitation in the Gethsemane episode include John Paul Heil, *The Gospel of Mark as Model for Action: A Reader-Response Commentary* (New York: Paulist Press, 1992), 301; Adela Yarbro Collins, *Mark*, Hermeneia (Minneapolis: Fortress, 2007), 681.

60. Bond, *Biography of Jesus*, 209–11.

61. Cornelis Bennema, "Character Analysis and Miracle Stories in the Gospel of Mark," in

Peter's mother-in-law. When Jesus hears that Peter's mother-in-law is in bed with a fever, he heals her without uttering a word. She also says nothing but begins to serve Jesus and the disciples (1:29–31). Her response to Jesus is limited to one action, "to serve" or "to care for" (διακονεῖν), but this verb gains significance in the Markan story where it occurs five times (1:13, 31; 10:45 [2x]; 15:40–41). It is not farfetched to suggest that by serving Jesus and the disciples, Peter's mother-in-law demonstrates one aspect of discipleship because 1:31 shares significant similarities with 15:40–41. First, in both episodes, women are the subject of διακονεῖν and Jesus the object, i.e., women serve Jesus. Second, in 15:40–41, two simultaneous actions characterize the women's relationship with Jesus—"they used to follow him and serve him." Since "to follow" is the primary indicator of discipleship, the corresponding action "to serve" would also be part of the semantic domain of discipleship. Mark reiterates that service is a characteristic of discipleship through two episodes, in 9:33–37 and 10:35–45. In the first, Jesus's exhortation to be a servant (διάκονος; 9:35) relates to discipleship because this episode happens "on the way" (ἐν τῇ ὁδῷ; 9:33–34)—a well-recognized Markan shorthand for discipleship. In the second, following James and John's self-serving request, Jesus points out the principle of being a servant/slave (διάκονος/δοῦλος; 10:43–44). Mark then uses διακονεῖν to describe Jesus's ultimate act of sacrificial service on behalf of humanity (10:45). Thus, Jesus's servant-identity and sacrificial service is a model for his followers to imitate (see also section 4.2.2 on the mimesis in 10:43). In sum, διακονεῖν is an important discipleship term for Mark and Peter's mother-in-law is the first character in the Markan story to demonstrate this key aspect of discipleship in response to Jesus.[62]

The Gerasene Demoniac. In 5:18, the ex-demoniac begs Jesus to let him stay with him. His request "to be with" Jesus (εἶναι μετ' αὐτοῦ) is essentially a request to become a disciple. In 3:14, Jesus appoints twelve disciples/apostles (1) to be

---

Hermeneutik der frühchristlichen Wundererzählungen: Historische, literarische und rezeptionsästhetische Aspekte, ed. Bernd Kollmann and Ruben Zimmermann, WUNT 339 (Tübingen: Mohr Siebeck, 2014), 413–26. For the exemplary value of the gentile minor characters, see Cornelis Bennema, "Gentile Characters and the Motif of Proclamation in the Gospel of Mark," in *Character Studies and the Gospel of Mark*, ed. Matthew Ryan Hauge and Christopher W. Skinner, LNTS 483 (New York: Bloomsbury T&T Clark, 2014), 215–31. Others have also noted the idea of the Markan characters as models for readers: Joel F. Williams, *Other Followers of Jesus: Minor Characters as Major Figures in Mark's Gospel*, JSNTSup 102 (Sheffield: JSOT Press, 1994); Elizabeth Struthers Malbon, *In the Company of Jesus: Characters in Mark's Gospel* (Louisville: Westminster John Knox, 2000).

62. See also Joel Marcus, *Mark 1–8*, AB 27 (New York: Doubleday, 2000), 196, 199. Robert H. Gundry disagrees because "the definition of discipleship as service lies a long way off in 9:35; 10:43–45" (*Mark: A Commentary on His Apology for the Cross* [Grand Rapids: Eerdmans, 1993], 91). However, it is reasonable to assume that a reader or listener will notice these echoes in subsequent readings or performances of the gospel.

with him (εἶναι μετ' αὐτοῦ) and (2) to send them to proclaim (κηρύσσειν) [the good news] (see also 13:10). While Jesus does not permit the ex-demoniac to stay, he seems to recognize the intent behind the request because he sends the man to tell his people about what the Lord has done for him (5:19), reflecting the second purpose for appointing the twelve disciples in 3:14. The ex-demoniac obeys and begins to proclaim (κηρύσσειν) Jesus's deeds, thus actualizing an important aspect of discipleship (5:20).[63] There is an implicit contrast between this man and the disciples—the disciples are called and appointed by Jesus to be with him, but the ex-demoniac makes this request without any prompting.[64] Then, while 6:6b–13 is the first opportunity for the disciples to actualize 3:14–15, including public proclamation (6:12), the ex-demoniac does so before them. In sum, Jesus grants the gentile ex-demoniac's request to be his disciple, not by allowing the man to stay with him but by sending him to proclaim the message. He obeys and actualizes this aspect of discipleship before the "professional" disciples.

Bartimaeus. Jesus's question to Bartimaeus, "What do you want me to do for you?" (10:51) echoes his question to the sons of Zebedee in the previous episode (10:36). However, unlike James and John, who request personal power (which is denied), Bartimaeus asks for sight (which is granted). While James and John fail to grasp a key aspect of discipleship (servanthood), Bartimaeus shows he is ahead by asking for sight—in order to follow Jesus (10:52). The episode peaks when Bartimaeus receives his sight and follows Jesus on the way (10:52). Scholars have noted the dramatic contrast between Bartimaeus's starting position as a blind beggar who "was sitting beside the way" (ἐκάθητο παρὰ τὴν ὁδόν; 10:46), and his final position as a seeing disciple who "was following Jesus on the way" (ἠκολούθει τῷ Ἰησοῦ ἐν τῇ ὁδῷ; 10:52).[65] "On the way" (ἐν τῇ ὁδῷ) is Markan shorthand for "on the way of discipleship."

Indeed, this phrase occurs five out of six times in 8:22–10:52, Mark's major section on discipleship (8:27; 9:33, 34; 10:32, 52). Four of those speak of the disciples accompanying Jesus on the road. In 8:27–29, Jesus asks his disciples "on the way" about their understanding of his identity, and although Peter's confession on behalf of the disciples is accurate, it soon becomes clear that their understanding does not include suffering, rejection, and death, or that the road of discipleship is

---

63. While the proclamation of the swineherds causes fear and prompts Jesus's departure (5:14–17), the ex-demoniac's proclamation results in amazement (5:20).

64. Contra Moloney, who claims that the ex-demoniac's request is impossible because "discipleship results from the initiative of Jesus" and "Jesus must determine the agenda" (*Mark*, 105).

65. E.g., Ludger Schenke, *Die Wundererzählungen des Markusevangeliums*, SBB 5 (Stuttgart: Katholisches Bibelwerk, 1974), 355; Christopher D. Marshall, *Faith as a Theme in Mark's Narrative*, SNTSMS 64 (Cambridge: Cambridge University Press, 1989), 140; Gundry, *Mark*, 593; Moloney, *Mark*, 211; Peter Dschulnigg, *Das Markusevangelium*, THKNT 2 (Stuttgart: Kohlhammer, 2007), 290.

4. Mimesis in the Synoptics and Acts

the road of self-denial and the cross (8:31–35). The disciples continue to misunderstand what true discipleship is because they argue about greatness "on the way," and Jesus has to clarify what true greatness means (9:33–35). Finally, while "on the way" again (10:32), Jesus explains what the road of discipleship holds (10:33–34). But James and John misunderstand, and Jesus provides correction yet again (10:35–45). This is why the contrast is so apparent when following this episode and closing Mark's major section on discipleship, we encounter Bartimaeus, who, being blind and stationary, immediately follows Jesus "on the way" after his miraculous healing (10:52). Bartimaeus outperforms the disciples in following Jesus on the way of discipleship. In showing understanding, faith, and discipleship, Bartimaeus proves an exemplary disciple.[66]

Simon of Cyrene. While Simon of Cyrene only features in one verse, his literal carrying of Jesus's cross (αἴρειν τὸν σταυρὸν αὐτοῦ; 15:21) is significant and exemplifies the figurative cross-bearing that Jesus demands from his followers in 8:34 (ἀράτω τὸν σταυρὸν αὐτοῦ).[67] As Kelly Iverson puts it, "By carrying the cross, Simon is depicted as one who understands the nature and cost of discipleship, becoming the idyllic portrait of what it means for a disciple to 'deny themselves, take up their cross, and follow' Jesus (8.34)."[68] Simon's action brings the disciples' failure into sharp focus because they have neither taken up their cross nor are available to carry Jesus's cross.[69] Iverson perceptively notes that the Simon who carries Jesus's cross is not Simon Peter, who, along with other disciples, is admonished to take up his cross, but a gentile, Simon from Cyrene.[70]

---

66. See also Marshall, *Faith*, 124, 140–44; Williams, *Followers*, 152–67; Dschnulnigg, *Markusevangelium*, 288. While Schenke surely attributes too much insight to Bartimaeus when he states, "Der Blinde glaubt, daß Jesu Leidensweg nach Jerusalem der Heilsweg ist" ("The blind man believes that Jesus's path of suffering to Jerusalem is the path of salvation") (*Wundererzählungen*, 360), Gundry seems to downplay Bartimaeus's discipleship in that his following is "a kind of following less than that required of disciples" (*Mark*, 595).

67. Williams argues that Luke makes the connection between cross-bearing and following Jesus in 14:27 more explicit by adding that Simon carried the cross "*behind* Jesus" (ὄπισθεν τοῦ Ἰησοῦ) in 23:26 (*Other Followers*, 182–83). Bond, however, contends that Simon does *not* provide a model of discipleship because Simon's act is involuntary, and the focus is not on Simon but on Jesus, who remains the true model for discipleship (*Biography of Jesus*, 214–16). However, the minor characters do not need to provide an exact fit to be exemplars; the verbal correspondence between 15:21 and 8:34 and the name "Simon" are sufficient to understand that Simon of Cyrene performs an act of authentic discipleship for imitation. On Bond's skepticism about the mimetic value of the minor characters, see our discussion at the beginning of section 4.2.4.

68. Kelly R. Iverson, *Gentiles in the Gospel of Mark: "Even the Dogs Under the Table Eat the Children's Crumbs,"* LNTS 339 (London: T&T Clark, 2007), 164.

69. Williams, *Other Followers*, 183.

70. Iverson, *Gentiles*, 141.

PART 2   MIMESIS IN EARLY CHRISTIANITY

The Markan minor characters, when taken together, are influential in shaping mimetic discipleship because they function as *literary examples* for Mark's audience to imitate. In imitating the commendable aspects of Mark's minor characters, Mark's audience can learn about and practice discipleship. Admittedly, this is mimesis at a different level; rather than a direct disciple–Jesus mimesis, we have an indirect, believer–literary character–Jesus mimesis.[71] In chapters 2–3, we noted this mode of *textually mediated mimesis* in Greco-Roman and Jewish literature.

4.2.5. Conclusion

Mark is not preoccupied with mimesis. At most, we can say that Mark's Gospel shows a "weak" or latent concept of mimesis. With regard to following Jesus, we find only notional traces of mimesis, and nowhere does Mark explicitly state that the purpose of following Jesus is to become like him. Mark makes only two possible references to mimesis by means of other linguistic expressions (10:15, 43), and even there, the case is not strong. In Gethsemane, when Jesus sets an example for the disciples to stay alert and pray to withstand testing, there is perhaps a stronger case for mimesis. Regarding the possible content of the disciple–Jesus mimesis, Mark refers to the activities of mission (proclamation, exorcism), cross-bearing, receptivity, self-denial, service, alertness, and prayer. In addition, Mark communicates the believer–Jesus mimesis to his audience through the minor characters. It must be noted that wherever mimesis occurs in Mark, whether with Jesus being an example for the disciples or Markan characters being examples for Markan readers, the context is always discipleship. In other words, mimesis is a means for shaping discipleship, even if it does not feature strongly.

Regarding the place of mimesis in Markan ethics, there is little to say because Mark's Gospel does not have many ethical instructions.[72] For Mark, "ethics" is virtually equivalent to discipleship, and even then, he focuses on the imminence of the kingdom of God (1:15, 38–39; 9:1) and how to receive or enter it (4:1–34; 10:14–15, 23–25; 12:34) rather than on how to live as a citizen of this kingdom as we find in Matthew's Sermon on the Mount. While Mark frequently mentions Jesus's teaching, he does not specify its content (1:21; 2:13; 6:2, 6, 34; 10:1; 14:49). The only

---

71. Regarding the minor characters of the Gerasene demoniac and the Syrophoenician woman, for example, O'Connor focuses on Jesus's actions and concludes that these do not present the idea of imitating him (*Moral Life*, 98, 101). However, if O'Connor's focus had been on the actions of the minor characters, he might have recognized that Mark is drawing attention to their mimetic potential for the reader.

72. However, see now the first volume of essays on Markan ethics: Michael Labahn and Martin Meiser, eds., *Ethics in the Gospel of Mark*, WUNT (Tübingen: Mohr Siebeck, 2025).

exceptions are 8:31 and 9:31, where Jesus's teachings about his suffering, betrayal, death, and resurrection serve to correct the disciples' misunderstanding. Where there is ethical instruction (3:33–35; 10:1–12; 12:13–17), the concept of mimesis is not in view. Thus, most "ethical" instruction is linked to the concept of following Jesus, where mimesis is only rarely in view, so we conclude that *mimesis is peripheral to Markan ethics*.[73]

4.3. Mimesis in the Gospel of Matthew

Several scholars have detected mimetic notions in Matthew. Samuel Byrskog argues that Matthew's emphasis on the intertwined didactic duties of "hearing and doing" Jesus's teaching implies that Jesus is an ethical model to be imitated.[74] Studying the concept of discipleship in Matt 8–11, Ulrich Luz concludes that "discipleship means conforming to the life of Christ and emulating his model."[75] Collinson observes that "Jesus also taught by modelling in his own life the qualities he sought to inculcate," referring to the desirable characteristics listed in the Beatitudes (5:2–12), as well as to humility and prayer (6:1–18; 11:25–27; 14:23; 26:36–44).[76] Likewise, Matera sketches how Jesus provides an example of righteous behavior that he holds up for his followers in the Sermon on the Mount.[77] Outlining Matthew's ethics, Burridge briefly discusses discipleship and imitation, arguing that Jesus is the model of the new righteousness in the kingdom of heaven.[78] Henry Pattarumadathil contends that Jesus exemplifies in his own life the virtues he demands from the disciples, such as resisting temptation, seeking God's glory, fearless proclamation of the good news of the kingdom, and surrendering to God's will.[79] Hood mentions numerous parallels between Jesus and the disciples in Mat-

---

73. O'Connor is more negative about mimesis in Mark. While he notes that Jesus's actions present some imitable traits, the disciples are unable to imitate Jesus and hence the idea that Mark presents an *imitatio Christi* ethic for discipleship is problematic (*Moral Life*, 107–8, 119, 141–42).

74. Samuel Byrskog, *Jesus the Only Teacher: Didactic Authority and Transmission in Ancient Israel, Ancient Judaism and the Matthean Community*, ConBNT 24 (Stockholm: Almqvist & Wiksell, 1994), 326–31.

75. Ulrich Luz, *The Theology of the Gospel of Matthew* (Cambridge: Cambridge University Press, 1995), 62–80 [quotation from p. 80]).

76. Collinson, *Making Disciples*, 50–51.

77. Matera, *New Testament Ethics*, 50–53.

78. Burridge, *Imitating Jesus*, 218–24.

79. Henry Pattarumadathil, *Your Father in Heaven: Discipleship in Matthew as a Process of Becoming Children of God*, AnBib 172 (Rome: Pontifical Biblical Institute, 2008), 196–202.

PART 2   MIMESIS IN EARLY CHRISTIANITY

thew, showing that Jesus was a model to be emulated.[80] While there is merit in their efforts to show Jesus as a model for imitation, they often do not demonstrate how the texts they refer to denote mimesis other than by loose association.[81]

Reinhard Feldmeier, on the other hand, is probably too cautious in his brief study of the Gospels. He argues that the Old Testament does not speak of imitating God in the sense of becoming like him, although this changes in early Judaism to reflect the assimilation or imitation of the divine in contemporary Hellenistic philosophy.[82] In the Gospels, Feldmeier contends that God's "perfect" love (Matt 5:48; John 13:34), as well as God's kindness and mercy (Luke 6:35b–36), indicate ethical conduct that speaks more of a correspondence to God rather than an imitation of him.[83] I would argue, however, that there is more to these texts than Feldmeier would have us believe. After all, the correspondence in these texts seems to be a *mimetic* correspondence indicated by the comparative particle ὡς or καθώς: just as God shows love, kindness, and mercy to people, so followers of Jesus should behave likewise to others (see further below).

Daniel Patte examines various hermeneutical approaches to the Matthean Sermon on the Mount, two of which relate to the idea of discipleship as imitation. In one approach, the focus is on imitating the person who exemplifies the ideals of the kingdom. Consequently, believers should primarily imitate Jesus as the one who ideally manifested the principles of the Sermon on the Mount in his ministry, but also other believers insofar as their attitudes and behaviors reflect those of Jesus. In this approach, to imitate Christ is to be both like him and unlike him; disciples are to strive towards perfection by imitating Christ but will never achieve that perfection. In the other approach, which Patte himself supports, the focus is on imitating a specific attitude of the exemplar. Believers should imitate Jesus's moral discernment and thus, like the wise housebuilder (7:24–27), build their lives on a solid moral foundation. Rather than imitating Jesus, this approach

---

80. Hood, *Imitating of God*, 77–79.

81. Byrskog, for example, contends that 5:17 points to Jesus's own behavior as the model for the behavior expected of disciples in 5:21–48 (*Jesus the Only Teacher*, 328–29), but there is no specific mimetic language to underpin this view. Burridge simply states that the Matthean Jesus is an example for imitation, citing other scholars rather than establishing this from the Matthean text (*Imitating Jesus*, 222–24). Regarding Hood's many examples, there is often no mimetic language to affirm these connections. While he notes, for example, the connection between Jesus's exhortation to others to be meek (5:5) and Jesus's own meekness (11:29) (*Imitating God*, 77), these verses are far removed from each other without a mimetic expression to connect them. He makes a better case for seeing notions of imitating God, especially in showing generous love (5:43–48) and forgiveness (6:12; 18:23–35) (*Imitating God*, 84–88).

82. Feldmeier, "Heavenly Father," 432–35. We argued similarly in chapter 3.

83. Feldmeier, "Heavenly Father," 438–44.

4. Mimesis in the Synoptics and Acts

advocates imitating Jesus's moral discernment and his pattern of behavior.[84] In my view, we should hold both approaches together. Mimesis involves imitating Jesus's attitude and behavior. However, since mimesis is a creative and cognitive process, moral discernment is needed to determine what the imitation of Jesus will look like in each context.

Like Burridge and Capes (see also section 1.2), Dale Allison recognizes the mimetic aspect of the Gospels as ancient biographies.[85] Early Christians, whether Jew or gentile, had made a change of allegiance, resulting in new beliefs, new behavior, and, accordingly, new models. Allison contends that Matthew, in keeping with the moral aims of the ancient biography, holds Jesus up as a model for imitation. He notes the mimetic correspondence between Jesus's words and deeds. For example, Jesus exhorts others to be meek (5:5), merciful (5:7), faithful to the Mosaic law (5:19–20), and cross-bearers (16:24), just as he is meek (11:29), merciful (9:27), faithful to the law (8:4), and crucified (27:26). In imitating Jesus, his followers may meet the demand for the perfect imitation of God (5:48) because he himself is the perfect example of and for such imitation. Hence, Matthew supplies a story where "the crucial moral imperatives are imaginatively and convincingly incarnated" in Jesus; Jesus embodies what he teaches.[86] As in my critique of Hood (see n. 81), the verses that are deployed to show a connecting idea are far removed from each other without a mimetic expression to link them.

4.3.1. Conceptual Traces of Mimesis in Following Jesus

As in Mark's Gospel, discipleship is a major theme in Matthew. The concept of "following Jesus," expressed by the verb ἀκολουθεῖν, is used of a variety of people: the (twelve) disciples (4:20, 22; 8:23; 9:9), the crowd (4:25; 8:1, 10; 12:15; 14:13; 19:2; 20:29), would-be followers (8:19–20; 19:21), two blind men (20:34), and some women (27:55). The expression of a person coming "behind" (ὀπίσω) Jesus is synonymous with the concept of following him as 4:19–20; 10:38; 16:24 indicate. Matthew specifies the various demands of following: homelessness (8:19–20), priority over family (8:21–22; 10:37), cross-bearing (10:38; 16:24), self-denial (16:24), and giving up everything (19:21, 27). Matthew indicates several rewards for following

---

84. Daniel Patte, *Discipleship according to the Sermon on the Mount: Four Legitimate Readings, Four Plausible Views of Discipleship, and Their Relative Values* (Valley Forge, PA: Trinity Press International, 1996), 312–50; Patte, *The Challenge of Discipleship: A Critical Study of the Sermon on the Mount as Scripture* (Harrisburg, PA: Trinity Press International, 1999), 86–117.

85. Dale C. Allison, *Studies in Matthew: Interpretation Past and Present* (Grand Rapids: Baker Academic, 2005), 147–55.

86. Allison, *Studies in Matthew*, 154–55 (quotation from p. 154).

PART 2   MIMESIS IN EARLY CHRISTIANITY

Jesus: a high return rate on what has been given up, everlasting life, and a share in Jesus's glory and reign (19:28–29; see also 10:39; 16:25). Often, people follow at Jesus's invitation (4:19, 21; 9:9; 19:21), and we must again examine whether Matthew's concept of following Jesus includes the idea of emulating Jesus in order to become like him.

As in Mark, I can only find traces of mimesis in a few instances where the Matthean Jesus sets an example that his disciples can "imitate." First, Jesus's purpose in calling the disciples is to make them "fishers of people" (4:19), which primarily consists of proclaiming the good news and performing exorcisms and healings (10:1, 7–8). This is an echo of Jesus's purpose for coming to the world: to proclaim the good news and perform mighty acts (4:23–24; 8:16–17) and "fish" for people (4:19, 21; 9:9, 13; 10:1; 19:21).[87] Second, Jesus practices self-denial and cross-bearing (26:39; 27:31, 35), and so should his disciples (10:38; 16:24). Third, the implication of 8:21–22 is that just as Jesus has no permanent home, his followers should expect to be itinerant. Fourth, just as Jesus's ministry takes priority over his biological family (12:46–50), so should that of his followers (8:21–22; 10:37). Fifth, just as Jesus made disciples, so also his disciples should make other disciples (28:19). However, just as in my earlier critique, the verses in question are far removed from each other, so the connection is tenuous at best. I therefore conclude that there is no explicit mention of mimesis in the Matthean concept of following Jesus—only traces of implied mimesis.

These conceptual traces of mimesis are still useful steps to understanding the full extent to which believers can imitate Jesus, but we will need a sound textual basis for mimesis on which to build. So, we search Matthew's vocabulary to find more explicit instances of mimesis. The most prominent particles in Matthew are ὥσπερ (ten occurrences), οὕτως (thirty-two occurrences), ὡς (forty occurrences), and the ὁμοι* group (twenty occurrences). The first instances of this potential mimetic language occur in the Sermon on the Mount. In fact, the Sermon on the Mount contains twenty out of these 102 occurrences or 20 percent of Matthew's potential mimetic language.[88] Hence, we will start there.

4.3.2. Mimesis in the Sermon on the Mount

The Sermon on the Mount outlines life in the kingdom of God or heaven. It is well recognized that Matthew presents Jesus as the new Moses and Jesus's teaching

---

87. See also Byrskog, *Jesus the Only Teacher*, 327; Patte, *Challenge of Discipleship*, 93.
88. The Sermon on the Mount contains two out of ten occurrences of ὥσπερ, seven out of thirty-two occurrences of οὕτως, eight out of forty occurrences of ὡς, and three out of twenty occurrences of the ὁμοι* group.

4. Mimesis in the Synoptics and Acts

as a reprise of the giving of the law, regulating life with God. Jesus's audience consists of his disciples and the crowd (5:1; 7:28), so the Sermon on the Mount is intended for both disciples and would-be disciples. While ἀκολουθεῖν does not feature in Matt 5–7, the term occurs in 4:25 and 8:1 with reference to large crowds following Jesus, effectively creating an *inclusio*. Since "following Jesus" suggests the potential for pledging allegiance to Jesus in discipleship, the Sermon on the Mount is also intended for would-be disciples. In Matt 5–7, Jesus's teaching about how one is expected to live in the realm where God is king is, therefore, both for those who are already following him and for those who might be interested in doing so. The Sermon on the Mount contains terms that may prove to be mimetic language—ὥσπερ (6:2, 7), οὕτως (5:12, 16, 19; 6:9, 30; 7:12, 17), ὡς (5:48; 6:5, 10, 12, 16, 29; 7:29 [2x]), and ὁμοιοῦν (6:8; 7:24, 26). We will first eliminate those that do *not* indicate mimesis and then examine the ones that do.

Non-Mimetic Occurrences. In most instances, the above-mentioned terms in the Sermon on the Mount do not constitute mimesis. In 5:12, the adverb οὕτως indicates analogy in that the persecution foreseen for followers of Jesus is likened or analogous to that of Old Testament prophets rather than suggesting that Jesus's followers seek to imitate the prophets (M&A criterion 1 is not met). Then, having stated that his followers are the light of the world (5:14), Jesus exhorts them to let their light shine before others in the same way (οὕτως) as a lamp on a lampstand illuminates a house (5:15–16). Jesus's theoretical example uses a non-descript person, so the correspondence is more analogous than mimetic (M&A criterion 2 is not met). In 5:19, Jesus speaks of a non-specific person (ὃς ἐάν) who breaks or annuls a commandment and teaches others to do likewise (οὕτως). Again, Jesus uses an analogous illustration rather than holding up a person who can be observed and imitated. In 6:10, ὡς denotes analogy to express that God's will be done on earth just as in heaven. In 6:29, ὡς denotes a comparison between the splendor of Solomon's clothes and the natural beauty of flowers, followed by the proposition in 6:30 that God does something similar (οὕτως) to both flowers and people, thus expressing analogy rather than mimesis (M&A criterion 2 is not met). In 7:12, Jesus's exhortation to treat others in the same way as (οὕτως) people wish to be treated is about reciprocal rather than mimetic behavior.[89] In 7:17, οὕτως is used to liken the teaching of false prophets to bad fruit on a bad tree. In

---

89. Nevertheless, Hans Dieter Betz contends that "all that you wish" (7:12) should be patterned on what God wishes (6:10), so the disciples are to emulate God's initiative of generosity, forbearance, and forgiveness to others in the hope that they will receive similar treatment (*The Sermon on the Mount: A Commentary on the Sermon on the Mount*, Hermeneia [Minneapolis: Fortress, 1995], 518).

PART 2   MIMESIS IN EARLY CHRISTIANITY

7:24 and 7:26, Matthew uses ὁμοιοῦν to refer to analogy, to compare non-specific people in imaginary situations. Finally, the twofold ὡς in 7:29 indicates that Jesus's teaching is authoritative, unlike the teaching of the scribes. We now turn to those occurrences that do indicate mimesis in the Sermon on the Mount.

Mimesis in Matthew 5. Schulz argues that 5:44–45 (// Luke 6:27–28, 35) contains mimesis in that love for an enemy, as the pinnacle of neighborly love, imitates God's impartial care for people.[90] Syntactically, however, the connection between 5:45b and 5:44 is causal (ὅτι) rather than comparative (as Schulz himself observes), so God's behavior is the basis for similar behavior by his children. Nevertheless, there is a "weak" idea of mimesis in that God's children should reflect their Father's impartiality and generosity towards people.

In 5:48, however, we find an explicit example of disciple–God mimesis: Jesus exhorts his audience to be perfect (τέλειος) just as (ὡς) their heavenly Father is perfect, calling them to imitate God.[91] We must ask, however, in what way God is an example for his children to imitate. The οὖν in 5:48 relates Jesus's exhortation to his teaching on love in 5:43–47. In seeking to correct or surpass the oral tradition of the Pharisees (ἠκούσατε ὅτι ἐρρέθη, "you have heard that it was said")—after all, the righteousness of God's children must exceed that of the scribes and Pharisees (5:20)—Jesus advocates the higher ethic of loving one's enemy, an *impartial* love that reflects or resembles the Father's behavior. Hence, the "perfection" that Jesus seeks from God's children is to imitate God in *being impartial in one's behavior towards others*.[92]

The "strong" idea of imitating God's impartiality in 5:48 certainly strengthens the "weak" idea of similar mimesis in 5:44–45. In fact, 5:48 is likely a fitting conclusion to the string of teachings in 5:21–47, "you have heard that it was said . . .

---

90. Schulz, *Nachfolgen und Nachahmen*, 226–30.

91. Feldmeier contends that 5:48 speaks more of a correspondence to God than an imitation of him ("Heavenly Father," 435). However, the correspondence in 5:48 is a *mimetic* correspondence indicated by the comparative particle ὡς.

92. Similarly, de Boer states that the imperative to imitate God's "perfection" is connected concretely with the love about which Jesus has just been speaking, so the disciples' love should also be all-embracing, complete, undivided, and universal (*Imitation of Paul*, 72). In keeping with his general thesis, Burridge notes that 5:48 exhorts people to emulate God's openness and inclusivity (*Imitating Jesus*, 216–21). See also Betz, *Sermon on the Mount*, 324–25; Griffiths, *Example of Jesus*, 42, 56; Charles H. Talbert, *Reading the Sermon on the Mount: Character Formation and Decision Making in Matthew 5–7* (Grand Rapids: Baker Academic, 2004), 96–98; Wesley G. Olmstead, "Jesus, the Eschatological Perfection of Torah, and the *Imitatio Dei* in Matthew," in *Torah Ethics and Early Christian Identity*, ed. Susan J. Wendel and David M. Miller (Grand Rapids: Eerdmans, 2016), 43–58, at 50–51. Olmstead then argues that the repeated phrase "I desire mercy, not sacrifice" (9:13; 12:7) alludes to Jesus imitating God's steadfast love in 9:1–13 and 12:1–8 ("Jesus," 53–58).

4. Mimesis in the Synoptics and Acts

but I say to you," to explain Jesus's demand for a righteousness that exceeds that of the scribes and Pharisees (5:20).[93] In which case, the imitation of God must apply to other forms of moral behavior affecting others, such as anger and reconciliation, lust and its radical solution, divorce and remarriage, truthful speech, retaliation, and generosity. As Dick France asserts, rather than laying out rules of conduct, Jesus points to *God's character* as the inspiration for ethical living.[94] This is the only Matthean example and one of the few in the New Testament that indicates a direct believer–God mimesis. More often, the imitation of God is mediated through the imitation of Christ so that the one who imitates Christ imitates God.

Most scholars have noted that 5:48, ἔσεσθε ... τέλειοι ὡς ὁ πατὴρ ὑμῶν ὁ οὐράνιος τέλειός ἐστιν ("Be perfect, therefore, as your heavenly Father is perfect," NRSV), echoes Lev 19:2, ἅγιοι ἔσεσθε ὅτι ἐγὼ ἅγιος κύριος ὁ θεὸς ὑμῶν ("You shall be holy, for I the LORD your God am holy," NRSV; see also 11:44–45).[95] What has received less attention, however, is that Matthew has redacted Lev 19:2 in three ways. First, the personal name for the God of Israel, YHWH Elohim (יְהוָה אֱלֹהִים [MT]) or LORD God (κύριος ὁ θεός [LXX]), has become more intimate—"heavenly Father." Second, Matthew has changed the divine moral standard of "holiness" to "perfection," although arguably, this is to provide a fitting climax to the teaching of 5:17–48, where Jesus explains the demand for a righteousness that surpasses the Pharisees by a series of teachings "you have heard that it was said." The term τέλειος ("perfection") refers to a disciple's wholehearted allegiance to God rather than moral perfection.[96] Third, and more importantly, Matthew has changed the causal

---

93. See also Schulz, *Nachfolgen und Nachahmen*, 231; Betz, *Sermon on the Mount*, 321, 325; R. T. France, *The Gospel of Matthew*, NICNT (Grand Rapids: Eerdmans, 2007), 228; David L. Turner, *Matthew*, BECNT (Grand Rapids: Baker Academic, 2008), 177; Jonathan T. Pennington, *The Sermon on the Mount and Human Flourishing: A Theological Commentary* (Grand Rapids: Baker Academic, 2017), 203–4.

94. France, *Matthew*, 228.

95. The connection to Leviticus is strengthened by the partial quotation of Lev 19:18 in Matt 5:43 (ἀγαπήσεις τὸν πλησίον σου).

96. Many scholars support this view of τέλειος in 5:48 in light of its use in Deut 18:13 LXX ("be τέλειος before the Lord your God"). For example, John Nolland understands τέλειος here as wholeheartedness or loyalty (*The Gospel of Matthew: A Commentary on the Greek Text*, NIGTC [Grand Rapids: Eerdmans, 2005], 271). France contends that τέλειος is a broader term than moral flawlessness and denotes spiritual maturity, and thus suitably sums up the demand for the "greater righteousness" in 5:20 (*Matthew*, 228–29). For Pennington, τέλειος denotes holistic holiness or integrity/righteousness that has a bearing on the entire person—mind, heart, and body. Hence, 5:48 calls not for moral perfection but a wholehearted orientation toward God (*Sermon on the Mount*, 204–5). Ulrich Luz suggests that τέλειος in 5:48 refers to the unity of heart and

PART 2   MIMESIS IN EARLY CHRISTIANITY

particle כִּי (MT) or ὅτι (LXX) in Lev 19:2 to the *comparative* particle ὡς to denote the mimetic relation between God's holiness/perfection and that of his people.[97] In other words, 5:48 introduces the shift from God as the basis or reason for holy living to *God as a parental example* for life in the divine family. However, this begs the question of how the invisible, "absent" God can be an example for imitation. I suggest that the answer lies in Matthew's concept of Jesus as "Immanuel," meaning "God is with us" (1:23, quoting Isa 7:14). Consequently, Jesus functions as the "living example" of the invisible God to facilitate mimesis.[98]

Mimesis in Matthew 6. There are arguably seven potential instances of mimesis in the literary unit 6:1–18. In 6:1, Jesus warns his followers about practicing their righteousness publicly for others to see. Instead, Jesus exhorts his audience to act in secret so only God can see and reward them. Structurally, each section (6:2–4, 5–6, and 16–18) opens with an imperative not to imitate (ὥσπερ in 6:2 and ὡς in 6:5, 16) the "hypocrites," which is primarily a reference to the Pharisees and scribes (15:7; 22:18; 23:13, 15, 23, 25, 27, 29), and ends with the exhortation to do one's act of righteousness (almsgiving, prayer, fasting) in secret, where only God can see and reward. Only section 6:5–6, on prayer, extends into 6:7–15, where twice more Jesus commands his followers not to imitate others in the way they pray through the use of ὥσπερ (6:7) and ὁμοιοῦν (6:8). However, instead of the hypocritical Jewish authorities, the reference this time is to gentiles and their wordiness in prayer.[99] In short, regarding the three "acts of righteousness" (almsgiving, prayer, fasting), the terms ὥσπερ (6:2, 7), ὡς (6:5, 16), and ὁμοιοῦν (6:8) are used synonymously to

---

totality of obedience (*Matthew 1–7: A Commentary*, Hermeneia [Minneapolis: Fortress, 2007], 289). In contrast, Jacques Dupont contends that τέλειος is not a divine attribute in the Bible but comes from the Greek traditions and projects a human ideal onto God. Moreover, while Luke is more theological in 6:36, focusing on God's behavior, Matthew is more ethical in 5:48, focusing on human behavior ("L'Appel à Imiter Dieu en Mt 5,48 et Lc 6,36," in idem, *Études sur les Évangiles Synoptiques*, vol. 2, BETL 70 [Leuven: Leuven University Press, 1985], 529–50). However, this contrast is too stark and flawed. First, the cognate verb τελειοῦν is used with reference to God in 2 Sam 22:16 (Nolland, *Matthew*, 271n279). Second, Luz contends that a Jewish background to τέλειος is more suitable than a Greek background (*Matthew*, 289). Third, Betz shows that, in the context of Matt 5–7, God's "perfection" refers to his impartial generosity, bestowing the benefits of his creation continuously on all people (*Sermon on the Mount*, 323–24). Hence, in Matthew too, the focus is on God's behavior as an example for imitation.

97. We will see in section 7.2 that 1 Pet 1:15–16 has preserved the causal ὅτι in Lev 19:2.

98. Unfortunately, Matthew does not elaborate on the term Ἐμμανουήλ in his Gospel, so we cannot push the idea of Jesus exemplifying the invisible God for imitation.

99. This probably indicates that 6:1–18 is the conflation of two sources or traditions, one found in 6:1–6, 16–18 and another in 6:7–15. Matthew then merges Jesus's teachings on two different occasions to create one theological unit.

4. Mimesis in the Synoptics and Acts

indicate that Jesus's followers should not imitate the hypocritical Jewish authorities or the gentiles in their behavior.[100] While these five instances (6:2, 5, 7, 8, 16) clearly speak of mimesis, they are not relevant to our understanding of the disciples–Jesus/God mimesis because they are an injunction against imitating the hypocritical Jewish authorities and the gentiles. We now turn to the two relevant instances of mimesis—in 6:9 and 6:12.

In 6:9–13, Jesus presents his audience with a model prayer that they can imitate. I contend that οὕτως in 6:9a denotes mimesis rather than analogy because Jesus presents them with a memorable prayer that functions as an example to follow.[101] Generations of Christians have imitated this so-called "Lord's Prayer"— mostly by repeating it literally in public. I suggest, however, that this was not Matthew's intention. In the entire section 6:1–18, Jesus explicitly and repeatedly warns against practicing one's righteousness *in public* in order to be seen by others and instead exhorts his followers to do it *in secret* where only God can observe it. Especially when it comes to prayer, Matthew finds it necessary to warn against both the desire for public praise that the Jewish authorities seek and the verbosity that gentiles use in their prayers. I contend that Jesus taught the model prayer in 6:7–15 on another occasion (as we find in Luke 11:1–4), and Matthew placed it in a context of practicing one's righteousness in private, indicating that in his view Jesus's model prayer should not be used publicly.[102]

Given that Jesus provides a concrete example of prayer to be imitated by his followers in private, the issue is whether Jesus intended that this prayer be recited verbatim or be a template for private prayer. I argue that the latter is nearer to Jesus's intention. If Jesus had intended literal replication, Matthew would probably have used the demonstrative pronoun οὗτός rather than its adverb οὕτως and have Jesus say, pray "this" rather than "like this" or "in this manner." Nevertheless,

---

100. While the evidence of mimesis in 6:2, 5, 7, 16 is strong, in 6:8 the phrase "do not be/become like them" could simply denote analogy (see the use of ὁμοιοῦν in 7:24, 26). However, since 6:8 is an extension of 6:7, I consider it a "weak" or "medium" case of mimesis.

101. Similarly, Betz states, "The adverb 'thus' (οὕτως) does not introduce the Lord's Prayer as a new entity but as an example well known to the readers already," suggesting that the Lord's Prayer is a model for all prayers (*Sermon on the Mount*, 370).

102. For two reasons I contend that 6:7–15 is from another source or occasion in Jesus's ministry. First, vv. 7–15 disrupt the neat structure where, following the topic statement in v. 1, vv. 2–4, 5–6, and 16–18 have the same structure and equal length. Second, Jesus warns his audience here against the verbose prayers of the gentiles (see also Mark 12:40) rather than the attention-seeking prayers of the Pharisaic hypocrites. By placing it in a context that seeks to promote living out one's practical moral life "in secret," Matthew considers that the Lord's Prayer should be used privately. To use this passage to build a case against communal prayers would be to miss the point.

the use of οὕτως does not conclusively determine whether the intended mimesis involves literal replication or creative expression, so the issue must be resolved on other grounds.[103] First, Jesus would expect his followers to pray with intent and understanding rather than mindlessly repeating words. This implies that content takes priority over form. Next, by way of three imperatives on how not to pray in 6:5, 7–8, Jesus indicates that prayer must be accompanied by the right attitude, namely one that avoids being performative and verbose. Thus, how (in what manner) and what Jesus's followers pray seem more important than the precise form of prayer. As the thesis statement of 6:1 indicates, Jesus wants his followers to pay conscious attention (προσέχειν) to their piety—to think about how they give alms, pray, and fast.

When Jesus provides an example of prayer to imitate, it is likely that this mimesis involves a cognitive aspect that affects the content and form of prayer as well as the attitude with which people pray. In short, the prayer is a ὑπόδειγμα or τύπος ("example," "pattern," "model") to follow; instead of elaborate teaching on prayer, Jesus gives them a sample prayer on which to model their own. It is unlikely that Jesus intends that his followers clone the prayer but use it as a template or model for their own prayers. While I do not object to reciting the Lord's Prayer, this does not exhaust the ways in which Jesus's followers can use it. Regardless of the form, if believers do not think about what they say while praying, they will miss the point. In other words, with this paradigmatic prayer, Jesus primarily intends that his audience imitate a particular attitude to prayer rather than simply repeat the literal words.

The content of 6:12–13 raises the issue of whether Jesus himself used this prayer and, therefore, whether the disciples imitate Jesus in the way he prays or simply "use" the prayer Jesus gives them. Since Jesus presents here a tangible example of prayer that the disciples can use by praying it at least once in their presence, there is a sense of the disciples' observing Jesus pray and being able to imitate him.[104] Similarly, in John 13, Jesus washes his disciples' feet only once, but he clearly expects his disciples to imitate him (13:15). Looking ahead in Matthew, we note that both Jesus's prayer in Gethsemane and his encouragement for the disciples to pray reflect aspects of the Lord's Prayer. Jesus's resolve to submit to God's will in 26:39, 42 corresponds to the request in 6:10b, and Jesus's exhortation to his disciples to

---

103. France, however, contends that the adverb οὕτως indicates liturgical repetition of the words rather than a pattern for prayer (*Matthew*, 241).

104. In Luke, however, there may be a hint that Jesus himself prayed this kind of prayer because the prayer that Jesus taught his disciples in Luke 11:2–4 may not differ from what he himself prayed in Luke 11:1.

4. Mimesis in the Synoptics and Acts

pray in order to avoid testing in 26:41a echoes the plea in 6:13a.[105] The fact that Jesus's prayer in Gethsemane is modeled on the Lord's Prayer strengthens the case that 6:9 denotes mimesis.[106]

It must be noted that within this mimetic prayer, there is another possible instance of mimesis. In 6:12, the comparative conjunction ὡς is used to ask God to forgive the petitioner just as the petitioner has forgiven others who have sinned against him (see also 6:14–15). The issue is whether God "imitates" or reciprocates people's attitude in forgiveness. On the one hand, the request to God to imitate the petitioner's behavior of forgiving others is odd, and 6:12 more likely indicates that God behaves in a similar manner to people who forgive (analogous behavior) rather than that he intentionally seeks to imitate them. God reciprocating people's record on forgiveness in 6:12 is elaborated in 6:14–15, using a conditional construction. On the other hand, in Jesus's parable on forgiveness in 18:23–35, there is potential evidence of mimesis: (1) in 18:33, ὡς καί indicates that the unforgiving slave should have imitated his master's merciful attitude expressed as debt cancellation—so, by implication, the disciples should imitate God in merciful forgiveness, and (2) in 18:35, moving from the level of story to the level of narrative, Jesus indicates that God acts like the master in the parable (οὕτως καί), which probably indicates analogy since the master in the parable is not a real person to be observed and imitated. Hence, since the comparative particle ὡς in 18:33 indicates mimesis in relation to forgiveness, ὡς in 6:12 may arguably also connote mimesis.[107] However, the possible case for mimesis in 6:12 does not explicitly relate to a believer–God mimesis, so I will not consider this instance.

In conclusion, we noted that the Sermon on the Mount contains twenty out of 102 occurrences (i.e., 20 percent) of Matthew's potential mimetic language (see n. 88). Our study suggested that seven of these twenty occurrences (i.e., 35 percent) actually express mimesis, albeit with varying levels of mimetic strength

---

105. See also Sandnes, *Discourses*, 146. Sandnes contends that the Gethsemane story provided a narrative background for the particular petition "Your will be done" in the Lord's Prayer (*Discourses*, 259). That Jesus, in his request to God, uses slightly different wording—οὐχ ὡς ἐγὼ θέλω ἀλλ' ὡς σύ in 26:39 versus γενηθήτω τὸ θέλημά σου in 26:42 (the latter are the exact words of 6:10)—poses no problem but simply shows that exact replication is not required to qualify as mimesis.

106. Did. 8:2 echoes Matt 6:8–13 and Did. 8:3 indicates that the early church "imitated" the Lord's Prayer three times a day (see also Peter J. Tomson, "The Lord's Prayer at the Faultline of Judaism and Christianity," in *Studies on Jews and Christians in the First and Second Centuries*, WUNT 418 [Tübingen: Mohr Siebeck, 2019], 261–77, at 265–66). Tomson also notes that in form and content the Lord's Prayer is a typical Jewish "short prayer."

107. Schulz, oddly, contends that Matt 18:23–35 illustrates God's mercy in Luke 6:36 (*Nachfolgen und Nachahmen*, 237).

PART 2   MIMESIS IN EARLY CHRISTIANITY

(5:48; 6:2, 5, 7, 8, 9, 16). However, when we consider our focus—the imitation of Jesus or God—there are only *two* instances in the Sermon on the Mount where relevant mimesis is in view: (1) 5:48 with reference to the imitation of God's impartial love ("strong" mimesis), and (2) 6:9 with reference to the imitation of Jesus's prayer ("medium" mimesis). We must note that Matthew 5–7 uses familial imagery where God is predominantly presented as (the heavenly) Father,[108] and those in his kingdom as his "sons" or children (5:9, 45). The sermon's envisaged morality, therefore, is that of family behavior, implying that *the context of mimesis is behavior in the divine family*. We will see in the next chapter that in John, mimesis is much more prominent in regulating the believers' behavior in the divine family.

4.3.3. Mimetic Language in the Rest of Matthew

Having examined the idea of mimesis in Matt 5–7, we will now look at the remaining part of the Gospel, starting with the most frequently occurring conjunctions or particles ὥσπερ, οὕτως, ὡς, and the ὁμοι* group. Matthew uses a ὥσπερ ... οὕτως construction four times (12:40; 13:40; 24:27, 37). However, only in 12:40 is there a "weak" case of mimesis (it could also simply denote analogy), though it is one that is not in the interest of this study because the idea of Jesus imitating Jonah is outside the realm of ethics. The other three occurrences express analogy. In 13:40–42, the similarity is between the collection and fate of the "weeds" and of evildoers rather than the angels imitating the imaginary reapers; in 24:27, the return of the Son of Man is likened to the spectacular appearance of lightning; and in 24:37, the circumstances surrounding the coming of the Son of Man resemble those in Noah's time (24:38–39 expands 24:37 with a similar, analogous ὡς ... οὕτως construction).

Of the four occurrences of ὥσπερ on its own, three denote analogy rather than mimesis: in 18:17, one should regard an unrepentant believer like a gentile and tax collector rather than the sinner seeking to imitate a gentile or tax collector; in 25:14, one's readiness for the kingdom of God is likened to a master who had left his property in the hands of his slaves and returns to settle accounts with them; in 25:32, the Son of Man sorting out people at his return is likened to a shepherd separating the sheep from the goats rather than the shepherd being a tangible example that Jesus seeks to imitate (several M&A criteria are not met). Following the episode where the sons of Zebedee present a self-serving request to Jesus, we find in 20:26–28 a "medium" case of the disciple–Jesus mimesis. After telling his

---

108. Πατήρ occurs nineteen times (5:16, 45, 48; 6:1, 4, 6 [2x], 8, 9 [2x], 14, 15 [2x], 18 [2x], 26, 32; 7:11, 21) over against six occurrences of θεός (5:8, 9, 34; 6:24, 30, 33).

4. Mimesis in the Synoptics and Acts

disciples that they should not imitate gentile rulers (οὕτως is used in 20:26), Jesus points out the importance of servanthood and presents himself as an example to imitate (ὥσπερ is used in 20:28).[109] While the disciples' servanthood and self-giving may not have the same scope or effect as Jesus, he nevertheless presents himself as an example for imitation (see also section 4.2.2 on Mark 10:43–45).[110]

Οὕτως does not indicate mimesis, except for 6:9, 12:40, and 20:26 (see above). Often οὕτως simply refers to something preceding or following in the narrative (e.g., 1:18; 2:5; 3:15). In 17:12, we find the thought that people will treat Jesus similarly to Elijah, hence expressing analogy rather than mimesis (M&A criterion 2 is not met). Likewise, 13:47–50 describes the analogy between the kingdom of heaven and a fishing net to explain the eschatological collection of people and subsequent separation of the wicked from the righteous (the adjective ὅμοιος and the conjunction οὕτως are used). In 18:35, οὕτως expresses analogous behavior—God will act like the master in the parable toward unforgiving people—rather than that God seeks to imitate the hypothetical person. Similarly, Jesus likens the scribes and Pharisees to white-washed tombs in 23:28 rather than suggesting that the scribes and Pharisees are engaged in mimesis.

The particle ὡς occurs most often in Matthew (forty times), sometimes to refer to something that has been said (1:24; 26:19; 28:15) but more often to analogy (6:10, 29; 7:29; 10:16; 13:43; 17:2, 20; 22:30; 26:55; 28:3–4). Occasionally, however, ὡς denotes mimesis. In addition to the disciple–God mimesis in 5:48, the exhortation not to imitate certain others in 6:5, 16, and the mimesis of merciful forgiveness in 18:33 (see section 4.3.2), ὡς denotes mimesis twice more. In 10:25, Jesus indicates that a disciple is like (ὡς) his teacher in that his followers will experience the same slander as Jesus. This might be a "weak" case of "existential mimesis," where Jesus's followers will be subjected to a reality in imitation of their teacher. In 18:1–4, when the disciples are preoccupied with greatness, Jesus presents them with a child (the tangible example) and exhorts them to imitate the low social status of a child (ὡς is used twice) if they want to achieve greatness.[111]

Except for ὁμοιοῦν in 6:8 (see section 4.3.2), Matthew uses the ὁμοι* group in cases of analogy, either to compare people with others in hypothetical situations (11:16; see also 7:24, 26) or parables to liken the kingdom of God with something

---

109. Matthew presents a stronger case for mimesis here than Mark, who links 10:43–44 and 10:45 with a causal conjunction (γάρ) (see section 4.2.2).
110. See also France, *Matthew*, 761; Nolland, *Matthew*, 823–24; Turner, *Matthew*, 487.
111. The idea is not so much to seek the intellectual virtue of humility (which children often do not model) but to embrace the low status children had in society (France, *Matthew*, 679; Turner, *Matthew*, 435–36).

PART 2   MIMESIS IN EARLY CHRISTIANITY

(13:24, 31, 33, 44, 45, 47; 18:23; 20:1; 22:2; 25:1), or to denote repeated speech (22:26; 26:35; 27:41; see also ὡσαύτως below).[112]

There are a few remaining occurrences of Matthew's mimetic language. Matthew uses καθώς only three times and, as in Mark, it always refers to something that has been said, ordered, or written (21:6; 26:24; 28:6). The comparative conjunction ὡσαύτως simply denotes that a person repeats a particular action or speech (20:5; 21:30, 36; 25:17). Finally, the comparative conjunction ὡσεί always denotes analogy in Matthew: in 3:16, the Spirit's descent resembles that of a fluttering dove (analogy) rather than suggesting that the Spirit observes a dove and then imitates it; in 9:36, Jesus compares the crowd to sheep without a shepherd (analogy), whereas mimesis would require that the crowd seeks to imitate a flock of sheep; and in 14:21, ὡσεί is used to approximate the size of the crowd.

In conclusion, we have found *five* further instances of mimesis beyond the Sermon on the Mount: in 10:25 (an existential disciple–Jesus mimesis); 18:3–4 (disciples imitating the lowly status of children); 18:33 (a "weak" disciple–God mimesis by implication); 20:26 (disciples not to imitate gentile rulers); and 20:28 (a "medium" disciple–Jesus mimesis).

4.3.4. Further Concepts of Mimesis

Matthew contains a few instances of conceptual mimesis that are not linked to any mimetic language. Matthew's account of the event in Gethsemane (26:36–46) closely resembles that in Mark, so arguably, there is a case for mimesis in that believers seek to imitate Jesus in being watchful in prayer to avoid testing (see section 4.2.3). In Mark, however, the mimetic connection is stronger, with Mark 13:11 stating that the divine Spirit will aid believers in testing times, which is absent from Matt 24:9–14. Then, Matt 11:29 contains a possible concept of mimesis. Taking ὅτι explicatively, Jesus urges his audience to learn from him *that* he is gentle and humble in heart.[113] Beyond an intellectual assent to this assertion, Jesus surely intended his audience to become like him. In fact, the imperatival phrase "take my yoke upon you" suggests this learning is by imitation because, in antiquity, a yoke symbolized union in that a young ox was put in a yoke alongside a mature ox in order to learn. Finally, while Mark's minor characters have mimetic potential,

---

112. In 22:39, ὅμοιός simply likens two commandments in terms of their significance.

113. Ὅτι usually indicates content after verbs that denote mental or sense perception, or the transmission of such perception, or an act of the mind, to indicate the content of what is said and so on (BDAG, s.v.).

Matthew uses this literary strategy less. Nevertheless, some characters unique to his account could function as "literary examples" for Matthew's audience.[114]

4.3.5. Conclusion

As in Mark, we found that the Matthean concept of following Jesus only contained traces of mimesis. Examining other potential mimetic language, we found that a few occurrences denote mimesis in relation to ethics. The comparative conjunction ὥσπερ indicates mimesis three out of ten times—twice to indicate that the disciples should not imitate certain others (6:2, 7), and once to indicate a disciple–Jesus mimesis (20:28). Οὕτως indicates mimesis only two out of thirty-two times—once to indicate those the disciples should not imitate (20:26), and once to say that disciples should imitate Jesus's prayer (6:9). Although ὡς occurs forty times in Matthew, it only indicates mimesis in three texts (5:48; 10:25; 18:3–4). Considering our interest in the believer–Jesus/God mimesis, we find a disciple–Jesus mimesis thrice (indicated by οὕτως in 6:9, ὡς in 10:25, and ὥσπερ in 20:28) and a disciple–God mimesis once (indicated by ὡς in 5:48). There is also a disciple–child mimesis (indicated by ὡς in 18:3–4). I thus conclude that Matthew has a "weak" to "medium" concept of the believer–Jesus/God mimesis. As for the content of mimesis, Matthew emphasizes the activities of being impartial, engaging in mission (proclamation, exorcism, healing), prayer, servanthood, self-denial, cross-bearing, forgiveness, and humility.

Matthew is clearer about the place of mimesis in ethics than Mark. For Matthew, the primary ethical context is the kingdom of heaven/God. For example, he starts his account of Jesus's public ministry by focusing on how to live as a citizen of the kingdom of heaven/God in the Sermon on the Mount (Matt 5–7).[115] The familial imagery in the Sermon on the Mount (see n. 108) implies that the instances of mimesis are situated in the context of the divine family. Elsewhere he also provides instruction for ethical living or discipleship (e.g., 10:16–42; 15:10–20; 16:24–26; 17:24–27; 18:1–9, 15–35; 19:1–12; 20:20–28; 24:36–25:46). Although all examples of mimesis occur within Matthew's ethical material, these mimetic examples are sporadic so we must conclude that also for Matthew, mimesis is peripheral to his ethics.

---

114. See also Patte, who states that other characters are "models of discipleship only insofar as their attitude and behavior reflects Jesus' and his teaching" (*Sermon on the Mount*, 339–41 [quotation from p. 339]). Likewise, Burridge, *Imitating Jesus*, 223–24.

115. Although Matthew uses the phrase ἡ βασιλεία τοῦ θεοῦ six times, one of which is in the Sermon on the Mount (6:33), he prefers the phrase ἡ βασιλεία τῶν οὐρανῶν (thirty-eight times, of which ten occur in the Sermon on the Mount).

4.4. Mimesis in Luke–Acts

Just as in Mark and Matthew, some scholars have noticed notions of mimesis in Luke–Acts, but these have rarely been developed. Matera asserts that Jesus functions as a model for moral behavior for his followers (e.g., in seeking God's will, praying constantly, being inclusive, and overcoming evil by doing good).[116] Collinson contends that in Luke's Gospel, the disciples are expected to imitate Jesus in, for example, purity of life (6:40), prayer (11:1–14), being lights (11:33–36), and forgiving one's enemies (23:34).[117] However, Matera and Collinson do not elaborate on how the texts they refer to indicate mimesis.

Based on Jesus's command "go and do likewise" (Luke 10:37) and taking the Johannine footwashing as a test case, William Spohn suggests that Christians are invited to use their imaginations creatively and analogically to re-enact Jesus's action faithfully rather than merely repeating or copying it.[118] According to him, "Analogies exercise a normative function by implying actions and ways of living that are congruent with the prototype."[119] While Spohn does not use the terms imitation or mimesis, his concept of "creative, analogical imagination" corresponds closely to our understanding of mimesis as a creative cognitive process (see especially our chapter 5), even though I consider analogy to be broader than mimesis (see section 1.5).

Like Spohn, Burridge considers Jesus's instruction to the lawyer to follow the example of the Good Samaritan, "go and do likewise" (Luke 10:37), as representative of the numerous examples to follow (or avoid) for moral conduct in Luke–Acts. Regarding the Gospel, some parables unique to Luke feature two people, one to imitate and one to avoid (the rich man and Lazarus, the widow and the unjust judge, the Pharisee and the tax collector). Likewise, Acts presents several characters whose behavior readers can emulate, such as Barnabas, Dorcas, Lydia, Stephen, and Paul.[120] Burridge also sees the idea of imitating Jesus's open attitude to others in Luke–Acts.[121]

Hood suggests that Luke 14:12–14 provides a model for hospitality, and Luke 15 exemplifies God's forgiveness, mercy, and hospitality as qualities to be imitated.[122]

---

116. Matera, *New Testament Ethics*, 86–89.
117. Collinson, *Making Disciples*, 69. In Acts, she notes that Paul reminds the Ephesian elders of the example of his own life (20:18) (*Making Disciples*, 111, 115).
118. William C. Spohn, *Go and Do Likewise: Jesus and Ethics* (New York: Continuum, 2007), 50–54.
119. Spohn, *Go and Do Likewise*, 55.
120. Burridge, *Imitating Jesus*, 280–81.
121. Burridge, *Imitating Jesus*, 282.
122. Hood, *Imitating God*, 89–90.

4. Mimesis in the Synoptics and Acts

When it comes to Acts, Hood notes two patterns of imitation and participation: (1) actions or experiences of Jesus's followers (e.g., Stephen and Paul) echo those of Jesus, and (2) Jesus's followers obey commands given by Jesus in the Gospel and serve as models of obedience for later readers (e.g., the church rejoices in suffering [Acts 5:41] just as Jesus commanded [Luke 6:23]).[123] While I endorse Hood's first pattern (see section 4.4.4), his second pattern refers simply to obedience to Jesus's teaching rather than mimesis.

In a non-academic book on the imitation of Jesus in Luke's Gospel, Jimmy Agan presents three features in Luke as evidence that the imitation of Jesus is intended: (1) in Luke's world, people expected their lives to be shaped by the example of their teachers; (2) in ancient biographies, like Luke, readers were encouraged to imitate the central character; and (3) the interplay of prescriptive and descriptive material encourages the imitation of Jesus.[124] Beyond these general features, Agan suggests four guidelines for identifying which aspects of Jesus's life are intended for imitation: (1) a correspondence between Jesus's teaching and his own conduct; (2) a contrast between Jesus and other leaders; (3) consistency with the purpose of Luke's Gospel; and (4) the principle/practice distinction.[125] The remainder of his book then applies these guidelines. While I commend Agan for deploying a method for deciding what to imitate about Jesus, it often is insufficiently grounded in the Lukan text. For example, Agan states that just as Jesus was aware of the need for Scripture for his spiritual life (Luke 2:46, 49; 4:4), so should we be.[126] Or, like Jesus, we should become a "friend of sinners" and welcome those estranged from God or marginalized in society into God's family.[127] These are more general lessons drawn from Jesus's life, based on loose association. Elsewhere, Agan asserts that Luke 9:23 denotes imitating Jesus in self-denial and cross-bearing and goes on to explain how this would look today.[128] However, he fails to establish how 9:23 indicates imitation.

4.4.1. Conceptual Traces of Mimesis in Following Jesus

As in the other Gospels, discipleship is one of the main themes in Luke's account. The concept of "following Jesus," expressed by the verb ἀκολουθεῖν, applies to a variety of people: the (twelve) disciples (5:11, 28; 22:39), the crowd (7:9; 9:11; see also

123. Hood, *Imitating God*, 141–46.
124. Agan, *Imitation of Christ*, 38–43.
125. Agan, *Imitation of Christ*, 43–48.
126. Agan, *Imitation of Christ*, 74–75.
127. Agan, *Imitation of Christ*, 108–11.
128. Agan, *Imitation of Christ*, 139–44.

14:25; 23:27), would-be followers (9:57, 59, 61; 18:22), a blind beggar (18:43 [identified as Bartimaeus in Mark]), and some women (8:2–3; 23:27, 49). The expression of a person coming "behind" (ὀπίσω) Jesus is synonymous with the concept of following him, as 9:23 and 14:27 indicate. Luke specifies certain characteristics related to following: it requires "leaving everything" (5:11, 28; 14:33; 18:22, 28); it involves self-denial and cross-bearing, which may demand one's life (9:23–24; 14:27) and homelessness (9:58); and it takes precedence over family (9:59–62; 14:26). Luke indicates two kinds of rewards for following Jesus: (1) a disproportionately high rate of return on what one has given up in one's present life and (2) everlasting life in the age to come (18:30). Once again, we must examine whether Luke's concept of following Jesus includes the idea of mimesis, i.e., imitating Jesus in order to become like him.

As in Mark and Matthew, we can find some indications of a disciple–Jesus mimesis in Luke, where Jesus sets the example for his followers to "imitate." First, Jesus has come to "catch" people (5:31–32) by proclaiming the good news and conducting healings and exorcisms (4:15, 18–19, 35; 6:17–49). Likewise, Jesus's purpose in calling the disciples is to make them "fishers of people" (5:4, 10) by proclaiming the kingdom of God, exorcising demons, and healing (9:1–2; see also 10:9, 17). Second, Jesus sets the example for what he expects from his followers: Jesus has left everything—his trade, hometown, and family—in order to do God's work (3:23; 4:16, 29); he practices self-denial and cross-bearing, which ultimately costs him his life (22:42; 23:33, 46); he experiences homelessness (9:58); and his work takes priority over his biological family (8:19–21). Nevertheless, like Mark and Matthew, there is no explicit mention of mimesis in the Lukan concept of following Jesus, only conceptual traces.

Sverre Bøe, for example, examines the calls to cross-bearing in 9:23 and 14:27 and concludes that there is no link between Jesus's cross and the disciples' crosses, so the idea of imitation is absent.[129] Admittedly, Jesus's cross is not identical to that of the disciples (e.g., regarding the aspect of atonement), but aspects of suffering, shame, and sometimes even death, which are inextricably related to cross-bearing, are similar. Jesus's followers are to imitate Jesus's attitude of being willing to suffer, deny themselves, and be self-giving. Authentic mimesis demands a close resemblance but not always a one-to-one correspondence. While the cross-bearing of his followers is not identical to Jesus's own, and there is no mimetic language connecting these ideas at a conceptual level, Luke nevertheless presents Jesus as an implicit example for imitation.

---

129. Sverre Bøe, *Cross-Bearing in Luke*, WUNT 2/278 (Tübingen: Mohr Siebeck, 2010), 79–196.

4.4.2. The Lukan Mimetic Language

The most frequent comparative particles in Luke–Acts are καθώς (twenty-eight occurrences), οὕτως (forty-eight occurrences), and ὡς (114 occurrences). The comparative conjunction καθώς refers most often to something that has been said, written, handed down, commanded, and so on (Luke 1:2, 55, 70; 2:20, 23; 5:14; 19:32; 22:13; 24:24; Acts 2:4, 22; 7:17, 42, 44, 48; 15:15), and on a few occasions it denotes analogy or reciprocity rather than mimesis (Luke 6:31; 11:1; 17:26, 28; 24:39; Acts 15:8; 22:3).[130] However, in three instances, the concept of mimesis is evident. First, in Luke 6:36, καθώς denotes a disciple–God mimesis in that a disciple, like God, must be merciful or compassionate.[131] This verse is the Lukan equivalent of Matt 5:48, where believers are exhorted to imitate the Father's "perfection" in terms of impartial love and righteous behavior towards others (see section 4.3.2).[132] While Luke typically uses the terms ἔλεος ("mercy/compassion") and ἐλεεῖν ("to have mercy/compassion") (ten occurrences), in 6:36, he employs the unusual term οἰκτίρμων, which is more common in the LXX and Second Temple Judaism.[133] This is a strong case of mimesis and significant for our focus on the believer–Jesus/God mimesis. As Betz rightly states, "Not heavenly reward [6:35] but imitation of God is the higher and more important doctrine motivating Christian ethics."[134]

---

130. For example, Luke 6:31 speaks of reciprocal rather than mimetic behavior and 17:26, 28 indicate an analogy in circumstances. In Luke 11:1, the disciples request Jesus to teach them to pray *just as* John the Baptist *also* taught his disciples. The idea of the καθώς . . . καί construction, however, is not so much that Jesus observed and emulated John in how he taught his disciples to pray but that Jesus would teach his disciples in a similar or analogous manner as John taught his disciples.

131. See also John Nolland, *Luke 1–9:20*, WBC 35a (Dallas: Word, 1989), 300, 303. Contra Feldmeier, who states, "Mercy . . . is not so much a quality of God that is to be imitated as it is our experience of God's loving care and response to it" ("Heavenly Father," 440). Michael Wolter merely sees analogy in the καθώς construction (*Das Lukasevangelium*, HNT 5 [Tübingen: Mohr Siebeck, 2008], 260).

132. Betz also notes that Greco-Roman antiquity knew of imitating the gods in being merciful (*Sermon on the Mount*, 613). Based on Matt 5:44–45, Schulz sees implicit mimesis in the Lukan parallel 6:27–28, 35 (*Nachfolgen und Nachahmen*, 226–30). However, like Matt 5:45, Luke 6:35 has a causal conjunction (ὅτι) to express the connection between the expected behavior of disciples and God's character.

133. See further Schulz, *Nachfolgen und Nachahmen*, 234–36; Darrell L. Bock, *Luke*, 2 vols., BECNT 3 (Grand Rapids: Baker Academic, 1994, 1996), 1:604. Joel B. Green suggests that Luke may be echoing Tg. Ps.-J. on Lev 22:28, "My people, children of Israel, since our Father is merciful in heaven, so should you be merciful on the earth" (*The Gospel of Luke*, NICNT [Grand Rapids: Eerdmans, 1997], 275).

134. Betz, *Sermon on the Mount*, 614.

The imitation of God's kind and generous mercy does not only apply to what goes before (6:27–35) but also to what follows (6:37–42).[135] God's extravagant mercy is modeled in various Lukan parables (e.g., 14:15–24; 15:11–32).[136] Second, in Luke 11:30, the καθώς ... οὕτως (καί) construction indicates that Jesus will imitate Jonah in becoming a sign for the people of his time. However, this instance of "weak" mimesis does not relate to ethical behavior and, hence, is not relevant to our study. Third, the comparative conjunction καθώς in Luke 22:29 indicates a Jesus–Father mimesis in bestowing the right to rule.

The adverb οὕτως most often refers to something that precedes or follows in the narrative (e.g., Luke 1:25; 2:48; 9:15; 10:21; 12:38, 43, 54; 19:31; 24:24, 46), but can also indicate analogy (e.g., 12:21; 17:24, 26; 23:11). On four occasions, however, we can make a case for mimesis. First, in Luke 11:30, the καθώς ... οὕτως (καί) construction indicates a "weak" case of Jesus–Jonah mimesis but this is outside the realm of ethics (see above). Second, Luke 17:10 indicates a "weak" instance of a disciple–slave mimesis in that a disciple should imitate the faithful service of a slave to his master. Third, in Luke 22:25–26a, Jesus urges his disciples not to imitate gentile kings and those in authority who rule people. Fourth, in Acts 20:34, Paul reminds the Ephesian elders of his policy to support himself and his coworkers through manual labor. Then, in Acts 20:35, Paul states that he has set this example so that they would, likewise, support the weak among them. The mimesis is established by the ὑποδείκνυμι ... οὕτως construction ("to show [as an example] ... [to do] likewise").[137]

The particle ὡς has 114 occurrences in Luke–Acts, often as a temporal conjunction ("when," "after"; e.g., Luke 1:23, 41, 44; 2:15, 39; 4:25; 5:4; Acts 1:10; 3:12) or a reference to analogy (e.g., Luke 3:22; 10:3, 18, 27; 11:36, 44; 12:27; 15:19; 17:6; 18:11; 21:35; 22:31; Acts 3:22; 7:37, 51; 10:47; 23:11).[138] A few times, however, mimesis may be in

---

135. See also Joseph A. Fitzmyer, *The Gospel according to Luke*, 2 vols., AB28–28a (Garden City, NY: Doubleday, 1981, 1985), 1:641; Bock, *Luke*, 1:587. Schulz states that Matt 5:48 functions as a conclusion to the section 5:21–47 on righteous living, but Luke 6:36 introduces the section 6:37–42 on judging (*Nachfolgen und Nachahmen*, 231).

136. See also Hood, *Imitating God*, 89–90.

137. In 2 Thess 3:7–9, Paul refers to his record of working for a living when establishing the Thessalonian church, as an example to imitate (see section 6.2.3).

138. In Luke 15:19, the prodigal son's plea to his father to make him like (ὡς) one of the hired workers could hint at existential mimesis, but it is more likely that the son asks his father to treat him analogously to the hired workers (M&A criterion 2 is not met). Acts 10:47 states that the household of Cornelius had received the Spirit in the same manner as the believers at Pentecost in Acts 2. Acts 3:22 and 7:37 evoke the prediction in Deut 18:15, 18 that God will raise up a prophet like, i.e., analogous or similar to, Moses, and there is no hint at active imitation. In Acts 7:51, Stephen points out the analogy between the Sanhedrin authorities and their Israelite ancestors

4. Mimesis in the Synoptics and Acts

view. In Luke 6:40, Jesus indicates that a disciple is not above (ὑπέρ) the teacher, but when fully trained, he will be like (ὡς) his teacher. I rate this instance as a "weak" case of mimesis in that a fully qualified disciple will have the same status as the teacher and probably resembles him (see also section 4.3.3 on Matt 10:25).[139] In Luke 18:17, Jesus urges his disciples to imitate the receptivity of children in order to enter the kingdom of God (the presence of children in 18:15 presents a tangible example). A clearer example of mimesis is indicated by the threefold ὡς in 22:26–27. Here we find a disciple–slave and disciple–Jesus mimesis in that a disciple must imitate Jesus in humble service. Responding to the disciples' dispute about greatness (22:24), Jesus urges them not to "imitate" the gentile kings in lording it over their subjects and so-called "benefactors" in exercising their authority (22:25). Instead, if a disciple aspires to greatness, he must imitate (γενέσθαι ὡς) the least (see also the child in 9:48) and the servant (22:26). Jesus then refers to himself as a servant—ἐγὼ δὲ ἐν μέσῳ ὑμῶν εἰμι ὡς ὁ διακονῶν (22:27). Thus, Jesus not only wishes that the disciples imitate a servant but also sets the example, so that by implication the disciples can observe and imitate him.[140]

Among the Synoptics, Luke is the only one who uses the term τύπος ("type," "copy," "pattern," "example"). Of the three occurrences of τύπος (Acts 7:43, 44; 23:25), only 7:44 denotes mimesis in that Moses replicated the example of the tabernacle he had observed (presumably in a vision provided by God; see also Exod 25:9 LXX). The Israelite tabernacle, then, was a copy and reflection of the

---

in their resisting the work of the Holy Spirit—the Sanhedrin in rejecting the Spirit-endowed Messiah and Israel in killing the Spirit-inspired prophets who foretold the coming Messiah (7:52–53). In Acts 23:11, there is no exemplar and observer; rather, it indicates that Paul will testify in Rome in a similar manner as he had done in Jerusalem (M&A criterion 2 is not met).

139. While Witmer makes a passing reference to Luke 6:40 as an example of disciples imitating their teacher, he does not explain it (*Divine Instruction*, 98). Neither does Jon Ruthven, "The 'Imitation of Christ' in Christian Tradition: Its Missing Charismatic Emphasis," *JPT* 16 (2000): 60–77, at 68–69 (Ruthven also seems to understand "imitation" simply as "exact duplication"). Based on Acts, Collinson argues that although some disciples became teachers in the early Christian community, Jesus remained the ultimate master (*Making Disciples*, 109–11). Hence, in Luke 6:40, Jesus may have been speaking proleptically of the post-Easter reality where his disciples become teachers (see, e.g., Acts 2:42; 5:28; 13:12; 17:19).

140. See also Peter K. Nelson, *Leadership and Discipleship: A Study of Luke 22:24–30*, SBLDS 138 (Atlanta: Scholars Press, 1994), 159–60; François Bovon, *Luke 3: A Commentary on the Gospel of Luke 19:28–24:53*, Hermeneia (Minneapolis: Fortress, 2012), 174–75. Looking at the Synoptic parallels regarding servanthood (Mark 10:43–45 // Matt 20:25–28 // Luke 22:25–27), Matthew presents the strongest case for a disciple–Jesus mimesis, followed by Luke and then Mark. Holly Beers sets Luke 22:24–27 in the context of the Isaianic servant (*The Followers of Jesus as the "Servant": Luke's Model from Isaiah for the Disciples in Luke–Acts*, LNTS 535 [New York: Bloomsbury T&T Clark, 2015], 115–16).

heavenly original.¹⁴¹ However, to copy a given design does not really involve ethical behavior, so we will disregard this instance. Of the remaining potential mimetic language in Luke (ὡσαύτως, ὡσεί, ὥσπερ, ὁμοι* group), actual mimesis may be in view on two occasions. In 18:11, ὥσπερ could denote mimesis but refers more likely to analogy. In 10:37, Jesus urges a Mosaic scholar to "imitate" (ποιεῖν ὁμοίως) the so-called "good Samaritan" in being merciful (see also 6:36). While the hypothetical scenario in the parable arguably points to analogy rather than mimesis, Jesus's vivid description in 10:30–35 could readily enable his audience to visualize the events and imitate the protagonist in the parable.¹⁴² Luke–Acts also provides some instances of mimesis that are not expressed by specific mimetic language, and to these we now turn.

4.4.3. Further Concepts of Mimesis—the Lord's Supper and Gethsemane

While the Synoptics all recount the so-called "Lord's Supper," only Luke has recorded Jesus's instruction, "Do this in remembrance of me" (22:19).¹⁴³ Jesus reenacts the traditional Jewish Passover meal that we know from Old Testament traditions (see also 22:15) and gives it new significance, indicating that his imminent death will establish a new covenant.¹⁴⁴ "Do this" refers to imitating Jesus in breaking bread, and "in remembrance of me" implies remembering the significance of Jesus's words and actions. Focusing on the injunction "do this," John Laurance asserts that in the Lord's Supper, Christians perform the very actions of Jesus—to

---

141. Heinrich Schlier, "δείκνυμι, κτλ.," in *TDNT* 2:25–33, at 33.
142. Spohn's claim that Jesus invites his audience to think creatively and analogically (*Go and Do Likewise*, 4) comes close to our concept of mimesis. Burridge overstates his case that "go and do likewise" is Luke's most explicit statement of mimesis (*Imitating Jesus*, 280). Most occurrences of ὡσαύτως, ὡσεί, ὥσπερ, and the ὁμοι* group denote analogy. For example, in Luke 5:33, ὁμοίως simply denotes that both John's disciples and those of the Pharisees partake in similar activities rather than the former imitating the latter. In 6:31, ὁμοίως (and καθώς) indicate reciprocal rather than mimetic behavior. In 6:47–49, ὅμοιος is used analogously to show that someone who hears Jesus's teaching and acts on it resembles a "wise" person and someone who hears but does not follow it through in action resembles a "foolish" person (see also 7:31–32). In 11:4, the plea to God to forgive the petitioner in proportion to the petitioner's forgiveness of others echoes Matt 6:12, where we discussed the issue of whether God "imitates" or reciprocates people's attitude in forgiveness (see section 4.3.2). In 13:3, Jesus uses ὁμοίως analogously to warn that his audience may suffer a similar fate as the Galileans. In two brief parables, five occurrences of the ὁμοι* group denote an analogy of the kingdom of God (13:18–21).
143. Paul applies this remembrance language to both the bread and the cup in 1 Cor 11:23–25.
144. See also Fitzmyer, *Luke*, 2:1391–92, 1401.

take up the bread and cup—and thus make him present in his saving deeds.¹⁴⁵ As Donald L. Williams explains, "To remember is not an intellectual discipline, 'to re-member' is to re-create, 'to re-member' is to become involved, 'to re-member' is to actualize, 'to re-member' is to re-present, 'to re-member' is to respond... 'This do in remembrance of me' must mean, 'so that you may participate in the sufferings and death of our Lord and respond to them.'"¹⁴⁶ For Williams, "The Lord's Supper is the re-enactment of the Christian Exodus-event, the historical beginning which continues to give the church life."¹⁴⁷ Hence, re-enacting the Lord's Supper involves imitation—the replication of Jesus's act of breaking bread and repeating his words.¹⁴⁸ However, this is not a mindless replication; it involves cognition and volition because in the re-enactment, believers remember, participate in, and respond to Jesus's sacrificial death.¹⁴⁹

In section 4.2.3, I suggested that the Gethsemane event in Mark (and Matthew) has a mimetic dimension in that believers should imitate Jesus's watchfulness in prayer to avoid testing situations. In the Markan (and Matthean) account, there are both biographical aspects (describing Jesus's unique experience) and exemplary aspects (exhorting believers to imitate Jesus). In Luke, these biographical and exemplary dimensions are presented in two versions of the event through the textual variant in 22:43–44. While these verses are textually uncertain and probably a later addition, Watson contends that the two versions of Luke's Gethsemane account circulated from early in its history—at least as early as the mid-second century.¹⁵⁰ According to Watson, the two versions are at odds with each other: the

---

145. John D. Laurance, "The Eucharist as the Imitation of Christ," *TS* 47 (1986): 286–96, at 291–92.

146. Williams, "Israelite Cult," 121. Contra Bock, who views the Lord's Supper only as a memorial meal (*Luke*, 2:1724–26).

147. Williams, "Israelite Cult," 121.

148. Kurz calls this "the imitation of a stylized liturgical action in a set ritual" ("Narrative Models," 175).

149. Green states that the recollection of Jesus's life should also include "his openness to outsiders, his comportment as a servant, his indifference towards issues of status, honor, and the like—so that these features of his life would come to be embodied in the community of those who call him Lord" (*Gospel of Luke*, 762). At another level, based on his examination of various Eucharist traditions, Bruce Chilton argues that two factors were the impetus for the emergence of the Eucharist as a mimetic surrogate of sacrifice within Jesus's practice. First, Jesus's meals with people were a sign of the eschatological banquet, enacting the kingdom of God (Matt 8:11; Luke 13:28–29). Second, during the last meal with his followers ("the Last Supper"), which comes after the cleansing in the temple, Jesus asserts that his blood and flesh provide a better sacrifice than what was offered in the temple ("The Eucharist and the Mimesis of Sacrifice," in *Sacrifice, Scripture, and Substitution: Readings in Ancient Judaism and Christianity*, ed. Ann W. Astell and Sandor Goodheart, CJAS 18 [Notre Dame: Notre Dame University Press, 2011], 140–54).

150. Watson, *Fourfold Gospel*, 139.

longer version stresses the biographical dimension because there is nothing exemplary about 22:43–44, while the shorter version supports the exemplary dimension in that believers are called to imitate Jesus when facing testing situations.[151]

Contra Watson, Sandnes contends that Gethsemane holds both the biographical and exemplary dimensions together. When importance is given to the biographical view, Jesus's agony comes to the fore, while Jesus's embracing of God's will is easily understood as an example to imitate.[152] According to Sandnes, 22:43–44 even enhances Jesus as an example of one who embraced God's will despite his internal turmoil.[153] In other words, there are aspects of the Gethsemane event that are unique to Jesus, but other aspects function as an example to imitate.[154] Nevertheless, Luke's omission of the dominical proverb in Mark 14:38 (τὸ μὲν πνεῦμα πρόθυμον ἡ δὲ σὰρξ ἀσθενής) from his compressed account of the Gethsemane episode is surprising, considering his clear interest in the divine Spirit. Luke also omits Mark 13:11 from 21:12–19, so he has effectively omitted the double reference to the divine Spirit in Mark 13–14. Consequently, Luke seems to de-emphasize the mimetic dimension of the Gethsemane story found in Mark.[155]

4.4.4. Mimetic Characters

While some Lukan characters undoubtedly have mimetic potential or value for his audience, they do not play the same role as do the Markan characters.[156] Nevertheless, Burridge observes that the parables unique to Luke feature two people, one

---

151. Watson, *Fourfold Gospel*, 141–42.

152. Sandnes, *Discourses*, 309–11. Bock contends that Luke 22:42 exemplifies what Jesus taught in 22:27 (*Luke*, 2:1759).

153. Sandnes, *Discourses*, 172.

154. Bock comes very close to stating that how Jesus responds to crisis is an example to follow (*Luke*, 2:1763).

155. Kurz, however, contends that the Lukan redaction actually strengthens the portrayal of Jesus as a model for imitation: (1) 22:39 mentions that *all* the disciples (not just Peter, James, and John) *follow* Jesus into the garden, (2) Jesus's repeated instruction to his disciples, "pray that you may not come into a time of testing" (22:40, 46), frames his own example of prayer in 22:41–45, (3) Jesus's prayer in 22:42 has echoes of the Lord's Prayer in 11:1–4 ("Narrative Models," 185–86). However, 22:42 has no verbal echoes of 11:1–4; rather, Jesus's twofold instruction in 22:40, 46 echoes the petition "do not bring us into a time of testing" in 11:4.

156. For example, Luke uses several characters to teach on wealth ethics, and they may function as implied models for imitation (see Cornelis Bennema, "The Rich Are the Bad Guys: Lukan Characters and Wealth Ethics," in *Characters and Characterization in Luke–Acts*, ed. Frank E. Dicken and Julia A. Snyder, LNTS 548 [New York: Bloomsbury T&T Clark, 2016], 95–108). In an extensive discussion, Brian E. Beck concludes that Luke in some way holds up the characters in his Gospel for imitation (*Christian Character in the Gospel of Luke* [London: Epworth, 1989],

4. Mimesis in the Synoptics and Acts

to imitate and one to avoid (the rich man and Lazarus, the widow and the unjust judge, the Pharisee and the tax collector),[157] which reminds us of the characters in Plutarch's *Lives*, who often have mimetic qualities (see section 2.2.4). Likewise, we have Kurz's perceptive observation about the scene in Gethsemane, "Because the disciples in the story missed much of Jesus's example by sleeping, the paradigm is clearly addressed to the implied readers, who are the only witnesses of the entire scene that the narrator depicts."[158] In Acts, however, it is more evident that Luke presents some of his main characters as imitating (aspects of) Jesus and, hence, as models for the readers.

For Tinsley, the main mimetic element is the emphasis on the disciples as witnesses (μάρτυρες), imitating Jesus, the model witness (μάρτυς).[159] Regarding Peter, Tinsley notes a deliberate parallelism between Jesus's healing the paralytic in Luke 5:17–26 and Peter's healing the lame man in Acts 3:1–10: the language of "getting up" and "walking"; the audience's reaction of wonder and praise; and the healings causing a clash with the Jewish authorities.[160] He also notes that Peter's mission imitates that of Jesus: Peter's endowment with the Spirit; his speeches; his healing of Aeneas and raising of Dorcas; his arrest on the day of unleavened bread (Acts 12:3 // Luke 22:1); the disbelief at his reappearance and his having to calm other believers (Acts 12:15–17 // Luke 24:36–38).[161]

Tinsley also shows how Luke's account of Stephen's mission, speech, and death is a striking early example in Acts of the concept of the *imitatio Christi*. Like Jesus, Stephen is full of grace and power (Acts 6:8), leaving his opponents unable to withstand the wisdom and the Spirit with which he speaks (Acts 6:10; see

---

105–26). For the most comprehensive argument that the Lukan characters function as narrative models for imitation, see Kurz, "Narrative Models," 171–89.

157. Burridge, *Imitating Jesus*, 280.

158. Kurz, "Narrative Models," 186.

159. Tinsley, *Imitation of God*, 112–13. Similarly, Swartley contends that Luke presents Jesus's conduct before the authorities as an example for Christian witness in their trials before Roman authorities (*Covenant of Peace*, 370–71). Griffiths also notes that the apostles imitate Jesus's mannerisms, such as looking straight at people (Acts 3:4; 14:9) and laying hands on sick people (Acts 5:12; 14:3; 19:11; 28:8) (*Example of Jesus*, 50–51). Others mention more parallels between Jesus and his followers in general (Hood, *Imitating God*, 143–46; Charles H. Talbert, "Discipleship in Luke–Acts," in *Discipleship in the New Testament*, ed. Fernando F. Segovia [Philadelphia: Fortress, 1985], 62–75). Mathias Nygaard contends that Luke stresses the paradigmatic function of Jesus in the parallels between Jesus's prayers and those of his followers in Acts (Luke 3:21–22 // Acts 1:14; 2:1–4; Luke 6:12–13 // Acts 1:24–26; 13:2–3; Luke 23:34 // Acts 7:60) (*Prayer in the Gospels: A Theological Exegesis of the Ideal Pray-er*, BINS 114 [Leiden: Brill, 2012], 211).

160. Tinsley, *Imitation of God*, 109.

161. Tinsley, *Imitation of God*, 111. He gives no text references for Peter's speeches.

PART 2   MIMESIS IN EARLY CHRISTIANITY

also Luke 21:15). Instead, they stir up people against him and bring false charges (6:12–14). Stephen's speech echoes that of Jesus in the Nazareth synagogue, and his death resembles that of Jesus (cf. Luke 22:69 with Acts 7:55–56; Luke 23:34 with Acts 7:60; Luke 23:46 with Acts 7:59; Luke 23:50 with Acts 8:2; and Luke 23:27 with Acts 8:2). For Luke, Jesus is the model martyr, and his disciples are called to imitate him in the "way" of suffering, which is precisely what Stephen does.[162]

Tinsley contends that Paul's mission is also patterned on that of Jesus: Paul is sent on his mission by the Spirit; Paul's healing of the lame man at Lystra echoes Jesus's raising the paralytic in Luke 5:17–26; and Paul's passion is very similar to that of Jesus.[163] Hood highlights more parallels between Jesus and Paul: they both cite Isaiah 6:9–10 to explain their rejection (Luke 8:10; Acts 28:26–27); both are recognized by demons (Luke 4:34–35, 41; 8:28; Acts 16:17; 19:15); both are law-observant (Luke 2:21–24, 41–42; 16:17; Acts 16:3–4; 18:18, 21; 20:6, 16; 21:21–24); and both are charged with four offenses and have four trials.[164]

The parallels between Jesus and Peter, Stephen, and Paul are indeed striking, although we cannot be certain they intentionally imitated Jesus or if Luke shaped his account in a way that key people in the early church are patterned on Jesus. Moss supports the latter idea, arguing that "Luke labors to present Stephen in the same way as he narrated the passion of Jesus."[165] She goes so far as to assert that an element has been added to Jesus's death to align it with that of Stephen. Regarding the parallel prayer for forgiveness of others in Acts 7:60 and Luke 23:34, Moss notes that 23:34a is absent in many key manuscripts and is most likely a later addition to the text. This would make Stephen not simply a perfect imitator of Christ but more Christly since the death of Jesus is edited to resemble that of Stephen.[166] Instead, it is safer to conclude that, *narratively*, Peter, Stephen, and Paul imitate aspects of Jesus's life. In other words, it is more likely that Luke models

---

162. Tinsley, *Imitation of God*, 109–10. Others have also noted the parallels in the experiences of Stephen and Jesus (Schulz, *Nachfolgen und Nachahmen*, 268–69; Griffiths, *Example of Jesus*, 54, 59–60, 82; Moss, *Other Christs*, 34, 54–55). Regarding Acts 8, Tinsley argues that Philip imitates Jesus's manner of reasoning from Scripture and apostolic proclamation (*Imitation of God*, 108–9).

163. Tinsley, *Imitation of God*, 111–12. Ruthven claims that Peter and Paul imitate Jesus's miracles in many more instances ("Imitation of Christ," 74–75).

164. Hood, *Imitating God*, 144–45. Differently, Jean-François Landolt argues that Paul's exemplarity is his journey of conversion to Christianity ("'Soyez mes imitateurs, frères' (Ph 3,17): Paul comme figure exemplaire dans le corpus paulinien et les Actes des apôtres," in *Reception of Paulinism in Acts/Reception du paulinisme dans les Actes des apôtres*, ed. Daniel Marguerat, BETL 229 [Leuven: Peeters, 2009], 261–94, at 273–94).

165. Moss, *Other Christs*, 34.

166. Moss, *Other Christs*, 54–56. Alternatively, even if the logion in Luke 23:34 is a later

4. Mimesis in the Synoptics and Acts

the lives of Peter, Stephen, and Paul on that of Jesus than that they intentionally imitated Jesus.[167]

Even so, we must consider whether these parallels between Jesus and Peter, Stephen, and Paul indicate mimesis and to what extent these leading characters are models for imitation for other believers. De Boer's word of caution is helpful when he critiques Tinsley's view on imitation in Acts, taking Stephen as an example. Seeking to determine the scope of imitation, that is, whether "every parallelism, likeness, similarity, resemblance, and conformity between Christ and the believer come under the heading 'imitation of Christ,'" de Boer distinguishes between active imitation and experiences or events that echo one's life.[168] According to de Boer, "Stephen was an imitator of Christ in his faithful witness, his forgiving love toward his persecutors, and his committal of himself at the point of death to God's care. He was *not* an imitator in receiving a heavenly vision, in being martyred, buried by devout men, or lamented."[169]

We can use de Boer's strategy to examine how Peter and Paul imitate Jesus. The reactions of the audience and authorities to Peter's healing of the lame man, his endowment of the Spirit, and his arrest and reappearance are circumstances that parallel those of Jesus but simply happen *to* Peter rather than Peter intentionally imitating Jesus. However, we can say that Peter imitates Jesus in healing or raising the dead. With Paul, again, there are external circumstances analogous to those in Jesus's ministry, such as being sent on his mission by the Spirit, being recognized by demons, or having a similar pattern of trial, but they do not count as instances where Paul intentionally seeks to imitate Jesus. Paul does arguably imitate Jesus in doing miraculous works (e.g., healing the lame man at Lystra or raising Eutychus), being law-observant, and citing Isa 6:9–10 to explain people's rejection.

---

addition, it may still be an original saying of Jesus spoken on another occasion (see, e.g., Luke 11:4; 12:10; see also Luke 6:27–29) rather than plucked from the lips of Stephen, as Moss claims.

167. In an extensive study, David P. Moessner places the parallels between Jesus and Peter, Stephen, and Paul in the context of Moses's prophetic calling to Israel ("'The Christ Must Suffer': New Light on the Jesus–Peter, Stephen, Paul Parallels in Luke–Acts," *NovT* 28 [1986]: 220–56). Differently, Beers argues that the disciples, Stephen, Philip, and Paul embody similar aspects of the vocation of the Isaianic servant as Jesus, such as (1) to be witnesses, (2) to experience persecution, arrest, and sometimes death, and (3) to divide opinion amongst their audience about them and their message (*Followers of Jesus*, 119–75). While these parallels would suggest a more typological relationship between the Isaianic servant and Jesus and his followers than a mimetic relationship, perhaps one could argue that key people in the early church imitated (aspects of) Jesus in his Isaianic servant role.

168. De Boer, *Imitation of Paul*, 65–66 (quotation from p. 65).

169. De Boer, *Imitation of Paul*, 66 (emphasis added).

Having established that Peter, Stephen, and Paul imitated Jesus in certain ways, they can, in turn, be held up as models for other believers. In chapter 8, for example, we will see that Stephen, as the first Christian martyr, probably fueled the second-century concept of martyrdom as the ideal imitation of Christ.[170] We also noted this mode of *textually mediated mimesis* where characters in the narrative hold mimetic potential for the audience in Mark (see section 4.2.4) as well as Greco-Roman and Jewish antiquity (see chapters 2–3).

4.4.5. Conclusion

Just as in the other Synoptic Gospels, when speaking of the concept of following Jesus, Luke's account only hints at mimesis. Regarding other potential mimetic language, Luke's Gospel contains a few examples where mimesis is more clearly in view: a disciple–God mimesis in 6:36 (καθώς) on being merciful (see also 10:37); a disciple–slave/Jesus mimesis in 17:10 (οὕτως) and 22:26–27 (ὡς) about service; a disciple–child mimesis in 18:17 (ὡς) regarding receptivity; and a disciple–Jesus mimesis in relation to the Lord's Supper. On examining Acts, we found one example where Paul presents himself as an example to the Ephesian elders (20:34–35). At another level, however, we see that Luke considers Peter, Stephen, and Paul to have mimetic potential for his audience because he presents aspects of their lives that mirror that of Jesus. I thus conclude that Luke presents a "weak" to "medium" concept of mimesis. When we consider the place of mimesis in Lukan ethics, it appears similar to that in Matthew, and like Matthew, Luke's primary ethical context is "the kingdom of God."[171] Luke's Sermon on the Plain (6:17–49), for example, provides ethical instruction for life in the kingdom of God or discipleship, but so does the long section on Jesus's journey to Jerusalem (9:51–19:27). While most allusions to mimesis occur within Luke's ethical material, they are sporadic, so we conclude that also for Luke mimesis is at the margins of his ethics.

---

170. See also Tinsley, *Imitation of God*, 110; de Boer, *Imitation of Paul*, 14–15; Kurz, "Narrative Models," 187; Moss, *Other Christs*, 34, 53–59. Irenaeus states that "Stephen . . . was the first to follow the footsteps of the martyrdom of the Lord" (*Haer.* 3.12.10). Greg Stirling argues that Luke reworked Jesus's death and presented it as an exemplary martyr death, rooted in Socrates as a model for the noble death, thus paving the way for later Christian martyrology ("*Mors philosophi*: The Death of Jesus in Luke," *HTR* 94 [2001]: 383–402).

171. The phrase ἡ βασιλεία τοῦ θεοῦ occurs fifty-five times in the Synoptics, of which thirty-five times in Luke's Gospel.

4.5. Conclusion

In our study of the concept of mimesis in the Synoptic Gospels and Acts, we found that it barely features in Mark and appears occasionally in Matthew and Luke–Acts. While several scholars link the concepts of mimesis and following/discipleship too readily, we saw no explicit linguistic expression that ties ἀκολουθεῖν to mimesis, only conceptual traces of mimesis. As for other linguistic expressions, they occasionally denote mimesis. Nevertheless, we need not be as uncompromising as Schulz. In his extensive study on mimesis in the New Testament, he settles on Mark 10:43–45 (// Matt 20:26–28) as the *only* occurrence of imitating Jesus in the Synoptics and concedes to a few more occurrences of the imitation of God (e.g., Matt 5:48 // Luke 6:36; Matt 18:33).[172] Admittedly, instances of imitation of Jesus and God are scarce in the Synoptics, but there are more than Schulz allows for. Besides, it is sometimes evident that the Evangelists were intentional about mimesis. For example, both Matt 5:48 and Luke 6:36 echo Lev 19:2. But where Leviticus shows a causal relation (כִּי), Matthew and Luke have changed it to a comparative one (ὡς and καθώς, respectively). Nevertheless, I concede that mimesis is not a dominant aspect of discipleship in the Synoptics. As Ernest Best asserts, "The total relationship of the disciple to the Lord is too complex to be resolved into imitation alone."[173] We noted that Matthew and Luke–Acts contain more instances of mimesis than Mark and show a slightly stronger concept of mimesis than Mark, which leads me to conclude that the Synoptics manifest a "weak" to "medium" concept of mimesis. When we consider the various ethical material in the Synoptics, we find that mimesis is only peripheral to ethics in the Synoptics.

The following table presents our findings, and the device "mimetic strength" with its indicators "weak," "medium," and "strong" is used heuristically to convey our degree of certainty of the presence of mimesis in a particular passage.

---

172. Schulz, *Nachfolgen und Nachahmen*, 248–49, 303–5.
173. Best, *Following Jesus*, 41.

PART 2   MIMESIS IN EARLY CHRISTIANITY

	Reference	Mimetic Indicator	Content of Mimesis	Mimetic Strength
Mark	1:17; 8:34; 10:28	ἀκολουθεῖν	possible conceptual traces of mimesis regarding mission, self-denial, cross-bearing	weak
	10:15	ὡς	to imitate a child's receptivity	weak
	10:43–45	οὕτως	disciples should *not* imitate gentile rulers, but imitate Jesus in servanthood	medium/weak
	14:32–42	conceptual	disciple–Jesus mimesis regarding watchfulness in prayer to avoid testing	medium
		mimetic characters	various minor characters exemplify aspects of discipleship	medium
Matthew	4:19; 10:38; 16:24	ἀκολουθεῖν	possible conceptual traces of mimesis regarding mission, self-denial, cross-bearing	weak
	5:48	ὡς	believer–God mimesis in "being perfect"	strong
	6:2, 5, 7, 8, 16	ὡς, ὥσπερ, ὁμοιοῦν	warning *not* to imitate the Jewish authorities or gentiles	strong
	6:9	οὕτως	to imitate Jesus's prayer	medium
	10:25	ὡς	disciple–Jesus mimesis of defamed status	medium
	18:3–4	ὡς	disciples imitating the humble status of children	medium
	18:33	ὡς καί	an implied disciple–God mimesis regarding forgiveness (see also 6:12)	weak
	20:26	οὕτως	disciples are *not* to imitate gentile rulers	medium
	20:28	ὥσπερ	disciple–Jesus mimesis regarding servanthood	medium
	26:36–46		disciple–Jesus mimesis regarding watchfulness in prayer to avoid testing	weak
Luke–Acts	5:10–11; 9:23; 14:27	ἀκολουθεῖν	possible conceptual traces of mimesis regarding mission, self-denial, cross-bearing	weak

4. Mimesis in the Synoptics and Acts

Reference	Mimetic Indicator	Content of Mimesis	Mimetic Strength
6:36	καθώς	disciple–God mimesis in being merciful	strong
6:40	ὡς	disciple–Jesus mimesis in having the status of a teacher	weak
10:37	ὁμοίως	disciple–"good Samaritan" mimesis in being merciful	medium
17:10	οὕτως	disciple–slave mimesis in giving faithful service	weak
18:17	ὡς	disciples are to imitate a child's receptivity	medium
22:19		implied believer–Jesus mimesis in re-enacting the Lord's Supper	medium/strong
22:25–26a	οὕτως	disciples are *not* to imitate gentile rulers	medium
22:26b–27	ὡς	disciple–Jesus mimesis regarding servanthood	medium
22:29	καθώς	Jesus–God mimesis in granting the right to rule	medium
22:39–46		disciple–Jesus mimesis regarding watchfulness in prayer to avoid testing	weak
Acts 20:34–35	ὑποδείκνυμι ... οὕτως	Paul presents self-support as an example for the Ephesian elders	medium
	mimetic characters in Acts	Luke presents Peter, Stephen, and Paul as imitating aspects of Jesus's life	medium

In several instances, we found traces of mimesis in the concept of following Jesus, but these could not, on their own, make a strong case for imitating Jesus. However, together with the more robust instances of mimesis, these mimetic hints can nevertheless be useful for considering the full extent to which believers can imitate Jesus. Accordingly, the Synoptics indicate the following mimetic activities in the believer's relationship with Jesus or God:

PART 2   MIMESIS IN EARLY CHRISTIANITY

Believer–Jesus/ God Mimesis	Mark	Matthew	Luke
proclamation	3:13–15; 6:7–13 (related to 1:17)	10:1–8 (related to 4:19)	9:1–2; 10:9 (related to 5:10–11)
exorcism and healing	3:13–15; 6:7–13 (related to 1:17)	10:1–8 (related to 4:19)	9:1–2; 10:17 (related to 5:10–11)
self-denial	8:34; 10:28	10:38; 16:24	9:23; 14:27
cross-bearing	8:34; 10:28	10:38; 16:24	9:23; 14:27
receptivity	10:15		18:17
servanthood/self-giving/service	10:43–45	20:26–28	17:10; 22:26–27
prayer (alertness; how to pray)[174]	14:32–42	6:9–13; 26:36–46	22:39–46
impartiality		5:48	
forgiveness		6:12; 18:33	
humility		10:25; 18:3–4	
being merciful			6:36; 10:37
re-enacting Jesus's sacrificial death			22:19

While these tables present a fair amount and range of potential mimetic activities across the Synoptics, we identified them mostly as "weak" to "medium," and they do not collectively constitute a "strong" ethical concept. Nevertheless, we noted the mimetic potential of three significant events in Jesus's life and ministry. First, regarding the *Lord's Prayer*, Matthew's account shows "medium" mimesis, while there is no mimesis in Luke's version. Luke 11:1 indicates an analogy between John the Baptist and Jesus rather than Jesus imitating John. In Matt 6:9–13, however, Jesus provides an exemplary prayer on which his followers can model their own. Second, regarding the *Lord's Supper*, Mark and Matthew's accounts do not indicate mimesis, but there is a case of "medium" mimesis in Luke. In Luke 22:19, Jesus's instruction, "Do this in remembrance of me," calls for the re-enactment

---

174. I consider prayer an ethical activity. The model prayer in Matt 6:9–13, for example, has moral content and potential for transformation as a person aligns oneself with God's values and purposes.

4. Mimesis in the Synoptics and Acts

or imitation of Jesus's words and actions. Finally, the *Gethsemane* scene has a mimetic dimension. Mark presents Jesus's watchfulness and prayer in Gethsemane as an example for believers to imitate. In Matthew, the Gethsemane event has a weaker mimetic dimension than in Mark and lesser still in Luke, where it is complicated by a variant reading. Nevertheless, we noted that Matthew's account of Gethsemane has two parallels with the Lord's Prayer (the petition "do not lead us into testing" and Jesus's resolve to submit to God's will) and Luke's Gethsemane scene has one parallel with the Lord's Prayer (the petition "do not lead us into testing").

The patchy evidence of mimesis in the Synoptics and Acts is an inadequate basis for constructing a model of mimesis, so we cannot draw a relevant comparison with our Greco-Roman mimetic model. Nevertheless, we detect similar forms or modes of mimesis that we noted in Greco-Roman and Jewish antiquity. The most common form that remains is *direct observation*, where the imitator directly observes the exemplar for imitation. In addition, the Synoptics and Acts contain instances of *mediated mimesis*, where the exemplar is mediated to the imitator by other means. Matthew alludes to *personally mediated mimesis* in that Jesus as "Immanuel" is the "living example" of the invisible God to enable imitation. Mark and Luke especially use *textually mediated mimesis* to promote discipleship as they present literary characters in their writings for their audience to visualize, study, and imitate. Luke also employs *mnemonic mimesis* regarding the Lord's Supper, where believers are exhorted to recount Jesus's actions and words in order to remember, and thus visualize, Jesus's death and its significance.

Having concluded that the Synoptics and Acts only provide a weak to medium concept of mimesis, we are compelled to look further in the New Testament for a more robust notion of mimesis, so we proceed to the Johannine literature.

5

Mimesis in John's Gospel and Letters

The study of mimesis in the Johannine literature is challenging for two reasons.[1] First, Johannine ethics was a problematic area for a long time. The contention of many scholars was that the Johannine writings had little or no ethical content (except for the love command) and that they had an inward-looking or sectarian perspective. In 2012, however, the first volume on Johannine ethics provided scholarship with a new impetus to explore this subject.[2] This landmark study became the starting point for Johannine ethics as a recognized subject, and there has been a surge of interest in the subject since.[3] Despite this renaissance of Johannine ethics, mimesis remains a neglected topic (section 5.1).[4] This is unsurprising and takes us to the second challenge—that the lexeme μιμεῖ-σθαι occurs only once in the Johannine literature, in 3 John 11. This means that if

---

1. I will examine both the Gospel and Letters of John and refer to the author(s) of these writings as "John." The similarities in language, style, and thought in the Gospel and Letters warrant an examination of both writings. While common authorship and order of composition are debated, I take the Gospel and Letters to represent the so-called "Johannine tradition," where the social setting of the Letters concerns a later period than that of the Gospel. While Hugo Méndez agrees that the Johannine writings represent a single literary lineage, with the Gospel predating the Letters, he argues that these writings are pseudepigrapha and unreliable bases for historical reconstruction ("Did the Johannine Community Exist?," *JSNT* 42 [2020]: 350–74). His challenge does not affect our study because we focus on the shared (ethical) thought of the Johannine writings and call attention to issues only when these writings present discrepancies of thought.

2. Jan G. van der Watt and Ruben Zimmermann, eds., *Rethinking the Ethics of John: "Implicit Ethics" in the Johannine Writings*, CNNTE 3, WUNT 291 (Tübingen: Mohr Siebeck, 2012).

3. See the list of publications on Johannine ethics between 2012–2022 in Cornelis Bennema, "A Model of Johannine Ethics," *SCE* 35 (2022): 433–56, at 453–56.

4. Due to our focus on mimesis as an ethical concept, I will not consider Keith L. Yoder's study of John 13:1–17 being a literary mimesis of Luke 7:36–50 ("Mimesis: Foot Washing from Luke to John," *ETL* 92 [2016]: 655–70).

5. Mimesis in John's Gospel and Letters

the concept of mimesis features in the Johannine literature, John uses different language to express it.

After outlining the Johannine mimetic language (section 5.2), we will explore the concept of mimesis in the Godhead (section 5.3) and between the believer and Jesus or God (section 5.4). Once we understand the workings of Johannine mimesis, we can determine its place in Johannine ethics (section 5.5) and see if we can construct a Johannine model of mimesis that has affinities with our Greco-Roman model (section 5.6). Finally, we will address how Johannine Christians in the late first century could imitate an "absent" Jesus, that is, a Jesus they could no longer directly observe (section 5.7).

The reader may observe that, methodologically, we approach the Johannine literature somewhat differently than the Synoptics and Acts. In the Synoptics and Acts, where mimesis is less apparent, we had to explore every linguistic and conceptual avenue: first, the language of "following Jesus," then other potential mimetic language, and lastly, the possible concepts of mimesis. In John, we will also move from mimetic language (section 5.2) to mimetic concepts (sections 5.3–5.4), but we have grouped the examination of the language of "following Jesus" together with the typical Johannine language of "remaining in Jesus" and the concept of filial mimesis under the broader concept of discipleship in section 5.4.1.

Adapting the definition in section 1.5, we would say the term "Johannine ethics" refers to the moral values and principles that govern the conduct and character of a particular group of "believers" or Christians in relation to their God and fellow human beings, as envisaged by the Johannine writings. While ethics is usually limited to the realm of human interactions, I broaden Johannine ethics to the divine realm because the Johannine writings (1) present God as a moral being who extends various divine commodities to people and operates at the human level through the incarnation, and (2) use the human category of "family" to explain the divine–human relationship.

5.1. Mimesis in Johannine Scholarship

In 2017, I produced the first full-length study on the subject of Johannine mimesis.[5] I argued that mimesis is a cognitive, creative hermeneutical process that is

---

5. Cornelis Bennema, *Mimesis in the Johannine Literature: A Study in Johannine Ethics*, LNTS 498 (London: Bloomsbury T&T Clark, 2017). Nevertheless, a few studies touched on Johannine mimesis prior to 2017: Burridge, *Imitating Jesus*, 343–45 (he merely mentions the mimetic aspect in the footwashing and the love command rather than explaining the concept); Dirk G. van der Merwe, "*Imitatio Christi* in the Fourth Gospel," *Verbum et Ecclesia* 22 (2001): 131–48 (he

central to Johannine ethics, shaping both the believer's behavior and identity within the context of the divine family. In subsequent articles, I sketched a trajectory of mimesis from John's Gospel to his letters to the martyr traditions in the second century and how mimesis might have worked in Johannine Christianity in the late first century.[6] This chapter weaves together these works and engages with recent scholarship on the subject.

Lindsey Trozzo uses a rhetorical approach to examine the moral change that the Johannine narrative can bring about in its audience.[7] While Trozzo notes the presence of mimesis in John's Gospel, she does not consider it prevalent and contends that the participation of the believers in the unity between Jesus and God is the central focus of Johannine ethics.[8] In a study on mimesis in 1 John, Mavis Leung responds to my 2017 book on Johannine mimesis, arguing that the imitation of Jesus in 1 John 2:6; 3:3, 16; 4:17 is rooted in the Old Testament idea of imitating God.[9] While Leung presents a good case for the imitation of God in the Old Testament and early Judaism, she does not go beyond our findings in chapter 3.[10] I endorse her conclusion that "the implicit concept of the imitation of God in the OT has become expressly perceptible in the Jewish ethical thought of the Second Temple period"[11] but maintain that this shift came about precisely because of prolonged contact with Greek thought and culture. Michael Gorman explores the concept of missional theosis in John's Gospel, referring to the process of becoming like God by participating in the life and mission of God.[12] For him, theosis includes

---

treats mimesis in John's Gospel only cursorily and often fails to anchor the concept in concrete Johannine words); Jan G. van der Watt, "The Ethos of Being Like Jesus: Imitation in 1 John," in *Ethos und Theologie im Neuen Testament: Festschrift für Michael Wolter*, ed. Jochen Flebbe and Matthias Konradt (Neukirchen-Vluyn: Neukirchener Verlag, 2016), 415–40; van der Watt, "Reciprocity, Mimesis and Ethics in 1 John," in *Erzählung und Briefe im johanneischen Kreis*, ed. Uta Poplutz and Jörg Frey, WUNT 2/420 (Tübingen: Mohr Siebeck, 2016), 257–76. In his *New Testament Ethics,* Matera has a section on Jesus as a model for moral behavior for each of the Synoptics but has not done so for John, which is surprising given that mimesis features more significantly in John than in the Synoptics.

6. Cornelis Bennema, "Moral Transformation through Mimesis in the Johannine Tradition," *TynBul* 69 (2018): 183–203, at 197–203; Bennema, "Imitation in Johannine Christianity," *ExpTim* 132 (2020): 101–10, at 106–9.

7. Lindsey M. Trozzo, *Exploring Johannine Ethics: A Rhetorical Approach to Moral Efficacy in the Fourth Gospel Narrative*, WUNT 2/449 (Tübingen: Mohr Siebeck, 2017).

8. Trozzo, *Johannine Ethics*, 80, 85–96.

9. Leung, "Ethics," 111–31.

10. Leung, "Ethics," 114–24. See also the references to Leung in chapter 3 in this volume.

11. Leung, "Ethics," 123–24.

12. Michael J. Gorman, *Abide and Go: Missional Theosis in the Gospel of John* (Eugene, OR: Wipf and Stock, 2018), xvii, 8, 16, 21, 23.

5. Mimesis in John's Gospel and Letters

both imitation and participation.[13] Gorman notes that my language of mimesis, participation, and transformation is similar to his language of missional theosis as transformative participation in the life of God. His sole critique is my hesitancy in the use of theosis.[14] I concede his point and will clarify my understanding of theosis in relation to mimesis in section 5.6.

In his study on Johannine ethics, Sookgoo Shin argues that John's Gospel presents two stages of moral progress as part of discipleship: (1) John 1–12 promotes coming to faith in Jesus, and (2) John 13–17 invites readers to the next level of discipleship by imitating Jesus.[15] In the chapter that outlines the second stage of moral progress, Shin first argues that the footwashing episode establishes the idea of imitation as instrumental for moral progress. He then focuses on the use of the comparative conjunction καθώς ("just as") to identify traits of Jesus that disciples should imitate—love (13:34; 15:12), unity (17:11, 21–22), mission (17:18; 20:21), and "otherworldliness" (17:14, 16).[16] I take issue with his notion of imitation as the "next level," "culmination," or "second phase" of discipleship.[17] The Johannine mimetic injunctions of serving and loving one another (13:15, 34) are fundamental to discipleship rather than its "next level." In fact, mimesis takes one to the "next level" in that believers gradually become more Christlike through imitation.[18]

Jan van der Watt's magnum opus (in two parts) on Johannine ethics is of great importance.[19] While the first volume (on John's Gospel) does not feature mimesis prominently, he does explain how Jesus sets the ethical example for imitation. He identifies Jesus's washing of the disciples' feet and Jesus's death as the primary examples to imitate, but other examples include Jesus's obedience to God, his seeking God's glory, and his care for God's flock.[20] He then explains how mimesis shapes behavior: in following Jesus, believers observe his words and deeds, which

---

13. Gorman, *Abide and Go*, 158–59.
14. Gorman, *Abide and Go*, 17n62, 187–89.
15. Shin, *Ethics in the Gospel of John*.
16. Shin, *Ethics in the Gospel of John*, 131–91. While Shin refers to my 2017 work regarding the importance of καθώς and the identification of Jesus's imitable traits (*Ethics in the Gospel of John*, 141n44, 142n46), he fails to do so when he unpacks these imitable traits in the rest of the chapter, although I deal with these traits at length.
17. Shin, *Ethics in the Gospel of John*, 49, 192, 194.
18. Shin's conclusion is more on target: "Readers are not simply called to believe in Jesus but to be Jesus-like" (*Ethics in the Gospel of John*, 196).
19. Jan G. van der Watt, *A Grammar of the Ethics of John: Reading John from an Ethical Perspective*, 2 vols., WUNT 431, 502 (Tübingen: Mohr Siebeck, 2019, 2023). Van der Watt has doggedly pursued the topic of Johannine ethics since the 1980s and is also one of the editors of the pioneering 2012 volume (see n. 2).
20. Van der Watt, *Grammar*, 1:244–50.

informs what they say or do and leads to their imitating him.[21] In his second volume (on the Johannine Letters), van der Watt explores five instances of mimesis in 1 John: (1) to walk in the light as God is (in) the light (1:5–7, 2:8–11); (2) to live like Jesus (2:6); (3) to be righteous like God/Jesus (2:29; 3:7); (4) to be pure like Jesus (3:3); and (5) to love like God/Jesus and to die like Jesus (3:16–17).[22] He argues that in reflecting its Greco-Roman milieu, Johannine mimesis is not a mechanical duplication but a creative expression of the character and attitude of the model in the context of God's family.[23] Van der Watt considers mimesis and reciprocity to be key mechanisms in Johannine ethics.[24]

Most recently, Paul Hartog has built on my work and added the aspect of "desiderative mimesis" (i.e., imitation in relation to desire).[25] He shows that the Johannine literature lacks propositional ethics (there are very few ethical imperatives, rules, or maxims) and instead promotes exemplary or mimetic ethics through the vocabulary of ὀφείλειν ("ought"), καθώς, ἐντολή ("commandment"), and ὑπόδειγμα.[26] Hartog endorses my emphasis on the cognitive and behavioral aspects of Johannine mimesis and proposes adding to my model a desiderative aspect that links being (identity) with behavior (actions).[27] He explores desiderative aspects of inclination, desire, and motivation in John 3:19–21; 8:39–44; 1 John 2:15–17 to argue that John's key moral category "love" is not only a facet of one's identity and behavior but also "a desiderative orientation of one's affections, attractions, and attachments."[28]

Statement of the Problem. Our survey reveals some areas of disagreement. First, there is disagreement about whether Johannine mimesis is rooted in the

---

21. Van der Watt, *Grammar*, 1:257–62. While van der Watt contends that Johannine mimesis is rooted in Greco-Roman antiquity (*Grammar*, 1:257, 589–602), he is critical of my attempt to draw parallels between Johannine ethics and Greco-Roman virtue ethics (*Grammar*, 1:228–29, 326–27).

22. Van der Watt, *Grammar*, 2:89–100. See also n. 5 for his earlier work on 1 John. In my view, however, 1 John 1:7 is not an example of mimesis but of the analogous idea that both the believers' behavior and God's existence occur in the realm of light. He also looks briefly at the explicit mention of mimesis in 3 John 11 (*Grammar*, 2:360–61).

23. Van der Watt, *Grammar*, 1:257–61; 2:84–86, 271–73, 389–94.

24. Van der Watt, *Grammar*, 1:257–62, 525, 636; 2:88–89, 273, 393–94, 417. In his articles on 1 John (see n. 5), van der Watt constantly seeks to clarify whether a phrase is predominantly reciprocal or mimetic.

25. Paul Anthony Hartog, "Johannine Ethics: An Exegetical-Theological Summary and a 'Desiderative' Extension of Mimesis," *Religions* 13 (2022): 1–18, https://doi.org/10.3390/rel13060503.

26. Hartog, "Johannine Ethics," 3–7.

27. Hartog, "Johannine Ethics," 7–8.

28. Hartog, "Johannine Ethics," 10–13 (quotation from p. 13). Oddly, Hartog does not engage René Girard's theory of mimetic desire.

Old Testament (Leung) or the Greco-Roman mimetic traditions (Bennema, van der Watt, Shin). Second, I consider the concept of mimesis central to Johannine ethics, but for Trozzo it is peripheral, and van der Watt views mimesis and reciprocity to be on par.[29] Third, Gorman's work indicates that I must clarify the relation between mimesis and theosis. This chapter has one limitation: we will not deal with the mimetic aspect of Johannine characters as we did with the Synoptics because unpacking the concept of Johannine mimesis will take all our attention. However, I have explained the mimetic qualities of the Johannine characters elsewhere.[30]

5.2. The Johannine Mimetic Language

We noted at the start that the lexeme μιμεῖσθαι occurs only once in the Johannine writings (in 3 John 11), so I must show *that* mimesis exists in the Johannine literature and that we can legitimately speak about it. In section 1.5, we suggested that outlining the semantic domain of mimesis need not be limited to explicit mimetic language and should include the terms for "example" (e.g., τύπος, ὑπόδειγμα, ὑπογραμμός) and comparative particles (e.g., καθώς, ὥσπερ, οὕτως, ὡς, ὥσπερ, ὅμοιος, ὁμοίως). We must bear in mind that a comparative particle itself does not necessarily indicate mimesis; only a literary context can do that. The following examination of the Johannine writings will reveal eight different linguistic expressions that indicate mimesis. While a full list of mimetic occurrences appears at the end of the section, I will present here representative examples for each category and unpack the concept in more detail in the remainder of the chapter.

1. μιμεῖσθαι. Of the literal terms for mimesis, only the verb μιμεῖσθαι turns up in the Johannine literature—once, in 3 John 11 as a general ethical imperative to imitate good and not evil:

3 JOHN 11

Ἀγαπητέ, μὴ μιμοῦ τὸ κακὸν ἀλλὰ τὸ ἀγαθόν. ὁ ἀγαθοποιῶν ἐκ τοῦ θεοῦ ἐστιν· ὁ κακοποιῶν οὐχ ἑώρακεν τὸν θεόν.

---

29. For the difference between mimesis and reciprocity, see section 1.5.

30. Bennema, *Mimesis*, 153–54 (with references to my other work on Johannine characters). See also van der Watt, *Grammar*, 1:229–32. Olivia L. Rahmsdorf, however, contends that the Johannine characters merely serve to help us have confidence in the cross-event (*Zeit und Ethik im Johannesevangelium: Theoretische, methodische und exegetische Annäherungen an die Gunst der Stunde*, CNNTE 10, WUNT 2/488 [Tübingen: Mohr Siebeck, 2019], 438–40).

PART 2   MIMESIS IN EARLY CHRISTIANITY

> Beloved, do not <u>imitate</u> what is evil but imitate what is good. Whoever does good is from God; whoever does evil has not seen God.

John's exhortation to Gaius to imitate τὸ ἀγαθόν ("that which is good") seems abstract, impersonal, and seemingly fails to qualify for our definition of mimesis. However, the substantive participle ὁ ἀγαθοποιῶν ("the one who does good") "personalizes" the imitation. Besides, in the immediate context (3 John 9–12), "that which is evil" and "that which is good" find application in the conduct of Diotrephes and Demetrius, respectively. It seems legitimate, therefore, to extend John's imperative to Gaius (to imitate what is good in Demetrius) to believers, exhorting them to imitate what is good (in other people's lives).[31]

2. καθώς. The comparative conjunction καθώς on its own denotes mimesis in twelve instances (John 8:28; 10:14b–15a; 14:27; 15:10, 12; 17:11b, 14b, 16, 22b; 1 John 3:3, 7, 12). The following examples will clarify the mimetic idea.

JOHN 8:28
ἀπ' ἐμαυτοῦ ποιῶ οὐδέν, ἀλλὰ <u>καθὼς</u> ἐδίδαξέν με ὁ πατὴρ ταῦτα λαλῶ.

I do nothing on my own, but I speak these things <u>just as</u> the Father taught me.

Although this text may not indicate mimesis beyond doubt—καθώς could simply be used comparatively to express that Jesus's teaching is rooted in the Father's instruction—I contend a good case can be made for the presence of mimesis in Jesus's teaching when we consider similar texts, such as John 3:34; 5:19; 7:16; 8:26; 12:49–50; 14:24; 15:15; 17:8. In section 5.3.1, I will explain more fully the mimetic idea that Jesus speaks what he hears from the Father and does what he sees in the Father's presence.

JOHN 17:22B
[κἀγὼ τὴν δόξαν ἣν δέδωκάς μοι δέδωκα αὐτοῖς,] ἵνα ὦσιν ἓν <u>καθὼς</u> ἡμεῖς ἕν·

[The honor that you have given me I have given them,] so that they may be one, <u>just as</u> we are one.

---

31. See also de Boer, *Imitation of Paul*, 85; I. Howard Marshall, *The Epistles of John*, NICNT (Grand Rapids: Eerdmans, 1978), 92; Rudolf Schnackenburg, *The Johannine Epistles*, trans. R. and I. Fuller (London: Burns & Oates, 1992), 299–300. Differently, Raymond E. Brown suggests that this is not a general directive to do good but to practice hospitality as a specific application of the Johannine love command (*The Epistles of John*, AB 30 [Garden City, NY: Doubleday, 1982], 721).

5. Mimesis in John's Gospel and Letters

Jesus expresses his desire for believers to imitate the unity that exists between him and the Father (see also John 10:30). The mimetic idea is that a particular state of being or existence is imitated among believers. One could argue that the idea here is one of analogy rather than mimesis because no tangible act seems to be in view (see section 1.5, M&A criterion 3). However, the disciples will have heard Jesus speak of his unity with the Father and observed the tangible reality of Jesus's relationship with the Father (see, e.g., John 10:30, 38; 14:10–11, 20; 17:21–23), so it would be a perceptible reality. Similarly, the believers' unity with the Father and Son is a verifiable (and hence tangible) reality rather than something surreal or ethereal (see, e.g., 1 John 4:12–13, 15).

1 JOHN 3:7
ὁ ποιῶν τὴν δικαιοσύνην δίκαιός ἐστιν, καθὼς ἐκεῖνος δίκαιός ἐστιν·

The one who does what is right is righteous, just as he is righteous.

It is unclear whether the referent of ἐκεῖνος is God or Jesus. On the one hand, a similar phrase in 1 John 2:29 (δίκαιός ἐστιν) could refer to God since the last part of the verse, ἐξ αὐτοῦ γεγέννηται, undoubtedly refers to God. On the other hand, since Jesus is the subject in 1 John 3:4–6 (perhaps even in 3:2b–3), he is probably also in view in 3:7 (see also 1 John 2:1). In which case, Jesus is the example to emulate with regard to doing/being what God requires.

3. καθώς . . . καί. The comparative conjunction καθώς in the protasis with the correlative καί in the apodosis to form a καθώς . . . καί construction occurs nine times to denote mimesis (John 6:57; 13:15, 34; 15:9; 17:18, 21; 20:21; 1 John 2:6; 4:17b).

JOHN 13:15
ὑπόδειγμα γὰρ ἔδωκα ὑμῖν ἵνα καθὼς ἐγὼ ἐποίησα ὑμῖν καὶ ὑμεῖς ποιῆτε.

For I have set you an example, so that just as I have done to you, you also should do.

This is arguably the clearest instance of the believer–Jesus mimesis in the Johannine literature and occurs, appropriately, at the beginning of the farewell discourses, where Jesus prepares his disciples for the time when he will return to his Father. This is a complex verse, and scholarship is divided on whether the mimesis refers to a literal washing of feet or the general idea of loving, humble service (see further section 5.4.2).

PART 2   MIMESIS IN EARLY CHRISTIANITY

JOHN 13:34
Ἐντολὴν καινὴν δίδωμι ὑμῖν, ἵνα ἀγαπᾶτε ἀλλήλους, <u>καθὼς</u> ἠγάπησα ὑμᾶς ἵνα <u>καὶ</u> ὑμεῖς ἀγαπᾶτε ἀλλήλους.

> I give you a new commandment, that you love one another. <u>Just as</u> I have loved you, you <u>also</u> must love one another.

The love command represents the most recognized (for some, even only) Johannine ethic. Jesus introduces the love command in 13:34a and then explains it in 13:34b using a mimetic καθώς . . . καί construction. Given the centrality of the love command in Johannine theology or ethics, we will return to this topic in section 5.4.3.

JOHN 17:18
<u>καθὼς</u> ἐμὲ ἀπέστειλας εἰς τὸν κόσμον, <u>κἀγὼ</u> ἀπέστειλα αὐτοὺς εἰς τὸν κόσμον·

> <u>Just as</u> you have sent me into the world, I <u>also</u> have sent them into the world.

This verse expresses a double mimesis. First, Jesus imitates the Father in sending others into the world. The second mimetic idea presented here is an implied "existential" mimesis in that it describes the disciples' state of being sent into the world by Jesus in imitation of Jesus's state of being sent into the world by the Father.

JOHN 17:21
<u>καθὼς</u> σύ, πάτερ, ἐν ἐμοὶ κἀγὼ ἐν σοί, ἵνα <u>καὶ</u> αὐτοὶ ἐν ἡμῖν ὦσιν,

> <u>Just as</u> you, Father, are in me and I am in you, may they <u>also</u> be in us,

The mimetic idea here is that the believers' indwelling of the Father and Son is patterned on the mutual indwelling of the Father and Son—an example of "existential" mimesis describing a particular state of being or existence.

1 JOHN 2:6
ὁ λέγων ἐν αὐτῷ μένειν ὀφείλει <u>καθὼς</u> ἐκεῖνος περιεπάτησεν <u>καὶ</u> αὐτὸς [οὕτως] περιπατεῖν.

> <u>Just as</u> he walked, the one who claims to abide in him must <u>also</u> walk [similarly].

I contend that this is a mimetic καθώς . . . καί construction rather than a καθώς . . . οὕτως construction. Καί here cannot be a coordinate conjunction ("and") but must function as an adverb ("also"). This makes the οὕτως superfluous since the comparison is already established by the καθώς... καί construction. The referent of ἐν αὐτῷ μένειν is either Jesus (see also John 15:4–10; 1 John 2:28) or God (see also 1 John 1:6). Virtually all scholars agree that the referent of ἐκεῖνος here is Jesus. Also, since περιπατεῖν ("to walk") is shorthand for "way of life" or behavior, this most likely refers to Jesus's life on earth that had been observed—and hence could be imitated.[32] While historically the disciples would have observed Jesus's life for themselves, later believers have access to Jesus's earthly life through John's written accounts (see further in section 5.7).

4. καθώς... οὕτως. The comparative conjunction καθώς in the protasis with the correlative οὕτως in the apodosis to form a καθώς... οὕτως construction denotes mimesis twice (John 12:50; 15:4).

JOHN 12:50
[ἃ οὖν ἐγὼ λαλῶ,] καθὼς εἴρηκέν μοι ὁ πατήρ, οὕτως λαλῶ.

[What I speak, therefore,] just as the Father has spoken to me, so I speak.

The mimetic idea is that Jesus's teaching is rooted in God's instruction—Jesus's words are the very words of God (see also John 3:34; 8:28). This mimesis of speech is a specific instance of the general Son–Father mimesis in John 5:19 (see category 8 below and section 5.3.1).

5. οὕτως... καί. The οὕτως... καί construction denotes mimesis in one instance.

1 JOHN 4:11
Ἀγαπητοί, εἰ οὕτως ὁ θεὸς ἠγάπησεν ἡμᾶς, καὶ ἡμεῖς ὀφείλομεν ἀλλήλους ἀγαπᾶν.

Dear friends, since God loved us in this manner, we also must love one another.

The conjunction καί here does not function as a coordination marker ("and") but as an adverb ("also"). This is the first of two occurrences where the believer is urged to imitate God himself (the other occurrence is in 1 John 4:17; see category 3 above). The believers' love for each other is rooted in and patterned after God's love for them (see also John 13:34).

6. καί. A singular adverbial καί can also denote mimesis, arguably seven times in the Johannine writings (John 12:26; 13:14; 14:3, 12, 19; 17:24; 1 John 3:16).

---

32. Leung contends that "to walk" as a reference to the whole of living is a Semitism and sees parallels with "walking in the way of the Lord" in the Old Testament ("Ethics," 125–26).

PART 2   MIMESIS IN EARLY CHRISTIANITY

JOHN 14:3
ἵνα ὅπου εἰμὶ ἐγὼ <u>καὶ</u> ὑμεῖς ἦτε.

so that where I am, you <u>also</u> may be.

The mimetic concept "to be where Jesus is" refers to existential mimesis or mimesis of being (see also John 12:16; 17:24), but the spatial location ὅπου refers to is unclear. In section 5.4.4, we will discuss whether the believer's eternal residence in heaven or God's family on earth is in view.

1 JOHN 3:16
ἐν τούτῳ ἐγνώκαμεν τὴν ἀγάπην, ὅτι ἐκεῖνος ὑπὲρ ἡμῶν τὴν ψυχὴν αὐτοῦ ἔθηκεν <u>καὶ</u> ἡμεῖς ὀφείλομεν ὑπὲρ τῶν ἀδελφῶν τὰς ψυχὰς θεῖναι.

We know love by this, that he laid down his life for us; <u>likewise</u>, we must lay down our lives for one another.

John extends Jesus's saying in John 15:13 by creating a new mimetic imperative: just as Jesus laid down his life for his followers' sake, so believers must lay down their lives for each other's sake. While καί could be a coordinate conjunction ("and"), it functions more likely as an adverbial καί ("likewise," "also"), thus strengthening the general idea of mimesis in this verse.

7. ὥσπερ . . . οὕτως καί. The comparative conjunction ὥσπερ occurs twice in the Johannine literature and denotes mimesis as part of the expression ὥσπερ . . . οὕτως καί.

JOHN 5:21
<u>ὥσπερ</u> γὰρ ὁ πατὴρ ἐγείρει τοὺς νεκροὺς καὶ ζωοποιεῖ, <u>οὕτως καὶ</u> ὁ υἱὸς οὓς θέλει ζωοποιεῖ.

For <u>just as</u> the Father raises the dead and gives them life, <u>so also</u> the Son gives life to whomever he wishes.

JOHN 5:26
<u>ὥσπερ</u> γὰρ ὁ πατὴρ ἔχει ζωὴν ἐν ἑαυτῷ, <u>οὕτως καὶ</u> τῷ υἱῷ ἔδωκεν ζωὴν ἔχειν ἐν ἑαυτῷ.

For <u>just as</u> the Father has life in himself, <u>so also</u> he has granted the Son to have life in himself.

5. Mimesis in John's Gospel and Letters

While 5:19 speaks of the Son–Father mimesis in a broad, general sense—the Son imitates the Father in everything (see category 8)—5:21 and 5:26 express a specific mimetic activity, namely the Son's prerogative to be a source of life in imitation of the Father (see also John 1:4).

8. ὁμοίως/ὅμοιος. The adverb ὁμοίως ("similarly," "likewise") denotes imitation in one instance and the adjective ὅμοιος ("similar") arguably also once.

> JOHN 5:19
> Ἀπεκρίνατο οὖν ὁ Ἰησοῦς καὶ ἔλεγεν αὐτοῖς· ἀμὴν ἀμὴν λέγω ὑμῖν, οὐ δύναται ὁ υἱὸς ποιεῖν ἀφ᾽ ἑαυτοῦ οὐδὲν ἐὰν μή τι βλέπῃ τὸν πατέρα ποιοῦντα· ἃ γὰρ ἂν ἐκεῖνος ποιῇ, ταῦτα καὶ ὁ υἱὸς <u>ὁμοίως</u> ποιεῖ.
>
> Jesus said to them, "Very truly, I tell you, the Son can do nothing on his own, but only what he sees the Father doing; for whatever the Father does, the Son does these things <u>likewise</u>."

This verse is foundational for the Son–Father mimesis (see further section 5.3.1). The mimesis is unspecified—the Son imitates whatever he sees the Father doing. The Son can do so because the Father loves the Son and shows him all that he does (ὁ γὰρ πατὴρ φιλεῖ τὸν υἱὸν καὶ πάντα δείκνυσιν αὐτῷ ἃ αὐτὸς ποιεῖ; 5:20 [see also John 3:35]).

> 1 JOHN 3:2
> οἴδαμεν ὅτι ἐὰν φανερωθῇ, <u>ὅμοιοι</u> αὐτῷ ἐσόμεθα ὅτι ὀψόμεθα αὐτὸν καθώς ἐστιν.
>
> We know that when he is revealed, we will be <u>like</u> him because we will see him as he is.

The subject of φανερωθῇ in 3:2b is probably Jesus because he often is the subject of the passive form of φανεροῦν in this letter (1 John 1:2; 2:28; 3:5, 8). Although the essence of the verse is clear—believers will be transformed at the Parousia—the difficult issue is whether this transformation is one of resemblance (believers will seem like Jesus) or contains a mimetic element (believers will be like Jesus). In light of the presence of mimesis in the immediate context (3:3 and 3:7; see category 2 above), mimesis could be in view here too. The believers' mimetic transformation probably refers to becoming like Jesus in his humanity—to become truly human.

In addition to these eight categories, sometimes the concept of imitation is present or implied even when no comparative term or phrase is used (John 8:26,

PART 2 MIMESIS IN EARLY CHRISTIANITY

38–39; 14:16; 15:15; 16:13–15; 17:22a).[33] The following table shows all mimetic occurrences and their most significant aspects in the Johannine writings.[34]

Reference	Mimetic Expression	Who Imitates Whom?	Type of Mimesis	Mimetic Strength	Aspect of Mimesis
John 5:19	ἃ γὰρ ἂν ἐκεῖνος ποιῇ, ταῦτα καὶ ὁ υἱὸς <u>ὁμοίως</u> ποιεῖ	Jesus, Father	performative	strong	to do (anything)
John 5:21	<u>ὥσπερ</u> ὁ πατὴρ . . . ζῳοποιεῖ, <u>οὕτως καὶ</u> ὁ υἱὸς οὓς θέλει ζῳοποιεῖ	Jesus, Father	performative	strong	to give life
John 5:26	<u>ὥσπερ</u> γὰρ ὁ πατὴρ ἔχει ζωὴν ἐν ἑαυτῷ, <u>οὕτως καὶ</u> τῷ υἱῷ ἔδωκεν ζωὴν ἔχειν ἐν ἑαυτῷ	Jesus, Father	quasi-existential	strong	to possess life
John 6:57	<u>καθὼς</u> ἀπέστειλέν με ὁ ζῶν πατὴρ κἀγὼ ζῶ διὰ τὸν πατέρα, καὶ ὁ τρώγων με <u>κἀ</u>κεῖνος ζήσει δι' ἐμέ	disciples, Jesus	quasi-existential	weak	to live, to have life
John 8:26	κἀγὼ ἃ ἤκουσα παρ' αὐτοῦ ταῦτα λαλῶ εἰς τὸν κόσμον	Jesus, Father	performative	weak	to speak
John 8:28	<u>καθὼς</u> ἐδίδαξέν με ὁ πατὴρ ταῦτα λαλῶ	Jesus, Father	performative	medium	to speak/teach
John 8:38–39	ἃ ἐγὼ ἑώρακα παρὰ τῷ πατρὶ λαλῶ· καὶ ὑμεῖς οὖν ἃ ἠκούσατε παρὰ τοῦ πατρὸς ποιεῖτε . . . εἰ τέκνα τοῦ Ἀβραάμ ἐστε, τὰ ἔργα τοῦ Ἀβραὰμ ἐποιεῖτε	οἱ Ἰουδαῖοι, God and Abraham	performative (tentatively)	weak	to behave (οἱ Ἰουδαῖοι imitate the devil rather than God and Abraham)

33. For an explanation of these occurrences, see Bennema, *Mimesis*, 54–56.
34. For a detailed explanation of each mimetic occurrence, see Bennema, *Mimesis*, 40–56 (the table comes from pp. 207–9).

168

5. Mimesis in John's Gospel and Letters

Reference	Mimetic Expression	Who Imitates Whom?	Type of Mimesis	Mimetic Strength	Aspect of Mimesis
John 10:14–15	γινώσκω τὰ ἐμὰ καὶ γινώσκουσί με τὰ ἐμά, <u>καθὼς</u> γινώσκει με ὁ πατὴρ κἀγὼ γινώσκω τὸν πατέρα	Jesus and disciples, Father and Jesus	quasi-existential	weak	mutual knowing
John 12:26	ὅπου εἰμὶ ἐγὼ ἐκεῖ <u>καὶ</u> ὁ διάκονος ὁ ἐμὸς ἔσται	disciples, Jesus	existential	strong	to be in a specific place (where Jesus is)
John 12:50	<u>καθὼς</u> εἴρηκέν μοι ὁ πατήρ, <u>οὕτως</u> λαλῶ	Jesus, Father	performative	strong	to speak
John 13:14	εἰ οὖν ἐγὼ ἔνιψα ὑμῶν τοὺς πόδας ... <u>καὶ</u> ὑμεῖς ὀφείλετε ἀλλήλων νίπτειν τοὺς πόδας	disciples, Jesus	performative	medium	to serve one another
John 13:15	<u>καθὼς</u> ἐγὼ ἐποίησα ὑμῖν <u>καὶ</u> ὑμεῖς ποιῆτε	disciples, Jesus	performative	strong	to serve one another
John 13:34	<u>καθὼς</u> ἠγάπησα ὑμᾶς ἵνα <u>καὶ</u> ὑμεῖς ἀγαπᾶτε ἀλλήλους	disciples, Jesus	performative	strong	to love one another
John 14:3	ἵνα ὅπου εἰμὶ ἐγὼ <u>καὶ</u> ὑμεῖς ἦτε	disciples, Jesus	existential	strong	to be in a specific place (where Jesus is)
John 14:12	ὁ πιστεύων εἰς ἐμὲ τὰ ἔργα ἃ ἐγὼ ποιῶ <u>κἀ</u>κεῖνος ποιήσει	disciples, Jesus	performative	medium	to do miraculous works
John 14:16	ἄλλον παράκλητον δώσει ὑμῖν	Spirit, Jesus	performative	weak	the Spirit will imitate Jesus's functions
John 14:19	ὅτι ἐγὼ ζῶ <u>καὶ</u> ὑμεῖς ζήσετε	disciples, Jesus	quasi-existential	weak	to live
John 14:27	οὐ <u>καθὼς</u> ὁ κόσμος δίδωσιν ἐγὼ δίδωμι ὑμῖν	Jesus, *not* the world	performative	medium	to give peace

PART 2   MIMESIS IN EARLY CHRISTIANITY

Reference	Mimetic Expression	Who Imitates Whom?	Type of Mimesis	Mimetic Strength	Aspect of Mimesis
John 15:4	καθὼς τὸ κλῆμα οὐ δύναται καρπὸν φέρειν ἀφ' ἑαυτοῦ ἐὰν μὴ μένῃ ἐν τῇ ἀμπέλῳ, <u>οὕτως</u> οὐδὲ ὑμεῖς ἐὰν μὴ ἐν ἐμοὶ μένητε	disciples, branches	performative (tentatively)	weak	to bear fruit (through abiding)
John 15:9	<u>καθὼς</u> ἠγάπησέν με ὁ πατήρ, <u>κἀγὼ</u> ὑμᾶς ἠγάπησα	Jesus, Father	performative	strong	to love
John 15:10	ἐὰν τὰς ἐντολάς μου τηρήσητε, μενεῖτε ἐν τῇ ἀγάπῃ μου, <u>καθὼς</u> ἐγὼ τὰς ἐντολὰς τοῦ πατρός μου τετήρηκα καὶ μένω αὐτοῦ ἐν τῇ ἀγάπῃ	disciples, Jesus	performative	strong	to be obedient in order to remain in a loving relationship
John 15:12	ἵνα ἀγαπᾶτε ἀλλήλους <u>καθὼς</u> ἠγάπησα ὑμᾶς	disciples, Jesus	performative	strong	to love one another
John 15:15	πάντα ἃ ἤκουσα παρὰ τοῦ πατρός μου ἐγνώρισα ὑμῖν	Jesus, Father	performative	medium	to speak
John 16:13–15	οὐ γὰρ λαλήσει ἀφ' ἑαυτοῦ, ἀλλ' ὅσα ἀκούσει λαλήσει . . . ἐκ τοῦ ἐμοῦ λαμβάνει καὶ ἀναγγελεῖ ὑμῖν	Spirit, Jesus	performative	medium	to speak (teach)
John 17:11	ἵνα ὦσιν ἓν <u>καθὼς</u> ἡμεῖς	disciples, Father and Son	existential	strong	unity
John 17:14	οὐκ εἰσὶν ἐκ τοῦ κόσμου <u>καθὼς</u> ἐγὼ οὐκ εἰμὶ ἐκ τοῦ κόσμου	disciples, Jesus	existential	strong	not a member of the world
John 17:16	ἐκ τοῦ κόσμου οὐκ εἰσὶν <u>καθὼς</u> ἐγὼ οὐκ εἰμὶ ἐκ τοῦ κόσμου	disciples, Jesus	existential	strong	not a member of the world
John 17:18	<u>καθὼς</u> ἐμὲ ἀπέστειλας εἰς τὸν κόσμον, <u>κἀγὼ</u> ἀπέστειλα αὐτοὺς εἰς τὸν κόσμον	Jesus, Father disciples, Jesus	performative existential	strong strong	to send into the world to be sent into the world

5. Mimesis in John's Gospel and Letters

Reference	Mimetic Expression	Who Imitates Whom?	Type of Mimesis	Mimetic Strength	Aspect of Mimesis
John 17:21	καθὼς σύ, πάτερ, ἐν ἐμοὶ κἀγὼ ἐν σοί, ἵνα καὶ αὐτοὶ ἐν ἡμῖν ὦσιν	disciples, Father and Son	existential	strong	mutual indwelling
John 17:22a	κἀγὼ τὴν δόξαν ἣν δέδωκάς μοι δέδωκα αὐτοῖς	Jesus, Father	performative	weak	to honor
John 17:22b	ἵνα ὦσιν ἓν καθὼς ἡμεῖς ἕν	disciples, Father and Son	existential	strong	unity
John 17:24	Πάτερ, ὃ δέδωκάς μοι, θέλω ἵνα ὅπου εἰμὶ ἐγὼ κἀκεῖνοι ὦσιν μετ' ἐμοῦ	disciples, Jesus	existential	strong	to be in a specific place (where Jesus is)
John 20:21	καθὼς ἀπέσταλκέν με ὁ πατήρ, κἀγὼ πέμπω ὑμᾶς	Jesus, Father / disciples, Jesus	performative / existential	strong / strong	to send into the world / to be sent into the world
1 John 2:6	ὁ λέγων ἐν αὐτῷ μένειν ὀφείλει καθὼς ἐκεῖνος περιεπάτησεν καὶ αὐτὸς [οὕτως] περιπατεῖν	believers, Jesus	performative	strong	to conduct oneself
1 John 3:2	ὅμοιοι αὐτῷ ἐσόμεθα	believers, Jesus	existential	medium	to be like Jesus
1 John 3:3	καὶ πᾶς ὁ ἔχων τὴν ἐλπίδα ταύτην ἐπ' αὐτῷ ἁγνίζει ἑαυτόν, καθὼς ἐκεῖνος ἁγνός ἐστιν	believers, Jesus	performative	medium	to purify oneself
1 John 3:7	ὁ ποιῶν τὴν δικαιοσύνην δίκαιός ἐστιν, καθὼς ἐκεῖνος δίκαιός ἐστιν	believers, Jesus	existential (with a performative aspect)	strong	to be righteous
1 John 3:12	οὐ καθὼς Κάϊν ἐκ τοῦ πονηροῦ ἦν καὶ ἔσφαξεν τὸν ἀδελφὸν αὐτοῦ	believers, *not* Cain	performative	strong	not to imitate the devil

PART 2   MIMESIS IN EARLY CHRISTIANITY

Reference	Mimetic Expression	Who Imitates Whom?	Type of Mimesis	Mimetic Strength	Aspect of Mimesis
1 John 3:16	ἐκεῖνος ὑπὲρ ἡμῶν τὴν ψυχὴν αὐτοῦ ἔθηκεν; <u>καὶ</u> ἡμεῖς ὀφείλομεν ὑπὲρ τῶν ἀδελφῶν τὰς ψυχὰς θεῖναι	believers, Jesus	performative	medium	to lay down one's life
1 John 4:11	εἰ <u>οὕτως</u> ὁ θεὸς ἠγάπησεν ἡμᾶς, <u>καὶ</u> ἡμεῖς ὀφείλομεν ἀλλήλους ἀγαπᾶν	believers, God	performative	strong	to love one another
1 John 4:17	<u>καθὼς</u> ἐκεῖνός ἐστιν <u>καὶ</u> ἡμεῖς ἐσμεν ἐν τῷ κόσμῳ τούτῳ	believers, God	existential	strong	to be in the world
3 John 11	μὴ <u>μιμοῦ</u> τὸ κακὸν ἀλλὰ τὸ ἀγαθόν	Gaius, good not evil	performative	strong	to imitate what is good

The most significant findings and inferences from our analysis are as follows:

1. The Johannine literature yields approximately *forty-four examples of mimesis*.[35] Even if one disputes some of the findings, sufficient mimetic occurrences remain to speak of it as a prominent Johannine concept.
2. Since mimesis is not equally strong or clear in every candidate passage, the heuristic device "mimetic strength" aids us in gauging the likelihood of mimesis in each passage (see also section 1.5). In most cases (twenty-seven out of forty-four mimetic occurrences, or 61 percent), the mimetic strength is "strong," implying that these passages most likely indicate mimesis.
3. John uses *a broad semantic domain* to indicate mimesis—besides the literal term μιμεῖσθαι, mimesis is conveyed by seven other linguistic expressions.
4. The comparative conjunction καθώς, either on its own or in the protasis with either the correlative καί or οὕτως in the apodosis, communicates the Johannine concept of mimesis most often (twenty-three out of forty-four occurrences, or 52 percent).

---

35. Schulz mentions about fifteen mimetic occurrences, which is more than Johannine scholars have noted (*Nachfolgen und Nachahmen*, 243–47, 298–304). However, I do not endorse all his examples: in 1 John 1:7, the different verbs, "to walk" versus "to be," indicate general comparison rather than the imitation of a particular action; in 1 John 4:19, ὅτι is a causal conjunction, providing the reason or basis for particular behavior, rather than constituting mimesis.

5. Mimesis in John's Gospel and Letters

5. The vast majority of mimetic occurrences in the Johannine literature fall into *two categories*: (1) the believer–Jesus/God mimesis (59 percent of all occurrences)[36] and (2) the Son–Father mimesis (25 percent of all occurrences).[37] The believer–Jesus/God mimesis can refer to the believer's imitation of Jesus, God, or both, of which the believer–Jesus mimesis is most prevalent.[38]

6. Most examples of mimesis occur in *paraenetic* or *didactic* material—the farewell discourses in John 13–17, where Jesus teaches on aspects of discipleship, and in 1 John, where John urges believers to behave according to the truth. Thus, mimesis seems to be an important feature or instrument of moral instruction in the teaching of both Jesus and John. This is not surprising because early Christian mimesis is an ethical concept.

7. There are two types of Johannine mimesis. Most often, mimesis involves the imitation of an action (twenty-eight out of forty-four occurrences, or 64 percent). This refers to *"performative mimesis,"* where a person imitates the exemplar in a particular activity. The second type of mimesis is less common (sixteen out of forty-four occurrences, or 36 percent) and can be called *"existential mimesis,"* where a person "imitates" the exemplar in a particular state of being (usually the verb "to be" is used).

8. The Johannine writings contain a large number of *mimetic imperatives* (ten out of forty-four mimetic occurrences, or 23 percent).[39] Looking specifically at the believer–Jesus/God mimesis, we observe that 27 percent (seven out of twenty-six occurrences) are mimetic imperatives (going up to 35 percent if we include 1 John 3:12 and 3 John 11).[40] The implication is that mimesis is not optional but a crucial aspect of the believer's relationship with the Father and Son.

Summary. An extensive survey of mimetic occurrences in the Johannine literature shows that John uses eight different linguistic constructions to indicate about forty-four occurrences of mimesis.[41] This provides the basis to speak legitimately

---

36. See John 6:57; 10:14–15; 12:26; 13:14, 15, 34; 14:3, 12, 19; 15:10, 12; 17:11, 14, 16, 18, 21, 22b, 24; 20:21; 1 John 2:6; 3:2, 3, 7, 16; 4:11, 17.

37. See John 5:19, 21, 26; 8:26, 28; 12:50; 15:9, 15; 17:18, 22a; 20:21.

38. The believer–God mimesis occurs in 1 John 4:11, 17, although it is debatable whether the object of imitation in 1 John 4:17 is God or Jesus. John 8:38–39 constitutes a "weak" case of an implied believer–God mimesis. The believer's imitation of both the Father and Son occurs in John 10:14–15; 17:11, 21, 22b.

39. John 8:38–39; 13:14, 15, 34; 15:12; 1 John 2:6; 3:12, 16; 4:11; 3 John 11.

40. John 13:14, 15, 34; 15:12; 1 John 2:6; 3:16; 4:11. 1 John 3:12 refers to the believers' non-imitation of Cain, and 3 John 11 to Gaius's imitation of good (people).

41. Only John 1–4 and 2 John do not contain mimetic occurrences.

of a Johannine concept of mimesis. Realizing that not every occurrence shows mimesis with equal clarity, we used the heuristic device of mimetic strength to situate each occurrence on a mimetic spectrum with a sliding scale of "weak," "medium," and "strong" to express our certainty of the presence of mimesis in each passage. Even if there is uncertainty about some texts, it would not negate the prevalence of the concept of mimesis in the Johannine literature. The Johannine literature presents two types of mimesis—performative mimesis and existential mimesis—and the two prominent mimetic categories are the Son–Father mimesis and the believer–Jesus/God mimesis. The latter category occurs primarily in paraenetic sections of the Johannine literature and contains many mimetic imperatives, suggesting that mimesis is a prominent instrument of ethical instruction for the believer's relationship with the Father and Son. Thus, I conclude that mimesis is both *varied* (in terms of different mimetic expressions) and *widespread* (in terms of where mimesis occurs) in the Johannine literature.

A final note on the Johannine mimetic language. Except for 3 John 11, John does not use the typical language of the Greek mimetic traditions—the lexeme μιμεῖσθαι. Instead, John develops his own vocabulary, with a broad semantic domain, in which the comparative conjunction καθώς (on its own or with the correlative καί or οὕτως) communicates the concept of mimesis most often. Interestingly, καθώς rarely features in "secular" (i.e., not Judeo-Christian) Greek literature from the fifth century BCE to the first century CE (see the Thesaurus Linguae Graecae database).[42] While the term frequently occurs in the LXX, the pseudepigrapha, the New Testament, and Josephus's *Antiquities*, generally it does *not* indicate mimesis. In this Judeo-Christian tradition, John's choice of making καθώς, instead of the lexeme μιμεῖσθαι, central to his mimetic language is rather unique.

5.3. Divine Mimesis

Having shown that mimesis is a legitimate and prevalent concept in the Johannine literature, we can begin to unpack the mimesis within the Godhead, comprising a dominant Son–Father mimesis (section 5.3.1) and a latent Spirit–Jesus mimesis (section 5.3.2). It is appropriate to start with divine mimesis for two reasons. First, the initial occurrences of mimesis in the Gospel of John (5:19, 21, 26) all refer to divine mimesis. Second, the Son–Father mimesis is paradigmatic for the believer–Jesus mimesis. This divine mimesis relates to ethics because the activities in which

---

42. In fact, Phrynichus and the Atticists strongly oppose the use of καθώς (in favor of καθά and καθό) (see BDAG, s.v. "καθώς").

the Son imitates the Father are moral activities that benefit people and mediate moral goods such as life, love, and truth. In other words, the Son–Father mimesis exemplifies and informs the mimetic behavior that is expected from believers as part of God's family.

5.3.1. The Son–Father Mimesis

The relationship between God and Jesus must be understood in the context of the family because, throughout the Johannine writings, God relates to Jesus as Father and Jesus to God as Son.[43] The filial relationship between the Father and Son is primarily characterized by the attributes of life, light, love, truth, and honor.[44] This relationship between the Father and Son, however, is not exclusive; believers are drawn in and participate in this divine relationship through the birth of God when they accept, that is believe in, Jesus (John 1:12–13; 3:3–5; 1 John 5:1). One advantage of depicting the relationship between Jesus and God in familial terms is its natural capacity for expansion and inclusivity. John thus uses the language of "birth" ("to be born," the passive form of γεννᾶν, occurs twenty-six times in the Johannine literature) and "children" (τέκνα/τεκνία) to show that people can be included in this divine family (e.g., John 1:12–13; 3:3, 5; 1 John 3:9; 5:1). But the Son–Father relationship is also characterized by another important dynamic, namely mimesis, and to this aspect we now turn.

The Paradigm of the Son–Father Mimesis. The first occurrence of mimesis in the Gospel of John occurs in 5:19 and specifies (appropriately) the paradigm for the Son–Father mimesis. In general and unqualified terms, Jesus claims that he cannot do anything by himself—he "merely" does what he sees the Father doing. The adverb ὁμοίως ("likewise") denotes mimesis in that the Son imitates whatever he observes from the Father.[45] This raises various questions: What kind of things

---

43. The term πατήρ ("father") occurs 154 times in the Johannine literature (37 percent of all occurrences in the New Testament), of which about 137 (almost 90 percent) refer to God. The term υἱός ("son") occurs seventy-nine times in the Johannine writings, of which sixty-seven occurrences (85 percent) refer to Jesus as the Son, Son of Man, or Son of God.

44. Bennema, *Mimesis*, 65–66.

45. Tinsley also notes the Son–Father mimesis (*Imitation of God*, 124). In contrast, Jan G. van der Watt explains the Son–Father dynamic in John 5:19–23 in terms of analogy: "Was Gott Jesus vormacht, ist daher nur *analog* dem, was ein gewöhnlicher Vater seinem Sohn vormacht. In der Parabel wird nur mittels einer Analogie ausgesagt, *dass* der Vater zeigt, gibt und tut, aber die Aufmerksamkeit konzentriert sich nicht darauf, *wie* er das genau tut" ("What God shows Jesus is therefore only *analogous* to what an ordinary father shows his son. In the parable, it is only stated by analogy *that* the Father shows, gives and does, but the attention is not focused on *how* exactly he does this") ("Der Meisterschüler Gottes (von der Lehre des Sohnes)—John 5,19–23," in

does he see the Father do? Where does Jesus observe the Father's actions? How is he able to do so? Before answering these questions, we must consider the circumstances that caused Jesus to make this extraordinary claim.

In John 5, the controversy between Jesus and "the Jews" revolves around Jesus's healing an invalid at the pool of Bethesda on the Sabbath (5:1–16). As Steven Bryan explains, what is at issue is the legitimacy of using *God's* power on the Sabbath.[46] In reply to the accusations, Jesus claims in 5:17 that it is legitimate for him to be working on the Sabbath because even God is at work on the Sabbath. This remains an enigmatic claim until we reach 5:19, where Jesus explains that he simply does what he sees the Father doing. In 5:20, Jesus then gives a rationale for this Son–Father mimesis. The Father's love for the Son is the motive or driving force behind him showing the Son all his ἔργα ("works"). We must note the verbal and conceptual parallels between 5:19–20 and 3:34–35. In 3:34–35, the Father's love for the Son results in his giving πάντα ("everything"—the entire revelation) to the Son so that he can speak God's words on earth. In 5:19–20, the Father's love for the Son results in his showing the Son πάντα (all his ἔργα) so that he can do them on earth.[47] "Showing" is one of the first steps in the mimetic process because usually, someone does something concrete that the imitator can observe and emulate.[48]

I return to the question: What kind of things does the Son see the Father do that he can emulate? While the actions in John 5:19 are unspecified, the immediate and wider Johannine context clarifies (1) the kind of activities that are associated with ποιεῖν ("to do, act, make") and (2) the reference of the unspecified τι ("what"), ἃ ἄν ("whatever"), and ταῦτα ("these things") in 5:19. Regarding ποιεῖν, Jesus is

---

Kompendium der Gleichnisse Jesu, ed. Ruben Zimmermann [Gütersloh: Gütersloher Verlagshaus, 2007], 745–54, at 747 [original emphasis]).

46. Steven M. Bryan, "Power in the Pool: The Healing of the Man at Bethesda and Jesus' Violation of the Sabbath (John 5:1–18)," *TynBul* 54 (2003): 7–22, at 14–16.

47. C. K. Barrett draws attention to scholars' observation that 5:19–20a contains a parable: "A son . . . apprenticed to his father does only what he sees his father doing, but his father shows him all the processes that belong to his craft" (*The Gospel according to St John*, 2nd ed. [Philadelphia: Westminster, 1978], 259). This mimetic dependency resembles the son–father relationship in antiquity with reference to their trade (Raymond E. Brown, *The Gospel according to John*, 2 vols., AB 29–29a [Garden City, NY: Doubleday, 1966, 1970], 1:218). Jo-Ann A. Brant also notes that mimesis is the key pedagogical method of instruction in antiquity (*John*, Paideia [Grand Rapids: Baker Academic, 2011], 105–6).

48. In turn, the Son "shows" the invisible Father to people so that they may know him, indicating that the Son is the Father's self-revelation (1:18; 10:32; 14:8–9). As the Son imitates the Father, it is natural that those who observe the Son, "see" the Father. In 5:20, there must have been a visual demonstration because this is coupled with the use of βλέπειν in 5:19. The Father's audible instruction to the Son occurs in texts such as 8:26, 28; 12:50; 15:15.

the subject of various actions in John 5: ποιεῖν ὑγιῆ (5:11, 15); ποιεῖν τὰ ἔργα (τοῦ πατρός) (5:19–20, 36); ποιεῖν κρίσιν (5:27); ζῳοποιεῖν (5:21). It seems reasonable to infer that the activity of ποιεῖν ὑγιῆ (5:11, 15) is included in ποιεῖν τὰ ἔργα τοῦ πατρός (5:19–20, 36) and synonymous with ἐργάζεσθαι (5:17). While πάντα ("all things") in 5:20a does not clarify the mimesis in 5:19, 5:20b reveals that the unspecified τι, ἃ ἄν, and ταῦτα in 5:19 and πάντα in 5:20a are ἔργα. Although the kind of work is unspecified, the wider Johannine context will resolve this. Jesus's purpose for coming into the world is to do the will (θέλημα) of the Father, that is, to complete his work (ἔργον) (4:34).[49] Since the θέλημα of the Father is that people believe in the Son and have eternal life (6:40), the implication is that the Father's ἔργον is salvific in nature. It consists of drawing people to Jesus and saving them, by what Jesus does and completes at the cross (6:39–40, 44; 12:32; see also the use of τελειῶσαι in 4:34 and 17:4; 19:30). Hence, I suggest that the Son–Father mimesis in 5:19 refers to the work of restoring people—physically, socially, and spiritually (salvation). In short, the Son imitates the life-giving or salvific works of the Father. Then, the answer to the question at hand —"What kind of things does the Son see the Father do that he can emulate?"—is "all the activities the Father does in order to restore or save people." Before I can answer the other questions about the where and how of this Son–Father mimesis, we must examine further occurrences of this divine filial mimesis.

Specific Occurrences of the Son–Father Mimesis. While John 5:19–20 describes the general Son–Father mimesis, other texts mention specific mimetic activities in the Son–Father relationship:

1. *To Be a Source of Life (John 5:21, 26).* We find a specific Son–Father mimesis in 5:21 and 5:26, both by means of a ὥσπερ ... οὕτως καί construction. John 5:21 states that just as the Father has the ability to give life (ζῳοποιεῖν), so does the Son. The idea is that the Son, in imitation of the Father, is a source of life to people. In addition, the Son has control over the distribution of life (οὓς θέλει ζῳοποιεῖ). John 5:26 expresses a similar mimetic idea in that just as the Father has life in himself (ἔχει ζωὴν ἐν ἑαυτῷ), so also the Son has life in himself (see also 1:4).[50]

---

49. I take καί in John 4:34 as epexegetical, explaining what doing the Father's will involves.

50. The phrase "to have life in himself" (ἔχειν ζωὴν ἐν ἑαυτῷ) is a unique divine prerogative, hence reserved for the Father and Son (John 5:26). Although the phrase occurs in 6:53 with reference to believers, this is qualified by the prerequisite of accepting Jesus. Similarly, in the parallel verse 6:54, the phrase that believers "have" (eternal) life means something like them "having *a share in* the divine life of the Father and Son." Believers do not have life independent of their relationship with Jesus. This becomes clear in 6:57, where a mimetic construction clarifies that believers depend on Jesus for life, just as Jesus depends on the Father. Nevertheless, while the Father has granted that the Son is a source of life, believers only have (access to) the divine life as long as they partake in their relationship with the Father and Son. As such, they can be a

The Son is so closely associated with the divine ζωή that he can claim εἶναι ἡ ζωή (11:25; 14:6), that is, he embodies or represents life and is able to distribute it at will. While the Son's ability in 5:21 to *give* life in imitation of the Father denotes a performative mimesis, the Son's ability in 5:26 to *have* life in himself in imitation of the Father refers to existential mimesis or imitation of being. However, we need not distinguish too sharply between the types of mimesis in 5:21 and 5:26 because the shared idea is that the Son is a source of life in imitation of the Father. Thus, the Son is a source of life and has autonomy over its distribution but not independently of the Father (see also 6:57).[51]

2. *To Speak/Teach (John 8:26, 28; 12:50; 15:15)*. In John, Jesus is depicted as a God-sent teacher (1:38; 3:2; 8:4; 11:28; 13:13–14; 20:16) and, as such, speaks the very words of God (3:34). Indeed, Jesus repeatedly claims that he only speaks and teaches what the Father tells him (7:16–17; 8:26, 28, 38; 12:49–50; 14:24; 15:15; 17:8, 14). Some of these texts show a mimetic dynamic where the Son speaks what the Father tells him. The Son–Father mimesis of speaking is most explicit in 8:28 and 12:50 (indicated by καθώς and καθώς ... οὕτως, respectively), to a lesser extent in 8:26 and 15:15, and possibly in 8:38. This mimesis creates congruent speech—the Son's words are the Father's words (3:34; 14:14; 17:8) and the Son's teaching is the Father's teaching (7:16).[52] There are linguistic indicators that Jesus's imitation of the Father's words is a specific case of the general Son–Father mimesis mentioned in 5:19. In 8:28, the phrase ἀπ' ἐμαυτοῦ ποιῶ οὐδέν ("I do nothing from myself"), immediately followed by the mimetic construction καθὼς ἐδίδαξέν με ὁ πατὴρ ταῦτα λαλῶ, echoes 5:19 where Jesus first states that he can do nothing by himself before he proclaims the general Son–Father mimesis. In 12:49, the phrase ἐγὼ ἐξ ἐμαυτοῦ οὐκ ἐλάλησα ("I have not spoken from myself"), followed by the mimetic construction in 12:50, also reflects the order and content of 5:19. There is a further connection between the mimesis of speech and the mimesis of praxis referred to in 5:19. Jesus's revelatory words or teaching have a soteriological dimension in that they contain liberating, life-giving truth about the divine reality (6:63, 68; 8:31–32; 12:49–50). So, just as the Son–Father mimesis of doing relates to life-giving work, the Son–Father mimesis of speaking also relates to life-giving teaching.

---

derivative source of life to others (7:38). Whereas the Son can give life (ζῳοποιεῖν) because he is a direct, autonomous source of life, believers can only pass on this life as a derivative source (7:38).

51. It still is the Father who "gives" or "draws" people to the Son (John 6:37, 39, 44, 65; 17:2, 6, 9). Hence, the Son's choice to give life to whomever he wishes (5:21) is still dependent on the Father's choice to give whomever he wishes to the Son (17:2) (see also J. Ramsey Michaels, *The Gospel of John*, NICNT [Grand Rapids: Eerdmans, 2010], 312).

52. Witmer also mentions that imitation in ancient education is common (*Divine Instruction*, 96–98).

3. *To Love* (*John 15:9*). Just as the Father loves the Son, so also the Son loves the disciples (15:9; καθώς . . . καί construction). The Son imitates the Father in that Jesus's love for the disciples is patterned after the Father's love for him. The love between the Father and Son is not just reciprocal (3:35; 5:20; 14:31) but is extended to others through the dynamic of mimesis. In essence, the reciprocal love between the Father and Son operates or remains within the boundaries of the divine nucleus, but mimetic love breaks this mold open and includes others in this shared love of the Father and Son. We saw a similar dynamic in 5:21, 26: the divine life that the Father and Son share is extended to believers who are subsequently drawn into this life-giving relationship with the Father and Son. I will elaborate on this mimetic chain of love in section 5.4.3.

4. *To Send* (*John 17:18; 20:21*). The καθώς . . . καί construction in both verses creates a mimesis of sending, where Jesus's sending the disciples into the world is patterned after his own sending into the world by the Father. The Johannine concept of sending has a clear soteriological dimension in that the Father has sent Jesus into the world to save it (John 3:17; 6:29; 1 John 4:9–10, 14). Based on the mimesis of sending, the Father's salvific work, which is Jesus's salvific mission, is continued through the disciples' salvific mission (see also John 17:20). The mimesis of sending refers to the imitation of purpose, intent, and message. Just as the Father sent Jesus into the world as his agent to do what he does and speak what he says in order to save people, Jesus sends the disciples into the world as his agents to continue the same work and proclaim the same message (John 4:38; 14:12; 15:27; 17:20).

5. *To Honor* (*John 17:22*). Δόξα ("honor") was the most significant indicator of one's status or worth in ancient societies.[53] Honor also characterizes the relationship of the Father and Son. Similar to life and love, honor is extended to those who have entered the divine family by means of mimesis. Just as the Father has honored the Son, Jesus honors the disciples—and, by extension, future believers (17:22).[54] This is an ascribed honor that affirms the believer's status in the divine family (see also 20:17, where Jesus calls the disciples ἀδελφοί for the first time).

---

53. The translation of δόξα as "honor" rather than "glory" fits better with the Johannine concept of the divine family. See also those who resort to the social sciences, such as Jerome H. Neyrey, *The Gospel of John*, NCBC (Cambridge: Cambridge University Press, 2007), 16–21. However, this choice does not negate a complementary meaning of "glory," with connotations of splendor and exaltation. Jesper Tang Nielsen makes a good case that *both* meanings of δόξα are in view in the Johannine writings ("The Narrative Structures of Glory and Glorification in the Fourth Gospel," *NTS* 56 [2010], 343–66).

54. The table in section 5.2 shows that John 17:22a is not a clear case of mimesis, so I will not make too much of this text. Besides the possible idea of mimetic honor, there is recipro-

PART 2   MIMESIS IN EARLY CHRISTIANITY

In sum, while John 5:19 speaks of the Son–Father mimesis in broad, general terms (the Son imitates the Father in all he does), specific mimetic activities include giving life, speaking, loving, sending, and honoring. Having outlined the scope and content of the Son–Father mimesis, we can now examine the precise mechanics and nature of this divine mimesis.

I now return to two issues raised earlier but not yet discussed: the questions about the where and how of this Son–Father mimesis. First, where does Jesus see the Father's actions and hear the Father's words so that he can imitate them? In John's dualistic worldview, there are only two spatial locations or spheres: heaven (οὐρανός) or the realm above (ἄνωθεν or ἐκ τῶν ἄνω), and the created world (κόσμος) or realm below (ἐκ τῶν κάτω) (see, e.g., John 3:31; 8:23). God the Father, who is invisible, resides in heaven (1:18; 12:28; 17:4); hence this must be the place where he operates and shows everything to the Son. However, this creates a problem because there is no natural contact between the two realms (3:13). While the invisible Father resides in heaven, the visible Son (Jesus) is on earth to carry out the Father's work. So, how is Jesus on earth able to observe the Father's actions and hear the Father's words in heaven? The answer lies in the uniqueness of the incarnation. The one who has come to earth and taken on humanity is, according to John, in the unique position to testify to what he has seen and heard in the heavenly realm (3:12–13, 31–32) and, therefore, able to reveal the Father (1:18; 6:46; 8:38).

This could suggest that prior to the incarnation, the Father showed the blueprint of his work to the Son, who subsequently carried it out on earth. While this is certainly possible, John presents an alternative scenario: that Jesus on earth has continuous access to heaven, so is in constant communication with his heavenly Father, and that this dynamic is realized through the Spirit. First, Jesus is presented as the point of contact between heaven and earth; he has continuous, open access to heaven (John 1:51).[55] Next, the present participle ποιοῦντα in 5:19b indicates that the action occurs simultaneously with the action in the main verb so that Jesus asserts that he can only do "what he sees the Father (*presently*) doing." Hence, the use of the future tense in 5:20b, "He *will* show him greater works than these (i.e., those in 5:1–18)," would indicate the Father's ongoing unfolding of his plan to the Son, who subsequently actualizes it on earth.[56] The force of 5:19–20 is that the Son continuously does on earth what he continuously sees the Father doing in

---

cal honor between the Father and Son in that they mutually honor each other (17:1; see also 13:31–32; 17:4–5).

55. The present tense of the participles ἀναβαίνοντας and καταβαίνοντας in 1:51 probably denotes that the access to heavenly revelation is an ongoing, current activity.

56. See also Hartwig Thyen, *Das Johannesevangelium*, 2nd ed., HKNT 6 (Tübingen: Mohr Siebeck, 2015), 309.

5. Mimesis in John's Gospel and Letters

heaven because the Father continuously shows the Son his ἔργα (see also 11:41–42; 12:27–28).[57] Therefore, I suggest that a reference to a "pre-incarnational blueprint" where the Father and Son talked through every detail of what the Son would do and say on earth is unlikely because John seems to indicate that Jesus on earth was in continual communication with his Father in heaven.

Regarding the "how" of the Son–Father mimesis, I suggest that the Son is in constant communication with the Father and can observe the heavenly reality by means of the Spirit. If Jesus's anointing with the Spirit in John 1:32 alludes to the coming of the Spirit on the Messiah in Isaiah 11:2 (as many scholars concede), then the Spirit would be expected to provide Jesus specifically with revelatory wisdom and knowledge to carry out his messianic ministry.[58] This would include being informed about the Father's works, which Jesus will then carry out on earth. This coincides with the information in 3:34 that Jesus can speak God's words *because* God has given Jesus the Spirit.[59] Thus, John probably understood that during his earthly ministry, Jesus was continuously in communication with his Father—through the Spirit—in which Jesus received information concerning what to do, speak, reveal, and so on.

While this clarifies the mechanics of the Son–Father mimesis to a great extent, one last question remains. If mimesis is instrumental to accomplishing the Father's work on earth, in what manner does Jesus imitate the Father? Would Jesus have repeated the Father's words verbatim on every occasion? According to 3:34, Jesus can speak the very words of God *because* he has received the Spirit, suggesting that the Spirit functions as the channel of communication between the Father and the Son. Therefore, it is unlikely that Jesus simply reiterated on earth what the Father had dictated to him in heaven or reproduced on earth what the Father had shown him in heaven. It is more likely that Jesus *on earth* was in continual communication with his Father *in heaven* through the Spirit. The main Johannine thought seems to be that Jesus does nothing independent of the Father, and the Son–Father mimesis has more to do with Jesus's faithfully acting as or on behalf of God than a cloning of God's words and actions. In other words, the Son–Father mimesis refers not so much to the Son's literal replication of the Father's words and actions but to a creative retelling and re-enaction. Putting all this together,

---

57. Although in 8:26, 28, 38, and 12:49–50, the Father's instruction is expressed by aorist and perfect tenses and Jesus's telling by present tenses, this simply shows that Jesus's words come *after* hearing the Father's words, but these instances of hearing–speaking probably occur *during* Jesus's ministry.

58. See Bennema, *Power of Saving Wisdom*, 163.

59. The subject of διδόναι is most likely God rather than Jesus (Bennema, *Power of Saving Wisdom*, 164–65).

the idea emerges that *John presents a perpetual Son–Father mimesis where Jesus continuously does on earth what he sees the Father do in heaven by means of the Spirit through which he has open and continuous access to the heavenly realm.*

5.3.2. The Spirit–Jesus Mimesis

The Spirit not only plays a crucial role in the Son–Father mimesis but is also part of another mimetic relationship within the divine family. Although no specific family label is given to the Spirit in the Johannine literature, there are ample reasons to consider the Spirit part of the divine family. First, among the Spirit's functions are ζῳοποιεῖν ("to give [divine] life"; John 6:63)—a unique divine prerogative (see also 5:21). Second, the Spirit is sometimes called "the Spirit of truth"—a functional label for the Spirit's role of communicating the truth, that is, to reveal the divine reality (14:17; 15:26; 16:13; see also 1 John 5:6). Third, the Spirit appears to be the channel of communication between the Father in heaven and Jesus on earth (see section 5.3.1). Fourth, the Spirit is instrumental in facilitating entry into the divine family (3:5), mediates the presence of Father and Son to the believer (14:17–18, 23; 1 John 3:24; 4:13), and is sent by the Father and Son to the human members of the divine family (14:26; 15:26). Hence, it is difficult to deny that the Spirit is an essential member of the divine family.

With his departure from this world imminent, Jesus promises his followers the Spirit, who will replace him and assist them in their ongoing mission. There are several indicators that the Spirit is patterned on Jesus. When Jesus tells his disciples that he will give them ἄλλος παράκλητος ("another advocate/counselor"; John 14:16), the implication is that he is the first παράκλητος (see also 1 John 2:1) and the Spirit is modeled after him and will take over Jesus's functions as παράκλητος after his departure.[60] In other words, the Spirit will "imitate" Jesus in his role as παράκλητος. The Spirit will specifically "imitate" Jesus in his teaching function. In John 14:26, Jesus informs his disciples that the Spirit will teach them everything and remind them of everything that he has told them. The Spirit will not bring unfamiliar teaching because both occurrences of πάντα are qualified by the phrase ἃ εἶπον ὑμῖν [ἐγώ]. Hence, the Spirit's teaching consists of what Jesus has taught. Similarly, the Spirit will not speak on his own but only what he hears from Jesus (16:13–15). Hence, just as Jesus spoke what he simultaneously heard the Father say,

---

60. Rudolf Bultmann (*The Gospel of John: A Commentary*, trans. G. R. Beasley-Murray [Oxford: Blackwell, 1971], 566–67) and Raymond E. Brown ("The Paraclete in the Fourth Gospel," *NTS* 13 (1966–1967): 113–32, at 113–14, 126–27) were the first to point out the numerous functional parallels between Jesus and the Spirit.

so the future tense of the verbs ἀκούειν and λαλεῖν in 16:13 refers to simultaneous activities—the Spirit will speak what he hears Jesus say. The precise nature of the Spirit's mimesis of Jesus's didactic function probably lies between two extremes: while the Spirit does not provide new teaching *independent of* Jesus's historical teaching, neither does the Spirit simply reiterate the literal words of Jesus. The Spirit's didactic role is most likely to explain the meaning and significance of Jesus's historical teachings in any culture and time.[61]

In sum, the Spirit–Jesus mimesis refers, more broadly, to the Spirit's imitation of Jesus as a παράκλητος and, specifically, to speaking/teaching. In fact, there seems to be a mimetic chain—the Son speaks what he hears from the Father, and in turn, the Spirit speaks what he hears from Jesus. This mimetic chain of teaching ensures that people hear God's very words.[62] Compared to the Son–Father mimesis, however, the Spirit–Jesus mimesis is more latent.

5.3.3. Conclusion

The Johannine literature depicts a concept of a divine family comprising the Father, Son, and Spirit. Within this divine family, the Son–Father mimesis is dominant but there is also a latent Spirit–Jesus mimesis. The Spirit–Jesus mimesis refers to the following mimetic actions: broadly, to be a παράκλητος and, specifically, to speaking. The Son–Father mimesis includes the imitation of the following actions: generally, to do "everything," and specifically, to give life, to speak, to love, to send, and to honor. In fact, Jesus's main activities of doing/working and speaking/teaching are rooted in the concept of mimesis—Jesus does what he sees the Father do and speaks what he hears the Father say. Regarding the where and how of mimesis, the Son continuously observes what the Father does and says in heaven by means of the Spirit so that he can imitate it on earth. Regarding the nature of mimesis, I suggest that it has more to do with a creative, faithful retelling and re-enactment of what the Father says and does rather than cloning.

The divine family depicted in the Johannine writings is not exclusive. When people accept or believe in Jesus, they become part of the divine family through a birth of God or the Spirit. While we will examine the believer–Jesus/God mimesis in the following sections, I draw attention to some implications of the Son–Father

---

61. See Bennema, *Power of Saving Wisdom*, 228–34.

62. Witmer arrives at the same conclusion via another route. He focuses on how the prophecy of Isa 54:13 quoted in John 6:45a ("and they shall all be taught by God") is fulfilled in the teaching of Jesus. As Jesus receives direct, divine instruction from God and imitates him (e.g., 5:19–20; 7:16; 8:26, 28), so Jesus's teaching perfectly mediates God's word to people (*Divine Instruction*, 94–106).

PART 2 MIMESIS IN EARLY CHRISTIANITY

mimesis for believers as the human members of the divine family. Our study shows that many attributes that characterize the relationship of the Father and Son (life, light, love, truth, honor) play a part in mimesis. We have seen that in imitation of the Father, Jesus is a source of life, love, and honor for his followers. Even in the case of "truth," it could be argued that Jesus imitates the Father in being a source of truth for people if we recognize the following syllogism: (1) Jesus speaks the Father's words, and (2) Jesus's words contain truth (John 8:31–32; 18:37), hence (3) Jesus reiterates the truth that the Father speaks. Thus, "truth" as the content of the Father and Son's speech to people is linked to the specific mimetic activity of speaking. This means that the fundamental attributes and activities that characterize the Father–Son relationship are extended or made available to people by means of mimesis (see also section 5.5). In other words, *mimesis is instrumental for the divine–human relationship*.

In fact, the Son–Father mimesis takes place *for the sake of* people. All the Son's mimetic activities benefit people. The Son imitates the Father in giving life, speaking the truth, loving, sending into the world, and sharing his honor in order to reveal God and mediate the things of God to people. *Mimesis is a device or mechanism for mediating the divine reality of the world above to the world below*. Through the Son–Father mimesis, people can experience the divine life, love, truth, and so on. Whereas reciprocity is exclusive and refers to a mutual exchange of goods and services between the benefactor and the recipient, mimesis is *inclusive* in that goods or benefits are passed down a mimetic chain from the originator to the imitator–recipient to the recipient. Hence, *an imitator is a mediator*. The perpetual flow of life, love, truth, and honor between the Father and Son is extended to believers through the Son's mimesis of the Father. Thus, mimesis is an essential tool or mechanism in mediation. Jesus is the mediator between God and humanity, between the inaccessible realm above and the realm below, and he functions as such through mimesis. People can know and experience the divine reality through Jesus's mediatory-mimetic activities. Mimesis, therefore, is instrumental in revealing the divine reality to people and making it tangible or accessible to them. It is as the imitator of God that Jesus is also the revealer of God.

In imitating the Father, the Son actualizes the Father's work on earth. As such, the Son is the visible and audible manifestation of the Father himself. In the mimetic act, the Son unveils, on earth, the Father in heaven. The Son–Father mimesis thus impacts humanity. In imitating the Father, the Son opens up the heavenly realm and reveals the Father on earth so that people can "hear" and "see"—that is, experience—God for themselves. Thus, Jesus represents the invisible God on earth by means of mimesis. We must now examine the extent to which believers are expected to imitate Jesus (and God).

5.4. The Believer–Jesus/God Mimesis

In this section, I will examine the prevalent believer–Jesus mimesis and occasional believer–God mimesis.[63] Human–divine mimesis makes up the majority of mimetic occurrences in the Johannine literature, so this section takes up the largest part of the chapter.

5.4.1. Discipleship and Mimesis

Discipleship undoubtedly involves relationship (personal attachment to the teacher), loyalty (allegiance to the teacher), and learning (adherence to the teacher's instruction). While it may seem obvious that a disciple seeks to imitate the teacher, the question is whether the verbs ἀκολουθεῖν ("to follow") and μένειν ("to remain"), which are central to John's understanding of discipleship, suggest imitation. I will first examine the concept of following Jesus, then look at the idea of remaining with Jesus, and finally, at possible filial mimesis in John 8:30–47.

Following Jesus. In section 4.1, we noted that scholarship is divided on whether following Jesus is related to imitating him. De Boer is most nuanced, arguing that the language of "following Jesus" in the Gospels has connotations of imitation.[64] He also notes that "following Jesus" has an additional aspect, namely participation in his life and fate (see, e.g., John 12:25–26), which would require a measure of imitation.[65] Indeed, in John's Gospel, the disciples' act of following Jesus is not just about going where he goes but also observing him (see also 1:37–39) and participating in his life (6:66 shows that some could or would no longer follow Jesus because of his teaching). According to de Boer, John 13:36–38 and 21:18–19 indicate that Peter's following of Jesus has a mimetic dimension—Peter will "follow" (i.e., imitate) Jesus in laying down his life for his master. De Boer concludes that while "following Jesus" does not mean "imitating him," in practice imitation is implied or will develop.[66] I concur. John 21:18–19 expresses the idea that Peter's following Jesus leads to imitating Jesus in laying down his life for his master. While Peter's following Jesus in itself does not amount to imitation, it brings him to a position where he can imitate Jesus. Regarding 12:26, although following Jesus arguably has a mimetic aspect in that the believer goes where Jesus goes, strictly speaking, the mimetic aspect is connected to the verb εἶναι in 12:26b rather than ἀκολουθεῖν

---

63. See section 5.2, n. 38, for the rare references to a direct believer–God mimesis.
64. De Boer, *Imitation of Paul*, 51–54.
65. De Boer, *Imitation of Paul*, 52.
66. De Boer, *Imitation of Paul*, 53–54.

in 12:26a. That is, the believer arrives at the same place as Jesus (mimesis) as the result of following him. Thus, mimesis seems to be an *effect* of following. Similar to the Synoptics, no explicit linguistic expression in John ties ἀκολουθεῖν to mimesis; there are only conceptual traces of mimesis. In other words, following Jesus *facilitates* mimesis. It is *as* people follow Jesus that they observe and imitate him. Therefore, ἀκολουθεῖν is only conceptually linked to mimesis in so far as following Jesus as a disciple *facilitates* imitating him.[67]

Remaining with Jesus. There is marginally more evidence in John's Gospel that μένειν has mimetic connotations. The verb μένειν is logically related to ἀκολουθεῖν in that following Jesus implies remaining with or in him (only in John 1:37–40 are the two terms directly related). Of the sixty-seven occurrences of μένειν in the Johannine literature, only three hint at mimesis—John 15:4; 15:10; and 1 John 2:6. The καθώς . . . οὕτως construction in 15:4 perhaps indicates mimesis: Just as (καθώς) a branch can only bear fruit when it abides in the vine, so (οὕτως) the disciples can only bear fruit when they abide in Jesus. Jesus exhorts the disciples to observe the vine and its branches and "imitate" the branches in abiding, as it were, in order to be fruitful. Even so, this is not an occurrence of the believer–Jesus mimesis. Again, in 15:10, we find the comparative conjunction καθώς (but now without the correlative οὕτως) to indicate the mimetic idea that just as (καθώς) Jesus has been obedient and abides in the Father's love, so the disciples will abide in Jesus's love when they are obedient. Jesus's obedience to the Father (and the corollary aspect of abiding in the Father's love) is the example for the disciples to imitate. In 1 John 2:6, the imperative to imitate Jesus's way of life (the mimesis is indicated by a καθώς . . . καί construction) applies to those who claim to abide in Jesus. In both John 15:10 and 1 John 2:6, the primary objects for imitation are Jesus's obedience and Jesus's way of life rather than remaining with him. Therefore, just as following Jesus should inspire imitation, the idea here also is that remaining with Jesus should *result* in imitating him.

Filial Mimesis. The most poignant exchange in the conflict between Jesus and οἱ Ἰουδαῖοι ("the Jews" or Judeans) is to be found in John 8, with οἱ Ἰουδαῖοι alleging that Jesus is demon-possessed (John 8:48) and Jesus calling his opponents children of the devil (8:44).[68] Notwithstanding the harsh allegations, the conflict between Jesus and οἱ Ἰουδαῖοι is a "family" debate, where Jesus addresses οἱ Ἰου-

---

67. See also the discussion in section 4.1. Van der Merwe equates "following Jesus" too easily with "imitating him" ("*Imitatio Christi*," 133–34).

68. The term Ἰουδαῖοι refers to a subset of the Jewish people in Jesus's time, namely an overtly religious group of Torah- and temple-loyalists, found especially in Judea (Cornelis Bennema, "The Identity and Composition of οἱ Ἰουδαῖοι in the Gospel of John," *TynBul* 60 [2009]: 239–63).

5. Mimesis in John's Gospel and Letters

δαῖοι, who had been disciples (8:30–31), and explains the existence of two mutually exclusive families with different fathers (8:39–47). The first hint of mimesis may be seen in 8:38. Jesus's claim in 8:38a that he speaks of what he has seen in the Father's presence echoes the mimetic pattern revealed in 5:19–20. If this mimetic idea lies behind Jesus's claim in 8:38a, then his exhortation in 8:38b could also echo the concept of mimesis: "Therefore, you should also do what you have heard from the Father."[69] In which case, just as Jesus mimics the Father, so also οἱ Ἰουδαῖοι should imitate the Father. It soon becomes clear, however, that οἱ Ἰουδαῖοι imitate another father (8:39–44). Jesus points out that their behavior suggests they are children of the devil and choose (θέλειν) to emulate their father (8:44).[70] Indeed, the immediate context shows that οἱ Ἰουδαῖοι imitate their father the devil: like the devil, they sin (8:24; see also 1 John 3:8), lie (8:44, 55), seek to kill (8:37, 40, 44, 59), and do not accept the truth (8:44–46). True followers of Jesus, however, are expected to imitate his father—God (see also 8:38b).[71]

Summary. Although some occurrences of ἀκολουθεῖν and μένειν arguably allude to mimesis, it would not be judicious to force our case. The terms ἀκολουθεῖν and μένειν only hint at mimesis rather than having clear mimetic connotations. Similarly, a good case can be made that John 8 indicates the concept of family mimesis within a discipleship context, but I conclude that it lies beneath the surface. This means that we must look elsewhere if we wish to speak more confidently of a believer–Jesus mimesis in the Johannine writings.

5.4.2. The Footwashing

The first clear evidence of the believer–Jesus mimesis is found in the footwashing episode in John 13.[72] The focus of this section is Jesus's mimetic imperative to his disciples in John 13:15: ὑπόδειγμα γὰρ ἔδωκα ὑμῖν ἵνα καθὼς ἐγὼ ἐποίησα ὑμῖν καὶ ὑμεῖς

---

69. The textual variant ὑμῶν after τοῦ πατρός is most probably a scribal refinement to show a contrast between God as the father of Jesus and the devil as the father of οἱ Ἰουδαῖοι, but this contrast is only introduced in 8:41 (Bruce M. Metzger, *A Textual Commentary on the Greek New Testament*, 2nd ed. [Stuttgart: Deutsche Bibelgesellschaft, 1994], 193). Besides, it would be odd for Jesus to *exhort* οἱ Ἰουδαῖοι to imitate the devil (even though 8:44 indicates that this is what they are doing).

70. Θέλειν here denotes a volitional act motivated either by desire (to wish, to want) or resolve (to will, to intend). Hartog focuses on the term ἐπιθυμία ("desire") as part of his effort to add a "desiderative" dimension to my Johannine model of mimesis ("Johannine Ethics," 11–12).

71. Against the backdrop of ancient education, van der Watt explains that children did what their father did ("Ethics Alive in Imagery," 424–28; *Grammar*, 1:615–19).

72. For a detailed discussion of mimesis in the footwashing episode, see Cornelis Bennema, "Mimesis in John 13: Cloning or Creative Articulation?," *NovT* 56 (2014): 261–74.

ποιῆτε ("For I gave you an example, that you also should do just as I have done to you"). The footwashing pericope consists of two parts, each conveying a distinct but related meaning: (1) in 13:1–11, Jesus performs the footwashing and explains it in terms of the disciples' spiritual cleansing that he will complete for them on the cross (soteriology); and (2) in 13:12–17, Jesus explains the footwashing in terms of humble, loving service that needs ongoing repetition (ethics).[73]

Although scholarship has examined the footwashing pericope extensively, the focus has been on 13:1–11, and the topic of mimesis has received little consideration. In the following examination, I will stress the cognitive and creative aspects of mimesis and, in so doing, mediate between two conflicting views. Scholars are divided on whether the mimetic imperative in John 13:15 calls for a literal duplication of the footwashing or if it is a directive to humble (loving) service. Of the proponents of the first view, Christopher Thomas has offered the most extensive case, but we will see that it has its weaknesses.[74] And while most scholars take

---

73. It is well recognized that the verbs θεῖναι and λαβεῖν used in 13:4, 12 to describe Jesus's taking off and putting on his clothes echo 10:18, where Jesus speaks of his ability to lay down and pick up his life of his own accord—which, of course, he does on the cross and in the resurrection. Robert L. Brawley contends that the idea of imitation in John 13 is "overblown" because (1) if the footwashing is an example to imitate, Jesus would not need to inform Peter that he will understand the footwashing only later; (2) ὑπόδειγμα refers not to an example for imitation but a revelatory pattern; and (3) Jesus reiterates the meaning of the footwashing not as an example for imitation but as a new command to love one another (13:34) ("Jesus as the Middle Term for Relationships with God in the Fourth Gospel," in *Biblical Ethics and Application: Purview, Validity, and Relevance of Biblical Texts in Ethical Discourse*, ed. Ruben Zimmermann and Stephan Joubert, CNNTE 9, WUNT 384 [Tübingen: Mohr Siebeck, 2017], 121–37, at 124–26). However, Jesus's remark in 13:7 that Peter will understand the footwashing only later refers to its salvific meaning in 13:1–11, while he expects his disciples to understand its ethical meaning in 13:12–17 already now (see on 13:12 below). Moreover, the love command has a clear mimetic structure too (see section 5.4.3), so that John 13 contains two related mimetic imperatives. Similarly, Rahmsdorf argues that the footwashing has a clear temporal reference and is not a timeless example for imitation (*Zeit und Ethik*, 387–95). While I endorse her argument for the soteriological section 13:1–11, the imperative to imitate Jesus's example in the ethical section 13:12–17, however, *is* timeless. Both Brawley and Rahmsdorf insufficiently distinguish between the different parts of the footwashing.

74. John Christopher Thomas, *Footwashing in John 13 and the Johannine Community*, JSNTSup 61 (Sheffield: JSOT Press, 1991), 110, 128. Other supporters of a literal replication of the footwashing (but with symbolic meaning) include Christoph Niemand, *Die Fusswaschungserzählung des Johannesevangeliums: Untersuchungen zu ihrer Entstehung und Überlieferung im Christentum*, SA 114 (Rome: Pontificio Ateneo S. Anselmo, 1993), 383–86, 411 (to initiate and welcome John the Baptist's disciples into the Johannine community); Mary L. Coloe, "Welcome into the Household of God: The Foot Washing in John 13," *CBQ* 66 (2004): 400–415, at 411–15 (to welcome believers into God's family); van der Watt, "Ethics and Ethos," 167–74; van der Watt, *Grammar*,

the latter view, they rarely substantiate their position or explain the mechanics of the mimesis.[75] They do not ask if, perhaps, Jesus *did* intend the exact replication of the footwashing. The central question, therefore, is: Did Jesus, by his mimetic imperative, intend that the disciples literally replicate the act of footwashing or that they creatively express the idea underlying the footwashing? It is clear from 13:1 that the footwashing is also an act of love; that is, Jesus is showing the disciples the extent of his love—proleptically in what he is going to do on the cross (13:6–11) and at this moment in humble service (13:12–17).[76] I shall focus on 13:4–5 and 12–17, which are the verses relevant to the Johannine concept of mimesis.

A close examination of 13:4–5, 12–17 shows a mimetic pattern that consists of four aspects. First, 13:4–5, 12a describes the physical act of footwashing. Three successive verbs describe Jesus's actions at the start (Jesus gets up from the table, takes off his outer garment, and washes the disciples' feet) and in reverse order at the finish (having washed the disciples' feet, he puts on his outer garment, and reclines again at the table). This explicit account of Jesus's actions builds up to the mimetic imperative that follows in 13:14–15, which suggests that one can only imitate what is *observed* first. Second, when Jesus returns to the table after the footwashing, he does not immediately command his disciples to imitate his example. Instead, he asks in 13:12b, γινώσκετε τί πεποίηκα ὑμῖν? Here, γινώσκειν has the force of "to understand"—Jesus challenges the disciples to see whether they have understood what he did for them. Thus, the disciples must *interpret* Jesus's original act in order to imitate him. This implies that mimesis cannot simply be a

---

1:305–8 (to express unreserved love for one another during the habitual sharing of meals); Richard Bauckham, "Did Jesus Wash His Disciples' Feet?," in idem, *The Testimony of the Beloved Disciple: Narrative, History, and Theology in the Gospel of John* (Grand Rapids: Baker Academic, 2007), 91–206, at 195; Lisa P. Stephenson, "Getting Our Feet Wet: The Politics of Footwashing," *JPT* 23 (2014): 154–70, at 166–70 (to express several political acts such as reconciliation and economic solidarity).

75. Scholarship supporting this view includes Fernando F. Segovia, "John 13:1–20, The Footwashing in the Johannine Tradition," *ZNW* 73 (1982): 31–51, at 45–46; Francis J. Moloney, "A Sacramental Reading of John 13:1–38," *CBQ* 53 (1991): 237–56, at 244–45, 254 (to love unto death); R. Alan Culpepper, "The Johannine *Hypodeigma*: A Reading of John 13," *Semeia* 53 (1991): 133–52, at 141–44 (to imitate Jesus's virtuous death); Jörg Augenstein, *Das Liebesgebot im Johannesevangelium und in den Johannesbriefen*, BWANT 134 (Stuttgart: Kohlhammer, 1993), 35; Jean Zumstein, "Le Lavement des Pieds (Jean 13,1–20): Un Exemple de la Conception Johannique du Pouvoir," *RTP* 132 (2000): 345–60, at 354; Burridge, *Imitating* Jesus, 300–301, 343–44 (to love unto death and to provide loving service); Jörg Frey, "Love-Relations in the Fourth Gospel: Establishing a Semantic Network," in *Repetitions and Variations in the Fourth Gospel: Style, Text, Interpretation*, ed. G. van Belle, M. Labahn, and P. Maritz, BETL 223 (Leuven: Peeters, 2009), 171–98, at 192.

76. For the connection between John 13:1–11 and 13:12–20, see further Thomas, *Footwashing*, 116–25; Niemand, *Fusswaschungserzählung*, ch. 2.

PART 2   MIMESIS IN EARLY CHRISTIANITY

mindless replication. Third, 13:14–15 contains Jesus's ethical imperative and naturally requires *a volitional act* from the disciples—they must act in response to the imperative. Jesus explicitly states that he expects his followers to do for one another what he did for them. Fourth, according to 13:17, understanding should result in doing as well as being. Obedience to Jesus's mimetic imperative leads to a state of blessedness or happiness (μακάριος εἶναι). Thus, 13:4–17 shows a mimetic pattern or process that comprises four stages: showing→knowing→doing→being. I will now examine more closely the nature of mimesis in this episode.

Jesus's explicit mimetic imperative occurs in John 13:14–15. Both 13:14 ("If I did this, you also ought to do this") and 13:15b ("Just as I did, you also must do") indicate the intended mimesis. In 13:14, the adverbial use of the second καί, the imperatival force of ὀφείλειν, and the repetition of the verb νίπτειν create a mimetic imperative: "[If I have washed your feet], you must also wash one another's feet." Then, the conjunction γάρ logically connects 13:15 with 13:14 and most likely functions as an explanatory conjunction ("for, you see"; see also 3:16; 4:8) rather than a causal conjunction ("because," "since"). John 13:15 can hardly provide the basis or grounds for the action in 13:14; rather, 13:15 builds on the information in 13:14; hence, it explains. The term ὑπόδειγμα ("example," "model," "pattern") occurs only here in John's Gospel and harks back to the footwashing as the visible example or model that Jesus presents for his disciples to imitate. In 13:15b, the comparative conjunction καθώς in the protasis with the correlative καί in the apodosis denotes the mimesis. So, mimesis is indicated by the καθώς ... καί construction and ὑπόδειγμα refers to the footwashing as "showing," that is, the visible example or model for imitation. However, the exact mode of imitation (whether literal replication or faithful expression of the underlying idea) is not specified and must be determined by the context.[77]

We now turn to whether the mimetic imperative invites exact replication or creative, truthful representation. A few factors count against the former option. First, exact replication (or even mimesis) is not inherent in ὑπόδειγμα, which here simply denotes "example," "pattern," or "model" of behavior used for purposes of moral instruction.[78] Second, although the syntax of the καθώς ... καί construction denotes

---

[77]. Thomas disagrees, saying that if there is an explicit command in 13:14 that the disciples are to wash one another's feet, 13:15 should be taken likewise (*Footwashing*, 110). However, Jesus often uses ordinary or physical events to point to an underlying spiritual reality. For example, Jesus moves from the request for literal water to the offer of "living water" (4:7–10), from literal food to the "food" that sustains his mission (4:31–34), from physical bread to the "true bread" (6:31–32), and from physical sight (or lack of it) to spiritual insight (9:39–41). Likewise, Jesus may have used the physical act of footwashing to point to the spiritual reality behind it, namely humble, loving service.

[78]. BDAG, s.v. "ὑπόδειγμα." Thomas's argument that 13:15 contains the only ὑπόδειγμα Jesus

comparison (here even mimesis), it does not automatically demand exact replication. Hence, I object to Thomas's argument that the καθώς ... καί construction simply assumes literal replication.[79] Missing in Thomas's treatment of the footwashing (and that of many others) is the vital distinction between the interpretation of the original act and the consequent mimetic act. Third, the phrase νίπτειν τοὺς πόδας had already acquired a figurative sense of providing humble service or showing hospitality by the first century (see also Gen 18:4; 1 Sam 25:41; Jos. Asen. 13:12; 20:3).[80] Fourth, the footwashing has two intertwined meanings—a spiritual cleansing that Jesus will complete on the cross and humble, loving service—of which the first cannot be replicated. Hence, any imitation of the footwashing can only be partial. Fifth, for John, it is unlikely that Jesus simply desired the exact replication of the visible act because to wash someone's feet without an attitude of humility and love would certainly be to miss the point. Sixth, since mimesis requires understanding (so 13:12b, 17a), it cannot be mechanical copying. If it did, Jesus would simply have said in 13:17, "Amen, amen, I tell you, you must do exactly as I did." Instead, he adds εἰ ταῦτα οἴδατε and gives an explanation in 13:14, 16. Thomas ignores the significance of Jesus's question in 13:12b and, hence, the cognitive dimension of mimesis.

As we have seen, Jesus's question in 13:12b adds a cognitive aspect to the concept of mimesis. This suggests that mimesis consists of two components: (1) the interpretation of the original act and (2) the resulting mimetic act. For John, mimesis is a *hermeneutical process* where the disciple interprets Jesus's original act in order to imitate it.[81] Consequently, the imitator must understand the intent of the original act *and* express this understanding in a corresponding mimetic act. This implies that the mimetic act cannot be limited to a replication of the original act but can be a creative expression of that act. While I have no objection to the practice of washing someone's feet as an expression of humble, loving service (to kneel before a person and perform a demeaning task may aid the person's attitude), it does not exhaust the scope of what Jesus meant.[82] The significance of the

---

gives (*Footwashing*, 110) is a truism that still begs the question of what the precise nature of Jesus's example is.

79. Thomas, *Footwashing*, 110.

80. BDAG, s.v. "νίπτω"; Konrad Weiss, "πούς," in *TDNT* 6:624–31, at 631; Thomas, *Footwashing*, 26–56; Bauckham, "Did Jesus Wash," 192–93; Bincy Mathew, *The Johannine Footwashing as the Perfect Sign of Love: An Exegetical Study of John 13:1–20*, WUNT 2/464 (Tübingen: Mohr Siebeck, 2018), 74–122 (she uncovers figurative meanings of hospitality, intimacy, and love in ancient Jewish, Greek, and Roman practices of footwashing).

81. Van der Watt also asserts that imitating Jesus is not about mechanical copying but involves interpretation ("Reciprocity," 267–76; *Grammar*, 1:250, 595–97).

82. Within the New Testament, 1 Tim 5:10 is the only other reference to the practice of washing the feet of fellow believers. Thomas traces the literal practice of footwashing in early

footwashing in John 13 lies in understanding the concept (the need for humble, loving service to one another) *and* a resulting tangible expression that creatively but truthfully articulates this understanding.[83]

It appears that most scholars have neglected the significance of Jesus's question in 13:12b and consequently the cognitive aspect of mimesis. They have overlooked the distinction between the interpretation of the original act and the mimetic act, so they are faced with the question of whether mimesis refers to exact replication or creative representation. I contend that instead of an either/or, we have a both/and situation. Mimesis involves the understanding of the original act and the articulation of the subsequent mimetic act that creatively but faithfully articulates this understanding. This is not to say that the exact replication of the act is always invalid, but it is not limited to it. Nevertheless, there must be a close correspondence between the creative articulation and the original example in order to qualify as mimesis. For John, the mimetic act must have a tangible form that can convey the same meaning as the original in order to be authentic and effective.[84]

An authentic and effective imitation of the footwashing would include the adoption of a slave identity,[85] thereby retaining a counterculutral aspect since menial, servile service runs counter to human aspirations.[86] The strong connec-

---

Christian communities, although he admits that it is unfortunate that the Johannine Epistles do not refer to the practice (*Footwashing*, 128–46).

83. Van der Watt stresses that footwashing is primarily an example of love rather than humility (*Grammar*, 1:308–9). This dichotomy seems too stark; rather, both love and humility are in view.

84. In my view, for example, showing compassion for a homeless person by picking him up and providing him with a shower and a meal belongs to the conceptual mimetic domain of the footwashing, whereas throwing a coin at him does not. As long as the idea of humble loving service is in view, I would also approve the literal washing of feet to welcome new believers into God's family (see also the positions of Niemand and Coloe in n. 74 above). Similarly, Spohn states that "although there are no rules for the precise application of analogies, there are boundaries beyond which the original pattern, or 'prime analogate,' is no longer recognizable" (*Go and Do Likewise*, 62).

85. Jesus's rationale for the mimetic imperative in 13:13–14, 16 contains a threefold *argumentum a maiore ad minus* for why the disciples are not exempt from imitating Jesus: what the person of higher status (master, teacher, sender) has done must also be done by the one of lower status (slaves, disciples, messengers). The scandal of the footwashing lies in the reversal of status and role, where ὁ κύριος καὶ ὁ διδάσκαλος acts as, and identifies with, δοῦλος. Allegiance to this δοῦλος–κύριος then demands that οἱ μαθηταί must be δοῦλοί to one another too. The implication is that the disciples' mimesis involves participation in Jesus's slave identity. Contra van der Watt's critique of me (*Grammar*, 1:308–9n132). Matthew Nantlais Williams's conclusion that "the foot washing is more fundamentally one of *participation* than mimesis" (original emphasis) distinguishes too sharply between these two aspects ("'Good News to the Poor?' Socio-Economic Ethics in the Gospel of John" [PhD diss., Durham University, 2021], 129).

86. Bauckham, "Did Jesus Wash," 206. Spohn mentions the shocking reversal of a well-

5. Mimesis in John's Gospel and Letters

tion between the believer's mimesis and Jesus's original example also means that the mimetic act serves as a reminder of Jesus's humble, loving service (supremely seen at the cross). To stretch this idea, the imitator and the mimetic act become a channel through which the beneficiary can experience Jesus and his humble, loving service for himself (see also 13:20).[87]

5.4.3. Actualizing the Love Command through Mimesis

When Johannine ethics was still considered problematic, scholarship assumed that Jesus's love command in John 13:34 was virtually the only (explicit) ethic (albeit perhaps as the *précis* of his commandments) in the Gospel or even the entire Johannine corpus. As a result, scholars all too often emphasize *that* believers should love one another and rarely address the *means* by which Jesus's command can be carried out.[88] The focus of this section, therefore, is on the *practice* of the love command. Our central question is this: How can believers *actualize* Jesus's ethical imperative "to love one another"? In answer to this, I wish to argue that, for John, believers should and are able to love one another through *mimesis*. The mimetic chain looks like this: just as the Father loves Jesus, Jesus loves the disciples (15:9); just as Jesus loves the disciples, they should love one another (13:34; 15:12; 1 John 4:11). The concept of mimesis does not simply address why the love command must be carried out but also how it can be achieved or realized. Since

---

educated white pastor shining the shoes of old African Americans as an appropriate exercise of analogical imagination because it tried to re-enact Jesus's action without merely repeating it (*Go and Do Likewise*, 53–54). For an even broader countercultural application of the footwashing, see Klaus Scholtissek, "'Ein Beispiel habe ich euch gegeben ...' (Joh 13,15): Die Diakonie Jesu und die Diakonie der Christen in der johanneischen Fußwaschungserzählung als Konterkarierung römischer Alltagskultur," in idem, *Textwelt und Theologie des Johannesevangeliums: Gesammelte Schriften (1996–2020)*, WUNT 452 (Tübingen: Mohr Siebeck, 2020), 303–22.

87. See also Thomas, *Footwashing*, 150. Considering the meaning of the literal practice of footwashing for the Johannine community, Thomas argues that it functioned as an extension of their water baptism and signified their continual cleansing from sin in continued fellowship with Jesus. Although this interpretation may have merit, Thomas seems to have disregarded the aspect of humble service.

88. For the vast amount of literature on the Johannine subject of love, see Ruben Zimmermann, "Is there Ethics in the Gospel of John? Challenging an Outdated Consensus," in *Rethinking the Ethics of John: "Implicit Ethics" in the Johannine Writings*, ed. Jan G. van der Watt and Ruben Zimmermann, CNNTE 3, WUNT 291 (Tübingen: Mohr Siebeck, 2012), 44–80, at 47–48n14; Michael Labahn, "'It's Only Love'—Is That All? Limits and Potentials of Johannine 'Ethic'—A Critical Evaluation of Research," in *Rethinking the Ethics of John: "Implicit Ethics" in the Johannine Writings*, ed. Jan G. van der Watt and Ruben Zimmermann, CNNTE 3, WUNT 291 (Tübingen: Mohr Siebeck, 2012), 3–43, at 20n82.

mimesis is relational, believers can actualize the love command based on their relationship with Jesus, for it is precisely Jesus's love for the believers (the original example or ὑπόδειγμα) that is the basis that motivates and empowers believers to love one another. I will argue my case in relation to four passages (John 13:34–35; 15:9–17; 1 John 3:11–18; 4:7–21) because these contain the most pertinent references to the love command and its mimesis.[89] Another issue of debate is the scope of the love command. Many Johannine scholars contend that John has an inward or sectarian outlook (due to the hostility of "the world") so that the believer's love is aimed exclusively at fellow believers (a specific conventicle ethic). After all, the Johannine Jesus "merely" commands his followers to love one another (ἀλλήλων), that is, fellow believers, without mentioning one's neighbor (see Mark 12:31), let alone one's enemies (Matt 5:44). I will discuss this issue after we have examined the four "love" passages.

The Giving of the Love Command (John 13:34–35). Knowing that his departure from this world is imminent, Jesus retreats to have a final meal with his disciples and to dispense his final teachings (John 13–17). After Judas leaves Jesus's company (13:30), the time comes for Jesus's final instructions, the first of which is the love command. In 13:34, Jesus tells his disciples, ἐντολὴν καινὴν δίδωμι ὑμῖν, ἵνα ἀγαπᾶτε ἀλλήλους, καθὼς ἠγάπησα ὑμᾶς ἵνα καὶ ὑμεῖς ἀγαπᾶτε ἀλλήλους. The first ἵνα clause is epexegetical, explaining the content of the commandment: "I give you a new commandment, *namely that* you love one another." The second ἵνα clause with the subjunctive has an imperative force, "You *should/must* love one another." The comparative conjunction καθώς in the protasis with the correlative καί in the apodosis constitutes a mimetic construction: "*Just as* I loved you, you *also* should love one another." While 13:34a provides the love command, 13:34b expands 13:34a with a mimetic imperative.

The significance of this is that the love command is not given in a vacuum but has a precedent. That is, the disciples' love for one another is based on their experience of Jesus's love for them—as they have, for example, experienced in the foot-washing (see 13:1). Echoing the language of 13:15, we may say that Jesus's love for his disciples is the ὑπόδειγμα for their love of one another. But Jesus's ὑπόδειγμα of love is more than just an object lesson or practical example that the disciples must

---

89. Twelve of the sixteen references to the love command occur in our selected passages through various means: (1) the use of ἐντολή (and its cognate verb ἐντείλασθαι) (John 13:34; 15:12, 17; 1 John 3:23; 4:21; 2 John 5); (2) an explicit imperative (1 John 2:15; 3:16; 4:11); (3) occasions where ἵνα and the subjunctive have an imperatival force (John 13:34; 15:17; 1 John 3:11, 23; 4:21); and (4) an exhortatory subjunctive sometimes functions as a command (1 John 3:18; 4:7). *All* occurrences of mimesis regarding the love command occur in our selected passages: (1) mimesis indicated by καθώς (... καί) (13:34; 15:9, 10, 12; 1 John 4:17); and (2) mimesis that is implied (1 John 3:16; 4:11).

5. Mimesis in John's Gospel and Letters

repeat. They have seen this love in action and experienced it for themselves. This implies that Jesus's love for his disciples is not simply the example he sets but also the *basis* that motivates and empowers them to do likewise. This is a significant aspect of mimesis. Mimesis springs from a relationship with Jesus where believers have observed and experienced his love *for themselves*.[90] The mimesis believers are called to is not simply imitating something Jesus did objectively but what he did *for* them. Jesus's showing his love *for* or *to* the disciples *enables* them to love one another.[91] Hence, Jesus's example is not simply the model to imitate but also the *empowering and motivational basis* from which believers can imitate him.

Finally, we learned from our study of the footwashing scene that Jesus's example of humble, limitless self-giving must translate into a corresponding tangible act by the imitator. John 13:35 confirms that the mimetic love act must be concrete or tangible; it must be observable by outsiders. Since love is the hallmark of discipleship and the command to love one another is expressed as a mimetic imperative, it follows that mimesis serves discipleship because it promotes and enacts acceptable family behavior. However, love does not only serve as an identity marker within the circle of believers, but it also has a missional focus because observing the love among believers could cause non-believers to be drawn to Jesus.

Abiding and Supreme Love (John 15:9–17). The second farewell discourse portrays two contrasting groups and attitudes: the disciples who are to exemplify love (15:1–17) and the world which is characterized by hate (15:18–16:4a). Significant for our purposes is 15:9a, where Jesus proclaims a mimesis of love: καθὼς ἠγάπησέν με ὁ πατήρ, κἀγὼ ὑμᾶς ἠγάπησα (*"Just as* the Father has loved me, I *also* have loved you"). Then, in 15:9b, there is Jesus's imperative to the disciples to abide in his love, that is, the shared love between the Father and Son.[92] Therefore, mimesis is, at heart, a *relational* concept: the imitator must rely on the one who shows the example. The answer to the question, "How can the disciples abide in Jesus's love?" is given in 15:10a—by keeping his commandments (see also 14:15, 21, 23).

---

90. See also de Boer, *Imitation of Paul*, 56–57.

91. See also D. François Tolmie, *Jesus' Farewell to the Disciples: John 13:1–17:26 in Narratological Perspective*, BINS 12 (Leiden: Brill, 1995), 201; Xavier Léon-Dufour, *Lecture de l'Évangile selon Jean*, 3 vols. (Paris: Seuil, 1988, 1990, 1993), 3:83; Volker Rabens, "Johannine Perspectives on Ethical Enabling in the Context of Stoic and Philonic Ethics," in *Rethinking the Ethics of John: "Implicit Ethics" in the Johannine Writings*, ed. Jan G. van der Watt and Ruben Zimmermann, CNNTE 3, WUNT 291 (Tübingen: Mohr Siebeck, 2012), 114–39, at 120–27.

92. See also Hans Weder, who uses the concept of the believer remaining in "ein dynamischer Lebensraum der Liebe" ("a dynamic habitat of love") ("Das neue Gebot: Eine Überlegung zum Liebesgebot in Johannes 13," in *Studien zu Matthäus und Johannes/Études sur Matthieu et Jean*, ed. Andreas Dettwiler and Uta Poplutz, ATANT 97 [Zürich: TVZ, 2009], 187–205, at 199–200).

John 15:10b clarifies that the keeping of Jesus's commandments is not meant to be a legalistic exertion of one's will but once again a mimetic act: *just as* (καθώς) Jesus has kept his Father's commandments and (hence) abides in his love, so the disciples should imitate Jesus. Jesus shows the example first, and his disciples can then (and therefore) imitate him. For those who are part of God's family, it is not (or should not be) arduous to love one another (1 John 5:3–4) because they have experienced Jesus's love for themselves and are thus empowered to imitate Jesus and articulate this love to one another. Hence, in the act of mimesis, believers experience (perhaps even receive afresh) the divine love and pass it on to others. While 15:12 simply repeats 13:34, the verses that follow provide a significant expansion. In 15:13, Jesus tells his disciples that the supreme or ultimate expression of love is to give up (literally, "to lay down") one's life for one's friends, that is, fellow believers. Through the use of θεῖναι τὴν ψυχὴν αὐτοῦ ὑπὲρ τῶν φίλων αὐτοῦ, Jesus builds a connection with 10:11, where he speaks of laying down his life for the sheep, and with 13:4, where he "lays down" his robe (proleptic of laying down his life on the cross) in order to wash his disciples' feet. Through this complex web of ideas, Jesus indicates that, at its heart, love is sacrificial and limitless—it may demand all. In sum, there is a mimetic chain of love: the starting point is the Father's love, which is directed towards his Son; the Son imitates the Father and directs his love towards the disciples; and the disciples are to imitate Jesus and express this divine love towards one another.[93]

Love in Action (1 John 3:11–18). The first reference to Jesus's love command in the Johannine Epistles occurs in 1 John 3:11, and in the verses thereafter, John elaborates on what this love should look like.[94] Cautioning his audience against imitating the behavior of Cain, John reminds his audience that they know what love is because Jesus has demonstrated it in laying down his life for the sheep (1 John 3:16; see also John 15:13; 10:11). Moreover, 1 John 3:16 includes an implicit mimetic imperative: "He laid down his life for us—likewise (καί) we ought to lay down our lives for our fellow believers." Believers ought to (ὀφείλειν) imitate Jesus in laying down their lives for their fellow believers (οἱ ἀδελφοί), that is, they should demonstrate a love that is self-giving and limitless. John then stresses that love must be tangible and should be demonstrated *in action* (1 John 3:17). He sets a very practical test before his audience: if you see a fellow believer with a need

---

93. See also Fernando F. Segovia, *The Farewell of the Word: The Johannine Call to Abide* (Minneapolis: Fortress, 1991), 152–55; Frey, "Love-Relations," 194; Augenstein, *Liebesgebot*, 70. While van der Watt also recognizes that love in John is a chain, he considers it primarily reciprocal rather than mimetic (*Grammar*, 1:311–15, 328).

94. Although ἡ ἀγγελία is used rather than ἡ ἐντολή, undoubtedly John harks back to John 13:34.

and you have the means to help (ἔχειν τὸν βίον τοῦ κόσμου), you cannot refuse to show compassion (κλείειν τὰ σπλάγχνα αὐτοῦ).[95] John effectively reasons that if God's love truly resides in a believer, the person must express this love in concrete action. He sums it up with the exhortation to love ἐν ἔργῳ καὶ ἀληθείᾳ (in action-and-truth or truthful action) rather than by word or speech (1 John 3:18; see also 2 John 1; 3 John 1). John's point is that love must be both demonstrable and truthful—*a tangible act of limitless self-giving*. The Johannine literature only provides two concrete examples of love in action (the footwashing in John 13 and economic assistance in 1 John 3:17), but believers do not need a list of potential actions. Instead, for John, love becomes the dominating moral force and attitude of the believers' behavior so that *all* their actions should be informed and characterized by love. Besides, love is a primary identity marker of God in relationships, and such a relationship cannot be spelled out in every detail.[96]

God's Love Compels (1 John 4:7–21). John starts the section with the exhortation to love one another, appealing this time not to a commandment (as in 1 John 3:11) but to God's very nature (1 John 4:7–8; see also 4:16b). The logic is that those who belong to God (who is love) will also love because those who love are born of God and know God (in relationship). From 1 John 4:9–11, I infer three principles. First, God's initiative to love precedes that of believers (see also 1 John 4:19). The implication is that believers *can* love *because* (they have experienced that) God loves them.[97] Second, believers *should* love because God loves them.[98] The combination of the verb ὀφείλειν and the phrase οὕτως . . . καί in 1 John 4:11 provides a mimetic imperative, "If [as is the case] God loves us in this way [described in 1 John 4:9–10],

---

95. Judith M. Lieu remarks that the situation envisaged here may not have been unusual because the economic realities of the early Roman Empire were such that most the population lived close to the breadline and were particularly vulnerable to the uncertainties of unemployment or food supply (*I, II & III John: A Commentary* [Louisville: Westminster John Knox, 2008], 151).

96. See also Paul's ethical exhortations "to keep in step with the Spirit" and "to be guided by the Spirit." Similarly, van der Watt concludes that the relational nature of the Johannine concept of love "elevates ethics above a list of rules to reciprocal *interpersonal relationship*-orientated loyalty" ("Ethics and Ethos," 165 [original emphasis]).

97. See also Schulz, who states that "Die gegenseitige ἀγάπη der Christen gründet in der persönlich erfahrenen, zuvorkommenden Liebe Gottes" ("The mutual ἀγάπη of Christians is based on the personally experienced, accommodating love of God") (*Nachfolgen und Nachahmen*, 247). Similarly, Udo Schnelle remarks that "Gottes Gabe der Liebe ermöglicht die Liebe der Glaubenden zueinander" ("God's gift of love enables believers to love one another") (*Die Johannesbriefe*, ThHK 17 [Leipzig: Evangelische Verlagsanstalt, 2010], 152).

98. God's proactive love for "us" creates the obligation to love one another in turn, that is, those who are fellow recipients of God's love (Lieu, *I, II & III John*, 184).

we also ought to love one another." Third, believers should love *in action* because God did, too. God's visible demonstration of his love in sending his only Son into the world as an atoning sacrifice to provide forgiveness and life (1 John 4:9–10) speaks of a love that is tangible, limitless, and sacrificial.

The latter part of the passage continues to unpack the mimetic concept of love. The καθώς . . . καί construction in 1 John 4:17 expresses an "existential" mimesis: "Just as he is, we also are in this world." Contra the majority of scholars who contend that the referent of ἐκεῖνος is Jesus, I tentatively suggest it is God.[99] Admittedly, all other occurrences of ἐκεῖνος in 1 John most likely refer to Jesus (2:6; 3:3, 5, 7, 16), but the focus in 1 John 4:7–21 is God rather than Jesus. In the light of the entire passage, verse 17 can then be paraphrased as "Just as God is love and has shown it, we also are to be characterized by love in action in this world." The significance of this mimesis is that the believers are to imitate *on earth* the God who is in heaven. In 1 John 4:20, John pushes this idea further when he indicates that one cannot (claim to) love the unseen God and hate fellow believers who can be seen, so love for God and love for one another are inextricably linked. John effectively stresses that there must be *a mimetic correspondence between the believer on earth and God in heaven* in that the believer must reflect God's nature through tangible acts of love. In their mimesis of God's love, believers provide a visible, concrete expression on earth of who God is.[100] The logical conclusion is that whoever claims to love God must (the ἵνα with the subjunctive has an imperative force) love their fellow believer also (1 John 4:21).

The Scope of the Love Command (and Other Forms of Mimesis). One issue that we must discuss is the scope of the intended objects or beneficiaries of the love command. This relates to the referent of ἀλλήλων in the command ἀγαπᾶν ἀλλήλων in John 13:34 (and other texts where the love command occurs). The same applies to the footwashing episode where Jesus commands his disciples ἀλλήλων νίπτειν τοὺς πόδας (13:14). Hence, when Jesus commands his disciples to wash one another's feet and to love one another, we must ask to whom such service and love should be extended. Since ἀλλήλων is a reciprocal pronoun, the referent seems to be fellow believers or members of God's family.[101] This idea is strengthened by the

---

99. See also Fernando F. Segovia, *Love Relationships in the Johannine Tradition: Agapē/Agapan in 1 John and the Fourth Gospel*, SBLDS 58 (Chico, CA: Scholars Press, 1982), 256n137.

100. Just as Jesus was God's representative on earth (e.g. John 1:18), so believers are now the representatives of God and Jesus on earth. Contra Leslie J. Houlden, who claims that "for John the believer has no duties towards 'the world'" (*Ethics in the New Testament* [Harmondsworth: Penguin, 1973], 36).

101. Regarding the use of ἀλλήλων, van der Watt observes that where this term is linked to love in antiquity, the context is virtually always that of family or friends in order to express "an

5. Mimesis in John's Gospel and Letters

use of other ingroup language, such as ἀδελφός ("brother," i.e. fellow believer), τὰ τέκνα τοῦ θεοῦ ("children of God"), and φίλος ("friend") in the context of the love command (15:13; 1 John 2:8–11; 3:10–17; 4:20–21).[102] However, while the mimetic acts of service and love are intended for the community of believers, it does not imply an inward or sectarian outlook.

I present a threefold argument that John or Jesus did intend a broader group of recipients concerning the mimetic acts of service and love than just the community of believers. First, Jesus washed Judas's feet even though he had already been identified as an outsider (John 6:70–71; 13:2). While one could argue that Judas was an outsider and the footwashing did not benefit him (13:10–11)—suggesting that we should not extend humble service to outsiders—the point is that Jesus extends his salvific service to everyone and does not exclude anyone. That Jesus's salvific service does not benefit everyone to whom it is offered is another issue.

Second, John 13:35 indicates that the love command has an effect beyond the community of faith; that is, ἀγαπᾶν ἀλλήλων (insider-love) benefits πάντες (outsiders). Besides, if divine love has a cosmic scope (John 3:16; 1 John 3:16; 4:9–10), it naturally follows that the believer's love for fellow believers must also have an outward aspect.

Third, for John, mimesis has a centrifugal effect. In section 5.3, we learned that the Son–Father mimesis occurs for the sake of others so that through mimetic acts such as sending, speaking, giving life, and so on, Jesus makes God known to people and extends to them divine benefits such as life, love, and salvific truth. It would then be logical that the believer–Jesus mimesis also has an outward aspect in that various mimetic acts are done not just for the sake of believers but also for others. Indeed, we noted that believers' imitating Jesus by loving one another also has an outward dimension. In addition, the purpose of believers' being sent into the world just as Jesus was sent (John 17:18; 20:21) is to testify about Jesus (15:27) and continue his life-giving mission so that people may come to believe (17:20).

---

egalitarian relationship expecting common reciprocation within that particular group" ("Ethics and Ethos," 159). See also Michael Wolter, "Die ethische Identität christlicher Gemeinden in neutestamentlicher Zeit," in *Woran Orientiert Sich Ethik?*, ed. Wilfried Härle and Reiner Preul, MJT 13 (Marburg: Elwert, 2001), 61–90, at 84–86.

102. Differently, Wolfgang Schrage states cautiously that "everyone is 'potentially' included in 'one another'" (*The Ethics of the New Testament*, trans. David E. Green [Edinburgh: T&T Clark, 1988], 318). Others even argue that the term "brother" in 1 John is sometimes synonymous for "neighbor" (Rudolf Bultmann, *The Johannine Epistles*, Hermeneia [Minneapolis: Fortress, 1973], 28; Schnackenburg, *Johannine Epistles*, 110–14; Victor Paul Furnish, *The Love Command in the New Testament* [London: SCM, 1972], 152–54). While I am sympathetic to these views, they seem textually untenable.

Likewise, the mimetic unity among believers (their unity is modeled on the unity of the Father and Son) attests to outsiders that Jesus is sent by God, that he is God's authorized agent (17:21).

It thus seems reasonable to conclude that John and Jesus intended the mimetic acts of service and love primarily for the community of faith, but a broader group of recipients should not be excluded.[103] While John focuses on the mimetic dynamics within the divine family, by no means does he deny that such behavior should be extended to outsiders. Perhaps the idea is that believers should first learn or practice serving and loving fellow believers before they can extend such demanding ethics beyond their circle. John's focus on how believers should exist and behave in God's family is not in tension with the cosmic scope of his narrative.

Summary. Our central question was how believers can realize in action Jesus's ethical imperative "to love one another." I have argued that the love command is actualized through mimesis, where Jesus's own love for the disciples is the basis (ὑπόδειγμα), motivation, and empowerment for believers to imitate Jesus by loving one another. In fact, in the act of mimesis, believers likely experience Jesus's love afresh in order to extend it to others—first to fellow believers but also to those outside the Christian group. The mimetic love act has three main characteristics: (1) it must be a sacrificial and limitless act of self-giving; (2) it must be a concrete, tangible, observable act; and (3) it must be a truthful act—it should reflect the true nature of divine love. Actualizing Jesus's love command through mimesis serves two main causes. First, it is a vital identity marker of the members of God's family. Second, it provides a concrete expression of God's love on earth, and this tangible testimony may attract others to know and experience God for themselves.

5.4.4. Existential Mimesis

The previous sections explored how believers might imitate Jesus through actions, which we call "performative mimesis," but the Johannine literature also contains many examples of mimesis where believers imitate Jesus in a particular state of existence or being through the use of the verb εἶναι. This "existential mimesis" appears mostly in John 17 and 1 John 3–4.

To Be One. Both in John 17:11 and 17:22, Jesus uses the near identical phrase

---

103. See also Beth M. Stovell, "Love One Another and Love the World: The Love Command and Jewish Ethics in the Johannine Community," in *Christian Origins and the Establishment of the Early Jesus Movement*, ed. Stanley E. Porter and Andrew W. Pitts, TENTS 12 (Leiden: Brill, 2018), 426–58; Gorman, *Abide and Go*, 156–78 (he even speaks of "enemy-love"); Shin, *Ethics in the Gospel of John*, 154–58; van der Watt, *Grammar*, 1:320–24.

ἵνα ὦσιν ἓν καθὼς ἡμεῖς ἕν ("that they may be one just as we are one") to describe the unity that he desires among believers. The comparative conjunction καθώς indicates that the oneness or unity among believers is patterned on the oneness or unity of the Father and Son (see also 10:30).[104] Thus, 17:11, 22 contain a mimetic construction indicating that the unity among believers is an imitation of the unity in the Godhead. I suggest that while the expression εἶναι ἕν ("to be one") is primarily functional or relational language for the intimate relationship between the Father, Son, and believers, an ontological dimension in terms of a mystical union cannot be ruled out. Indeed, using the category of "relational ontology," 17:11, 22 speaks of a quasi-literal union between the believers and God. The significance of understanding the mimetic union among believers in terms of relational ontology is that John depicts this reality not so much in either static ontological or fluid relational categories but as a dynamic and transformative communion or relationship, which affects both the believers' identity and behavior, both their being and doing in the world. The unity among believers and with the Father and Son is a tangible unity of love that can be observed by outsiders; it is a testimony to the world (17:23; see also 17:21; 13:35).

Not to Be of the World. In John 17:14 and 17:16, the identical phrase οὐκ εἰσὶν ἐκ τοῦ κόσμου καθὼς ἐγὼ οὐκ εἰμὶ ἐκ τοῦ κόσμου shows that Jesus's followers no longer have their origins in this world. Any person, by physical birth, belongs to the natural world but a birth of God or the Spirit propels them into the world of God (1:13; 3:5). The preposition ἐκ frequently denotes origin in John's Gospel, where John's dualistic scheme depicts a contrast between those who are ἐκ θεοῦ/πνεύματος (1:13; 3:5) and those who are ἐκ τοῦ κόσμου (8:23) or ἐκ τοῦ διαβόλου/πονηροῦ.[105] Thus, believers "imitate" or mirror Jesus's existence in that they are no longer ἐκ the world because they have become ἐκ God. Shin aptly states, "ἐκ-status in John's Gospel is not primarily concerned with promoting sociopolitical separation from the world but rather presupposes active engagement with the world while keeping oneself pure from the worldly pressures and temptations for the purpose of influencing the world."[106]

To Be Sent. The καθώς ... καί construction in John 17:18 indicates a mimesis where Jesus's sending of the disciples into the world imitates God's sending of

---

104. Jesus's claim that he and the Father are "one" may be a modification of Israel's Shema in Deut 6:4 (Craig S. Keener, *The Gospel of John: A Commentary* [Peabody, MA: Hendrickson, 2003], 826), thus showing his awareness of being included in the divine identity. One could object, however, because εἷς in Deut 6:4 LXX is masculine whereas ἕν in John 10:30 is neuter, so ontological unity is probably not in view in John. In 1 Cor 8:6, referring to εἷς θεὸς ὁ πατήρ and εἷς κύριος Ἰησοῦς Χριστός, it is more certain that Paul intends a deliberate modification of the Shema.

105. See also van der Watt, *Grammar*, 1:157–60.

106. Shin, *Ethics in the Gospel of John*, 177.

Jesus into the world (see also 20:21). In other words, 17:18 and 20:21 depict a mimetic agency in that just as Jesus is God's agent in the world, so the believers are Jesus's agents in the world. Although the active construction in Greek indicates a performative mimesis—Jesus's act of sending the disciples imitates the Father's act of sending him—the corollary is an implied existential mimesis where the disciples find themselves in the same situation Jesus was in. The significance of this mimetic construction is that the disciples are ultimately God's ambassadors in the world and might have the same effect Jesus had as God's first agent. Indeed, Jesus indicates in 17:20 that people will believe in him based on the disciples' words, which probably refers to their Spirit-informed testimony (15:26–27).

To Be in the Father and Son. While John 17:21a expresses Jesus's desire for unity among believers, 17:21b expands on this pithy phrase by means of a mimetic construction: just as the Father and Son indwell each other, so may all believers also indwell the Father and Son (καθὼς σύ, πάτερ, ἐν ἐμοὶ κἀγὼ ἐν σοί, ἵνα καὶ αὐτοὶ ἐν ἡμῖν ὦσιν). John 17:21–23 clarifies that "to be one" and "to be in" are synonymous existential concepts. This appears to be a kind of existential mimesis where the indwelling of believers by the Father and Son is patterned on and is a part of the unity between the Father and Son. The existential concepts of oneness and indwelling go to the heart of the believers' identity because they are shaped as they share in the divine identity. Identity has to do with the notion of self (personhood) or a set of qualities, values, characteristics, and behavior that distinguishes one person from another. The concept of communion best captures the essence of God's identity. While the literal term κοινωνία occurs only in 1 John 1:3–7, the concept of communion is widespread in the Johannine literature through the terms for oneness/unity (ἕν εἶναι) and indwelling (μένειν ἐν; [εἶναι] ἐν). Hence, communion (fellowship, oneness, unity, indwelling) appears to be the most significant identity marker of the divine family, and mimesis is an important mechanism through which identity is shaped.

To Be Where Jesus Is. In John 17:24, Jesus expresses the desire that all future believers will also be where he is (ὅπου εἰμὶ ἐγὼ κἀκεῖνοι ὦσιν μετ' ἐμοῦ). The word καί, here, does not function as a coordinating conjunction ("and") but as an adverb ("also"). Since Jesus does not clarify, the reader may wonder what location ὅπου refers to. The phrase ὅπου εἰμὶ ἐγὼ also occurs in 7:34, 36; 12:26; 14:3, and it is the mimetic construction in 14:3 (ἵνα ὅπου εἰμὶ ἐγὼ καὶ ὑμεῖς ἦτε) that particularly sheds light on the referent of ὅπου. Usually, 14:2–3 is taken to mean an eschatological, heavenly abode where believers will be reunited with Jesus after death,[107] but

---

107. See, for example, Steven M. Bryan, "The Eschatological Temple in John 14," *BBR* 15 (2005): 187–98.

5. Mimesis in John's Gospel and Letters

Coloe makes a better case for seeing 14:2–3 as a reference to God's household or family on earth, which Jesus makes ready for believers through his death and resurrection.[108] Via the cross, Jesus prepares a permanent place for his followers, and therefore, after the resurrection, he can, for the first time, call them "brothers" (20:17) to affirm their family membership. Therefore, the mimetic expression that believers will be in the same place where Jesus is refers to their place in God's family. Just as Jesus is part of God's household, so too will believers reside in that household (see also 8:34–36).

To Be Like Jesus. The subject of φανερωθῇ in 1 John 3:2b is probably Jesus because he often is the subject of the passive form of φανεροῦν in this letter (1:2; 2:28; 3:5, 8). While Jesus's being revealed in 1:2; 3:5, 8 refers to the incarnation, the reference in 2:28 is the Parousia (παρουσία), and this idea is key in the entire section 2:28–3:3. The essence of 3:2, therefore, seems clear: believers are God's children in the present but anticipate their future existence—for only at the Parousia will they be transformed into the likeness of Christ. The difficulty is in deciding on the nature of the believers' transformation. Since mimesis is present in the immediate context (3:3, 7), it is perhaps in view here, too, and indicated by the comparative adjective ὅμοιος ("like," "of the same nature"). Regarding the issue of how believers will be like Jesus at the Parousia, I suggest the idea is not so much to become divine but to become like him in his humanity—to become truly human (but see further section 5.6 on theosis). This would not only refer to the resurrection body spoken of elsewhere in the New Testament but also to Jesus's character displayed in his humanity—characteristics such as love, obedience, humility, and so on.[109] In light of the prominent Johannine connection between identity and behavior, this transformation will most likely be a gradual process, starting with a person's entry into God's family (εἶναι τέκνον θεοῦ) and culminating at the final day (εἶναι ὅμοιοι αὐτῷ).

To Be Righteous. First John 3:7 contains the mimetic idea that believers are (expected to be) righteous just as he is righteous, where the comparative conjunction καθώς indicates the mimesis. Again, while it is unclear whether the referent of ἐκεῖνος is God or Jesus, since Jesus is the subject in 3:4–6, 8 (and probably also in 3:2b–3), he is most likely also in view in 3:7 (see also 2:1). In which case, Jesus is the example to emulate regarding being and behaving in accordance with what God requires.

---

108. Mary L. Coloe, *Dwelling in the Household of God: Johannine Ecclesiology and Spirituality* (Collegeville, MN: Liturgical Press, 2007), 108–12, 145–48.
109. The idea of believers becoming like Jesus is also present in Paul (e.g., Rom 8:29; 2 Cor 3:18; 4:11; Phil 3:21) and Peter (2 Pet 1:4).

To Be in the World. The καθώς ... καί construction in 1 John 4:17 expresses an existential mimesis: "Just as he is, we are also in this world" (καθὼς ἐκεῖνός ἐστιν καὶ ἡμεῖς ἐσμεν ἐν τῷ κόσμῳ τούτῳ). Contra the majority of scholars, I maintain that the referent of ἐκεῖνος is God rather than Jesus.[110] Although the demonstrative pronoun ἐκεῖνος in 1 John, in five out of seven instances, clearly refers to Jesus (2:6; 3:3, 5, 7, 16; in 5:16, the referent is sin), the focus throughout 1 John 4:7–21 is God. Besides, if there is a mimetic idea in this text, the phrase ἐν τῷ κόσμῳ τούτῳ must be matched by a corresponding spatial location with reference to God—heaven. The verse can, therefore, be paraphrased as follows: "Just as God in heaven is characterized by love, so believers on earth are to be characterized by love." In other words, believers are to imitate God in one of his chief attributes so that this loving, invisible God can be made known on earth.[111]

Summary. Although performative mimesis remains the prominent category in the Johannine writings, existential mimesis nevertheless accounts for a third of all mimetic occurrences (see section 5.2). We noted that the Johannine concept of existential mimesis, as far as it relates to people, comprises no less than eight different modes of being: to be one; to be not of the world; to be sent; to be in God; to be where Jesus is; to be like Jesus; to be righteous; to be in the world. These modes of being can be aggregated into three clusters. *Relationally*, believers are where Jesus is (in God's family), which means being in (relationship with) God and being united with him and fellow believers. *Missionally*, believers are not of the world, yet they are sent into the world to be representatives of God's love in the world. *Existentially*, in imitation of Jesus, believers are expected to be righteous (through right behavior) and, by extrapolation, develop other characteristics that God approves of, and eventually be transformed into the true humanity of Jesus.[112] The significance of the category of existential mimesis is that John envisages the believers' existence to be patterned on the person of Jesus. Existential mimesis

---

110. In fact, Segovia is the only modern scholar who views God as the referent (*Love Relationships*, 256n137). Centuries earlier, Reformer John Calvin commented on this verse, "By these words [as he is] ... [John] means that we in our turn are required to resemble the image of God. Therefore, what God is in heaven, He bids us be in this world" (*The Gospel according to St John 11–21 and the First Epistle of John*, trans. T. H. L. Parker [Edinburgh: Saint Andrew Press, 1961], 295).

111. If, however, the referent is Jesus, the mimetic idea is most likely that just as Jesus is in the Father's love, so are believers in Jesus's love.

112. Shin, who follows me closely, identifies four traits of Jesus for imitation: love (which we discussed in section 5.4.3), unity, mission, and ἐx-status (*Ethics in the Gospel of John*, 138, 141–42). The reason that Shin finds fewer examples of mimesis than we do is that he only looks at καθώς to identify Jesus's imitable traits. Williams also notes the relational and missional aspects in John 17, and links these with the cross to create the concept of "cruciform mimetic participation" ("Good News," 164–77).

is transformational in that the believer's life and character are being shaped by that of the Father and Son.

5.4.5. Conclusion

In this section, we explained the scope, nature, and mechanics of the believer's mimesis of Jesus and, in some instances, God. Although we found only conceptual traces of mimesis in our examination of ἀκολουθεῖν, μένειν, and family, it nevertheless points to the idea that mimesis occurs within the context of discipleship in the divine family. It is to those who have come to Jesus and pledged allegiance to him that Jesus outlinzes the kind of behavior and character he expects where mimesis proves to be instrumental. The most explicit and elaborate evidence for the believer–Jesus mimesis in the Johannine literature is found in the footwashing pericope and the love command in John 13.

The footwashing proved instrumental in our understanding of mimesis in John because of its explicit mimetic model of observing and interpreting the example that needs imitating, and the consequent carrying out of a recontextualized mimetic act, which indicates for John that *mimesis is a cognitive and creative process*. This mimetic model of showing → understanding → doing → being is also present in the passages where the love command occurs: (1) the disciples have seen and experienced Jesus's love; (2) they have to understand or interpret Jesus's love as being a concrete act of limitless self-giving; (3) they have to perform a tangible mimetic act of love; and (4) the actualization of Jesus's love command through mimesis ensures they will be or abide in Jesus's love.

Even though this mimetic model is not reiterated in its entirety elsewhere in the Johannine literature, we can detect certain aspects. For example, the disciples have probably "observed" the unity of the Father and Son that they must emulate among themselves from hearing Jesus speak about it on numerous occasions (e.g., John 10:30; 14:10; 17:21–23). So, when Philip asks Jesus about showing them the Father, Jesus expresses his incredulity by referring to the time the disciples spent with him, during which they could have deduced that his tangible unity with the Father meant that seeing him equals seeing the Father (14:8–9; see also 12:45). The disciples must have discerned from Jesus's teaching that he was sent by God and was not of the world so that when Jesus holds out these examples to them in 17:14, 16, 18 to explain their being in the world in imitation of him, they would have understood it. Or, when John reminds his readers in 1 John 2:6 that they should behave like Jesus, no explicit behavior is mentioned precisely because this causes them to reflect on Jesus's life and think through how they can imitate him.

The Johannine mimetic model indicates that mimesis is a relational concept. Mimesis springs from a relationship where Jesus sets himself as an example to imitate for his disciples. The disciples' observation and experience of Jesus's original act probably also motivates and empowers them to imitate him. At the same time, the believers' imitation of Jesus sustains and strengthens their relationship with Jesus and with one another and ensures continued access to various divine benefits. Mimesis thus affirms and reinforces the social fabric of the divine family. Yet, although mimesis primarily occurs in and for the community of believers, it also has a broader scope of recipients and aims to draw people into this community.

Our mimetic model also indicates that mimesis is a sensory, cognitive, and volitional process. Mimesis involves both sensory and cognitive perception in that the imitator must observe the original act or state and interpret it. Then, the imitator must determine the appropriate form that a corresponding mimetic act can take and decide to carry it out. The broad array of mimetic expressions in John can be reduced to two basic types of mimesis: *performative mimesis* and *existential mimesis*. Performative mimesis is the most prevalent form (accounting for two-thirds of all mimetic occurrences), and understandably so because mimesis is usually associated with the imitation of an activity. Yet, the category of existential mimesis is remarkably frequent (accounting for a third of all mimetic occurrences) and varied (eight kinds of clear existential mimesis and two kinds of quasi-existential mimesis). In addition, existential mimesis is significant in that it directly contributes to John's understanding of the believer's identity, whereas performative mimesis does so indirectly (habitual mimetic behavior leads to becoming like Jesus over time).

In section 5.3, we saw that mimesis mediates the divine reality to people, and in this section, we also noted the mediatory function of mimesis in that *authentic mimesis mediates Jesus*. Regarding the commands to serve and love one another, for example, mimesis *mediates* the original experience of Jesus to the beneficiaries, who can thus experience Jesus for themselves. There must be a strong correspondence between the believer's mimetic act and Jesus's original act, so much so that the believer's mimetic act becomes a channel through which the beneficiaries can experience both Jesus and his humble, loving service for themselves. This also explains John 13:20, where Jesus declares that "whoever receives one whom I send, receives me." In short, mimesis mediates the original experience of Jesus to the recipient, who can then possibly respond to him.[113] This indicates that mimesis benefits both the imitator and the recipient of the mimetic act (mimesis for the sake of others).

The paradigm for the believer–Jesus mimesis is the Son–Father mimesis, thus logically linking sections 5.3 and 5.4. The significance of this is twofold. First, Jesus's method of using personal example to move his followers towards the kind

---

113. Although the idea that a person could experience Jesus himself through the believer's mimesis can seem fanciful, this was the testimony of those dying on the streets of Calcutta about Mother Teresa.

of behavior and character he expects from them by means of mimesis did not arise in a vacuum but was learned from his Father. Second, we can detect a mimetic chain where Jesus imitates the Father and, in turn, becomes the example for the disciples to imitate.[114] Having outlined in detail the Son–Father and believer–Jesus/God mimesis, we now turn to the issue of what role mimesis plays in Johannine ethics.[115]

5.5. The Place of Mimesis in Johannine Ethics

The aim of this section is to determine the place that mimesis occupies in Johannine ethics. The central question is this: Is mimesis central or peripheral to Johannine ethics? I will pursue two lines of argument to suggest that mimesis occupies a central place in Johannine ethics.[116]

The Statistical Argument. I will focus on the most prominent form of mimesis in John to argue my case, namely the believer's mimesis of Jesus and, occasionally, God.[117] I suggest a simple two-step procedure to determine the place of mimesis in Johannine ethics. First, taking the most rewarding route into Johannine ethics—to study the values, norms, and behavior embedded in the Johannine narrative—I will identify a list of verbs that indicate moral behavior or existence in the Johannine writings. Second, I will determine which of these moral activities mimesis is linked to. This should give an indication of the place of mimesis in Johannine ethics. An examination of the Johannine writings reveals the following behavioral and existential activities in relation to believers that involve mimesis:

---

114. Trozzo rejects a simple imitation of Jesus and claims that "it is not Jesus' direct actions in the Gospel that serve as an ethical example. Rather, the audience is called to imitate Jesus' unity with God and his response to God" (*Johannine Ethics*, 96). We have shown, however, that the Johannine writings mention a wide range of concrete actions of Jesus suited to imitation.

115. There are a few further instances of the believer–Jesus mimesis in the Johannine literature: "to live" (John 6:57); mutual knowing (10:14b–15a); "to obey" (15:10); to do Jesus's works (14:12); "to behave" (1 John 2:6); "to purify oneself" (1 John 3:3). For these, see Bennema, *Mimesis*, 135–39.

116. For a broader understanding of Johannine ethics, see Bennema, "Model of Johannine Ethics," 433–56. For a more extensive case that mimesis is the center of Johannine ethics, see Bennema, "Centre of Johannine Ethics," 142–62.

117. I could make a case regarding the Son–Father mimesis, but it is difficult, methodologically, to relate this intra-divine mimesis to ethics as ethics usually relates to human relationships. I will, however, stress that, for John, divine mimesis is expressed in a variety of behaviors. So, while John 5:19–20 speaks of the Son–Father mimesis in a broad, general sense (Jesus imitates the Father in everything), specific mimetic activities include giving life (5:21), speaking (8:26, 28; 12:50; 15:15), loving (15:9), honoring (17:22a), and sending (20:21). Hence, we may conclude that mimesis is central to divine interaction.

PART 2   MIMESIS IN EARLY CHRISTIANITY

Activities of Behavior or Existence	Mimesis	Mimetic Strength
to abide or remain	—	
to ask (the Father in Jesus's name)	—	
to be in or sent into the world	17:18; 20:21; 1 John 4:17	strong
to be like Jesus	1 John 3:2	medium
to be not of the world	17:14, 16	strong
to be one or in	17:11, 21, 22	strong
to be righteous	1 John 3:7	strong
to be where Jesus is	12:26; 14:3; 17:24	strong
to bear fruit[118]	—	
to believe[119]	—	
to do a particular action[120]	14:12 (do Jesus's works)	medium
to follow Jesus	—	
to forgive sins[121]	—	
to harvest or draw people[122]	—	
to know or be in the know	10:14–15	weak
to live or be alive	6:57; 14:19	weak
to love one another	13:34; 15:12; 1 John 4:11	strong
to obey	15:10	strong
to purify oneself	1 John 3:3	medium
to serve or lay down one's life for one another	13:14–15; 1 John 3:16	strong/medium
to testify	—	
to walk in the light or truth[123]	1 John 2:6	strong

118. I do not count the mimesis in 15:4 as this does not relate to the believer–Jesus/God mimesis but to believers being likened to or "imitating" branches.
119. In John 6:29, πιστεύειν is identified as ἔργον.
120. See also ποιεῖν in John 13:15; 14:12; 15:14; 1 John 1:6; 2:29; 3:7, 22; 5:2.
121. John 20:23.
122. John 4:35–38; 21:6–8.
123. John uses "truth" as an ethical category because it refers to the reality of who God is

5. Mimesis in John's Gospel and Letters

I observe that fourteen of these twenty-two activities (i.e., 64 percent) are related to, or actualized by, mimesis. Although these have various degrees of mimetic strength, it seems reasonable to conclude that mimesis is a dominant aspect of Johannine ethics. This shows that Jesus (and sometimes God) sets the example for appropriate family existence and behavior that he expects his disciples to adopt through mimesis.

The Argument from the Nature of the Divine–Human Relationship. In addition to the statistical evidence, another argument for the centrality of mimesis in Johannine ethics is that it is integral to the divine–human relationship. I will argue that the divine identity and behavior are modeled to believers by means of mimesis. The claim that mimesis is central to the dynamics of the divine family is based on the initial finding in section 5.3 of a mimetic chain where the Father sets the example for the Son to imitate, and in turn, the Son sets the example for his followers to imitate. We learned that through the Son–Father mimesis, believers share in the divine identity characterized by the moral goods of life, light, love, truth, and honor because in imitating the Father, Jesus mediates these moral commodities to people. While we suggested this in the conclusion to section 5.3, I will now expand on this.[124]

The relationship between the Father and Son, in which believers come to share, is characterized by the moral qualities of life, light, love, truth, and honor. Believers can share in these divine qualities or attributes because they are extended to them *through mimesis,* shaping both their identity and behavior. Regarding *life,* just as the Son is a source of life in imitation of the Father (John 5:21, 26), so believers become a derivative source of life in imitation of Jesus (4:14; 7:38–39; 17:20). In other words, just as the Son lives because of the Father, so believers live because of the Son (6:57; 14:19). For example, when the Samaritan woman has drunk from the life-giving water that Jesus offers her, she becomes a mimetic source of life in leading her fellow villagers to the source of life (4:28–30, 39). Likewise, the disciples' testimony will stimulate life-giving belief (17:20) because they have become a derivative source of life (7:38–39). Access to the divine life is "passed on," as it were, via a mimetic chain from the Father to the Son to believers to potential believers.

As for *love,* Jesus imitates the Father in a sacrificial act motivated by love: just as the Father's love for the world compelled him to give up his Son, so Jesus's love for

---

(14:6), and "to do the truth" (1 John 1:6) and "to walk in the truth" (2 John 4; 3 John 3–4) refer to a way of life that reflects the divine reality.

124. Van der Watt only examines love, light, and truth as the main ethical concepts (*Grammar,* 1:287–362).

PART 2   MIMESIS IN EARLY CHRISTIANITY

the world led him to give up his life. The mimetic chain of love is also evident: the Son loves the disciples just as the Father loves him (15:9), so the disciples (should) love one another, imitating Jesus's love for them (13:34; 15:12). Regarding *truth*, Jesus imitates the Father's words (John 8:26, 28; 12:50). Since truth is the essence of divine speech (8:31–32), Jesus imitates the Father and is a source of truth for people through his teaching. Believers, in turn, become a source of truth for others because their testimony is modeled on Jesus's teaching, when the Spirit of truth, who imitates Jesus's speech, communicates the truth to them (15:26–27; 16:12–15; 17:20). The mimetic aspect of truth is more abstract or derivative because despite being rooted in the mimetic language at the textual level, it surfaces more at the conceptual level of John's theology.

While the Johannine literature does not mention a Son–Father mimesis regarding *light* (light is linked to God only in 1 John 1:5), there is arguably an implied mimesis in the depiction of John the Baptist as a derivative "light" imitating Jesus as he faithfully testifies to the Light. In 5:35, John is characterized as a "lamp" (λύχνος) that shines (the verb φαίνειν occurs in John's Gospel only here and in 1:5 in reference to the Logos) and provides "light" (except for this occurrence, φῶς is used exclusively with reference to Jesus or God). John providing light refers to his activity of testifying to the Light, which elicits belief (1:7; 1:35–37; 10:41–42). By extension, believers are also called to testify to the Light (15:27), and since their testimony has the potential to provide light (17:20), it could be argued that believers "imitate" Jesus as light. Nevertheless, we must not push this idea too far. Regarding *honor*, just as the Father honors the Son, so also the Son honors believers (17:22), although we noted that this is a "weak" case of mimesis.

In sum, the core attributes and activities that characterize the Father–Son relationship also inform and shape the believers' identity and behavior through the mechanism of mimesis.[125] Thus, divine identity and behavior are modeled to believers by mimesis, so mimesis is instrumental in the divine–human relationship. In other words, the Son–Father mimesis is *for the sake of* people—the Son imitates the Father in order to extend various moral goods to people. So, it is reasonable to conclude that mimesis is central to John's family ethics because mimesis largely shapes the believer's relationship with God. The mimetic chain operates as follows: (1) the Son–Father mimesis benefits believers, and (2) the

---

125. Other mimetic activities of the Son–Father dynamic also inform the mimetic behavior of believers. For example, in the activity of sending, there is a mimetic chain where the Father sends the Son into the world and the Son, in turn, sends his followers into the world. Jesus's mission to carry out the Father's work is the model for the disciples' mission to continue this divine work (John 17:18; 20:21).

5. Mimesis in John's Gospel and Letters

believer–Jesus/God mimesis benefits other believers and non-believers. We can thus speak of a family identity and behavior shaped by mimesis.

This idea of mimesis as a critical mechanism in shaping believers' identity and behavior is pervasive in John. Concerning the footwashing, for example, merely *imitating* the actions of Jesus as a δοῦλος (behavior) within the "slave–Lord" relationship (John 13:14–16) would fall short of what is intended; the disciples must also *become* δοῦλοί to one another (identity).[126] Sacrificial service is inextricably related to adopting a δοῦλος identity, and conversely, the mimetic act of serving others affirms and shapes one's δοῦλος identity. We also see a correlation between mimetic behavior and identity elsewhere. Jesus's mimetic imperative in 13:34 serves to guide the disciples' behavior but also confirms their identity since 13:35 states, "By this everyone will know that you are my disciples (identity), if you have love for one another (behavior)." In 17:20–22, the mimetic unity among believers (identity), modeled on the unity of the Father and Son, is linked to testifying about Jesus (behavior).

The Johannine letters present a similar picture. For example, 1 John 3:7 reveals that the practice of doing what is right transforms the person into being right(eous) in imitation of Jesus. In 1 John 3:16, the imperative to believers to lay down their lives for each other, just as Jesus did, is directed at believers who have experienced a transformative relocation from death to life (1 John 3:14). In addition, practicing this sacrificial love-in-action (1 John 3:17–18) will affirm and enhance their transformation (see also 3 John 5–8). In 1 John 3:2, the transformation of believers into the likeness of Christ at the Parousia very likely results from a lifetime of imitating Jesus. Mimesis thus shapes both the believer's identity and behavior and is crucial for Johannine ethics.

Gorman largely endorses my view that mimesis is central to the Johannine ethical life.[127] Volker Rabens's position also aligns with mine. For him, loving, intimate relationships are central to Johannine ethics, with mimesis as one of the "connecting mechanisms" between what he calls "initial love" and "responsive love."[128] Since mimesis is the *primary* mechanism that drives several aspects of these intimate relationships, it sits at the heart of John's ethics. Somewhat differently, van der Watt asserts that both mimesis and reciprocity are key to Johannine ethics.[129] However, I maintain that mimesis has the edge over reciprocity. For

---

126. Van der Watt also stresses the intrinsic connection between identity and behavior, so it is surprising that he refutes the idea of the disciples becoming slaves (*Grammar*, 1:308–9n132).

127. Gorman, *Abide and Go*, 187–89.

128. Volker Rabens, "The Dilemma of Human Agency in John: Ethics and Anthropology in the Fourth Gospel," in *Images of the Human Being*, ed. Cosmin Pricop, Karl-Wilhelm Niebuhr, and Tobias Nicklas, WUNT 521 (Tübingen: Mohr Siebeck, 2024), 257–81.

129. Van der Watt, *Grammar*, 1:257–62, 525, 636; 2:88–89, 273, 393–94, 417.

PART 2   MIMESIS IN EARLY CHRISTIANITY

example, there is no clear reference to reciprocal love between God and believers, but a fair number of texts refer to mimetic love (e.g., John 13:34; 15:9, 12; 1 John 4:11).[130] While I acknowledge that the believers' love for one another in response to God's love for them has a reciprocal aspect, it is predominantly mimetic in that believers are to love one another, imitating God's love for them. In addition, we noted in section 5.3 that the reciprocity between the Father and Son is exclusive and remains within the boundaries of the Godhead, whereas mimesis is inclusive and benefits people with divine goods that are passed down a mimetic chain from the Father to the Son to believers.

Trozzo and I disagree on what goes to the heart of Johannine ethics. Trozzo contends that mimesis does not seem to be the controlling concept because of Jesus's elevated and unique status and because Jesus does not offer concrete examples for ethical living. For her, it is the unity between Jesus and God, in which believers participate, that is central to Johannine ethics.[131] It seems Trozzo has failed to consider the wide range of concrete actions that Jesus models for his followers to imitate. Besides, it is no coincidence that the first reference to mimesis in John's Gospel is the Son–Father mimesis in 5:19, which then fittingly becomes the paradigm for the believer–Jesus mimesis. Finally, if Trozzo had also considered the Johannine letters (she does so briefly in her conclusion), she may have noted that John introduces *new* forms of imitating Jesus, rooted in the life and teachings of Jesus as recorded in his Gospel (see section 5.7.3). This reveals that mimesis is more critical to Johannine ethics than Trozzo would have us believe.

Summary. What connects Johannine mimesis and ethics is that mimesis is the primary mechanism to direct the believer's identity and behavior within the context of the divine family. The core attributes and activities that characterize the Son–Father relationship (to give life and light, show love, speak truth, and bestow honor) inform and shape the believers' identity and behavior through the Son–Father mimesis. In effect, the Johannine concept of mimesis is fundamental to the divine family dynamics where Jesus imitates the Father and sets the example for believers to imitate. Based on our findings, I draw two conclusions. First, mimesis is *central* to Johannine ethics; hence, Johannine ethics is specifically *mimetic ethics*. This may seem to be an audacious claim at first, but not when we consider that the most prominent forms of Johannine ethics—service and love—are expressed by mimetic imperatives (John 13:15, 34; 15:12; 1 John 3:16; 4:11). Second, if it is the

---

130. Van der Watt admits that "there are no direct statements in John referring to believers' love for the Father," although he argues that believers' *obedience* reciprocates God's love (*Grammar*, 1:311–12, quotation from p. 311).

131. Trozzo, *Johannine Ethics*, 80, 85–96, 178–79.

primary means by which John envisages the believers' identity and behavior will be shaped, then *mimesis is instrumental to moral transformation*.

5.6. A Model of Johannine Mimesis

In this section, we will line up our findings on Johannine mimesis against our Greco-Roman model of mimesis. The footwashing episode is a fitting starting point for understanding Johannine mimesis because (1) John 13:14–15 contains Jesus's first explicit mimetic imperative to the disciples, and (2) the pericope 13:1–17, in which this imperative is embedded, describes the mechanics of mimesis. Indeed, our analysis of the footwashing in John 13 showed a four-stage process of showing→knowing→doing→being (see section 5.4.2).[132] These four stages readily correspond to stages 2–5 in our Greco-Roman model of mimesis. Adding a first stage, "Selection and Association," drawn from the Johannine writings, we can articulate a model of Johannine mimesis that is consistent with our Greco-Roman model:

1. *Selection and Association.* At the level of story, Jesus sets things in motion—he chooses his disciples and invites them to associate with him (1:39; 6:70; 15:16).[133] At the level of narrative, John encourages his audience to select and associate ("remain") with Jesus (e.g., 6:35–40, 60–71; 7:37–38; 15:1–7; 20:31). This is the crux of discipleship, and Jesus, as an example for imitation, plays a key role.

2. *Observation.* The act of footwashing is described in 13:4–12a, which has a chiastic structure:

A [v. 4] ἐγείρεται ἐκ τοῦ δείπνου
   B καὶ τίθησιν τὰ ἱμάτια καὶ λαβὼν λέντιον διέζωσεν ἑαυτόν·

---

132. Van der Watt claims that I define Johannine mimesis on the basis of my analysis of John 13 (*Grammar*, 1:257n205). On the contrary, my understanding of Johannine mimesis is based on extensive analysis of the various expressions that indicate mimesis (section 5.2) and I simply suggest that John 13 *best* shows how Johannine mimesis works.

133. In Greco-Roman antiquity and Judaism, pupils usually selected and attached themselves to a teacher or rabbi. Nevertheless, the Greek philosophical tradition also contains call stories (Shiner, *Follow Me*, 176–82). Piecing together information from John and the Synoptics creates a more complete picture. In John 1, Jesus arguably does not call any of his disciples (he only extends an invitation in 1:39) and would-be disciples seem to take the initiative. However, when Jesus says in John 6:70 and 15:16 that he took the initiative, this very likely refers to a later calling of the disciples, which is recorded in the Synoptics (Cornelis Bennema, "How Readers Construct New Testament Characters: The Calling of Peter in the Gospels in Cognitive-Narratological Perspective," *BibInt* 29 [2021]: 430–51, at 447–49).

PART 2   MIMESIS IN EARLY CHRISTIANITY

    C [v. 5]   εἶτα βάλλει ὕδωρ εἰς τὸν νιπτῆρα καὶ ἤρξατο νίπτειν τοὺς πόδας τῶν
             μαθητῶν καὶ ἐκμάσσειν τῷ λεντίῳ ᾧ ἦν διεζωσμένος.
    D [vv. 6–11]   Jesus's interaction with Peter
    C' [v. 12a]   Ὅτε οὖν ἔνιψεν τοὺς πόδας αὐτῶν
   B' [καὶ] ἔλαβεν τὰ ἱμάτια αὐτοῦ
  A' καὶ ἀνέπεσεν πάλιν

The bookends in 13:4–5 and 13:12a are significant for our understanding of mimesis because they vividly describe Jesus's movements. Instead of merely *telling* the disciples to wash one another's feet, Jesus *shows* them what to imitate.

    3. *Discernment/Interpretation.* When Jesus returns to the table after washing his disciples' feet, he does not just command his disciples to imitate his example. Instead, he asks in 13:12b whether they have *understood* what he did for them (γινώσκετε τί πεποίηκα ὑμῖν;). Jesus's question constitutes a cognitive challenge for the disciples; they must interpret Jesus's actions in order to imitate him.

    4. *Imitation.* Sandwiched between the rationale for imitation in 13:14 and 13:16 is 13:15, the fulcrum of the passage: ὑπόδειγμα γὰρ ἔδωκα ὑμῖν ἵνα καθὼς ἐγὼ ἐποίησα ὑμῖν καὶ ὑμεῖς ποιῆτε. The term ὑπόδειγμα ("example," "model," "pattern") occurs just this once in John and refers to the footwashing as the visible example that Jesus presents for his disciples to imitate. The prescribed actions in 13:14–15, "You also ought *to wash* one another's feet" and "You should also *do*," make it clear that the mimetic imperative must be expressed by a *tangible action*—a visible demonstration that is then emulated in a corresponding, concrete act. For John, mimesis is not a mindless cloning but a hermeneutical process that involves the interpretation of the original act and deciding on an appropriate mimetic act.[134]

    5. *Transformation/Assimilation.* John 13:17 indicates that mimesis results in transformation: "If you understand these things, you are μακάριοί if you do them." The term μακάριος ranges in meaning from "fortunate/happy" to "recipient of divine favor" (at times approaching the Hebrew שָׁלוֹם). We can extend this state of "blessedness" to the concept of moral transformation because the goal of mimesis is for the imitator to become like the exemplar (see also 1 John 3:2). Believers imitate Jesus in service and love for one another so that they become people characterized by love and service. From 13:14, 16, we learn that imitating Jesus the

---

134. Whether the mimetic act is a replication or faithful expression of the original act is less important; an authentic mimetic act must stay within the conceptual domain of the original act. In washing his disciples' feet, Jesus's intention is that the disciples understand the need for humble, loving service to one another *and* produce a tangible act that creatively but truthfully articulates this understanding.

5. Mimesis in John's Gospel and Letters

δοῦλος–κύριος requires not just performing acts of sacrificial service but that the disciples *become* δοῦλοί to one another, which implies transformation.

While this mimetic model does not appear in its entirety elsewhere in the Johannine literature, other texts confirm individual aspects. For instance, John 5:19–20 states that the Son can imitate the Father only because the Son *observes* (βλέπειν) all that the Father *shows* (δεικνύειν) him. While 5:19–20 speaks of the Son–Father mimesis in a general sense, other passages mention specific instances of the Son imitating the Father, such as giving life (5:21, 26), speaking (8:26, 28, 38; 12:49–50; 15:15), loving (15:9), honoring (17:22), and sending (20:21). The Son can imitate the Father because he is closely *associated* with the Father (1:18; 10:30). However, the Son does not simply replicate the Father; he *interprets* (ἐξηγηθῆναι) the Father (1:18). In turn, Jesus is able to "show" (δεικνύειν) the (invisible) Father to his followers (14:8–9). In other words, the Jesus–God mimesis is paradigmatic for the believer–Jesus mimesis.

We also noted that John 13:34b expands the love command in 13:34a with a mimetic imperative (<u>καθὼς</u> ἠγάπησα ὑμᾶς ἵνα <u>καὶ</u> ὑμεῖς ἀγαπᾶτε ἀλλήλους). This means that the love command is not given in a vacuum but is derived from a precedent, such as the footwashing where the disciples have *observed* and experienced Jesus's love for them. Echoing 13:15, Jesus's love for his disciples is the ὑπόδειγμα for their love for one another. The mimetic actions that demonstrate the believers' love for one another in different situations require interpretation.

First John 3:7 shows that the regular practice of what is right *transforms* the person—as they grow in righteousness and become more like Jesus. The mimetic transformation of believers into the likeness of Christ on the final day (1 John 3:2) is unlikely to be an instant metamorphosis from one state into another and more likely a gradual, evolutionary transformation resulting from a lifetime of imitating Jesus.

In 1 John 3:14–18, we find the mimetic model in a veiled form. In 1 John 3:16, John creates a new call for mimesis (believers are to lay down their lives for each other in imitation of Jesus), which is very likely based on his personal observation and interpretation of what Jesus taught and exemplified (see 15:13; 19:35). From this imperative to imitate Jesus's sacrificial love in 1 John 3:16, John makes the leap to the specific mimetic act of giving material aid to a fellow believer in 1 John 3:17, which certainly shows interpretation. Finally, John states in 1 John 3:14 that this regular practice of mimetic love-in-action affirms (and perhaps enhances) the fundamental transformation believers have experienced.

We will now discuss the concepts of moral reasoning and theosis in relation to our mimetic model.

Moral Reasoning. On becoming members of God's family, believers must start to think in keeping with their new environment. This new thinking, which I call "moral reasoning," should inform their behavior. Moral reasoning is to think in line with God's character and purposes and to reason according to the beliefs, values, and norms of the divine family. Moral reasoning is not optional. The list of explicit moral instructions in the Johannine writings is not exhaustive, so believers must learn to think morally in line with the divine family code, and this moral reasoning should direct their behavior.[135] Moral reasoning also applies to mimesis because Johannine mimesis is not a simplistic replication but a dynamic and creative hermeneutical process. Regarding the footwashing, we noted that Jesus's question in John 13:12b amounts to a cognitive challenge for the disciples, indicating that from observation must come understanding. They must comprehend, for example, that if their κύριος–διδάσκαλος has become a δοῦλος, no one is exempt from humble service and that they are to become δοῦλοί as well.

Other instances of Johannine mimesis reiterate the need for moral reasoning. Regarding the mimetic love command in John 13:34, any mimetic action that expresses the believers' love for one another in different situations will involve interpretation. Likewise, when believers are sent into the world by Jesus just as he was sent into the world by the Father (17:18; 20:21), it will look different for each believer. Interpretation of the mimetic unity between believers and the Father and Son (17:11, 21–22) should guide how this is worked out in the corporate life of the believing community. The generic mimetic imperative to "walk" like Jesus walked in 1 John 2:6 requires interpretation, as indicated by other expressions of περιπατεῖν in 1 John 1:6–7; 2 John 4, 6; 3 John 3–4. Hence, authentic mimesis entails moral reasoning so that Jesus's intention and attitude are interpreted and translated into a corresponding mimetic act.[136] Moral reasoning may even lead to *new forms* of mimesis. I say this because John himself does so in his first letter, creating several new forms of mimetic behavior from Jesus's teaching and personal example (see section 5.7.3).

---

135. Nico J. Grönum also argues that practicing moral deliberation is important for behavioral change; otherwise people simply fall back on instinctive behavior guided by cultural schemata ("A Return to Virtue Ethics: Virtue Ethics, Cognitive Science and Character Education," *Verbum et Ecclesia* 36.1 [2015]: 1–6, http://dx.doi.org/10.4102/ve.v36i1.1413). Likewise, Trozzo asserts that "Johannine ethics engages the audience in moral deliberation rather than delivering explicit ethical propositions" (*Johannine Ethics*, 178). Van der Watt uses the concept of discernment, referring to "*reflection* on an issue in the light of certain *ethical criteria*, leading to a motivated *decision*" (*Grammar*, 1:425–29, 529–33, 636 [quotation from p. 426; original emphasis]).

136. While Noël Lazure simply lists a few examples of mimesis in John's Gospel and 1 John without sufficient explanation, he captures the concept well when he concludes that Johannine mimesis does not refer to the literal copying of Jesus's actions but to the *translation* of what each situation requires in order to participate in Jesus's life (*Les Valeurs Morales de la Théologie Johannique* [Paris: Gabalda, 1965], 154–57).

5. Mimesis in John's Gospel and Letters

Having to interpret Jesus's example (stage 2), we came to the concept of moral reasoning, but other stages in the mimetic process also require moral reasoning. Regarding stage 1, the Johannine invitation to "come and see" (John 1:39, 46; 4:29) and the concept of "seeking Jesus" (e.g., 1:38; 6:24; 7:18; 20:15) invite the reader to discover and discern who Jesus is and whether it is appropriate to associate oneself with him. Regarding stage 3, moral reasoning is required for *both* the interpretation of the original act *and* shaping the resulting mimetic act. In other words, we might call moral reasoning the "cognitive engine" of John's mimetic ethics, driving and regulating mimetic behavior within the believing community.

Transformation and Theosis. The aim of mimesis as it relates to human behavior is transformation in that someone imitates an exemplary person in order to become like that person. The Johannine writings refer to mimetic transformation in two ways. First, when believers become members of God's family, they also share in the divine attributes of life, love, light, truth, and honor through mimesis. Participation in these divine qualities will shape and transform the believers' thinking and behavior in such a way that the believers' identity is shaped along the lines of the divine identity. Second, the concept of existential mimesis contains three expressions that involve transformation: "to be *one* with the Father and Son," "to be *in* the Father and Son," and "to be *like* Jesus" (see section 5.4.4). John's language of "oneness" (εἶναι ἕν) and "indwelling" (μένειν ἐν; [εἶναι] ἐν) is a functional or relational language describing the intimate relationship between the Father, Son, and believer. Nevertheless, an ontological dimension cannot be ruled out. While the believer may not be indwelled by or be one with God ontologically—in the sense of sharing the divine essence (and hence cross the creator/creation divide)—a divine indwelling or unity in terms of an intimate relationship with God can still be viewed in a quasi-ontological sense. Using the category of "relational ontology" (over against substance ontology), John has in mind a quasi-literal or mystical union between the believer and God.[137]

The significance of using the category of relational ontology to understand the Johannine concepts of "oneness" and "indwelling" is that John depicts this reality not so much in either static-ontological or fluid-relational categories but as a dynamic and transformative relationship that affects both the believers' being and doing in the world. Regarding the nature of the believers' transformation into the likeness of Christ at the Parousia in 1 John 3:2, we must discount the idea of believers becoming divine, lest the creator/creation divide becomes blurred.[138] Rather, the idea is to become like him in his humanity—to become truly human.

---

137. See further Bennema, *Mimesis*, 126–28.
138. See also the deceptive promise to Eve in the Garden—ἔσεσθε ὡς θεοί (Gen 3:5).

While this could refer to the resurrection body spoken of elsewhere in the New Testament, it will most likely include Jesus's character displayed in his humanity—characteristics such as love, obedience, humility, and so on. If someone opts for the term "theosis" or "deification" to describe the believer's transformation, it should probably be understood in terms of participation in God's life and character in order to become *like* God (*homoiousios*) rather than participating in God's essence in order to become God (*homoousios*). Gorman critiques my earlier hesitancy about the use of theosis,[139] and I now agree that, without crossing the creator/creation divide, the term "theosis" can be used to denote the believers' transformative participation in the life and attributes of God.[140]

Summary. The Johannine writings show a model of mimesis that is remarkably similar to that found in the Greco-Roman traditions, even though John's mimetic language does not employ the lexeme μιμεῖσθαι. Our model shows that Johannine mimesis is a complex, cognitive, creative, and participatory hermeneutical process to which believers must apply moral reasoning to interpret Jesus's examples and teaching and determine what constitutes a proper mimetic act. The transformative potential of Johannine mimesis is such that we can use the terms theosis or deification for it, albeit carefully nuanced.

5.7. The Practice of Mimesis in Johannine Christianity

Our study raises three questions regarding the workings of mimesis in Johannine Christianity. First, when John wrote his Gospel and Letters in the late first century, Jesus was long gone, so how could Johannine believers imitate an "absent" Jesus whom they could not observe?[141] By Jesus's "absence," I mean the spatial separation between Jesus in heaven and his followers on earth, even though he is "present" or accessible through the Spirit. Second, what were Johannine believers supposed to imitate about Jesus—his teachings, character, or entire lifestyle? Third, was imitation limited to the examples Jesus gave in his own life? To answer these questions, I will turn to the Johannine Letters and delineate how John's mimetic ethics might have worked among Johannine Christians in the late first century.

---

139. Gorman, *Abide and Go*, 17n62, 187–89.
140. Andrew J. Byers also carefully suggests that there is a link between mimesis and theosis (*Ecclesiology and Theosis in the Gospel of John*, SNTSMS 166 [Cambridge: Cambridge University Press, 2017], 202–6).
141. Leung, who focuses on mimesis in 1 John, does not consider this crucial issue in her "Ethics."

5. Mimesis in John's Gospel and Letters

5.7.1. The Mimesis of an "Absent" Jesus

Mimesis is a sensory process where someone usually observes an exemplar to discern what needs imitating. So how could Johannine Christians imitate Jesus when he had returned to the Father? Did mimesis mutate from first-hand observation to second-hand instruction on what to imitate? Not necessarily. In chapter 2, we noted the study by David Capes, where he showed that in antiquity, the lives of notable people were upheld as models for imitation. And while living models were preferred, the lives of great men from the past could also be "observed" (and imitated) through spoken and published accounts. Capes then explained how the Gospels, as ancient biographies of Jesus, provided early Christians with a script for imitation.[142] John's writings reveal that he also knew of living and literary examples for imitation.

The Imitation of Living Examples. While Paul presents himself and others regularly as examples for imitation (see chapter 6), John never does so in his letters. Nowhere does John tell his audience, "imitate me," as Paul does. Nevertheless, as Jeffrey Brickle notes, John's assertion, "'Our κοινωνία is with the Father and with the Son Jesus Christ' (1 John 1:3)," implies that he lived out a Christlike life before his community.[143] Only once does John explicitly refer to living examples—in 3 John 11, the only place in the Johannine writings where the lexeme μιμεῖσθαι occurs. John's exhortation to Gaius to imitate "that which is good" seems abstract, but the latter half of the verse "personalizes" the imitation: "the one who does good" most likely indicates the one who imitates "that which is good." So, considering the immediate context (3 John 9–12), John directs Gaius to Demetrius as a living example for imitation and to Diotrephes as one whose behavior should be avoided.[144] We can extend John's exhortation to all believers, instructing them to imitate what is good in the lives of other Christians.

The Imitation of Literary Examples. John has recorded the life and teachings of Jesus in his Gospel and Letters so that his audience can reconstruct this "remembered" Jesus.[145] In other words, Johannine Christians can observe and imitate

---

142. Capes, "*Imitatio Christi*," 1–19.

143. Jeffrey E. Brickle, "Transacting Virtue within a Disrupted Community: The Negotiation of Ethics in the First Epistle of John," in *Rethinking the Ethics of John: "Implicit Ethics" in the Johannine Writings*, ed. Jan G. van der Watt and Ruben Zimmermann, CNNTE 3, WUNT 291 (Tübingen: Mohr Siebeck, 2012), 340–49, at 346.

144. De Boer, *Imitation of Paul*, 85. Van der Watt seems to ignore that Demetrius is presented as an exemplar and argues that "to imitate what is good" refers to imitating God (who is good) (*Grammar*, 2:361).

145. The Johannine writings assert they are based on eyewitness testimony (note the "we"

the "reconstructed" Jesus from the Johannine text. We will see below that 1 John mentions several new ways of imitating Jesus, showing that John clearly expects his audience to be able to imitate Jesus. John draws attention to Spirit-enabled remembrance and interpretation (14:26; 16:12–15). The Spirit's role is to enable the remembrance of Jesus and guide Johannine believers in "visualizing" a reconstructed Jesus from the text to aid their imitation of him. The Johannine text thus functions as the basis for mimesis in that readers can "observe" the example of Jesus in the text and imitate him. Besides Jesus, other characters in the Johannine narrative can also function as models for readers to imitate (see also n. 30).[146] The portrayal of Thomas in John 20 especially shows that we need not distinguish between the historical disciples and later generations of believers. What the original disciples observed and remembered about Jesus's life and teaching is accessible to later believers as they hear or read the Johannine accounts. So, the "absence" of Jesus is not an obstacle to imitating him as far as John is concerned.

5.7.2. The Content of Mimesis

Considering the Johannine text as the basis for mimesis, what aspects of Jesus should Johannine Christians imitate? Should they imitate specific actions, the intentions behind those actions (resulting in a general mindset of moral discernment), or Jesus's entire lifestyle? We saw that Trozzo claims that Jesus's actions do not serve as an ethical example for imitation because they are not specific or tangible (see nn. 8 and 131). Similarly, Rahmsdorf is skeptical of Jesus as an example for imitation because (1) his actions lack concreteness and (2) are *einmalig* ("unique," "one-off") and therefore cannot be repeated.[147] I consider their claims untenable. First, the Johannine writings provide many more concrete examples for imitation than Trozzo

---

in John 1:14; 21:24; 1 John 1:1–3; see also John 19:35). In 1 John 1:1–3, John explains that he is communicating the divine realities he and others have observed firsthand (he refers to the senses of hearing, sight, and touch) to an audience that has not had this experience but can "know" (and experience) these realities through his written testimony. Before John had produced his Gospel, the oral tradition about Jesus would have been the means for "visualizing" and imitating Jesus.

146. See Cornelis Bennema, "Virtue Ethics in the Gospel of John: The Johannine Characters as Moral Agents," in *Rediscovering John: Essays on the Fourth Gospel in Honor of Frédéric Manns*, ed. L. Daniel Chrupcała, SBFA 80 (Milan: Edizioni Terra Santa, 2013), 167–81, at 174–79; Bennema, "Virtue Ethics and the Johannine Writings," in *Johannine Ethics: The Moral World of the Gospel and Epistles of John*, ed. Sherri Brown and Christopher W. Skinner (Minneapolis: Fortress, 2017), 297–317, at 277–78. For the representative value of the Johannine characters, see Cornelis Bennema, *Encountering Jesus: Character Studies in the Gospel of John*, 2nd ed. (Minneapolis: Fortress, 2014), 366–70.

147. Rahmsdorf, *Zeit und Ethik*, 432–38.

5. Mimesis in John's Gospel and Letters

and Rahmsdorf have us believe (see, for example, the table in section 5.5). Second, the cognitive tool of moral reasoning intends to guide the imitator regarding what exactly needs imitation and how to translate this into a concrete mimetic act. Third, John's application of moral reasoning to introduce new forms of mimesis in 1 John (a letter neither Trozzo nor Rahmsdorf considers) shows that he considers the ongoing imitation of Jesus to be essential, appropriate, and feasible.

Others propose a broader, flexible approach to the imitation of Jesus. Kille, for example, suggests that the issue is not what people should imitate from the accounts of Jesus's life but what values they can learn from Jesus's way of living.[148] Burridge advocates that people should imitate Jesus's open attitude to others.[149] For Hood, imitating Jesus is primarily about adopting a mindset.[150] While these scholars are careful not to depict mimesis as a mindless replication of Jesus's actions and recognize the need to discern the underlying intentions and attitudes, their concept of imitation is arguably too broad and insufficiently controlled by the text. They often do not outline which literal terms feed into their concept of imitation, nor do they develop criteria to distinguish between imitation, analogy, and reciprocity. I therefore propose a tighter hermeneutical control and that we should consider only those aspects of Jesus's life that are indicated by the Johannine text for imitation (see also section 5.2).

In doing so, we must hold together the imitation of Jesus's specific actions, its underlying intentions, and perhaps his lifestyle. The footwashing, for example, provides a concrete example of mimesis, yet the mimetic act should also embody the intention and attitude underlying the original example. John's exhortation that believers conduct themselves like Jesus (1 John 2:6) contains no explicit instructions precisely because this will require them to reflect on Jesus's entire life and contemplate how they can imitate him by applying moral reasoning. While people cannot imitate every aspect of Jesus's life, such as dying on the cross for the sake of humanity, John nevertheless takes Jesus's saying in 15:13 to mean that Jesus's sacrificial death becomes an example for imitation (1 John 3:16).[151] Hence, believers should embody Jesus's life and teachings or his lived-out ethos of God's world as it is preserved in the Johannine text.

---

148. Kille, "Imitating Christ," 263.

149. Burridge, *Imitating Jesus*, 77. He then sees this pattern in John's Gospel (*Imitating Jesus*, 343–45).

150. Hood, *Imitating God*, 12, 74, 132. Surprisingly, Hood's biblical theology of mimesis hardly pays attention to the Johannine literature. Oddly, only in the conclusion does he answer various general questions with reference to the Johannine Epistles (*Imitating God*, 209–20), as if the Johannine Epistles can address all aspects of imitation.

151. For Jesus's death as an example to follow, see van der Watt, *Grammar*, 1:245–48, 310–19.

PART 2   MIMESIS IN EARLY CHRISTIANITY

5.7.3. Applied Hermeneutics

The answer to the third question, "Is imitation limited to the examples Jesus gave in his life?" is both "yes" and "no." "Yes," in that Jesus's example preserved in the text remains the basis and boundary for our imitation of Christ. Jesus's instruction to abide in his words (John 15:7; see also 14:23; 16:12–15; 17:8) requires us not only to study and observe them but also to remain *within their boundaries*. Likewise, in 2 John 9, John warns his audience not to go beyond the teaching of Christ. However, the answer is also "no," in that John himself applied moral reasoning and created *new* forms of imitation by extending Jesus's example and teaching. Here are some examples:

- 1 John 2:6: "*Just as* [Jesus] walked, the one who claims to abide in him must *also* walk [similarly]." "To walk" is shorthand for "way of life," referring to Jesus's life on earth as a model for imitation. John may have derived this command from Jesus's saying in John 14:6 that he is the "way of life" in which people should walk. How this might look in various situations will, of course, require moral reasoning.
- 1 John 3:3: "All who have this hope in him purify themselves, *just as* [Jesus] is pure." This call to mimesis is perhaps rooted in John 17:19. Although the idea of imitation is weak—it does not say that believers must purify themselves just as Jesus purified himself (because Jesus *is* pure)—it nevertheless urges believers to imitate Jesus's purity.
- 1 John 3:7: "The one who does what is right is right(eous), *just as* [Jesus] is right(eous)." This example of mimesis may be influenced by John 5:30; 7:24.
- 1 John 3:16: "We know love by this, that [Jesus] laid down his life for us; *likewise*, we must lay down our lives for one another." John does not simply remind his audience of Jesus's saying in John 15:13 but turns it into a new form of mimesis: just as Jesus laid down his life for the sake of his followers, so they should lay down their lives for each other. John's subsequent progression from imitating Jesus's sacrificial love in 1 John 3:16 to the concrete mimetic act of giving economic help to a fellow believer in 1 John 3:17 clearly displays moral reasoning.
- 1 John 4:11: "Since God loved us in this manner, we *also* must love one another." This mimetic command is a conflation of John 3:16 and 13:34.

In sum, 1 John contains several instances of moral reasoning where John develops new forms of mimetic behavior from Jesus's life and teaching. This suggests that Johannine Christians (and later believers) may also create new forms of mimesis—as long as these are rooted in Jesus's example and teaching rather than the product of a person's subjective imagination disconnected from the biblical text. Indeed, when we follow the Johannine tradition into the second century, we find examples of mimesis that are arguably rooted in the life of the Johannine Jesus. In the Apostolic Fathers, martyrdom was viewed as the *ideal* imitation of Christ (e.g., Ign. *Rom.* 6:1–3; Mart. Pol. 17:3; 19:1; see further chapter 8). Although it is not certain, a good case can be made that Ignatius and Polycarp were acquainted with the apostle John.[152] If that be the case, the parallels between Jesus's death and those of some apostolic fathers can be traced back via John's new mimetic command in 1 John 3:16 to Jesus's own saying in John 15:13.

5.7.4. Conclusion

To sum up, Jesus's absence was not an insurmountable problem for Johannine Christians because people in antiquity were familiar with the idea of imitating living, dead, or literary examples. While John occasionally uses living examples (exemplary Christians) to encourage the *imitatio Christi* among the believing community, his written eyewitness testimony about Jesus formed the basis for mimesis. Johannine Christians were to reconstruct and imitate the Jesus whom John had observed, remembered, and preserved in his writings. The Johannine text, therefore, is the *basis* and *boundary* for mimesis. John's new forms of mimesis in 1 John do not contradict this principle because they are extrapolated from and remain within the boundaries of Jesus's life and teaching. The possible reception history of the Johannine tradition in the second century suggests that the notion of martyrdom as the ideal *imitatio Christi* can be traced back via John (in 1 John) to Jesus (in John's Gospel).

We also drew attention to the hermeneutical role of the Spirit. The Johannine writings depict the Spirit as an interpreter (14:26; 16:12–15; 1 John 2:20, 27; 2 John 9), implying that the Spirit will aid believers in reconstructing Jesus from the text.[153]

---

152. Kenneth Berding, "John or Paul? Who Was Polycarp's Mentor?," *TynBul* 58 (2007): 135–43; Hermut Löhr, "The Epistles of Ignatius of Antioch," in *The Apostolic Fathers*, ed. Wilhelm Pratscher (Waco, TX: Baylor University Press, 2010), 91–115, at 101–2; Murray J. Smith, "The Gospels in Early Christian Literature," in *The Content and Setting of the Gospel Tradition*, ed. Mark Harding and Alanna Nobbs (Grand Rapids: Eerdmans, 2010), 181–208, at 204. L. Stephanie Cobb also considers that the "cup" in *Mart. Pol.* 14:2 alludes to John 18:11 ("Polycarp's Cup: *Imitatio* in the *Martyrdom of Polycarp*," *JRH* 38 [2014]: 224–40, at 226). Differently, Justin Buol stresses a tradition of imitation from Jesus to the bishop martyrs via Paul (*Martyred for the Church: Memorializations of the Effective Deaths of Bishop Martyrs in the Second Century CE*, WUNT 2/471 [Tübingen: Mohr Siebeck, 2018], 237–43).

153. For a detailed explanation of the hermeneutical role of the Spirit, see Cornelis Bennema, "The Hermeneutical Role of the Spirit in the Johannine Writings," in *The Spirit Says: Inspiration*

Hence, the two interrelated hermeneutical devices available to believers for imitating Jesus are *the text* and *the Spirit*. Jesus's life and exemplary behavior are preserved in the text, and readers must, guided by the Spirit, reconstruct "observable behavior" from the text. The Spirit aids believers in (1) reconstructing Jesus from the text, (2) interpreting Jesus's example and enabling mimesis, and (3) possibly inferring new forms of mimesis from Jesus's teaching. While the main hermeneutical aids to the believer's imitation of Jesus are the text and the Spirit, mature believers may function as living examples for imitation.[154]

In a recent study based on cognitive psychology, Cockayne recognizes the transformative aspect of mimesis but argues that this requires an experience of Christ *in the present* through the indwelling Spirit, in which the imitator can perceive Christ's intentions and behavior.[155] The danger of any mimesis rooted in the *contemporary* experience of Christ is that it can lead to uncontrolled, subjective interpretations. Instead, I suggest that the imitation of Jesus should be text-centered, i.e., controlled by Jesus's examples and behavior preserved in the text. Hermeneutically, the "contemporary" Jesus of personal experience must correspond to the Jesus reconstructed from the text.

Glen Lund is one of few scholars who consider how Jesus may have functioned as an ethical model within the believing community:

> For all their nobility and wide-ranging application the ethical principles of the fourth gospel certainly lack specificity. Other than in the foot-washing ceremony, none of Jesus' commands are fleshed out by detailed instructions indicating how they might be practically applied. Each command ultimately refers to the example of Jesus as the basis of their application which is a dynamic tradition that is neither fixed nor systematic. The ultimate test for Johannine moral acceptability could perhaps be described as intimate connection to Jesus/God through belief and faithfulness to his testimony within the Spirit-guided community....
>
> In practice, the moral conduct in the Johannine community would not have been governed by the fourth gospel but would have been fleshed out by their corporate memory of Jesus and supplemented by remembered, internalized values from the Torah.... This would mean that Johannine ethical practice

---

and Interpretation in Israelite, Jewish, and Early Christian Texts, ed. Ron Herms, Jack Levison, and Archie Wright, Ekstasis 8 (Berlin: de Gruyter, 2021), 169–88. For the role of the Spirit in Johannine mimesis, see Bennema, *Mimesis*, 186–91.

154. We will examine the use of living examples more clearly in Paul, in chapter 6.

155. Cockayne, "Imitation Game," 3–24.

would be based on relational unity and communal values, not written texts and fixed laws.[156]

There is much to commend in Lund's view of a Torah-based, Spirit-guided community ethics, but it does not, in my view, go to the heart of Johannine ethics. Rather, *the personal example of Jesus*, preserved in the text of John's Gospel and extrapolated in his Letters, is the basis for Johannine ethics, with mimesis regulating its inner workings.[157]

5.8. Conclusion

The aim of this chapter was to establish that mimesis is a valid Johannine concept, explain its particulars, and show that it is integral to Johannine ethics. In section 5.2, we found that the Johannine mimetic language consists of eight different linguistic constructions accounting for about forty-four occurrences of mimesis. We noted that the Johannine literature presents two types of mimesis—performative mimesis and existential mimesis—and that the two prominent categories are the Son–Father mimesis and the believer–Jesus/God mimesis. Noting that many references to the believer–Jesus/God mimesis use imperatives, we inferred that mimesis is not optional but a critical aspect of the believer's relationship with Jesus/God. In sum, we concluded that the concept of Johannine mimesis is *varied* with regard to the different mimetic expressions, *widespread* across the Johannine literature, and *distinctive* because the comparative conjunction καθώς is central to the Johannine mimetic language. This meant we had a strong case to explore the concept further.

In section 5.3, we noted that John's depiction of the divine family presents a dominant Son–Father mimesis and a latent Spirit–Son mimesis in the Godhead. This divine mimesis, rather than being mere duplication, is a creative, faithful representation of God's words and works on earth. We learned that divine mimesis is instrumental in the God–human relationship because certain fundamental attributes and activities that characterize the Father–Son relationship are extended

---

156. Glen Lund, "The Joys and Dangers of Ethics in John's Gospel," in *Rethinking the Ethics of John: "Implicit Ethics" in the Johannine Writings*, ed. Jan G. van der Watt and Ruben Zimmermann, CNNTE 3, WUNT 291 (Tübingen: Mohr Siebeck, 2012), 264–89, at 278, 280. For the idea of intimate relationships enabling ethical living, see Rabens's essay in the same volume ("Johannine Perspectives," 114–39).

157. Even though Lund mentions the idea of imitating Jesus, he does not see its centrality in Johannine ethics ("Joys," 277, 283, 287–88).

to people by means of mimesis. In other words, the Son–Father mimesis (and Spirit–Jesus mimesis) are on display for the sake of people, implying that mimesis is a vital mechanism for mediating the divine reality to the earthly realm.

In section 5.4, we unpacked the prevalent believer–Jesus mimesis and occasional believer–God mimesis, revealing that John presents mimesis as a cognitive, creative, and participatory process that is concerned with both the interpretation of the original act and the formulation of a corresponding mimetic act. We argued that for John, mimesis is primarily the creative, faithful, tangible articulation of the idea and attitude that lie behind the original act rather than its literal replication (cloning). While performative mimesis is the most prevalent form of the believer–Jesus/God mimesis, existential mimesis features prominently, indicating that the believer's mimesis of Jesus or God is not simply related to behavior but also involves the shaping of identity.[158] We also learned that the believer–Jesus/God mimesis does not only benefit the believer but also others because some expressions of mimesis, such as serving one another, loving one another, and being sent into the world, mediate Jesus/God to the beneficiary of the mimetic act. We noted a similar dynamic in the Son–Father mimesis and the believer–Jesus mimesis, such that we could speak of a mimetic chain where Jesus imitates God (the Spirit imitates Jesus) and the believer imitates Jesus, in which divine moral goods such as life, love, light, truth, and honor are passed along the chain.

In section 5.5, we addressed the place of mimesis in Johannine ethics. We argued that mimesis is central to Johannine ethics and instrumental in the believers' moral transformation. To put it differently, mimesis is the primary mechanism for directing appropriate character and conduct in the divine family.[159] The aim of mimesis is to shape the believer's identity and behavior towards the ethos (i.e., beliefs, values, and norms) of God's family that is embedded in the Johannine narrative. We noted that the goal of mimesis in antiquity was moral transformation, where the imitator sought to become (gradually) like the exemplar. Hence, believers imitate Jesus in serving, loving, being one, and so on, in order to *become* people characterized by service, love, and unity. A pattern emerges of transformation through mimesis where Jesus demonstrates ethical living, and his followers then (and therefore) imitate him.

---

158. Most recently, Hartog has expanded my model by adding desiderative facets (desires, motivations, affections) to John's mimetic ethics, although he admits this is less prominent ("Johannine Ethics," 7–13).

159. Contra Shin's conclusion that "imitating Jesus is expected of those who have already achieved a significant progress in their journey of faith" (*Ethics in the Gospel of John*, 195). Instead, imitating Jesus is expected at every stage of discipleship (see also my critique of Shin in section 5.1).

5. Mimesis in John's Gospel and Letters

In section 5.6, we outlined a Johannine model of mimesis that is similar to the one we found in the Greco-Roman traditions. While the footwashing episode embodies this model most vividly, other texts reinforce several aspects. The model stresses that Johannine mimesis is a complex, cognitive, and creative process in which believers must apply moral reasoning to interpret the example of Jesus and translate this into an appropriate mimetic act. With the necessary caution, we can use the term "theosis" to indicate the transformation that mimesis has the potential to bring about.

The advantage of having the Gospel and Letters as part of the Johannine tradition, where the Letters describe a later period than the Gospel, is that we can reconstruct how mimesis might have worked in Johannine Christianity (section 5.7). John's creation of new forms of mimesis based on the example and teaching of Jesus indicates that he expected his audience to be able to imitate Jesus. While John can use living examples for imitation, the main basis for mimesis is the recorded example and teaching of Jesus in the Johannine text. Albeit implied, the Spirit's hermeneutical role enables mimesis in the Christian community.

We can infer three modes of mimesis from the Johannine writings. First is the mode of *direct observation*, where the imitator has direct access to observe and imitate the exemplar. While this mode of mimesis was available to the disciples because Jesus was present with them, John mentions this mode only sporadically elsewhere. In 3 John, we noted that John pointed Gaius to the example of Demetrius for imitation and, by implication, believers could observe other exemplary Christians for imitation. John, however, deploys another mode of mimesis for Johannine Christians in the late first century who could no longer directly observe Jesus, namely *textually mediated mimesis*. In this mode, the Johannine text is the primary basis for mimesis where Johannine Christians, aided by the Spirit, can "observe" and imitate a Jesus reconstructed from the text. We noted that characters in the Johannine narrative also have mimetic value. The third mode of mimesis in the Johannine writings is *mnemonic mimesis*, which is linked to the previous mode. The Spirit's role includes enabling the believers' memory and guiding them in "visualizing" a reconstructed Jesus from the text to help them imitate him.

6

Mimesis in the Pauline Letters

In this chapter, we will explore the concept of mimesis in the Pauline tradition. Most of the work on mimesis in the New Testament has focused on the Pauline corpus, which is where we find eight of the eleven occurrences of the lexeme μιμεῖσθαι ("to imitate") in the New Testament (1 Thess 1:6; 2:14; 2 Thess 3:7, 9; 1 Cor 4:16; 11:1; Phil 3:17; Eph 5:1). Understandably, most scholars gravitate towards these letters, but we will examine whether Paul's understanding of mimesis is broader than this lexeme (e.g., τύπος and καθώς). We will also scrutinize two specific claims about Pauline mimesis. First, there is the assertion that Paul only exhorts those churches he has personally founded to imitate him. Second, there is the contention that Paul's call to imitate him (2 Thess 3:7, 9; 1 Cor 4:16; 11:1; Phil 3:17; see also 1 Thess 1:6; Gal 4:12) is unique in antiquity. Nevertheless, the more important issue for our study is to establish whether mimesis is peripheral or central to Pauline ethics. We will include both the undisputed and disputed Pauline letters as representing the Pauline tradition and call attention to issues only when these two epistolary clusters present different concepts of mimesis. Nevertheless, the focus of the investigation will be on the undisputed letters 1 Thessalonians, 1 Corinthians, and Philippians, where the concept of mimesis is most pervasive, whereas it appears to play a lesser role in the disputed letters (2 Thess, Eph, Col, the Pastorals).

It is important to remember that Paul had to develop an extensive code of ethics for his churches as most of his converts came from pagan backgrounds and were unfamiliar with Jewish-Christian values. Adapting our broad definition of New Testament ethics (see section 1.5), I suggest that Pauline ethics refers to "the moral beliefs, values, and norms that govern the conduct and character of Paul's churches in relation to God and fellow human beings." Paul's goal in ministry was not simply to proclaim the gospel, win converts, and plant churches wherever

6. Mimesis in the Pauline Letters

he went but to foster the moral formation of believers.[1] As a working definition, "moral formation" refers to the shaping of people's character and conduct according to the beliefs, values, and norms held out for their shared life. As his letters often attest, Paul's ambition was to present "blameless" churches before God at the Parousia (1 Thess 3:13; 5:23; 1 Cor 1:8; Phil 1:10; Col 1:22; Eph 1:4).[2] Within this broad context of Pauline ethics, our task is to discover the place of personal example and imitation.

Our strategy to determine the contours of Pauline mimesis unfolds in five steps. First, a survey of Pauline scholarship on the subject will highlight the issues we must address (section 6.1). Second, we will examine the explicit mimetic language in Paul's letters to the Thessalonians, Corinthians, Philippians, and Ephesians to erect the main scaffolding of Paul's notion of mimesis (sections 6.2–6.5). We will do this in chronological order of the letters (while recognizing that there may not be a consensus on this) to detect possible variations or development. Third, we will explore the mimetic connotations of the term "example" (τύπος, ὑποτύπωσις) in the Pastorals (section 6.6). Fourth, because we learned in previous chapters that the concept of mimesis is broader than the lexemes μιμεῖσθαι and τύπος, we will search for other possible mimetic expressions in the remaining letters in the Pauline tradition—Galatians, Romans, Colossians, and Philemon (section 6.7). Fifth, we will consider the overall evidence in the Pauline letters to articulate a model of Pauline mimesis (section 6.8) and determine whether mimesis is peripheral or central to Pauline ethics (section 6.9).

6.1. Mimesis in Pauline Scholarship

6.1.1. A Survey of Pauline Studies

There is a surplus of Pauline studies on mimesis, so this overview represents the most significant studies that have looked at mimesis across multiple letters in the Pauline corpus to identify interpretative possibilities and pertinent issues that deserve closer examination.[3] At the outset, we must identify one approach to Pauline

---

1. James W. Thompson, *Moral Formation according to Paul: The Context and Coherence of Pauline Ethics* (Grand Rapids: Baker Academic, 2011), 2.
2. Paul uses different terms (ἄμεμπτος, ἀνέγκλητος, ἀπρόσκοπος, ἄμωμος) for the concept of "blameless."
3. In this chapter, we will re-engage the relevant studies on mimesis in early Christianity that we identified in chapter 1, such as those by Tinsley, de Boer, Schulz, Betz, Burridge, and Hood. For

mimesis that has not stood the test of time, namely to view Pauline mimesis in terms of hierarchy and power, where Paul's call to imitation is viewed as a call to obey Paul's apostolic authority.[4] Instead, we will see that most scholars regard Paul's call to the imitation of himself as a call to imitate Christ, especially in humility, self-denial, and self-giving.[5] While mimesis can relate to hierarchy (see also section 1.5), we saw in the previous chapter in relation to the footwashing in John 13 that the "superior" exemplar (Jesus the Lord and Teacher) adopts the identity of a subordinate to set an example to imitate. Hence, Jesus uses the mechanism of mimesis to subvert rather than establish or affirm power structures. Similarly, we will see in this chapter that Paul's exhortation to imitate him is free from explicit power structures.

Focusing on the imitation of Paul, Willis Peter de Boer notes that Paul's call to imitate him is only directed to churches that he has founded and where he is personally known. Running through this call to imitation are the qualities of humility, self-denial, and self-giving for the sake of Christ and others.[6] De Boer notes that the concept of imitation in Pauline Christianity occurs primarily in the overlapping areas of education, family, and ethics.[7] Paul uses his conduct and personal example for pedagogical purposes when teaching about Christianity. As he considers himself the spiritual father of those who had turned to Christianity through his preaching, Paul's plea to imitate him comes in light of this spiritual father–child relationship. Paul is, therefore, a vital link in the process by which his converts learn to express Christ and Christianity in their lives.[8]

---

a popular work on the subject, see Rodney Reeves, *Spirituality according to Paul: Imitating the Apostle of Christ* (Downers Grove, IL: IVP Academic, 2011).

4. For example, Michaelis, "μιμέομαι," 4:666–74; Betz, *Nachfolge und Nachahmung*, 155–57, 178–80; Adele Reinhartz, "On the Meaning of the Pauline Exhortation: '*Mimētai Mou Ginesthe*— Become Imitators of Me,'" *SR* 16 (1987): 393–403; Castelli, *Imitating Paul*; Joseph A. Marchal, *Hierarchy, Unity, and Imitation: A Feminist Rhetorical Analysis of Power Dynamics in Paul's Letter to the Philippians*, SBLAB 24 (Atlanta: Society of Biblical Literature, 2006). De Boer critiques at length Michaelis's limiting Paul's usage of μιμεῖσθαι (and its cognates) to obedience (*Imitation of Paul*, 206, 209–11). While Castelli's view still has a following (see, e.g., Moss, *Other Christs*, 23–28), it has not gained widespread support. For a critique of Castelli, see Copan, *Saint Paul*, 181–218; Ehrensperger, *Paul*, 137–54. For a broader discussion on the concept of power and Paul (including a critique of Castelli), see Andrew D. Clarke, *A Pauline Theology of Church Leadership*, LNTS 362 (Edinburgh: T&T Clark, 2008), 104–30.

5. See also Stephen E. Fowl, "Imitation of Paul/of Christ," in *Dictionary of Paul and His Letters*, ed. Gerald F. Hawthorne and Ralph P. Martin (Downers Grove, IL: InterVarsity Press, 1993), 428–31; Linda L. Belleville, "'Imitate Me, Just as I Imitate Christ': Discipleship in the Corinthian Correspondence," in *Patterns of Discipleship in the New Testament*, ed. Richard N. Longenecker (Grand Rapids: Eerdmans, 1996), 120–42.

6. De Boer, *Imitation of Paul*, 206–7.

7. De Boer, *Imitation of Paul*, 211.

8. De Boer, *Imitation of Paul*, 214–16. He provides a detailed exegesis of nine Pauline passages

6. Mimesis in the Pauline Letters

For Werner Wolbert, the issue with Pauline imitation is that Paul intentionally recommends *himself* as an example for imitation, thus placing himself between Christ and the believers.[9] He argues that the imitation of Paul is a general call to *sittlichem Ernst* ("moral seriousness"), a call to follow Paul's commandments about leading a Christian life.[10] This echoes Michaelis's view in his influential *TDNT* article that the imitation of Paul is mainly about obedience (see n. 4).[11] As a result, Wolbert takes the *imitatio Pauli* very generally, asserting that it does not refer to any specific behavior (except in 2 Thess 3:7–9) but to do good, to do God's will.[12] While Wolbert's support for Michaelis is open to challenge and his ensuing view of Pauline imitation as a general call to obedient living is arguably too broad, he is more constructive when he says that imitation has both a cognitive and volitional aspect and is not about copying an example but about realizing the moral good in appropriate deeds.[13]

In his 1986 monograph, Benjamin Fiore examines the hortatory device of personal example (and its relation to imitation) in Greco-Roman literature and the Pauline tradition, focusing especially on the Socratic and Pastoral Epistles.[14] He finds that the Pastoral Epistles stand in the tradition of Greco-Roman hortatory letters, which often use personal examples to complement direct exhortation.[15] Almost twenty years later, in an article on Paul's call to imitate his example (in the undisputed Pauline letters), Fiore shows that the use of example and call to imitation was widespread in Greco-Roman antiquity and draws specific attention to Seneca's hortatory epistles, which allowed the audience to conceptualize virtue from past examples of great men.[16] He then shows that Paul too uses a range of examples (e.g., Christ, himself, his coworkers, scriptural examples) as a literary strategy to instruct his audiences. In these letters, Paul explicitly appeals to his audience to be like him on six occasions (Gal 4:12; 1 Thess 1:5–6; 2:14–16; Phil 3:17;

---

that refer to imitation: 1 Thess 1:6; 2 Thess 3:7–9; 1 Cor 4:16; 11:1; Phil 3:17; Gal 4:12; 1 Tim 1:16; 2 Tim 1:13; 3:10 (*Imitation of Paul*, 92–201).

9. Werner Wolbert, "Vorbild: Zum Problem der Nachahmung des Paulus," *MTZ* 32 (1981): 249–70, at 250.

10. Wolbert, "Vorbild," 252.

11. Wolbert's critique of Michaelis is merely one of nuance: while Michaelis views the imitation of Paul as obedience to his *apostolic* authority, Wolbert understands it as obedience to Paul's *paraenetic* authority, which is rooted in love, freedom, and Paul's personal example ("Vorbild," 262–63).

12. Wolbert, "Vorbild," 257–58.
13. Wolbert, "Vorbild," 255–56.
14. Fiore, *Personal Example*.
15. Fiore, *Personal Example*, 191–92.
16. Fiore, "Paul," 228–57.

PART 2   MIMESIS IN EARLY CHRISTIANITY

1 Cor 4:16; 11:1), while the Pastoral Epistles mention Paul's example on three occasions (1 Tim 1:3–20; 2 Tim 1:3–18; 3:1–4:8).[17]

Adele Reinhartz focuses on Paul holding himself up as an example in 1 Cor 4:16; 11:1; 1 Thess 1:6; Phil 3:17 to address the paradox between the inherent superiority implied by Paul's appeal and the statements of humility found in the same context.[18] From a quick glance at μιμεῖσθαι in classical, Hellenistic, and early Christian literature, she concludes that Paul's exhortation to imitate him seems unique in antiquity.[19] For Reinhartz, Paul's call to imitate him ([συμ]μιμηταί μου γίνεσθαι) denotes a process where a change of state occurs—a transformation from one's present state into one that is characterized by imitating Paul.[20] She resolves the paradox by arguing that in all cases, Paul's call to imitate him occurs in the context of defending his status as an apostle and seeking to stress his apostolic authority not only to his churches but also to his opponents.[21]

Jo-Ann Brant looks at the mimetic process or activity that Paul exhorts his audience to engage in.[22] First, she notes that mimesis in Greek antiquity is not mere copying but a process in which the imitator is actively involved in bringing an idea to expression.[23] She then argues that, in keeping with the understanding of mimesis in classic Greek literature, Paul sees an active role for the imitator in the process of mimesis, especially in relation to the ethic of self-renunciation. Paul's concern is that the believer's words and deeds conform to (i.e., imitate) a life in Christ. Mimesis is a creative process where the imitator is actively involved by subordinating their own interests to those of others. Brant finds this notion of mimesis in 1 Thessalonians, 1 Corinthians, and Philippians. While Christ represents the ideal for the ethic of self-renunciation, Paul also serves as an example for the imitator because of the evidence of his own behavior.[24]

Andrew Clarke notes that Paul does not simply urge his readers to imitate certain examples (e.g., himself, Christ, God, other believers, and even churches) but

---

17. Fiore, "Paul," 237–44. He does not look at 2 Thess 3:7–9 since this is a disputed Pauline letter. While Fiore mentions several differences in the use of personal examples between the undisputed Pauline letters and the Pastorals (*Personal Example*, 223), we will see that these are differences in nuance rather than kind.

18. Reinhartz, "Meaning," 393–403. She does not consider 2 Thess 3:7–9 because of the doubt regarding its authenticity, or Gal 4:12 because it does not contain the lexeme μιμεῖσθαι.

19. Reinhartz, "Meaning," 394–96.

20. Reinhartz, "Meaning," 396.

21. Reinhartz, "Meaning," 403. For viewing Pauline mimesis in terms of power, see n. 4 above.

22. Brant, "*Mimēsis*," 285–300.

23. Brant, "*Mimēsis*," 286–88.

24. Brant, "*Mimēsis*," 288–98. She does not consider mimesis in 2 Thess and Eph because of their disputed status amongst scholars.

exhorts them also to become examples for others to imitate.[25] Clarke's contribution is his informed, comprehensive discussion of the main imitation and example texts across the Pauline corpus. He concludes that the imitation of Christ is primary and that Paul's role as an example for imitation is not unique but one that he shares with other named believers. Moreover, the position of the exemplar is not one of authority (contra Castelli) but of one who models oneself on Christ.[26]

Examining the *imitatio Christi* passages in 1–2 Thessalonians, 1 Corinthians, and Philippians (he does not look at imitating God in Eph 5:1), Otto Merk contends that the Pauline concept of imitating Christ is not rooted in the moral exemplary life of the historical Jesus but in the post-Easter life of the risen Christ.[27] However, the risen Christ is none other than the historical Jesus, so Merk concludes that the early Church took the theological-ethical step from following Jesus to imitating him.[28] Merk appears to pick up the quest from the 1960s that compared the concepts "following Jesus" in the Gospels and "imitating Christ" in the Pauline letters, assuming that the Gospels contain no significant notion of mimesis and that "following Jesus" is the near equivalent (see section 1.2). From our studies of the Gospels, we realize that this quest was partially misleading.

Brian Dodd explores how Paul uses his personal example as a literary strategy in the undisputed letters 1 Corinthians, Galatians, Philippians, 1 Thessalonians, Philemon, and Romans. He contends that Paul's written appeal to personal example "reflects his leadership style of modelling and embodying the teaching he propagated, and this is further underlined by the epistolary theory of the time, which urged the creation of a letter as an alter ego, a surrogate for one's personal presence with one's readers" (see also Fiore, above).[29] Dodd concludes that Paul's strategy of using this leadership and literary strategy was "sound pedagogy and effective psychagogy" because imitation was familiar in surrounding culture(s) and this leadership style was not unique to him.[30]

Philippe Nicolet examines 1 Thess 1:6; 2:14 (but not 2 Thess 3:7–9); 1 Cor 4:16; 11:1; Phil 3:17; and Gal 4:12 to argue that the calls to imitate Paul are not about power (contra Castelli) but refer to Christ being made evident through Paul's proclamation.[31] Like Merk, Nicolet contends that Paul speaks of imitating the risen Christ

---

25. Andrew D. Clarke, "'Be Imitators of Me': Paul's Model of Leadership," *TynBul* 49 (1998): 329–60.
26. Clarke, "Imitators," 359. See also Clarke, *Pauline Theology*, 104–30, 173–82.
27. Merk, "Nachahmung Christi," 333–34.
28. Merk, "Nachahmung Christi," 335.
29. Brian Dodd, *Paul's Paradigmatic "I": Personal Example as Literary Strategy*, LNTS 177 (Sheffield: Sheffield Academic Press, 1999), 237–38.
30. Dodd, *Paul's Paradigmatic "I,"* 238.
31. Philippe Nicolet, "Le concept d'imitation de l'apôtre dans la correspondance paulini-

rather than the earthly Jesus.[32] For Nicolet, to imitate Christ (through imitating Paul) does not mean to consider him an example for imitation but to participate in his life, to live one's life "in Christ."[33]

Drawing on contemporary educational theories, Andrew Kille argues that the mimesis Paul is calling for is not a slavish replication but a cognitive process where an action is observed, interpreted, and internalized in order to produce subsequent mimetic behavior.[34] Regarding imitating Paul, Kille states that "the 'Paul' that we now encounter in the epistles . . . is a symbolic construct . . . mediated through the vehicle of texts."[35] Concerning Paul's admonition to imitate him as he imitates Christ (1 Cor 11:1), Kille contends that the model of Christ that Paul holds up is not the historical Jesus but a "symbolic" Jesus reconstructed from the text. He concludes that the issue is not what readers should imitate from the accounts of Jesus's life but what values they can learn from Jesus's way of living.[36]

Victor Copan examines the imitation of Paul in 1 Thessalonians, 1 Corinthians, and Philippians, arguing that Paul's call for people to imitate him was in keeping with the common understanding of mimesis in Greek and Jewish antiquity. Imitating Paul could mean imitating the totality of Paul's life or specific virtues with a Christocentric orientation and reflecting a cruciform life.[37] This call to imitate Paul was mediated through three different means: (1) a letter (Paul's call to imitation came through written correspondence when he was not present with his audience); (2) memory recall (Paul asks his audience to remember their experience of him); or (3) a representative of Paul (Paul sends a coworker to show a Christlike life to his audience).[38] As for the application of Pauline imitation for contemporary contexts, Copan employs the idea of "metaphor-making." Rather than an analogical understanding or one-to-one correspondence of imitation, he argues that "the metaphorical understanding of imitation, in which two dissimilar items are compared, leads to comprehension on a deeper level, whereby the different contexts are acknowledged, forcing the reader to make a metaphoric leap in the transference from one unique situation to the reader's unique situation."[39]

---

enne," in *Paul, une théologie en construction*, ed. Andreas Dettwiler, Jean-Daniel Kaestli, and Daniel Marguerat, Le Monde de la Bible 51 (Geneva: Labor et Fides, 2004), 393–415.

32. Nicolet, "Le concept d'imitation," 400.
33. Nicolet, "Le concept d'imitation," 412–13.
34. Kille, "Imitating Christ," 253–54.
35. Kille, "Imitating Christ," 257.
36. Kille, "Imitating Christ," 257, 262–63.
37. Copan, *Saint Paul*, 223–25.
38. Copan, *Saint Paul*, 227–28.
39. Copan, *Saint Paul*, 242. Copan understands his applied hermeneutics to be in line with

6. Mimesis in the Pauline Letters

Susan Eastman has done innovative work on mimesis in Galatians and Philippians. Regarding Galatians, she argues that Paul's imperative in 4:12, "Become like me, for I also have become like you," denotes mimesis and that 4:12–20 envisions a communal life rooted in the "mimetic" relationship that Christ has established with humanity.[40] Speaking of Philippians, Eastman argues that Christ's imitation of humanity in 2:6–11 (Christ "putting on" Adam and enacting Adam's story of humanity enslaved to sin) precedes and is the basis of the believer's imitation of Christ.[41] Eastman's distinctive take on the concept of Pauline mimesis is her argument (regarding both Galatians and Philippians) that the incarnation and crucifixion present a *mimetic reversal*, where Christ's mimetic participation in the human plight is the basis for the believer's mimetic participation in Christ. In her latest work on Paul's anthropology, Eastman returns to Phil 2:6–11 to unpack the concept of "reciprocal mimetic participation" as Christ's participation in the human plight by adopting the likeness of Adam (humanity enslaved to sin) so that humans can participate in Christ and become like him.[42] In short, Christ's imitation of the human condition initiates a reciprocal human imitation of God.[43] Hence, for Eastman, mimesis begins with God and is a subset or aspect of divine–human participation.

Michael Jensen looks at the Pauline corpus (excluding Ephesians and the Pastorals) to explore the concepts of (1) imitating Christ (Rom 15:1–9; Phil 2:1–11; Col 3:13), (2) imitating Paul (1 Cor 4:16; 11:1; 1 Thess 1:6; 2 Thess 3:6–13), and (3) imitating the church (2 Cor 8:1–15; Phil 3:1–21; 1 Thess 2:13–15).[44] Based on this textual analysis, Jensen draws seven themes regarding ethical mimesis. First, imitation involves observation of the exemplar, and in the absence of Paul, his letters mediate the patterns of life and attitudes that he wants emulated. Second, imitation involves a pattern of authority derived from the model and mediated to the imitator. Third, identity precedes imitation; that is, based on their identification with Christ, believers are called to imitate him. Fourth, imitation is a cognitive and

---

that of Richard B. Hays, *The Moral Vision of the New Testament: A Contemporary Introduction to New Testament Ethics* (New York: HarperCollins, 1996), 298–99.

40. Susan Eastman, *Recovering Paul's Mother Tongue: Language and Theology in Galatians* (Grand Rapids: Eerdmans, 2007), 25–61.

41. Susan Eastman, "Imitating Christ Imitating Us: Paul's Educational Project in Philippians," in *The Word Leaps the Gap: Essays on Scripture and Theology in Honor of Richard B. Hays*, ed. J. Ross Wagner, C. Kavin Rowe, and Katherine Grieb (Grand Rapids: Eerdmans, 2008), 427–51. See also Susan Eastman, "Philippians 2:6–11: Incarnation as Mimetic Participation," *JSPL* 1 (2010): 1–22.

42. Susan Grove Eastman, *Paul and the Person: Reframing Paul's Anthropology* (Grand Rapids: Eerdmans, 2017), 129–40.

43. Eastman, *Paul*, 141.

44. Jensen, "Imitating Paul," 18–28.

imaginative activity; believers have to work out what actions result from Paul's ethic of imitation. Fifth, Paul's focus is on "passive" virtues; that is, in imitating Christ, believers wait patiently for God to work out various virtues in them (e.g., humility, generosity, patient endurance, forgiveness, forbearance, suffering with joy). Sixth, imitating Christ is for the benefit of others. Seventh, the goal of imitating Christ is the edification of the church.[45] For Jensen, the imitation of Christ is mediated via an imitation of Paul or an imitation of churches for the sake of others and the edification of the church.[46]

While most scholars look at Paul's concept of mimesis through the lens of ancient Greco-Roman education, where pupils imitate their teacher, James Harrison focuses on the *civic* context of Greco-Roman mimesis to explain Paul's urban ministry.[47] Based on an extensive survey of eulogistic inscriptions, statues, and literary evidence, he demonstrates the prevalence of a mimetic ethos or culture of imitation in Greco-Roman civic life, where "great men" were presented as examples for imitation in perpetuity—especially the emperor in the early imperial period.[48] He then shows how Paul uses mimetic language to subvert the adulatory imitation of the "great man" in Greco-Roman civic ethics and promote the imitation of an alternative model—the crucified Christ—for discipleship and social relations in his house churches.[49] Harrison views his contribution as complementing rather than contradicting other Pauline models of imitation.[50]

Suzan Sierksma-Agteres examines Greco-Roman philosophical education as the context for Paul's model of mimesis, specifically his use of "faith(fulness)" language.[51] Like Harrison, she notes the widespread culture of imitation in the early Roman Empire—in the spheres of family, education, and civic life. She notes that πίστις ("faith," "faithfulness") in Greco-Roman literature has a dual role in character formation, where it is both an attitude that enables imitation and a virtue to imitate.[52] Turning to Greco-Roman philosophical education, she discovers a "mimetic chain," where "the trustworthiness or credibility of the model (its disposition) should generate trust or credence in the imitators (an attitude), who ought

---

45. Jensen, "Imitating Paul," 28–33.
46. Jensen, "Imitating Paul," 33–34.
47. Harrison, "Imitation," 213–54.
48. Harrison, "Imitation," 222–45.
49. Harrison, "Imitation," 249–54.
50. Harrison, "Imitation," 222.
51. Sierksma-Agteres, "Imitation in Faith," 119–53.
52. Sierksma-Agteres, "Imitation in Faith," 122–24.

to become trustworthy (qua disposition) themselves."[53] With God at the origin of the mimetic chain, it is unsurprising that the ultimate goal in Greco-Roman ethics was to become like or assimilate to the divine nature, with πίστις as a prominent divine quality suitable for human imitation.[54] Turning to Paul's letters, she also finds a mimetic chain comprising Christ (mediating the imitation of God), Paul, and the addressed community who in turn can become an example for others (e.g., 1 Thess 1:6–8), and πίστις language is the basis or means for imitation.[55]

In his seminal work on Pauline ethics, David Horrell devotes one chapter to the topic of imitation, focusing on Phil 2, 1 Cor 9, and 2 Cor 8–9 rather than the explicit imitation passages to show that imitation is an important theme in Pauline ethics.[56] Horrell views Phil 2 as the foundational ethical text that guides the interpretation of 1 Cor 9 and 2 Cor 8–9. Advocating for an ethical (rather than theological) reading of Phil 2:5–11, he argues that Christ's "self-lowering other-regard" is the paradigm for Christian imitation, supported by the examples of Paul and his coworkers.[57] Taking 1 Cor 9 and Paul's example of setting aside one's rights out of concern for the other, Horrell focuses on 9:14–15 and echoes Hays's interpretation to argue that, for Paul, the imitation of Christ is a metanorm or fundamental ethical principle: "Paul allows the *imitatio Christi* paradigm to override all particular ethical rules and prescriptions, even when the rule is a direct command of the Lord Jesus."[58] He then looks at the phrase "the law (νόμος) of Christ" in Gal 6:2 and, more implicitly, 1 Cor 9:21, arguing that Christ's example of burden-bearing or self-giving is a normative pattern (νόμος) for Christian practice.[59] Finally, Horrell examines 2 Cor 8–9 (with a focus on 8:9–15), showing that Christ's self-lowering or self-giving is once again a model to imitate—seen here in giving generously to the Jerusalem collection.[60] He concludes that the explicit *imitatio Christi* passages in Paul are just the tip of the iceberg, revealing "other-regard" as a normative pattern of Christian conduct that is rooted in the moral paradigm of Christ's self-giving.[61]

---

53. Sierksma-Agteres, "Imitation in Faith," 124–27.
54. Sierksma-Agteres, "Imitation in Faith," 127–34.
55. Sierksma-Agteres, "Imitation in Faith," 135–41.
56. David G. Horrell, *Solidarity and Difference: A Contemporary Reading of Paul's Ethics*, 2nd ed. (London: Bloomsbury T&T Clark, 2016), 225–70.
57. Horrell, *Solidarity and Difference*, 227–36.
58. Horrell, *Solidarity and Difference*, 236–44 (quotation from p. 244).
59. Horrell, *Solidarity and Difference*, 244–54. Horrell is once again indebted to Richard Hays.
60. Horrell, *Solidarity and Difference*, 254–65.
61. Horrell, *Solidarity and Difference*, 265–66.

PART 2   MIMESIS IN EARLY CHRISTIANITY

6.1.2. A Statement of the Problem

Based on this survey, I identify six issues that divide Pauline scholarship or have been inadequately addressed:

1. *Scope of Mimesis*. While many scholars limit their studies to the explicit Pauline mimetic passages in 1(–2) Thessalonians, 1 Corinthians, and Philippians, scholars such as Fiore, Dodd, Eastman, and Horrell have mined other Pauline letters. Hence, the issue is whether mimesis is limited to the lexeme μιμεῖσθαι and the churches that Paul himself founded or is a broader concept found throughout the Pauline corpus.[62]

2. *The Nature and Content of Mimesis*. We must examine whether Pauline mimesis is a creative and cognitive process (de Boer, Wolbert, Brant, Copan, Jensen) similar to what we noticed in the Johannine corpus. We must also consider what believers are called to imitate about Paul, Christ, and other exemplars. In addition, we shall determine whether the concept of mimesis is consistent or developing across the Pauline corpus and even whether there is a discernible pattern or model.

3. *The Uniqueness of Paul's Call to Imitate Him*. A few scholars, such as Reinhartz, have claimed that Paul's call to imitate him is unique in antiquity. Since we have already looked at mimesis in antiquity in part 1, we can immediately address whether the injunction "imitate me" is uniquely Paul's at the end of this section.

4. *Modes of Imitation*. Since mimesis results from a sensory process of observing the exemplar to imitate, it raises the issue of how Paul can expect his audience to imitate him *in absentia*, or the unseen Christ or God. Scholars like Fiore, Dodd, Copan, Jensen, and Harrison each suggest ways in which recipients of Paul's letters could imitate an absent Paul or unseen Christ/God. This seems to indicate that there are modes of imitation other than direct observation of the exemplar.

5. *The Imitation of Which Jesus?* Scholars such as Merk and Nicolet contend that Paul refers to the imitation of the risen Christ rather than the earthly Jesus. For them, to imitate the risen Christ is to participate in Christ's life, to live one's life "in (the sphere of) Christ."[63] Differently, Kille argues that Pauline mimesis

---

62. Blanton also notes that mimesis can be present in texts where the literal terms do not occur (Fiore and Blanton, "Paul," 182). Blanton has revised part II of Fiore's earlier article "Paul."

63. See also Victor Paul Furnish, who concludes that the Pauline imitation passages indicate conformity to the risen Christ in humility, selfless service, and obedient love rather than

6. Mimesis in the Pauline Letters

does not hold up the historical Jesus for imitation but a "symbolic" Jesus constructed from the text.
6. *Role of Mimesis.* While there are a number of studies on Pauline mimesis, scholars do not address whether mimesis is central or peripheral to Pauline ethics. We thus need to examine whether we can speak of mimetic ethics in Paul, as we saw in John.

We will pay particular attention to these issues as we analyze the concept of mimesis in each Pauline letter (or set of letters) and return to them in a more systematic manner as we gather our findings in sections 6.8–6.9. First, however, we will turn to the issue of whether Paul's call to imitate him was unique in antiquity.

Six of the eight occurrences of the lexeme μιμεῖσθαι in the Pauline corpus refer to imitating Paul (1 Cor 4:16; 11:1; 1 Thess 1:6; 2 Thess 3:7, 9; Phil 3:17). Of these, two have Paul issuing the explicit injunction to imitate him, μιμηταί μου γίνεσθε (1 Cor 4:16; 11:1). In addition, Gal 4:12 contains a call to imitate Paul, even though the lexeme μιμεῖσθαι is not used. Some scholars claim that Paul's injunction "imitate me" is unique in antiquity.[64] Jin Ki Hwang argues extensively that Paul is unique in attaching the lexeme μιμεῖσθαι to a first-person pronoun, that is, as a self-reference "imitate me," although he notes a few exceptions in Greek and Hellenistic Jewish literature (4 Macc. 9:23; Plato, *Apol.* 23C; Ps.-Diogenes, *Ep.* 14.4; Ps.-Crates, *Ep.* 20.13).[65] However, we saw in chapter 2 that Isocrates, Cicero, and Seneca could occasionally also present themselves as examples for imitation,[66] so there are more examples of exhortations to self-imitation in antiquity than Hwang would have us believe. Other scholars concur. Fiore, for example, notes that although ancient philosophers and rhetoricians mostly refer to the example of others for their pupils to imitate, they can also offer themselves as models for

---

imitating specific actions of the earthly Jesus (*Theology and Ethics in Paul* [Nashville: Abingdon, 1968], 218–23). Similarly, Yung Suk Kim asserts that imitation is a way of life rooted in the image of Christ crucified ("'Imitators' (*Mimetai*) in 1 Cor 4:16 and 11:1: A New Reading of Threefold Embodiment," *HBT* 33 [2011]: 147–70).

64. Reinhartz, "Meaning," 395–96; Brant, "*Mimēsis*," 285 (Brant simply follows Reinhartz); Angela Standhartinger, "Weisheitliche Idealbiografie und Ethik in Phil 3," *NovT* 61 (2019): 156–75, at 157.

65. Jin Ki Hwang, Mimesis *and Apostolic* Parousia *in 1 Corinthians 4 and 5: An Apologetic-Mimetic Interpretation* (Lewiston, NY: Mellen, 2010), 33–35, 43, 53. For the text of Ps.-Diogenes and Ps.-Crates, see Abraham J. Malherbe, *The Cynic Epistles: A Study Edition*, SBLSBS 12 (Missoula, MT: Scholars Press, 1977).

66. See, e.g., Isocrates, *Panath.* 16; Cicero, *Off.* 1.78; Seneca, *Ep.* 98.13.

PART 2   MIMESIS IN EARLY CHRISTIANITY

their pupils (e.g., Isocrates, *Antid.* 239; Ps.-Diogenes, *Ep.* 38.25–30; 46.6–11).[67] Yun Lee Too points out that Isocrates presents himself as a model for imitation or that he is aware that others imitated him (*Ep.* 8.10; 9.15; *Panath.* 16; *Antid.* 7, 13, 28, 54, 88, 141).[68] In sum, there are several instances across Greco-Roman and Hellenistic literature where people present themselves as an example for imitation, even though this concept is not widespread. Hence, it is more accurate to say that Paul's injunction to imitate him is *uncommon but not unique*.

6.2. 1–2 Thessalonians

The Thessalonian letters are among Paul's earliest,[69] and have a strong ethical interest.[70] His primary concern is to instruct his audience on how to live in view of persecution and the Parousia (1 Thess 1:9–10; 2:12; 3:13; 4:1). The Thessalonian correspondence contains half of the Pauline instances of the lexeme μιμεῖσθαι (1 Thess 1:6; 2:14; 2 Thess 3:7, 9) and a quarter of the references to τύπος ("example," "pattern," "model"; 1 Thess 1:7; 2 Thess 3:9), so these early letters are instructive for understanding the place of imitation and example in Pauline thought.

Scholars have noted that in 1 Thess 1:6 and 2:14, Paul uses the indicative form of γίνεσθαι ("to be," "to become") to describe an existing or resulting state of imitation, while in 2 Thess 3:7–9 and elsewhere in his letters (1 Cor 4:16; 11:1; Eph 5:1;

---

67. Fiore, *Personal Example*, 176–77.
68. Too, *Rhetoric of Identity*, 188–89.
69. Paul probably wrote 1–2 Thess around 50–51 CE during his long stay in Corinth. Pauline authorship of 2 Thess is disputed, but it is hard to dismiss (1) the author's self-identification in 1:1; (2) his "signature" in 3:17, which parallels that in the undisputed letters (1 Cor 16:21; Gal 6:11; Phlm 19); and (3) the unease of the early church towards pseudonymous writings (see, e.g., Eusebius, *Hist. eccl.* 6.12.1–6). For an informed case for Pauline authorship, see Paul Foster, "Who Wrote 2 Thessalonians? A Fresh Look at an Old Problem," *JSNT* 35 (2012): 150–75. For Paul appending his autographic subscription as a means of authenticating and authorizing the letter, see Steve Reece, *Paul's Large Letters: Paul's Autographic Subscription in the Light of Ancient Epistolary Conventions*, LNTS 561 (London: Bloomsbury T&T Clark, 2017). Regardless of authorship, I consider 2 Thess to be part of the Pauline tradition and I call attention to issues only when 2 Thess presents a different notion of imitation from 1 Thess.
70. Paul's moral language revolves around παρακαλεῖν ("to exhort"; 1 Thess 2:12; 3:2, 7; 4:1, 10, 18; 5:11, 14; 2 Thess 2:17; 3:12) and περιπατεῖν ("to walk"; 1 Thess 2:12; 4:1, 12; 2 Thess 3:6, 11). While Abraham J. Malherbe considers 1 Thess to be a paraenetic letter ("Exhortation in First Thessalonians," *NovT* 25 [1983]: 238–56, at 238), Karl Paul Donfried contends that it is more a paracletic letter ("The Theology of 1 Thessalonians as a Reflection of Its Purpose," in *Paul, Thessalonica, and Early Christianity* [London: T&T Clark, 2002], 119–38, at 120). I will simply view 1 Thess as a letter of exhortation with paraenetic/paracletic material.

Phil 3:17) he uses the imperative form to exhort his audience to imitation. Betz remarks that the Thessalonians have already achieved what the early church is called to do.[71] Be that as it may, if we accept that imitation is a sensory process where someone usually observes an exemplar in order to imitate that person, then 1 Thessalonians poses a twofold challenge. First, the passive morphology in 1:6 and 2:14 (ἐγενήθητε μιμηταί; "you became imitators") seems to suggest that the Thessalonians had no active role in the mimetic process.[72] Second, we would have to ask how the Thessalonians served as an example for imitation to believers in Greece who could not have observed them (1:7), and conversely, how the Thessalonian church could be imitators of Judean churches they had never encountered (2:14). This would suggest that imitation does not require direct observation of an exemplar and can be mediated through other means.

Once we examine the relevant texts (sections 6.2.1–6.2.3), we will outline how example and imitation feature in Paul's ethics for the Thessalonians (section 6.2.4). Our study will reveal that mimesis is central to Paul's strategy for the moral formation of the Thessalonian church and that emulating Paul's (and Christ's) lifestyle of self-giving holds together the relevant texts in 1–2 Thessalonians. We will also learn that there are modes of imitation other than direct observation.

6.2.1. Being Imitators and Being Imitated (1 Thess 1:5–8)

First Thessalonians 1:2–10 is characterized by a mimetic chain regarding the gospel or "word of the Lord" involving (1) Paul, his team, and Christ; (2) the Thessalonian believers; and (3) believers across Macedonia and Achaia. Regarding the passive morphology surrounding mimesis in 1:6 (ἐγενήθητε μιμηταί), Paul most likely uses the indicative middle-passive γίνεσθαι to stress the result (the Thessalonians have become imitators) rather than the process (how they became imitators).[73] Even so, the process is not passive; rather, the idea is that the Thessalonian believers (intentionally) behaved in a particular way that led them to become imitators. Hence, we must determine what activity or activities the Thessalonians engaged in that caused them to be seen as imitators of Paul. When Paul says that the Thessalonians have become imitators of "us" (ἡμῶν; 1:6), he most likely includes his coworkers Silvanus and Timothy (1:1; see also Acts 16–17). We must also consider

---

71. Betz, *Nachfolge und Nachahmung*, 143.

72. See Schulz, *Nachfolgen und Nachahmen*, 314–16; Nicolet, "Le concept d'imitation," 399; Dodd, *Paul's Paradigmatic "I,"* 212–13; Jane M. F. Heath, "Absent Presences of Paul and Christ: *Enargeia* in 1 Thessalonians 1–3," *JSNT* 32 (2009): 3–38, at 12.

73. Cornelis Bennema, "Paul's Paraenetic Strategy of Example and Imitation in 1–2 Thessalonians," *ETL* 98 (2022): 219–38, at 220–23.

in what sense the Thessalonians have become imitators of Christ (καὶ τοῦ κυρίου; 1:6). Finally, we must resolve how the Thessalonian believers could have been an example to other believers across Greece when they had never encountered one another (1:7).

The Content of the Thessalonians' Imitation. De Boer argues that Paul does not make a generic reference to imitation in 1:6 but to the Thessalonians' joyful endurance of suffering on account of their faith. The Thessalonians had not only observed this in Paul when he was with them but were also aware of Jesus's sufferings through Paul's accounts, which means they were imitators of both Paul and the Lord.[74] Brant, however, notes Paul's exemplary behavior in 1:5; 2:7–9 and concludes (contra de Boer) that the imitation relates to Paul's overall lifestyle: "Paul stands as the principal example. He has adopted an ethic of self-renunciation in order to manifest a life in Christ and has provided the concrete example of how one should go about being an imitator."[75] Clarke lists possible ways in which the Thessalonians imitated Paul, his team, and the Lord in 1:6: (1) they received the word; (2) they received the word amidst persecution; and (3) they received the word with the joy of the Holy Spirit. Rejecting the first option, Clarke then finds the other two wanting because while persecution and joy characterized the mission of Paul and Jesus, it is unlikely that Paul intended imitation of these characteristics (contra de Boer).[76] Instead, Clarke proposes that 1:6 refers to the Thessalonians' imitation of the lifestyle of Paul, his team, and the Lord (like Brant): "The Thessalonians had become imitators by responding to the gospel in a way which reflected and was consistent with both Paul's and the Lord's conduct in living and proclaiming that message."[77] It is in this lifestyle of receiving, living out, and proclaiming the gospel that the Thessalonians have become a model for other believers to emulate (1:7–10).[78]

Hence, the main options for the content of the Thessalonians' imitation in 1:6a are (1) their steadfast and joyful endurance of suffering on account of their faith in

---

74. De Boer, *Imitation of Paul*, 114–23. For more recent support of this idea, see Matera, *New Testament Ethics*, 127; Nicolet, "Le concept d'imitation," 399; Swartley, *Covenant of Peace*, 360; Claude Coulot, "Les Thessaloniciens accueillent l'évangile: Un premier bilan (1 Th 1,2–10)," *BLE* 112 (2011): 29–40, at 36–37, 39–40; Hajnalka Ravasz, *Aspekte der Seelsorge in den paulinischen Gemeinden: Eine exegetische Untersuchung anhand des 1. Thessalonicherbriefes*, WUNT 2/443 (Tübingen: Mohr Siebeck, 2017), 47–48.

75. Brant, "*Mimēsis*," 292.

76. Clarke, "Imitators," 334–36.

77. Clarke, "Imitators," 337.

78. Clarke, "Imitators," 338. Copan analyzes the same options and agrees with Clarke (*Saint Paul*, 81–87).

1:6b (de Boer) or (2) an adoption of Paul's general lifestyle in 1:5b (Brant, Clarke). In my view, 1:5b provides the example for imitation, while 1:6b mentions the starting point of imitation. I take the aorist participle δεξάμενοι ("having received") in 1:6b to mean that the Thessalonians became imitators of Paul (and his team) *after* they had accepted the word amidst persecution. However, this persecution from their fellow citizens (see 2:14) was not limited to when the Thessalonians' church was first formed; rather, it became an ongoing reality (3:1–5; see also 2 Thess 1:4). As such, the Thessalonians experienced persecution just as Paul, Jesus, and the Judean churches had (see 2:14–16). Sharing the same experience, however, does not make one an imitator; otherwise, the proponents of the idea of passive imitation (see n. 72) would be correct. Rather, in order to be imitators, the Thessalonians must have engaged in a particular behavior that provoked opposition. Their ongoing experience of persecution on account of their faith is what makes Paul realize that they had been imitating him.[79] We must now determine in what way the Thessalonians had imitated Paul.

In 1:5a, Paul speaks of how the word came to the Thessalonians through his own ministry and that of his team, and in 1:5b, he reminds them of the kind of people he and his coworkers were for their sake. This implies that the Thessalonians had been able to observe Paul and his team during their visit, and this was intentional for their benefit (δι' ὑμᾶς). Besides establishing a correlation between the trustworthiness of the message and the messenger, the added benefit of putting his life on display was that the Thessalonians could observe and imitate it. While Paul does not provide details about his observable lifestyle in 1:5b, he does so in 2:1–12.[80] Paul's time with the Thessalonians was characterized by (1) proclaiming the gospel despite opposition (2:2); (2) seeking to please God rather than people (2:3–6); (3) showing a deep parental concern (2:7, 11–12); (4) sharing his entire life (τὰς ἑαυτῶν ψυχάς; 2:8); and (5) working for a living so as not to burden others (2:9). In short, Paul had modeled for the Thessalonians *a lifestyle of self-giving* as an example to be imitated.[81] Indeed, when Paul states that they have observed (ὑμεῖς

---

79. Similarly, Ben Witherington states that following the example of Paul (and Christ) led to persecution (*1 and 2 Thessalonians: A Socio-Rhetorical Commentary* [Grand Rapids: Eerdmans, 2006], 72).

80. De Boer also notes that 2:1–12 elaborates on 1:5 and repeatedly recalls what the Thessalonians already knew about Paul's conduct (e.g., οἴδατε ["you know"] in 2:1, 2, 5, 11 and μνημονεύετε ["you remember"] in 2:9) (*Imitation of Paul*, 112). See also Michael Martin, "'Example' and 'Imitation' in the Thessalonians Correspondence," *SwJT* 42 (1999): 39–49, at 43.

81. See also Matera, *New Testament Ethics*, 128–29. Differently, Daniel Marguerat takes 2:1–12 as "apostolic self-recommendation" (rather than paraenesis), in which Paul recalls his past conduct as an example to imitate in order to strengthen the beleaguered Thessalonians (*Paul in Acts*

μάρτυρες) his life as "blameless" (ἀμέμπτως) (2:10), he is implying that his life exemplified the goal for the Thessalonians' moral formation (3:13; 5:23). In sum, the lives of Paul and his coworkers had been on display for the Thessalonians to observe and imitate. Presenting himself as the spiritual parent of the Thessalonians, Paul models the kind of life that he wants them to emulate.[82] The content of imitation mentioned in 1:6a, therefore, is not found in 1:6b but in 1:5b and is elaborated in 2:1–12 when Paul describes his past visit and the lifestyle he had modeled.[83]

Imitators of the "Unseen" Lord. Besides being imitators of Paul and his team, the Thessalonians were also imitators of the Lord, whom they had never seen (1:6). Some scholars have suggested that this imitation refers to the Thessalonians' corporate life "in Christ" or the emulation of the risen Christ rather than the life of the historical Jesus.[84] In my view, however, Paul does not make a sharp distinction between the historical and risen Christ, and more importantly, this suggestion fails to explain how the Thessalonians could have observed the Lord. To explain how the Thessalonians were also imitators of the unseen Christ, Michael Jensen sees the phrase καὶ τοῦ κυρίου (1:6) as conveying result ("and so of the Lord") in that the Thessalonians effectively imitated Christ through imitating Paul and his team. The specific content of imitation here is a way of life characterized as the faithful response to the word of God amidst affliction.[85] While 1 Cor 11:1 supports Jensen's idea that the imitation of Christ can be mediated through Paul, I contend that his view of the content of imitation is too narrow (see our discussion above). The gospel that Paul presented to the Thessalonians would most likely have included various Jesus traditions.[86] Consequently, the Thessalonians could visualize aspects

---

and Paul in His Letters, WUNT 310 [Tübingen: Mohr Siebeck, 2013], 220–43). However, I view this self-recommendation as part of Paul's paraenesis.

82. For the idea of Paul as parent to the Thessalonians, see Jennifer Houston McNeel, *Paul as Infant and Nursing Mother: Metaphor, Rhetoric, and Identity in 1 Thessalonians 2:5–8*, SBLECL 12 (Atlanta: SBL Press, 2014).

83. See also Brant, "*Mimēsis*," 292; Clarke, "Imitators," 338–39; Copan, *Saint Paul*, 85–87; Fiore, "Paul," 239–40. Contra many commentators who regard 1:6b to express the content of imitation: e.g., Charles A. Wanamaker, *The Epistles to the Thessalonians: A Commentary on the Greek Text*, NIGTC (Grand Rapids: Eerdmans, 1990), 80–82; Gordon D. Fee, *The First and Second Letters to the Thessalonians*, NICNT (Grand Rapids: Eerdmans, 2009), 37–39; Jeffrey A. D. Weima, *1–2 Thessalonians*, BECNT (Grand Rapids: Baker Academic, 2014), 100.

84. E.g., Betz, *Nachfolge und Nachahmung*, 143–44; Merk, "Nachahmung Christi," 323–24; Nicolet, "Le concept d'imitation," 400.

85. Jensen, "Imitating Paul," 25. Similarly, Furnish also contends that the *only* aspect of imitation in view is that of "patient and loyal obedience even in the midst of suffering" (*Paul*, 221).

86. For a comprehensive case that Paul knew various Jesus traditions, see David Wenham, *Paul: Follower of Jesus or Founder of Christianity?* (Grand Rapids: Eerdmans, 1995); Wenham,

of Jesus's life and pattern their lives after it. While modeling a life of self-giving, Paul would also have stressed Christ's self-giving (see, e.g., 5:10).[87]

Research supports the idea of being able to "observe" and imitate someone who is absent. In chapter 2, we noted the important study by Capes, showing that in antiquity the lives of notable people were upheld as models for imitation, and while living models were preferred, the lives of great men from the past could also be "observed" (and imitated) through spoken and published accounts.[88] Similarly, Copan notes that people in antiquity had no difficulty with the concept of imitating deceased ancestors whose image had been preserved in written and oral tradition.[89] He suggests two complementary ways in which the Thessalonians could have imitated the Jesus of history they had never seen: (1) an *orally mediated imitation*, in which the Thessalonians could have visualized Jesus from Paul's oral account, and (2) a *personally mediated imitation*, where the Thessalonians could "see" Jesus through the life of Paul, who himself was an imitator of Christ (1 Cor 11:1).[90] In sum, the Thessalonians could visualize and imitate the Lord through (1) *hearing* Paul's account of Jesus and (2) *observing* Paul's life, which embodied Jesus.[91] The important principle to note is the concept of *mediated* imitation, where the imitator can visualize and "observe" the exemplar from oral tradition, written accounts, or embodied lives.[92]

The Example of the Thessalonians. The Thessalonians did not just imitate the example of Paul (and the Lord) but, in turn, became exemplars for other believers

---

Paul and Jesus: The True Story (London: SPCK, 2002). See also Burridge, *Imitating Jesus*, 139–43. De Boer contends that Paul was aware of the Jesus traditions specifically through the Antioch church, which was founded by Jerusalem Christians who were surely well informed about Jesus's life and teachings (*Imitation of Paul*, 159–60).

87. Paul frequently refers to Christ's self-giving (e.g., Rom 5:6–8; 1 Cor 11:24; 15:3; 2 Cor 5:15; Gal 1:4; 2:20; Phil 2:5–8; see also Eph 5:2, 25; 1 Tim 2:6; Titus 2:14).

88. Capes, "*Imitatio Christi*," 1–19. In chapter 5, I applied Capes's insights to the Johannine tradition, arguing that the author had recorded Jesus's life and teachings in his Gospel and Letters so that his audience could reconstruct this "remembered" Jesus from the Johannine text and imitate him.

89. Copan, *Saint Paul*, 47, 102.

90. Copan, *Saint Paul*, 102–4. Instead of Copan's "textually mediated imitation," the description "orally mediated imitation" fits better. Peter Orr also contends that Christ's earthly life is the content of imitation (*Christ Absent and Present: A Study in Pauline Christology*, WUNT 2/354 [Tübingen: Mohr Siebeck, 2014], 163).

91. Similarly, Abraham J. Malherbe asserts that Paul preached and embodied the gospel of the self-giving Lord (*The Letters to the Thessalonians*, AB 32b [New York: Doubleday, 2000], 127). Contra Ravasz, who contends that the Thessalonians' imitation of Christ was *unbewusst* ("unconscious") (*Aspekte der Seelsorge*, 48, 51).

92. See also Fiore, "Paul," 231–36; Harrison, "Imitation," 222–45.

in Macedonia and Achaia (1:7–8). In what way were they an example for imitation? Brant argues that the Thessalonians had engaged in missions in Macedonia and Achaia.[93] However, it is unlikely that the Thessalonians had evangelized all of Greece and that their missional methods had been observed so widely. If they had engaged in evangelism, it would probably have been locally. Instead, 1:8 states that it was the *report* of their acceptance of the gospel and their lived-out faith that had spread throughout Greece.[94] As we noted earlier, although imitation usually arises from direct observation of an exemplar, the example can be mediated through other means. In this case, oral reports about the Thessalonians that had spread throughout Greece would have enabled their recipients to visualize the life and enduring faith of the Thessalonian community. These accounts about the Thessalonian church could have functioned as the basis for imitation, where the recipients reconstructed and "observed" the example of the Thessalonians from the reports.

6.2.2. Imitating the Unseen Judean Churches (1 Thess 2:13–16)

First Thessalonians 1:4–10 and 2:13–16 are not only conceptually linked by the notions of imitation, example, the reception of the gospel, and persecution but also confront us with similar issues. First, 2:14 uses a passive morphology of γίνεσθαι, although we suggested in 1:6 that this does not necessarily translate into "passive" imitation.[95] Second, imitation usually requires that the imitator can observe the exemplar. Hence, we must explain how the Thessalonians could be imitators of the Judean churches that they have never seen. The idea in 2:14 seems to be merely one of analogy in that the Thessalonian and Judean churches share the same experience of being persecuted on account of their faith.

Others reject this view of passive imitation. De Boer, for example, asserts that the Thessalonians were imitators of the Judean churches in their steadfast endurance of religious persecution. Acknowledging that imitation requires an intentional following of an example, he explores how the Thessalonians could have been aware of the conduct of the Judean Christians. De Boer suggests that Paul may well have shared how he and the Judean believers had suffered at the hands of their own people.[96] Be that as it may, this needs clarification because imitation

---

93. Brant, "*Mimēsis*," 292–93. Malherbe also supports this view, albeit taking Paul's language of "all" and "everywhere" in 1:7–8 as approaching hyperbole (*Thessalonians*, 116–17).
94. See also the discussion in Weima, *1–2 Thessalonians*, 105–6.
95. Contra Wanamaker, *Thessalonians*, 112; Witherington, *Thessalonians*, 87.
96. De Boer, *Imitation of Paul*, 99–107.

6. Mimesis in the Pauline Letters

typically requires someone to *observe* the exemplar, whereas de Boer suggests that the Thessalonians had only *heard* Paul's report about the Judean churches. Differently, Brant argues that the Thessalonians were engaged in preaching the gospel in Macedonia and Achaia (1:8) and consequently experienced opposition as Paul and the Judean churches did (2:14–16).[97] While I agree with her view on 1:6, her claim that the Thessalonians had become imitators of the Judean churches by actively engaging in the same activity (to preach the gospel) is unconvincing. First, 1:8 does not indicate that the Thessalonians had evangelized the whole of Greece, and second, 2:13–16 does not imply that the Judean churches had engaged in preaching the gospel.

Instead, the imitation in 2:14 has a corresponding dynamic to that in 1:6. The assertion that the Thessalonian church had become imitators of the Judean churches in 2:14a is explained by the comparative conjunction καθώς ("just as") and the repeated preposition ὑπό ("from") in 2:14b: "You *also* suffered the same things from your people, *just as* they did from the Judeans." They shared similar experiences because of the effectiveness of God's word in their respective communities of faith. The Thessalonians accepted God's word (παραλαμβάνειν λόγον θεοῦ) from Paul (2:13a) and began to experience God's word at work (ἐνεργεῖν λόγον θεοῦ) among them (2:13b). The conjunction γάρ ("for, because") causally connects 2:13 and 2:14, clarifying that the experience of God's word at work leads to the experience of persecution on account of their faith. God's word at work would have been a corporate living out of the gospel in a hostile world and not limited to the private sphere of the community of believers.[98] In 2:2, Paul recalls the hostility of the Thessalonian Jews to his preaching of the gospel (see also Acts 17). In imitating Paul, the emergent Thessalonian church also suffers persecution from their own people because of the gospel. Hence, God's word at work among the Thessalonians is seen in (1) their active way of life that pleases God (4:1) and (2) their corporate church life, which becomes a testimony throughout Greece (1:8). We noted earlier that the Thessalonians had learned from Paul and his coworkers how to live out the gospel (see also 4:2).

We must now resolve how the Thessalonian church imitated the life of the Judean churches if we concede that sharing the same experience does not constitute imitation.[99] We return to de Boer, who rightly notes that imitation re-

---

97. Brant, "*Mimēsis*," 292–93.

98. For the nature of the conflict between the Thessalonian believers and their non-believing neighbors, see John M. G. Barclay, "Conflict in Thessalonica," *CBQ* 55 (1993): 512–30.

99. Simon Légasse seeks to counter the issue that imitating a *community* in 2:14 contrasts with its use in other Pauline passages where the idea is of imitating Christ and/or Paul himself, but his appeal to Paul's flexible use of vocabulary and ideas is unconvincing ("Paul et les Juifs

quires an intentional following of an example. He first argues that, by reason of their primacy of origin, the Jerusalem mother-church and the surrounding Judean churches were the template for Christian living.[100] He then suggests that the Thessalonians would have been familiar with the experiences of the Judean churches through Paul's reporting (see also the use of ἡμᾶς in 2:15–16).[101] While de Boer's argument points us in the right direction, we must explain how Paul's account facilitated imitation, so we return to our argument in 1:6–8. Essentially, Paul's reports about the Judean churches enabled the Thessalonians to visualize the lifestyle of the Judean Christians and emulate it. Based on Paul's portrayal of the Judean Christians, the Thessalonians are able to imitate them by re-creating their conduct, resulting in the parallel experience of being persecuted by their own people. As Jensen states, this is an example of "collective imitation," where one group imitates another.[102]

Summary of Imitation in 1 Thessalonians. Paul's use of the indicative in 1:6 and 2:14 stresses the current state of the Thessalonians as imitators of Paul and the Judean churches. For de Boer, the common element of imitation in 1:6 and 2:14 is the manner in which the Thessalonians endured suffering, namely with steadfastness and joy.[103] For Brant, however, it relates to the Thessalonians' willingness to proclaim the gospel despite persecution. While de Boer's focus is too narrow, Brant's argument that the Thessalonians actively proclaimed the gospel throughout Greece is unconvincing. Instead, our close reading of 1 Thess 1–2 shows that the actions of the Thessalonians involve the acceptance of the gospel, the observance

---

d'après 1 Thessaloniciens 2,13–16," *RB* 104 [1997], 572–91, at 575, 577). More convincing is the argument that Paul had already spoken of imitating communities in 1:7, and Paul also refers to this idea in 2 Cor 8 (see n. 101 below and section 6.3.4).

100. De Boer, *Imitation of Paul*, 104–5, 125. This assumes that Paul remained under the oversight of Jerusalem, which depends largely on how one resolves the aftermath of the Antioch crisis and the Jerusalem Council (see Cornelis Bennema, "The Ethnic Conflict in Early Christianity: An Appraisal of Bauckham's Proposal on the Antioch Crisis and the Jerusalem Council," *JETS* 56 [2013]: 753–63).

101. De Boer, *Imitation of Paul*, 106. De Boer notes how Paul in 2 Cor 8:1–7 upholds the Macedonian churches as an example for the Corinthian church on the matter of giving, so Paul's endorsement of the exemplary conduct of the Judean churches to the Thessalonians is not unusual (*Imitation of Paul*, 106).

102. Jensen, "Imitating Paul," 28.

103. De Boer, *Imitation of Paul*, 124. Castelli also notes that the Thessalonians' suffering ties their experience to that of others in the mimetic economy (Paul, the Lord, other persecuted communities). But unlike de Boer, she contends that Paul's discourse of imitation articulates a particular set of power relations within the social nascent structures of early Christian communities (*Imitating Paul*, 15, 90–95). For a critique of Castelli, see n. 4 above.

of the life of Paul and the Judean churches, and the emulation of their lifestyle, corporately and publicly, resulting in persecution. Hence, I reject Brant's implied mimetic chain from Paul to the Judean churches to the Thessalonian church revolving around preaching the gospel despite persecution. Instead, I suggest the mimetic chain involves Paul, the Judean churches, the Thessalonian church, and the believers throughout Greece regarding receiving and living out the gospel amidst persecution.[104] In short, the imitation Paul describes in 1 Thessalonians has more to do with *ethics* than mission.[105] If we remember that Paul's purpose in writing to the Thessalonians is a moral one, we start to see that imitation is in service of Paul's ethics. In this case, example and imitation are vital aspects of Paul's strategy for the moral formation of the Thessalonian church, and Paul's ethics here is specifically *mimetic ethics*.

Our findings have some affinity with Jane Heath's study on Paul's use of verbal ἐνάργεια ("vividness," "immediacy"), where "Paul seeks by words to render the apostolic presence vivid to the senses."[106] She notes that in 1:2–2:16, Paul does not describe in detail his past visit to the Thessalonians; rather, he has them *remember* it (note the frequent use of "you know" in 1:5; 2:1–2, 5, 11) as a means of actualizing his past presence.[107] This technique of evoking the audience's memory to make them experience something absent as if it were present was commonly used by ancient orators to achieve ἐνάργεια.[108] While Heath focuses on the concept of ἐνάργεια rather than imitation, her study helps us identify another mode of imitation. When Paul, in 1:2–2:16, appeals to the Thessalonians' memory of his lifestyle when he was with them, they can visualize Paul and imitate him. Hence, it is entirely fitting that he uses imitation language in this section of the letter. Having said this, Paul's use of the indicative in 1:6 and 2:14 shows that the Thessalonians already *are* imitators of him and the Judean churches. More precisely then, by appealing to their memory of his visit, Paul evokes mental images of him in the present and thus implicitly encourages them to *continue* their imitation. Thus, in addition to the concept of *mediated* imitation (see section 6.2.1), we have now found a second mode of imitation, namely *mnemonic* imitation, where remembrance can aid visualization and imitation.[109]

---

104. Fiore speaks of "the Thessalonians' mimetic endurance" ("Paul," 240).

105. In fairness, Brant does mention behavior as part of the imitation, but mainly related to 1:6.

106. Heath, "Presences," 5.

107. Heath, "Presences," 7–8.

108. Heath, "Presences," 8–11.

109. Where Heath and I differ is regarding Paul's purpose for evoking the Thessalonians' collective memory. While Heath argues that in invoking his past visit to the Thessalonians, Paul

6.2.3. A Neglected Aspect of Imitation (2 Thess 3:6–13)

When we turn to 2 Thessalonians, we see that some Thessalonian Christians had failed to imitate one aspect of Paul's lived example, namely, to work for a living for the sake of others. While Paul uses the indicative in 1 Thess 1:6; 2:14 to describe what they were already imitating, in 2 Thess 3:7–9, he uses the imperative to exhort the Thessalonians to imitate him (and his team) and earn a living in order to counter the ongoing issue of ἀτάκτως. The adverb ἀτάκτως has a general sense of "disorderly, undisciplined" and occurs in the New Testament only in the Thessalonian correspondence and always in the context of work. Contra common belief,[110] de Boer argues that ἀτάκτως does *not* take on the meaning "idle, lazy" because Paul calls these people "busybodies" who need to calm down (2 Thess 3:11–12). Hence, the issue is not inactivity but frenzied activity that causes them to be dependent on others for a living.[111]

The highest concentration of "work"-related words (ἔργον ["work"], ἐργάζεσθαι ["to work"], κόπος ["labor"], κοπιᾶν ["to labor"]) and the ἀτακτ* group occurs in 2 Thess 3:6–12, followed by 1 Thess 5:12–14.[112] In 1 Thess 4:11–12, Paul exhorts the Thessalonians to behave responsibly towards their non-Christian neighbors, including undertaking manual labor. This exhortation was probably based on his own example mentioned in 1 Thess 2:9. In light of the exhortation in 2 Thess 3:12 ("that as you work quietly, you may eat your own bread"), the threefold exhortation in 1 Thess 4:11 (to live quietly, to mind one's own affairs, and to take up physical work) probably refers to the single idea of working for a living. In 1 Thess 5:12–14, Paul reiterates that those who work should be commended, while those who do not should be admonished. When we come to 2 Thessalonians, the issue of disorderliness appears to have persisted or even worsened, given that Paul addresses the issue at length.[113]

---

reawakens his apostolic presence in order to evoke God's activity that the Thessalonians had experienced through Paul ("Presences," 20, 26, 29), I contend that Paul evokes the Thessalonians' memory so that they can continue their imitation of him (and Christ). In short, while Heath focuses on the Thessalonians' past experience of *God* made vivid in the present, I focus on their past experience of *Paul* made vivid in the present.

110. See, for example, Schulz, *Nachfolgen und Nachahmen*, 312 (he uses the term *Arbeitsscheu*); Clarke, "Imitators," 340–41; Weima, *1–2 Thessalonians*, 600. While many English Bibles translate ἀτάκτως as "idle" (e.g., CEV, ESV, ISV, NIV, NLT, NRSV), most German and French Bibles have "disorderly" (*unordentlich* and *désordre/désordonnée* respectively).

111. De Boer, *Imitation of Paul*, 127.

112. 1 Thess 5:12–14 features the terms κοπιᾶν, ἔργον, and ἄτακτος, while 2 Thess 3:6–12 includes ἀτάκτως (2x), ἀτακτεῖν, κόπος, and ἐργάζεσθαι (4x).

113. De Boer notes that the command to *admonish* the disorderly in 1 Thess 5:14 changes to a command to *separate* from them in 2 Thess 3:6 (*Imitation of Paul*, 127).

6. Mimesis in the Pauline Letters

Paul presents both a model to avoid (the "disorderly" who had ignored the tradition Paul had established in 3:6) and a model to imitate (Paul and his team, who worked for a living in 3:7–9).[114] The tradition (παράδοσις) that the disorderly group had ignored was Paul's moral teaching by example (the conjunction γάρ causally links 3:6 and 3:7–9). Paul promotes working for a living as the antidote to the issue of disorderliness in the Thessalonian church and reminds them of the visible example (τύπος) he had set while he was with them (3:7–9; see also 1 Thess 2:9).[115] The mimetic imperative to engage in physical labor to earn a living is not a command to duplicate the work Paul did but to be engaged *like* him in some kind of work to make a living and not live off fellow believers.

Harrison seeks to situate Paul's mimetic injunction in a specific social context, one where Paul exhorts the Thessalonians to abandon their dependence on Roman patronage and assume the role of benefactor to the needy through their house church networks.[116] While this suggestion is appealing, there is insufficient evidence to support it. The majority position is best represented by Clarke, who argues that Paul's mimetic injunction is for those Thessalonian believers who had "inappropriately chosen unemployment in their imminent expectation of the Parousia."[117] Besides taking issue with the notion of idleness (see above), de Boer critiques at length the idea that the believers' disorderliness relates to an excitement over the imminent Parousia.[118] Instead, he contends that these Thessalonians had become spiritual fanatics who had ceased to work for a living and had become reliant on the church.[119] While I agree that the issue is not idleness or inactivity, it is difficult to disconnect the disruptive conduct of this group from the strong eschatological outlook of both letters.

In my view, John Barclay makes a better case. He argues that when Paul provided the Thessalonian believers with an apocalyptic perspective (Christ's imminent return and the outpouring of God's wrath) to cope with the social harassment from their fellow citizens, some believers gave up their occupations to engage in provocative evangelism. This, combined with the conviction of some believers that the day of God's wrath has already begun, had the potential to exacerbate tensions between the church and the non-Christian citizens in Thessalonica, so Paul rebukes

---

114. See also Matera, *New Testament Ethics*, 136–37; Jensen, "Imitating Paul," 25.
115. Elsewhere, Paul uses his chosen lifestyle as an argument against being a stumbling block to others (1 Cor 9:1–18; 2 Cor 11:7–9).
116. Harrison, "Imitation," 250.
117. Clarke, "Imitators," 341.
118. De Boer, *Imitation of Paul*, 128–32.
119. De Boer, *Imitation of Paul*, 133.

those who have stopped working and are now interfering in others' affairs.[120] We can now gather our findings and explain the role of mimesis in Paul's strategy for the moral formation of the Thessalonian church.

6.2.4. The Place of Mimesis in Paul's Ethics for the Thessalonians

In Greco-Roman antiquity and early Christianity, letters often contained moral exhortation,[121] and the Thessalonian correspondence is no exception. Abraham Malherbe explains that "to provide concreteness to the exhortation, an example is offered for imitation," and the example often is a family member.[122] In fact, the spheres of family and education overlapped so that the teacher was considered a de facto parent who was expected to be a good example for his pupils.[123] Likewise, Paul presents himself as the spiritual parent of the Thessalonians (1 Thess 2:7, 11) and as an example to imitate (1 Thess 1:5–6; 2 Thess 3:7–9). His communication to the infant Thessalonian church focuses on how they should live in the face of persecution and in light of the Parousia. The moral goal he holds out for their shared life is described variously as (1) to be blameless (1 Thess 3:13; 5:23); (2) to live in a manner worthy of God (1 Thess 2:12); and (3) to live and please God in line with Paul's instructions (1 Thess 4:1–2).

Paul presents himself as an example for imitation, showing how his own blameless behavior during his stay in Thessalonica (2:10) exemplifies the moral goal of being blameless he holds out for the Thessalonians (3:13; 5:23).[124] The moral goal of living in a manner worthy of God (2:12) concludes a section that highlights various aspects of Paul's lifestyle (2:1–12), which serve as the example for the Thessalonians to emulate (1:5–6). Paul aimed to please God in his ministry (2:4) and exhorts the Thessalonians to do the same (4:1). Paul chooses to work for a living and not burden others (2:9), which is the basis for his exhortation in 4:11–12 and foreshadows his explicit language of example and imitation in 2 Thess 3:6–13.[125] It is evident that for Paul, example and imitation are crucial to the moral formation of the Thessalonian church.

---

120. Barclay, "Conflict," 516–29.

121. Malherbe, *Moral Exhortation*, 79, 124–25. Fiore even claims that epistolary presence could be more effective and purer than physical presence ("Paul," 236). Nonetheless, in 1–2 Thess, the mention of Paul as an example for imitation harks back to his presence with the Thessalonians in the past (1 Thess 1:5–6; 2:1–12; 2 Thess 3:7–10).

122. Malherbe, *Moral Exhortation*, 125. Elsewhere, he states, "A major part of ancient paraenesis was the offering of a model to be imitated" ("Exhortation," 240).

123. Fiore, "Paul," 234.

124. Wolbert also stresses that Paul's paraenetic authority is rooted in his personal example ("Vorbild," 263).

125. While 1 Thess 2:12; 4:1 presents the ideal kind of περιπατεῖν, 2 Thess 3:6, 11 refers to the wrong kind.

6. Mimesis in the Pauline Letters

In 1 Thessalonians, I see a four-stage process of mimesis: (1) some Thessalonians become Christians through the ministry of Paul and his team; (2) the newly-converted Thessalonians start to emulate Paul's lifestyle of self-giving (patterned after that of Jesus); (3) consequently, the Thessalonian Christians experience persecution as Paul (and Jesus) did; and (4) viewing this persecution as the sign that they have emulated him, Paul declares that the Thessalonians have become imitators of him (and Jesus). From 2 Thessalonians, we learn that some Thessalonian Christians were selective in imitating Paul's lifestyle, and Paul had to admonish them on the one aspect where they had neglected to imitate him, namely, to work for a living and not be dependent on others. In sum, it is Paul's lifestyle of self-giving (and that of Christ) that constitutes a coherent ethical template for mimesis in 1–2 Thessalonians.[126]

There is arguably a tension between Paul's assertion that the Thessalonians have already become imitators (1 Thess 1:6; 2:14) and his exhortation that they must press on in their moral life (παρακαλεῖν ... περισσεύειν μᾶλλον; 4:1, 10). When Paul uses the indicative mood in 1:6 to state that the Thessalonians have become imitators of him (and the Lord), he does not suggest that the process is complete. Rather, he appears to express his delight in how soon after their conversion they had successfully grasped the concept of imitation to grow in their Christian life— and his expectation that they will continue this imitation (and be examples to others). Indeed, by evoking the Thessalonians' memory of his past visit to them in 1:5 and 2:1–12, Paul appears to be encouraging them to *continue* their imitation of him. This corresponds to 4:1, where Paul commends the Thessalonians for living according to the ethical goal while also exhorting them to continue. The mention of the Thessalonians having "received" from Paul the notion of how to live (4:1) very likely refers to more than oral instructions and includes their observation of Paul's exemplary life. Similarly, the tradition that the Thessalonians had received from Paul (2 Thess 3:6) refers to the visible example of Paul working for a living (2 Thess 3:7–9). Hence, the receiving of traditions or instructions can extend beyond verbal to "embodied" instructions (see also Phil 4:9).[127]

---

126. Contra Merk, who states that imitation in 1 Thess 1:6; 2:14 is not about ethics but about sharing a particular Christian existence; only in 2 Thess 3:6–9 does imitation relate to ethics ("Nachahmung Christi," 323–27). Likewise, Nicolet asserts, "Imiter le Christ, ce n'est donc pas considérer ce dernier comme un modèle à imiter ... mais c'est vivre de la vie qu'il a inaugurée" ("To imitate Christ is therefore not to consider him as a model to imitate ... but to live the life that he has inaugurated") ("Le concept d'imitation," 412).

127. Malherbe also notes that, by referring to his exemplary behavior, Paul understands tradition to involve more than oral teaching (*Thessalonians*, 450). Likewise, Martin asserts that ancient philosophers taught with their *logos* (teaching) and their *ethos* (behavior) ("Example," 41).

6.2.5. Conclusion

We have sought to demonstrate that personal example and imitation are key aspects of Paul's paraenetic approach to the moral formation of the Thessalonian church. In keeping with the idea that the imitator typically has direct access to the exemplar, we inferred that the Thessalonians had observed Paul's life during his time in Thessalonica and imitated it. However, the Thessalonian correspondence also points to alternative modes of imitation because other exemplars (Jesus, the Judean churches, and Paul at the time of writing) were absent. First, there is the concept of *mediated* imitation, where the Thessalonians could visualize and "observe" Jesus and the Judean churches from Paul's accounts, as well as from Paul's own life (in the case of Jesus because Paul was an imitator of Jesus and hence embodied him). In turn, the Thessalonians continued the chain of mediated imitation by becoming an example to believers throughout Greece. The second mode of imitation we encountered was *mnemonic* imitation, where the Thessalonians were prompted to remember Paul as he was during a past visit in order to (continue to) "observe" and imitate his way of life.

We noted that, in antiquity, both living and literary examples could be held up for imitation. In the Thessalonian correspondence, Paul presents himself as a living example from the recent past, that is, as a remembered example. When Paul refers to himself as an example for imitation (1 Thess 1:5–6; 2 Thess 3:9), he reminds the Thessalonians of specific aspects of his lifestyle when he was with them to aid their recollection of him. Paul functions as a living example for imitation in that his letters evoke memories of the Thessalonians' first-hand experiences of him. In hearing or reading Paul's letters, Paul becomes in the minds of the Thessalonians a reconstructed exemplar whom they can imitate.

We learned that Paul's lifestyle of self-giving (modeled on that of Christ) is the ethical template for mimesis in 1–2 Thessalonians. However, although Paul mentions several expressions of such self-giving (e.g., in 1 Thess 2:1–12), there is no exhaustive list, so the implication is that the Thessalonians must discern what elements to imitate and how—a cognitive activity I call "moral reasoning." For example, Paul's mention of his "labor and toil, night and day" in 1 Thess 2:9 and 2 Thess 3:6–9 does not mean that the Thessalonians should all engage in the same kind of work or with the same intensity as Paul. Rather, they should imitate the principle that one should work for a living and avoid becoming a burden to others, and this will, of course, look different for different people. Hence, for Paul, mimesis is a cognitive, creative hermeneutical process rather than slavish copying.[128]

---

128. Similarly, Mary Ann Getty remarks that "the power of example is illustrated not in

6. Mimesis in the Pauline Letters

6.3. 1–2 Corinthians

Twice in 1 Corinthians, Paul issues the injunction to imitate him (μιμηταί μου γίνεσθε; 4:16; 11:1). Contrary to claims that Paul's injunction "imitate me" is unique in antiquity, I suggested that it is more accurate to say that Paul holding himself up as a model for imitation is uncommon but not unique (see section 6.1.1). With this understanding, we will examine Paul's twofold imperative μιμηταί μου γίνεσθε in 1 Cor 4:16; 11:1.[129] In addition to these explicit references, we will also explore possible traces of imitation in 1–2 Corinthians.

6.3.1. The Imitation of Paul Mediated through Timothy (1 Cor 4:16)

Most scholars agree that the church in Corinth was troubled by social divisions related to wealth and status. In 1 Cor 1–4, Paul seeks to promote unity and tackle divisions that had formed along the lines of loyalty to different leaders (Paul, Apollos, Peter).[130] Towards the end of this large section, we find Paul's imperative to imitate him, μιμηταί μου γίνεσθε (4:16).[131] However, Paul does not clarify what they are to imitate. Since 4:14–21 is most likely the conclusion to 1 Cor 1–4, it seems natural that Paul's injunction to imitate him looks back rather than forward.[132] We start, however, with the immediate context in which the mimetic imperative occurs.

---

duplicating the particularities of Paul's life but of assuring attitudes congruent both with his own and with Jesus' example" ("The Imitation of Paul in the Letters to the Thessalonians," in *The Thessalonian Correspondence*, ed. Raymond F. Collins, BETL 87 [Leuven: Peeters, 1990], 277–83, at 279). See also Ravasz, *Aspekte der Seelsorge*, 84.

129. For a Girardian interpretation of these passages where Paul seeks to correct the mimetic rivalry of the Corinthians that has caused them to be "puffed up" by presenting the right kind of mimesis—the imitation of him (and Christ) as victim and scapegoat, see Robert G. Hamerton-Kelly, "A Girardian Interpretation of Paul: Rivalry, Mimesis and Victimage in the Corinthian Correspondence," *Semeia* 33 (1985): 65–81. While Williams explores the possibilities for imitation in Jewish literature as a context for the imitation language in 1 Cor (see the references to Williams in our chapter 3), he does not really explain Paul's use of imitation ("Imitate Me," 209–24).

130. 1 Cor 1:10–17; 3:1–4:21 carries the main story line of personality cults, while 1:18–2:16 is a digression on the nature of true wisdom and power.

131. Except for 1 Thess 1:6 and 2:14, all other Pauline occurrences of the lexeme μιμεῖσθαι (1 Cor 4:16; 11:1; Eph 5:1; Phil 3:17; 2 Thess 3:7, 9) are in the imperative form.

132. Not all scholars agree that 4:16 looks back. Belleville, for example, contends that the injunction points forward in that "the Pauline exemplar is to be found in a common core of ethical teachings and norms of Christian practice that were routinely passed along to new congregations," such as we find in 7:17; 11:16; and 14:33 ("Imitate Me," 123). Dodd also takes 4:14–21 as introductory to what follows. He claims that just as παρακαλῶ in 1:10 introduces 1:10–4:13, so παρακαλῶ in 4:16 also introduces what is to come (*Paul's Paradigmatic "I,"* 65–67). How-

PART 2   MIMESIS IN EARLY CHRISTIANITY

It must be noted that 4:14–17 contains rich family language: (1) Paul describes himself as the (spiritual) father of the Corinthians (4:15); (2) the Corinthians are Paul's beloved children (4:14); and (3) Timothy is Paul's beloved and faithful child (4:17).[133] While 4:16 contains the mimetic imperative, 4:14–15 provides the grounds or basis for Paul's appeal to imitate him, where Paul presents himself as the spiritual parent of the Corinthians. We noted in chapter 2 that in antiquity, mimesis occurred in the overlapping spheres of family and education, where the teacher was a proxy parent who was expected to set the example for his pupils to imitate.[134] Paul frequently presents himself as a spiritual parent to his converts, as one who nurtures them in their religious-ethical life (see, e.g., on 1 Thess 2:7, 11 in section 6.2). By implication, Paul places the concept of imitation in the context of *family education*.[135] This needs elaboration.

The prepositional phrase διὰ τοῦτο ("for this reason") logically connects 4:17 to 4:16, expressing the idea that, in his absence, Paul is sending Timothy to help the Corinthian church in imitating him.[136] Paul's assertion that Timothy will remind them of his "ways in Christ Jesus" (ἀναμνήσει τὰς ὁδούς μου τὰς ἐν Χριστῷ [Ἰησοῦ])

---

ever, I contend that Paul's paraenetic exhortations παρακαλῶ in 1:10 and 4:16 form an *inclusio*, framing the unit 1:10–4:21. For a critique of Belleville's view (which also applies to Dodd), see Copan, *Saint Paul*, 110–11. Fiore is equivocal: in his monograph he implies that 4:16 looks back at 1:10–4:13 (*Personal Example*, 168–76), but in a later article he states that 4:16 and 11:1 form an *inclusio* ("Paul," 241).

133. Only 4:14–17 refers to Paul and the Corinthians as a spiritual family; all other family references are to God as father (1:13; 8:6; 15:24), to one's ancestors (10:1), and to human families (5:1; 7:14; 13:11; 14:20).

134. See also Fiore, *Personal Example*, 177; Ehrensperger, *Paul*, 145–46. For Castelli, however, the paternal metaphor does not evoke kindness and love but authority. She insists that the image of father must be understood in its Greco-Roman context where the father had total authority over children, so 4:16 reinforces that authoritative status of Paul (*Imitating Paul*, 98–111). While Ehrensperger recognizes that the metaphor of Paul as parent indicates a hierarchical relationship between the apostle and the Corinthian church, she does not understand it in terms of power (contra Castelli) but in terms of flexibility, responsibility, and supporting growth (*Paul*, 146–53). Indeed, in a section where Paul seeks to deconstruct "worldly" understandings of power, it would be odd if he were to stress a power-relationship in his mimetic language.

135. See also Brant, who explains that for Paul mimesis is an intentional process of education, in which he as a father seeks to move the Corinthians as his children from infancy to spiritual maturity ("*Mimēsis*," 295).

136. Contra Merk, who sees a "light break" (*leichte Zäsur*) between 4:16 and 4:17, arguing that 4:16 refers to Paul's lifestyle and points back to what has unfolded so far but 4:17 refers to Paul's teaching to strengthen the church and is *not* aimed at imitation. Hence, while 4:16 looks back, 4:17 looks forward. Merk's hesitation to see the same referent in 4:16 and 4:17 is based on his observation that Paul never points to himself and his life as the object of proclamation (see 2 Cor 4:5), which corresponds to how he rejects personality cults in 1 Cor 1–4, hence τὰς ὁδούς

is probably shorthand for his Christlike way of life or behavior patterned after Christ's (see also 11:1).[137] Timothy's remit most likely extends beyond conveying Paul's teachings to include how Paul's "ways in Christ" should be lived out. Surely, Paul would not send Timothy to simply repeat verbally what he teaches everywhere. Rather, ἀναμιμνῄσκειν most likely includes a *visible* reminder—an embodiment of Paul's cruciform way of life so that the Corinthians can imitate Paul by observing Timothy. In other words, Timothy would most likely exemplify the life Paul desires for the Corinthians.[138]

This is not new. Paul frequently uses Timothy as a surrogate example for imitation in his absence. In Phil 2:19–22, Paul intends to send Timothy to Philippi to model how to imitate Christ (see section 6.4.3), and in 1 Tim 4:12, Paul exhorts Timothy to be a τύπος for the Ephesian believers (see section 6.6). We should also note the parallels where Paul describes Timothy as his beloved child (μου τέκνον ἀγαπητόν; 1 Cor 4:17) and the Corinthians as his beloved children (τέκνα μου ἀγαπητά; 1 Cor 4:14). Paul is the spiritual parent of both Timothy and the Corinthians.

Consequently, by sending Timothy to help the believers in Corinth to imitate him, Paul presents Timothy as the *exemplary child* to his other "children." This means that Timothy will facilitate the imitation of Paul in two ways. First, he will evoke in the Corinthians the memory of Paul's past visit so that they can visualize Paul's "ways in Christ" and imitate Paul. Second, Timothy functions as a proxy for Paul so that the Corinthians can observe Timothy's way of life, which is patterned after that of Paul. We noted earlier that imitation is a sensory process, where the imitator usually observes the exemplar, so Paul's absence complicates matters when he instructs the Corinthians to imitate him. However, as we learned from the Thessalonian correspondence, we can infer in 1 Corinthians two alternative or complementary modes of imitation. First, there is *mnemonic mimesis*, where Timothy reminds the Corinthian Christians of what Paul taught and exemplified

---

μου does not refer to Paul's lifestyle but to his teaching ("Nachahmung Christi," 328–31). Schulz holds a similar position (*Nachfolgen und Nachahmen*, 309).

137. Similarly, Clarke contends that this phrase refers to "broad categories of Paul's life which are worthy of imitation" ("Imitators," 345). Tinsley sees echoes of the Old Testament idea of "the way of YHWH" in Paul's use in 4:17 (*Imitation of God*, 135). Betz sees a parallel with 1 Thess 4:1, where Paul asserts that the Thessalonians had learned from him (and the apostolic team) how they should live (*Nachfolge und Nachahmung*, 157).

138. See also Copan, *Saint Paul*, 119–21; Joseph A. Fitzmyer, *First Corinthians*, AYB 32 (New Haven, CT: Yale University Press, 2008), 223; Gordon D. Fee, *The First Epistle to the Corinthians*, rev. ed., NICNT (Grand Rapids: Eerdmans, 2014), 205–6. In this case, Paul's teaching is akin to that of ancient philosophers who taught with their *logos* (teaching) and their *ethos* (behavior) (Martin, "Example," 41). Likewise, Zimmermann states, "With eye contact and on the basis of living life together imitation can be particularly successful" (*Logic of Love*, 170).

during his one-and-half-year stay in Corinth (Acts 18:11) so that the Corinthians can visualize the remembered Paul. Second, there is *mediated imitation,* where the Corinthians are able to observe Timothy functioning as Paul's exemplary child. The Corinthians already knew Timothy (Acts 18:5) and most likely his trustworthiness (see Phil 2:22).

Although the imitation of Paul in 1 Cor 4:16 probably refers to his overall lifestyle, there is also a *specific* element. In 1:10–4:5, Paul addresses the social divisions in the Corinthian church based on personality cults. Deconstructing the Corinthians' misplaced ideas about wisdom and power, Paul also overturns their elevated ideas of leaders—they are servants in a line that goes back through to the Corinthian church to Christ and eventually to God (3:21–4:1). Paul then states in 4:6 that he has applied "these things" (ταῦτα) to Apollos and himself for the sake of the Corinthians (δι' ὑμᾶς; see also 1 Thess 1:5), in order that they may learn not to have an inflated image of themselves.[139] Copan states that the phrase ἵνα ἐν ἡμῖν μάθητε in 4:6 is "common imitation language and prepares ... for the explicit reference to imitation in 4:16."[140]

While it is clear that Paul and Apollos serve as examples for the Corinthians, the nature of the lesson is unclear and depends on how one understands the referent of ταῦτα in 4:6. De Boer contends that ταῦτα refers to the way Paul has spoken about himself and Apollos as servants and fellow-workers of God in 3:5, 9; 4:1 to counter any allegation of rivalry between them.[141] Likewise, Ehrensperger shows that despite the differing roles of Paul (the founding father of the Corinthians and hence their apostle) and Apollos (the one who contributed to building them up), their quest for cooperation (rather than competition) serves as an example for the Corinthians.[142] Subsequently, Paul continues with an extensive presentation of himself as, *inter alia,* publicly condemned, foolish, weak, dishonorable, physically

---

139. Likewise, Boykin Sanders contends that ταῦτα in 4:14 refers to 1:10–4:21 as a whole ("Imitating Paul: 1 Cor 4:16," *HTR* 74 [1981]: 353–63, at 353–55). For a discussion of the phrase τὸ μὴ ὑπὲρ ἃ γέγραπται ("not to go beyond the things that are written") in 4:6, see de Boer, *Imitation of Paul,* 142–43 (although his findings are inconclusive). See also our discussion of 2 John 9 in section 5.7.3 above.

140. Copan, *Saint Paul,* 113. Contra Dodd, who contends that Paul and Apollos are examples for the Corinthians' instruction (i.e., their examples serve as specimens for comparison) but not for imitation (*Paul's Paradigmatic "I,"* 33, 61, 64).

141. De Boer, *Imitation of Paul,* 140–42.

142. Ehrensperger, *Paul,* 148–49. While for Ehrensperger Paul's call for imitation in 4:16 does not result in sameness but preserves difference, for Castelli imitation is a movement towards sameness, and difference is perceived as problematic (Castelli, *Imitating Paul,* 21–22). I contend that sameness and difference can coexist in the concept of imitation. The aim of Christian mimetic ethics is not that Christians become clones of Christ but that they become *like* Christ in character and conduct.

6. Mimesis in the Pauline Letters

deprived, weary from toil, persecuted, slandered—in short, he has been deemed the scum of the earth (4:9–13).

Hence, Paul's injunction μιμηταί μου γίνεσθε refers *generally* to the imitation of his overall lifestyle (his "ways in Christ") and *specifically* to his extreme self-abasement and self-giving as the antidote for the Corinthians' arrogance and boasting in leaders.[143] Our findings that the content of imitation in 4:16 refers to Paul's self-giving and adopting a lowly status as the "father" of the Corinthians runs counter to Castelli's claim that the use of paternal metaphor stresses Paul's authoritative status.[144]

6.3.2. The Imitation of Christ Mediated through Paul (1 Cor 11:1)

The second occurrence of Paul's mimetic imperative μιμηταί μου γίνεσθε occurs in 1 Cor 11:1 as part of the conclusion 10:31–11:1 to chapters 8–10. In 1 Cor 8 and 10, Paul deals with the issue of eating food offered to idols in both public and private settings, with 1 Cor 9 expanding on Paul forsaking his personal rights for the sake of others as exemplifying the principle stated in 8:9.[145] Then, at the end of 1 Cor 8–10, the injunction to imitate Paul in 11:1 is a *general* call to ensure that Christian freedom does not cause offense to other believers. It refers to the entire literary unit 1 Cor 8–10, where Paul challenges an ethic of personal rights, promoting instead an ethic of other-oriented love that is demonstrated by voluntarily limiting one's freedom for the sake of others.[146] As Harrison states, "Paul's mimetic ethos [of

---

143. See also de Boer, *Imitation of Paul*, 146, 151; Clarke, "Imitators," 345; Jan Lambrecht, "Paul as Example: A Study of 1 Corinthians 4,6–21," in *Collected Studies in Pauline Literature and on The Book of Revelation*, AnBib 147 (Rome: Pontificio Instituto Biblico, 2001), 43–62, at 59–60; Copan, *Saint Paul*, 123–24; Zimmermann, *Logic of Love*, 171. Dodd, however, takes 4:14–21 as an introduction to what is to come (see n. 132) and argues that 4:16 is a call to execute discipline on the incestuous man in imitation of the judgment that Paul made in 5:3–5 (*Paul's Paradigmatic "I,"* 72). Differently, Sanders contends that the imitation Paul calls for is not the apostolic experience of suffering and humiliation but the communal principle of giving up the self-interest that causes divisions ("Imitating Paul," 358–63). In my view, however, both aspects can be held simultaneously.

144. Castelli, *Imitating Paul*, 98–111. Reinhartz sees both aspects—humility and authority—paradoxically at work in that "[Paul's] humility is a sign of his spiritual superiority, which he emphasizes by the call to imitation" ("Meaning," 397). Likewise, Hwang argues at length that in Paul's call to imitation not only does he offer himself as an example to follow but also seeks to re-establish his apostolic status/authority (Mimesis, 90–154).

145. While 1 Cor 8 deals with eating food offered to idols in the temple precincts, in 1 Cor 10 Paul discusses both public and private settings for such consumption.

146. See also Hays, *Moral Vision*, 42–43; Jensen, "Imitating Paul," 23–24; Zimmermann, *Logic of Love*, 172; J. B. Hood, "Imitation of Paul/of Christ," in *Dictionary of Paul and His Letters*, ed.

relinquishing one's rights to serve the 'weak'] restructures social relations in antiquity."[147] This corresponds to Paul's injunction to have regard for others in Phil 2:4 and presenting Christ as an example for imitation in 2:5–11 (see section 6.4.1).[148]

As was the case in 1 Cor 4:16, Paul's injunction to imitate him in 11:1 refers back *specifically* to 10:31–33, where Paul exhorts the Corinthians not to cause offense to anyone in service of the salvation of others.[149] While Copan largely agrees, he also asks how the Corinthians can imitate Paul when 1 Cor 8–10 hardly mentions any personal information about him.[150] His answer is that Paul expects the Corinthians to discern his reasoning about a particular ethos based on self-references to specific activities (e.g., in 9:6–7, 12–13).[151] Our analysis of the Johannine corpus showed that mimesis is a creative, cognitive process where believers must discern the appropriate act of imitation from the teaching and example of Jesus. Likewise, Paul may have expected the Corinthians to apply moral reasoning and discern what to imitate from his life and teaching.[152]

Paul's clarification καθὼς κἀγὼ Χριστοῦ indicates his awareness that he is "merely" a link in a mimetic chain in which Christ is the paradigmatic example for imitation. Wolbert, however, objects to the idea of Paul placing himself between Christ and Christians and states that in 1 Cor 11:1, Paul simply subordinates

---

Scot McKnight, Lynn Cohick, and Nijay Gupta, 2nd ed. (Downers Grove, IL: InterVarsity Press, 2023), 473–76, at 474.

147. Harrison, "Imitation," 251.

148. Similarly, Fiore states that, based on the pattern set by Christ, humility is at the heart of Paul's concept of imitation in 1 Corinthians and Philippians ("Paul," 242). See also Brant, "*Mimēsis*," 294. Likewise, for Horrell, Phil 2 is the foundational ethical text that guides the interpretation of 1 Cor 9 (*Solidarity and Difference*, 236–44).

149. For similar views, see de Boer, *Imitation of Paul*, 154–58; Schulz, *Nachfolgen und Nachahmen*, 285; Furnish, *Paul*, 220; Belleville, "Imitate Me," 126; Reinhartz, "Meaning," 398–99; Clarke, "Imitators," 346; Copan, *Saint Paul*, 130–37. Others take a slightly larger context (10:23–33) (e.g., Merk, "Nachahmung Christi," 331–32; Nicolet, "Le concept d'imitation," 404; Fee, *Corinthians*, 540). Differently (in a supplementary way), Dustin W. Ellington focuses on the phrase συγκοινωνὸς αὐτοῦ in 9:23, arguing that Paul's call to imitation exhorts the Corinthians to become, like him, partners of the gospel in the salvation of others and to allow its pattern and power to shape their shared life ("Imitating Paul's Relationship to the Gospel: 1 Corinthians 8.1–11.1," *JSNT* 33 [2011]: 303–15).

150. Copan, *Saint Paul*, 137.

151. Copan, *Saint Paul*, 137. Paul's positive example of renouncing his rights for the sake of others in 1 Cor 9 is contrasted with the negative example of those Corinthians whose knowledge-based behavior is destructive for other believers in 1 Cor 8:10–11.

152. Zimmermann recognizes that Paul was not seeking to create copies of himself; rather, "the goal of mimetic ethics is . . . to empower one's own behavior as it is informed or taught through the example of a role model" (*Logic of Love*, 173).

6. Mimesis in the Pauline Letters

himself to the same standard (Christ) that he applies to others.[153] I consider this a false dichotomy and contend that both aspects are in view. We saw earlier that Paul considers himself the spiritual parent of the Corinthians, so his call to imitate him as he imitates Christ should be understood within a familial context, where Paul, the parent, seeks to nurture his children in the ways of Christ, in which he is simply a little ahead of his converts.[154]

There is debate, however, on the exact referent of the imitation of Christ. Belleville contends that the direct imitation of Christ is not in view but the formation of Christ in Paul.[155] In light of 1 Cor 9:1, Reinhartz asserts that Paul is not thinking of an imitation of the earthly Jesus but of the risen Christ.[156] However, Paul does not sharply distinguish the earthly Jesus from the risen Christ. Based on our discussion of imitation in the Thessalonian correspondence (section 6.2.1), Paul would have had ample opportunity to share the Jesus traditions he knew with the Corinthians during his prolonged stay.[157] In 11:2, Paul commends the Corinthians for remembering everything about him (πάντα μου μέμνησθε) and for holding on to the traditions that he has passed on to them, which probably includes the Jesus tradition. As de Boer concludes, "There appears to be little reason to question that Paul's thoughts about Jesus' life and example were formed by the same tradition which we presently possess in the Synoptic Gospels.... *This Christ* Paul was bringing to expression in his imitation."[158]

Seyoon Kim also presents a strong case that "Paul knew and used effectively some concrete sayings and the example of Jesus for his teaching."[159] In addition, Copan explains that ancient writers assumed that the readers were familiar with the story of a hero from the past, so a simple reference to imitate such a person would be sufficient to recall the relevant tradition surrounding the exemplar. Hence, when Paul refers to his imitation of Christ, he assumes that the Corin-

---

153. Wolbert, "Vorbild," 261.

154. Contra Castelli, who views the hierarchy Christ–Paul–Corinthian church in terms of power relations (*Imitating Paul*, 111–15).

155. Belleville, "Imitate Me," 124.

156. Reinhartz, "Meaning," 399. Betz and Merk raise similar objections about Paul's declaration that the Thessalonians were imitators of the Lord in 1 Thess 1:6 (see n. 84).

157. It is thus surprising that Belleville, who essentially denies that Paul mediates the imitation of the *earthly* Jesus in 1 Corinthians ("Imitate Me," 124), claims that Paul draws on multiple examples of Jesus's life and ministry in 2 Corinthians (e.g., 4:10; 8:9; 10:1; 13:4) ("Imitate Me," 127).

158. De Boer, *Imitation of Paul*, 160 (emphasis added).

159. Seyoon Kim, "*Imitatio Christi* (1 Corinthians 11:1): How Paul Imitates Jesus Christ in Dealing with Idol Food (1 Corinthians 8–10)," *BBR* 13 (2003): 193–226. Kim sees specific references to Mark 7:15; 9:42–50; 10:45; 12:28–34 (and parallels) in 1 Cor 8–10. See also the work of David Wenham mentioned in n. 86 above.

thians would draw on the proper parallels in the Jesus tradition that correspond to Paul's example to inform their imitation.[160] In sum, the imitation of Christ is mediated through Paul *not* because Paul had seen the Lord and the Corinthians had not, nor because the Corinthians did not know about the earthly Jesus, but because the Corinthians were immature and needed to learn to imitate Christ through Paul.[161]

6.3.3. Traces of Imitation in 1 Corinthians

Besides the explicit references to imitating Paul in 4:16 and 11:1, 1 Corinthians contains a few instances of implicit imitation.

Not Imitating Israel (1 Cor 10). From the experience of Israel in the wilderness, Paul draws contemporary relevance for the Corinthian church through the Christological development in 10:4 ("and the rock was Christ") before pointing out the failings of the wilderness generation in 10:5. Paul then switches to mimetic language in 10:6 (the noun τύπος and comparative conjunction καθώς establish the imitation) to warn the Corinthian church not to imitate Israel's sinful conduct in the wilderness. The referent of ταῦτα in 10:6 cannot be found in 10:1–5 because these verses contain no mention of negative actions, so the referent must be in the verses that follow. Indeed, if we recognize that ταῦτα δὲ τύποι ἡμῶν ἐγενήθησαν (10:6) and ταῦτα δὲ τυπικῶς συνέβαινεν ἐκείνοις (10:11) form an *inclusio*, the τύποι to be avoided are found in 10:7–10—idolatry, sexual immorality, testing Christ, and grumbling.[162] The fourfold phrase "just as some of them did" (καθώς in 10:7–9 and καθάπερ 10:10) reinforces the imitation.

But how does this constitute authentic mimesis (as we defined it) when there was no direct observation of the exemplar? Paul's emphatic assertion that Israel's actions were τύποι ἡμῶν ("examples *for us*"; 10:6) and ἐγράφη πρὸς νουθεσίαν ἡμῶν ("written down to instruct *us*"; 10:11) is illuminating. As we learned earlier, David Capes has shown that in antiquity, the lives of notable people were upheld as models for imitation. While living models were preferred, the lives of great men

---

160. Copan, *Saint Paul*, 140. Copan then shows that those aspects in 10:32–33 that the Corinthians are to imitate, go back to the life of Jesus (*Saint Paul*, 140–41).

161. See also 2 Cor 4:10–11, where Paul stresses his desire to make the sufferings of Jesus visible in his life. For the idea of Paul as an image of Christ, see Jane Heath, "Corinth, a Crucible for Byzantine Iconoclastic Debates? Viewing Paul as an Icon of Christ in 2 Cor 4,7–12," in *Religiöse Philosophie und philosophische Religion der frühen Kaiserzeit: Literaturgeschichtliche Perspektiven*, ed. Rainer Hirsch-Luipold, Herwig Görgemanns, and Michael von Albrecht, STAC 51 (Tübingen: Mohr Siebeck, 2009), 271–84.

162. For a detailed exposition of these four examples, see Anthony C. Thiselton, *The First Epistle to the Corinthians*, NIGTC (Grand Rapids: Eerdmans, 2000), 733–43; Fee, *Corinthians*, 501–6.

from the past could also be "observed" (and imitated) through spoken and published accounts.[163] In line with Capes's study, Israel's conduct in the wilderness has been preserved in the Hebrew Bible and can be reconstructed, visualized, and imitated—or, in this case, act as a cautionary tale to be avoided.

We must consider the relation between the mimetic language in 10:1–13 and the mimetic injunction in 11:1 that looks back at all of 1 Cor 8–10. De Boer states that 10:1–13 anticipates Paul's warning in 10:14–22 that the Corinthians were not free to participate in pagan sacrificial feasts.[164] Differently, Copan suggests that 10:1–13 is a warning based on the example of Israel in the wilderness for those Corinthians who do not adopt the self-discipline that Paul did in 9:27.[165] De Boer seems to have the stronger case for two reasons. First, the references to food offered to idols (εἰδωλόθυτος; 8:1, 4, 7, 10; 10:19) and worshiping idols (εἰδωλολάτρης and εἰδωλολατρία; 10:7, 14) constitute a verbal connection between 10:1–13 and its surrounding chapters. Second, the conjunction διόπερ (10:14) logically connects 10:14–22 to 10:1–13. In this case, the Corinthians should not imitate the idolatrous behavior of Israel's wilderness generation and partake in public pagan festivals; rather, they are to imitate Paul (11:1).[166]

Imitation and the Lord's Supper (1 Cor 11). In 1 Cor 11:23–26, Paul refers to passing on the tradition he has received. As Paul recounts the events at Jesus's last supper, the Corinthians are able to visualize (i.e., form mental images of) what happened and emulate what Jesus did and said on the evening of his arrest. Focusing on the injunction "do this," John Laurance asserts that in the Lord's Supper, Christians perform the very actions of Jesus—to take up the bread and cup—and thus make him present in his saving deeds.[167] In short, Paul enables the Corinthians to imitate some of Jesus's last actions and words when re-enacting this constitutional practice of the church. The Lord's Supper is not simply a cognitive act of remembrance but a re-enactment of the new covenant in union and communion with Christ as the head of the church. As Donald Williams states, "To remember is not an intellectual discipline, 'to re-member' is to re-create, 'to re-member' is to become involved, 'to re-member'

---

163. Capes, "*Imitatio Christi*," 1–19. In light of his conviction that "the function of biblical texts ... is that of spiritual and ethical formation," Thiselton prefers to translate τύπος as "formative model" (*Corinthians*, 731).

164. De Boer, *Imitation of Paul*, 157.

165. Copan, *Saint Paul*, 129.

166. See also Zimmermann, *Logic of Love*, 168–69.

167. Laurance, "Eucharist," 291–92. Likewise, Smalley contends that the heart of Christian imitation is found in the sacraments of baptism (a mimesis of the death and resurrection of Christ) and the Eucharist (a mimesis of the Exodus and Israel's wilderness journey) ("Imitation of Christ in the New Testament," 17–18).

is to actualize, 'to re-member' is to re-present, 'to re-member' is to respond... 'This do in remembrance of me' must mean, 'so that you may participate in the sufferings and death of our Lord and respond to them.'"[168]

In the Synoptics, only Luke mentions the phrase "do this in remembrance of me" (Luke 22:19), so Paul and Luke probably had access to the same Jesus tradition, which is unsurprising given the contact Luke had with Paul (Phlm 24; Col 4:14; 2 Tim 4:11; see also the "we" passages in Acts).[169] Hence, just as Jesus instructed his followers to imitate him (Luke 22:19–20), so Paul continues this mimetic tradition (1 Cor 11:23–26). Earlier, we saw Paul inform the Corinthians that they are partners with Jesus during the Lord's Supper (κοινωνία/κοινωνός; 10:16, 20–21). So if Jesus is somehow present during the "holy communion," it is most likely that in the act of collective remembrance, believers re-experience their first encounter with Jesus. In fact, Paul considers this divine–human communion so sacred that he writes at length on the subject to the Corinthian church, where factions and abusive practices threatened to destroy this holy communion (1 Cor 11:27–34).

6.3.4. Imitating Other Churches (1 Cor 16; 2 Cor 8)

A significant part of Paul's ministry was dedicated to collecting money from the churches in Macedonia and Achaia to assist the impoverished Jerusalem church (Rom 15:25–27). The Corinthian church in Achaia was keen to participate in Paul's project but apparently slow to act. To help them act on their promise, Paul exhorts them to imitate other churches. In 1 Cor 16:1, Paul directs the Corinthian church to emulate the Galatian churches through a ὥσπερ... οὕτως καί construction: "Just as (ὥσπερ) I directed the Galatian churches, so also (οὕτως καί) you should do" (i.e., follow Paul's directives). Paul's detailed instructions in 16:2 are meant to assist the Corinthians in following the example of the Galatian churches. However, one could argue that this is merely an analogy in that Paul instructs the Corinthians to act in a similar manner as the Galatian churches rather than the Corinthian church being able to observe the Galatian churches and imitate them. Hence, the Corinthian church should do what the Galatian churches did, not by observing them but by following *Paul's instructions* for them. Nevertheless, the imitation could be *mediated* through Paul's instructions, and the detailed description of these instructions in 16:2 would help the Corinthians to visualize them. Hence, 16:1 perhaps contains a "weak" idea or a trace of mimesis.

---

168. Williams, "Israelite Cult," 121.
169. See also Bock, *Luke*, 2:1726.

6. Mimesis in the Pauline Letters

A stronger case for mimesis is found in 2 Cor 8, where Paul holds up the Macedonian churches as an example for the Corinthian church.[170] The Corinthian church had not followed through on their pledge (8:10–11), so Paul points to the example of the Macedonian churches, which had given generously despite their poverty and the persecution they faced (8:1–4). In fact, their sacrificial giving was based on the earlier act of giving themselves to the Lord (8:5). Paul's call for generous giving is rooted in the example of Christ's unreserved self-giving for their sakes (δι' ὑμᾶς) (8:9). Connecting the thoughts in 8:5 and 8:9, Paul's logic is that Christ's sacrificial self-giving for the sake of the Corinthians should be reciprocated in their self-giving—first to Christ and then to Paul and others, in this case the Jerusalem Christians. Hence, Christ's self-giving is an example to imitate.[171] As Horrell concludes, "The paradigm of Christ's self-giving thus plays a central role in Paul's appeal to the Corinthians to give generously to the collection."[172]

We have seen Paul state that the Thessalonian church had imitated the Judean churches (1 Thess 2:14), so it is not unusual for him to present some churches as examples for others to imitate.[173] We should also note the verbal parallel of self-giving in 1 Thess 2:8, where Paul says that he and his team had not only shared the gospel with the Thessalonians but also themselves (μεταδιδόναι τὰς ἑαυτῶν ψυχάς), and 2 Cor 8:4–5, where Paul states that the Thessalonians had not only shared their resources but also themselves (διδόναι ἑαυτούς). This commendation confirms that the Thessalonians had imitated Paul in self-giving, but not in the sense of literal replication or cloning. Notably, 1 Thess 2:8 stresses the sharing of the gospel as an expression of self-giving, whereas in 2 Cor 8, financial giving is a tangible articulation of self-giving.

---

170. Only few scholars (Belleville, Clarke, Jensen, and Horrell) have detected the potential mimesis in 2 Corinthians. For example, Belleville contends that Paul draws attention to the example of Jesus (e.g., in 4:10; 8:9; 10:1; 13:4) and himself (1:24; 4:5) ("Imitate Me," 127, 137), and Clarke endorses Belleville ("Imitators," 348). However, except for 4:10 and 8:9, none of the examples indicate imitation. While it is possible that someone's example can lead to imitation, in our study we explore imitation as an *intentional* concept, which requires that the text should contain some kind of mimetic language, which is not the case in Belleville's examples.

171. See also Jensen, "Imitating Paul," 26–27; Fiore and Blanton, "Paul," 186. Similarly, in Phil 2:6–11 Paul presents the example of Christ's self-giving (see section 6.4.1). Paul frequently refers to Christ's self-giving (e.g., Rom 5:6–8; 1 Cor 11:24; 15:3; 2 Cor 5:15; Gal 1:4; 2:20; Eph 5:2, 25; 1 Tim 2:6; Titus 2:14).

172. Horrell, *Solidarity and Difference*, 265.

173. Clarke notes that, in turn, Paul uses the Corinthian church as an example for the Macedonian church in 2 Cor 9:2 ("Imitators," 347n62).

6.3.5. Conclusion

The mimetic imperative in 1 Cor 4:16 harks back to 1 Cor 1–4 in general and to 4:6–17 specifically. In Paul's absence, the *imitatio Pauli* is mediated through Timothy. Similarly, the mimetic imperative in 1 Cor 11:1 goes back to 1 Cor 8–10 in general and to 10:31–33 specifically. Connecting 4:16–17 and 11:1, we detect a mimetic chain from Christ to Paul to Timothy to the Corinthian church. In both 4:16 and 11:1, the imitation of Paul has a *general* and *specific* content or reference.[174]

The main context of Paul's mimetic language in 1 Corinthians is family, where mimesis is instrumental in family education to nurture Christian maturity. As in 1 Thessalonians, Paul sets the language of imitation in 1 Corinthians within the context of family. De Boer explains that Paul's call to imitate him is "the call of a father to his children to walk in his ways and to become like him."[175] Paul's intention is that people learn through contact with him—a process in which he personally mediates the Christian life so that people can observe and imitate him.[176] Brant thus correctly stresses that mimesis must be an *intentional* educational process in order to progress from "infants" to spiritual maturity.[177]

Finally, Paul's idea of the imitation of Christ was not a "broad, nebulous, obscure, and vapid idea with him"; rather, it was firmly rooted in the life and ministry of the earthly Jesus, so "it would appear that in the early church there was much attention bestowed on capturing Christ's life and ways and bringing these to personal expression in individual Christian lives."[178] While the Thessalonian Christians had grasped this, the Corinthians still needed to put this into practice. Like 1–2 Thessalonians, it seems 1 Corinthians indicates that mimesis is central to Paul's ethics, albeit more implicit than in the Thessalonian correspondence. If 1 Cor 4:16 and 11:1 look back to 1 Cor 1–4 and 8–10, respectively, and if 1 Cor 11 and 16 also suggest mimesis, the inference is that most of the letter is permeated with mimetic thought.[179]

---

174. While Kim rightly rejects the idea of Pauline mimesis as copying or replication, his view that imitation in 4:16 and 11:1 refers to a Christlike way of life is too general ("'Imitators,'" 162–70). On the other hand, one can overstress the specific. Robert L. Plummer, for example, argues that Paul expected the Corinthians to imitate him *in evangelism* ("Imitation of Paul and the Church's Missionary Role in 1 Corinthians," *JETS* 44 [2001]: 219–35).

175. De Boer, *Imitation of Paul*, 153.

176. De Boer, *Imitation of Paul*, 153–54, 166–69.

177. Brant, "*Mimēsis*," 295. Contra Eastman, who contends that the imitation is mostly subconscious and unintentional (*Paul*, xii, 65–68).

178. De Boer, *Imitation of Paul*, 164–65.

179. In addition, Benjamin J. Lappenga argues that the language of ζῆλος, especially when it concerns people as the object, can convey "emulation" (e.g., in 1 Cor 12:31; 14:1, 12, 39; 2 Cor 7:7,

6.4. Philippians

Although the lexeme μιμεῖσθαι occurs only once in this letter (συμμιμητής in 3:17), we will see that the letter is saturated with mimetic ideas. All dimensions of Pauline mimesis—the imitation of Christ, Paul, and other exemplary believers—are found in this letter. Markus Bockmuehl captures it well when he writes, "The theme of imitation recurs as an integrating focus in every major section of Philippians."[180] Paul states the thesis or central case of his letter in 1:27, "live as citizens worthy of the gospel of Christ."[181] In essence, Paul's purpose in writing this letter is to instruct the Philippian church on how to live as good gospel citizens. In 2:3–4, Paul clarifies how such a life should look—where one considers others better than oneself and is concerned for others. Paul's strategy for inculcating such a mindset among the Philippian church is twofold: (1) to present Christ as the supreme example for imitation; (2) to present himself, Timothy, Epaphroditus, and other exemplary believers as models for imitation because each imitates certain aspects of Christ. As Witherington explains, Paul's call to imitate Christ and those who already live a life worthy of the gospel effects Christian identity and community formation.[182] In other words, to imitate Christ and Christlike examples is a community ethic that unites believers under Christ, shapes their shared identity and life, and effects moral transformation.

11; 9:2; 11:2), and hence relates to the concept of imitation (*Paul's Language of Ζῆλος: Monosemy and the Rhetoric of Identity and Practice*, BINS 137 [Leiden: Brill, 2016], 157–64). While I can see this in 2 Cor 7:7; 9:2, I find his other examples unconvincing and "zeal/jealousy" fits better in those cases. Buol argues that Paul employs *peristasis* ("hardship") catalogs in 1–2 Cor to show how his suffering imitates that of Jesus and, in turn, offer his sufferings as a model for imitation to others (*Martyred*, 102–10). I concur on 1 Cor 4:9–13 and possibly on 2 Cor 4:7–12 (see n. 161) but there are no mimetic ideas in 2 Cor 6:4–10; 11:23–33.

180. Markus Bockmuehl, *The Epistle to the Philippians*, BNTC (London: Black, 1997), 254. Matera states that Philippians, more than any other Pauline letter, presents an ethic of example and imitation (*New Testament Ethics*, 174). Likewise, Ben Witherington declares that Philippians is "a clarion call to imitate good examples and avoid bad ones" (*Paul's Letter to the Philippians: A Socio-Rhetorical Commentary* [Grand Rapids: Eerdmans, 2011], 14).

181. The verb πολιτεύεσθαι in 1:27 has political overtones, referring to one's public life as a citizen (see also 3:20). "Christians, then, are to adopt a way of life that is in keeping with their corporate citizenship as constituted in Christ and the gospel" (Bockmuehl, *Philippians*, 98). Others who identify 1:27–30 as the *propositio* or thesis statement with the imperatival verb πολιτεύεσθαι as the key include Timothy C. Geoffrion, *The Rhetorical Purpose and the Political and Military Character of Philippians: A Call to Stand Firm* (Lewiston, NY: Mellen, 1993), 23; Witherington, *Philippians*, 96–98; Smit, *Paradigms*, 79–80.

182. Witherington, *Philippians*, 77, 117.

6.4.1. Christ as the Supreme Example for Imitation

Paul desires that the Philippian believers will live as good gospel citizens, but instead of describing in detail what this means, he points them to various examples that they can observe and follow. In 2:5–11, Paul presents Christ as the supreme example for imitation, and as Bockmuehl states, "verse 5 is [sic] many ways the linchpin of the whole argument of 1.27–2.18: the key to a citizenship 'worthy of the gospel of Christ' is in fact none other than to adopt the mind of Christ."[183] This so-called "Christ hymn" probably originated in the early church, which Paul took over and perhaps adapted.[184] In the first part of the hymn, the focus is on Christ's humiliation in the incarnation and crucifixion, while Christ's exaltation in the resurrection and ascension governs the second. It is important to note that while the hymn may have been created for Christological or even soteriological reasons, Paul uses it for an *ethical* purpose, namely to present Christ as the supreme model for moral behavior in the Philippian church.[185]

Michael Gorman has done ground-breaking work on the concept of participation in Paul's writings. In his participatory model of Paul's theology and spirituality, Gorman identifies the Christ hymn in Phil 2:6–11 as Paul's "master story."[186] Recognizing that 2:5 is critical for understanding the connection between this hymn's theological foundation and the letter's key exhortation in 1:27–2:4, Gorman devotes an entire chapter to this verse.[187] Scholarship is divided on whether 2:5 should be taken as an imperative to adopt the attitude or mindset of Christ or an indicative to state that the Philippians already possess Christ's attitude or mindset.[188] As an alternative to these imitative (ethical) and locative

---

183. Bockmuehl, *Philippians*, 121. See also Hays, *Moral Vision*, 28–30; Witherington, *Philippians*, 117–18; Smit, *Paradigms*, 102.

184. For an informed discussion about the origin and form of the Christ hymn, see Ralph P. Martin, *A Hymn of Christ: Philippians 2:5–11 in Recent interpretation and in the Setting of Early Christian Worship*, 3rd ed. (Downers Grove, IL: InterVarsity Press, 1997); Witherington, *Philippians*, 132–36; Smit, *Paradigms*, 85–89; Gregory P. Fewster, "The Philippians 'Christ Hymn': Trends in Critical Scholarship," *CurBR* 13 (2015): 191–206, at 192–98.

185. Gerald F. Hawthorne, *Philippians*, WBC 43 (Dallas: Word, 1983), 79. We should be careful, however, not to create false dichotomies because 2:5–11 does, of course, contain Christology and in 2:12–18 Paul connects the imitation of Christ with (the outworking of) the Philippians' salvation (see also Smit, *Paradigms*, 106).

186. Michael J. Gorman, *Participating in Christ: Explorations in Paul's Theology and Spirituality* (Grand Rapids: Baker Academic, 2019), 33–38 (the term "master story" comes from p. 77). For Horrell, Phil 2:6–11 is also foundational for other *imitatio Christi* texts (*Solidarity and Difference*, 261–62).

187. Gorman, *Participating*, 77–95.

188. Gorman, *Participating*, 79–81. For other informed discussions whether the hymn is pri-

(kerygmatic) interpretations, Gorman offers a third option, a participatory interpretation with the resulting translation, "Cultivate this mindset—this way of thinking, feeling, and acting—in your community, *which is in fact a community in the Messiah Jesus*."[189]

Gorman's suggestion that "in Christ Jesus" refers to the church and not to Christ is intriguing but has several issues. While I agree that participation is the "big" theological category for Paul, Gorman appears at times to hold participation and imitation in opposition or tension,[190] whereas I contend that imitation is a *subset* of participation. Participation involves imitating the crucified Christ; as believers participate in Christ, they (can) imitate him. Contra Gorman's participatory interpretation of 2:5 at the expense of imitation, I suggest that both participation and imitation are in view in 2:5(-11).[191]

I take greater issue with Gorman's suggestion that ὃ καί in 2:5 (although I agree it is secondary whether ὃ is a relative pronoun or article) is an *id est* phrase ("that is") "referring not to *touto* but to the nearest neuter, or neutral, linguistic item—namely, the phrase ἐν ὑμῖν/*en hymin*."[192] Gorman claims that neuter relative pronouns can refer to "grammatical constructions or other generic, nongendered linguistic or semantic entities."[193] In support of this interpretation, he refers to BDAG (s.v. "ὅς" 1 g α, β) and to James Boyer's study that cites the examples of Acts 2:39; 2 Tim 1:5; Heb 12:25–26. Gorman then argues that the singular relative pronoun ὃ ("that") refers back to the plural ἐν ὑμῖν ("in you all") to create the equation "in your community" is "a community in the Messiah Jesus."[194] My dispute with Gorman's interpretation of ὃ is not its gender (a neuter relative pronoun referring to a nongendered semantic entity) but its number (a singular relative pronoun referring to a plural entity). None of the examples cited in BDAG and Boyer mention a *singular* relative pronoun referring to a *plural* antecedent. While I agree with Gorman that the antecedent of a relative pronoun can be a prepositional phrase, I contend that ὃ refers back to the phrase τοῦτο φρονεῖτε ἐν ὑμῖν, that

---

marily ethical or kerygmatic, see Fewster, "Christ Hymn," 198–203; Stephen E. Fowl, *The Story of Christ in the Ethics of Paul: An Analysis of the Function of the Hymnic Material in the Pauline Corpus*, JSNTSup 36 (Sheffield: JSOT Press, 1990), 77–102 (Fowl himself supports an ethical reading).

189. Gorman, *Participating*, 78, 81–93 (quotation from p. 78 with emphasis added to spotlight the unique part of Gorman's translation).

190. See Gorman, *Participating*, 15–17, 93–94. He states, for example, "Paul is describing *not* an ethic of imitation but a spirituality of participation" (p. 93, emphasis added).

191. Michael J. Gorman holds participation and imitation better together in his "minicommentary" on Philippians (*Apostle of the Crucified Lord: A Theological Introduction to Paul and His Letters*, 2nd ed. [Grand Rapids: Eerdmans, 2017], 501–13).

192. Gorman, *Participating*, 89.

193. Gorman, *Participating*, 88.

194. Gorman, *Participating*, 89–90.

PART 2   MIMESIS IN EARLY CHRISTIANITY

is, to the singular mindset of the Philippian church. I thus propose the translation (largely using Gorman's words), "Cultivate in your community this mindset—this way of thinking, feeling, and acting—which is also in the Messiah Jesus."[195]

With 2:5 looking both backward and forward, connecting the exhortation in 1:27–2:4 to the example in 2:6–11, I maintain that an *imitative* interpretation best explains the syntax and semantics of 2:5. Yet, the *imitatio Christi* can only occur while participating in Christ. Hence, in 2:5, Paul urges the Philippian church to adopt (i.e., imitate) the mindset that Christ displayed. Then, in 2:6–8, Paul describes Christ's mindset or attitude: (1) he did not consider his status as something to hold on to (2:6);[196] (2) he put himself totally at the disposal of others by taking on a slave-identity (2:7);[197] (3) he humbled himself and was obedient to the point of death by crucifixion (2:8).[198] It must be noted that 2:6–8 refers to a mindset or attitude that is *demonstrated in concrete actions*.[199] Just as Christ's mindset is demonstrated

---

195. I take the phrase ἐν ὑμῖν as "among you (plural)" to refer to the Philippians' corporate life as a church. Witherington notes that, later, Polycarp also urges the Philippians to imitate Christ's example in his letter *Phil.* 8:2; 10:1 (*Philippians*, 138).

196. The noun ἁρπαγμός can mean (1) something that one does not possess but violently grasps or forcefully seizes, or (2) something that one already possesses but does not cling to or exploit. The latter meaning is more likely, in that Christ did not take advantage of his divine status (so also Witherington, *Philippians*, 141). If Adam typology is intended in the Christ hymn, one could say that while the first Adam tried to grasp equality with God, the second Adam already possessed this but did not cling to it and instead chose incarnation and humiliation (Ralph P. Martin, *Philippians*, TNTC 11 [Leicester: Inter-Varsity Press, 1987], 103–4).

197. Instead of taking the phrase κενοῦν ἑαυτοῦ ("to empty himself") as referring to Christ putting aside aspects of his nature, status, or attributes (so Witherington, *Philippians*, 143; Raymond Bryce, "Christ as Second Adam: Girardian Mimesis Redeemed," *New Blackfriars* 93 [2012]: 358–70, at 364–67), which could lead to erroneous Christologies, I contend that Hawthorne is more on target, arguing that the phrase means Christ "poured himself out" or "drained himself," in that he put himself totally at the disposal of humanity, and hence "taking the nature of a slave" qualifies this pouring out (*Philippians*, 85–86).

198. "He humbled himself" refers to Christ's entire life on earth in perfect obedience and surrender to the Father, which reaches its climax with his death on a cross. More generally, R. Gregory Jenks explores the concept of imitating Christ in his death in the Pauline Corpus, arguing that this imitation can vary from sacrificial service and suffering to facing death (*Paul and His Mortality: Imitating Christ in the Face of Death*, BBRSup 12 [Winona Lake, IN: Eisenbrauns, 2015], 194–227). However, I contend that Jenks uses the concept too loosely and most texts he refers to speak of identification or participation rather than imitation. There is a greater case to be made for imitating Christ's death as martyrdom in the second century (see our chapter 8).

199. While Bockmuehl rightly notes that imitating the incarnation, or even the moral attitude behind it, is problematic, he is in danger of creating a false dichotomy when he states that the imitation of Christ refers not to the replication of particular actions but to the emulation of equivalent attitudes (*Philippians*, 122–23). Similarly, Jensen states Christ is an exemplar in attitude or mindset rather than some specific behavior ("Imitating Paul," 21). See also Eve-Marie

6. Mimesis in the Pauline Letters

in concrete actions, an authentic imitation of Christ requires a similar mindset demonstrated in matching actions. While mimesis in antiquity was not about literal replication, it nonetheless required close correspondence. Hence, imitating Christ is about emulating his *attitude-in-action*. As the second part shows, such a life of obedient submission is pleasing to God (2:9–11). We must note that the verb φρονεῖν ("to think," "to have a mindset") in 2:5 relates to moral reasoning, indicating that the imitation of Christ is not about mindless cloning or simplistic repetition.[200]

Christ's voluntary kenosis in 2:6–7 implies that the imitation of Christ relates to both identity and behavior. Instead of saying that Christ *exchanged* the μορφή of God for the μορφή of a slave, it is probably better to state that he *manifested* the μορφή of God *in* or *as* the μορφή of a slave.[201] Hence, the idea is not so much of Christ "putting aside" something but of emptying himself in taking on the identity of a slave, *as God*.[202] Referring to social identity theory, Witherington states that Christ assumed a "secondary identity" at the incarnation, which became primary while he was on earth. Similarly, in imitating Christ, the Philippians should make their identity as heavenly citizens their primary identity and live accordingly as good gospel citizens (1:27; 3:20).[203]

In presenting Christ to the Philippian believers as an example for imitation, Paul implies that their church life together should be modeled on Christ's way of thinking and result in corresponding behavior. Jesus Christ, the divine slave–Lord, had selflessly poured himself out for the sake of others. Similarly, in imitation of Jesus, the Philippians must express humility and self-giving through appropriate actions for the sake of others and for the sake of a flourishing unity in the church.[204]

Becker, "Mimetische Ethik im Philipperbrief: Zu Form und Funktion paulinischer *exempla*," in *Metapher–Narratio–Mimesis–Doxologie: Begründungsformen frühchristlicher und antiker Ethik*, ed. Ulrich Volp, Friedrich W. Horn, and Ruben Zimmermann, CNNTE 7, WUNT 356 (Tübingen: Mohr Siebeck, 2016), 219–34, at 232–33.

200. The verb φρονεῖν has no less than ten occurrences in this letter (1:7; 2:2 [2x], 5; 3:15 [2x], 19; 4:2, 10 [2x]). Others also link φρονεῖν to the idea of moral reasoning (Wayne A. Meeks, "The Man from Heaven in Paul's Letter to the Philippians," in *The Future of Early Christianity: Essays in Honor of Helmut Koester*, ed. Birger A. Pearson et al. [Minneapolis: Fortress, 1991], 329–36, at 332–33; Horrell, *Solidarity and Difference*, 235).

201. F. F. Bruce, *Philippians*, NIBC 11 (Peabody, MA: Hendrickson, 1983), 70.

202. See also Hawthorne, *Philippians*, 85–86. Likewise, in John 13, Jesus did not simply perform the task of a slave but also took on a slave-identity, as Lord and Teacher (see section 5.4.2). If Paul had the footwashing episode in mind, this is one more indication of his awareness of and ability to draw on the Jesus tradition.

203. Witherington, *Philippians*, 144.

204. Horrell points out that this "self-lowering other-regard" was *not* commended or perceived virtuous in Greco-Roman ethics (*Solidarity and Difference*, 232).

PART 2   MIMESIS IN EARLY CHRISTIANITY

Eastman notes that the phrase ἐν ὁμοιώματι ἀνθρώπων γενόμενος in 2:7 also points to mimesis in that Christ "imitates" the plight of humanity in the incarnation. She argues that Christ's imitation of humanity—Christ "putting on" Adam and enacting Adam's story of humanity enslaved to sin—precedes and is the basis of the believer's imitation of Christ.[205] Connecting imitation to education, she notes that, in ancient education, mimesis was relational, participatory, and creative in that the student had to participate in the teacher's life in order to acquire skills and become more like the teacher (but not through mere repetition).[206] While in ancient education mimesis has the notion of an upwardly mobile assimilation, Eastman observes that Christ's downward mobility in 2:6–11 causes a mimetic reversal or anti-education, in which Christ imitates fallen humanity, and believers are to imitate Christ's downward trajectory.[207] Eastman's main contribution is her observation that Christ's mimetic participation in the human plight is the basis for the believer's mimetic participation in Christ.

In her latest work on Pauline anthropology, Eastman returns to 2:6–11 to unpack the concept of "reciprocal mimetic participation" as Christ's participation in the human plight by assimilating the likeness of Adam, that is, a humanity enslaved to sin, so that humans can participate in Christ and become like him. In other words, Christ's joining Adamic humanity through mimetic assimilation in a mimetic reversal of Adam's creation in God's likeness is the basis for participatory union with God and each other. Hence, Christ's imitation of the human condition initiates a reciprocal human imitation of God.[208]

Although Christ was "absent" to the Philippian church and could not be observed, Paul still considered that the imitation of Christ was possible because Christ's attributes had been preserved in this hymn. Consequently, when the letter was read out, Christ could be visualized in the mind and be "observed" and imitated.[209] In 2:12–13, following the Christ hymn, Paul effectively urges the Philippians to emulate

205. Eastman, "Imitating Christ," 427–51. See also Eastman, "Philippians," 1–22. The latter article is an in-depth examination of the terms "form," "likeness," and "appearance" to illuminate the mimetic aspect of the incarnation.

206. Eastman, "Imitating Christ," 430–34.

207. Eastman, "Imitating Christ," 434–38. Sierksma-Agteres also notes that Christ's imitation of humanity as necessary for humanity's imitation of Christ is an unprecedented move in Greco-Roman antiquity, especially in its drastic form of Christ taking on slavery and suffering ("Imitation in Faith," 139–40).

208. Eastman, *Paul*, 129–41.

209. As in the Thessalonian and Corinthian correspondence, here too the issue is whether the Philippians seek to imitate the risen-ascended Christ or the historical Jesus (see also n. 202). I concur with Horrell's assessment that we need not distinguish between the heavenly Christ and earthly Jesus in this regard (*Solidarity and Difference*, 233–34).

6. Mimesis in the Pauline Letters

the model of Christ in their corporate church life.[210] At first sight, I am inclined to limit the believers' imitation of Christ to 2:6–8 rather than 2:6–11 for two reasons.[211] First, if we were to take the entire hymn as a model for ethical living, it could lead to the mistaken idea that one should seek humiliation *in order to* be exalted or that vindication will always follow in this life if one suffers humiliation for the sake of Christ. However, if Christ arguably did not seek self-humiliation for the purpose of being exalted, then neither should his followers. Second, Christ is the subject in 2:6–8, so believers should seek to imitate what he has demonstrated, whereas God is the subject in 2:9–11, where vindication and exaltation happen to Christ. However, there may be scope to speak of "existential mimesis" in 2:9–11, in that just as Christ was exalted, so believers will be "exalted" in the eschaton (2:15–16; 3:14–15, 21).[212]

---

210. Ὥστε in 2:12 logically links the Christ hymn with his instruction to show the outworking of the gospel (a life as good gospel citizens) in their corporate church life (μετὰ φόβου καὶ τρόμου τὴν ἑαυτῶν σωτηρίαν κατεργάζεσθε) with the knowledge that God effectively works among them to achieve this (2:13). See Hawthorne, *Philippians*, 98–100; Gordon D. Fee, *Paul's Letter to the Philippians*, NICNT (Grand Rapids: Eerdmans, 1995), 230–38. Smit argues that the entire section 2:12–18 has its basis in 2:5–11 and stresses the imitation of obedience, suffering, and future glorification (*Paradigms*, 95–100).

211. Most scholars contend that Paul only presents the humility and obedience of Christ as exemplary (e.g. Schulz, *Nachfolgen und Nachahmen*, 273; David M. Stanley, "Imitation in Paul's Letters: Its Significance for His Relationship to Jesus and to His Own Christian Foundations," in *From Jesus to Paul: Studies in Honour of Francis Wright Beare*, ed. Peter Richardson and John C. Hurd (Waterloo, ON: Wilfrid Laurier University Press, 1984), 127–41, at 137; Fiore, "Paul," 240; Clarke, "Imitators," 350).

212. While Bockmuehl notes that Christ's vindication is not something he produced and therefore no longer an example to be emulated, he nevertheless contends that God's response to the Christian's obedience is analogous to that of Christ, in that just as Christ was vindicated, so those who adopt the mind of Christ will also be vindicated (*Philippians*, 123). Likewise, Jensen states that the believers' obedient humility will also result in exaltation, albeit on a lesser scale ("Imitating Paul," 21). Horrell admits that although Christ's story in 2:6–11 is inimitable in many ways, "the pattern of faithful endurance through suffering leading to resurrection glory" can be reproduced in the Christian life (*Solidarity and Difference*, 231, 234). In light of Rev 3:21, Moss contends that the imitation of Christ could result in exaltation on the heavenly throne (*Other Christs*, 26). Arguing that the imitation of Christ in 2:6–11 contains both active and passive elements, Peter Wick remarks, "*Imitatio Christi* ist also nicht nur etwas, was der Gläubige aktiv tun kann, sondern auch etwas, was mit ihm geschieht und zu dem er durch göttliches Wirken wird: Ein Nachahmer Christi durch Teilhabe" ("*Imitatio Christi* is therefore not only something that the believer can actively do, but also something that happens to him and that he becomes through divine action: An imitator of Christ through participation") ("'Ahmt Jesus Christus mit mir zusammen nach!' (Phil 3, 17): *Imitatio Pauli* und *imitatio Christi* im Philipperbrief," in *Der Philipperbrief des Paulus in der hellenistisch-römischen Welt*, ed. Jörg Frey and Benjamin Schliesser, WUNT 353 [Tübingen: Mohr Siebeck, 2015], 309–26, at 318–22 [quotation from p. 320]). See also Fowl, *Story of Christ*, 90–92, 95, 99–100; Smit, *Paradigms*, 141–42.

As Paul Cable states, "Of course, there are important differences between Paul's and Christ's stories, not least in Paul's initial status vis-à-vis Christ's, but the point of contact between the examples is their *trajectory*," from suffering to exaltation.[213] I concur—believers cannot actively imitate Christ's exaltation. Yet, if God behaves analogously toward Christlike believers as he did to Christ—whether in this life or the eschaton—there is a "passive" mimesis where the believers' eschatological vindication or glorification will be patterned on that of Christ. We may call this mimesis of a particular state of existence in the eschaton "existential mimesis" (see also section 5.4.4). In essence, I consider the entire hymn, 2:6–11, as a paradigmatic example for imitation, where 2:6–11 contain aspects for "active" or "performative" mimesis and 2:9–11 refer to "passive" or "existential" mimesis.

6.4.2. Paul as an Imitator of Christ

In this letter, Paul presents himself to the Philippian church as an example for imitation, sometimes explicitly (3:17a; 4:9) but more often implicitly. We will explore six such occasions.[214]

Servitude (1:1). In his opening remarks, Paul introduces himself as δοῦλος Χριστοῦ Ἰησοῦ (1:1). I contend that the translation of δοῦλος is "slave" rather than "servant" (contra most Bible translations) because we would then expect the term διάκονος. While Paul's self-reference here is not unique, it is unusual. The Pauline corpus introduces Paul in different ways: (1) nine times as an *apostle* of Christ (Rom [but also as a slave], 1–2 Cor, Gal, Eph, Col, 1–2 Tim, Titus [but also as a slave]); (2) three times as a *slave* of Christ (Rom and Titus [but also as an apostle], Phil); (3) twice no status is mentioned (1–2 Thess); (4) once as a *prisoner* of Christ (Phlm). Philippians is the only letter where Paul introduces himself solely as a slave of Christ. If the opening of a letter serves to set the tone, we must ask why Paul refers to himself in this way. Martin contends that Paul's self-designation echoes that of God's servants in the OT (e.g., Moses [Exod 14:31]; prophets [Jer. 25:4]), and hence stresses instrumentality and calling/authority (God chose to work *through* his servants) rather than humble service.[215] However, when Paul wants to stress his calling or authority, he usually refers to his apostolic status. A more likely reason is that Paul intentionally identifies himself with the slave-status of Christ in 2:7 (δοῦλος only

---

213. Paul S. Cable, "*Imitatio Christianorum*: The Function of Believers as Examples in Philippians," *TynBul* 67 (2016): 105–25, at 117.

214. In his otherwise excellent article, Cable only identifies three occasions ("*Imitatio Christianorum*," 114–20).

215. Martin, *Philippians*, 57.

6. Mimesis in the Pauline Letters

occurs in 1:1 and 2:7) to show the Philippians that he is an imitator of Christ. This also strengthens the credibility of his exhortation to the Philippians to imitate Christ in 2:4–5 and to imitate him in 3:17a.[216]

Prioritizing Others (1:20–25). In two sections, Paul shares details from his current imprisonment: in 1:12–18, Paul informs the Philippians that his imprisonment has (surprisingly) aided in the spread of the gospel, and in 1:19–26, he considers the outcome of his imminent trial. The phrase "whether by life or by death" at the end of 1:20 seems to trigger an asymmetric reflection on the two alternatives in 1:21–24:

1:21a   *to live* is Christ (everything is about and for Christ),
1:21b   *to die* is gain (a more personal and permanent relationship with Christ),
1:22   *to live* means fruitful work,
1:23   *to die* is to be with Christ, which benefits Paul,
1:24   *to live* benefits the Philippians.

While both possible outcomes have distinct advantages, Paul's turmoil ends with the balance tipping towards the desire to live in order to serve. Weighing both options, Paul is selfless in choosing one that is less profitable to him but more profitable to the Philippians. Paul thus exemplifies what he is about to urge the Philippians to do in 2:4, which is to imitate the attitude of Christ in 2:6–8—to prioritize the interest of others. Paul ultimately chooses not what is best for him but what is best for the Philippian church. Paul is convinced that the Philippians need him, so he knows that God intends that for the immediate future he should live (1:25).[217]

Self-Sacrifice (2:17). In 2:12–18, Paul expresses confidence that, with God's help, the Philippian church will pattern its corporate life on that of Christ and that he is willing to help the Philippians achieve this. Martin takes the phrase of Paul being "poured out as a libation over the sacrifice" in 2:17 as a reference to a martyr's death—a violent, bloody death where Paul "likens his life-blood shed in death to the libation of wine or perfume which was poured out in the concluding rites of a sacrifice to a pagan deity."[218] Hawthorne, however, has the better case, arguing that a

---

216. See also Hawthorne, *Philippians*, 4–5; Bockmuehl, *Philippians*, 50–51; Witherington, *Philippians*, 42.

217. See also Hawthorne, *Philippians*, 44–53. Bradley Arnold contends that in the entire passage 1:12–26 Paul presents himself as an example to be imitated by drawing parallels between his circumstances and those of the Philippians, especially how to behave in times of hardship (*Christ as the* Telos *of Life: Moral Philosophy, Athletic Imagery, and the Aim of Philippians*, WUNT 2/371 [Tübingen: Mohr Siebeck, 2014], 153–56).

218. Martin, *Philippians*, 123.

libation accompanies and *completes* the sacrifice. Hence, when Paul uses the libation metaphor, he is not alluding to his own imminent death (in 2:24, he speaks of his confidence that he will see the Philippians soon) but to his sufferings as a seal on the Philippians' sacrificial service.[219] Bockmuehl does not go as far as Martin (Paul's libation = martyrdom), but he goes further than Hawthorne (Paul's libation = apostolic sufferings), arguing that Paul states his *willingness* to sacrifice his life in order to *complete* the Philippians' offering to God.[220] Thus, the focus is on the sacrificial service of the Philippians, and Paul is willing to sacrifice his life to perfect or complete the Philippians' sacrifice. Paul's willingness to pour out his life for the sake of the Philippians echoes Christ pouring out his life for the sake of humanity in 2:7.

Discarding Privileges (3:4–7). In 3:1–11, Paul warns the Philippians against the harmful beliefs and practices of a group of Jewish opponents and positions himself as an authentic Jew who is supremely qualified and competent to address the issue at hand. In 3:4–6, Paul stakes his claim to greater personal advantages than his Jewish opponents.[221] However, as Hawthorne explains, in reassessing his life as a Jew from the viewpoint of Christ, Paul gathers all his former privileges in one parcel called "profits" and writes them off as a single "loss" (3:7). All the good things Paul enjoyed, all the advantages he had from birth and from his own efforts, he now counts not as assets but as liabilities.[222] In a sense, Paul imitates Christ in 2:6–7, who did not take advantage of his position but relinquished it for the sake of humanity.[223] In showing the Philippians that his story of relinquishing his

---

219. Hawthorne, *Philippians*, 105–6.
220. Bockmuehl, *Philippians*, 160–61.
221. Smit wittily remarks that Paul presents himself as "superdog," in contrast to the opponents as "dogs" (*Paradigms*, 122).
222. Hawthorne, *Philippians*, 135.
223. William S. Kurz calls this "kenotic imitation" ("Kenotic Imitation of Paul and of Christ in Philippians 2 and 3," in *Discipleship in the New Testament*, ed. Fernando F. Segovia [Philadelphia: Fortress, 1985], 103–26). Similarly, Smit argues that 3:7 is unpacked in 3:8–11 and contributes to Paul's kenotic Christian identity, where he despises what he once valued and strives for what he once persecuted (*Paradigms*, 126–31). This is, of course, not a one-to-one correspondence (Christ did not relinquish his privileges to obtain something better, nor did Paul renounce his privileges to save others), but the concept of mimesis does not require that. Some note an additional notion of mimesis: Paul's desire to adopt the form of Christ's death in 3:10 emulates Christ having taken the form of a slave and become obedient to death (Bockmuehl, *Philippians*, 216; Witherington, *Philippians*, 205). Likewise, Cable notes that the trajectory of Paul's life in 3:4–14, 20–21 runs parallel to that of Christ's in 2:6–11 ("*Imitatio Christianorum*," 116–17). Van Kooten also notes the idea of the imitation of Christ in 3:10, 21, but compares this to the Platonic notion of assimilation to god (*Paul's Anthropology*, 210–11). It is thus possible to take 3:4–11, or even 3:4–16, as exemplary of Paul's imitation of Christ, in which case Paul's injunction to the Philippians to imitate him in 3:17a is the natural trajectory.

6. Mimesis in the Pauline Letters

privileges is modeled on Christ's story, Paul implicitly appeals to the Philippians to imitate his example when the opponents show up.[224]

Example for Imitation 1 (3:17a). Paul urges the Philippians to become fellow imitators of him (γενέσθαι συμμιμηταί μου), that is, to join with one another in imitating him.[225] As Peter Oakes asserts, "Of course, if Paul presents himself as a model, he would always see Christ standing behind this as a prior model. In 2:6–8, Christ is the pattern for the Philippians' behaviour."[226] Nevertheless, Paul's command to the Philippians to be co-imitators of him would sound supercilious unless we consider the following: (1) although there is mimetic language in *all* of Paul's letters, Paul only issues the explicit injunction to imitate *him* to churches he has founded; (2) as such, Paul sees himself as a father whose task it is to nurture his spiritual children; (3) Christ remains the supreme example for imitation, and just as Paul imitates Christ he wants to teach his spiritual children to do the same by imitating him. As de Boer states, "Paul's aim is to cultivate in his readers a living experience of the Christian way as he knows it. Hence, he calls them to be his imitators."[227] As they progress, they can go on to imitate Christ directly.[228] Paul is not claiming to be better than the Philippians. Rather, "like an experienced craftsman who shows an apprentice how to do a difficult job ... or like a scout who knows the way ... [Paul] is in no way ashamed to say, 'Follow me!'"[229]

---

224. Witherington, *Philippians*, 182–83.

225. Most scholars uphold this interpretation rather than the idea of joining with Paul in imitating Christ (see the discussions in de Boer, *Imitation of Paul*, 177–79; Copan, *Saint Paul*, 160–61). Bockmuehl is probably right to note that Paul already invites the Philippians to imitate him in 3:15–16 (*Philippians*, 224–28). Indeed, the recurring phrase τοῦτο φρονεῖν in 2:5 and 3:15 would strengthen this idea (Reinhartz, "Meaning," 400; Swartley, *Covenant of Peace*, 363; Cable, "*Imitatio Christianorum*," 117–18). While Paul's call to imitation is directed at the whole Philippian church, he is especially thinking of the "mature ones" who were prone to wander from the Christian way (3:15–16) (de Boer, *Imitation of Paul*, 174–77). Standhartinger disputes this, saying that Paul cannot have presented himself as an object for imitation in 3:17 because there is no reference to self-imitation in ancient literature ("Weisheitliche Idealbiografie," 157, 174). However, her claim is based on a wrong premise (see section 6.1.1). Brant is also skeptical: "The Philippians do not mimic Paul; they take the ideal that Paul's actions represent and apply it to their own behaviour" ("*Mimēsis*," 297).

226. Peter Oakes, *Philippians: From People to Letter*, SNTSMS 110 (Cambridge: Cambridge University Press, 2001), 103–4.

227. De Boer, *Imitation of Paul*, 186.

228. Fiore suggests that 3:17–18 corroborates the link between the cross, imitation, and authentic apostolic preaching (*Personal Example*, 185n63). Contra those who view the relationship Christ–Paul–Philippian church more in terms of hierarchy, authority, and power (Castelli, *Imitating Paul*, 95–97; Marchal, *Hierarchy*, 123, 135–37, 144–47, 152).

229. Hawthorne, *Philippians*, 161.

While some scholars contend that 3:17a refers to a general call to imitate Paul's way of life,[230] Copan argues that Paul's intention is for the Philippians to imitate the specific content of 3:4–14: (1) to put confidence in Christ and not in human accomplishments and external factors; (2) to pursue the ultimate goal of knowing Christ and share in his sufferings and resurrection power.[231] Since we have noted various occasions where Paul presented himself as an example, including 3:4–7 (see above), it is better to take 3:17a as a *general* call to imitate Paul as far as his audience has understood it (including those aspects in 3:4–14 where Paul imitates Christ, see also n. 223).[232]

Scholars have noticed that Paul's use of συμμιμεῖσθαι is unique—it does not occur elsewhere in the New Testament and only once in Greco-Roman literature (Plato, *Pol.* 274d), although the prefix συν is common in Philippians.[233] As we noted earlier, Paul uses the concept of mimesis to unite the Philippian church under Christ and transform them into his likeness (see also 3:20–21).[234] Arnold thus writes, "Those who are imitating Paul's way of thinking and living, or those who are living similarly, are joined together and demonstrate that they are members of this heavenly community because their lives are governed by a particular pattern of life."[235] Likewise, Brant asserts that by calling the Philippians συμμιμεῖσθαι, Paul stresses their united effort of engaging in the same mimesis with a single aim—to become Christlike.[236] We must note that although the imitation of a teacher's example is a classic didactic theme in both Greco-Roman and Jewish antiquity,[237] Paul is unusual in saying to his audience, "imitate *me*" (see also section 6.1.1). Smit explains that the self-promotion of an orator or writer as an

230. For example, de Boer, *Imitation of Paul*, 186; Hawthorne, *Philippians*, 159–60.

231. Copan, *Saint Paul*, 163–64. See also Furnish, *Paul*, 221 (to imitate "the Paul who has shared in Christ's sufferings and has been conformed to his death" [3:10–11]); Kurz, "Kenotic Imitation," 115 (to imitate Paul in surrendering his credentials and being conformed to Christ's death); Harrison, "Imitation," 253 (to imitate Paul's refusal to boast in his ancestry and achievements, thus countering the boasting culture of Greco-Roman antiquity).

232. Contra Landolt's narrower view that Paul's journey of conversion in Phil 3 is paradigmatic for the conversion of all believers ("'Soyez mes imitateurs,'" 262–69, 286).

233. De Boer mentions seven terms prefixed with συν as an indication of the close fellowship between Paul and the Philippians (*Imitation of Paul*, 170n231). See also Fee, *Philippians*, 19nn53–54; Copan, *Saint Paul*, 148–49, 160.

234. As Reinhartz asserts, συμμιμηταί μου γίνεσθε is "a call not only to imitation but to unity" ("Meaning," 400). See also Nicolet, "Le concept d'imitation," 407; Moss, *Other Christs*, 25.

235. Arnold, *Christ*, 207.

236. Brant, "*Mimēsis*," 297.

237. See, e.g., de Boer, *Imitation of Paul*, 6, 10, 25–26, 42–44; Brant, "*Mimēsis*," 287–88; Geoffrion, *Rhetorical Purpose*, 125–27; Hawthorne, "Imitation," 163–64, 172; Bockmuehl, *Philippians*, 229; Witherington, *Philippians*, 214; Arnold, *Christ*, 73–96; Fiore, "Paul," 228–37; Smit, *Paradigms*, 16–30.

example is legitimate if he possessed an appropriate ἦθος ("moral character") and could present himself effectively as an example to be followed—and suggests this is the case in Philippians.[238]

Example for Imitation 2 (4:9). In his final instructions to the Philippian believers, Paul commends various moral qualities (4:8) and urges them to keep on doing the things that they have learned, received, heard, and *seen* in him (4:9).[239] While "learned" and "received" very likely refer to Paul's authoritative teaching, "heard" to information from his letter and from Timothy or Epaphroditus, "seen" refers to Paul's personal example.[240] Paul's directive to practice what the Philippians have seen in him echoes his command to imitate him in 3:17a.[241] Whatever ἅ and ταῦτα refer to with regard to Paul's personal example in 4:9, they would certainly refer to what the Philippians had observed about Paul's life during his visit to Philippi (see Acts 16; see also the use of ὁρᾶν in 1:30). Hence, although Paul is absent when writing the letter to the Philippians, the "remembered" Paul could still function as an example for imitation. Copan makes a similar observation (albeit related to ἀκούειν rather than ὁρᾶν): "even third party information about Paul—how he lived, how he thought, what he taught—would be useful to the Philippians to shape their own thinking and lifestyle. This would indicate a *mediated* Pauline imitation, but imitation of Paul nonetheless."[242] Noting the connection between 4:9 and 1:29–30; 2:17–18; 1 Thess 2:2, Oakes suggests that "the most likely area for imitation is Paul's behaviour under suffering."[243] Be that as it may, we should not limit the scope too quickly. Rather, as de Boer asserts, "this statement indicates the breadth of scope in which Paul conceived of himself as being an example to his converts. In effect his whole life constituted an example to be followed."[244]

Summary. While Paul presents Christ as the supreme example for imitation, he also presents himself as being worthy of imitation because he imitates Christ.[245]

---

238. Smit, *Paradigms*, 120–21.

239. Bockmuehl states that 4:9 is a further and specific elaboration of 4:8 (*Philippians*, 254). See also Copan, *Saint Paul*, 171–72.

240. Fee, *Philippians*, 420.

241. See also Kurz who contends that the call to imitate Paul in 3:17a and 4:9 form an inclusio ("Kenotic Imitation," 114).

242. Copan, *Saint Paul*, 175 (emphasis added).

243. Oakes, *Philippians*, 106.

244. De Boer, *Imitation of Paul*, 187. Similarly, Fiore states that the call to imitate Paul in 4:9 refers to "Paul's previous presence, practice, and teaching among them as well as what they learned about him in his trials and imprisonment. As such, the Christian life finds embodiment in Paul himself" ("Paul," 241).

245. Kurz goes as far as to suggest that the calls to imitate Christ and Paul in Philippians 2–3 are an expansion of 1 Cor 11:1 ("Kenotic Imitation," 106, 118).

PART 2   MIMESIS IN EARLY CHRISTIANITY

Dodd, however, has a twofold objection to seeing Paul as an example for imitation. First, it is not possible to fully identify Paul's model for imitation: (1) some aspects of Paul are inimitable (e.g. the description of 3:4–6); (2) besides his epistolary exemplification (see also 3:17a), Paul also refers to his historical example (4:9), which is outside the text and hence unknown to us; (3) Paul includes other examples who can model proper doctrine and practice (3:17b).[246] Second, Dodd argues that Paul's presentation of himself as an example is *not* derived from the Christ hymn in 2:6–11 because (1) most elements in 2:6–11 are inimitable (e.g., the incarnation and exaltation) and (2) there are limited parallels between the content of Paul's personal example and Christ's.[247]

In my view, Dodd operates with a mistaken notion of example and imitation. In antiquity, including early Christian literature, authentic mimesis required faithful correspondence but not one-to-one replication (see our chapter 2). Moreover, while modern readers may not know exactly what Paul's example in 4:9 refers to, the Philippians would surely have been familiar with it. Finally, it is unclear why Dodd finds it problematic that Paul points to other examples beyond himself since Paul does not claim to be the paradigmatic model or sum total of imitation. Instead, Christ is the primary model for imitation (something Dodd denies), and Paul simply points to human models such as himself, Timothy, and Epaphroditus, who each model aspects of Christ.[248] This is not to say that Paul's call to imitation is without problems. After all, the Philippians have never seen Christ, and Paul is not present either. Hence, Paul sends Timothy and Epaphroditus to Philippi because each of them imitates Christ in different ways. We will now examine how Timothy and Epaphroditus can function as living examples for the Philippian church.[249]

6.4.3. Timothy and Epaphroditus as Imitators of Christ

Timothy. While Paul must wait for his release from prison to visit the Philippians, his plan is to send his close coworker Timothy ahead—not immediately but when

---

246. Dodd, *Paul's Paradigmatic "I,"* 182–83.

247. Dodd, *Paul's Paradigmatic "I,"* 191–93. Elsewhere, Dodd makes a similar case, arguing that while Christ models the Christian life, Paul simply mirrors Christ's example ("The Story of Christ and the Imitation of Paul in Philippians 2–3," in *Where Christology Began: Essays on Philippians 2*, ed. Ralph P. Martin and Brian J. Dodd [Louisville: Westminster John Knox, 1998], 154–61). I fail to see, however, how this is different from saying that Paul imitates Christ's example.

248. See also Smit's critique of Dodd (*Paradigms*, 137–38). Similarly, Geoffrion states, "since it is Christ, not Paul, who is the ultimate model, Paul does not think that he needs to be the only one to model appropriate behaviour . . . in his thinking, any Christian or church can be a model" (*Rhetorical Purpose*, 149).

249. See also Bockmuehl, *Philippians*, 175; Witherington, *Philippians*, 169–70.

6. Mimesis in the Pauline Letters

he has a clearer view of his affairs (2:19, 23). "I have no one like-minded" (2:20) suggests he has no one with him who shares his concerns about the Philippians except Timothy.[250] Besides, the Philippians know Timothy and his record, that is, his ongoing commitment to the advance of the gospel in close fellowship with Paul (2:22), because he had accompanied Paul on his first visit to Philippi (Acts 16:1–3; 17:14–15). Timothy's genuine concern for the Philippians reflects the ideal of 2:4 and "imitates" Christ's concern for others in 2:6–8. Moreover, we see Paul introduce Timothy, like himself, as a slave (δοῦλος) of Christ (1:1), thus endorsing Timothy's participation in the work of the gospel in terms of servanthood (δουλεύειν is "to serve or work like a slave"). Hence, Timothy imitates Christ in the aspects of servitude and prioritizing others. In sending Timothy, Paul provides the Philippians with a living example they can observe and imitate (see also 1 Tim 4:12).[251]

Epaphroditus. While Timothy is Paul's coworker, Epaphroditus is a member of the Philippian church. Epaphroditus is sent to Paul with a monetary gift as the expression of the Philippians' partnership in the gospel (1:5; 4:10–20), probably with the intention that he stay with Paul for an indefinite time.[252] In which case, Epaphroditus did not simply bring a financial gift—*he himself was the gift* from the Philippian church to Paul. It appears that Epaphroditus had fallen ill, either on his journey to Paul or when he arrived, but by God's mercy, he had recovered (2:26–27). Paul does not mention the nature of the illness except to say that it was serious (he nearly died) and was connected to the work of Christ and in service of Paul (2:30). Hence, Epaphroditus had risked his life for the work of Christ, in the interest of Paul, on behalf of the Philippian church.[253] This implies that Epaphroditus imitated Christ in being selfless and willing to die for others (see also the recurrent phrase μέχρι θανάτου in 2:8 and 2:30).[254] Just as Christ gave himself up for humanity, Epaphroditus was also willing to give himself up for the gospel and Paul. While Dodd recognizes this correspondence, he rejects the idea that

---

250. Martin suggests that this is a general statement from Paul: in a world of selfishness and self-seeking it is rare to find a person like Timothy who is really anxious to promote the welfare of other people (*Philippians*, 129). Hawthorne, however, makes the better argument, suggesting that Paul's coworkers were primarily concerned about their own churches instead of the distant Philippian church (*Philippians*, 111).

251. While Smit contends that Timothy is not explicitly presented as an example, he acknowledges that aspects of Paul's presentation of Timothy take on a paradigmatic quality (*Paradigms*, 110–11).

252. Paul's use of the word "send" rather than "send back" in 2:25 may indicate that Epaphroditus had come to Paul intending to remain with him (Hawthorne, *Philippians*, 117).

253. Martin, *Philippians*, 137.

254. Smit notes that the phrase μέχρι θανάτου occurs often within the martyrological contexts of 2–4 Maccabees (*Paradigms*, 113–14n189).

PART 2   MIMESIS IN EARLY CHRISTIANITY

Epaphroditus is presented to the Philippians as an example to imitate because there is a significant difference between the life patterns of Christ and Epaphroditus.[255] Smit, however, rightly notes that this is not necessarily a problem in light of first-century conventions about the function of *exempla*.[256] As we have shown, mimesis in antiquity did not require a one-to-one correspondence in all aspects or a literal replication; most often, faithful representation is in view (see chapter 2). Hence, Paul presents Epaphroditus as an example of the kind of attitude he wants to foster among the Philippians.[257]

6.4.4. Other Believers as Examples for Imitation

In 3:17a, Paul urges the Philippians to join together in imitating him (see section 6.4.2), but perhaps realizing that some may find it difficult to do this in his absence, he points them to other examples that are accessible for observation.[258] In 3:17b, Paul instructs the Philippians to observe closely (σκοπεῖν)—and surely imitate—τοὺς οὕτως περιπατοῦντας ("those who thus live") in keeping with (καθὼς) the example or pattern (τύπος) they have in ἡμᾶς ("us"). There is some disagreement on the referent of ἡμᾶς—Witherington suggests that "us" refers, besides Paul, to his coworkers Timothy and Epaphroditus, who are on their way to Philippi,[259] but de Boer contends the reference is to the "whole apostolic team" (including Silas and Timothy).[260] Since Paul has presented Timothy and Epaphroditus as examples for imitation in his letter, it seems that ἡμᾶς refers to them rather than Paul's entire apostolic team.[261]

More importantly, however, is the referent of the phrase τούς ... περιπατοῦντας. While de Boer argues that the phrase refers to exemplary leaders,[262] Bockmuehl contends that "the scope of reference is undoubtedly wider."[263] I concur with Bockmuehl and others that τούς ... περιπατοῦντας refers to "all people who live in

255. Dodd, *Paul's Paradigmatic "I,"* 190.
256. Smit, *Paradigms*, 114.
257. Similarly, Smit concludes that Timothy and Epaphroditus are "living embodiments of the values that Paul cherishes and recommends, which suits the demand from rhetorical theory that *exempla* should be as close to the audience as possible" (*Paradigms*, 115).
258. Hawthorne, *Philippians*, 162; Witherington, *Philippians*, 214; Jensen, "Imitating Paul," 27.
259. Witherington, *Philippians*, 215.
260. De Boer, *Imitation of Paul*, 182–83.
261. So also Copan, *Saint Paul*, 166–67.
262. De Boer, *Imitation of Paul*, 181–82.
263. Bockmuehl, *Philippians*, 229. So also Betz, *Nachfolge und Nachahmung*, 151; Fee, *Philippians*, 366; John Reumann, *Philippians*, AYB 33b (New Haven, NY: Yale University Press, 2008), 592; Copan, *Saint Paul*, 165–66.

6. Mimesis in the Pauline Letters

line with the lifestyle of Paul."[264] Regarding Paul's injunction to imitate this nameless group defined solely by their way of life, Cable remarks, "For Paul, it is not status, power or wealth but Christlikeness . . . that makes a worthy exemplar."[265] Hawthorne captures it well:

> Paul was urging the Philippians to join in imitating him and the lives of other worthy examples, not because he considered that he and they were such great and important people, better than anyone else—and certainly not because he believed that they had already reached perfection (note his own disclaimer of this in 3:12)—but only because he knew that they had been continually patterning their lives after Christ, the example par excellence (cf. 1 Cor 11:1; 1 Thess 1:6; 2 Thess 3:7). Only for this reason, and only insofar as they continued to imitate Christ, could they be considered people worthy of being imitated.[266]

Paul's instruction to the Philippian believers to imitate either him (in absentia) or other mature believers (who were present) shows the importance of personal examples for the early church. Many of the first Christians came from a pagan background and were unfamiliar with Jewish-Christian values. They had to observe the values embodied in the lives of Christian workers.[267] This reveals the concept of *transformation through imitation*. As Martin writes, "For Christianity, the pattern of ethical teaching is embodied not in a written code of precepts and maxims covering every possible contingency of life, but in a life—pre-eminently the life of the Lord Jesus, and secondarily in the lives of his earliest and closest followers."[268] Bockmuehl notes that to identify other believers worthy of imitation requires discernment, as 3:18–19 shows.[269]

---

264. Quotation from Copan, *Saint Paul*, 166. Copan rightly notes that περιπατεῖν refers to the totality of the lifestyle that is intended to be imitated (*Saint Paul*, 165). The repetition of περιπατεῖν in 3:17–18 creates a sharp contrast between those living according to Paul's example and the "enemies of the cross of Christ" (Kurz, "Kenotic Imitation," 114). As Fowl aptly notes, the "enemies of the cross of Christ" are unwilling to imitate the Christ of 2:6–8 and only accommodate the exalted Christ of 2:9–11 (*Story of Christ*, 100).

265. Cable, "*Imitatio Christianorum*," 125.

266. Hawthorne, "Imitation," 177.

267. Hawthorne, *Philippians*, 162. As Reumann notes, "Paul sets forth a method: *take note of*, observe carefully, even critically, people for reflection of Paul's gospel. They can be models only after inspection" (*Philippians*, 592 [original emphasis]).

268. Martin, *Philippians*, 159.

269. Bockmuehl, *Philippians*, 229.

6.4.5. Conclusion

Paul's primary concern in this letter is to instruct the Philippian believers about their corporate life as citizens worthy of the gospel, and his main strategy for their spiritual formation involves mimesis. In other words, Paul uses mimesis as the main didactic instrument to instruct the Philippian church on how to live together as good gospel citizens.[270] Fee correctly notes that Paul's concern in this letter has not been the (doctrinal) content of the gospel but its lived-out expression in the world.[271] Hence, Paul's didactic strategy of using mimesis is apt. For Paul, Christ is the supreme example for imitation, but he also presents Christlike examples such as himself, Timothy, Epaphroditus, and others who imitate Christ and show the life of good gospel citizenship.[272] In short, Paul's ethics in his letter to the Philippians is primarily *mimetic ethics*.

Regarding the content of mimesis, we saw that imitating Christ includes humility, sacrificial service, voluntary surrender of privileges, and prioritizing the "other." Hence, as Witherington explains, Paul uses mimetic language to promote stepping down, humility, and concern for others rather than a power move to enforce his authority over his converts (contra Castelli).[273] As in Greco-Roman antiquity, mimesis is a creative, cognitive process in Paul, so it comes as no surprise that moral reasoning is vital in this process. Moral reasoning is required to determine how imitating Christ's mindset-in-action looks in various situations and which living examples are modeling Christ and, hence, worthy of imitation.[274] Moreover, if Christ is the supreme model for imitation, the implication is that imitating Christ or those who exemplify Christ results in moral transformation—becoming like Christ.[275]

---

270. Some of the Christian values and behaviors Paul calls the Philippians to, such as self-sacrificial love and humility, are countercultural (Witherington, *Philippians*, 27).

271. Fee, *Philippians*, 419–20.

272. See also Smit, who concludes that for Paul, identity in Christ is an embodied affair, that is, the issue of patterning one's life on the *exempla* of Christ, Paul, and other Christlike believers (*Paradigms*, 162).

273. Witherington, *Philippians*, 126–28.

274. For an ethical reading of Philippians that holds together cognition and behavior in relation to role models, see Jae Hyun Lee, "'Think' and 'Do' Like the Role Models: Paul's Teaching on the Christian Life in Philippians," in *The Language and Literature of the New Testament*, ed. Lois Fuller Dow, Craig A. Evans, and Andrew W. Pitts, BINS 150 (Leiden: Brill, 2017), 625–43.

275. See also van Kooten, who argues that "the *homoiōsis Christōi* is the intermediary stage in the process of assimilation to God" (*Paul's Anthropology*, 213). While Sierksma-Agteres endorses this, she also argues that in order to allow for this assimilation, Christ must take on human likeness first ("Imitation in Faith," 139–40). This position resembles Eastman's concept of "reciprocal mimetic participation" (see n. 207 above).

6. Mimesis in the Pauline Letters

Like the Thessalonian and Corinthian correspondence, Philippians also presents several modes of mimesis. First, the imitator can have *direct access* to the exemplar for observation and imitation, such as Paul's directive to the Philippians to look for accessible exemplars in 3:17b. While this mode of mimesis is most common because the exemplars are naturally available in the imitator's environment, other modes of mimesis apply especially if the exemplar is absent. Hence, second, there is *textually mediated mimesis*, for example, in 2:5–11, where Paul presents Christ as a "literary example" whom the Philippians can visualize and imitate as Paul's letter is read out to them. Third, there is *personally mediated mimesis* in that Paul presents the Philippians with several "living examples" for imitation (Timothy, Epaphroditus). Fourth, there is *mnemonic mimesis*, where Paul reminds the Philippians on several occasions that he, as an imitator of Christ, is now a "remembered example" for the Philippians to visualize and imitate. These mimetic modes are not necessarily mutually exclusive, and some overlap exists. For example, the remembered Paul is also the literary Paul because the remembering is mediated or activated through the letter; the living examples of Timothy and Epaphroditus are also directly accessible for observation as they return to the Philippians, similar to the mature believers Paul points to in 3:17b.

De Boer's conclusion on imitation in Philippians is worth quoting:

> [Paul] reminds the Philippians of what true Christianity is by presenting his own Christian experiences, beliefs, and attitudes. The accent is strongly on a total and continuing humiliation of self in favor of gaining Christ and the goal in him. This is basic Christianity, and the appeal is to imitate Paul in this. . . . Imitation is a call to bring to personal expression the Christianity which Paul had portrayed to them. It is a means by which Paul seeks to lead the Philippians to mature and steadfast Christian faith and life.[276]

The standard of Christian belief and conduct before the composition of the New Testament was embodied in the teachings and personal examples of Christ, the apostles, and other exemplary believers.[277] With the formation of the New Testament, these normative teachings and personal examples have been preserved for

---

276. De Boer, *Imitation of Paul*, 188.

277. While Reumann sometimes appears skeptical or cautious about imitation in Paul (*Philippians*, 588, 591), he nevertheless states, "Yet for Paul what alternative was there, to communicate with an audience hundreds of miles from where Jesus lived and Christianity began, in a world of few and scattered Christians and an ascended Lord—except to point to those who brought the message and lived by it? What option but to include themselves and other churches as examples and embodiments of the gospel?" (*Philippians*, 591).

later generations of believers to "observe" and imitate these "literary examples." Nevertheless, this does not imply that there is no longer a need for normative "living examples" for imitation. Although the imitation of a teacher was standard practice in Greco-Roman and Jewish antiquity, Bockmuehl remarks that Paul's exhortation to imitate him derives "both its authority and its limitations from his own faithfulness to the prior example of Christ, who is himself the prototype and measure of all Christian discipleship."[278] This implies that the success or effectiveness of someone being a role model for others depends on how closely the person extending the invitation imitates Christ.

6.5. Ephesians

The only explicit reference to mimesis in Ephesians is found in 5:1, the injunction to be imitators of God (γίνεσθε οὖν μιμηταὶ τοῦ θεοῦ). This is the only one in the Pauline corpus where believers are commanded to imitate God (but see on Col 3:13 in section 6.7.3), and it poses a twofold challenge. First, we must resolve how believers can imitate the invisible God whom they cannot see. Second, it is not clear what believers are asked to imitate about God. I suggest that the immediate context, where 4:32–5:2 forms a small mimetic unit, provides important clues to address these issues:

4³² γίνεσθε [δὲ] εἰς ἀλλήλους χρηστοί, εὔσπλαγχνοι, χαριζόμενοι ἑαυτοῖς, <u>καθὼς καὶ</u> ὁ θεὸς ἐν Χριστῷ ἐχαρίσατο ὑμῖν. 5¹ Γίνεσθε οὖν <u>μιμηταὶ τοῦ θεοῦ</u> ὡς τέκνα ἀγαπητὰ ² καὶ περιπατεῖτε ἐν ἀγάπῃ, <u>καθὼς καὶ</u> ὁ Χριστὸς ἠγάπησεν ἡμᾶς καὶ παρέδωκεν ἑαυτὸν ὑπὲρ ἡμῶν προσφορὰν καὶ θυσίαν τῷ θεῷ εἰς ὀσμὴν εὐωδίας.

4³² Be [morally] good and compassionate to one another by forgiving one another, <u>just as</u> God in Christ <u>also</u> forgave us. 5¹ Be <u>imitators of God</u>, as beloved children, ² and so live in love, <u>just as</u> Christ <u>also</u> loved us and gave himself up for us as a fragrant offering and sacrifice to God.

In 4:32, the injunction to be morally good in dealing with fellow believers is clarified by the exhortation to imitate God in forgiveness, while 5:1–2 forms a single mimetic injunction to imitate God by imitating Christ in self-giving love.[279] Schulz

---

278. Bockmuehl, *Philippians*, 254.
279. The command to imitate God's forgiving attitude echoes the imitation of a merciful God in the Synoptic tradition (Matt 6:12, 14–15; 18:33, 35; Luke 6:36), while the mimetic injunction

6. Mimesis in the Pauline Letters

rightly notes that the believers' experience of God's forgiveness in Christ is the ground or basis for forgiving others.[280] I take the coordinating conjunction καί that links 5:1 and 5:2 as explicative ("in that," "namely," "and so"). Hence, Paul exhorts believers to imitate God primarily in sacrificial love and forgiveness.[281]

Clarke notes a parallel with the parental motif in 1 Cor 4:14–16, except that God (rather than Paul) is the father.[282] In which case, the idea of imitating God is an extension of the natural child–parent mimesis and is now placed in the context of a spiritual family. Moreover, the imitation of the invisible God is mediated through the imitation of Christ because believers have tangibly experienced God's forgiveness and love in Christ. As van Kooten notes, "As Christ is the image of God, and man, by becoming of the same form as Christ participates in this image, the *homoiōsis Christōi* is the intermediary stage in the process of assimilation to God,"[283] While Christ is also "absent," we have seen that the imitation of Christ is mediated through Paul (and other mature Christians).

Besides the mimetic unit of love and forgiveness in 4:32–5:2, there are two other mimetic occurrences. First, in 4:17, Paul exhorts the Ephesian believers not to imitate the Gentiles (καθὼς καί indicates the mimesis), who live without God because of their obstinacy and lack of knowledge (4:17–19). Instead, the Ephesians are to align themselves with God and be transformed in accordance with the Christian teaching they have received (4:20–24; see also Rom 12:2).[284] Paul

---

in 5:2 may be rooted in Jesus's mimetic love-command in John 13:34. This would indicate that Paul was not simply aware of various Jesus traditions but also the mimetic ideas in them (see also de Boer, *Imitation of Paul*, 76–77).

280. Schulz, *Nachfolgen und Nachahmen*, 239.

281. See also Clinton E. Arnold, *Ephesians*, ZECNT 10 (Grand Rapids: Zondervan, 2010), 309. This corresponds to Wolbert's assertion that one can only imitate God's moral attributes ("Vorbild," 269–70). Contra Markus Barth, who contends that 5:1 could refer to imitating a broad range of God's qualities (*Ephesians: Translation and Commentary on Chapters 4–6*, AB 34a [Garden City, NY: Doubleday, 1974], 555–56). His remark that περιπατεῖν in 5:2 shows that imitation in 5:1 aims at ethical conduct is more on target (*Ephesians*, 556).

282. Clarke, "Imitators," 351. See also Schulz, *Nachfolgen und Nachahmen*, 239–40.

283. Van Kooten, *Paul's Anthropology*, 213. Likewise, Barth notes that the imitation of God in 5:1 shares with Greek antiquity the idea that people cannot directly imitate God, except when it is mediated (*Ephesians*, 591).

284. De Boer notes that the "new person" being created in the image of God sets the stage for the idea of imitating God (*Imitation of Paul*, 75). Robert A. Wild connects the idea of imitating God in 5:1 and the phrase "in accordance with God" (κατὰ θεόν) in 4:24 with the Greek ethical telos of "assimilation to God" in Platonic and Philonic traditions (e.g., Plato, *Theaet.* 176a–b; Philo, *Fug.* 63). Unlike Philo, however, the Pauline imitation of God is not a Platonic flight of the soul from earth to heaven but is achieved and manifested in living responsibility in this world ("'Be Imitators of God': Discipleship in the Letter to the Ephesians," in *Discipleship in the*

then spells out how such a transformed life should look in 4:25–5:5, of which the mimetic unit 4:32–5:2 is part. Second, in the so-called "household code" or *Haustafel* (5:21–6:9), the instructions for husband–wife relationships contain mimetic traces. While 5:24 may contain a "weak" idea of existential mimesis, in that wives should "imitate" the church (ὡς ... οὕτως καί), 5:25 contains a stronger case, indicating that husbands should imitate Christ in self-sacrificial love (καθὼς καί). This idea closely resembles the imitation in 5:2 so that the husband–Christ mimesis is a *specific* application of the more general believer–Christ mimesis.[285]

In sum, besides the explicit mimetic injunction γίνεσθε μιμηταὶ τοῦ θεοῦ, the comparative phrase καθὼς καί also indicates mimesis on several occasions (4:17, 32; 5:2, 25). In effect, all three mimetic units (4:17–24; 4:32–5:2; 5:21–33) relate to the believers' new life in Christ that Paul seeks to explain from 4:1 onwards (see also the use of περιπατεῖν in 4:1, 17; 5:2, 8, 15), so once again Paul's ethics is *mimetic ethics*.[286]

6.6. The Pastoral Epistles

In the Pastoral Epistles (1–2 Tim, Titus), Paul writes to individuals (rather than churches), instructing them about organizing church life in his absence. The authorship and historical situation of the Pastorals are highly contentious, and I must stress that my analysis of example and mimesis in the Pastorals does not depend on any particular historical reconstruction. Nevertheless, a good case can be made for Pauline authorship and the possibility that 1 Timothy and Titus reflect Paul's second Aegean journey—after his release from Roman imprisonment about 62 CE and possible return from Spain around 64 CE.[287] For Paul's release from Roman imprisonment, we have (1) *internal evidence* from Phil 1:19–26, an undisputed

---

New Testament, ed. Fernando F. Segovia [Philadelphia: Fortress, 1985], 127–43, at 128–38). For the concept of assimilation and likeness to God in Greco-Roman antiquity, Philo, and Paul, see van Kooten, *Paul's Anthropology*, 92–219.

285. The phrase καθὼς καὶ ὁ Χριστὸς ἠγάπησεν ἡμᾶς καὶ παρέδωκεν ἑαυτὸν ὑπὲρ ἡμῶν in 5:2 closely parallels καθὼς καὶ ὁ Χριστὸς ἠγάπησεν τὴν ἐκκλησίαν καὶ ἑαυτὸν παρέδωκεν ὑπὲρ αὐτῆς in 5:25. Eph 5:28–29, however, does not denote mimesis but analogy—husbands should behave similarly towards their wives as to their own bodies. Further on in the household code, in 6:9, Thompson contends that slave-masters are to imitate divine impartiality (*Pauline Slave Welfare*, 260–61).

286. Likewise, Thompson concludes that "imitation of God and/or Christ underpins much of the epistle's ethics" (*Pauline Slave Welfare*, 251–53 [quotation from p. 253]).

287. See, for example, Stanley E. Porter, *The Apostle Paul: His Life, Thought, and Letters* (Grand Rapids: Eerdmans, 2016), 423–31.

6. Mimesis in the Pauline Letters

letter, and possibly Phlm 22 (although Philemon could have been written from Ephesus); and (2) *external evidence* from the late first century (1 Clem. 5:7), the second century (The Muratorian Fragment, lines 38–39; Acts of Pet. 3.1–3), and the fourth century (Eusebius, *Hist. eccl.* 2.22.2–8).

In this scenario, the Pauline congregations around the Aegean coastal area had multiplied and now included Crete, Miletus, and Nicopolis (Titus 1:5; 3:12; 2 Tim 4:20). As Ellis explains, instead of sending letters to these churches, he sent letters to his trusted coworkers—Titus in Crete and Timothy in Ephesus—which "served both as instruments of personal communication and encouragement and also as vade mecums to give apostolic authorization for their teaching."[288] This might explain that the mimetic language in the Pastoral Epistles is limited to the use of the term "example" (τύπος and ὑποτύπωσις).[289]

Paul as Example. Fiore argues that Paul's personal examples in 1 Tim 1:3–20, 2 Tim 1:3–18, and 3:1–4:8 embody the very qualities and actions advanced in these letters so that Paul effectively becomes the implicit example for imitation.[290] In my view, Fiore sees too much exemplary material in these passages. In 1 Tim 1:16, when Paul refers to himself as an example (ὑποτύπωσις), it is to show that the salvation that Paul, the superlative sinner, had received was available to all future believers.[291] Christ's demonstration of extreme patience in dealing with Paul, an egregious sinner, made Paul a model for those who would come to faith.[292] Luke Timothy Johnson rightly states that "it is God's power and grace that are exemplary, rather than any action of Paul's."[293] Indeed, Paul does not suggest others imitate him; rather, Paul's experience of Christ's extreme patience will also be replicated in the lives of future believers.[294] In short, Paul is *not* an example for

---

288. E. Earle Ellis, "Pastoral Letters," in *Dictionary of Paul and His Letters*, ed. Gerald F. Hawthorne, Ralph P. Martin, and Daniel G. Reid (Downers Grove, IL: InterVarsity Press, 1993), 658–66, at 661.

289. The phrase οὕτως καί in 2 Tim 3:8 indicates analogy rather than imitation, and the conjunction ὡς is also used to express analogy (e.g., 1 Tim 5:1–2; 2 Tim 1:3; Titus 1:5).

290. Fiore, "Paul," 244–45; Fiore, *Personal Example*, 198–211.

291. Fiore, *Personal Example*, 199. See also Clarke, "Imitators," 354. However, while Fiore takes the whole of 1:3–20 as referring to Paul's example, I consider only 1:12–17 relevant.

292. Raymond F. Collins, *1 & 2 Timothy and Titus: A Commentary*, NTL (Louisville: Westminster John Knox, 2002), 44–45.

293. Luke Timothy Johnson, *The First and Second Letters to Timothy*, AB 35a (New York: Doubleday, 2001), 181.

294. Philip F. Towner, *The Letters to Timothy and Titus*, NICNT (Grand Rapids: Eerdmans, 2006), 149. Likewise, Martin Dibelius and Hans Conzelmann state that Paul's conversion serves as a prototype: "Paul is the typical representative of those who have received the mercy which a sinner can experience" (*The Pastoral Epistles*, Hermeneia [Philadelphia: Fortress, 1972], 30).

PART 2   MIMESIS IN EARLY CHRISTIANITY

imitation here. In 2 Tim 1:13, the referent of ὑποτύπωσις is the "sound teaching" that Paul proclaimed rather than Paul himself (ὑποτύπωσιν ἔχε ὑγιαινόντων λόγων ὧν παρ' ἐμοῦ ἤκουσας). Nevertheless, Towner seems to hint at some imitation when he states, "The message Timothy is to adhere to in his preaching is the one Paul himself proclaimed."[295] In other words, while Paul presents himself as an example (although not for imitation) in 1 Tim 1:16, this is at most implied in 2 Tim 1:13. Regarding Fiore's third passage (2 Tim 3:1–4:8), while 2 Tim 3:10 contains no explicit mimetic language, the verb παρακολουθεῖν ("to follow closely") implies the idea of mimesis. When Paul, towards the end of his life, remarks that Timothy has "closely followed" his teaching, way of life, purpose, faith, patience, love, and perseverance, he surely implies that it went beyond close observation of Timothy's practice of carefully patterning his life after Paul's (see also the similar usage in 1 Tim 4:6).[296] Hence, Clarke's translation of σὺ παρηκολούθησάς as "you have observed" is too weak, whereas de Boer's translation "you did follow" is better because it implies action.[297] De Boer thus aptly concludes, "'Following' here is a concept which includes the phenomenon of imitation."[298] In sum, both occurrences of ὑποτύπωσις, in 1 Tim 1:16 and 2 Tim 1:13, do not present Paul as an example for imitation; only in 2 Tim 3:10 do we find a "weak" idea of implied mimesis.

Timothy as Example. 1 Timothy indicates that Paul and Timothy had been together in Ephesus and that Paul traveled to Macedonia, leaving Timothy in Ephesus to teach, deal with false teaching, and help the Ephesians to order their church life (1:3–7; 3:14–15; 4:11–16; 6:2, 20–21).[299] Hence, Timothy functions as a proxy for Paul until he returns (4:13). In his absence, Paul charges Timothy to organize the church in keeping with his teaching.[300] In 4:12, Paul commands Timothy to be a trustworthy example (τύπος γίνου τῶν πιστῶν) for the Ephesian believers in speech, conduct, love, faith, and purity.[301] As Fiore asserts, "Virtues dominate

---

295. Towner, *Timothy and Titus*, 477. Similarly, Fiore argues that although the example in 2 Tim 1:13 is not personal, it has personal aspects since Paul is the source of the "sound teaching" (*Personal Example*, 203–5).

296. While I agree with Fiore that 3:10–12 indicates mimesis, I disagree that 4:6–8a presents Paul as an example to follow (*Personal Example*, 205–6).

297. Clarke, "Imitator," 355; de Boer, *Imitation of Paul*, 200.

298. De Boer, *Imitation of Paul*, 201.

299. Gorman, *Apostle*, 633.

300. Gorman, *Apostle*, 633.

301. William D. Mounce contends that the idea is not so much that Timothy is an example for imitation but "a mold that should be pressed into the lives of others so that they attain the same shape" (*Pastoral Epistles*, WBC 46 [Nashville: Nelson, 2000], 259). However, if Timothy is exhorted to actively develop certain qualities, it would follow that others must also actively engage in emulating Timothy in order to attain these qualities. Interestingly, in Titus 2:7, Mounce does view Titus as a model to be followed (*Pastoral Epistles*, 413).

6. Mimesis in the Pauline Letters

over teaching as constituents of the desired model (*typos*) to be imitated."[302] For ancient moral teachers, speech and behavior go together.[303] As Towner remarks, "To be a model or set an example meant more than simply presenting a pattern that others were to mimic.... It was a case of living out life as faith in the gospel had shaped it."[304] Paul continues to urge Timothy to practice the public reading of Scripture, exhortation, and teaching so that everyone will note his progress and be saved (4:13–16). As one of Paul's most trusted coworkers, Timothy has been a frequent example for imitation to the believers in Thessalonica, Corinth, and Philippi (see sections 6.2–6.4).

Titus as Example. While Timothy remained in Ephesus, Paul left Titus in Crete to look after the church there (Titus 1:5). Besides organizing church life (1:5–16), Paul charges Titus to provide sound teaching (2:1–15). In Titus 2:6–8, Paul commands Titus to exhort the young men to be of sound mind (σωφρονεῖν) in two ways: (1) in conduct, by showing himself to be an example of good works (τύπον καλῶν ἔργων); and (2) in teaching, by showing integrity, seriousness, and speech beyond reproach. Paul does not spell out how Titus must show exemplary behavior that will count as "good works," but καλῶν ἔργων also occurs in 2:14 when speaking of Christ having redeemed a people zealous for good works. Hence, Paul charges Titus to demonstrate to the Cretan believers the kind of people Christ has chosen and redeemed.[305] Quinn notes a mimetic chain of exemplary behavior from Paul to Titus to the Cretan believers: "[Paul] has placed Titus among the younger men of the congregation.... Titus is not only to leave 'a pattern' on his peers but is also a living *typos* stamped out of the life and teaching of the Pauline model.... The apostolic succession in right conduct is refracted through the Christian life of Paul's coworker."[306]

Summary. An examination of the Pastoral Epistles showed that the mimetic language is limited to the use of τύπος ("example") with reference to Timothy and Titus.[307] Both Timothy and Titus are thus presented as vital links in the chain of

---

302. Fiore, "Paul," 245.

303. Johnson, *Letters to Timothy*, 252.

304. Towner, *Timothy and Titus*, 315. Towner notes that while modeling behavior was usually the responsibility of teachers, leaders, and elders in the community, Timothy qualifies as a model for others *despite* his youth (*Timothy and Titus*, 731n70).

305. Clarke notes that throughout the Pastoral Epistles, the use of personal example has a Christological orientation in that Christ is both the grounds and motivation for the conduct of Paul, Timothy, and Titus ("Imitators," 357).

306. Jerome D. Quinn, *The Letter to Titus*, AB35 (New York: Doubleday, 1990), 141.

307. The references to ὑποτύπωσις ("example") with reference to Paul in 1 Tim 1:16 and 2 Tim 1:13 do not indicate mimesis.

Christian exemplars.[308] Johnson's evaluation of Timothy (and we should include Titus) is worth quoting in length:

> Timothy is to make himself a *typos* whose moral progress is manifest to all believers and whose dedication to the good news can be emulated by them. We are reminded of how seriously ancient philosophers regarded the responsibility of teachers to live in accord with what they professed.... Since philosophy in the Hellenistic period was considered to be essentially a matter of integrity of life, and since virtue was thought to be learned first and best by the imitation of living models, the teacher had no greater duty than to live in a manner consonant with the principles he enunciated.[309]

Looking across the Pauline corpus, we find that of all his coworkers, Paul most often presents Timothy as an example for imitation—to the churches in Thessalonica, Corinth, Philippi, and Ephesus. This is unsurprising given that Timothy is designated to succeed Paul (2 Tim 3:10–4:8). By holding up Timothy and Titus as exemplars, Paul indicates that they will replace him as links in the mimetic chain from Christ to the believers in Ephesus and Crete. Seeing Paul repeatedly addresses Timothy and Titus as his "genuine children" (1 Tim 1:2; 2 Tim 1:2; Titus 1:4), we are reminded that, similar to the other Pauline letters, family is the context of mimesis in the Pastoral Epistles.

6.7. Other Pauline Letters

We will now examine the remaining letters in the Pauline corpus (Gal, Rom, Col, Phlm) to see if they contain some mimetic ideas.

6.7.1. Galatians

There is no explicit mimetic language in Galatians, but several scholars have noted an implied mimesis in 4:12, where Paul urges the Galatians, "Become like me, for I also have become like you" (γίνεσθε ὡς ἐγώ, ὅτι κἀγὼ ὡς ὑμεῖς).[310] Susan Eastman suggests that although Paul's imperative in 4:12 does not use explicit mimetic lan-

---

308. Collins, *Timothy and Titus*, 128. Collins made this remark about Timothy, but it obviously applies to Titus also.
309. Johnson, *Letters to Timothy*, 255.
310. In 3:6–7, Paul presents Abraham's response of trusting God as the paradigmatic response to God for all believers, to be consequently identified as Abraham's offspring. While it is possible to detect a trace of mimesis here, in that believers "imitate" Abraham's faith response,

guage, it nevertheless denotes mimesis because it resembles mimetic texts such as "Become imitators of me" in 1 Cor 4:16 and 11:1.[311] She argues that Paul and the Galatians had a shared past in slavery (to the law and the *stoicheia*, respectively) and a shared present experience in Christ.[312] In this dynamic, relational matrix, "Christ moves into the human situation [through the incarnation, effecting a 'mimetic reversal'], Paul moves via Christ into the Galatians' sphere, and they move into his."[313] "The resultant communal life that Paul envisions with his converts is to display the profoundly transformed and transformative 'mimetic' relationship that Christ has established with humanity."[314]

Dodd, however, contends that 4:12 is not a broad call to imitate Paul's lifestyle but a specific call to imitate his single-minded response to the gospel, especially in how to resist "people-pleasers" such as the Judaizers and not to be enslaved by them.[315] Somewhat differently, Clarke follows Dunn in saying that the Galatians are called to emulate Paul specifically in being deemed as falling outside the law.[316] De Boer agrees that the phrase "become as I am" means "become free from the law as I am," but also notes the familial language that follows in 4:19, where Paul addresses the Galatians as τέκνα μου ("my [little] children") and expresses his parental desire to produce well-formed children. Hence, "the Galatians are being called by their father to be real children of his, and to show this by their likeness to him."[317]

Horrell examines the phrase "the law (νόμος) of Christ" in 6:2 (and the related phrase ἔννομος Χριστοῦ in 1 Cor 9:21), supporting Richard Hays's argument that Christ's example of burden-bearing or self-giving is a normative pattern (νόμος) for Christian practice.[318] While this idea has validity, I contend that 6:2 could simply refer to obedience or adherence rather than imitation. There is no mimetic language

---

this is too weak to pursue. Then, in 2:20, the idea is largely one of reciprocity rather than mimesis (contra Sierksma-Agteres, "Imitation in Faith," 140).

311. Eastman, *Paul's Mother Tongue*, 26–29.

312. Eastman, *Paul's Mother Tongue*, 39–40. See also Nicolet, "Le concept d'imitation," 408–9.

313. Eastman, *Paul's Mother Tongue*, 57.

314. Eastman, *Paul's Mother Tongue*, 60.

315. Dodd, *Paul's Paradigmatic "I,"* 163–64. See also Fiore, "Paul," 238–39.

316. Clarke, "Imitators," 352; Clarke, *Pauline Theology*, 176–77; James D. G. Dunn, *The Epistle to the Galatians*, BNTC (London: A&C Black, 1993), 232. See also Schulz, *Nachfolgen und Nachahmen*, 322; Hans Dieter Betz, *Galatians*, Hermeneia (Philadelphia: Fortress, 1979), 222; Ben Witherington, *Grace in Galatia: A Commentary on St Paul's Letter to the Galatians* (Grand Rapids: Eerdmans, 1998), 307–8.

317. De Boer, *Imitation of Paul*, 191, 194 (quotation from p. 194). Differently, J. Louis Martyn puts 4:12 in the context of mutual friendship (*Galatians*, AB 33a [New York: Doubleday, 1997], 420).

318. Horrell, *Solidarity and Difference*, 244–54. Horrell is indebted to Richard B. Hays, "Christology and Ethics in Galatians: The Law of Christ," *CBQ* 49 (1987): 268–90, at 275, 287.

in the immediate context to speak confidently of mimesis being implied in 6:2. Moss reads Paul's statement in 6:17 about carrying the marks (στίγματα) of Jesus on his body in light of his being crucified with Christ in 2:20 to suggest that Paul imitates the sufferings of Christ.[319] While the idea is attractive, it is at most implied.[320]

6.7.2. Romans

De Boer and others rightly assert that Paul does not issue a call to imitate him in his letter to the Romans because he did not found this church and hence was not their spiritual father.[321] However, this does not mean Paul is unable to use the idea of mimesis as part of his paraenetic strategy. While the lexeme μιμεῖσθαι does not occur, the letter contains other expressions that could indicate mimesis.

In 4:1–12, Paul argues that Abraham is an example of the right response to God for all people. Paul first argues that Abraham could be regarded as the πατήρ ("father") of all uncircumcised believers precisely because his belief-response to God came *before* he was circumcised (4:11). Subsequently, Paul asserts that Abraham is also the πατήρ of circumcised believers who imitate Abraham's belief-response (4:12). The idiomatic expression στοιχεῖν τοῖς ἴχνεσιν denotes "to imitate" (lit. "to walk/follow in someone's footsteps"; see also 1 Pet 2:21). Hence, Paul upholds Abraham as an example for his response of trusting God, for both Jewish and Gentile believers to imitate.[322]

In Rom 5–6, we encounter the recurring construction ὥσπερ . . . οὕτως καί (5:12, 19, 21; 6:4) that potentially indicates mimesis. However, in most cases, it is analogy that is in view rather than mimesis. In 5:12, the universal stain of death corresponds or is analogous to the universal stain of sin. In 5:19, the disobedience of Adam and the obedience of Christ have far-reaching but opposite effects.[323] Likewise, 5:21 also contains an analogy of opposites; both sin and grace have powerful but opposite influences. It is only in 6:4 that we can find a possible trace of mimesis. The believers' union with Christ in baptism–death leads them to expe-

---

319. Moss, *Other Christs*, 27–28.

320. Differently, Thompson sees the concept of imitating God's impartiality in Gal 2:1–4:7 as rooted in the Jewish divine impartiality principle (*Pauline Slave Welfare*, 219–29). However, there is no specific language supporting his idea.

321. De Boer, *Imitation of Paul*, 206; Clarke, "Imitators," 353.

322. See also the informed discussion in Richard N. Longenecker, *The Epistle to the Romans: A Commentary on the Greek Text* (Grand Rapids: Eerdmans, 2016), 476–80.

323. Benjamin Schliesser is adamant that Christ's faith(fulness) or obedience is not the model for Christians to imitate (*Abraham's Faith in Romans 4: Paul's Concept of Faith in Light of the History of Reception of Genesis 15:6*, WUNT 2/224 [Tübingen: Mohr Siebeck, 2007], 269–71).

6. Mimesis in the Pauline Letters

rience a similar reality as Christ. Since Christ's experience is expressed through a passive construction ("he was raised from the dead by God"), there is possibly a "weak" idea of existential mimesis so that just as Christ lives now, believers also will live (see also 6:5, 8).[324]

The so-called "divided I" in 7:14–25 has led to intense debate. Dodd contends that while Paul is not excluded from "I," he is not writing directly about himself. Using this device of "I," Paul refers to the earlier contrast between life "in Adam" and life "in Christ" (5:12–6:23) but also draws a new contrast between the effects of the law (death) and the effects of the Spirit (life) in Rom 7–8.[325] I agree in part, but think that Paul is not included in the "I." Rather, the "I," from Paul's Christian viewpoint, refers to the Jew who seeks to please God by keeping the law but finds himself unable to do so. I do not see an aspect of mimesis here.

The clearest case of mimesis is found in Rom 15:7 through a καθώς . . . καί construction: "Therefore, accept one another, just as (καθώς) Christ also (καί) has accepted you."[326] Jensen argues that ὑμᾶς ("you" plural) particularly refers to Gentile Christians and their acceptance in Christ. In light of 15:5–9, Paul indicates that the Roman Christians should overcome the Jew–Gentile divide by mutual acceptance of one another just as Christ has done.[327] This fits the commonly held view of Romans, namely that Jewish Christians had started to return to Rome after 54 CE (after emperor Claudius had issued an edict around 48/49 CE to expel all Jews from Rome [see also Acts 18:2]) and found themselves marginalized in a now predominantly Gentile church.[328] Jensen also sees mimesis in 15:3, arguing that Christ is presented as a model for the twofold exhortation in 15:1 in that he does not please himself but bears the insults of the whole world directed at God.[329] While this idea is appealing, specific mimetic language is missing in 15:1–3. Instead, it would be better to understand the mimetic injunction in 15:7 *in light of* 15:1–3 so that Paul specifically exhorts the "strong" Roman believers to accept the "weak" in imitation of Christ accepting them.[330]

---

324. See also Smalley, "Imitation of Christ in the New Testament," 17; van Kooten, *Paul's Anthropology*, 208; Fiore and Blanton, "Paul," 184–85.

325. Dodd, *Paul's Paradigmatic "I,"* 234.

326. See also Michael B. Thompson, *Clothed with Christ: The Example and Teaching of Jesus in Romans 12.1–15.13*, LNTS 59 (Sheffield: Sheffield Academic Press, 1991), 230; Joseph A. Fitzmyer, *Romans*, AB 33 (New York: Doubleday, 1992), 705–6.

327. Jensen, "Imitating Paul," 20.

328. See, for example, Schulz, *Nachfolgen und Nachahmen*, 281.

329. Jensen, "Imitating Paul," 19. See also Schulz, *Nachfolgen und Nachahmen*, 279. Thompson even sees the idea of imitating Christ throughout 15:1–13 (*Clothed with Christ*, 234–36).

330. So Tinsley, *Imitation of God*, 138; de Boer, *Imitation of Paul*, 62; Clarke, "Imitators," 353.

PART 2   MIMESIS IN EARLY CHRISTIANITY

I draw attention to a study by Antonio Pitta who sees a pervasive pattern of human mimesis in Romans.[331] He starts by examining the noun ὁμοίωμα ("likeness," "image," "appearance"), which generally points to reproduction and appears four times in Romans (1:23; 5:14; 6:5; 8:3). Except for 1:23 where ὁμοίωμα refers to the representation of an idol, he sees mimesis in the other three instances. In 5:14, ὁμοίωμα refers to the outcome of a mimetic process, namely the condition of those who are not assimilated to Adam's transgression. In 6:5, Pitta argues for the idea of assimilation as the result of a mimetic process, where Christ's death is reproduced in the believers' existence so that they may share in his resurrection. In 8:3, ὁμοίωμα also refers to assimilation (as in 6:5 and Phil 2:7), in this case, the assimilation of the sinful flesh in the incarnate Christ.[332] Then, in 13:14, Pitta argues that the concept of "putting on Christ" is rooted in being assimilated to Christ in his death (6:4–5).[333] Finally, in light of 15:1–3, the conjunction καθώς in 15:7 indicates that Christ is "the model for a mutual acceptance in constant reproduction among believers."[334] Pitta's systematic gathering of his findings is worth quoting:

> The use of ὁμοίωμα in Rom 6:5 and 8:3 shows that human mimesis is carried out first of all by Christ in his taking on sinful flesh and then by the believers, so that they are assimilated in a natural way into Christ's death. It is out of this being assimilated that the Pauline exhortation to "put on the Lord Jesus Christ" (Rom 13:14) flows.... In a human mimesis, Christ, precisely as the archetype (cf. Rom 15:7), assimilates himself to human beings right up to the paradoxical assimilation of sinful flesh; and all believers are assimilated into his death in the unbridgeable gap that produces an endless mimesis.[335]

While Pitta's comprehensive analysis of human mimesis is impressive, I have some critical comments. First, 5:14 simply refers to those who are unlike Adam in their transgressions, and there is no concept of (intentional) mimesis. Pitta's analysis of 6:5 supports our understanding of "existential" mimesis in 6:4. I also accept Pitta's understanding of 8:3, which echoes Eastman's interpretation of Christ

---

331. Antonio Pitta, "The Degrees of Human Mimesis in the Letter to the Romans," in *Non mi vergogno del Vangelo, potenza di Dio*, ed. Francesco Bianchini and Stefano Romanello, AnBib 200 (Rome: Gregorian and Biblical Press, 2012), 221–38.

332. Pitta, "Human Mimesis," 225–30.

333. Pitta, "Human Mimesis," 231–32. See also Thompson, *Clothed with Christ*, 149–58; James D. G. Dunn, *The Theology of Paul the Apostle* (Grand Rapids: Eerdmans, 1998), 194.

334. Pitta, "Human Mimesis," 233.

335. Pitta, "Human Mimesis," 235.

imitating humanity in Phil 2:7. However, as Pitta himself states, 13:14 is *based on* the reality of 6:4–5, so "to put on Christ" is not a mimetic activity. More generally, Pitta's analysis highlights the concept of assimilation rather than mimesis because he sees assimilation as the outcome of a mimetic process, which means the idea of mimesis is implied and not described in Romans. In fact, Pitta's concept of assimilation corresponds to our concept of transformation as the goal of mimesis. But while for Pitta, assimilation is the result of a mimetic process, I contend that assimilation/transformation is *part of* the mimetic process as its last stage (see further section 6.8).

In sum, we find two clear cases of mimesis in Romans, in 4:12 and 15:7, where Abraham and Christ are examples for imitation. In 6:4–5, there is a trace of (existential) mimesis, in that believers will "imitate" Christ in experiencing the same reality of new life through God's agency rooted in their assimilation to Christ in his death. Finally, in 8:3, Christ "imitates" human existence by taking on "sinful flesh" (see also Phil 2:7).[336]

6.7.3. Colossians

In Colossians, there is one mimetic occurrence in 3:13, where Paul's exhortation to forgive each other is expanded to become a mimetic imperative. The καθώς ... οὕτως καί construction in 3:13b indicates that believers should imitate "the Lord" in extending forgiveness to others. The textual difficulty in 3:13 is whether κύριος refers to Christ or God. While the textual variant Χριστός has a better attestation than θεός, the latter brings the mimetic exhortation in line with the mimetic injunction in Eph 4:32. In addition, Schulz contends that the New Testament never presents Christ as the source of forgiveness.[337] Jensen, however, contends that Christ's death on the cross and the ensuing forgiveness in 2:13–14 (and see also 1:14) inform the mimetic practice required of the Colossians in 3:13.[338] However,

---

336. I disregard Hood's suggestion that Rom 12:1–2 refers to imitating a crucified Messiah because the text contains no mimetic language (*Imitating God*, 120). He also argues that Paul works out this imitation of Jesus in the remainder of Rom 12–15 (*Imitating God*, 121–22). I agree with him on some texts he refers to (e.g., 15:7), but other texts he mentions do not indicate mimesis (e.g. 15:23–27). Generally, my issue with Hood is that his views on imitation are too often insufficiently grounded in the text.

337. Schulz, *Nachfolgen und Nachahmen*, 240. F. F. Bruce also opts for God as the reference (*The Epistles to the Colossians, to Philemon, and to the Ephesians*, NICNT [Grand Rapids: Eerdmans, 1984], 155).

338. Jensen, "Imitating Paul," 22. Others who opt for Christ as the reference include James D. G. Dunn, *The Epistles to the Colossians and to Philemon: A Commentary on the Greek Text*, NIGTC (Grand Rapids: Eerdmans, 1996), 231; Douglas J. Moo, *The Letters to the Colossians and to*

1:13–14 speaks of God's salvation in terms of transferring people into the kingdom of his Son, *in whom* we have forgiveness of sins, indicating that Christ is the sphere or realm of redemption. More importantly, 2:13–14 explicitly states that God is the source of forgiveness, but of course, in relation to the cross. As God and the work of Christ are inseparable, I prefer to speak of God's forgiveness in Christ. Finally, if the Synoptic teaching on forgiveness (e.g., Matt 6:12–15; 18:21–35) is in the background here, as many scholars contend (including those who support Christ as the reference), it would support the idea of God as the reference in 3:13. In essence, forgiveness is actualized through mimesis as the Colossians' forgiveness of each other is rooted in and patterned after God's forgiveness of them (in Christ). In other words, God's forgiveness (in Christ) is not simply the model to imitate but also the *empowering* and *motivational basis* from which believers can forgive each other.[339]

6.7.4. Philemon

While Philemon does not contain mimetic language, it arguably hints at mimesis. Paul does not give specific commands to Philemon but appeals to his volition to choose the right thing (8–9, 14, 17, 20). Dodd argues that Paul paradigmatically presents himself as one who renounces his authority (14) and as an example of generosity, love, and compassion (9, 12, 18–19) regarding other members of the community of believers, with the expectation that Philemon will emulate his example in his relationship with Onesimus (21b).[340] In short, Paul's restraint in exercising his authority, combined with a display of love and generosity, shows paradigmatically how Philemon should treat Onesimus.[341] Likewise, Fiore contends that Paul's appeal to Philemon to choose voluntarily, combined with an undercurrent of compulsion, is the "paradigmatic attitude of interaction that Paul wishes Philemon to adopt vis-à-vis Onesimus."[342] In sum, Paul implicitly exhorts

---

Philemon (Grand Rapids: Eerdmans, 2008), 280; Paul Foster, *Colossians*, BNTC (London: Bloomsbury T&T Clark, 2016), 350–51.

339. The same dynamic occurs in John 13:34, where the love command in 13:34a is expanded as a mimetic imperative in 13:34b (see section 5.4.3). Thompson also sees mimesis in 3:25–4:1, where slave masters are urged to imitate God's impartial treatment ("you also") (*Pauline Slave Welfare*, 246–49). However, there is insufficient mimetic language to support this; 4:1b has a causal conjunction (ὅτι) rather than a comparative one.

340. Dodd, *Paul's Paradigmatic "I,"* 203–5.

341. Dodd, *Paul's Paradigmatic "I,"* 211.

342. Fiore, "Paul," 244. While Wolbert does not understand the imitation of Paul as obedience to his apostolic authority (contra Michaelis, Castelli, et al.) and recognizes that Paul trusts

6. *Mimesis in the Pauline Letters*

Philemon to imitate his self-restraint and show love and generosity. For Dodd, the letter to Philemon is the apex of Paul's rhetorical use of exemplification because the implicit paradigmatic aspects are woven into his nuanced epistolary persuasion.[343] If Dodd is right in his assessment, it becomes harder to identify mimesis because it is implicit and has become so much a part of Paul's thinking that it has been integrated into his rhetorical style.

6.8. A Model of Pauline Mimesis

Paul had to develop extensive ethics for his churches since most of his converts came from pagan backgrounds and were unfamiliar with Jewish-Christian values. For Paul, mimesis was a crucial mechanism for moral transformation, and we can infer a model of mimesis from his writings that resembles what we found in Greco-Roman antiquity. This is not to say that Paul had such a systematic understanding of the workings of mimesis or that I am imposing a Greco-Roman model on Paul. Rather, I seek to infer a model of mimesis from the Pauline writings.[344] The following examples are not exhaustive but serve to illustrate the various stages in the Pauline concept of mimesis. While I recognize that the authorship of several letters is disputed, this section will show that the concept of mimesis is sufficiently coherent across the Pauline tradition.

1. *Selection and Association.* The Pauline tradition often presents Paul as an example for imitation, using the lexeme μιμεῖσθαι (1 Cor 4:16; 11:1; Phil 3:17a; 1 Thess 1:6; 2 Thess 3:7, 9), the noun τύπος (2 Thess 3:9), or other mimetic language (Gal 4:12; Phlm; 2 Tim 3:10). Where Paul is unable to visit a church, he holds up coworkers as examples for his audience, either as his surrogate during a temporary absence (e.g., Timothy in 1 Cor 4:17; Phil 2:19–24; Epaphroditus in Phil 2:25–30) or to continue the mimetic chain after his death (Timothy in 1 Tim 4:12; Titus in Titus 2:7). Paul even exhorts his audience to select mature Christians as examples for imitation (Phil 3:17b). Occasionally, Paul employs the concept of "corporate imitation," where he presents one church as a collective example for other churches (1 Thess 1:7; 2:14; 1 Cor 16:1; 2 Cor 8:1–11). Paul also uses examples from the past (e.g., rebellious Israel in 1 Cor 10:1–13).

However, Christ is, without doubt, the supreme example for imitation for Paul

---

Philemon to know his Christian duties towards Onesimus, he nevertheless views imitation as obedience to Paul's *paraenetic* authority rooted in Paul's personal example ("Vorbild," 262–63).

343. Dodd, *Paul's Paradigmatic "I,"* 212.

344. I first developed this model in Bennema, "Model of Mimesis," 184–87.

PART 2   MIMESIS IN EARLY CHRISTIANITY

(1 Thess 1:6; 1 Cor 11:1, 23–26; Rom 15:7; Phil 2:5–11), and it is natural that Christians (should) closely associate themselves with Christ.³⁴⁵ Paul rarely spells out the example of Christ (Phil 2:5–11 is an important exception), but this is probably because Paul's converts are still "young in the faith" and had to learn to imitate Christ from Paul. Thus, the imitation of Christ is primarily mediated through Paul (1 Cor 11:1), which explains the frequent call to imitate Paul himself (six out of the eight occurrences of the lexeme μιμεῖσθαι refer to the *imitatio Pauli*). In his absence, the imitation of Paul is mediated through trusted coworkers, who function as surrogates of Paul in the mimetic chain that runs from Christ through Paul and his coworkers to Paul's converts.

2. *Observation*. When Paul urges his converts to imitate him, it typically follows that they are able to observe him. For example, in addressing the ongoing issue of disorderliness in the Thessalonian church, Paul reminds them of the visible example (τύπος) he had been as he worked for a living while he was with them (2 Thess 3:6–13; see also 1 Thess 2:9–10). In Phil 4:9, Paul urges the Philippians to keep on doing (i.e., imitating) the things that they had *seen* (ἰδεῖν) when he was with them.

However, Paul also presents other living examples to his churches. In 1 Cor 4:16–17, Paul urges the Corinthians to imitate him, but as he is absent and cannot be observed (διὰ τοῦτο provides the causal connection between the verses), he is sending Timothy to provide a visible example of the Christlike life that he wants the Corinthians to adopt. Likewise, in Phil 2:6–11, Paul presents Christ as the supreme example for imitation, but to help the church model their corporate life on that of Christ (2:12), he sends Timothy and Epaphroditus as living examples for the Philippians to observe and imitate because each imitates aspects of Christ. In his personal letters to Timothy and Titus, Paul urges them to be a visible example (τύπος) of a Christlike life for other believers (1 Tim 4:12; Titus 2:7). Timothy (and Titus by implication) can do this because they have observed and imitated Paul closely (2 Tim 3:10). Paul can even tell the Philippians in 3:17b that in his absence they should observe (σκοπεῖν) other mature Christians in their surroundings who can provide a visible example for imitation.

Besides direct observation, the Pauline corpus points to other modes of "observation." For instance, Paul holds up an example for his audience in an oral report (e.g., Christ or the Judean churches for the Thessalonian church in 1 Thess 2:14) or in a letter (e.g., himself in an earlier personal visit [1 Thess 1:6; 1 Cor 4:16], a coworker [Timothy, Titus, Epaphroditus], or another church [1 Cor 16:1; 2 Cor 8:1–11]). In hearing Paul's report or his letter being read out, his audience could remember and reconstruct (in the case of Paul) or create a mental picture of the example for imitation. Hence, Paul

---

345. On Paul's participatory theology of believers being and partaking "in Christ," see Gorman, *Participating*.

presents his audience with an array of living, literary, and remembered examples they could observe from embodied lives, oral tradition, or written accounts.

3–4. Interpretation and Imitation. The model for imitation (whether Christ, Paul, Paul's trusted coworkers, or other mature Christians) was not simply to be observed but also examined in order to avoid a reductionist concept of mimesis. For Paul, mimesis is not about simplistic, literal replication but an interpretative, creative task in which the mimetic act corresponds to the original act. We have labeled this cognitive aspect in the mimetic process as "moral reasoning," where the imitator must interpret *what* to imitate and *how* to articulate this in a corresponding mimetic act.[346] For example, in proclaiming the gospel in Macedonia and Achaia, the Thessalonian believers imitated Paul's cruciform life and ministry, and in doing so, became a corporate example (τύπος) to be imitated by other Christians (1 Thess 1:6–8). The imitation in view is more likely a creative resemblance rather than an exact replication of Paul's actions. In 2 Thess 3:7–9, the mimetic imperative to engage in physical labor to earn a living is not a command to do the same work Paul did but to engage, *like* Paul, in work to earn a living and not burden fellow believers by living off them.

Paul's audience in Galatia must discern what Paul's mimetic imperative in 4:12, "Become like me, for I also have become like you," entails and should look like. Likewise, Paul's injunction to the Corinthians to imitate him in 1 Cor 4:16; 11:1 is (partly) referring to the imitation of Paul's overall lifestyle, and while the immediate context mentions some specific activities or attitudes of Paul, they do not constitute an exhaustive list. Paul probably expected the Corinthians to apply moral reasoning and discernment in determining what to imitate, based on their memories of him during his extended stay in Corinth (see Acts 18:11).

When Paul presents Christ as the paradigmatic example for imitation in Phil 2:5–11, he does not expect the Philippians to imitate Christ in every aspect. Rather, he urges them to contemplate (φρονεῖν) Christ's mindset (2:5) and work out (κατεργάζεσθαι) what Christlike living would look like in their corporate church life (2:12; note the causal conjunction ὥστε). Similarly, when Paul urges the Philippians in 4:8 to think (λογίζεσθαι) about various aspects of a virtuous lifestyle, he does not spell these out (note the repeated use of ὅσα in 4:8) but exhorts them in 4:9 to imitate what they have observed (ἰδεῖν) and understood (μαθεῖν) about his life.

5. Transformation/Assimilation. In antiquity, the notion that people would become like the ones they sought to imitate was driven by the idea of moral transformation. We noted that the Pauline corpus presents a mimetic chain that starts with Christ as the supreme example—the template for moral transformation. The

---

346. Likewise, Jensen refers to the reader's "deliberative process" to work out what mimetic actions result from imitating Christ's mindset/phronesis ("Imitating Paul," 31).

next link in the chain is Paul or a surrogate of Paul (usually a trusted coworker, but it could also be a mature Christian), who mediates the imitation of Christ to his converts as the last link. Hence, the goal of Pauline mimesis is that believers become Christlike. I do not object to using the terms "theosis," "Christosis," or "deification" for the believer's transformation as long as this refers to participating in Christ's or God's life and character in order to become *like* Christ or God (*homoiousios*) rather than participating in their essence in order to become God (*homoousios*).[347]

In the Pauline writings, the passive form of the verb μεταμορφοῦσθαι ("to be transformed") is found in two passages. Rom 12:2 speaks of transformation through the renewal of the mind, and 2 Cor 3:18 refers to transformation through contemplation, which also points to a cognitive aspect as it relates to the "unveiled mind" (2 Cor 3:15–16).[348] While these passages do not mention mimesis, the concept of transformation through observation and intellectual contemplation corresponds to stages two to five in our mimetic model, where close scrutiny and examination of an exemplar, followed by ongoing creative, cognitive mimetic acts will naturally lead to being transformed into the likeness of the exemplar.

Regarding the Thessalonian correspondence, for example, we noted that Paul's goal for the Thessalonian church is to present them "blameless" before God at the Parousia and that mimesis is instrumental in or central to Paul's paraenetic strategy to achieve this moral transformation. Paul's mimetic imperative in Gal 4:12, "Become like me, for I also have become like you," implies moral transformation as a result of mimesis. Philippians, a letter saturated with mimetic ideas, most clearly alludes to the believer's transformation as a result of imitation. We noted earlier that Paul, when he could not be present, points the Philippians to other individuals they could observe and imitate (3:17), but identifying those believers worthy of imitation requires discernment (3:18–19). Consequently, a life of imitating Christ (mediated through others) will result in being transformed into Christ's

---

347. See the helpful discussions in van Kooten, *Paul's Anthropology*, 199–219; Volker Rabens, "The Holy Spirit and Deification in Paul: A 'Western' Perspective," in *The Holy Spirit and the Church according to the New Testament*, ed. Predrag Dragutinovic, Karl-Wilhelm Niebuhr, and James Buchanan Wallace, WUNT 354 (Tübingen: Mohr Siebeck, 2016), 187–220; Michael J. Gorman, *Becoming the Gospel: Paul, Participation, and Mission* (Grand Rapids: Eerdmans, 2015), 2–14, 261–94; Gorman, *Participating*.

348. Rom 8:29 also refers to the believer's transformation (σύμμορφος) into the likeness of Christ. Regarding 2 Cor 3:18, Volker Rabens explains how believers are transformed into the image of Christ through pneumatic contemplation (*The Holy Spirit and Ethics in Paul: Transformation and Empowering for Religious-Ethical Life*, 2nd ed., WUNT 2/283 [Tübingen: Mohr Siebeck, 2013], 174–203).

likeness: μετασχηματίσει τὸ σῶμα τῆς ταπεινώσεως ἡμῶν σύμμορφον τῷ σώματι τῆς δόξης αὐτοῦ (3:21).[349]

In conclusion, the Pauline tradition depicts a model of mimesis that is similar in its workings to what we found in the Greco-Roman traditions.[350] Paul considers himself the spiritual father of those who became Christians through his ministry (see especially 1 Thess 2:7, 11; 1 Cor 4:14–16, but also Gal 4:12, 19). In this spiritual father–child relationship, Paul calls those he sees as his offspring in the Christian faith to imitate him so they can reach maturity in Christ. In his absence, he sometimes presents others as examples for imitation. It is worth noting that the only explicit mention of imitating God in the Pauline writings is also found in a familial context (Eph 5:1). In Romans, Paul presents Abraham as the "father" of all (Jewish and Gentile) believers (Rom 4:1–12). Hence, also in the Pauline tradition, the concept of mimesis is developed primarily in the context of *family education*.

6.9. Conclusion

At the outset, we noted that many scholars have limited their investigation of Pauline imitation to either the undisputed Pauline letters or those letters where the lexeme μιμεῖσθαι occurs. In this chapter, we have explored a broader concept of mimesis across the entire Pauline tradition. Early on in this chapter, based on a review of Pauline scholarship, we identified several issues that needed addressing (see section 6.1.1), so we will summarize our findings under the same headings.[351]

6.9.1. The Scope of Pauline Mimesis

The Pauline mimetic language is varied and includes: (1) the lexeme μιμεῖσθαι (1 Cor 4:16; 11:1; Eph 5:1; Phil 3:17; 1 Thess 1:6; 2:14; 2 Thess 3:7, 9); (2) the noun τύπος (1 Thess 1:7; 2 Thess 3:9; 1 Cor 10:6; Phil 3:17; 1 Tim 4:12; Titus 2:7) and adverb τυπικῶς

---

349. Others have also seen the idea of Paul imitating Christ in his death in Phil 3:10 (συμμορφιζόμενος τῷ θανάτῳ αὐτοῦ; see n. 223).

350. Jensen's seven themes related to Pauline mimesis have similarities with our model ("Imitating Paul," 28–33 [see also section 6.1]). While Ravasz applies Albert Bandura's modern model of mimetic learning to Paul, she acknowledges that Bandura's theory is in keeping with the ancient mimetic theories of Quintilian, Seneca, Plutarch, and Epictetus (*Aspekte der Seelsorge*, 64, 72–77, 83–85).

351. The issue of which Jesus to imitate—the historical, risen, or reconstructed Jesus (issue 5 in section 6.1.1)—is addressed here together with issue 2, "The Nature and Content of Pauline Mimesis." Issue 3 (the uniqueness of Paul's call to imitate him) was dealt with in section 6.1.1.

(1 Cor 10:11); (3) comparative constructions such as καθώς/ὥσπερ ... (οὕτως) καί (Rom 6:4; 15:7; 1 Cor 16:1; Col 3:13; Eph 4:17, 32; 5:2, 25) or stand-alone comparative conjunctions such as καθώς (1 Cor 10:7–9), ὡς (Gal 4:12), and καθάπερ (1 Cor 10:10); and (4) other expressions such as παρακολουθεῖν (2 Tim 3:10) and στοιχεῖν τοῖς ἴχνεσιν (Rom 4:12).

While Christ is the ultimate object of imitation, the imitation of Paul is most frequent. The lexeme μιμεῖσθαι to express the concept of the *imitatio Pauli* occurs in 1–2 Thessalonians, 1 Corinthians, and Philippians (1 Thess 1:6; 2 Thess 3:7, 9; 1 Cor 4:16; 11:1; Phil 3:17). In other letters, however, Paul could also call for his audience to imitate him using other mimetic language (Gal 4:12; 2 Tim 3:10; possibly Phlm).[352] We noted that while Paul's injunction to imitate him is not unique in antiquity, it is unusual (see section 6.1.1). Even so, the imitation of Christ is always the ultimate focus (see, e.g., 1 Cor 11:1). While 1 Cor 11:1 simply mentions that the imitation of Paul is based on the imitation of Christ, the latter aspect is not spelled out, and one has to turn to texts such as Phil 2:5–11 to find specific content of the imitation of Christ (but see also Rom 6:4–5; 15:7; Eph 5:25).

Since Christ remains the supreme example for imitation, Paul appears to have created a unique mimetic chain of Christ–Paul–believer. Instead of Paul, trusted coworkers such as Timothy or Titus, and even other mature believers (e.g., Epaphroditus or those mentioned in Phil 3:17b), can become links in the chain in order to mediate the imitation of Christ to Paul's converts. These surrogate exemplars thus expand the mimetic chain to Christ–Paul–(surrogates for Paul)–believer. Occasionally, the scope of mimesis extends to corporate mimesis, where Paul holds up one church as an example for another church to imitate (1 Thess 1:7; 2:14; 1 Cor 16:1; 2 Cor 8:1–11). References to imitating God are rare (Eph 5:1 and possibly Col 3:13).[353]

While we noted that Paul could sometimes recommend to his churches other exemplary Christians as models to imitate, the issue is how closely these are tied to Paul's example. For example, regarding 1 Corinthians, Clarke suggests that Timothy is an appropriate ethical model for the Corinthians (4:17), not because he models Paul but because he models appropriate behavior. Clarke also considers Stephanas, Fortunatus, and Achaicus to be appropriate models for the Corinthians because they exemplify appropriate behavior (15:15–18).[354] Clarke submits that

---

352. For a history of reception of the *imitatio Pauli*, see Michael Motia, "Three Ways to Imitate Paul in Late Antiquity: Ekstasis, Ekphrasis, Epektasis," *HTR* 114 (2021): 96–117.

353. The imitation of God is presumably mediated through the imitation of Christ, especially since Christ is "the image of [the invisible] God" (2 Cor 4:4; Col 1:15).

354. Clarke, *Pauline Theology*, 177–78.

"Paul's underlying concern is not the privileging of his own model, but the reinforcement of appropriate ethical standards, *regardless* of who is the model."[355]

While Clarke's suggestion has validity, I nevertheless contend that the exemplary Christians Paul recommends to his churches to promote and facilitate appropriate ethical behavior are closely patterned on Paul's own life. First, we showed that the examples set by Timothy and Titus are accurate extensions of Paul's example (see sections 6.3.1 and 6.6). Second, Paul's recommendation in Phil 3:17b to closely observe other mature believers is still regulated by the phrase "the example you have in us" (ἔχετε τύπον ἡμᾶς). Paul understands his responsibility to lead his churches to moral maturity (to be "blameless"), and personal example and mimesis are crucial instruments in achieving this moral goal. As such, he is careful in selecting surrogate examples for his churches to emulate to ensure that they do not deviate from his own life and standards. I therefore tie those Christians that Paul recommends as examples to emulate more closely to Paul's life than Clarke does. Besides, Paul's "control" was not so much characterized by coercion or domination to consolidate hierarchy (contra Castelli et al.) but by paternal supervision and direction (e.g., de Boer, Copan, et al.).[356] In other words, Paul does not claim to be the only model worthy of imitation (under the supreme model of Christ), but the other Christians he holds up as examples are most likely those whom he had mentored and who had reached the maturity to imitate Christ for themselves. In this, I agree with Clarke that "Paul draws attention to the model of Christ that he is following, and privileges this over his own, and urges others to follow Christ."[357]

Scholars have noted that Paul uses the injunction to imitate him only in churches where he is personally known—the churches in Thessalonica, Corinth, and Philippi. For example, de Boer notes that Paul only speaks of *imitation of himself* to churches he has founded, i.e., to believers who personally knew him. While de Boer acknowledges that there is mimetic language in Romans, Ephesians, and Colossians, none of it is about imitating *Paul*.[358] He argues that Paul presents himself as a spiritual father who nurtures his children and sets them an example to imitate, as he imitates Christ. Paul's aim is that as his children become mature, they will imitate Christ for themselves.[359] Similarly, Matera asserts that "Paul was addressing people who did not know Jesus of Nazareth personally, and

---

355. Clarke, *Pauline Theology*, 178 (added emphasis).
356. While Moss supports Castelli's views, she is more moderate in stating that Paul constructs a hierarchy of imitation (from Christ to himself to his churches) to regulate behavior and promote conformity to Christ *and himself* among his unruly churches (*Other Christs*, 23).
357. Clarke, *Pauline Theology*, 180.
358. De Boer, *Imitation of Paul*, 206. See also Clarke, *Pauline Theology*, 174, 180. Interestingly, Paul does not use the lexeme μιμεῖσθαι in Galatians.
359. De Boer, *Imitation of Paul*, 214–15.

PART 2   MIMESIS IN EARLY CHRISTIANITY

many of them had little acquaintance with Jewish morality. In calling others to imitate him, therefore, Paul was providing them with a concrete example of the Christian moral life."[360] While I largely agree, it is worth noting that Paul includes the concept of mimesis in *all* his correspondence with churches: (1) he uses the *lexeme* μιμεῖσθαι in the churches in Thessalonica, Corinth, Philippi, and Ephesus; (2) he refers to the *concept* of mimesis in the churches in Galatia (Gal 4:12), Rome (Rom 4:12; 6:4; 15:7), Ephesus (Eph 4:32; 5:25), and Colossae (Col 3:13); and (3) he uses τύπος to refer to personal examples for imitation in the churches in Philippi (Phil 3:17b), Thessalonica (2 Thess 3:9), Ephesus (1 Tim 4:12), and Crete (Titus 2:7), or even to corporate mimesis where Paul holds up one church as an example for other churches (1 Thess 1:7; 2:14; 1 Cor 16:1; 2 Cor 8:1–11). It is apparent that personal example and imitation play a key role in Paul's ethics for all his churches, and hence, we can justifiably speak of *mimetic ethics* in Paul.

6.9.2. The Nature and Content of Pauline Mimesis

Regarding the content of Pauline mimesis, what must Christians imitate about Paul or Christ?[361] Hwang, for example, contends that when Paul makes a call to imitate his example (e.g., 1 Cor 4:16; 11:1; Phil 3:17), he is quite ambiguous about what his readers are to imitate about him.[362] While Tinsley lists various aspects of the Christian life in the Pauline writings, such as service, patience, humility, suffering, obedience, trouble, love, and poverty, and shows that these attributes apply to Christ, he does not always show how these qualities are developed through mimesis.[363] Burridge sees the imitation of Jesus's "open pastoral practice" also reflected in the Pauline letters, where Paul points to imitating the example of Christ's self-giving love, humility, and concern for others.[364] While Burridge makes a better case for Paul than he does on the Gospels (see our chapters 4–5), his overriding idea of "imitating Jesus's open acceptance of others" is still too general and needs refinement.

Horrell also notes that Pauline mimesis is a corporate endeavor in the service of others, stressing that imitating Christ's self-giving and self-lowering is for the

---

360. Matera, *New Testament Ethics*, 252.
361. The issue of which Jesus to imitate—the historical Jesus, the risen Christ, or a symbolic Christ (see section 6.1.1)—does not cause the dispute one would expect. For Paul, the risen Christ is the historical Jesus, and he shows awareness of the Jesus tradition in his letters (see our discussions on 1 Thess 1:6; 1 Cor 11:1–2, 23–26; Eph 4:32).
362. Hwang, Mimesis, 49.
363. Tinsley, *Imitation of God*, 143–46, 150–54.
364. Burridge, *Imitating Jesus*, 144–48.

6. Mimesis in the Pauline Letters

sake of the other:[365] "Other-regard is primarily a community-focused virtue, practiced in relation to 'one another' . . . by which unity and equality can be created and sustained within the community."[366] Like Burridge, Kille asserts that the issue is not what readers should imitate from the accounts of Jesus's life but what values they can learn from Jesus's lifestyle.[367] Similarly, Hood notes that Pauline imitation is not a matter of producing exact copies or clones but about sharing a mindset, direction, or pattern.[368] While I partially concur, the danger is that mimesis either remains at the level of ideas without being shown in action or becomes too general, where anything can be viewed as mimesis.[369] I suggest that Pauline mimesis is about emulating a particular mindset or attitude that is actualized or demonstrated in specific actions, demonstrating for example humility, self-giving love, and other-regard. It calls Christians to adopt a slave-identity, work for a living, and provide financial support for the poor.

While the content of Paul's call to mimesis focuses on humility, self-giving love, and other-regard, he does not spell out an exhaustive list of mimetic activities for his audience, and this is where *moral reasoning* comes in. After carefully observing and studying the lives of Christ, Paul, and other exemplars, Christians must discern how a godly mindset translates into daily life through a creative, cognitive hermeneutical process where the imitator must determine what to imitate about the exemplar—a process of discernment we call "moral reasoning." Regarding Philippians, for example, Paul instructs the Philippian church to cultivate moral reasoning (φρονεῖν; 2:5) by examining Christ's paradigmatic example (2:6–11) and deliberating how this should be applied to the corporate life of the Philippian church (2:12).[370]

The uniqueness of the Pauline call to mimesis lies in Paul inserting himself in the mimetic chain (see also section 6.9.1). Presenting oneself as an example for imitation is unusual but not unique in antiquity, but Paul's call to his audience to imitate him creates a unique practice in early Christian mimesis because the mimetic chain is extended from the believer–Christ mimesis that we saw in our

---

365. Horrell, *Solidarity and Difference*, 267.
366. Horrell, *Solidarity and Difference*, 270.
367. Kille, "Imitating Christ," 262–63.
368. Hood, *Imitating God*, 132–33. See also Kim, "'Imitators,'" 147–70.
369. Hood's views on imitation in Paul are often merely conceptual without sufficient textual support (*Imitating God*, 117–35; "Imitation," 473–76).
370. Admittedly, the lexemes φρονεῖν (thirty-four occurrences in the Pauline corpus) and δοκιμάζειν (seventeen occurrences), which mainly convey the concept of moral reasoning in Paul, are not often linked to mimetic texts.

PART 2   MIMESIS IN EARLY CHRISTIANITY

previous chapters to the believer–Paul–Christ mimesis. By extension, readers can also replace "Paul" with mature believers.

We learned that when Paul inserts himself into the mimetic chain it comes from seeing himself as a surrogate parent to his converts, whom he seeks to bring to spiritual maturity. Hence, for Paul, mimesis is a critical tool in family education. That is, within the context of a spiritual family, mimesis is a didactic instrument for moral development, shaping the character and conduct of Jesus followers. As Witherington states, "The family language and the pedagogical call to imitation reveal Paul as the spiritual parent who has responsibility for and authority over his children, and Paul the teacher and persuader who has a moral duty to instruct his audience with a view to their making progress in Christian character."[371]

Paul's primary mimetic model is a parent–child one, and as a spiritual father he exemplifies the imitation of Christ in order to achieve spiritual maturity and conformity among his converts. Paul's ultimate goal is to present his churches, made up of Gentile and Jewish believers, pure and blameless before Christ at the Parousia. In short, Paul adopts a *familial* model of mimesis, where he functions as a spiritual father for his converts to imitate so he can present them spotless to God on the day of Christ.[372] Imitating Christ, through the imitation of Paul, is a vital didactic mechanism to achieve this moral goal. In John, we also noted that mimesis is a crucial mechanism for moral transformation.

Mimesis in early Christianity, including Pauline Christianity, had countercultural implications. Harrison has shown that Paul's mimetic ethos subverts Greco-Roman conventions of the power of patronage. Paul's mimetic model, where Christ is the supreme paradigm/example for imitation, counters and subverts the mimetic ethos of Greco-Roman culture in which early Christianity was embedded.[373] Like-

---

371. Witherington, *Philippians*, 30–31. Similarly, Ravasz asserts, "Wie in der Antike der größte Teil der moralischen Erziehung durch Nachahmung in der Familie geschah, so wollte Paulus seine Gemeindefamilien durch den Ruf in seine Nachahmung erziehen und führen" (*Aspekte der Seelsorge*, 66).

372. De Boer states that love relationships are the most effective environment for imitation (*Imitation of Paul*, 78). See also Rabens, who stresses that intimate love relationships empower the religious-ethical life (*Holy Spirit*, 133–38, 203–42). While he recognizes there is a role for mimesis in the religious-ethical life (*Holy Spirit*, 138n54, 235; Volker Rabens, "Sein und Werden in Beziehungen: Grundzüge relationaler Theologie bei Paulus und Johannes," in *Relationale Erkenntnishorizonte in Exegese und Systematischer Theologie*, ed. Walter Bührer and Raphaela Meyer zu Hörste-Bührer, MThSt 129 [Leipzig: Evangelische Verlagsanstalt, 2018], 91–143, at 106), he does not develop this (he does more so on John [see our chapter 5]) and hence does not fully recognize that mimesis lies at the heart of these empowering love relationships and is central to both Johannine and Pauline ethics.

373. Harrison, "Imitation," 249–52.

6. Mimesis in the Pauline Letters

wise, Thomas Blanton notes that while the Romans had made Jesus a negative example by crucifying him as a revolutionary messianic pretender, Paul prompts an ideological reversal by reinterpreting Jesus's crucifixion to present him as a positive example for imitation.[374] Instead of the "great men" represented in the Greco-Roman traditions, Paul presents Christ as God's visible "statue" for imitation.[375] However, while Christ is "the image of [the invisible] God" (2 Cor 4:4; Col 1:15), Christ is also "unseen" for Pauline believers, and hence Paul mediates the imitation of Christ by presenting himself as an exemplar (see section 6.9.1).

Our study of the Johannine literature revealed two types of mimesis—"performative mimesis," where a person intentionally and actively emulates another person, and "existential mimesis," where a person emulates a state of being of another person or where a person's identity or experience is emulated. And although performative mimesis is the dominant type, existential mimesis still accounts for about a third of all mimetic references in the Johannine literature. In the Pauline writings, however, existential mimesis rarely features—we only see implicit references in Rom 6:4–5 and Phil 2:9–11 in relation to the imitation of Christ. As Blossom Stefaniw states with regard to the imitation of the divine, "Now we are talking in a more complex way about ethics as ontology, about acquiring a certain ethical state through a process of assimilation."[376] This transformation or assimilation is the ultimate stage in the mimetic process with Christ/God as the ideal (see also our model of Pauline mimesis in section 6.8).

I return to Jensen's study because his findings come from a rich theological understanding of Paul's mimetic ethics that has a close affinity to ours.[377] Our findings endorse Jensen's theme 1, that in his absence, Paul's letters convey the patterns of life and attitudes that he wants his audience to emulate. On the issue of authority (theme 2), I agree that the concept of mimesis naturally assigns a level of authority to the exemplar, but we also see that the paradigmatic exemplars (Christ, Paul) explicitly present themselves as slaves, thus emptying themselves of any strong sense of authority (contra Castelli et al.). Regarding theme 3, Jensen's observation that imitation is rooted in identity is important because it refutes the idea that imitation can lead to salvation, that by imitating Christ, one can become a Christian. Instead, Pauline mimesis is for those who already belong to Christ; it aims at directing the character and conduct of those "in Christ" to become more like Christ. Our findings endorse theme 4, that mimesis is a creative and cognitive

---

374. Fiore and Blanton, "Paul," 183.
375. Harrison, "Imitation," 254.
376. Stefaniw, "Disciplined Mind," 243.
377. See Jensen's seven themes in "Imitating Paul," 28–33, summarized in section 6.1.

process where believers must work out what actions result from Paul's ethic of imitation. However, I dispute the "passive" aspect Jensen ascribes to the mimetic process, where believers wait patiently for God to develop various virtues in them (theme 5). While it is, of course, God who brings about change, the imitator actively and intentionally *participates* in this process of theosis by imitating Christ and Christlike believers. Finally, I endorse Jensen's themes 6 and 7, where he asserts that imitating Christ is for the benefit of others and aimed at edifying the church and that imitation is ultimately for the sake of the other.

Finally, I draw attention to Eastman's innovative work on Pauline mimesis. In her latest work, focusing on Paul's anthropology as participation (the self-in-relation-to-others), Eastman states that she has come to understand Pauline mimesis primarily as "nonvolitional participatory mimesis."[378] To arrive at this understanding of Pauline mimesis, she partly draws on contemporary research into infant development in the fields of neuroscience and experimental psychology, which reveals that infants largely relate and develop through unconscious imitation.[379] While endorsing her emphasis on mimesis as relational and participatory, I disagree with the nonvolitional, unconscious aspect of her model of Pauline mimesis. Although Paul views his new converts as "spiritual children," their imitation of him as their spiritual father is not automatic or subconscious. Paul's explicit exhortations for them to imitate him refute such notions. Paul's use of mimetic imperatives shows that he wants his readers to consciously choose whom and what to imitate. Without denying that a great deal of mimesis is nonvolitional or unconscious (whether in infant development or human behavior in general), I contend that early Christian writers, such as Paul and John, sought to bring mimesis into the Christians' volitional and conscious realm. In other words, early Christian authors promoted an *intentional* imitation of Christ among his followers so they would grow in Christlikeness or "spiritual" maturity.[380] In this, they were not unique; in antiquity, personal example and imitation were advocated as means of human improvement in pursuit of perfection.

6.9.3. Modes of Pauline Mimesis

Mimesis is a sensory process where the imitator usually observes and imitates an exemplar. However, Paul is absent when he refers to the concept of mimesis in his letters, and we examined various scholars' views on how Paul's audience

---

378. Eastman, *Paul*, xii.
379. Eastman, *Paul*, 64–76.
380. See also de Boer, *Imitation of Paul*, 214–16. Brant makes a similar observation based on 1 Cor 4:16 ("*Mimēsis*," 295).

6. Mimesis in the Pauline Letters

could imitate an absent Paul.[381] Based on our study of the Pauline writings, we can infer five modes of mimesis (see also stages 1–2 of our model of Pauline mimesis in section 6.8):

1. *Direct observation.* In this mode, the imitator can observe and imitate the exemplar directly. As Paul founded various churches, he was with his converts as an example they could observe, whether for a brief time (e.g., in Philippi and Thessalonica) or a longer period (e.g., in Corinth). However, when he was absent, there were surrogate exemplars such as a trusted coworker or mature believers for direct observation (e.g., 1 Cor 4:16–17; Phil 2:19, 25; 3:17b; 1 Tim 4:12; Titus 2:7). While direct observation is the common mode of mimesis where exemplars are naturally available in the imitator's environment, in the Pauline tradition this is often not the case. The supreme exemplar, Christ, is unseen, and Paul, who mediates the example of Christ, is often absent, so the following modes of mimesis apply if the exemplar is absent.
2. *Mnemonic mimesis.* Paul sometimes reminds his audience of his example from earlier visits, so they can reconstruct the remembered Paul (see, e.g., 1 Thess 1:5–6 in relation to 2:1–12; 2 Thess 3:6–9; 1 Cor 4:9–13; 11:1–2; Phil 4:9).
3. *Textually mediated mimesis.* In his letters, Paul sometimes presents the unseen Christ to his audience as a "literary example" to be studied and emulated (see especially Phil 2:5–11 but also Rom 15:7; 1 Cor 11:23–26). When Paul describes aspects of his lifestyle (e.g., 1 Thess 2:1–12; 1 Cor 4:9–13), he effectively presents himself as a "literary example" for imitation.[382]
4. *Personally mediated mimesis.* The supreme exemplar (Christ) is not visible to Paul's converts, so Paul mediates the example of Christ to them (see, e.g., 1 Cor 11:1). In his own absence, Paul sends trusted coworkers (especially Timothy) who exemplify the kind of behavior and thinking that he seeks to model for his churches.
5. *Orally mediated mimesis.* The Pauline correspondence implies that, based on oral reports or tradition, an audience could construct a mental picture of an exemplar to "observe" and imitate (e.g., 1 Thess 1:6–8; 2:14–16; 1 Cor 11:1–2).

---

381. See especially the work of Fiore, Dodd, Capes, Copan, and Jensen. Like us, Jensen notes that usually imitation involves observation of the exemplar but the absence of Christ (and Paul) necessitates mediation of the original exemplar. He then mentions several modes of mediation: (1) recalling the examples of the apostolic band; (2) a brief description of the Christological drama (e.g., Phil 2:5–11); and (3) a believer or even a church can represent Christ to others ("Imitating Paul," 28–29).

382. Based on his study of Seneca's moral epistles, Fiore goes as far as suggesting that epistolary presence might be even more effective than physical presence ("Paul," 235–36; *Personal Example*, 88).

These mimetic modes are not mutually exclusive, so there is an overlap. For example, the remembered Paul is also the literary Paul because the remembering is mediated through the letter. The living example of Timothy is directly accessible for observation as he is sent to a particular church as a surrogate to mediate Paul's example. Paul's epistolary/literary example reinforces his living example from past visits. The "reconstructed" Paul from the text (mediated imitation) also complements the "remembered" Paul (mnemonic imitation). As Dodd states, Paul's past presence had left his churches with "a concrete and specific model that he could refer to and expect them to remember, implying that his epistolary exemplification . . . serves to complement the personal example he set when previously present with them. . . . Paul's exhortation to imitation, then, may recall his personal example when physically present with his churches, but also includes his selective, literary self-portrait."[383] Hence, Paul uses an array of living, literary, and remembered examples.

We also keep in mind Copan's explanation that ancient writers assumed that the readers were familiar with the story of a hero from the past, so a simple reference to imitate such a person would be sufficient to recall the relevant tradition surrounding the exemplar. For example, when Paul refers to his imitation of Christ in 1 Cor 11:1, he assumes that the Corinthians would draw on the right parallels in the Jesus tradition that correspond to Paul's example to inform their imitation (see also 1 Cor 11:2).

Christos Karakolis asserts that while Paul could envisage the imitation of Christ mediated not only through his own example but also through his faithful coworkers, "he did not go as far as to speak of what has later become known as *imitatio sanctorum*, an imitation that is not only necessarily based on personal acquaintance but also on just reading the vitae of saints or more generally by listening to narratives about them within the ecclesial social space."[384] I have to disagree. We noted that both in Greco-Roman antiquity and Paul's ministry, letters and other writings can mediate an example for imitation (textually mediated mimesis). We also saw in previous chapters that the written Gospels can mediate the example of Jesus to audiences that have not personally encountered him (see, e.g., section 5.7.1).

We must note that these modes or forms of mimesis did not originate with Paul but are rooted in the Greco-Roman traditions, which knew the value of living, literary, and remembered examples.

---

383. Dodd, *Paul's Paradigmatic "I,"* 32.
384. Christos Karakolis, "Personal Relationship as a Prerequisite for Moral Imitation according to the Apostle Paul," in *Personhood in the Byzantine Christian Tradition: Early, Medieval, and Modern Perspectives*, ed. Alexis Torrance and Symeon Paschalidis (London: Routledge, 2018), 9–18, at 15.

6.9.4. The Place of Mimesis in Pauline Ethics

We have seen that the concept of mimesis is central to Paul's ethics in 1–2 Thessalonians, 1 Corinthians, and Philippians. The main difference between these letters is that the language of example and imitation is explicit and prevalent in 1–2 Thessalonians but more implicit in 1 Corinthians and Philippians, although still permeating these letters with mimetic thought. In Ephesians, the concept of mimesis is present only in three small segments (4:17–24; 4:32–5:2; 5:21–33), but since these occur in the largely ethical part of the letter, we can maintain that mimesis is key to Paul's ethics. Scholars such as Fiore, Dodd, Eastman, and Horrell have shown that other Pauline letters (e.g., 2 Cor, Gal, and the Pastorals) contain an implied concept of mimesis. In sum, there is sufficient evidence in the Pauline corpus to conclude that Paul's ethics is to a large extent *mimetic ethics*. This is not to say that all of Pauline ethics is about mimesis, but that personal example and imitation are key aspects in Paul's ethical thought.[385]

It seems that there is no significant development of Paul's concept of mimesis across the letters. We noted that already in the early Thessalonian correspondence, mimetic language is evident, and the Corinthian and Philippian correspondence, reflecting the middle and later periods of Paul's ministry, do not show a significant change or additions to Paul's earliest concept of mimesis. Besides, the various modes of Pauline mimesis (see section 6.9.3) are found in Paul's earliest letters (1–2 Thess), a middle letter (1 Cor), and a late letter (Phil), which confirms that there is no discernible development in Paul's concept of mimesis.

6.9.5. Conclusion

Our findings have led us to conclude that the concept of Pauline mimesis reflects largely the Greco-Roman mimetic traditions in terms of language and workings (see section 6.8), but it is uniquely Christ-centered.[386] While the Greco-Roman orators

---

385. Hays states that, for Paul, the imitation of Christ is "a basis for Christian ethics" (*Moral Vision*, 413). Douglas A. Campbell also notes the importance of mimesis for Pauline ethics (*Pauline Dogmatics: The Triumph of God's Love* [Grand Rapids: Eerdmans, 2020], 226, 233–35).

386. While Larsson considers the Jewish rabbi–pupil relationship to be the basis for the Pauline concept of imitating Christ (*Christus als Vorbild*, 15–28), others contend that the Greek concept of mimesis is the proper background to Pauline mimesis (e.g., Schulz, *Nachfolgen und Nachahmen*, 202–4, 332–35; Betz, *Nachfolge und Nachahmung*, 137–42, 186–89). De Boer holds an intermediate position: while he recognizes the notion of imitation in the Jewish rabbi–pupil relationship, he sees that it is, like Paul's concept of mimesis, due to the influence of Greek thought (*Imitation of Paul*, 15–16, 23, 89–91, 211–12).

PART 2 MIMESIS IN EARLY CHRISTIANITY

and philosophers would have recommended multiple exemplars to their audiences, for Paul, Christ is the sole exemplar—although the imitation of Christ sometimes had to be mediated through the imitation of himself (and other Christlike believers). The following table summarizes our findings.

Aspects of mimesis	1–2 Thessalonians	1–2 Corinthians	Philippians	Ephesians	Pastorals	Other Letters
Mimetic language	μιμεῖσθαι, τύπος	μιμεῖσθαι, τύπος/τυπικῶς, other mimetic language (ὥσπερ … οὕτως καί; καθώς; καθάπερ)	μιμεῖσθαι, τύπος, other mimetic language	μιμεῖσθαι, other mimetic language (καθὼς καί)	τύπος, παρακολουθεῖν	Other mimetic language (καθώς/ ὥσπερ … [οὕτως] καί; ὡς; στοιχεῖν τοῖς ἴχνεσιν)
Nature and content of mimesis	Self-giving; Paul's overall lifestyle Moral reasoning Family context	General (Paul's overall lifestyle) and specific content (humility, self-giving, not causing offence) Moral reasoning Family context	Humility, self-giving, other-regard Moral reasoning	Love, forgiveness Family context	Speech and conduct Family context	Forgiveness (Col) Family context (Gal, Rom) Family context (Phlm)
Modes of mimesis	Direct access, mediated, mnemonic	Direct access, mediated, mnemonic	Direct access, mediated, mnemonic	Mediated	Direct access	
Place of mimesis in Pauline ethics	Central	Central	Central	Prominent	Peripheral	Peripheral

314

7

Mimesis in the Rest of the New Testament

An examination of the rest of the New Testament—Hebrews, the Catholic Epistles (barring 1–3 John), and Revelation—yields few results that show evidence of mimesis.

In James, the ὥσπερ ... οὕτως καί ("just as ... so also") construction in 2:26 and the phrase οὕτως καί in 3:5 indicate analogy rather than mimesis. In 5:7–8, James's audience is exhorted to be patient regarding the coming of the Lord, like the farmer waiting patiently for his crop. While this may contain a "weak" idea of mimesis, it more likely indicates analogy. Finally, in 5:10, James's exhortation to take the prophets from Israel's past as an example (ὑπόδειγμα) of suffering and patience possibly hints at James encouraging his audience to imitate them. Robert Foster explores four exemplars in James, arguing that Abraham and Rahab are exemplars of faith-at-work, Job is an exemplar of steadfast endurance, and Elijah is an exemplar of effective prayer.[1] However, what James says about these exemplars (see 2:21–23, 25; 5:11, 17) is so minimal that it is doubtful whether he intends for his audience to emulate them. Nevertheless, James may be trying to evoke the fuller narratives about these exemplars in the Hebrew Bible, where the audience might discern aspects for emulation.[2] This coheres with our position that characters in a narrative can function as literary examples to be emulated or avoided. On the whole, however, James contains no significant notion of mimesis.

Regarding the Book of Revelation, Richard Hays contends that Jesus, as a faithful martyr, is a model for imitation.[3] Similarly, Moss notes that Revelation is the

---

1. Robert J. Foster, *The Significance of Exemplars for the Interpretation of the Letter of James*, WUNT 2/376 (Tübingen: Mohr Siebeck, 2014).

2. Copan, for example, explains that ancient writers assumed that the readers were familiar with the story of a hero from the past, so that a simple suggestion to imitate such a person would be sufficient to recall the relevant tradition surrounding the exemplar (*Saint Paul*, 140).

3. Hays, *Moral Vision*, 176–78. See also Hood, *Imitating God*, 149–50. In Rev 14:4, the phrase

PART 2   MIMESIS IN EARLY CHRISTIANITY

first book to use ὁ μάρτυς ("witness," "martyr") in a titular sense with reference to both Christ, the protomartyr (1:5; 3:14), and other martyrs who imitate Christ in his death (2:13; 17:6).[4] While there is merit in these views, there is no mimetic language to support them, and I only see a "weak" concept of mimesis that is not elaborated. Only Hebrews and 1 Peter present unequivocal instances of mimesis, but an examination of these instances hardly warrants a separate chapter. We must, however, scrutinize them for the sake of completeness.[5]

7.1. Hebrews

We will first deal with any possible instances of mimesis before moving on to more certain ones. In 4:10, the comparative conjunction ὥσπερ could denote mimesis in that God's people can experience God's rest by ceasing from their work just as God ceased from his. We saw earlier that in Exod 20:8–11 the prohibition to work on the Sabbath is patterned on God's example of taking rest (section 3.1.2). However, 4:10 could merely express an analogy, so there is, at most, a "weak" instance of mimesis. Then, in 4:11, the noun ὑπόδειγμα ("example," "model," "pattern") could be taken as the author cautioning his audience against imitating Israel's past disobedience, but again, the idea of mimesis is "weak."

The noun ὑπόδειγμα denotes mimesis in two instances, but these do not relate to ethical mimesis (i.e., the imitation of a particular human behavior). In 8:5, the author explains that the tabernacle was an inferior copy or imitation (ὑπόδειγμα) of the heavenly template (τύπος) shown to Moses on Mount Sinai. Likewise, in 9:23–24, the earthly sanctuary is identified as a copy (ἀντίτυπος) of the heavenly example (ὑπόδειγμα). The idea of the tabernacle (and temple) being a copy of a heavenly template goes back to the LXX (Exod 25:9, 40; 1 Chr 28:11–12) and continued in early Judaism (Philo, *Leg.* 3.102; Wis 9:8) (see sections 3.2.1 and 3.2.3).

There are arguably a few instances of mimesis related to Christ: (1) 2:17 mentions that Christ became like (ὁμοιοῦν) a human being in every respect; (2) 5:4–5 states that just as Aaron did not seek the high priesthood, so also (οὕτως καί) Christ

---

that the undefiled group of redeemed people "follow the Lamb wherever he goes" may facilitate mimesis but does not in itself denote mimesis (see the discussion in section 4.1).

4. Moss, *Other Christs*, 38–39. Moss also sees a mimetic idea in Rev 3:21, in that Christians can "emulate the conquest of Christ in their own sufferings and death and receive the same heavenly reward as a result" (*Other Christs*, 39).

5. Jude 7 refers to the divine destruction of Sodom and Gomorrah for their sexual immorality as an example (δεῖγμα, a *hapax legomenon* in the New Testament) of what will happen to the immoral false teachers, but there is no notion of mimesis.

7. Mimesis in the Rest of the New Testament

did not; and (3) 7:15 presents Jesus as a priest resembling or emulating (κατὰ τὴν ὁμοιότητα) Melchizedek. However, our interest lies in believers imitating Christ. In this regard, Phillip Davis mentions several instances where Jesus's behavior is presented as exemplary, such as his faithfulness (3:1–2), sinlessness (4:15; 7:26), prayers, and obedience (4:14–16; 5:7–8).[6] Likewise, Brian Small argues that the characterization of Jesus in Hebrews draws attention to actions and traits that the audience is to imitate.[7] While the idea of Jesus as an exemplar in Hebrews is difficult to deny, the similarities between Jesus and believers mentioned by Davis and Small are not based on explicit mimetic language but on an implied notion of mimesis.[8] Bryan Dyer presents a stronger text-based case for Jesus as an exemplar of endurance amidst suffering and death.[9]

There are instances where there is clearer evidence of mimesis in relation to ethics. In 10:25, the author uses the comparative conjunction καθώς ("just as") to warn his audience not to "imitate" those believers who neglect their meetings. In Heb 11, the author recalls the faith(fulness) of many great Israelites from the past as examples for his audience. As Davis asserts, "The author does not leave the audience with just the warning, but gives a host of examples of those who received approval because of their faithful lives."[10] Moreover, in 12:2–3, the audience is urged to observe (ἀφορᾶν) and consider (ἀναλογίζεσθαι) the example of Jesus's enduring suffering.[11] As Moss asserts, "The model of Jesus crucified is held up as the supreme model for fidelity," and, "The paranetic purpose of invoking the example of Jesus is an attempt to arouse them to greater perseverance."[12] In short, while Heb 11–12 contains no explicit mimetic language, there is the implied idea that the audience is to imitate the faith(fulness) of Jesus and Israel's past heroes.[13] We

---

6. Phillip A. Davis, *The Place of Paideia in Hebrews' Moral Thought*, WUNT 2/475 (Tübingen: Mohr Siebeck, 2018), 35, 46, 66–67.

7. Brian C. Small, *The Characterization of Jesus in the Book of Hebrews*, BINS 128 (Leiden: Brill, 2014), 312–16.

8. Admittedly, Small concedes that mimetic language is only used twice (6:12; 13:7) but maintains that in other places it is clear that believers are urged to follow the example of Jesus (*Characterization of Jesus*, 312).

9. Bryan R. Dyer, *Suffering in the Face of Death: The Epistle to the Hebrews and Its Context of Situation*, LNTS 568 (New York: Bloomsbury T&T Clark, 2017), 167–74.

10. Davis, *Paideia*, 37 (see further pp. 97–100).

11. See also Buol, *Martyred*, 70–71, 90. Buol also sees the idea of Jesus's suffering as a model to follow in Heb 13:13 (*Martyred*, 88). The phrase "to fix one's eyes on Jesus" in Heb 12:2 finds a parallel in Quintilian's exhortation to fix one's eyes on Cicero as a model to follow (*Inst.* 10.1.112; see section 2.2.3).

12. Moss, *Other Christs*, 37.

13. See also de Boer, *Imitation of Paul*, 81–83; Swartley, *Covenant of Peace*, 365; Hood, *Imitating God*, 147; Macaskill, *Union with Christ*, 186–87.

should note Carl Mosser's remark that "the heroes are not presented for imitation because they believe right doctrine or display generic faithfulness, but for specific *deeds* intended as precedent for a community in deliberation."[14]

In 6:12, we have the first explicit mention of mimesis. The author urges his audience to become imitators (μιμηταί) of those who received God's promises by exemplifying faithfulness and endurance (such as Abraham in 6:13–15).[15] Besides the example of Abraham, 6:12 probably anticipates those who exemplified faithfulness and endurance listed in Heb 11.[16] Then, in 13:7, the author instructs his audience to carefully observe (ἀναθεωρεῖν) the outcome of the lives of their religious leaders and imitate (μιμεῖσθαι) their faith(fulness).[17] Dyer explains that the emphasis is not on *how* these leaders died but on their way of life up until their death (they did not abandon the faith), and it is the latter that is worthy of imitation.[18] Differently, Wolbert states that the imitation of leaders refers to their obedience to the faith, not to specific behavior.[19] However, this appears to be a strange dichotomy, as faithfulness or faithful obedience *is* a specific behavior.

In conclusion, while there are just two instances of explicit mimesis related to human behavior (6:12; 13:7), there are sufficient instances of implied mimesis to conclude that the author of Hebrews was familiar with the concept of mimesis. Like Paul, the author of Hebrews can point to both past examples (6:12–15; 11:4–38) and living examples (10:25; 13:7) for imitation.[20] Davis thus concludes, "The plethora of exemplars model not only the proper faithful and trusting disposition expected of the audience, but also the right action that expresses it."[21] We do not go as far as Tinsley, who claims that Hebrews presents the Christian life as a mimesis of Christ's veritable journey to heaven.[22] All things considered, mimesis seems to have a significant but not central role in the ethics of Hebrews.

---

14. Carl Mosser, "Rahab Outside the Camp," in *The Epistle to the Hebrews and Christian Theology*, ed. Richard Bauckham et al. (Grand Rapids: Eerdmans, 2009), 383–404, at 387–88.

15. See also de Boer, *Imitation of Paul*, 81; Martin Karrer, *Der Brief an die Hebräer*, ÖTK 20/2 (Gütersloh: Gütersloher Verlagshaus, 2008), 48–49.

16. See also Craig R. Koester, *Hebrews: A New Translation with Introduction and Commentary*, AB 36 (New York: Doubleday, 2001), 317–18; Dyer, *Suffering*, 151.

17. See also Harold W. Attridge, *The Epistle to the Hebrews*, Hermeneia (Philadelphia: Fortress, 1989), 392; Davis, *Paideia*, 70–71.

18. Dyer, *Suffering*, 166.

19. Wolbert, "Vorbild," 251.

20. See further Dyer, who examines three groups of exemplars in Hebrews to be imitated—figures from Jewish history, the community that is addressed in Hebrews, and Jesus Christ (*Suffering*, 147–74).

21. Davis, *Paideia*, 117.

22. Tinsley, *Imitation of God*, 168–70. Likewise, Smalley contends that *the imitatio Christi*

7. Mimesis in the Rest of the New Testament

7.2. 1 Peter

First Peter has a few references to mimesis. The comparative conjunction ὡς ("as," "like") arguably implies mimesis (1:14; 2:2, 5, 11, 25) when the Petrine audience is likened to obedient children, newborn infants, living stones, aliens/strangers, and sheep in particular behavior, although these are just "weak" cases of mimesis. It is inviting to see mimesis in the call to holy living in 1:15–16, but the quotation of Lev 19:2 indicates a causal rather than a comparative relationship—Christians should be holy *because* (ὅτι) God is holy (see also section 3.1.2). In 5:3, Peter urges elders to be examples (τύποι) to the flock. In light of 5:4, the shepherd-elders are to imitate the example of Christ (see also 2:25), and arguably, believers can imitate their humility, which may amount to a "weak" case of mimesis.[23]

A few scholars are too ready to see evidence of mimesis in 1 Peter. Tinsley states, "If one had to choose a single book from the New Testament to illustrate the Christian conception of the imitation of God, none could be better than the First Epistle of St Peter."[24] According to him, the Petrine Christians are new Israelites who follow a path that Christ, as Israel himself, had pioneered.[25] While Tinsley's idea of "the way" is rightly rooted in the idiomatic expression "to follow in Christ's footsteps" (2:21), he then reads this mimetic concept into other passages that do not support this alleged pattern. Influenced by Tinsley, Smalley claims that 1 Peter is dominated by the *imitatio Christi* theme.[26] According to Smalley, the theme of imitating Christ is aimed at holiness in character and conduct, especially through imitating Christ's suffering (2:21–25) in baptism (3:18–4:1).[27] Like Tinsley, he reads mimesis into too many texts.[28]

A clearer case of mimesis is found in 2:21, where Christ's patient suffering when mistreated is an example for believers to imitate—literally, "an example, so that you may follow in his footsteps" (ὑπογραμμόν, ἵνα ἐπακολουθήσητε τοῖς ἴχνεσιν

---

in Hebrews focuses on Jesus being the way and the journey ("Imitation of Christ in the New Testament," 20).

23. See also Paul J. Achtemeier, *A Commentary on First Peter*, Hermeneia (Minneapolis: Fortress, 1996), 328–29; John H. Elliott, *1 Peter: A New Translation with Introduction and Commentary*, AYB 37b (New Haven, CT: Yale University Press, 2000), 832–33. Gregory E. Lamb contends that Peter encourages his fellow-elders to imitate his own example and that, in turn, believers will imitate their elders ("Saint Peter as '*Sympresbyteros*': Mimetic Desire, Discipleship, and Education," *Christian Education Journal* 15 [2018]: 189–207, at 191, 202–4).

24. Tinsley, *Imitation of God*, 166.

25. Tinsley, *Imitation of God*, 166–68.

26. Smalley, "Imitation of Christ in the New Testament," 19.

27. Smalley, "Imitation of Christ in 1 Peter," 172–76.

28. Likewise, contra Schulz (*Nachfolgen und Nachahmen*, 318), 1 Pet 3:6 does not constitute mimesis; rather, Sarah is simply an example of the kind of woman that is commended in 1 Pet 3:5.

αὐτοῦ).²⁹ For de Boer, however, Christ's suffering is inimitable; rather, this suffering is the foundation of the Christian life that is exemplified in Christ.³⁰ In my view, this is too general, and Swartley is more on target when he states that the content of the example is the non-retaliatory conduct of Jesus when threatened and abused.³¹ Katie Marcar is more specific, arguing that 2:22–25 depicts Jesus as the Isaianic suffering servant who is held up in 2:21 as a model for Christian slaves and even for all believers.³² Noting that *exempla* permeated spoken and written discourse and operated across all levels of Greco-Roman society, she asserts that early Christians may have used Roman exemplary discourse to model distinct Christian values.³³ The Romans' preference for Roman *exempla* and the conviction that the best *exempla* came from one's own family especially suit the description of Christians in ethnic and familial language in 1 Peter 2.³⁴ She then explains how Christ's suffering provides a model of endurance in the face of unjust suffering, first for slaves but second for all believers to imitate.³⁵ Marcar's argument that the new familial and ethnic identity for believers in the first half of the letter is connected to the moral exhortation in the second half through *exempla* supports our findings that, in John and Paul, mimesis functions primarily as education in God's family.

Clifford Barbarick also makes an important contribution. Against the backdrop of the function of *exempla* in ancient moral discourse, he argues that the example of Christ in 1 Peter is both pattern and power; that is, it is not only the

---

29. Contra Achtemeier, who states that 2:21 is a call to discipleship rather than a call to imitation (*First Peter*, 199). While Macaskill's assessment of 4:1 may be correct ("Peter is not calling for mimesis of an exemplary suffering"), he overlooks 2:21 (*Union with Christ*, 279). Elliott is more on target, stating that "this Petrine formulation appears to be a creative blending of the motifs of both imitation and discipleship" (*1 Peter*, 527). Even firmer, Reinhard Feldmeier asserts that Jesus's behavior is the necessary model to imitate rather than just a call to endure suffering (there is no concept of discipleship here) (*The First Letter of Peter: A Commentary on the Greek Text*, trans. Peter H. Davids [Waco, TX: Baylor University Press, 2008], 173).

30. De Boer, *Imitation of Paul*, 58. See also Simon J. Kistemaker, *Exposition of the Epistles of Peter and of the Epistle of Jude*, NTC (Welwyn: Evangelical Press, 1987), 108–9.

31. Swartley, *Covenant of Peace*, 364. See also Moss, *Other Christs*, 36; Buol, *Martyred*, 90–91.

32. Marcar, "Footsteps," 253–73.

33. Marcar, "Footsteps," 257–59. She builds on the works of Matthew Roller, James Petitfils, and Rebecca Langlands (for their works, see our chapter 2).

34. Marcar, "Footsteps," 257–65.

35. Marcar, "Footsteps," 266–72. See also Elritia Le Roux, *Ethics in 1 Peter: The* Imitatio Christi *and the Ethics of Suffering in 1 Peter and the Gospel of Mark—a Comparative Study* (Eugene, OR: Wipf and Stock, 2018), 126, 370–72, 394–95, 496–502.

7. Mimesis in the Rest of the New Testament

model for Christian life but also facilitates the moral transformation needed to live that life.[36] He explains that, in ancient (Stoic) paraenesis, *exempla* are not mere illustrations for moral transformation; they compel and enable it through the process of "transformation by vision." *Exempla* presented a pattern for imitation, and when a student contemplates that pattern, either by studying a living example or by "picturing" a past example, the vision could affect moral transformation, and the student would reflect that pattern in their own life.[37] Similarly, while the recipients of 1 Peter cannot see Jesus himself, they have access to his example through Peter's account of Christ, and this pattern of Christ (especially his faithful suffering that leads to vindication) enables imitation by transforming those who adhere to the pattern.[38] In a later article, Barbarick relates the imitation of Christ to the concept of theosis, in that conformity to the holiness of God (1:15) occurs through conformity to the example of Christ, so Christosis is theosis.[39] While our study of mimesis in Greco-Roman, Johannine, and Pauline literature supports Barbarick's idea of imitating the unseen Christ, Barbarick sees more mimesis in 1 Peter than the text warrants.[40]

7.3. Conclusion

The latter part of the New Testament contains some traces and instances of mimesis, but these do not add to our understanding of the concept, which has been shaped mainly by the Johannine and Pauline writings. While James and Revelation show a few instances of "weak" mimesis, the concept is more explicit in Hebrews and 1 Peter, although we cannot claim that mimesis is central to the ethics of

---

36. Clifford A. Barbarick, "The Pattern and the Power: The Example of Christ in 1 Peter" (PhD diss., Baylor University, 2011). See also Elliott, *1 Peter*, 528.

37. Barbarick, "Pattern," 49–69.

38. Barbarick, "Pattern," 182–83, 204–34.

39. Clifford A. Barbarick, "'You Shall Be Holy, for I Am Holy': Theosis in 1 Peter," *JTI* 9 (2015): 287–97. Like Gorman and others (see our discussion on theosis in sections 5.6 and 6.8), Barbarick explains that Christian theosis or deification does not mean an ontological fusion with the divine essence but to participate in the divine and take on certain divine attributes.

40. For example, there is no textual basis for Barbarick's claim that in 2:4–8, Peter calls his audience to imitate Christ's example ("Pattern," 207). Similarly, Barbarick's argument that 3:18–22 presents a mimetic pattern of Christ's endurance through suffering and shame that ends in glory, is not warranted by the text ("Pattern," 215–25). Barbarick also perceives Sarah (3:5–6) and Noah (3:20–21) as examples for imitation ("Pattern," 236–39). However, since mimetic language is absent, these are mere illustrative examples.

PART 2   MIMESIS IN EARLY CHRISTIANITY

these writings. Nevertheless, it shows that mimesis, especially the imitation of Christ, is a pervasive ethical concept in early Christianity. In 1 Peter, mimesis is placed in the context of divine family education, as we saw in John and Paul. We will now turn our attention to the first half of the second century, where we find a new development in the concept of mimesis among the apostolic fathers.

8

Mimesis in the Apostolic Fathers

Mapping the concept of mimesis in the New Testament would have been a well-defined project, but I wish to include the Apostolic Fathers in our investigation for three reasons. First, the apostolic writings present abundant mimetic language: besides eighteen occurrences of the lexeme μιμεῖσθαι,[1] we also find potential mimetic terms such as τύπος, ὑπόδειγμα, ὑπογραμμός, the ὁμοι* group, and comparative conjunctions such as ὡς and ὥσπερ.[2] Second, these writers were acquainted with some of the apostles, so there is the possibility of influence. Third, during this time (the first half of the second century), the idea of martyrdom as the ideal *imitatio Christi* emerged. De Boer, for example, notes that these writers saw a connection between imitation and martyrdom, and martyrs were seen as imitators of Christ.[3] This idea of martyrdom as the ideal imitation of Christ's suffering and death came about through particular historical circumstances in the first half of the second century when Christianity was on a collision course with the Roman Empire.[4]

We will examine the following apostolic fathers and their writings: Clement of Rome (1 Clem.), Ignatius of Antioch (his letters *To the Ephesians, To the Mag-*

---

1. The lexeme μιμεῖσθαι occurs in 1 Clem. 17:1; Diogn. 10:4–6 (4 times); Ign. *Eph.* 1:1; 10:2, 3; Ign. *Magn.* 10:1; Ign. *Trall.* 1:2; Ign. *Rom.* 6:3; Ign. *Phld.* 7:2; Ign. *Smyrn.* 12:1; Pol. *Phil.* 1:1; 8:2; Mart. Pol. 1:2; 17:3; 19:1.

2. De Boer notes that although the term τύπος occurs frequently in the Apostolic Fathers, it refers mostly, typologically, to the position of the bishop, whereas τύπος is replaced by ὑπόδειγμα and ὑπογραμμός when personal example is in view (*Imitation of Paul*, 22–23).

3. De Boer, *Imitation of Paul*, 14–15. For the concept of martyrological mimesis in the first four centuries, see especially Moss, *Other Christs*.

4. For the confrontation between early Christianity and the Roman Empire, see, for example, Cornelis Bennema, "Early Christian Identity Formation Amidst Conflict," *JECH* 5 (2015): 26–48, at 36–39.

nesians, *To the Trallians, To the Romans, To the Philadelphians, To the Smyrnaeans,* and *To Polycarp*), Polycarp of Smyrna (*To the Philippians*), and the anonymous authors of the Martyrdom of Polycarp, the Letter of Barnabas, the Letter to Diognetus, the Didache, and the Shepherd of Hermas. Our examination of the Apostolic Fathers will (1) explore the concept of mimesis in the writings mentioned above, (2) determine how prevalent the concept of mimesis was in these writings, and (3) assess whether we can trace the apostolic idea of martyrdom as the ideal imitation of Christ back to the New Testament.[5]

8.1. Clement of Rome

First Clement, addressed to the church in Corinth, was probably written by bishop Clement 1 at the end of the first century, whereas 2 Clement was traditionally attributed to Clement 1 but no longer.[6] Besides, while 1 Clement contains some mimetic ideas, 2 Clement contains none, and hence it is not relevant to our study. In 1 Clement, comparative conjunctions that could potentially indicate mimesis (e.g., καθώς, ὡς, ὥσπερ, οὕτως) only denote reciprocity (e.g., 13:2) or analogy (e.g., 16:3, 6–7; 29:3; 32:2; 56:14–15), but not mimesis.[7] The mimetic language in 1 Clement includes a single occurrence of the noun μιμητής (17:1) and several occurrences of ὑπόδειγμα (5:1; 6:1; 46:1; 55:1; 63:1) and ὑπογραμμός (5:7; 16:17; 33:8).

In seeking to address the envy, strife, and division that characterized the Corinthian church (e.g., 3:1–4), part of Clement's strategy is to introduce examples from both past and present for imitation.[8] Examining ancient (Stoic) paraenesis,

---

5. Although Sandnes contends that Christian martyrdom was more sporadic and piecemeal than is often assumed (*Discourses*, 53n41), he is less skeptical about its historicity than Candida Moss, who holds that Christian martyrdom was more a matter of rhetoric than real experience (*The Myth of Persecution: How Early Christians Invented a Story of Martyrdom* [New York: HarperOne, 2013]). Moss is less skeptical about the historicity of early Christian martyr accounts in her earlier work *Other Christs*.

6. Clayton N. Jefford, *Reading the Apostolic Fathers*, 2nd ed. (Grand Rapids: Baker Academic, 2012), 106–9, 125–27. Clare K. Rothschild, however, contends that 1 Clem. is also pseudepigraphal (*New Essays on the Apostolic Fathers*, WUNT 375 [Tübingen: Mohr Siebeck, 2017], 61).

7. The closest Clement comes to the idea of mimesis is with the use of ὡς in the comparison of Christians and sheep in their tendency to go astray (16:6), and of Christ being led to the slaughter like a sheep (16:7), but even there the notion may be one of analogy.

8. See also Barbarick, "Pattern," 92–94, 107–8. Petitfils mentions nine lists of *exempla* in 1 Clem. (*Mos Christianorum*, 151). Rothschild contends that στάσις, which refers to "faction" or "schism" rather than "strife or discord," is the key issue that threatens the church's peace. She also argues that the letter refers to some sort of second-century church schism but not to a specific

8. Mimesis in the Apostolic Fathers

Barbarick shows that *exempla* are a means to achieve "transformation by vision." *Exempla* are literary devices that present a pattern for imitation, where a student contemplates that pattern, either by studying a living example or by "picturing" a past example. This vision can affect moral transformation when the student starts to display that pattern in their own life.[9] Barbarick sees this link between *exempla* and imitation at work in 1 Clement: "The myriad *exempla* not only define the Christian life and call for imitation; they are an important tool the author employs to enable the moral transformation needed to achieve peace and harmony."[10] He then shows how several *exempla* in 1 Clement, especially of the created order and the example of Christ, compel and enable the process of "transformation by vision" to promote peace and harmony in the Corinthian church.[11] We will examine some examples Clement presents and how they affect moral transformation through imitation.

Having presented examples from Israel's past of those who were persecuted out of envy, such as Abel, Jacob, Joseph, Moses, and David (4:1–13), Clement turns to the more recent examples (ὑπόδειγμα) of Peter and Paul, who suffered martyrdom because of envy (5:1–7). The phrase "let us set before our eyes the good apostles" (λάβωμεν πρὸ ὀφθαλμῶν ἡμῶν τοὺς ἀγαθοὺς ἀποστόλους; 5:3) alludes to the idea of observing an exemplar in the mind's eye. Paul is specifically held up as an example (ὑπογραμμός) of steadfast endurance (5:7).[12] In addition to the apostles, Clement speaks of a multitude of Christians who also suffered martyrdom because of envy, and he presents them collectively as an excellent example (ὑπόδειγμα κάλλιστον) to follow (6:1).[13]

---

church in Corinth that had lapsed back into the same rival factions that Paul addressed in 1 Cor (*Apostolic Fathers*, 64–66). However, if the letter was written by Clement (which Rothschild disputes) and earlier than Rothschild claims, it would not be inconceivable that the Corinthian problem in the mid-50s had continued into the 90s.

9. Barbarick, "Pattern," 49–69. See also Langlands, *Exemplary Ethics*, 86–111; and chapter 2 of this volume.

10. Barbarick, "Pattern," 111.

11. Barbarick, "Pattern," 111–56.

12. Andreas Lindemann notes that the description of Paul as a ὑπομονῆς . . . μέγιστος ὑπογραμμός exceeds that of Peter and matches the description of Christ as ὑπογραμμός in 1 Pet 2:21; 1 Clem. 16:17; 33:8; Pol. *Phil.* 8:2 (*Die Clemensbriefe*, HNT 17 [Tübingen: Mohr Siebeck, 1992], 39). Moss's claim that it is not Christ but Peter and Paul who are the "greatest example" for Clement's audience (*Other Christs*, 40) is overstated given that Christ is presented as an example in 16:17. She is more on target in her assertion that the martyred Peter and Paul have themselves become models for imitation because they are successful imitations of the suffering and death of Christ (*Other Christs*, 40).

13. Regarding the reference to a contest in the arena in 7:1, even if this refers to a figurative

PART 2   MIMESIS IN EARLY CHRISTIANITY

In 1 Clem. 16, Clement elaborates on Christ's humility amidst suffering, concluding that Christ has presented an example (ὑπογραμμός) to follow (16:17). Clement then exhorts the Corinthian Christians to be imitators (μιμηταί; 17:1) of Israel's ancient heroes who exemplified humility, such as the prophets Elijah, Elisha, and Ezekiel, as well as Abraham, Moses, Job, and David (17:1–18:17).[14] Having reminded the Corinthian church of these many great examples, Clement exhorts them to the practice of peace (i.e., harmony, unity) through the contemplation of God (lit. "to gaze at God with the mind") (19:1–3).[15] In keeping with the general principle of being able to "observe" the one whom one seeks to imitate, Clement urges the Corinthian Christians to look to God the creator as an example (ὑπογραμμός) of good works (33:8). Elsewhere, he addresses the issues of strife and division in the Corinthian church by presenting worthy examples for imitation (46:1; 63:1)—even pagan examples (55:1).

In sum, Clement presents several examples from the past and present who have shown (1) steadfast endurance amidst persecution and martyrdom, (2) humility, and (3) good works to counter a potential schism in the Corinthian church. Petitfils concludes that while 1 Clement generally reflects the Roman model of exemplary leadership, it promotes a distinct ancestral tradition where the main *exempla* are heroes from Israel's sacred tradition, the apostles, and Christ. In addition, Clement deviates from traditional Roman moral values by preserving largely Pauline traditions in emphasizing the virtues of love and humility.[16] However, love and humility are also virtues to be imitated in the Johannine tradition (see sections 5.4.2–5.4.3), so it is safe to say that Clement preserved a distinct *Christian* tradition. Likewise, Cilliers Breytenbach shows that "examples from the Greek Bible and from contemporary Christianity are thus fitted into Greek rhetorical tradition to form paradigmatic narratives for fellow Christians. *1 Clement*, therefore, reveals a mode of reference to biblical tradition that is highly influenced by contemporary culture."[17]

---

contest against the moral enemy of envy rather than a physical contest in a literal arena, the context still echoes Roman martial virtues (Petitfils, *Mos Christianorum*, 160n60). While the terms ὑπόδειγμα and ὑπογραμμός do not occur in 1 Clem. 9–11, the author presents Enoch, Noah, and Abraham as examples of obedience, Lot as an example of hospitality and piety, and Rahab as an example of faith and hospitality (Barbarick, "Pattern," 109).

14. For a detailed account of *exempla* of humility, see Petitfils, *Mos Christianorum*, 174–81.

15. The verb ἀτενίζειν ("to gaze") used in the context of contemplating behavior of others as a pattern to follow also occurs in 7:4 and 9:2 (see also Barbarick, "Pattern," 122, 137–40).

16. Petitfils, *Mos Christianorum*, 197–99.

17. Cilliers Breytenbach, "The Historical Example in 1 Clement," ZAC 18 (2014): 22–33, at 22.

8. Mimesis in the Apostolic Fathers

Barbarick's conclusion on the nexus of *exempla*, imitation, and moral transformation is worth quoting in full:

> In the Scriptures, Christian writings, and Christian history the audience of *1 Clement* is presented with patterns of the various virtues that the author wants to inculcate in his audience. The audience clings to these holy examples by diligently studying them; and by clinging to them, they are transformed, becoming like the *exempla* to which they have attended (46.1–2). This transformation enables them to imitate the examples of the biblical figures, and in this way they become types or imitators of the primary example, the archetype: Christ.[18]

Barbarick's extensive work on *exempla* in Greco-Roman antiquity is significant because it shows that 1 Clement echoes multiple aspects of the mimetic model we constructed from our study of Greco-Roman literature (see section 2.3), namely observing an exemplar (whether literally or mentally), interpreting what is observed, followed by imitation and resulting transformation.

8.2. Ignatius of Antioch

We have seven extant letters that Ignatius, the bishop of Antioch, wrote on his way to Rome, where he was martyred around 108 or 140 CE.[19] The dominant motif in Ignatius's letters is that of unity, which is primarily achieved through obedience to ecclesiological authority (especially the bishop, as the successor of the apostles, but also deacons) and the sacraments (the Eucharist and baptism).[20] A quick scan through Ignatius's letters shows that his mimetic language includes the lexeme μιμεῖσθαι, the noun τύπος (and its synonym ἐξεμπλάριον), and the comparative conjunctions ὥσπερ and ὡς (but not καθώς). Several denote analogy rather than mimesis (e.g., *Eph.* 4:1 [= *Phld.* 1:2]; *Magn.* 5:2; *Trall.* 2:1; *Pol.* 2:3). In *Trall.* 3:1, Ignatius identifies the bishop (ἐπίσκοπος) as a τύπος of Christ, but this refers to the bishop as a type or representative of Christ rather than an imitator (see also *Trall.* 2:1).[21] The only other occurrence of τύπος, in *Magn.* 6:2, is in reference to

---

18. Barbarick, "Pattern," 154–55.
19. For the possible dates of Ignatius's martyrdom, see Buol, *Martyred*, 137n9.
20. In the New Testament, church leadership is more fluid and there appears to be no sharp distinction between elders (πρεσβύτεροι) and overseers/bishops (ἐπίσκοποι) (Cornelis Bennema, "Elders.NT," in *Encyclopedia of the Bible and Its Reception*, ed. Hans-Josef Klauck et al., vol. 7 [Berlin: de Gruyter, 2013], 586–88).
21. Jimmy Agan, however, does detect mimetic connotations in *the Didascalia Apostolorum*,

the exemplary life (and teaching) of the bishop and other leaders, and any idea of imitation is remote and in the background.[22] In *Eph.* 2:1, Ignatius mentions Crocus as an example (ἐξεμπλάριον, a Latin loanword for *exemplarium* [BDAG, s.v.] and synonymous with τύπος) of the Ephesians' love. The idea that Crocus might function as an example for imitation is no more than implied.[23] We will now turn to texts that more explicitly convey mimesis.

Various mimetic occurrences relate to unity, which is the dominant motif in the Ignatian corpus. In *Eph.* 5:1, Ignatius's assertion that the Church is united to Christ, as (ὡς) Christ is to God, indicates "weak" existential mimesis in that the unity between Christ and the Church is patterned on the unity between Christ and God. When Ignatius urges the Philadelphian Christians to be imitators of Christ, just as (ὡς) Christ is of God, he does so in a context of commending purity and unity (*Phld.* 7:2). In *Magn.* 7:1, Ignatius exhorts the Magnesian Christians to be obedient to the bishop, just as (ὡς) Christ was obedient to God (when he was on earth), so that there may be unity. A similar idea is found in the exhortation that everyone should follow (i.e., obey) the bishop just as (ὡς) Jesus Christ followed God (*Smyrn.* 8:1). As David Reis explains, unity is contingent upon the church imitating the bishop, and mirrors the unity between Jesus and God: "In Ignatius' view, the bishop represents the divine model that the community, as a copy of the model, should strive to imitate."[24] The idea of achieving unity through mimesis can be traced back to John 17, where existential mimesis occurs in relation to unity (see section 5.4.4).

Other Ignatian texts also contain mimetic ideas that can be traced back to John. In *Eph.* 6:1, Ignatius presents the bishop as a type of Christ, and the phrase "to receive the bishop as (ὡς) we would receive Christ who sent him" echoes Jesus's saying, "whoever receives one whom I send receives me" in John 13:20, at the end of the footwashing pericope that stresses the imitation of Jesus's humble, sacrificial service to his disciples. In *Magn.* 7:1, the idea that the Magnesian Christians should

---

saying "Christian leaders, and bishops in particular, should lead exemplary lives, with Christ as their pattern" (C. D. Agan, "Toward a Hermeneutic of Imitation: The Imitation of Christ in the *Didascalia Apostolorum*," *Presb* 37 [2011], 31–48, at 35). While this is a third-century document, there is arguably a conceptual parallel with the bishop being a τύπος in Ignatius.

22. William R. Schoedel, *Ignatius of Antioch: A Commentary on the Letters of Ignatius of Antioch*, Hermeneia (Philadelphia: Fortress, 1985), 115.

23. In *Trall.* 3:2, ἐξεμπλάριον is used in a similar fashion: Ignatius sees the example of the Trallians' love embodied in their bishop. In *Smyrn.* 12:1, however, ἐξεμπλάριον has mimetic connotations, due to the explicit use of the verb μιμεῖσθαι (see below).

24. David M. Reis, "Following in Paul's Footsteps: *Mimēsis* and Power in Ignatius of Antioch," in *Trajectories through the New Testament and the Apostolic Fathers*, ed. Andrew F. Gregory and C. M. Tuckett (Oxford: Oxford University Press, 2005), 287–305, at 302–3 (quotation from p. 303).

8. Mimesis in the Apostolic Fathers

not do anything without the permission of the bishop and elders, just as Jesus did nothing without the consent of the Father (a mimetic ὥσπερ ... οὕτως construction) is evidently derived from Jesus's mimetic saying in John 5:19 (see also *Phld.* 7:2). In *Phld.* 2:1, the phrase "where the shepherd is, there you, as sheep, follow" echoes the mimetic idea of "to be where Jesus is" in John 12:26; 14:3; 17:24 (see section 5.4.4).

The Ignatian corpus also shows influences from Paul regarding mimesis. In *Phld.* 11:1, Ignatius's gratitude that the Philadelphians have welcomed certain Christian workers (Philo of Cilicia and Rheus Agathopus), just as Christ had also (ὡς καί) welcomed the Philadelphians, echoes the Pauline mimetic imperative "welcome one another, just as Christ has welcomed you" in Rom 15:7. The mimetic expression "bear with all, as also (ὡς καί) the Lord does with you" (*Pol.* 1:2) resembles Gal 6:2, where there may be a "weak" idea of mimesis (see the discussion in section 6.7.1). In *Pol.* 5:1, the exhortation to husbands to love their wives as (ὡς) Christ loves the church is derived from Eph 5:25.[25]

At times, Ignatius holds up exemplary people for imitation. In *Eph.* 1:3, he expresses his desire for the Ephesian Christians to emulate (ἐν ὁμοιότητι εἶναι) their exemplary bishop Onesimus. In *Smyrn.* 12:1, Ignatius presents Burrhus as an exemplary minister of God (ἐξεμπλάριον θεοῦ διακονίας) and expresses the desire that everyone imitates (μιμεῖσθαι) him.[26] Elsewhere, Ignatius calls believers "imitators" (μιμηταί) of God (*Eph.* 1:1; *Trall.* 1:2) or Christ (*Eph.* 10:3; *Phld.* 7:2), but it is often unclear on what basis he makes that claim.[27] *Eph.* 10:1–3, however, provides some insight. Ignatius encourages the Ephesian Christians to show exemplary behavior (lit. "to teach by your works"; ἐκ τῶν ἔργων ὑμῖν μαθητευθῆναι) to win over unbelievers to become disciples (*Eph.* 10:1).[28] As Moss asserts, "Learning to be a disciple from the deeds of the Christians involves imitation."[29] Then, in contrast,

---

25. Jonathon Lookadoo also sees imitation in the phrase "care for the widows *after the Lord*" in *Pol.* 4:1 ("Categories, Relationships and Imitation in the Household Codes of 1 Clement, Ignatius and Polycarp: A Comparison with Household Codes in the Pauline Corpus," *Neot* 53 [2019]: 31–52, at 45–46). For other possible Pauline influences, see Buol, *Martyred*, 157, 163, 170, 175.

26. The only other occurrence of the verb μιμεῖσθαι in the Ignatian corpus is in *Magn.* 10:1, where Ignatius hypothetically refers to God imitating human behavior (as an implied threat of divine judgment) in order to encourage the Magnesians to be sensitive to God's goodness and learn about the Christian way of life (see also Schoedel, *Ignatius*, 126).

27. Regarding *Eph.* 1:1, Schoedel contends that Ignatius considers the affection of the Ephesians for him as an imitation of God's love for the world (*Ignatius*, 41). In both *Eph.* 1:1 and *Trall.* 1:2, Schoedel contends that "imitators of God" actually refers to the imitation of Christ (*Ignatius*, 41, 139). The phrase "the blood of God" in *Eph.* 1:1 seems to affirm the idea of a reference to Christ.

28. Schoedel views "attaining God," "becoming disciples," and "being imitators of Christ" as connected themes (*Ignatius*, 70).

29. Moss, *Other Christs*, 42.

Ignatius exhorts the Ephesians not to imitate (ἀντιμιμήσασθαι) the behavior of hostile unbelievers (10:2) but to be imitators (μιμηταί) of Christ (10:3) by showing gentleness, humility, and kindness in the face of violent opposition.

Ignatius's letter *To the Romans* conveys his desire to be a martyr in imitation of Christ. In martyrdom, Ignatius declares, "I will truly be a disciple of Jesus Christ" (ἔσομαι μαθητὴς ἀληθῶς Ἰησοῦ Χριστοῦ; 4:2). This craving for martyrdom is driven by his desire to be an imitator (μιμητής) of the suffering Christ (6:3).[30] As Paul Hartog asserts, "For Ignatius, imitation is the core of discipleship," and "The ultimate manifestation of discipleship was martyrdom."[31] Ignatius viewed martyrdom as a straight path to God.[32]

The Ignatian corpus thus shows a link between imitation and discipleship, in which martyrdom is the truest expression of the imitation of Christ. Based on an extensive lexical survey, Willard Swartley postulates that Ignatius's use of ethical terms (including the lexeme μιμεῖσθαι) is linked to his anxiety about unity in the Syrian church (*Phld.* 7:2 links imitation and unity). Once he knows that there is peace in his church in Syrian Antioch (*Phld.* 10:1), his anxiety about his imminent martyrdom (imitation relates primarily to suffering) subsides.[33] Swartley thus situates this language of imitation within the specific context of Ignatius's own discipleship. Imitating God/Christ in suffering, love, and unity characterizes Ignatius's life of discipleship, and unity in the church in Syria reveals that he is a genuine bishop, a worthy martyr, and thus a true disciple.[34] Drake Williams also notes that Ignatius speaks of imitation and discipleship in the context of suffering and possibly martyrdom.[35] He concludes, "Imitation ideas are less likely to enforce power as imitation passages refer to the suffering Christ and the sacrifice of individuals. Imitation is used to promote unity, humility, endurance, and patience.

---

30. The expression τὸ πάθος τοῦ θεοῦ ("the Passion of God") is most likely a reference to the suffering Christ (see also the numerous occurrences of πάθος with reference to Christ throughout the Ignatian corpus [e.g., *Magn.* 5:2]). Buol argues that Ignatius, in contemplating his sufferings and martyrdom, intentionally models himself on Paul (*Martyred*, 133, 149).

31. Paul A. Hartog, "*Imitatio Christi* and *Imitatio Dei*: High Christology and Ignatius of Antioch's Ethics," *Perichoresis* 17 (2019): 3–22, at 14. See also Moss, *Other Christs*, 42–43; Buol, *Martyred*, 153.

32. Henning Paulsen, *Die Briefe des Ignatius von Antiochia und der Brief des Polykarp von Smyrna*, HNT 18 (Tübingen: Mohr Siebeck, 1985), 76.

33. Willard M. Swartley, "The Imitatio Christi in the Ignatian Letters," *VC* 27 (1973): 81–103, at 91–100.

34. Swartley, "Imitatio Christi," 101.

35. H. H. Drake Williams, "'Imitate Me': Interpreting Imitation in 1 Corinthians in Relation to Ignatius of Antioch," *Perichoresis* 11 (2013): 75–93, at 78–83.

8. Mimesis in the Apostolic Fathers

Imitation involves suffering as the calling of all Christians in general."[36] The main difference is that Swartley situates Ignatius's language of imitation within the specific context of Ignatius's own discipleship, while Williams (who seems unaware of Swartley) extends it to general Christian discipleship.

David Reis offers a different perspective by exploring the dual ideas of ethical and literary mimesis in Ignatius. Regarding *ethical* mimesis, Reis shows how Ignatius's life imitates that of Paul: both were church leaders who wrote letters to instruct churches, were taken to Rome, and died as martyrs. However, Reis adopts Castelli's understanding of mimesis as having elements of hierarchy and power where the model is superior to the copy, so he contends that Ignatius (the copy) falls short of Paul (the model): "By constantly drawing attention to his subordinate status and his self-doubts about his Christian status, Ignatius exemplifies the coercive effect of Paul's rhetoric that Castelli has identified."[37] Setting aside the issues with Castelli's model of mimesis (see section 6.1), I contend that Ignatius's choice of Paul as an exemplar may simply be out of humility and a recognition that he himself was not an apostle.[38] Regarding *literary* mimesis, Reis sees that the Ignatian letters resemble the Pauline letters in vocabulary, ideas, and argumentation, in effect elevating Ignatius as the "new" Paul who speaks with a similar apostolic authority.[39]

Driving this ethical and literary mimesis is a strategy of establishing a "recognition of, and submission to, an authoritative hierarchy that naturally leads to unity."[40] Reis reasons that Ignatius could not present himself as a model for imitation, as Paul had done, among the churches in Asia Minor if he did not establish unity in his own church in Antioch.[41] Barring his Castellian views, Reis makes a strong case that Ignatius used mimesis (1) to promote unity among the churches and (2) to establish his own credibility as instrumental in bringing about this unity (see also Swartley, above). In support of Reis, Buol states that, in imitating Christ and Paul in death, Ignatius enters the mimetic chain where Christians are

---

36. Williams, "'Imitate Me,'" 83.

37. Reis, "Paul's Footsteps," 293–96 (quotation from p. 296).

38. While Reis acknowledges Ignatius's extreme humility and reverence of Paul and the apostolic age ("Paul's Footsteps," 293), he contends that this is the coercive effect of mimesis embedded in power as Castelli has outlined. Carl B. Smith also perceives Ignatius to be an imitator of Paul but without resorting to a Castellian model of mimesis. He notes that Paul is often self-effacing, and Ignatius may simply be imitating this aspect ("Ministry, Martyrdom, and Other Mysteries: Pauline Influence on Ignatius of Antioch," in *Paul and the Second Century*, ed. Michael F. Bird and Joseph R. Dodson, LNTS 412 [London: T&T Clark, 2011], 37–56, at 39, 55–56).

39. Reis, "Paul's Footsteps," 296–300, 305.

40. Reis, "Paul's Footsteps," 300.

41. Reis, "Paul's Footsteps," 300.

to imitate the bishop as he imitates Christ and God in order to achieve unity in the church.[42]

Conclusion. The concept of mimesis is evident in the Ignatian corpus and reveals the influence of John and Paul.[43] While mimesis is not prevalent in or central to Ignatian thought, it is nevertheless employed to support the central theme of unity. Common forms of Ignatian mimesis relate to humility, obedience, and love in service of unity. Ignatius can exhort Christians to imitate exemplary people as well as Christ and God. Just as in John, the Christ–God mimesis is often a motivational basis for other forms of mimesis.[44] For Ignatius, martyrdom is the supreme imitation of Christ and evidence of true discipleship. Behind Ignatius's use of mimesis is his overall strategy to bring unity among the Asian churches, beginning with his own Syrian church so that he would gain credibility among the churches he writes to.

8.3. Polycarp of Smyrna

We turn to Polycarp's letter *To the Philippians* and the anonymous writing Martyrdom of Polycarp.

To the Philippians. This is the only extant letter from Polycarp, bishop of Smyrna, dated around 120 CE.[45] Irenaeus, his disciple, asserts that Polycarp had been instructed by the apostles and had met many eyewitnesses of the risen Christ (*Haer.* 3.3.4).[46] Berding shows convincingly that Polycarp draws on both Johannine and Pauline traditions.[47] Several passages convey mimetic ideas. In *Phil.* 1:1, Polycarp expresses his delight that the Philippian Christians have "received the imitations of true love" (δεξαμένοις τὰ μιμήματα τῆς ἀληθοῦς ἀγάπης) and accompanied those who were bound in chains. If "true love" is a reference to Christ, those in chains are probably Ignatius and fellow prisoners who were on their way to

---

42. Buol, *Martyred*, 153–54, 174.
43. See also Löhr, "Epistles of Ignatius," 91–115, at 101–2.
44. As Hartog states, "The underlying foundation of mimesis concerns Jesus' imitation of the Father" ("*Imitatio Christi*," 14).
45. Berding, "John or Paul?," 136n6.
46. See further Buol, *Martyred*, 179–80.
47. Berding, "John or Paul?," 135–43. Angela Standhartinger contends that Polycarp was familiar with Paul's letter to the Philippians ("'Join in Imitating Me' (Philippians 3.17): Towards an Interpretation of Philippians 3," *NTS* 54 [2008]: 417–35, at 433). While Boudewijn Dehandschutter acknowledges Pauline influences on Pol. *Phil.*, he sees the case for Johannine influences as equivocal ("The Epistle of Polycarp," in *The Apostolic Fathers: An Introduction*, ed. Wilhelm Pratscher [Waco, TX: Baylor University Press, 2010], 117–33, at 124–26).

8. Mimesis in the Apostolic Fathers

martyrdom in Rome (see BDAG, s.v. "μίμημα"). In short, Polycarp may be referring to Ignatius and other prisoners as imitators of Christ in their sufferings (see also *Phil.* 1:2, which mentions Christ's martyrdom).

Abraham Malherbe has shown that it was common in ancient paraenetic letters to provide concrete examples for imitation to support the exhortation.[48] Polycarp mentions several such examples in chapters 8–10. In *Phil.* 8:2, he exhorts the Philippians to be(come) imitators (μιμηταί) of Christ's steadfast endurance amidst suffering because Christ himself has set this example (ὑπογραμμός) (see also 1 Clem. 5:7; 16:17). Then, in *Phil.* 9:1, Polycarp urges them, again, to practice this same endurance that they have observed (εἴδατε κατ' ὀφθαλμούς) in others, such as Ignatius, Zosimus, Rufus, Paul, and other apostles.[49] Finally, in *Phil.* 10:1 (which is preserved only in Latin), Polycarp urges the Philippians to follow the example of Christ (*domini exemplar sequimini*) in faithful endurance.

Martyrdom of Polycarp. This anonymous letter describes the death of Polycarp around 155–160 CE and presents martyrdom as the supreme imitation of Christ.[50] Moss notes that this writing is "the sine qua non of martyrological *imitatio Christi*."[51] The immediate effect of Polycarp's martyrdom is that it ended the Smyrnean persecution (1:1).[52] From the outset, the author presents Polycarp as an "imitator" of Christ in martyrdom (lit. "he waited to be handed over [to death], as the Lord had also done") in order to encourage other Christians also to become imitators (μιμηταί) of Christ in martyrdom (1:2).[53] As Sandnes explains, the opening of the letter, stating that martyrdom is "in accordance with the Gospel" (1:1–2), implies that the story follows a pattern set by Christ in the passion narrative and is expected to generate imitators.[54] Sandnes then shows how Polycarp's death is patterned on that of Christ:

---

48. Malherbe, *Moral Exhortation*, 124–25.

49. Paul Hartog, *Polycarp and the New Testament: The Occasion, Rhetoric, Theme, and Unity of the Epistle to the Philippians and Its Allusions to New Testament Literature*, WUNT 2/134 (Tübingen: Mohr Siebeck, 2002), 130. Hartog also notes that the phrase "before one's eyes" was common in paraenetic texts (e.g., Seneca, *Ep.* 6.5). This coheres with our findings in Greco-Roman antiquity and early Christian writers such as John and Paul that observing the example is vital for imitation.

50. Jefford, *Apostolic Fathers*, 90–93.

51. Moss, *Other Christs*, 47.

52. Buol, *Martyred*, 193.

53. Buol remarks that the phrase "looking not only to our own interests, but also to the interests of our neighbors" in Mart. Pol. 1:2 alludes to Phil 2:4 (*Martyred*, 204).

54. Sandnes, *Discourses*, 55. Shawn J. Wilhite argues that the phrase "in accordance with the Gospel" refers to both the imitation of the Gospel passions and the broader ethics of the

Narratively, Polycarp's martyrdom picks up details from the Passion Narrative that makes the Christ assimilation notably vivid: Polycarp is betrayed by one of his servants, whose destiny is said to be equal to that of Judas. The bishop was arrested by a police captain by the name of Herod. The arrest takes place on "the day of preparation," i.e. the day before the Sabbath and they came with arms "as though against a brigand," citing Matt 26:55 about the arrest of Jesus. Polycarp was led into the city sitting on an ass. These details underline what martyrdom is about, being an imitator of Christ in his sufferings.[55]

The purpose of this "narratological Gospel mirroring" (to use Wilhite's phrase) in the account of Polycarp's death is to continue the *imitatio Christi* motif.[56] Moss also notes the contrast with Quintus, who offered himself for martyrdom but was unable to see it to completion, so the narrator concludes that voluntary martyrdom is not in keeping with the teaching of the gospel (4:1).[57] "The gospel-worthy martyr does not offer him- or herself for martyrdom but eagerly embraces it once the sentence is passed."[58] As Buol asserts, the contrast between Polycarp and Quintus underscores the document's purpose "to instruct others regarding the proper manner in which to approach persecution and martyrdom."[59]

In 17:3, the author explicitly declares that a martyr is a disciple and imitator of Christ (μάρτυρας ὡς μαθητὰς καὶ μιμητὰς τοῦ κυρίου). In 19:1, Polycarp is depicted as a pre-eminent martyr, whom many desire to imitate in keeping with the Gospel of Christ (μάρτυς ἔξοχος οὗ τὸ μαρτύριον πάντες ἐπιθυμοῦσιν μιμεῖσθαι κατὰ τὸ εὐαγγέλιον

Gospel ("'That We Too Might Be Imitators of Him': The *Martyrdom of Polycarp* as *Imitatio Christi*," *Churchman* 129 [2015]: 319–36, at 328–29).

55. Sandnes, *Discourses*, 56. In addition, Sandnes sees parallels between Polycarp's prayer in Mart. Pol. 7 and that of Jesus in Gethsemane (*Discourses*, 60–61). Others have also noted the numerous gospel parallels in Mart. Pol.: e.g., Paul Middleton, *Radical Martyrdom and Cosmic Conflict in Early Christianity*, LNTS 307 (London: T&T Clark, 2006), 83; Moss, *Other Christs*, 57–58; Paul Hartog, "The Christology of the *Martyrdom of Polycarp*: Martyrdom as Both Imitation of Christ and Election by Christ," *Perichoresis* 12 (2014): 137–51, at 138; Cobb, "Polycarp's Cup," 224; Wilhite, "Imitators," 331–34; Buol, *Martyred*, 201. Michael W. Holmes, however, is skeptical about Gospel parallels informing imitation motifs in Mart. Pol. (*The Apostolic Fathers: Greek Texts and English Translations*, 3rd ed. [Grand Rapids: Baker Academic, 2007], 299–300).

56. Wilhite, "Imitators," 331–36. Interestingly, Moss notes that Polycarp's death deviates from Christ's in that Polycarp is bound, not nailed, to the stake and explains this in light of the "binding" traditions surrounding Isaac. Since the binding of Isaac foreshadows the sacrifice of Jesus, the binding of Polycarp thus augments the crucifixion and reinforces the *imitatio Christi* (*Other Christs*, 58–59).

57. Moss, *Other Christs*, 47–48.
58. Moss, *Other Christs*, 48.
59. Buol, *Martyred*, 209.

8. Mimesis in the Apostolic Fathers

Χριστοῦ γενόμενον).⁶⁰ As Gerd Buschmann asserts, "The imitation theme κατὰ τὸ εὐαγγέλιον is not secondary but central for the theology of MartPol."⁶¹ Buschmann contends that Mart. Pol. takes the Ignatian martyrdom theology in *Rom.* 6:3 to its logical conclusion, where salvation is mediated by the *imitatio Christi* in martyrdom.⁶² Although in a weaker form, the same idea is expressed in 22:1, where following the example of Polycarp (lit. "to be found in his steps"; τὰ ἴχνη εὑρεθῆναι) will lead martyrs into the kingdom of Christ. As Moss explains, "Polycarp is part of a mimetic chain, one that connects the audience of the martyrdom to Christ himself."⁶³ Likewise, Wilhite identifies Polycarp as an *imitatio*-mediator—when people imitate Polycarp, they are imitating Christ.⁶⁴ Hartog adds that Christ is not simply the "passive" historical exemplar for martyrdom but plays an active, contemporary role in selecting martyrs (20:1) and helping them to endure (2:2; 13:3).⁶⁵

There is, arguably, an implied idea of transformation through mimetic martyrdom in 11:1 (Polycarp uses the verb μετατίθεσθαι to refer to his imminent death) and 15:2 (the change in Polycarp is described in terms of precious refinement and pleasant fragrance).⁶⁶

8.4. The Letter of Barnabas

The Letter of Barnabas, written between 70 and 130 CE, is a Christocentric, allegorical interpretation of the Old Testament.⁶⁷ The letter does not mention the lexeme μιμεῖσθαι and only features the term τύπος, the ὁμοι* group, and a few comparative conjunctions. The use of the ὁμοι* group mainly indicates analogy or likeness, and τύπος is often used typologically with reference to Christ, for example, Isaac as a type (τύπος) of Christ in 7:3 (see also 7:7, 10–11; 8:1–2; 12:5–6). The comparative conjunctions do not indicate mimesis. In short, the Letter of Barnabas contains no mimetic ideas.

---

60. Moss even asserts that Polycarp's martyrdom trumps that of Christ (*Other Christs*, 48).
61. Gerd Buschmann, "The Martyrdom of Polycarp," in *The Apostolic Fathers: An Introduction*, ed. Wilhelm Pratscher (Waco, TX: Baylor University Press, 2010), 135–57, at 146.
62. Buschmann, "Martyrdom," 148–49.
63. Moss, *Other Christs*, 46. See also Buol, *Martyred*, 200, 203. For Moss, the death of Stephen in Acts and that of Polycarp in Mart. Pol. are the only martyr accounts that mimic the entire story line of Jesus's passion (*Other Christs*, 53).
64. Wilhite, "Imitators," 329–31.
65. Hartog, "Christology," 147.
66. For Buol, 15:2 refers to Polycarp being refined and changed into a pleasing sacrifice (*Martyred*, 196–98).
67. Jefford, *Apostolic Fathers*, 7–8, 11–13.

PART 2 MIMESIS IN EARLY CHRISTIANITY

8.5. The Letter to Diognetus

The Letter to Diognetus, possibly composed in the latter half of the second century, is an early example of Christian apologetics.[68] In terms of mimetic language, it features the lexeme μιμεῖσθαι (10:4–6), a few occurrences of the ὁμοι* group, and some comparative conjunctions, but these latter two groups do not indicate mimesis, so we turn our attention to 10:4–6. Chapter 9 stresses God's kindness/goodness (χρηστότητης; 9:1–2, 6), and 10:4–6 exhorts Diognetus to imitate God's kindness/goodness. The author reasons in 10:4 that love for God should lead to or be expressed through imitating his kindness/goodness (ἀγαπήσας δὲ μιμητὴς ἔσῃ αὐτοῦ τῆς χρηστότητος). Then, in 10:5, the author warns that lording it over others, accumulating wealth, or showing violence are not the means to flourish or be happy (εὐδαιμονεῖν) nor qualify as imitating God (μιμεῖσθαι θεόν) because these things are antithetical to God. Rather, as 10:6 continues, one is an imitator of God (οὗτος μιμητής ἐστι θεοῦ) when one bears another's burden, does good to others, and provides for the needy.[69]

In fact, the imitator becomes a god to the beneficiaries of these actions (θεὸς γίνεται τῶν λαμβανόντων; 10:6). Clayton Jefford states that theosis is in view here, in that Christians become deified through their imitation of the divine nature of God.[70] While this is possible, it is secondary. The genitive τῶν λαμβανόντων to indicate that the imitator becomes a god "of" (i.e., "to" or "for") others points in another direction. I contend that the phrase primarily indicates that the imitator is a mediator. In imitating God, the imitator mediates God or divine goods to the recipients (see also sections 5.3.3 and 5.4.5). As 10:7 asserts, then the people on earth will know (lit. "see") that (i.e., how) God lives in heaven (τότε θεάσῃ τυγχάνων ἐπὶ τῆς γῆς ὅτι θεὸς ἐν οὐρανοῖς πολιτεύεται). In essence, people can "observe" God through the Christians who imitate him.

At the same time, as William Horst points out, "The ability to 'look up to heaven' should likely also be understood as a necessary condition for divine imitation."[71]

---

68. Jefford, *Apostolic Fathers*, 168–70. Charles E. Hill provides an extensive case for Polycarp being the author of the Letter to Diognetus (*From the Lost Teaching of Polycarp: Identifying Irenaeus' Apostolic Presbyter and the Author of Ad Diognetum*, WUNT 186 [Tübingen: Mohr Siebeck, 2006], 128–65).

69. For a detailed study of the imitation of God's love/goodness as a key aspect of second-century discipleship, see Charles Theodore Mielke, "Christian Love and the Imitation of Christ in the *Epistle to Diognetus*: A Second-Century Example of Christian Discipleship" (D.Ed. diss., Southern Baptist Theological Seminary, 2017).

70. Clayton N. Jefford, *The Epistle to Diognetus (with the Fragment of Quadratus): Introduction, Text, and Commentary* (Oxford: Oxford University Press, 2013), 245.

71. William Horst, "The Secret Plan of God and the Imitation of God: Neglected Dimensions of Christian Differentiation in *Ad Diognetum*," *JECS* 27 (2019): 161–83, at 180.

This goes to the principle that imitation requires observation, even if this is mental imaging, as may be in view here. As Jefford declares, "It is the expression of the believer's participation in the 'God-filled life.'"[72] There are echoes of the mimetic language in 1 John 4:17, where believers make the invisible God in heaven known on earth by imitating him (see section 5.4.4).[73] There is the additional notion of martyrdom attached to imitation. As Horst explains, if Diognetus becomes an imitator of God, he will realize that true life is in heaven with God and come to admire those who embrace martyrdom (10:7–8).[74]

We have learned that there is a cognitive dimension to mimesis in several New Testament texts, and Diogn. 10:4–6 is no exception in that authentic imitation of God requires knowledge of him. Horst observes that the author of the Letter to Diognetus outlines a process by which Diognetus can become an imitator of God. Diognetus must first acquire an understanding of God, specifically God's love for humans (10:1–2), then respond with reciprocal love to God, and finally show God's benevolent love in his behavior toward other people (10:3–4).[75] Horst, too, recognizes that the imitation of God is not about cloning because Diognetus's behavior toward other humans differs from God's behavior toward humanity: "Imitation of God is less a matter of doing the same specific acts that God has done toward humans, and more a matter of behaving in accordance with God's character."[76] Horst also stresses that becoming an imitator of God requires divine initiative—"if God is willing" (10:4)—and thus, becoming an imitator of God is an expression of God's own goodness toward Christians.[77]

8.6. The Didache

This anonymous didactic writing, dated by most scholars somewhere between 80 and 110 CE, contains virtually no mimetic ideas.[78] In 4:11, the author states that slaves should submit to their masters with modesty and respect as to a type

---

72. Jefford, *Epistle to Diognetus*, 245.

73. Jefford notes further Johannine parallels: the phrases "for God loved humankind" and "he sent his only-begotten son" in 10:2 echo those in John 3:16, and "how will you love the one who first loved you?" in 10:3 resembles 1 John 4:19 (*Epistle to Diognetus*, 73). For a more extensive discussion of Johannine and Pauline influences in Diogn., see Mielke, "Christian Love," 79–98.

74. Horst, "Secret Plan," 179.

75. Horst, "Secret Plan," 177–78.

76. Horst, "Secret Plan," 178.

77. Horst, "Secret Plan," 180. While the personal pronoun αὐτοῦ in the phrase δύναται θέλοντος αὐτοῦ can refer to God or the human imitator, many scholars support a reference to God (Holmes, *Apostolic Fathers*, 303; Mielke, "Christian Love," 51).

78. Jefford, *Apostolic Fathers*, 26–30.

or example of God (ὡς τύπῳ θεοῦ), but there are no mimetic connotations. Some comparative conjunctions indicate analogy but not mimesis (e.g., ὥσπερ in 9:4 and ὡσαύτως in 11:11; 13:2). Only in 8:2–3, there is a "medium" case of mimesis (activated by οὕτω, "like this," "in this manner"), indicating that the early church repeated or "imitated" the Lord's Prayer three times a day.[79] Barring this occurrence, the Didache contains no mimetic ideas.

8.7. The Shepherd of Hermas

The Shepherd of Hermas, dated in the second century, contains five visions, twelve commandments, and ten parables.[80] The work does not contain the lexeme μιμεῖσθαι; only the term τύπος, the ὁμοι* group, and comparative conjunctions. The term τύπος is used typologically without mimetic connotations (Herm. Vis. 4 1:1; 2:5; 3:6) or simply to denote an example (Herm. Sim. 2 1:2). The comparative conjunctions indicate analogy rather than mimesis (see, e.g., ὥσπερ in Herm. Vis. 3 6:6; 11:3; Herm. Vis. 4 3:4; Herm. Mand. 12 6:2; Herm. Sim. 3 1:3; Herm. Sim. 9 20:3, καθώς in Herm. Vis. 3 8:7; Herm. Mand. 10 1:5; and ὡσαύτως in Herm. Sim. 2 1:7). In a few instances, however, there may be "weak" mimetic ideas. Herm. Vis. 3 9:7 contains a trace of mimesis in that the author warns its readers not to "imitate" or be like magicians or drugmixers (μὴ γίνεσθε ὅμοιοι τοῖς φαρμακοῖς) who carry poison in their hearts. In Herm. Mand. 1 4:9, there is a "weak" mimetic idea in the warning not to "imitate" pagans in committing adultery (ὃς ἂν τὰ ὁμοιώματα ποιῇ τοῖς ἔθνεσιν μοιχᾶται). They are so sporadic, however, that we must conclude that the Shepherd of Hermas has no concrete mimetic ideas.

8.8. Conclusion

Mimesis does not feature in all the literature of the apostolic fathers—2 Clement and the Letter of Barnabas contain no mimetic ideas, the hint of mimesis in the Shepherd of Hermas is negligible, and the Didache only has a single occurrence. More noteworthy are 1 Clement, the Ignatian corpus, Polycarp's letter *To the Philippians*, the Martyrdom of Polycarp, and the Letter to Diognetus. We have seen that several apostolic fathers (Ignatius, Polycarp, the author of Mart. Pol.) connect

---

79. See also chapter 4, n. 106, of this volume.
80. Jefford, *Apostolic Fathers*, 143–47.

8. Mimesis in the Apostolic Fathers

imitation and martyrdom, where the deaths of Christ and Paul are viewed as models for imitation. Moss notes that early Christian martyrs were not only exemplars in death but exemplified a range of virtues in the *manner* of their death, such as "obedience, endurance, piety, love, humility, forgiveness, and fearlessness."[81] In these writings, though not always explicit, we could detect several aspects of our model of mimesis that we constructed from the Greco-Roman traditions. The following table shows our findings:

	1 Clement	Ignatius	Pol. *Phil.*	Mart. Pol.	Diognetus
Mimetic language	μιμητής, ὑπόδειγμα, ὑπογραμμός	μιμεῖσθαι, μιμητής, ἐξεμπλάριον, ὥσπερ...οὕτως, ὡς	μιμητής, μίμημα, ὑπογραμμός	μιμεῖσθαι, μιμητής, τὰ ἴχνη εὑρεθῆναι	μιμεῖσθαι, μιμητής
Nature and content of mimesis	examples of endurance and humility to counter division in the church	martyrdom as the *imitatio Christi*; imitation to promote unity; imitation of the bishop, God, and Christ	martyrdom as the *imitatio Christi*; examples of endurance	martyrdom as the *imitatio Christi*	to imitate God in his goodness
Aspects of our model of mimesis	observation, interpretation, imitation, transformation	direct observation, imitation, transformation (unity)	direct observation, imitation	imitation, possibly transformation	observation, interpretation, imitation, transformation

Scholars have noted that the apostolic fathers' concept of martyrdom as the ideal *imitatio Christi* is a development from mimetic ideas in the New Testament. Agan, for example, traces the concept of martyrdom as the ideal imitation of Christ back to Paul's writings and Jesus's sayings in the Gospels.[82] Maarten Taveirne, who focuses on the concept of martyrdom as the ideal *imitatio Christi* in late Christianity (the 4th to 6th centuries), also traces it back to the New Testament and shows how the concept is subsequently deepened in the era of the apostolic fathers, especially the Martyrdom of Polycarp, by means of quoting from or alluding to

---

81. Moss, *Other Christs*, 105–7 (quotation from p. 105).
82. Agan, "Hermeneutic of Imitation," 41–43.

passion materials in the Gospels.[83] We noted that although Luke is the first to describe an imitation of Jesus's death in the martyrdom of Stephen, John is the first to make martyrdom a legitimate endeavor in keeping with Jesus's teachings when he creates a new mimetic command in 1 John 3:16 from Jesus's instruction in John 15:13. Indeed, I have argued that "a good case can be made that Ignatius and Polycarp had connections with the apostle John. In this case, the imitation of Jesus's death in the Apostolic Fathers can be traced back via John's newly-created imitative command in 1 John 3:16 to Jesus's own saying in John 15:13."[84] We saw that the Letter to Diognetus also contains Johannine influences. Likewise, Moss sees a trajectory from the Johannine concept of laying down one's life for another as an expression of love to the death of Polycarp (Mart. Pol. 1:2) and later martyr accounts.[85] Buol and Petitfils, however, stress a tradition of imitation from Jesus to the bishop martyrs via Paul.[86] There is no need to choose. Our findings show that possible influences of both the Johannine and Pauline mimetic traditions can be found in the Ignatian Corpus, Pol. *Phil.* (see n. 47), Mart. Pol. (see n. 53), and Diogn. (see n. 73). To find these influences in the Apostolic Fathers is unsurprising because John and Paul are the main "mimesis theologians" in the New Testament.[87]

In a stimulating, broad study on mimesis in antiquity, Anders Klostergaard Petersen argues that while most religions contain a notion of imitation of the gods (especially in the context of ritual), only in historical or utopian types of religion is this notion associated with the divinization of the religious adherents.[88] With regard to second- and third-century Christianity, he contends that early Christian writings such as the Martyrdom of Polycarp and Ignatius's letter *To the Romans* reveal the tendency to view martyrdom as a prime means for imitating Christ.[89]

---

83. Maarten Taveirne, "Das Martyrium als *imitatio Christi*: Die literarische Gestaltung der spätantiken Märtyrerakten und -passionen nach der Passion Christi," ZAC 18 (2014): 167–203, at 170–77.

84. Bennema, "Imitation in Johannine Christianity," 109. I refer specifically to Berding, "John or Paul?," 135–43; Löhr, "Epistles of Ignatius," 101–2; Smith, "Gospels," 204. Cobb also considers that the "cup" in Mart. Pol. 14:2 alludes to John 18:11 ("Polycarp's Cup," 226).

85. Moss, *Other Christs*, 50, 106.

86. Buol, *Martyred*, 237–43; Petitfils, *Mos Christianorum*, 197–99.

87. Beyond the apostolic period, Watson draws attention to Justin Martyr, who, in a brief description of early Christian worship, notes that the reading of the Gospels or Old Testament prophets, followed by expository teaching, should lead to imitating what was taught in daily life (*1 Apol.* 67.3–5). Watson concludes that the re-enactment of Jesus's actions and words is the basis for a broader mimesis of the Gospel practiced in daily life (*Fourfold Gospel*, 172–75).

88. Anders Klostergaard Petersen, "Attaining Divine Perfection through Different Forms of Imitation," *Numen* 60 (2013): 7–38, at 9–10.

89. Petersen, "Divine Perfection," 16–18.

8. Mimesis in the Apostolic Fathers

In contrast to locative religions (including ancient Israelite religion), utopian religions (including Christianity) offer divinization to their religious adherents as a means to leave this world and attain kinship with the divine in another world.[90] He concludes that in early Christianity, kinship with God or divinization was supremely achieved through martyrdom as the most radical form of imitation of God.[91] Moss, however, is less certain about the correlation between martyrdom and theosis: the martyr's "sharing the status of Christ does not say anything (positively or negatively) about ontological deification."[92] She argues that *ousia* was not a term or category used in the martyr acts; these texts were interested in status, not ontology.[93] I concur. While some apostolic writings (1 Clem., Mart. Pol., Diogn.) possibly convey the notion of transformation, it would be going too far to classify this as theosis.

---

90. Petersen, "Divine Perfection," 25–27.
91. Petersen, "Divine Perfection," 34–35.
92. Moss, *Other Christs*, 164, 277 (quotation from p. 277).
93. Moss, *Other Christs*, 266.

PART 3
SYNTHESIS

9

Summary—The Research Findings

This is the first comprehensive study on mimesis as a religious-ethical concept in early Christianity within the intellectual milieu of Jewish and Greco-Roman antiquity. In this part 3, I will summarize our findings (section 9.1), answer the four questions that had framed our inquiry (section 9.2), explain the complexities of early Christian mimesis as a hermeneutical process (section 10.1), explore the ongoing relevance of early Christian mimesis (section 10.2), and state the key takeaways of the book (section 10.3). While chapter 9 collates our research findings, chapter 10 will use these findings to draw conclusions about the concept of early Christian mimesis.

9.1. Summary of Our Findings

In chapter 1, we noted that mimesis or imitation is central to human life, but there are two particular challenges in studying this topic. First, contemporary Christianity is not in agreement about the importance and appropriateness of the idea of imitating Christ, so we had to demonstrate the validity of our study. Second, mimesis has evaded a precise definition throughout history, although it remained rooted in ancient Greek thought. Having noted these challenges, we then provided a brief sketch of the landscape. A peek into early Christian literature showed that mimesis features in the Pauline, Johannine, and Apostolic Fathers, but less so, if at all, in the Old Testament and other parts of the New Testament. A quick scan of scholarship showed that the 1960s and the last two decades were most fruitful in the study of early Christian mimesis. Out of these previews of primary and secondary literature, we articulated four research questions that have guided our study:

PART 3   SYNTHESIS

1. Where do the historical origins of the early Christian concept of mimesis lie?
2. What language did early Christian authors use to articulate the concept of mimesis?
3. Is the early Christian concept of mimesis consistent, varied, or developing—and what is its place in early Christian ethics?
4. How could early Christians imitate an absent Jesus or Paul—and what should they imitate about them?

Our working definition of mimesis, that "person B represents or emulates person A in activity or state X in order to become like person A," meant in most cases that early Christians sought to imitate Jesus in specific actions or a state of being in order to become like him. We clarified how mimesis differs from related concepts such as analogy and reciprocity. The overall thesis was that "early Christian mimesis was a dynamic, participatory, creative, and cognitive process within the context of divine family education with the goal for Christians to represent and resemble Christ in character and conduct." By implication, mimesis was a crucial didactic instrument for moral transformation in early Christianity, shaping people's conduct and character.

In chapter 2, we used our findings on mimesis in Greco-Roman antiquity to construct a model that could explain the mechanics of mimesis. Methodologically, this was a good starting point because (1) discourse on mimesis originated in this environment, and (2) various Greco-Roman authors explained how mimesis worked. We examined mimesis in the overlapping areas of religion, family, and education, featuring the imitation of gods, parents, and teachers. In classical Athenian drama, we found that mimesis had a moral role in the civic education of the spectators. We then outlined how Plato and Aristotle laid the foundations for the concept of mimesis in antiquity and found that Aristotle was more positive about the value of mimesis than Plato. Turning to ancient rhetorical education, we examined select moral discourses of Isocrates, Cicero, Seneca, Quintilian, and Plutarch. These Greco-Roman traditions revealed a shared discourse on mimesis that enabled us to construct a model of the workings of mimesis, comprising five aspects: (1) selecting and associating with an appropriate exemplar; (2) carefully observing the exemplar; (3) discerning what should be imitated; (4) imitating the exemplar's virtuous behavior; and (5) being transformed or making moral progress from imitating virtuous exemplars. We noted that besides direct observation, the exemplar could also be mediated through text and memory, enabling the imitator to create a mental picture of the exemplar. Our findings provided a basis for understanding the concept of mimesis in early Christianity.

In chapter 3, we searched for the concept of mimesis in ancient Jewish traditions (the Hebrew Bible, Hellenistic Judaism, and Rabbinic Judaism) in order

9. Summary—the Research Findings

to test whether the roots of early Christian mimesis lie in the Jewish traditions rather than Greco-Roman ones. We found that while the Hebrew Bible contains no explicit mimetic language, some texts (mainly in the Pentateuch) allude to the concept of imitating God. Once Greek culture started to influence Jewish thought, we found evidence that Hellenistic and Rabbinic Judaism had incorporated the ethical concept of mimesis from the Greek traditions. Nevertheless, Second Temple Judaism does not reveal a uniform concept of mimesis—Josephus and Philo, for example, refer to mimesis more extensively than the rabbis. We also noted that Jewish mimetic ethics was set in the context of the covenant (the religious-ethical life with God), while Greek ethics was set in civic life (the political-ethical life in the *polis*).[1] We concluded that the concept of mimesis was latent in the Hebrew Bible and came to fruition when Second Temple Judaism came into contact with Greek culture.

Chapters 1–3 prepared the ground for our main investigation of early Christian mimesis in chapters 4–8 in three ways: (1) a preview of primary and secondary literature on the topic helped articulate our main research questions; (2) we found that the origins of early Christian mimesis lie in the Greco-Roman traditions but the idea is latent in Hebraic thought; and (3) our examination of the Greco-Roman traditions yielded a composite model of the workings of mimesis. We will now summarize our findings on mimesis in the various sections of early Christian writings.

In chapter 4, we examined the idea of mimesis in the Synoptics and Acts. We found that the phrase "to follow Jesus," which is central to discipleship across the Synoptics, does not signify mimesis but can facilitate it when people observe and imitate Jesus as they follow him. Mark shows only "weak" evidence of mimesis: (1) "following Jesus" has notional traces of mimesis; (2) 10:15 and 10:43 are the only instances of mimetic language; (3) the Gethsemane event indicates mimesis; and (4) the "minor characters" have mimetic potential. In Matthew, "following Jesus" again contains only traces of mimesis, but overall, Matthew shows more and clearer instances of mimesis than Mark: (1) the Sermon on the Mount contains the greatest concentration of Matthew's mimetic language and presents mimesis in the context of divine family education; (2) beyond the Sermon on the Mount, there are six other instances of mimesis. While mimesis is peripheral to Matthew's ethics (as is the case in Mark), Matthew places mimesis in a clearer ethical context than Mark, namely family behavior in the kingdom of God. Luke also hints at mimesis in the notion of "following Jesus," has some instances of mimesis, and injects mimesis into his account of the Lord's Supper (but less so in the Gethsemane episode). Like Mark, Luke presents literary characters as examples to

---

1. Josephus related mimesis to the political life too (see section 3.2.2).

PART 3   SYNTHESIS

imitate in Acts. In sum, mimesis barely features in Mark and only sporadically in Matthew and Luke–Acts, resulting in a "weak" to "medium" concept of mimesis overall. Mimesis is not a dominant theme of discipleship in the Synoptics and Acts and is only peripheral to their ethics. Interestingly, the Lord's Prayer, the Lord's Supper, and the scene at Gethsemane have the most mimetic potential. Despite the patchy evidence for mimesis in the Synoptics and Acts, we found several forms or modes of mimesis—from direct observation to textually mediated mimesis (through the literary characters) to the occasional mnemonic mimesis (the Lord's Supper). We were thus compelled to continue our quest for a more robust concept of mimesis in early Christianity.

The Gospel and Letters of John were the focus of chapter 5. We found that the Johannine mimetic language is *varied* (mimesis is expressed by eight different expressions), *widespread* (there are about forty-four occurrences of mimesis), and *distinctive* (the comparative conjunction καθώς, rather than the lexeme μιμεῖσθαι, is central to John's mimetic language). John develops his concept of mimesis in the context of the divine family, where the Son–Father mimesis is paradigmatic for the believer–Jesus mimesis. The main attributes and actions that characterize the relationship between Jesus and God are extended to people by means of mimesis. When we unpacked the believer–Jesus (and occasional believer–God) mimesis, we found that Johannine mimesis is a creative, cognitive hermeneutical process rather than simplistic repetition. In this process, believers are expected to apply "moral reasoning" to interpret the example of Jesus (or sometimes God) and decide on an appropriate mimetic act. We demonstrated that mimesis is central to Johannine ethics in that mimesis is a crucial didactic tool for shaping appropriate behavior and character in the divine family. We constructed a model of Johannine mimesis consisting of five aspects (selection and association, observation, interpretation, imitation, and transformation), which is remarkably similar to our Greco-Roman model. We also explored how mimesis might have worked in Johannine Christianity when believers could not observe Jesus directly. We found that, besides direct observation, John presents two other means of mediating mimesis: (1) believers can visualize and imitate a Jesus reconstructed from the Johannine text, and (2) believers can visualize and imitate a remembered Jesus. In both cases, the Spirit aids the imitation—by guiding believers in reconstructing Jesus from the text and by enabling their memory of Jesus and his example.

In chapter 6, we examined the Pauline literature where the concept of mimesis is most apparent. Besides the lexeme μιμεῖσθαι (73 percent of the New Testament occurrences occur in Paul), the Pauline mimetic language includes the noun τύπος ("example"), some comparative constructions (καθώς/ὥσπερ . . . [οὕτως] καί) and stand-alone comparative conjunctions (καθώς, ὡς, καθάπερ), and a few

9. Summary—the Research Findings

other expressions (παρακολουθεῖν, στοιχεῖν τοῖς ἴχνεσιν). While the ideal is always the imitation of Christ, Paul often presents himself as the object of imitation and sometimes his trusted coworkers or mature believers, whose lives are closely patterned on that of Paul. Paul thus creates a unique mimetic chain of Christ–Paul (or surrogates for Paul)–Paul's converts. We constructed a model of mimesis from the Pauline tradition that resembles that in the Greco-Roman traditions. The Pauline mimetic model presents five modes of mimesis that can partially overlap: (1) direct observation of the exemplar; (2) mnemonic mimesis; (3) textually mediated mimesis; (4) personally mediated mimesis; and (5) orally mediated mimesis.

Pauline mimesis is not about cloning, but it often involves imitating Paul's general lifestyle or a particular mindset or attitude that finds expression in specific activities such as humility, self-giving love, other-regard, and forgiveness. Thus, the Pauline concept of mimesis is a creative, cognitive hermeneutical process where the imitator must apply "moral reasoning" to discern what needs imitating about the exemplar. The mimetic model Paul uses is that of a child and parent, where Paul is the spiritual father exemplifying the imitation of Christ for his converts. Hence, mimesis is a critical tool in family education in the Pauline tradition as well. It plays a key role in Paul's ethics for *all* his churches, so that his ethics is, to a degree, *mimetic* ethics.

We noted that mimesis is not uniformly present across the Pauline writings. It varies from being central to Paul's ethics in 1–2 Thessalonians, 1–2 Corinthians, and Philippians to prominent in Ephesians and peripheral in the Pastorals and other letters (Gal, Rom, Phlm, Col). The centrality and nature of mimesis in Paul's earliest letters (1–2 Thess), his middle letters (1–2 Cor), and a late letter (Phil) do not reveal any significant development of the concept of mimesis across the Pauline tradition.

Chapter 7 explored mimesis in the rest of the New Testament. While James and Revelation contained a few references to mimesis, the concept was more prevalent in Hebrews and 1 Peter. Like John and Paul, Peter also situated mimesis in the context of divine family education. We found that mimesis has a significant, but not a central, role in the ethics of Hebrews and 1 Peter.

Chapter 8 took us beyond the New Testament to the apostolic writings in the first half of the second century. The Apostolic Fathers are significant for understanding early Christianity because they are the bridge between the apostles and the next generation of early Christian leadership, and it is during this time that the concept of martyrdom as the ideal imitation of Christ emerged. While some apostolic writings contain little or no ideas of mimesis, other writings, such as 1 Clement, the Ignatian Letters, Polycarp's letter *To the Philippians*, Martyrdom of Polycarp, and the Letter to Diognetus, are more significant and reflect several aspects of the model of mimesis that we constructed from the Greco-Roman mimetic traditions. We also found evidence of influences from the Johannine and Pauline mimetic traditions that may explain the emergence of the concept of martyrdom as the ideal *imitatio Christi*.

9.2. Answering Our Primary Research Questions

We are now able to answer the four big questions that we formulated in chapter 1 and that have framed our inquiry.

Question 1: Where do the historical origins of the early Christian concept of mimesis lie?

We found that the majority of scholarship is right in claiming that the concept of mimesis originated in Greek antiquity and found its way into early Christianity (and Second Temple Judaism) through the process of Hellenization. Nevertheless, we also found that the Hebrew Bible or Christian Old Testament contained traces of the concept of mimesis, which prepared the ground for the assimilation of the Hellenistic concept of mimesis into Second Temple Jewish and early Christian literature. This is unsurprising because mimesis is fundamental to human life and hence features in all cultures and traditions. The explanation that accounts best for all the data, then, is that the Old Testament (mainly the Pentateuch) contains an implied concept of imitating God, and contact with Greek thought caused the concept to become pronounced in Judaism and early Christianity. Contra Tinsley and Hood, I contend that Boer is correct in concluding that the Old Testament only provides the "raw material" for the New Testament concept of mimesis. Hence, in terms of the origins of the early Christian concept of mimesis, there was a cross-fertilization of "latent mimetic ideas" in the Hebrew Bible and the Greco-Roman concept of mimesis.[2]

---

2. Differently, Stefaniw contends that the broad use of mimesis in Greek antiquity, linked to textuality and pedagogy, became conceptually constricted in early Christianity (read "Paul") to refer to the pedestrian notion of mimesis as the imitation of a moral exemplar, and broadened out again in late Christianity ("Disciplined Mind," 237–44). She concludes, "Mimesis [in early Christianity] is deployed as a rudimentary hortatory tool, with no link to textuality or pedagogy as in the classical [i.e., Greco-Roman] tradition. New Testament literature thus constitutes something of a conceptual bottle-neck in which mimesis is reduced to its most pedestrian conceptual form. From this it will become clear that later Christian authors, at the end of the fourth century, when Christianity found itself in a much different social position to that of Paul and his followers, did not derive their mimetic ethic so much from New Testament literature as from the classical tradition in which they had been educated" ("Disciplined Mind," 244). However, as we have shown, this is not quite accurate because the early Christian concept of mimesis is

9. Summary—the Research Findings

Continuity and Discontinuity with the Hebrew Bible. We learned in chapter 3 that the transcendence and holiness of God in the Hebrew Bible rendered it unthinkable to imitate him. We also saw how Petersen distinguishes between locative religions, which stress the gap between humans and the gods and hence do not consider the possibility of adherents becoming like gods, and utopian religions, where there is an inherent relationship between imitation of the gods and divinization of religious adherents.[3] He then notes that "Israelite religion as an example of a Near Eastern locative type of religion does not lay stress on the idea of imitation of the god."[4] In early Christianity, the idea of imitating God directly remains rare—it is only found in Matt 5:48; Luke 6:36; Eph 5:1; Col 3:13; 1 John 4:11, 17—and is developed Christologically where the imitation of God is mediated through the imitation of Jesus as the visible exemplar of the invisible God (see also section 3.1.2).[5]

We saw that early Christian authors developed instances of "embryonic" mimesis in the Hebrew Bible. With reference to the foundational holiness command in Lev 19:2, for example, we see two approaches in the New Testament. Peter quotes Lev 19:2 verbatim, and the call to holy living in 1 Pet 1:15–16 indicates a causal rather than mimetic relationship—Christians should be holy *because* (ὅτι) God is holy. In contrast, when Matthew and Luke allude to Lev 19:2, they change the causal particle (כִּי/ὅτι) to a comparative one (ὡς in Matt 5:48 and καθώς in Luke 6:36) to indicate that believers should imitate God in being impartial (so Matthew) and merciful (so Luke). More tenuously, the implicit call to mimesis in Deut 10:18–19 for Israel to love the sojourner, just as God does, combined with the command to love one's neighbor in Lev 19:18, may be the basis for the mimetic love command in John 13:34. More generally, the implicit notion of imitating some attributes of God in the Hebrew Bible (see section 3.1.3) becomes explicit in the New Testament exhortations to imitate Jesus, who visibly represents God on earth.[6]

Continuity and Discontinuity with Greco-Roman Mimesis. As in Greco-Roman antiquity, mimesis in early Christianity is almost exclusively a religious-ethical concept, operating in the overlapping areas of religion, education, and family. In God's family, mimesis is a didactic tool for the moral formation of early Christians. While the origins of early Christian mimesis lie in the Greco-Roman traditions,

---

equally broad, linked to textuality (textually mediated mimesis; see under question 4, below) and pedagogy (mimesis was a vital didactic tool).

3. Petersen, "Divine Perfection," 9–10, 25–27.
4. Petersen, "Divine Perfection," 34 (see also p. 26).
5. There is also the idea of the believer imitating both God and Jesus in John 10:14–15; 17:11, 21, 22b.
6. See also section 3.2, where Josephus, Philo, and the rabbis interpreted texts from the Hebrew Bible in terms of mimesis.

early Christians did not assimilate the Greek concept of mimesis into their ethical thinking and practices indiscriminately. They deployed mimesis as a crucial mechanism to regulate the religious-ethical life, but they also adapted it Christologically by elevating Christ as the primary example for imitation. In other words, the *imitatio Dei* is achieved through the *imitatio Jesu*.

Reinhard Feldmeier notes another important difference between the imitation of God in Greek antiquity and in Judaism and Christianity. In Stoicism and Middle Platonism, imitating God meant "the realization of the higher nature that is inherent in the human person," but in the Old Testament the goal is not "assimilation to the divine, but fellowship with God."[7] Hence, despite the influence of Greek thought, Judaism and Christianity remain close to the Old Testament idea that what is involved is a correspondence to God.[8] Likewise, Barton notes that the Judeo-Christian God is unlike both the Ancient Near Eastern and Greek gods: while the Ancient Near Eastern gods are the source of ethical obligation, they do not exemplify the behavior they require, and the Greek gods are morally inconsistent and sometimes even unethical.[9] Hence, in the Greco-Roman traditions, to imitate or assimilate to God means to realize one's inherent divine potential (see also section 2.1), whereas in the Judeo-Christian tradition, imitating God is relational, where a moral, godly life in relationship with and in proximity to a holy God is paramount.

We will mention a final instance of continuity/discontinuity between mimesis in the Greco-Roman and Judeo-Christian traditions. Meeks notes that the context of Jewish ethics is not the *polis*, as in Greek ethics, but "the people of God."[10] Hence, the orientation of early Jewish ethics is primarily covenantal (the religious-ethical life with God) rather than civic (the political-ethical life in the *polis*). However, there is also continuity in that Christian "civic" life relates to life in God's kingdom or the church. On the one hand, the covenantal context of Old Testament Israel as "the people of God" continues into the New Testament as God's renewed people centered around Christ. On the other hand, the theopolitical context of the Old Testament is somewhat spiritualized in the New Testament as the church of Christ. In essence, there is a close connection between their religious-ethical life and civic life so that early Christians were called to live well in both God's "society" (the church) and in the geopolitical societies in which the church exists; and mimesis proves to be a crucial mechanism to regulate the religious, ethical, and "political" aspects of the life of early Christians.[11]

---

7. Feldmeier, "Heavenly Father," 435.
8. Feldmeier, "Heavenly Father," 435.
9. Barton, *Ethics in Ancient Israel*, 263.
10. Meeks, *Moral World*, 65.
11. For the concept of mimesis in the political-ethical life of early Christians, see Cornelis

Question 2: What language did early Christian authors use to articulate the concept of mimesis?

When we explored early Christian literature, we realized that not every occurrence of potential mimesis indicated mimesis "beyond reasonable doubt." We, therefore, used the heuristic device of "mimetic strength" for texts that contain mimetic language and ideas, situating these on a sliding scale of the mimetic spectrum using "weak," "medium," and "strong" to indicate our confidence in the presence of mimesis in a particular text.

Examining the Synoptic Gospels and Acts, we found that the concept of mimesis barely features in Mark and sporadically in Matthew and Luke–Acts (see the table in section 4.5). While ἀκολουθεῖν, with reference to following Jesus, does not denote mimesis, in some instances the concept is evoked. The use of comparative language (e.g., καθώς, οὕτως, ὡς, and ὥσπερ) does occasionally indicate mimesis. The Synoptics and Acts thus present a "weak" to "medium" concept of mimesis.

The Johannine writings reveal an entirely different picture. Here, the mimetic language is *varied* (mimesis is expressed by eight different expressions), *widespread* (there are about forty-four occurrences of mimesis), and *distinctive* (the comparative conjunction καθώς, rather than the lexeme μιμεῖσθαι, is central to John's mimetic language) (see the table in section 5.2). Instead of using the standard mimetic language of Greek discourse (the lexeme μιμεῖσθαι), John is unique in using καθώς—either on its own or in the protasis with either the correlative καί or οὕτως in the apodosis—to communicate the concept of mimesis most often (52 percent of all mimetic occurrences in John). Nevertheless, he is familiar with the standard mimetic language (the term μιμεῖσθαι occurs in 3 John 11), and his concept of mimesis coheres with that in Greco-Roman antiquity. In sum, while his writings reveal a "strong" concept of mimesis that was familiar in his Hellenized environment, John uses non-standard language to articulate it.[12]

Bennema, "How to Live Well: Mimetic Ethics and Civic Education in Graeco-Roman Antiquity and Early Christianity," *TynBul* 74 (2023): 87–112.

12. We must also note that the genre of ancient biography lent itself to the idea of imitation (see Capes and Burridge in section 1.2). Smith, for example, notes that the title περὶ τοῦ βίου Μωυσέως indicates that Philo's *De vita Mosis* is a biography, like Plutarch's *Lives* (*Manufacture of Minds*, 104–8). Smith even contends that Isocrates's *Evagoras* is a biography/encomium (*Manufacture of Minds*, 78–80). Ancient Greco-Roman biographies had an ethical interest where the characters functioned as moral exemplars or object lessons for the moral formation of their audiences (Smith, *Manufacture of Minds*, 71; see also Capes, "Imitatio Christi," 3–7; Burridge, *Imitating Jesus*, 28–29, 73). In this case, Plutarch's *Lives*, Philo's *Lives of Abraham, Joseph, and Moses* (they are all identified as βίοι), possibly Isocrates's *Evagoras*, and the canonical Gospels (most scholars consider them βίοι) all stand in the same ethical tradition of the ancient biography.

PART 3   SYNTHESIS

The Pauline writings also show a "strong" concept of mimesis (see section 6.9.1). Besides the lexeme μιμεῖσθαι (73 percent of the New Testament occurrences occur in Paul), the Pauline mimetic language includes the nouns τύπος/τυπικῶς, some comparative constructions (καθὼς καί; καθώς/ὥσπερ ... οὕτως καί), some standalone comparative conjunctions (καθώς, ὡς, καθάπερ, ὁμοι*), and a few figurative uses of "following" (παρακολουθεῖν, στοιχεῖν τοῖς ἴχνεσιν). The Pauline concept of mimesis is not distributed evenly throughout the corpus—it is prevalent in 1–2 Thessalonians, 1–2 Corinthians, and Philippians; less so in Ephesians; and sporadic in the other letters (see the table in section 6.9.5).

Across the rest of the New Testament, James and Revelation show little evidence of the concept of mimesis, but it is more prevalent in Hebrews (the lexeme μιμεῖσθαι occurs twice and καθώς denotes mimesis once) and 1 Peter (τύπος and ὑπογραμμός each denote mimesis once, and ὡς a few times). When we get to the second century, the concept of mimesis is "medium" to "strong" in some writings by the apostolic fathers: μιμητής and ὑπόδειγμα/ὑπογραμμός feature in 1 Clement; μιμεῖσθαι, μιμητής, ἐξεμπλάριον, ὥσπερ ... οὕτως, and ὡς occur in the Ignatian corpus; μιμητής, μίμημα, and ὑπογραμμός appear in Polycarp's letter *To the Philippians*; and μιμεῖσθαι and μιμητής figure in Martyrdom of Polycarp and the Letter to Diognetus (see the table in section 8.8).

The appendix presents the range of mimetic language in early Christianity in more detail, but the following table shows a rudimentary distribution of mimetic language in the early Christian writings:

	Synoptics & Acts	John	Paul	Rest of the New Testament	Apostolic Fathers
Standard mimetic language of example and imitation	once[13]	twice[14]	frequent	occasional (in Heb and 1 Pet)	frequent
Language of "following Jesus"[15]	traces	traces	twice	once	once
Comparative language	rare	frequent	occasional[16]	rare	occasional

13. The term τύπος denotes mimesis once.
14. The verb μιμεῖσθαι occurs once and the single occurrence of ὑπόδειγμα relates to mimesis.
15. The figurative usage of "following/walking in the footsteps" in Rom 4:12; 2 Tim 3:10; 1 Pet 2:21; Mart. Pol. 22:1 denotes mimesis.
16. This is primarily restricted to the comparative conjunction καθώς.

9. Summary—the Research Findings

We conclude that the Synoptics and Acts reveal a "weak" to "medium" concept of mimesis, but John, Paul, and some Apostolic Fathers demonstrate a "strong" concept of mimesis, although they deploy different semantic domains. While Paul and the Apostolic Fathers mainly use the standard Greek mimetic language of μιμεῖσθαι and its cognates, John is unique in developing his characteristic mimetic καθώς language to express the concept. Besides, while Paul uses the term τύπος for people who model the Christian life and the Apostolic Fathers use ὑπόδειγμα/ὑπογραμμός for personal examples (e.g., 1 Clem.), John never uses the language of "example" to refer to people—ὑπόδειγμα in 13:15 refers to the example of the footwashing and the two occurrences of τύπος in 20:25 denote "scar." Nevertheless, these differences in the mimetic language should not be exaggerated. John is clearly aware of the standard Greek mimetic language (he uses μιμεῖσθαι once), and comparative language can denote mimesis in both Paul (e.g., καθώς on its own or with [οὕτως] καί) and the Apostolic Fathers (e.g., ὥσπερ ... οὕτως and ὡς in the Ignatian corpus). Besides, despite not using the language of "example," John refers to living examples (e.g., Demetrius in 3 John 12) and literary examples (the Johannine characters have mimetic value). Finally, unlike the Greco-Roman mimetic traditions, we see that early Christian literature does not use παράδειγμα but prefers ὑπόδειγμα (and ὑπογραμμός) to denote an example for imitation.

We noted in chapter 1 that in the 1960s, there was considerable interest in European scholarship regarding the relationship between "following Jesus" in the Gospels and "imitating Christ" in Paul, although no consensus was reached. While these studies asked questions that remain relevant, the quest was partially misdirected because scholars assumed that the Gospels contained no significant notion of mimesis and that "following Jesus" was the nearest equivalent. Our study has shown that following Jesus does not equate to imitating him and that mimesis does feature in the Gospels, especially John.

Question 3: Is the early Christian concept of mimesis consistent, varying, or developing—and what is its place in early Christian ethics?

Our findings show that the concept of mimesis in the early Christian traditions has several characteristics in common:

1. Mimesis in early Christianity functions as a didactic tool in the context of God's family. We saw in part 1 that mimesis in antiquity features in the spheres of religion, family, and education. Likewise, early Christian mimesis is found in the religious-ethical sphere at the intersection of family and education. In Matthew, the Sermon on the Mount describes how Christians should live in relation to their heavenly Father so that the few instances of mimesis are placed

PART 3   SYNTHESIS

within the context of the divine family. John draws a compelling familial model of mimesis where the Son imitates the Father, and Christians, as God's children, imitate the Son. Paul uses a parental model of mimesis, where he adopts the role of a spiritual parent instructing his converts toward appropriate behavior in God's household or family. The Petrine concept of imitating Christ is also linked to the familial language of God's household. Hence, for early Christians, mimesis is a crucial ethical instrument in the moral formation of God's people in the divine family.

2. Early Christian mimesis is a participatory, cognitive, creative hermeneutical process (rather than cloning or simplistic replication) that is significant or central to (much of) early Christian ethics. In selecting and associating with suitable exemplars, the imitator shares in their lives in order to study them and discern what to imitate.[17] Within the context of early Christianity, "moral reasoning" refers to thinking in line with God's character and purposes, to reason according to the beliefs, values, and norms of the divine family. It is the device of moral reasoning that enables early Christians to work out their mimetic ethics in different situations. We saw this dynamic especially in the writings of John, Paul, and some Apostolic Fathers.

3. A major reason for the scarcity of references to imitating God in the Hebrew Bible is the transcendence and holiness of God, coupled with the prohibition of creating a physical representation of the invisible God. The incarnation, however, resolves this issue, and early Christians could now "observe" God in Christ (e.g., John 1:18; 12:45; 14:9; 2 Cor 4:4; Col 1:15; 2:9; Heb 1:3). Consequently, the imitation of God in early Christianity is mediated through the imitation of Christ. Only rarely do we find a direct believer–God mimesis—in the Synoptics, Matt 5:48; Luke 6:36; in John, 1 John 4:11, 17; and in Paul, Eph 5:1; Col 3:13—and even then, there often is the implication that one imitates God by imitating Christ.[18]

4. The content of early Christian mimesis usually relates to virtues such as humility, sacrificial service, love, unity, other-regard, and forgiveness, and some of these values would have been countercultural. The early Christian mimetic model, where Christ is the supreme example for imitation, will have run counter to and subverted the mimetic ethos of Greco-Roman culture in which early Christianity

---

17. While "participation" can be conveyed by special vocabulary, such as the Pauline phrase "in Christ" (ἐν Χριστῷ) or the Johannine concept of "indwelling" (μένειν ἐν; [εἶναι] ἐν), I also use it more loosely in the sense of "involvement" or "association."

18. In John 10:14–15; 17:11, 21, 22b, there is also the idea of the believer imitating both God and Jesus.

was embedded. The Johannine footwashing, for example, is a case of status reversal where Christians, in imitation of Jesus, are to adopt a slave identity and provide loving service to one another. Harrison shows how Paul uses mimetic language to subvert civic ethics in Greco-Roman antiquity and promote the imitation of the crucified Christ as an alternative model.[19]

5. Both John and Paul recognize that the imitation of Christ should continue with the next generation of Christians. In his first letter, John creates new forms of mimesis, rooted in the example and teaching of Jesus, which expected Christians in the late first century to still be able to imitate an "absent" Christ. While Paul presents himself as an example to imitate for his new converts, he also realizes that he cannot be present with them all the time or be observed indefinitely. He, therefore, anticipates how the imitation of Christ could continue after his own death (see, for example, the Pastorals in section 6.6). Paul sometimes presents other exemplary Christians to his new converts so they can learn to imitate Christ and reach maturity or "Christlikeness." Hence, while Christ remains the fountainhead and focal point of the mimetic chain, Christians who faithfully exemplify the kind of life that the New Testament espouses can serve as models to be emulated.

6. Early Christianity is familiar with both personal and corporate mimesis that aims at becoming a better, i.e., Christlike, person or community. Nevertheless, early Christian mimesis is ultimately for the sake of others and not just a private matter. For example, John presents personal imitation, where a believer imitates Jesus in order to become like him, but this personal imitation is also for the sake of others (13:35 follows 13:34) and mediates Jesus to others. Paul stresses corporate imitation, whether it be the Thessalonian church imitating the Judean churches or his urging the Philippians collectively to imitate Christ and himself (2:12; 3:17). In sum, the moral goal of early Christian mimesis is to become part of the mimetic chain God–Christ–Paul (and mature Christians)–"young"/immature Christians, with the ideal outcome being the new Christian moving up from merely engaging in imitation to becoming an example to others.

Notwithstanding these common characteristics, we must conclude that the concept of mimesis is not homogeneous in early Christianity. To assess early Christian mimesis as a whole, we must also identify the variations and distinctions across early Christian literature. The following table shows the distribution and strength of the concept of mimesis in the various sections of early Christian literature and the place of mimesis in their ethics.

---

19. Harrison, "Imitation," 249–54. See also Eve-Marie Becker, *Paul on Humility*, trans. Wayne Coppins (Waco, TX: Baylor University Press, 2020).

PART 3   SYNTHESIS

	Synoptics & Acts	John	Paul	Rest of the New Testament	Apostolic Fathers
Distribution of mimesis	sporadic	prevalent	prevalent in most letters (1–2 Thess, 1–2 Cor, Phil, Eph); less so in the other letters	occasional in Heb and 1 Pet; rare in Jas and Rev	prevalent in some writings; none or rare in others
Strength of mimesis	weak to medium	strong	strong in most letters; medium in others	weak (Jas, Rev) to medium (Heb, 1 Pet)	medium to strong
Place of mimesis in ethics	peripheral	central	central in 1–2 Thess, 1–2 Cor, Phil; prominent in Eph; peripheral in the other letters	prominent (but not central) in Heb and 1 Pet	prominent in 1 Clem.; the Ignatian corpus; Pol. *Phil.*; Mart. Pol.; Diogn.

We note that John, Paul, and some apostolic fathers are the key authors in early Christianity who employ mimesis in their ethical discourse and practice.[20] However, while mimesis is prevalent across the Johannine writings and central to John's ethics, it varies in Paul's ethics (perhaps due to the different issues he addresses in his churches) and that of the Apostolic Fathers. We can distinguish how mimesis varies in the parts of early Christianity where it features most prominently—John, Paul, and the Apostolic Fathers.

John's mimetic ethics has the following distinct features:

- John develops a unique mimetic language centered on the comparative conjunction καθώς (see under question 2 or section 5.2).
- Besides the imitation of particular actions ("performative" mimesis), the Johannine writings contain a great deal of "existential" mimesis (36 percent of the Johannine mimetic occurrences), where the believer imitates Jesus (and God) in a particular state of being.
- Mimesis is central to John's ethics and a vital mechanism to regulate Christian behavior in the divine family.

20. Unsurprisingly, the distribution of mimetic language in the early Christian literature is also strongest in John, Paul, and the Apostolic Fathers (see the table under question 2).

9. Summary—the Research Findings

- John stresses the believer–Jesus mimesis because he views the personal example of Jesus as the main basis for imitation.[21] As Jesus imitates God, we are presented with a mimetic chain of God–Jesus–believer. Jesus thus "introduces" his followers to the concept of mimesis, something he himself practices in his relationship with God.
- Besides Jesus, the supreme example, John uses literary examples (the narrative characters in his Gospel) who function as personal examples for his audience.[22]
- Through the use of moral reasoning, John creates new forms of mimesis from Jesus's example and teaching in his first letter.

Paul's mimetic ethics has the following distinct features:

- The Pauline writings present a unique mimetic chain of Christ–Paul–believers or Christ–surrogates of Paul–believers. Apart from Phil 2:6–11, Paul rarely presents Christ as an explicit example for imitation, even though it is always implied (see 1 Cor 11:1). Instead, Paul presents himself as an example to be imitated (1 Cor 4:16; 11:1; Phil 3:17; 1 Thess 1:6; 2 Thess 3:7, 9), presumably because he considers himself a faithful imitator of Christ. While his mimetic imperative "imitate me" is not unique in antiquity, it is unusual (see section 6.1.1).
- Paul regularly holds up living examples for his converts to imitate because he had to convey Jesus's teachings to his predominantly Gentile converts who were unfamiliar with Jewish-Christian morality. Recognizing that the imitation of Christ, whom they had never met, was out of reach for them, he urged Gentile Christians to imitate him as he imitated Christ. Paul only issued such exhortations to churches he himself had founded, to believers he knew, and more importantly, to believers who knew him and had seen the example he had set for them. Paul also points his converts to worthy imitators of Christ, such as trusted coworkers and other mature believers, as living examples for his audiences to imitate.
- Pauline ethics is more varied than Johannine ethics. While mimesis is the singular device at the heart of Johannine ethics, for Paul, holiness/sanctification, the household code, virtue/vice lists, Scripture, and the Spirit play important roles in his ethics besides mimesis.

21. In 1 Peter too, Christ is the main example for imitation.
22. I explain the representative value of a broad array of Johannine characters in Bennema, *Encountering Jesus*, 366–70, but allude to the mimetic value of the Johannine characters in Bennema, *Mimesis*, 153–54; Bennema, "Virtue Ethics in the Gospel of John," 174–80; Bennema, "Virtue Ethics and the Johannine Writings," 277–78. Considering that most narrative material is present in the Gospels and Acts, we found that the mimetic value of literary characters is greater in Mark, John, and Acts but less so in Matthew and Luke.

PART 3   SYNTHESIS

The Apostolic Fathers' mimetic ethics also display some distinct features:

- The Apostolic Fathers drew frequently on the lexeme μιμεῖσθαι (eighteen times) and used the terms ὑπόδειγμα and ὑπογραμμός for personal example rather than τύπος.
- Influenced by the Johannine and Pauline mimetic traditions, some Apostolic Fathers go further and present martyrdom as the ideal imitation of Christ, thus introducing the concept of martyrological mimesis.[23]

Recognizing these distinctions, we must navigate between the Scylla of assuming that mimesis is a homogenous concept in early Christianity and the Charybdis of exaggerating the variations. First, we noted that while John develops his own mimetic language, he is aware of the standard Greek terminology because he uses the lexeme μιμεῖσθαι in 3 John 11. Conversely, Paul mainly uses the lexeme μιμεῖσθαι, but he also employs comparative language to indicate mimesis.[24] Second, Paul often presents himself as an example to imitate, whereas John never does so in his letters—nowhere does John tell his audience to "imitate me" as Paul does. Nevertheless, as Brickle notes, John's assertion "our κοινωνία is with the Father and with the Son Jesus Christ" in 1 John 1:3 implies that he modeled a Christlike life before his community.[25] Third, Paul presents a range of examples to imitate, from Christ (often implied) to himself, his coworkers, and mature Christians, while John mainly presents Jesus as the example to imitate. Nevertheless, John does occasionally refer to other living examples, such as Demetrius in 3 John 11–12, even if he does not use the term τύπος (see section 5.7.1).

In sum, although there are clear differences in the articulation of mimesis in the Johannine and Pauline traditions, I suggest that John and Paul's concepts of mimesis are situated on the same spectrum where (1) Paul uses "standard" mimetic language *more* than John; (2) Paul uses living examples *more* than John; and (3) John uses Jesus as the primary and explicit example *more* than Paul (where this is assumed). This leads us to conclude that although the early Christian traditions show variation in the concept of mimesis, we can nevertheless speak of a *unified* concept.

---

23. The concept of "martyrological mimesis" is also found in 4 Macc (see section 3.2.1).
24. For example, "just as (ὥσπερ) Christ was raised from the dead . . . so we also (οὕτως καί) might walk in newness of life" (Rom 6:4); "Therefore, accept one another, just as (καθώς) Christ also (καί) has accepted you" (Rom 15:7); "forgiving one another, just as (καθώς) God in Christ also (καί) has forgiven you" (Eph 4:32); "Husbands, love your wives, just as (καθώς) Christ also (καί) loved the church" (Eph 5:25); "just as (καθώς) Christ has forgiven you, so you also (οὕτως καί) must forgive" (Col 3:13); "to walk in the footsteps" (στοιχεῖν τοῖς ἴχνεσιν) denotes imitation (Rom 4:12).
25. Brickle, "Transacting Virtue," 346.

Question 4: How could early Christians imitate an absent Jesus or Paul—and what should they imitate about them?

Jesus and Paul were undoubtedly the most influential people in early Christianity and, hence, the primary models for imitation. Mimesis is a sensory process where someone usually observes an exemplar for imitation, which raises the issue that seems at odds with the concept: How could early Christians imitate an "absent" Jesus who had returned to heaven or an imprisoned Paul who could only write letters to his churches?[26] Did mimesis mutate from first-hand observation to second-hand instruction on what to imitate? Not necessarily. Our study has shown that the exemplar could be accessible through means other than direct observation.

In early Christianity, the primary "living examples" were Jesus, who was observed by the original disciples and eyewitnesses, and Paul, who was observed by his coworkers and converts (mimesis through observance). In the absence of Jesus and Paul, these Christians could draw on their first-hand experiences of Jesus or Paul, thus creating a "remembered" Jesus or Paul whom they could imitate (mimesis through memory recall). Another option in the absence of a primary living example is the concept of secondary living examples (mimesis through surrogates). In the absence of Christ, Paul mediated the imitation of Christ by urging his converts to imitate him. Then, in his own absence, he could send a trusted coworker, such as Timothy or Titus, to his converts or point to exemplary Christians who were accessible to them. Alternatively, living examples could become literary examples when an eyewitness preserved the living example in writing, whether that be the Evangelists recording Jesus in their Gospels or Paul presenting Jesus or himself in his letters. This meant that early Christians could reconstruct Jesus or Paul from the text they read or heard. This reconstructed Jesus or Paul can then be visualized, observed, and imitated by their audiences (mimesis through textual reconstruction).[27] Hence, the issue of imitating an absent Jesus and Paul is addressed by employing different

---

26. Jesus's "absence" refers to the spatial separation between Jesus in heaven and his followers on earth, yet he is "present" or accessible through the Spirit (see below). See also Orr's *Christ Absent and Present* where he deals with both Jesus's bodily absence and his mediated presence.

27. In section 5.7.1, we explained how John's written eyewitness testimony about Jesus enabled Johannine Christians in the late first century to imitate an "absent" Jesus. In Paul, his letters became the medium through which Pauline Christians could visualize and imitate a reconstructed Jesus or Paul. While Jesus rarely features as a literary example for imitation in Paul's letters (except for Phil 2:6–11), the imitation of Jesus is mediated through the imitation of Paul, who often presents himself as an example for imitation in his letters. In reading or hearing the letter, Paul's audience can reconstruct either the Paul whom they remembered from an earlier visit or from information in the letter itself. For example, when the Thessalonian Christians hear 1 Thess 2:1–12 being read out to them, they could recall these aspects of Paul's lifestyle when he had been with them. Likewise, Paul's willingness to be poured out to complete the Philippians'

PART 3   SYNTHESIS

modes of mimesis. Early Christians could observe and imitate (1) a "remembered" Jesus or Paul through memory recall; (2) a "modeled" Jesus in the lives of other believers; or (3) a "reconstructed" Jesus or Paul from the text or oral accounts.[28]

Looking across the various Greco-Roman, Jewish, and early Christian traditions, we have identified different modes of mimesis:

1. Direct observation: the imitator is able to observe the exemplar directly.
2. Mediated mimesis:
   a. *Mnemonic mimesis.* This is a form of mediated mimesis where a past exemplar is mediated to the present through memory, so that the imitator can reconstruct and visualize the remembered exemplar from the past.
   b. *Textually mediated mimesis.* An author can present an exemplar who is otherwise inaccessible to his audience (e.g., the exemplar is dead or absent) as a literary example to be reconstructed, visualized, and emulated.
   c. *Personally mediated mimesis.* A person can model an absent exemplar through their own life for others to imitate. Or, in one's own absence, one can suggest a surrogate exemplar who exemplifies the behavior that one seeks to model for the audience.
   d. *Orally mediated mimesis.* Based on oral reports or tradition, one can construct a mental picture of an exemplar to imitate (see section 6.9.3).

Mode of Mimesis		Greco-Roman Antiquity	Judaism	Early Christianity
Direct observation		✓	✓	✓
Mediated mimesis	Mnemonic mimesis	✓	✓	✓
	Textually mediated mimesis	✓	✓	✓
	Personally mediated mimesis			✓
	Orally mediated mimesis[29]			✓

---

sacrificial service (Phil 2:17) in imitation of Christ's being poured out into human form (Phil 2:7) could be visualized and emulated by Paul's audience.

28. We also noted earlier that narrative characters, especially in the Gospels and Acts, are a variant of textually mediated mimesis in that these have mimetic value and function as "literary examples."

29. This mode of mimesis was probably also present in Greco-Roman and Jewish antiquity.

9. Summary—the Research Findings

Having clarified that the physical absence of Jesus or Paul was not an obstacle to imitating them, we now address the issue of what exactly early Christians were expected to imitate about Jesus or Paul. Should they imitate (1) specific actions, (2) the underlying intentions or attitudes, or (3) a general mindset of moral discernment? Our findings lead us to conclude that all three options apply. At times, it is appropriate to replicate an action of Jesus, always recognizing that this must include the original intention or attitude in order to avoid mindless cloning. At other times, the mimetic act may differ from the original example while expressing the intention or attitude of the original act. As believers embrace a lifestyle of imitating Jesus, they must also align their thinking with the values and norms of God's world, that is, to develop *moral reasoning* and acquire a mindset of moral discernment. We noted that early Christians regularly applied moral reasoning: (1) John created new forms of mimesis based on Jesus's example and teachings; (2) Paul created a new mode of mimesis where he could exhort his audiences to imitate him (or surrogates of him); (3) early Christians in the second century developed a concept of martyrological mimesis from New Testament teachings. Moral reasoning drives the cognitive "engine" of mimetic ethics. In Greco-Roman antiquity and early Christianity, mimesis always had a cognitive component, and both were critical of mindless cloning or simplistic replication.

It goes without saying that there are aspects or acts of Jesus (and God) that cannot be imitated because while Jesus and God *are* the paradigm or model for human behavior, this is true *only* to the extent to which the biblical text indicates this. I contend that there can be adequate hermeneutical control in the mimetic process when we examine the mimetic language that each biblical author uses. Hence, we must "observe" and imitate only those aspects of the lives of Jesus (and Paul) that are indicated by the biblical authors. This requires determining the mimetic language used in each writing to avoid a subjective "pick and choose" approach. In this hermeneutical process, the mimetic act must embody the principle of the original act and have a recognizable resemblance or correspondence to the original act. The Spirit is given to the Christian to aid in the hermeneutical, mimetic process.

Having answered the main research questions, we will theorize about and systematize the concept of mimesis in early Christianity in the final chapter.

10

Conclusion—The Hermeneutics of Mimesis

Based on the summary of our findings in chapter 9, we will reflect further on the hermeneutical process of early Christian mimesis and its ongoing relevance today and finish by stating the key takeaways of the book.

10.1. Early Christian Mimesis as a Complex Hermeneutical Process

Having noted that mimesis in Greco-Roman antiquity and early Christianity is not about cloning or simplistic replication, I offer some reflections on our constructed model of early Christian mimesis and its complex hermeneutics. To sum up, we learned that early Christian mimesis is a complex hermeneutical process consisting of five aspects (see also sections 5.6 and 6.8):

1. *Selection and Association.* The aspiring imitator seeks an exemplary model for imitation and associates with that exemplar. In early Christianity, this meant becoming a follower of Jesus and beginning to model one's life on him.
2. *Observation.* Christians closely observe Jesus or those who exemplify a Christlike life. We noted in section 9.2 (under question 4) the different ways or modes in which they can do so.
3. *Interpretation.* By closely observing Jesus or Christlike exemplars, Christians discern what to imitate and how to avoid mindless replication.
4. *Imitation/Emulation.* Having observed and discerned what to imitate, the Christian articulates this in an appropriate mimetic act that authentically expresses the underlying attitude or motivation of the original act.
5. *Transformation.* The continual imitation of Jesus results in moral progress, with Christians gradually becoming more like Jesus.

10. Conclusion—the Hermeneutics of Mimesis

For early Christians, mimesis was a crucial mechanism for moral transformation, and their writings reveal a mimetic model similar to what we found in Greco-Roman antiquity. This is not to say that early Christians had such a systematic understanding of mimesis, nor are we seeking to impose a Greco-Roman model on early Christianity. Rather, we have inferred a model of early Christian mimesis from their writings and found that it corresponds to the common model of mimesis in Greco-Roman antiquity. Here are the various aspects of our model of early Christian mimesis.

The Selection and Use of Exemplars in Early Christian Mimesis. We saw that the Greco-Roman mimetic traditions deployed a rich catalog of exemplars, and people were encouraged to be eclectic in choosing role models. Early Christianity is *unique* in presenting Jesus as the supreme example for imitation, although mature Christians, who exemplify Christ in their lives, can also function as examples for imitation. In a way, the selection of Jesus as the chief example of moral behavior is *unusual*. Thomas Blanton notes that while the Romans made Jesus a negative example by crucifying him as a revolutionary messianic pretender, Paul caused an ideological reversal by reinterpreting Jesus's crucifixion and presenting him as a positive example for imitation.[1] This holds true across the early Christian movement. The crucified Christ, a negative example for both Jews and Gentiles, is held up as the paradigmatic example of imitation in early Christianity.

In both Greco-Roman antiquity and early Christianity, we see past/historical and present/living examples. In selecting past exemplars, Greeks and Romans drew on their own tradition for exemplary figures, preferring examples in keeping with their nationality and ethnicity. Hence, Romans preferred Roman heroes over Greek ones. Likewise, Hellenistic Jewish and early Christian authors found examples in their scriptural tradition and preferred heroes from Israel's past.[2] Paul, for example, holds up scriptural examples such as Abraham and the Israelite wilderness generation (the latter as an example to avoid), while Hebrews and 1 Clement present a whole catalog of scriptural examples. Nevertheless, in both Greco-Roman, Jewish, and early Christian traditions, living examples, especially from one's family, were preferred to historical examples. As Marcar states,

> Exemplarity was an adaptable medium. Though influenced by Greek traditions, Romans, Jews and Christians were able to deploy it for their own purposes. In

---

1. Fiore and Blanton, "Paul," 183.
2. Besides the relevant material in our chapters 2–3, see also Reed, "Construction," 191–95; Petitfils, *Mos Christianorum*, 24 (Romans favoring Roman *exempla*), 98–132 (the *exempla* of Moses in Josephus and Philo); Fiore and Blanton, "Paul," 186–89; Marcar, "Footsteps," 257–65.

sum, Greek, Latin, Jewish and Christian authors exhibit a strong preference to cite internal rather than external exempla. Such exempla were seen to carry more pedagogical, rhetorical, moral and/or political force, with the added likelihood of being better known to their audiences. Such internal exempla were effective at consolidating a sense of group identity and, concurrently, as a means of issuing moral exhortation based on group identity.[3]

Early Christians identified living examples from God's family. Paul, in particular, points to several living examples who faithfully imitate Jesus as role models for his converts, but John also uses the living example of Demetrius. The literary characters in the Gospels (esp. Mark and John) and Acts also function as examples either to be emulated or avoided. Hence, within the context of the divine family in early Christianity, Christ is the primary exemplar, but biblical heroes from the past, mature Christians in the present, and literary characters in the text could also serve as models for imitation. In sum, early Christians readily used the ideas of exemplarity and imitation that permeated Greco-Roman society to promote Christian values and behavior.

Interpretation and Imitation. Mimetic ethics in early Christianity is not about mechanically replicating certain commands or moral principles found in the New Testament but about closely observing an exemplar regarding their character, lifestyle, and conduct. In associating with and studying a suitable exemplar, the imitator "participates" in the exemplar's life. Hence, mimetic ethics is not concerned with abstract principles but with the lived-out or embodied values of exemplary people. Such mimesis requires a creative and cognitive dimension that understands the underlying attitudes and goals of the original act and can "translate" this meaning into a corresponding mimetic act. Early Christian mimesis, therefore, is both a volitional and cognitive process, in contrast to Eastman, who, based on infant development studies, argues that mimesis (in Paul) is nonvolitional and unconscious (see further section 6.9.2 and n. 9 below). Since early Christian mimesis is primarily about a faithful, creative expression of the original rather than literal replication or cloning, there is both continuity and discontinuity between the original example and the mimetic act. Arne Melberg explains how the passage of time creates both similarity and difference in mimesis. Mimesis involves both recollection or anamnesis (a movement backward in time) and repetition, that is, doing something again (a movement forward in time). Based on the principle that you cannot jump into the same river twice, any mimesis is a "new" act and, hence, a movement forward.[4]

---

3. Marcar, "Footsteps," 265.
4. Melberg, *Theories of Mimesis*, 1–6, 131–38.

10. Conclusion—the Hermeneutics of Mimesis

Mimetic Transformation and Theosis. I would like to consider the last aspect of the model of early Christian mimesis, namely transformation, a little more. Christian ethics, of which mimesis is part, flows out of identity. The Christian life begins with a change of allegiance to Jesus, the entry into God's family, and receiving a new identity (children of God). Once a person has become part of God's family, they have to learn how to live out this new identity—and this is where mimesis comes in. Much of the expected Christian behavior is modeled, rather than described, and learned by imitation. Mimesis, therefore, is a crucial didactic tool in Christian formation, and the primary context of Christian mimesis is divine family education. This is most evident in the Johannine and Pauline writings, as well as in 1 Peter. Mimesis is not simply related to behavior but also to identity because as mimesis shapes ethical behavior, one becomes like the exemplar. In short, mimesis enables Christians to become more Christlike. Therefore, with the necessary qualifications, the transformation resulting from imitating Jesus (and God) can be called theosis (see sections 5.6 and 6.8).

We can use the term "theosis" to describe this transformation because the aim of mimesis is to become *like* Jesus/God rather than become God. In the words of Hauerwas, Christians are "called upon to be *like* Jesus, not to *be* Jesus."[5] For Christians, the aim of imitating Jesus is not to become a clone but to express Jesus and his character in their lives. This will be an *authentic, creative,* and *personal exercise*: authentic because each seeks to imitate Jesus in a faithful way; creative because mimesis involves interpretation of the original act for a new context; and personal because Christ will be uniquely expressed through each individual. It is about *(re)generation*, too, because the original is reproduced in the copy—as Jesus is imitated, he "reproduces" himself in the Christian. While there is a tension between sameness and difference in the concept of mimesis (unless one understands mimesis in terms of mere copying or cloning), they can coexist. The ultimate aim of Christian mimetic ethics is not that Christians become clones of Christ but that they, in their unique way, gradually represent and become like Christ in character and conduct.[6]

---

5. Stanley Hauerwas, *The Peaceable Kingdom: A Primer in Christian Ethics* (Notre Dame: University of Notre Dame Press, 1983), 76 (original emphasis).

6. Stefaniw is partly right when she remarks, "If ethics is imitation of the divine, it is no longer about mere behaviour, as surely the divine is not subject to ethical imperatives and surely human beings cannot be required to behave as the divine behaves.... Now we are talking about ethics as ontology, about acquiring a certain ethical state through a process of assimilation" ("Disciplined Mind," 242–43). We saw that early Christian mimetic ethics involves all these aspects—imitating divine behavior, identity formation, and theosis—and while early Christianity only occasionally mentions the direct imitation of God (Matt 5:48; Luke 6:36; 1 John 4:11, 17; Eph 5:1; Col 3:13), divine behavior for imitation was primarily exemplified by Jesus.

PART 3   SYNTHESIS

Contemporary Theories of Mimesis. Our findings resonate with contemporary understandings of mimesis.[7] We saw that moral reasoning is required in the hermeneutical mimetic process, both in the Greco-Roman traditions as well as early Christianity (especially in John and Paul). Contemporary science affirms that mimesis is a complex, creative, and cognitive hermeneutical process. I mention here a selection of scholars whose contemporary studies echo this view. Christoph Wulf, for example, explains that the mimetic act is a reconstruction of the original by the imitator, thus leaving room for difference, particularity, and creativity.[8] Linda Zagzebski asserts that mimesis is not mere copying. For babies and infants, imitation is automatic, but as they mature, their moral sense develops, their imitation becomes more intentional, and they are able to discern what is deserving of imitation.[9] Based on contemporary cognitive theory, István Czachesz asserts that "imitation is accompanied by an understanding of the context and purpose of the imitated action."[10] From examining evolutionary human development, Jordan Zlatev concludes that mimesis is more complex than simply the re-enactment of the external event because it "requires grasping the purpose (intention) behind the modeled event."[11] Nico Grönum argues that fostering moral deliberation is important for behavioral change; otherwise, people are simply operating on instinct and driven by cultural schemata.[12]

According to Joachim Duyndam, imitation is a creative process, referring to the interpretation and translation of what is valuable from the exemplar's life to one's own, and must be strictly distinguished from aping, copying, or duplication.[13] He argues that ethical reasoning is required to determine what we translate or apply when imitating an exemplar's life. While ethical reasoning is based on principles, values, and virtues, these are neither available directly nor are they abstract but are embodied or expressed in the actions or behaviors of an inspiring exemplar.[14] Duyndam's description of the hermeneutical process of imitation corresponds to the mimetic model we reconstructed from Greco-Roman antiquity and is discernible in the

---

7. See also Campbell, who relates mimesis in Pauline ethics to contemporary research on mimetic learning (*Pauline Dogmatics*, 226–29, 233–35).
8. Wulf, "Mimetic Learning," 57–58.
9. Zagzebski, *Exemplarist Moral Theory*, 130, 136, 154.
10. Czachesz, "Mirror Neurons," 274.
11. Jordan Zlatev, "Mimesis: The 'Missing Link' between Signals and Symbols in Phylogeny and Ontogeny?," in *Mimesis, Sign and Language Evolution*, ed. Anneli Pajunen, Publications in General Linguistics 3 (Turku: University of Turku, 2002), 93–122, at 93–94.
12. Grönum, "Virtue Ethics," 1–6.
13. Duyndam, "Hermeneutics of Imitation," 11.
14. Duyndam, "Hermeneutics of Imitation," 9, 14, 16.

10. Conclusion—the Hermeneutics of Mimesis

early Christian traditions. His process of imitation includes (1) the inspiring appeal of the exemplar, indicating a certain kinship with the exemplar, and (2) the need to interpret the exemplar as a creative process where the imitator seeks to discern and appropriate the values that are embodied in the exemplar's concrete actions, words, and gestures. Duyndam thus considers imitation a practical form of hermeneutics—"hermeneutics-by-doing."[15] This naturally leads to the next section.

10.2. Early Christian Mimesis and Applied Hermeneutics

Extending the discussion in the previous section, we will now consider how early Christian mimesis has ongoing relevance for contemporary Christian thought and practice.[16] This section on applied hermeneutics is framed by four questions: (1) which Jesus should we imitate; (2) how can we imitate an unseen exemplar; (3) what should we imitate about Jesus; and (4) is imitation limited to the examples mentioned in the New Testament? We will address each question.

Which Jesus Should We Imitate? This question arises from scholars and Christians constructing different versions of Jesus: (1) the historical Jesus preserved in the Gospel texts (Capes); (2) a "symbolic" Jesus constructed from the text (Kille); and (3) the "contemporary" Jesus experienced today (Cockayne).[17] Arguably, options (1) and (2) merge because all we have today is a "remembered" Jesus from the past as he is preserved in the Gospel accounts and who can be constructed from the text by the modern interpreter. Hermeneutically, then, we must hold together a "constructed" Jesus from the text and a "contemporary" Jesus from personal experience. I will elaborate on this by returning to Joshua Cockayne's significant study on the hermeneutics of imitation, as mentioned in section 1.2.

In light of cognitive psychology, Cockayne explains the concept of imitating Christ as a radical transformative process that is rooted in the *contemporary* experience of Christ.[18] Cockayne's model of transformative imitation has three aspects. First, people were made in the image of God (Gen 1:27), and redemption is the process of people being restored to the image of God through Christ. This redemptive process of "becoming like Christ," or the *ordo salutis*, consists of justification, sanctification, and deification, with imitation being integral to

---

15. Duyndam, "Hermeneutics of Imitation," 14–15.
16. In section 5.7, we touched on this in relation to Johannine Christianity in the late first century, but we will now extend it to contemporary Christianity.
17. We raised this issue under question 4 in section 1.3 but did not address it in section 9.2.
18. Cockayne, "Imitation Game," 3–24.

PART 3   SYNTHESIS

the latter two stages.[19] Second, imitation has both a moral aspect (to behave like Christ) and a metaphysical aspect (to become more like Christ). If imitation is to be transformative, it needs to go beyond mere replication of behavior and include a focus on Christ's intentions.[20] Third, such transformative imitation requires an experience of Christ in the present through the indwelling Spirit so that the imitator can discern Christ's intentions and behavior.[21] The originality of Cockayne's model is the notion of mimesis as a metaphysical transformative process that is rooted in the contemporary experience of Jesus. While most scholars limit their understanding of imitation to the historical Jesus and his actions preserved in the early Christian writings, Cockayne argues that authentic imitation requires that Jesus be experienced in the present. While his theory of mimesis is built on insights from cognitive psychology, our study of early Christianity corroborates his findings. Nevertheless, while his idea of cultivating the presence of Christ so the imitator can "observe" Christ's intentions and behavior in order to imitate him is attractive, this could easily lead to uncontrolled and subjective interpretations. I contend that an authentic imitation of Jesus must correspond to the conceptual domain of imitation in the Bible. Hence, a robust model of text-centered early Christian mimesis (which Cockayne does not provide) must inform and direct contemporary expressions of imitating Christ. We will say more in a moment.

How Can We Imitate an Unseen Exemplar? We noted that the New Testament writers refer to the imitation of Jesus and Paul, though they were not present to early Christians, which presents the issue of *accessibility*. We have shown that the exemplar was accessible through means other than direct observation. The issue of how one can imitate a person who is absent arises in the Pauline letters when he exhorts his readers to imitate him though he is absent. We have the same issue with the Gospels because the exhortations to imitate Jesus would have been difficult for his followers after Jesus's ascension.[22] We must not assume that mimesis has mutated from first-hand observation to second-hand instructions on what to imitate. Early Christian literature does not address how one can imitate a person who is absent, but the Greco-Roman mimetic traditions offer valuable insights when we learn that "literary examples" could be imitated. Likewise, readers of the New Testament can "observe" Jesus's example in the text and construct a mental picture of him to imitate.

Nevertheless, we noted that "living examples" were preferred over "literary examples" in both Greco-Roman antiquity and Pauline Christianity. When Paul

19. Cockayne, "Imitation Game," 6–7.
20. Cockayne, "Imitation Game," 8–15.
21. Cockayne, "Imitation Game," 15–22.
22. In section 5.7, I discussed how Johannine Christians in the late first century could imitate an "absent" Jesus.

10. Conclusion—the Hermeneutics of Mimesis

was unable to visit his churches, he would send trusted workers such as Timothy, Titus, or Epaphroditus to model Christ for his converts. Alternatively, following his exhortation to the Philippians to become fellow imitators of him (Phil 3:17a), Paul encourages them to observe living examples accessible to them who, in his absence, can model the kind of behavior he holds out for them (Phil 3:17b). In short, rather than instructing his readers to construct a "symbolic" Paul from his letters (although Paul could remind his audience of his past example; see section 6.9.3), he instructs them to look for exemplary Christians around them and imitate them. Hence, an alternative strategy to studying a "literary" Jesus is finding living examples in the Christian community who model the absent Jesus. Just as Paul, in his role as spiritual father, models the imitation of Christ for his new converts (presumably until they can imitate Christ for themselves), mature believers can model the imitation of Christ to new believers. This corporate aspect of mimesis stresses the importance of *imitatio Christi* as a "community project" (see also Phil 2:12).

As stated earlier, we must hold together, hermeneutically, a "constructed" Jesus from the text and a "contemporary" Jesus from personal experience. The Spirit has a hermeneutical role in the life of Christians and can aid in holding these "two Jesuses" together. First, the "contemporary" Jesus can be experienced through the indwelling Spirit. In the Johannine farewell discourse, for example, as Jesus prepares his disciples for his imminent departure, he informs them that the Spirit will mediate his presence to them (14:23). For Paul, too, the indwelling Spirit is key to experiencing the divine (Rom 8:9–17; Gal 4:6–7). Second, the New Testament depicts the Spirit as an interpreter (see, e.g., John 14:26; 16:12–15), so it follows that the Spirit will aid the modern interpreter in constructing Jesus and his exemplary life from the text.[23] The expressions "walking" and "being led/guided" by the Spirit (Gal 5:16, 18, 25; Rom 8:4–5, 14) indicate that, for Paul, the Christian life must be under the direction of the Spirit. In sum, Jesus can be "present" to Christians and be a model for Christian living through the Spirit.

What Should We Imitate About Jesus? Under question 4 in section 9.2, we concluded that Christians could imitate several elements of Jesus: (1) specific actions, (2) the underlying intentions or attitudes, and (3) a general mindset of moral discernment. Just as moral reasoning powered the cognitive "engine" of mimetic ethics in early Christianity, contemporary Christians who seek to imitate Jesus must develop moral reasoning to determine what to imitate and how this will take shape in a specific situation. This prompts us to ask whether the imitation of Jesus today is limited to the examples that the New Testament provides, to which we now turn.

---

23. For a detailed explanation of the Spirit's hermeneutical role in the Johannine writings, see Bennema, "Hermeneutical Role of the Spirit," 169–88.

Is Imitating Jesus Limited to the Examples Mentioned in the New Testament? Based on our discussion in section 5.7.3, in relation to Johannine Christianity, we maintain that the answer is both "yes" and "no." "Yes" in that most Christians confess that Scripture, where the life and teachings of Jesus have been preserved, is the primary authority for Christian thought and practice. Hence, the numerous examples of imitation recorded in the New Testament, demonstrating values such as humility, love, forgiveness, unity, self-giving, and other-regard, should be adequate to inform our understanding and practice of imitating Jesus. However, the answer is also "no" because we saw John create new forms of mimesis in 1 John, based on Jesus's life and teaching, and Paul direct his new converts to the examples of mature Christians. If mimesis is a creative process in which moral reasoning guides the Christian's practice, then authentic mimesis is not limited to a fixed expression of a particular act or value.

At the same time, when contemporary Christians seek to imitate Jesus, whether a "constructed" Jesus from the text of the New Testament or Christ-like conduct that is observable in mature Christians, there must be adequate hermeneutical safeguards in place to avoid a subjective "cherry-picked" mimesis. In this regard, I suggest a twofold hermeneutical control along the lines of *text* and *Spirit*. First, we must stay within the *semantic domain* of the early Christian concept of mimesis; that is, any potential imitation of Jesus must be rooted in the mimetic language used in the New Testament to avoid imitation by loose association where no imitation is intended. Second, we should stay within the *conceptual domain* of the selected mimesis; that is, the contemporary mimetic act must bear faithful correspondence to the original example. For example, tossing money to a homeless person does not constitute an authentic mimetic act in keeping with the intended mimesis of humble, sacrificial service indicated in John 13:15, whereas sitting with them, listening, and perhaps providing them access to a shower and meal would fall within the conceptual mimetic domain of the footwashing. If Spirit-led moral reasoning is vital to the hermeneutical mimetic process (see above), then the Spirit is expected to guide the Christian in (1) discerning whether a particular text in the Bible indicates mimesis, and (2) articulating an authentic mimetic act that falls within the conceptual domain of the original act.

10.3. The Book's Takeaways

We finish by summing up (1) the study's contribution to scholarship, (2) the scope of contemporary mimesis, (3) recommendations for further study, and (4) some practical implications.

10. Conclusion—the Hermeneutics of Mimesis

Contribution to Scholarship. This first comprehensive study on the topic of mimesis as a religious-ethical concept in early Christianity makes several contributions to scholarship and Christian practice:

It has outlined the range of mimetic language of early Christianity, described the nature and workings of mimesis, and determined its place in the ethics of the various early Christian authors. For example, while Paul uses "standard" Greco-Roman mimetic terminology, John develops his own mimetic language. In addition, while mimesis plays a minor role in the Synoptics and Acts, it is central to both Johannine and Pauline ethics and important in some of the Apostolic Fathers (e.g., Ignatius, Polycarp).

It has shown that early Christian mimesis was not about literal replication or cloning but a creative, cognitive, and transformative didactic instrument that shaped the conduct and character of early Christians. In essence, it is a key religious-ethical concept in service of the moral education of early Christians.

It has situated the early Christian concept of mimesis in the broader Greco-Roman (and Jewish) environment of the first century. While there are differences in how early Christian authors understood mimesis, they did share a model of mimesis, and it resembled what we found in Greco-Roman antiquity. Just as the main spheres of Greco-Roman mimesis were religion, family, and education (i.e., the imitation of god, parent, and teacher), so the main context of early Christian mimesis is divine family education.

Finally, it has shown that early Christian authors used the mechanism of *mediated* mimesis to overcome the issue of imitating an unseen Jesus or Paul. For example, early Christians could visualize and imitate Jesus from reading or hearing the Gospel accounts. They could also imitate Paul by reading his letters or observing surrogates of Paul, such as Timothy, Titus, or other exemplary Christians. Sometimes, Paul reminds his converts of his visits to them so they can reconstruct this "remembered" Paul and imitate his way of life. Both living and literary examples could be held up for imitation.

Scope of Contemporary Mimesis. We identified three contexts in which early Christian mimesis operated and remains valid today. The *ethical context* of early Christian mimesis is virtue ethics, which was essentially the only form of ethics in Greco-Roman society (in Judaism, there was also divine command theory or deontology). Virtue ethics centers on the character of a moral agent as a driving force for ethical behavior and seeks to answer questions such as, "What is the good life?" and "How should I live it?" As a moral concept, mimetic ethics is a subset of virtue ethics because the goal of imitating an exemplary person is to become a better person and to live well. It would take further study to determine whether virtue ethics is a good heuristic framework for understanding early and contemporary Christian ethics (see below).

PART 3   SYNTHESIS

The *theological context* of early Christian mimesis is (divine) family education: (1) for John, family is a major theological category, and mimesis is the crucial mechanism that regulates Christian behavior and character; (2) Paul functions as a father who guides his spiritual children in imitating Christ; and (3) Peter provides Christians alienated from society with a new identity as part of God's people and mimesis is one mechanism that drives his family ethics. Understanding early Christian ethics as divine family education with mimesis as a key mechanism could shape contemporary Christian ethics.

The *sociopolitical context* of early Christian mimesis is "civic" education. While we noted that mimesis in Greco-Roman antiquity was often in service of civic education (to instruct people how to live well in society), we suggested that mimesis has a place in both the ethical and political life of Christians today (section 9.2 under question 1). Elsewhere, I have shown that the mechanism of personal example and imitation regulates the ethical-political life of early Christians—on how to live as good Gospel citizens in both the church and the sociopolitical milieu in which the church exists—but this needs further study.[24]

Recommendations for Further Study. Virtue ethics, deontology, and consequentialism are key approaches to contemporary normative ethics. While virtue ethics is the oldest form, originating in ancient Greek philosophy (with Plato, Aristotle), it was marginalized during the Enlightenment and only revived in the late twentieth century by scholars such as Stanley Hauerwas, Alasdair MacIntyre, Martha Nussbaum, James A. Donahue, and Linda Zagzebski.[25] In contradistinction to deontological ethics (duty to rules) and utilitarian/consequential ethics (deriving rightness or wrongness from the outcome of an action), virtue ethics emphasizes moral character and the virtues a person embodies as the grounds for defining or assessing ethical behavior. Virtue ethics seeks to answer questions such as, "What is the good life?" and "How should I live it?" Mimetic ethics belongs with virtue ethics because the goal of imitating an exemplar is to become a better person and live a good life.

Mimetic ethics has yet to surface in contemporary ethics. Joachim Duyndam notes (using his words) "the humble status of imitation in modern ethics," stating,

---

24. Bennema, "How to Live Well," 87–112.

25. See, for example, Arthur F. Holmes, *Ethics: Approaching Moral Decisions*, 2nd ed. (Downers Grove, IL: IVP Academic, 2007), 131–41; Julia Annas, "Ancient Eudaimonism and Modern Morality," in *The Cambridge Companion to Ancient Ethics*, ed. Christopher Bobonich (Cambridge: Cambridge University Press, 2017), 265–73; Rosalind Hursthouse and Glen Pettigrove, "Virtue Ethics," *The Stanford Encyclopedia of Philosophy*, ed. Edward N. Zalta and Uri Nodelman, https://plato.stanford.edu/archives/fall2023/entries/ethics-virtue; John-Stewart Gordon, "Modern Morality and Ancient Ethics," *The Internet Encyclopedia of Philosophy*, ed. James Fieser and Bradley Dowden, https://iep.utm.edu/modern-morality-ancient-ethics.

10. Conclusion—the Hermeneutics of Mimesis

"Although in the history of Western Culture, the imitation of exemplars has been both an important ethical principle and a widely extended moral practice—e.g. the exemplarily embodied virtues in Aristotelian ethics, the imitation of saints and of Christ himself in Christianity—in modern ethics, the role of exemplars seems to have been downgraded to the sole position of only instances, merely illustrating general and abstract moral rules and statements."[26] Noting the importance of mimesis in Paul and how contemporary science affirms mimetic learning, Douglas Campbell highlights the need to reclaim the centrality of mimesis: "We are learning rapidly today that imitation is an enormously powerful engine of change that bears an intimate relationship with the construction of our brains and the rest of our bodies and results in a directly relational pedagogy that many of us badly need to acknowledge and to recover."[27] Instead of developing an abstract moral philosophy, Linda Zagzebski uses exemplars to construct a comprehensive ethical theory: "I am proposing that the process of creating a highly abstract structure to simplify and justify our moral practices is rooted in one of the most important features of the pre-theoretical practices we want to explain—the practice of identifying exemplars, and in a kind of experience that most of us trust very much—the experience of admiration, shaped by narratives that are part of a common tradition."[28] Ethicists such as Zagzebski recognize the importance of exemplars for moral conduct in contemporary ethics, and I suggest that further study should contribute to restoring the role of mimetic or exemplary ethics in the quest for how to live well.

Practical Implications. The religious-ethical concept of mimesis in early Christianity centers on the imitation of Jesus, whose exemplary life and teachings have been preserved in the Bible. Many Christians hold the Bible to be authoritative for their beliefs and practice, so early Christian mimesis has ongoing relevance today. In addition, scholars have shown that the concept of mimesis has changed little from Greek antiquity to today.[29] Hence, by implication, we can situate the early Christian concept of mimesis on that trajectory and extend it to today. I mention three such extensions.

First, *authentic imitation involves creativity and applying our intellect.* As we saw, for early Christians, imitation required moral reasoning—to observe, interpret, and re-contextualize Jesus's original example. There is scope for creating

---

26. Duyndam, "Hermeneutics of Imitation," 10.
27. Campbell, *Pauline Dogmatics*, 233.
28. Zagzebski, *Exemplarist Moral Theory*, 15–16. Her mention of various ways to observe exemplars, including narration and personal experience (*Exemplarist Moral Theory*, 65–68), corresponds to our categories of literary and living examples.
29. See Gebauer and Wulf, *Mimesis*, 305, 309; Potolsky, *Mimesis*, 5.

PART 3   SYNTHESIS

new forms of imitation as long as they are rooted in the example and teaching of Jesus as recorded in Scripture.

Second, *authentic imitation mediates Jesus*. There must be a close correspondence between the Christian's imitative act and Jesus's original act so that the object or beneficiary of the Christian's imitation can experience Jesus for themselves. This would exemplify John 13:20 at the end of the footwashing episode, where Jesus says, "Whoever receives one whom I send, receives me." The idea that a person could experience Jesus through the believer's imitation may seem bizarre, but this was the testimony of those dying on the streets of Calcutta about Mother Teresa.

Third, *authentic imitation is other-oriented*. Jesus imitated the Father in order to mediate life, love, and God's revelation to humanity, and he is an exemplar for his followers to transform their character and conduct so that they become like him. A personal example is a great motivator for character formation, and while Jesus remains the primary role model, we, too, can function as role models for others. Whether as parents for our children, teachers for our students, or ministers for our congregants, we are potential role models for transformation. Ultimately, we must imitate Jesus not for our sake but for the sake of others.

Before the compilation of the New Testament, the standard for Christian living was embodied in the teachings and personal examples of Jesus and the apostles. The imitation of Jesus has not weakened over time. The combination of Scripture, where the life and teachings of Jesus have been preserved, and the divine Spirit, who mediates Jesus's presence and facilitates the interpretation of Scripture and moral reasoning, ensures that Christians today can imitate Jesus in a way similar to the eyewitnesses to Jesus's ministry or the first generation of Christians.[30] Although the New Testament articulates normative behavior, this does not mean that there is no longer a need for normative examples for imitation. We need mature Christians who can model authentic Christian behavior for younger Christians today.

---

30. Likewise, Orr states, "In the gospel and by the Spirit the believer can encounter the risen Lord Jesus and experiences the same form of glorious divine power that Paul did on the Damascus Road" (*Christ Absent and Present*, 152).

Appendix:
The Mimetic Language of Early Christianity

The following table shows the varied mimetic language of early Christianity as far as ethics is concerned. For each mimetic expression, the number of occurrences is mentioned and, in the case of non-explicit mimetic language, whether the expression indicates mimesis because this may not always be the case. For example, καθώς occurs three times in Matthew, but it does not indicate mimesis, whereas the term occurs forty-four times in the Johannine corpus, where it frequently indicates mimesis.

Mimetic Expression	Matthew	Mark	Luke–Acts	Johannine Writings	Pauline Writings	Hebrews, Catholic Writings, Revelation	Apostolic Fathers
\multicolumn{8}{c}{explicit mimetic language[1]}						
ἀντιμιμεῖσθαι							1
μιμεῖσθαι				1	2	1 (Heb)	4
μίμημα							1
μίμησις							
μιμητής					5	1 (Heb)	12
συμμιμητής					1		
\multicolumn{8}{c}{language of "example"}						
δεῖγμα						1 (Jude); no	3; no

1. The ζηλ* group (ζήλωσις, ζηλωτός, ζῆλος, ζηλῶσαι) occurs fifty times in the New Testament and Apostolic Fathers but without mimetic connotations.

APPENDIX: THE MIMETIC LANGUAGE OF EARLY CHRISTIANITY

Mimetic Expression	Matthew	Mark	Luke–Acts	Johannine Writings	Pauline Writings	Hebrews, Catholic Writings, Revelation	Apostolic Fathers
ἐξεμπλάριον							3; yes
παράδειγμα							
τύπος			3; no[2]	2; no	8; often	2; once (1 Pet)	24; rare
τυπικῶς					1; yes		
ὑποτύπωσις					2; no		
ὑπόδειγμα				1; yes		5; rare	6; yes
ὑπογραμμός						1 (1 Pet); yes	4; yes
language of "following"							
ἀκολουθεῖν	25; traces	18; traces	21; traces	19; traces	1; no	6; no	12; no
παρακολουθεῖν					1; yes		
ὀπίσω μου/ αὐτοῦ	5	5	2				
στοιχεῖν/ ἐπακολουθεῖν/ εὑρεθῆναι τοῖς ἴχνεσιν					1; yes	1 (1 Pet); yes	1; yes (Mart. Pol.)
comparative language							
καθάπερ					12; once	1; no	3; no
καθώς[3]	3; no	8; no	28; rare	44; often	88; occasional	11; once (Heb)	48; no
ὁμοι*[4]	20; once	2; no	25; once	6; occasional	11; once	36; rare	56; rare
οὕτως[5]	32; rare	10; once	48; rare	16; occasional	73; rare	28; once	172; occasional

2. While τύπος in Acts 7:44 indicates mimesis, it does not relate to ethical behavior.
3. Καθώς often occurs in combination with οὕτως or καί to create a mimetic construction.
4. The ὁμοι* group contains ὁμοιότης, ὁμοιοῦν, ὅμοιος, ὁμοίωμα, ὁμοίως, ὁμοίωσις.
5. Οὕτως occurs often in combination with καθώς or ὥσπερ to form a mimetic construction.

Appendix: The Mimetic Language of Early Christianity

Mimetic Expression	Matthew	Mark	Luke–Acts	Johannine Writings	Pauline Writings	Hebrews, Catholic Writings, Revelation	Apostolic Fathers
ὡς	40; rare	22; once	114; rare	34; no	157; once	137; rare	293; occasional
ὡσαύτως	4; no	2; no	3; no		8; no		6; no
ὡσεί	3; no	1; no	15; no		1; no	1; no	18; no
ὥσπερ	10; rare		5; no	2; yes	14; rare	5; no	39; occasional
ὡσπερεί					1; no		

379

Bibliography

Ancient Literature

Aristotle. *Nicomachean Ethics*. Translated by H. Rackham. LCL 73. Cambridge, MA: Harvard University Press, 1926.
———. *Poetics*. Translated by Stephen Halliwell. LCL 199. Cambridge, MA: Harvard University Press, 1995.
———. *Politics*. Translated by H. Rackham. LCL 264. Cambridge, MA: Harvard University Press, 1932.
Cicero. *On Duties*. Translated by Walter Miller. LCL 30. Cambridge, MA: Harvard University Press, 1913.
———. *On Old Age*. Translated by W. A. Falconer. LCL 154. Cambridge, MA: Harvard University Press, 1923.
———. *On the Orator: Books 1–2*. Translated by E. W. Sutton and H. Rackham. LCL 348. Cambridge, MA: Harvard University Press, 1942.
———. *On the Orator: Book 3*. Translated by H. Rackham. LCL 349. Cambridge, MA: Harvard University Press, 1942.
———. *Philippics 7–14*. Edited and translated by D. R. Shackleton Bailey. Revised by John T. Ramsey and Gesine Manuwald. LCL 507. Cambridge, MA: Harvard University Press, 2010.
———. *Pro Archia*. Translated by N. H. Watts. LCL 158. Cambridge, MA: Harvard University Press, 1923.
———. *Pro Murena*. Translated by C. Macdonald. LCL 324. Cambridge, MA: Harvard University Press, 1976.
———. *Pro Sestio*. Translated by R. Gardner. LCL 309. Cambridge, MA: Harvard University Press, 1958.
———. *The Verrine Orations. Volume I: Against Caecilius*. Translated by L. H. G. Greenwood. LCL 221. Cambridge, MA: Harvard University Press, 1928.

BIBLIOGRAPHY

———. *The Verrine Orations. Volume II: Against Verres, Books 3–5*. Translated by L. H. G. Greenwood. LCL 293. Cambridge, MA: Harvard University Press, 1935.

Dionysius of Halicarnassus. *Roman Antiquities*. Vol. 3. Translated by Earnest Cary. LCL 357. Cambridge, MA: Harvard University Press, 1940.

Epictetus. *Discourses, Books 1–2*. Translated by W. A. Oldfather. LCL 131. Cambridge, MA: Harvard University Press, 1925.

———. *Discourses, Books 3–4. The Encheiridion*. Translated by W. A. Oldfather. LCL 218. Cambridge, MA: Harvard University Press, 1928.

Euripides. *Helen*. Edited and translated by David Kovacs. LCL 11. Cambridge, MA: Harvard University Press, 2002.

Isocrates. *Evagoras. Letters*. Translated by La Rue Van Hook. LCL 373. Cambridge, MA: Harvard University Press, 1945.

———. *On the Peace. Areopagiticus. Against the Sophists. Antidosis. Panathenaicus*. Translated by George Norlin. LCL 229. Cambridge, MA: Harvard University Press, 1929.

———. *To Demonicus. To Nicocles. Nicocles or the Cyprians. To Philip. Archidamus*. Translated by George Norlin. LCL 209. Cambridge, MA: Harvard University Press, 1928.

Plato. *Laws*. 2 vols. Translated by R. G. Bury. LCL 187, 192. Cambridge, MA: Harvard University Press, 1926.

———. *Phaedrus*. Edited and translated by Christopher Emlyn-Jones and William Preddy. LCL 166. Cambridge, MA: Harvard University Press, 2022.

———. *Protagoras*. Translated by W. R. M. Lamb. LCL 165. Cambridge, MA: Harvard University Press, 1924.

———. *Republic*. 2 vols. Edited and translated by Christopher Emlyn-Jones and William Preddy. LCL 237, 276. Cambridge, MA: Harvard University Press, 2013.

———. *Theaetetus. Sophist*. Translated by Harold North Fowler. LCL 123. Cambridge, MA: Harvard University Press, 1921.

———. *Timaeus*. Translated by R. G. Bury. LCL 234. Cambridge, MA: Harvard University Press, 1929.

Plutarch. *Lives*. 11 vols. Translated by Bernadotte Perrin. LCL 46–47, 65, 80, 87, 98–103. Cambridge, MA: Harvard University Press, 1914–1926.

———. *Moralia. Volume I: How the Young Man Should Study Poetry. On Listening to Lectures. How to Tell a Flatterer from a Friend. How a Man May Become Aware of His Progress in Virtue*. Translated by Frank Cole Babbitt. LCL 197. Cambridge, MA: Harvard University Press, 1927.

———. *Moralia. Volume II: How to Profit by One's Enemies. Letter of Condolence to Apollonius*. Translated by Frank Cole Babbitt. LCL 222. Cambridge, MA: Harvard University Press, 1928.

---. *Moralia. Volume VI: On Being a Busybody.* Translated by W. C. Helmbold. LCL 337. Cambridge, MA: Harvard University Press, 1939.

---. *Moralia. Volume VII: On the Delays of the Divine Vengeance.* Translated by Phillip H. De Lacy and Benedict Einarson. LCL 405. Cambridge, MA: Harvard University Press, 1959.

Polybius. *The Histories.* Vols. 1, 4. Translated by W. R. Paton. Revised by F. W. Walbank and Christian Habicht. LCL 128, 159. Cambridge, MA: Harvard University Press, 2010, 2011.

Quintilian. *The Orator's Education.* Vol. 4. Edited and translated by Donald A. Russell. LCL 127. Cambridge, MA: Harvard University Press, 2002.

Seneca. *Epistles.* 3 vols. Translated by Richard M. Gummere. LCL 75–77. Cambridge, MA: Harvard University Press, 1917, 1920, 1925.

Xenophon. *Cyropaedia.* Vol. 2. Translated by Walter Miller. LCL 52. Cambridge, MA: Harvard University Press, 1914.

---. *Memorabilia.* Translated by E. C. Marchant and O. J. Todd. Revised by Jeffrey Henderson. LCL 168. Cambridge, MA: Harvard University Press, 2013.

Modern Literature

Achtemeier, Paul J. *A Commentary on First Peter.* Hermeneia. Minneapolis: Fortress, 1996.

Adam, A. K. M. "Walk This Way: Repetition, Difference, and the Imitation of Christ." *Int* 55 (2001): 19–33.

Agan, C. D. (Jimmy). "Departing from—and Recovering—Tradition: John Calvin and the Imitation of Christ." *JETS* 56 (2013): 801–14.

---. *The Imitation of Christ in the Gospel of Luke: Growing in Christlike Love for God and Neighbor.* Phillipsburg: P&R, 2014.

---. "Toward a Hermeneutic of Imitation: The Imitation of Christ in the *Didascalia Apostolorum.*" *Presb* 37 (2011): 31–48.

Allison, Dale C. *Studies in Matthew: Interpretation Past and Present.* Grand Rapids: Baker Academic, 2005.

Annas, Julia. "Ancient Eudaimonism and Modern Morality." Pages 265–80 in *The Cambridge Companion to Ancient Ethics.* Edited by Christopher Bobonich. Cambridge: Cambridge University Press, 2017.

Archee, Ray. "Æmulatio, Imitatio and Mimesis in Tertiary Education." *Procedia—Social and Behavioral Sciences* 174 (2015): 2418–24.

Arnold, Bradley. *Christ as the Telos of Life: Moral Philosophy, Athletic Imagery, and the Aim of Philippians.* WUNT 2/371. Tübingen: Mohr Siebeck, 2014.

Arnold, Clinton E. *Ephesians*. ZECNT 10. Grand Rapids: Zondervan, 2010.
Attridge, Harold W. *The Epistle to the Hebrews*. Hermeneia. Philadelphia: Fortress, 1989.
Auerbach, Eric. *Mimesis: The Representation of Reality in Western Literature*. Princeton: Princeton University Press, 1953.
Augenstein, Jörg. *Das Liebesgebot im Johannesevangelium und in den Johannesbriefen*. BWANT 134. Stuttgart: Kohlhammer, 1993.
Baban, Octavian. *On the Road Encounters in Luke–Acts: Hellenistic Mimesis and Luke's Theology of the Way*. Milton Keynes: Paternoster, 2006.
Barbarick, Clifford A. "The Pattern and the Power: The Example of Christ in 1 Peter." PhD diss., Baylor University, 2011.
———. "'You Shall Be Holy, for I Am Holy': Theosis in 1 Peter." *JTI* 9 (2015): 287–97.
Barclay, John M. G. "Conflict in Thessalonica." *CBQ* 55 (1993): 512–30.
Barrett, C. K. *The Gospel according to St John*. 2nd ed. Philadelphia: Westminster, 1978.
Barth, Markus. *Ephesians: Translation and Commentary on Chapters 4–6*. AB 34a. Garden City, NY: Doubleday, 1974.
Barton, John. *Ethics in Ancient Israel*. Oxford: Oxford University Press, 2014.
———. "Understanding Old Testament Ethics." *JSOT* 9 (1978): 44–64.
———. *Understanding Old Testament Ethics: Approaches and Explorations*. Louisville: Westminster John Knox, 2003.
Barton, Stephen. *Discipleship and Family Ties in Mark and Matthew*. SNTSMS 80. Cambridge: Cambridge University Press, 1994.
Bauckham, Richard. "Did Jesus Wash His Disciples' Feet?" Pages 191–206 in *The Testimony of the Beloved Disciple: Narrative, History, and Theology in the Gospel of John*. Grand Rapids: Baker Academic, 2007.
———. *Jesus and the Eyewitnesses: The Gospels as Eyewitness Testimony*. 2nd ed. Grand Rapids: Eerdmans, 2017.
Beck, Brian E. *Christian Character in the Gospel of Luke*. London: Epworth: 1989.
Becker, Daniel, Annalisa Fischer, and Yola Schmitz, eds. *Faking, Forging, Counterfeiting: Discredited Practices at the Margins of Mimesis*. Bielefeld: Transcript Verlag, 2018.
Becker, Eve-Marie. "Mimetische Ethik im Philipperbrief: Zu Form und Funktion paulinischer *exempla*." Pages 219–34 in *Metapher–Narratio–Mimesis–Doxologie: Begründungsformen frühchristlicher und antiker Ethik*. Edited by Ulrich Volp, Friedrich W. Horn, and Ruben Zimmermann. CNNTE 7. WUNT 356. Tübingen: Mohr Siebeck, 2016.
———. *Paul on Humility*. Translated by Wayne Coppins. Waco, TX: Baylor University Press, 2020.
Beers, Holly. *The Followers of Jesus as the "Servant": Luke's Model from Isaiah for the Disciples in Luke–Acts*. LNTS 535. New York: T&T Clark, 2015.

Belleville, Linda L. "'Imitate Me, Just as I Imitate Christ': Discipleship in the Corinthian Correspondence." Pages 120–42 in *Patterns of Discipleship in the New Testament*. Edited by Richard N. Longenecker. Grand Rapids: Eerdmans, 1996.

Bennema, Cornelis. "The Centre of Johannine Ethics." Pages 142–62 in *The Ethics of John: Retrospect and Prospects*. Edited by Jan G. van der Watt and Matthijs den Dulk. BINS 227. Leiden: Brill, 2025.

———. "Character Analysis and Miracle Stories in the Gospel of Mark." Pages 413–26 in *Hermeneutik der frühchristlichen Wundererzählungen: Historische, literarische und rezeptionsästhetische Aspekte*. Edited by Bernd Kollmann and Ruben Zimmermann. WUNT 339. Tübingen: Mohr Siebeck, 2014.

———. "Early Christian Identity Formation Amidst Conflict." *JECH* 5 (2015): 26–48.

———. "Elders. NT." Pages 586–88 in *Encyclopedia of the Bible and Its Reception*. Edited by Hans-Josef Klauck et al. Vol. 7. Berlin: de Gruyter, 2013.

———. *Encountering Jesus: Character Studies in the Gospel of John*. 2nd ed. Minneapolis: Fortress, 2014.

———. "The Ethnic Conflict in Early Christianity: An Appraisal of Bauckham's Proposal on the Antioch Crisis and the Jerusalem Council." *JETS* 56 (2013): 753–63.

———. "Gentile Characters and the Motif of Proclamation in the Gospel of Mark." Pages 215–31 in *Character Studies and the Gospel of Mark*. Edited by Matthew Ryan Hauge and Christopher W. Skinner. LNTS 483. New York: T&T Clark, 2014.

———. "The Hermeneutical Role of the Spirit in the Johannine Writings." Pages 169–88 in *The Spirit Says: Inspiration and Interpretation in Israelite, Jewish, and Early Christian Texts*. Edited by Ron Herms, Jack Levison, and Archie Wright. Ekstasis 8. Berlin: de Gruyter, 2021.

———. "How Readers Construct New Testament Characters: The Calling of Peter in the Gospels in Cognitive-Narratological Perspective." *BibInt* 29 (2021): 430–51.

———. "How to Live Well: Mimetic Ethics and Civic Education in Graeco-Roman Antiquity and Early Christianity." *TynBul* 74 (2023): 87–112.

———. "The Identity and Composition of οἱ Ἰουδαῖοι in the Gospel of John." *TynBul* 60 (2009): 239–63.

———. "Imitation in Johannine Christianity." *ExpTim* 132 (2020): 101–10.

———. "Mimesis in John 13: Cloning or Creative Articulation?" *NovT* 56 (2014): 261–74.

———. *Mimesis in the Johannine Literature: A Study in Johannine Ethics*. LNTS 498. London: T&T Clark, 2017.

———. "A Model of Johannine Ethics." *SCE* 35 (2022): 433–56.

———. "Moral Transformation through Mimesis in the Johannine Tradition." *TynBul* 69 (2018): 183–203.

———. "Paul's Paraenetic Strategy of Example and Imitation in 1–2 Thessalonians." *ETL* 98 (2022): 219–38.

———. *The Power of Saving Wisdom: An Investigation of Spirit and Wisdom in Relation to the Soteriology of the Fourth Gospel*. WUNT 2/148. Tübingen: Mohr Siebeck, 2002.

———. "The Referent of Πνεῦμα in Mark 2:8 and 8:12 in Light of Early Jewish Traditions: A Study in Markan Anthropology." *Neot* 52 (2018): 195–213.

———. "The Rich Are the Bad Guys: Lukan Characters and Wealth Ethics." Pages 95–108 in *Characters and Characterization in Luke–Acts*. Edited by Frank E. Dicken and Julia A. Snyder. LNTS 548. New York: T&T Clark, 2016.

———. "A Shared (Graeco-Roman) Model of Mimesis in John and Paul?" *JSNT* 43 (2020): 173–93.

———. *A Theory of Character in New Testament Narrative*. Minneapolis: Fortress, 2014.

———. "Virtue Ethics and the Johannine Writings." Pages 297–317 in *Johannine Ethics: The Moral World of the Gospel and Epistles of John*. Edited by Sherri Brown and Christopher W. Skinner. Minneapolis: Fortress, 2017.

———. "Virtue Ethics in the Gospel of John: The Johannine Characters as Moral Agents." Pages 167–81 in *Rediscovering John: Essays on the Fourth Gospel in Honor of Frédéric Manns*. SBFA 80. Edited by L. Daniel Chrupcała. Milan: Edizioni Terra Santa, 2013.

———. "Whose Spirit Is Eager? The Referent of Πνεῦμα in Mark 14:38 and the Intended Comparison." *ZNW* 110 (2019): 104–14.

Berding, Kenneth. "John or Paul? Who Was Polycarp's Mentor?" *TynBul* 58 (2007): 135–43.

Best, Ernest. *Disciples and Discipleship: Studies in the Gospel according to Mark*. Edinburgh: T&T Clark, 1986.

———. *Following Jesus: Discipleship in the Gospel of Mark*. JSNTSup 4. Sheffield: JSOT Press, 1981.

Betz, Hans Dieter. *Galatians*. Hermeneia. Philadelphia: Fortress, 1979.

———. *Nachfolge und Nachahmung Jesu Christi im Neuen Testament*. BHT 37. Tübingen: Mohr (Siebeck), 1967.

———. *The Sermon on the Mount: A Commentary on the Sermon on the Mount*. Hermeneia. Minneapolis: Fortress, 1995.

Black, C. Clifton. *The Disciples according to Mark: Markan Redaction in Current Debate*. JSNTSup 27. Sheffield: Sheffield Academic Press, 1989.

Bock, Darrell L. *Luke*. 2 vols. BECNT 3. Grand Rapids: Baker Academic, 1994, 1996.

Bockmuehl, Markus. *The Epistle to the Philippians*. BNTC. London: Black, 1997.

Bøe, Sverre. *Cross-Bearing in Luke*. WUNT 2/278. Tübingen: Mohr Siebeck, 2010.

Boer, Willis Peter de. *The Imitation of Paul: An Exegetical Study*. Kampen: Kok, 1962.

Böhl, Felix. "Das Rabbinische Verständnis des Handelns in der Nachahmung Gottes." *ZMR* 58 (1974): 134–41.

Bond, Helen. *The First Biography of Jesus: Genre and Meaning in Mark's Gospel.* Grand Rapids: Eerdmans, 2020.
Bonhoeffer, Dietrich. *Nachfolge.* Munich: Kaiser, 1958.
Bovon, François. *Luke 3: A Commentary on the Gospel of Luke 19:28–24:53.* Hermeneia. Minneapolis: Fortress, 2012.
Bowden, Chelsea Mina. "Isocrates' Mimetic Philosophy." MA diss., Ohio State University, 2012.
Brant, Jo-Ann A. *John.* Paideia. Grand Rapids: Baker Academic, 2011.
———. "The Place of *Mimēsis* in Paul's Thought." *SR* 22 (1993): 285–300.
Brawley, Robert L. "Jesus as the Middle Term for Relationships with God in the Fourth Gospel." Pages 121–37 in *Biblical Ethics and Application: Purview, Validity, and Relevance of Biblical Texts in Ethical Discourse.* Edited by Ruben Zimmermann and Stephan Joubert. CNNTE 9. WUNT 384. Tübingen: Mohr Siebeck, 2017.
Breytenbach, Cilliers. "The Historical Example in 1 Clement." *ZAC* 18 (2014): 22–33.
Brickle, Jeffrey E. "Transacting Virtue within a Disrupted Community: The Negotiation of Ethics in the First Epistle of John." Pages 340–49 in *Rethinking the Ethics of John: "Implicit Ethics" in the Johannine Writings.* Edited by Jan G. van der Watt and Ruben Zimmermann. CNNTE 3. WUNT 291. Tübingen: Mohr Siebeck, 2012.
Brown, Raymond E. *The Death of the Messiah: From Gethsemane to the Grave.* 2 vols. ABRL. London: Yale University Press, 1994.
———. *The Epistles of John.* AB 30. Garden City, NY: Doubleday, 1982.
———. *The Gospel according to John.* 2 vols. AB 29–29a. Garden City, NY: Doubleday, 1966, 1970.
———. "The Paraclete in the Fourth Gospel." *NTS* 13 (1966–1967): 113–32.
Bruce, F. F. *The Epistles to the Colossians, to Philemon, and to the Ephesians.* NICNT. Grand Rapids: Eerdmans, 1984.
———. *Philippians.* NIBC 11. Peabody, MA: Hendrickson, 1983.
Bryan, Steven M. "The Eschatological Temple in John 14." *BBR* 15 (2005): 187–98.
———. "Power in the Pool: The Healing of the Man at Bethesda and Jesus' Violation of the Sabbath (John 5:1–18)." *TynBul* 54 (2003): 7–22.
Bryce, Raymond. "Christ as Second Adam: Girardian Mimesis Redeemed." *New Blackfriars* 93 (2012): 358–70.
Buber, Martin. "Nachahmung Gottes." Pages 35–44 in *Schriften zum Judentum.* Edited by Michael Fishbane and Paul Mendes-Flohr. Vol. 20 of *Martin Buber Werkausgabe.* Gütersloh: Gütersloher Verlagshaus, 2018. Originally in *Der Morgen* 1 (1926): 638–47.
Bultmann, Rudolf. *The Gospel of John: A Commentary.* Translated by G. R. Beasley-Murray. Oxford: Blackwell, 1971.
———. *The Johannine Epistles.* Hermeneia. Minneapolis: Fortress, 1973.

BIBLIOGRAPHY

Buol, Justin. *Martyred for the Church: Memorializations of the Effective Deaths of Bishop Martyrs in the Second Century CE.* WUNT 2/471. Tübingen: Mohr Siebeck, 2018.

Burridge, Richard A. *Imitating Jesus: An Inclusive Approach to New Testament Ethics.* Grand Rapids: Eerdmans, 2007.

———. *What Are the Gospels? A Comparison with Graeco-Roman Biography.* 2nd ed. Grand Rapids: Eerdmans, 2004. Originally *What Are the Gospels? A Comparison with Graeco-Roman Biography.* SNTSMS 70. Cambridge: Cambridge University Press, 1992.

Buschmann, Gerd. "The Martyrdom of Polycarp." Pages 135–57 in *The Apostolic Fathers: An Introduction.* Edited by Wilhelm Pratscher. Waco, TX: Baylor University Press, 2010.

Byers, Andrew J. *Ecclesiology and Theosis in the Gospel of John.* SNTSMS 166. Cambridge: Cambridge University Press, 2017.

Byrskog, Samuel. *Jesus the Only Teacher: Didactic Authority and Transmission in Ancient Israel, Ancient Judaism and the Matthean Community.* ConBNT 24. Stockholm: Almqvist & Wiksell, 1994.

Cable, Paul S. "*Imitatio Christianorum*: The Function of Believers as Examples in Philippians." *TynBul* 67 (2016): 105–25.

Calvin, John. *The Gospel according to St John 11–21 and the First Epistle of John.* Translated by T. H. L. Parker. Edinburgh: Saint Andrew Press, 1961.

Campbell, Douglas A. *Pauline Dogmatics: The Triumph of God's Love.* Grand Rapids: Eerdmans, 2020.

Capes, David B. "*Imitatio Christi* and the Gospel Genre." *BBR* 13 (2003): 1–19.

Castelli, Elizabeth A. *Imitating Paul: A Discourse of Power.* Louisville: Westminster John Knox, 1991.

Chapman, Stephen B., and Laceye C. Warner. "Jonah and the Imitation of God: Rethinking Evangelism and the Old Testament." *JTI* 2 (2008): 43–69.

Chaze, Micheline. *L'Imitatio Dei dans le Targum et la Aggada.* Leuven: Peeters, 2005.

Chilton, Bruce. "The Eucharist and the Mimesis of Sacrifice." Pages 140–54 in *Sacrifice, Scripture, and Substitution: Readings in Ancient Judaism and Christianity.* Edited by Ann W. Astell and Sandor Goodheart. CJAS 18. Notre Dame: Notre Dame University Press, 2011.

Clarke, Andrew D. "'Be Imitators of Me': Paul's Model of Leadership." *TynBul* 49 (1998): 329–60.

———. *A Pauline Theology of Church Leadership.* LNTS 362. Edinburgh: T&T Clark, 2008.

Cobb, L. Stephanie. "Polycarp's Cup: *Imitatio* in the *Martyrdom of Polycarp.*" *JRH* 38 (2014): 224–40.

Cockayne, Joshua. "The Imitation Game: Becoming Imitators of Christ." *RS* 53 (2017): 3–24.
Collins, Raymond F. *1 & 2 Timothy and Titus: A Commentary*. NTL. Louisville: Westminster John Knox, 2002.
Collinson, Sylvia Wilkey. *Making Disciples: The Significance of Jesus' Educational Methods for Today's Church*. PTM. Milton Keynes: Paternoster, 2004.
Coloe, Mary L. *Dwelling in the Household of God: Johannine Ecclesiology and Spirituality*. Collegeville, MN: Liturgical Press, 2007.
———. "Welcome into the Household of God: The Foot Washing in John 13." *CBQ* 66 (2004): 400–415.
Copan, Victor A. "Μαθητής and Μιμητής: Exploring an Entangled Relationship." *BBR* 17 (2007): 313–23.
———. *Saint Paul as Spiritual Director: An Analysis of the Imitation of Paul with Implications and Applications to the Practice of Spiritual Direction*. Colorado Springs, CO: Paternoster, 2007.
Corbett, Edward P. J. "The Theory and Practice of Imitation in Classical Rhetoric." *College Composition and Communication* 22 (1971): 243–50.
Coulot, Claude. "Les Thessaloniciens accueillent l'évangile: Un premier bilan (1 Th 1,2–10)." *BLE* 112 (2011): 29–40.
Crouzel, Henri. "L'Imitation et la 'Suite' de Dieu et du Christ dans les Premiers Siècles Chrétiens ainsi que leurs Sources Gréco-Romaines et Hébraïques." *JAC* 21 (1978): 7–41.
Culpepper, R. Alan. "The Johannine *Hypodeigma*: A Reading of John 13." *Semeia* 53 (1991): 133–52.
Culy, Martin M. *Echoes of Friendship in the Gospel of John*. NTM 30. Sheffield: Sheffield Phoenix Press, 2010.
Czachesz, István. "From Mirror Neurons to Morality: Cognitive and Evolutionary Foundations of Early Christian Ethics." Pages 271–87 in *Metapher–Narratio–Mimesis–Doxologie: Begründungsformen frühchristlicher und antiker Ethik*. Edited by Ulrich Volp, Friedrich W. Horn and Ruben Zimmermann. CNNTE 7. WUNT 356. Tübingen: Mohr Siebeck, 2016.
Davies, Eryl W. "Walking in God's Ways: The Concept of *Imitatio Dei* in the Old Testament." Pages 99–115 in *In Search of True Wisdom: Essays in Old Testament Interpretation in Honour of Ronald E. Clements*. Edited by Edward Ball. JSOTSup 300. Sheffield: Sheffield Academic Press, 1999.
Davis, Philip G. "Christology, Discipleship, and Self-Understanding in the Gospel of Mark." Pages 101–19 in *Self-Definition and Self-Discovery in Early Christianity: A Study in Changing Horizons*. Edited by David J. Hawkin and Tom Robinson. SBEC 26. Lewiston: Edwin Mellen, 1990.

Davis, Phillip A. *The Place of Paideia in Hebrews' Moral Thought*. WUNT 2/475. Tübingen: Mohr Siebeck, 2018.

Dehandschutter, Boudewijn. "The Epistle of Polycarp." Pages 117–33 in *The Apostolic Fathers: An Introduction*. Edited by Wilhelm Pratscher. Waco, TX: Baylor University Press, 2010.

Dibelius, Martin, and Hans Conzelmann. *The Pastoral Epistles*. Hermeneia. Philadelphia: Fortress, 1972.

Dodd, Brian J. *Paul's Paradigmatic "I": Personal Example as Literary Strategy*. LNTS 177. Sheffield: Sheffield Academic Press, 1999.

———. "The Story of Christ and the Imitation of Paul in Philippians 2–3." Pages 154–61 in *Where Christology Began: Essays on Philippians 2*. Edited by Ralph P. Martin and Brian J. Dodd. Louisville: Westminster John Knox, 1998.

Donfried, Karl Paul. "The Theology of 1 Thessalonians as a Reflection of Its Purpose." Pages 119–38 in *Paul, Thessalonica, and Early Christianity*. London: T&T Clark, 2002.

Dschulnigg, Peter. *Das Markusevangelium*. THKNT 2. Stuttgart: Kohlhammer, 2007.

Duff, Tim. *Plutarch's Lives: Exploring Virtue and Vice*. Oxford: Clarendon Press, 1999.

Dunn, James D. G. *The Epistles to the Colossians and to Philemon: A Commentary on the Greek Text*. NIGTC. Grand Rapids: Eerdmans, 1996.

———. *The Epistle to the Galatians*. BNTC. London: A&C Black, 1993.

———. *The Theology of Paul the Apostle*. Grand Rapids: Eerdmans, 1998.

Dupertois, Rubén R. "Writing and Imitation: Greek Education in the Greco-Roman World." *Forum* 1 (2007): 3–29.

Dupont, Jacques. "L'Appel à Imiter Dieu en Mt 5,48 et Lc 6,36." Pages 529–50 in *Études sur les Évangiles Synoptiques*. Vol. 2. BETL 70. Leuven: Leuven University Press, 1985.

Duyndam, Joachim. "Hermeneutics of Imitation: A Philosophical Approach to Sainthood and Exemplariness." Pages 7–21 in *Saints and Role Models in Judaism and Christianity*. Edited by Marcel Poorthuis and Joshua Schwartz. JCPS 7. Leiden: Brill, 2004.

Dyer, Bryan R. *Suffering in the Face of Death: The Epistle to the Hebrews and Its Context of Situation*. LNTS 568. New York: Bloomsbury T&T Clark, 2017.

Eastman, Susan (Grove). "Imitating Christ Imitating Us: Paul's Educational Project in Philippians." Pages 427–51 in *The Word Leaps the Gap: Essays on Scripture and Theology in Honor of Richard B. Hays*. Edited by J. Ross Wagner, C. Kavin Rowe, and Katherine Grieb. Grand Rapids: Eerdmans, 2008.

———. *Paul and the Person: Reframing Paul's Anthropology*. Grand Rapids: Eerdmans, 2017.

———. "Philippians 2:6–11: Incarnation as Mimetic Participation." *JSPL* 1 (2010): 1–22.

———. *Recovering Paul's Mother Tongue: Language and Theology in Galatians*. Grand Rapids: Eerdmans, 2007.
Ehrensperger, Kathy. *Paul and the Dynamics of Power: Communication and Interaction in the Early Christ-Movement*. New York: T&T Clark, 2007.
Ellington, Dustin W. "Imitating Paul's Relationship to the Gospel: 1 Corinthians 8.1–11.1." *JSNT* 33 (2011): 303–15.
Elliott, John H. *1 Peter: A New Translation with Introduction and Commentary*. AYB 37b. New Haven, CT: Yale University Press, 2000.
Ellis, E. Earle. "Pastoral Letters." Pages 658–66 in *Dictionary of Paul and His Letters*. Edited by Gerald F. Hawthorne, Ralph P. Martin, and Daniel G. Reid. Downers Grove, IL: InterVarsity Press, 1993.
Evans, Craig A. "Judaism, Post-A.D. 70." Pages 605–11 in *Dictionary of the Later New Testament and Its Developments*. Edited by Ralph P. Martin and Peter H. Davids. Downers Grove, IL: InterVarsity Press, 1997.
Eve, Eric. *Relating the Gospels: Memory, Imitation and the Farrer Hypothesis*. LNTS 592. London: T&T Clark, 2021.
Fantham, Elaine. "Imitation and Decline: Rhetorical Theory and Practice in the First Century after Christ." *CP* 73 (1978): 102–16.
———. "Imitation and Evolution: The Discussion of Rhetorical Imitation in Cicero *De oratore* 2.87–97 and Some Related Problems of Ciceronian Theory." *CP* 73 (1978): 1–16.
Fee, Gordon D. *The First and Second Letters to the Thessalonians*. NICNT. Grand Rapids: Eerdmans, 2009.
———. *The First Epistle to the Corinthians*. Rev. ed. NICNT. Grand Rapids: Eerdmans, 2014.
———. *Paul's Letter to the Philippians*. NICNT. Grand Rapids: Eerdmans, 1995.
Feldmeier, Reinhard. "'As Your Heavenly Father Is Perfect': The God of the Bible and Commandments in the Gospel." *Int* 70 (2016): 431–44.
———. *The First Letter of Peter: A Commentary on the Greek Text*. Translated by Peter H. Davids. Waco, TX: Baylor University Press, 2008.
Fewster, Gregory P. "The Philippians 'Christ Hymn': Trends in Critical Scholarship." *CurBR* 13 (2015): 191–206.
Fiore, Benjamin. *The Function of Personal Example in the Socratic and Pastoral Epistles*. AnBib 105. Rome: Biblical Institute Press, 1986.
———. "Paul, Exemplification, and Imitation." Pages 228–57 in *Paul in the Greco-Roman World: A Handbook*. Edited by J. Paul Sampley. New York: Trinity Press International, 2003.
Fiore, Benjamin, and Thomas R. Blanton. "Paul, Exemplification, and Imitation." Pages 169–95 in *Paul in the Greco-Roman World: A Handbook*. Edited by J. Paul Sampley. London: T&T Clark, 2016.

Fitzmyer, Joseph A. *First Corinthians*. AYB 32. New Haven, CT: Yale University Press, 2008.

———. *The Gospel according to Luke: Introduction, Translation, and Notes*. 2 vols. AB 28–28a. Garden City, NY: Doubleday, 1981, 1985.

———. *Romans*. AB 33. New York: Doubleday, 1992.

Fletcher, Michelle Linda. *Reading Revelation as Pastiche: Imitating the Past*. LNTS 571. New York: Bloomsbury T&T Clark, 2017.

Fossheim, Hallvard. "Mimesis in Aristotle's Ethics." Pages 73–86 in *Making Sense of Aristotle: Essays in Poetics*. Edited by Øivind Andersen and Jon Haarberg. London: Bloomsbury Academic, 2001.

Foster, Paul. *Colossians*. BNTC. London: Bloomsbury T&T Clark, 2016.

———. "Who Wrote 2 Thessalonians? A Fresh Look at an Old Problem." *JSNT* 35 (2012): 150–75.

Foster, Robert J. *The Significance of Exemplars for the Interpretation of the Letter of James*. WUNT 2/376. Tübingen: Mohr Siebeck, 2014.

Fowl, Stephen E. "Imitation of Paul/of Christ." Pages 428–31 in *Dictionary of Paul and His Letters*. Edited by Gerald F. Hawthorne and Ralph P. Martin. Downers Grove, IL: InterVarsity Press, 1993.

———. *The Story of Christ in the Ethics of Paul: An Analysis of the Function of the Hymnic Material in the Pauline Corpus*. JSNTSup 36. Sheffield: JSOT Press, 1990.

France, R. T. *The Gospel of Matthew*. NICNT. Grand Rapids: Eerdmans, 2007.

Frey, Jörg. "Love-Relations in the Fourth Gospel: Establishing a Semantic Network." Pages 171–98 in *Repetitions and Variations in the Fourth Gospel: Style, Text, Interpretation*. Edited by G. van Belle, M. Labahn, and P. Maritz. BETL 223. Leuven: Peeters, 2009.

Friis, Martin. *Image and Imitation: Josephus' Antiquities 1–11 and Greco-Roman Historiography*. WUNT 2/472. Tübingen: Mohr Siebeck, 2018.

Furnish, Victor Paul. *The Love Command in the New Testament*. London: SCM, 1972.

———. *Theology and Ethics in Paul*. Nashville: Abingdon, 1968.

Garrels, Scott R. "Human Imitation: Historical, Philosophical, and Scientific Perspectives." Pages 1–38 in *Mimesis and Science: Empirical Research on Imitation and the Mimetic Theory of Culture and Religion*. Edited by Scott R. Garrels. East Lansing: Michigan State University Press, 2011.

Garrett, Susan R. *The Temptations of Jesus in Mark's Gospel*. Grand Rapids: Eerdmans, 1998.

Gebauer, Gunter, and Christoph Wulf. *Mimesis: Culture, Art, Society*. Berkeley: University of California Press, 1995.

Geoffrion, Timothy C. *The Rhetorical Purpose and the Political and Military Character of Philippians: A Call to Stand Firm*. Lewiston, NY: Mellen, 1993.

Gerhardsson, Birger. "Agape and Imitation of Christ." Pages 163–76 in *Jesus, the Gospels, and the Church: Essays in Honor of William R. Farmer*. Edited by E. P. Sanders. Macon, GA: Mercer University Press, 1987.

———. *Memory and Manuscript: Oral Tradition and Written Transmission in Rabbinic Judaism and Early Christianity*. Grand Rapids: Eerdmans, 1998. Originally Uppsala: Almquist & Wiksells, 1961.

Getty, Mary Ann. "The Imitation of Paul in the Letters to the Thessalonians." Pages 277–83 in *The Thessalonian Correspondence*. Edited by Raymond F. Collins. BETL 87. Leuven: Peeters, 1990.

Gill, Christopher. "The Transformation of Aristotle's Ethics in Roman Philosophy." Pages 31–52 in *The Reception of Aristotle's Ethics*. Edited by Jon Miller. Cambridge: Cambridge University Press, 2012.

Gloyn, Liz. *The Ethics of the Family in Seneca*. Cambridge: Cambridge University Press, 2017.

Gordon, John-Stewart. "Modern Morality and Ancient Ethics." *The Internet Encyclopedia of Philosophy*. Edited by James Fieser and Bradley Dowden. https://iep.utm.edu/modern-morality-ancient-ethics.

Gorman, Michael J. *Abide and Go: Missional Theosis in the Gospel of John*. Eugene, OR: Wipf and Stock, 2018.

———. *Apostle of the Crucified Lord: A Theological Introduction to Paul and His Letters*. 2nd ed. Grand Rapids: Eerdmans, 2017.

———. *Becoming the Gospel: Paul, Participation, and Mission*. Grand Rapids: Eerdmans, 2015.

———. *Participating in Christ: Explorations in Paul's Theology and Spirituality*. Grand Rapids: Baker Academic, 2019.

Green, Joel B. *The Gospel of Luke*. NICNT. Grand Rapids: Eerdmans, 1997.

Griffiths, Michael. *The Example of Jesus*. London: Hodder and Stoughton, 1985.

Grönum, Nico J. "A Return to Virtue Ethics: Virtue Ethics, Cognitive Science and Character Education." *Verbum et Ecclesia* 36.1 (2015): 1–6. http://dx.doi.org/10.4102/ve.v36i1.1413.

Gundry, Robert H. *Mark: A Commentary on His Apology for the Cross*. Grand Rapids: Eerdmans, 1993.

Halliwell, Stephen. *The Aesthetics of Mimesis: Ancient Texts and Modern Problems*. Princeton: Princeton University Press, 2002.

———. *Aristotle's Poetics*. London: Bloomsbury Academic, 1986.

Hamerton-Kelly, Robert G. "A Girardian Interpretation of Paul: Rivalry, Mimesis and Victimage in the Corinthian Correspondence." *Semeia* 33 (1985): 65–81.

Hariman, Robert. "Civic Education, Classical Imitation, and Democratic Polity."

Pages 217–34 in *Isocrates and Civic Education*. Edited by Takis Poulakos and David Depew. Austin: University of Texas Press, 2004.

Harrison, James R. "The Imitation of the 'Great Man' in Antiquity: Paul's Inversion of a Cultural Icon." Pages 213–54 in *Christian Origins and Greco-Roman Culture: Social and Literary Contexts for the New Testament*. Vol. 1 of *Early Christianity in Its Hellenistic Context*. Edited by Stanley E. Porter and Andrew W. Pitts. TENTS 9. Leiden: Brill, 2013. Repr. as pages 217–56 in James R. Harrison, *Paul and the Ancient Celebrity Circuit: The Cross and Moral Transformation*. WUNT 430. Tübingen: Mohr Siebeck, 2019.

Hartin, Patrick J. "Ethics in the Letter of James, the Gospel of Matthew, and the Didache: Their Place in Early Christian Literature." Pages 289–314 in *Matthew, James, and Didache: Three Related Documents in Their Jewish and Christian Settings*. Edited by Huub van de Sandt and Jürgen K. Zangenberg. SBL Symposium Series 45. Atlanta: Society of Biblical Literature, 2008.

Hartog, Paul Anthony. "The Christology of the *Martyrdom of Polycarp*: Martyrdom as Both Imitation of Christ and Election by Christ." *Perichoresis* 12 (2014): 137–51.

———. "*Imitatio Christi* and *Imitatio Dei*: High Christology and Ignatius of Antioch's Ethics." *Perichoresis* 17 (2019): 3–22.

———. "Johannine Ethics: An Exegetical-Theological Summary and a 'Desiderative' Extension of Mimesis." *Religions* 13 (2022): 1–18. https://doi.org/10.3390/rel13060503.

———. *Polycarp and the New Testament: The Occasion, Rhetoric, Theme, and Unity of the Epistle to the Philippians and Its Allusions to New Testament Literature*. WUNT 2/134. Tübingen: Mohr Siebeck, 2002.

Hauerwas, Stanley. *The Peaceable Kingdom: A Primer in Christian Ethics*. Notre Dame: University of Notre Dame Press, 1983.

Hauge, Matthew Ryan. "The Creation of Person in Ancient Narrative and the Gospel of Mark." Pages 63–72 in *Character Studies and the Gospel of Mark*. Edited by Christopher W. Skinner and Matthew Ryan Hauge. LNTS 483. London: Bloomsbury T&T Clark, 2014.

Hawthorne, Gerald F. "The Imitation of Christ: Discipleship in Philippians." Pages 163–79 in *Patterns of Discipleship in the New Testament*. Edited by Richard N. Longenecker. Grand Rapids: Eerdmans, 1996.

———. *Philippians*. WBC 43. Dallas: Word, 1983.

Hays, Richard B. "Christology and Ethics in Galatians: The Law of Christ." *CBQ* 49 (1987): 268–90.

———. *The Moral Vision of the New Testament: A Contemporary Introduction to New Testament Ethics*. New York: HarperCollins, 1996.

Heath, Jane M. F. "Absent Presences of Paul and Christ: *Enargeia* in 1 Thessalonians 1–3." *JSNT* 32 (2009): 3–38.

———. "Corinth, a Crucible for Byzantine Iconoclastic Debates? Viewing Paul as an Icon of Christ in 2 Cor 4,7–12." Pages 271–84 in *Religiöse Philosophie und philosophische Religion der frühen Kaiserzeit: Literaturgeschichtliche Perspektiven.* Edited by Rainer Hirsch-Luipold, Herwig Görgemanns, and Michael von Albrecht. STAC 51. Tübingen: Mohr Siebeck, 2009.

Heath, Malcolm. "Rhetoric and Pedagogy." Pages 73–83 in *The Oxford Handbook of Rhetorical Studies.* Edited by Michael J. MacDonald. Oxford: Oxford University Press, 2017.

Heil, John Paul. *The Gospel of Mark as Model for Action: A Reader-Response Commentary.* New York: Paulist Press, 1992.

Henderson, Suzanne Watts. *Christology and Discipleship in the Gospel of Mark.* SNTSMS 135. Cambridge: Cambridge University Press, 2006.

Hengel, Martin. *The Charismatic Leader and His Followers.* Translated by James C. G. Greig. Edinburgh: T&T Clark, 1981. Translation of *Nachfolge und Charisma.* BZNW 34. Berlin: de Gruyter, 1968.

Herrmann, Arnd. *Versuchung im Markusevangelium: Eine Biblisch-Hermeneutische Studie.* BWANT 197. Stuttgart: Kohlhammer, 2011.

Hill, Charles E. *From the Lost Teaching of Polycarp: Naming Irenaeus' Apostolic Presbyter and the Author of* Ad Diognetum. WUNT 186. Tübingen: Mohr Siebeck, 2006.

Holmes, Arthur F. *Ethics: Approaching Moral Decisions.* 2nd ed. Downers Grove, IL: IVP Academic, 2007.

Holmes, Michael W. *The Apostolic Fathers: Greek Texts and English Translations.* 3rd ed. Grand Rapids: Baker Academic, 2007.

Hood, Jason B. *Imitating God in Christ: Recapturing a Biblical Pattern.* Downers Grove, IL: IVP Academic, 2013.

———. "Imitation of Paul/of Christ." Pages 473–76 in *Dictionary of Paul and His Letters.* Edited by Scot McKnight, Lynn Cohick, and Nijay Gupta. 2nd ed. Downers Grove, IL: InterVarsity Press, 2023.

Hooker, Morna D. *The Gospel according to Saint Mark.* BNTC 2. London: A&C Black, 1991.

Hörcher, Ferenc. "Dramatic Mimesis and Civic Education in Aristotle, Cicero and Renaissance Humanism." *Aisthesis* 10 (2017): 87–96.

Horn, Friedrich W. "Mimetische Ethik im Neuen Testament." Pages 195–204 in *Metapher–Narratio–Mimesis–Doxologie: Begründungsformen frühchristlicher und antiker Ethik.* Edited by Ulrich Volp, Friedrich W. Horn, and Ruben Zimmermann. CNNTE 7. WUNT 356. Tübingen: Mohr Siebeck, 2016.

Horrell, David G. *Solidarity and Difference: A Contemporary Reading of Paul's Ethics.* 2nd ed. London: Bloomsbury T&T Clark, 2016.

Horst, William. "The Secret Plan of God and the Imitation of God: Neglected Dimensions of Christian Differentiation in *Ad Diognetum.*" *JECS* 27 (2019): 161–83.

Houlden, J. Leslie. *Ethics in the New Testament.* Harmondsworth: Penguin, 1973.

Houston, Walter J. "The Character of YHWH and the Ethics of the Old Testament: Is *Imitatio Dei* Appropriate?" *JTS* 58 (2007): 1–25.

Hursthouse, Rosalind, and Glen Pettigrove. "Virtue Ethics." *The Stanford Encyclopedia of Philosophy.* Edited by Edward N. Zalta and Uri Nodelman. https://plato.stanford.edu/archives/fall2023/entries/ethics-virtue.

Hurtado, Larry W. "Following Jesus in the Gospel of Mark—and Beyond." Pages 9–29 in *Patterns of Discipleship in the New Testament.* Edited by Richard N. Longenecker. Grand Rapids: Eerdmans, 1996.

Hwang, Jin Ki. Mimesis *and Apostolic* Parousia *in 1 Corinthians 4 and 5: An Apologetic-Mimetic Interpretation.* Lewiston, NY: Mellen, 2010.

Iverson, Kelly R. *Gentiles in the Gospel of Mark: "Even the Dogs Under the Table Eat the Children's Crumbs."* LNTS 339. London: T&T Clark, 2007.

Jedan, Christoph. "Metaphors of Closeness: Reflections on *Homoiōsis Theōi* in Ancient Philosophy and Beyond." *Numen* 60 (2013): 54–70.

Jefford, Clayton N. *The Epistle to Diognetus (with the Fragment of Quadratus): Introduction, Text, and Commentary.* Oxford: Oxford University Press, 2013.

———. *Reading the Apostolic Fathers.* 2nd ed. Grand Rapids: Baker Academic, 2012.

Jenks, R. Gregory. *Paul and His Mortality: Imitating Christ in the Face of Death.* BBRSup 12. Winona Lake, IN: Eisenbrauns, 2015.

Jensen, Michael. "Imitating Paul, Imitating Christ: How Does Imitation Work as a Moral Concept?" *Churchman* 124 (2010): 17–36.

Johnson, Luke Timothy. *The First and Second Letters to Timothy.* AB 35a. New York: Doubleday, 2001.

Joosten, Jan. *People and Land in the Holiness Code: An Exegetical Study of the Ideational Framework of the Law in Leviticus 17–26.* VTSup 67. Leiden: Brill, 1996.

Kaell, Hillary. "Under the Law of God: Mimesis and Mimetic Discipleship among Jewish-Affinity Christians." *JRAI* 22 (2016): 496–515.

Karakolis, Christos. "Personal Relationship as a Prerequisite for Moral Imitation according to the Apostle Paul." Pages 9–18 in *Personhood in the Byzantine Christian Tradition: Early, Medieval, and Modern Perspectives.* Edited by Alexis Torrance and Symeon Paschalidis. London: Routledge, 2018.

Karrer, Martin. *Der Brief an die Hebräer.* ÖTK 20/2. Gütersloh: Gütersloher Verlagshaus, 2008.

Käsemann, Ernst. "Kritische Analyse von Phil 2,5–11." Pages 51–95 in *Exegetische Versuche und Beginnungen I*. Göttingen: Vandenhoeck & Ruprecht, 1960.

Keener, Craig S. *The Gospel of John: A Commentary*. Peabody, MA: Hendrickson, 2003.

Kennedy, George A. *Classical Rhetoric and Its Christian and Secular Tradition from Ancient to Modern Times*. London: Croom Helm, 1980.

Kennedy, George A., trans. *Progymnasmata: Greek Textbooks of Prose Composition and Rhetoric*. WRGW 10. Leiden: Brill, 2003.

Kierkegaard, Søren. *Practice in Christianity*. Kierkegaard's Writings 20. Translated by Howard V. Hong and Edna H. Hong. Princeton: Princeton University Press, 1991.

Kille, D. Andrew. "Imitating Christ: Jesus as Model in Cognitive Learning Theory." Pages 251–63 in *Text and Community: Essays in Memory of Bruce M. Metzger*. Edited by J. Harold Ellens. NTM 19. Sheffield: Sheffield Phoenix Press, 2007.

Kim, Seyoon. "*Imitatio Christi* (1 Corinthians 11:1): How Paul Imitates Jesus Christ in Dealing with Idol Food (1 Corinthians 8–10)." *BBR* 13 (2003): 193–226.

Kim, Yung Suk. "'Imitators' (*Mimetai*) in 1 Cor 4:16 and 11:1: A New Reading of Threefold Embodiment." *HBT* 33 (2011): 147–70.

Kistemaker, Simon J. *Exposition of the Epistles of Peter and of the Epistle of Jude*. NTC. Welwyn: Evangelical Press, 1987.

Kittel, Gerhard. "ἀκολουθέω, κτλ." *TDNT* 1:210–16.

Koester, Craig R. *Hebrews: A New Translation with Introduction and Commentary*. AB 36. New York: Doubleday, 2001.

Kooten, George H. van. *Paul's Anthropology in Context: The Image of God, Assimilation to God, and Tripartite Man in Ancient Judaism, Ancient Philosophy and Early Christianity*. WUNT 232. Tübingen: Mohr Siebeck, 2008.

Kurz, William S. "Kenotic Imitation of Paul and of Christ in Philippians 2 and 3." Pages 103–26 in *Discipleship in the New Testament*. Edited by Fernando F. Segovia. Philadelphia: Fortress, 1985.

———. "Narrative Models for Imitation in Luke–Acts." Pages 171–89 in *Greeks, Romans, and Christians: Essays in Honor of Abraham J. Malherbe*. Edited by David L. Balch, Everett Ferguson, and Wayne A. Meeks. Minneapolis: Augsburg Fortress, 1990.

Kwon, Soon-Gu. *Christ as Example: The Imitatio Christi Motive in Biblical and Christian Ethics*. Uppsala Studies in Social Ethics 21. Uppsala: Uppsala University Press, 1998.

La Bua, Giuseppe. *Cicero and Roman Education: The Reception of the Speeches and Ancient Scholarship*. Cambridge: Cambridge University Press, 2019.

Labahn, Michael. "'It's Only Love'—Is That All? Limits and Potentials of Johannine 'Ethic'—A Critical Evaluation of Research." Pages 3–43 in *Rethinking the Ethics* of John: "Implicit Ethics" in the Johannine Writings. Edited by Jan G. van der Watt and Ruben Zimmermann. CNNTE 3. WUNT 291. Tübingen: Mohr Siebeck, 2012.

Labahn, Michael, and Martin Meiser, eds. *Ethics in the Gospel of Mark*. WUNT. Tübingen: Mohr Siebeck, 2025.

Lamb, Gregory E. "Saint Peter as '*Sympresbyteros*': Mimetic Desire, Discipleship, and Education." *Christian Education Journal* 15 (2018): 189–207.

Lambrecht, Jan. "Paul as Example: A Study of 1 Corinthians 4,6–21." Pages 43–62 in *Collected Studies in Pauline Literature and on The Book of Revelation*. AnBib 147. Rome: Pontificio Instituto Biblico, 2001.

Landolt, Jean-François. "'Be Imitators of Me, Brothers and Sisters' (Philippians 3.17): Paul as an Exemplary Figure in the Pauline Corpus and the Acts of the Apostles." Pages 290–317 in *Paul and the Heritage of Israel: Paul's Claim upon Israel's Legacy in Luke and Acts in the Light of the Pauline Letters*. Edited by David P. Moessner et al. Translated by Michael D. Thomas, Eric Gilchrest, and Timothy Brookins. London: T&T Clark, 2012. Translation of "'Soyez mes imitateurs, frères' (Ph 3,17): Paul comme figure exemplaire dans le corpus paulinien et les Actes des apôtres." Pages 261–94 in *Reception of Paulinism in Acts/Reception du paulinisme dans les Actes des apôtres*. Edited by Daniel Marguerat. BETL 229. Leuven: Peeters, 2009.

Langlands, Rebecca. *Exemplary Ethics in Ancient Rome*. Cambridge: Cambridge University Press, 2018.

Lappenga, Benjamin J. *Paul's Language of Ζῆλος: Monosemy and the Rhetoric of Identity and Practice*. BINS 137. Leiden: Brill, 2016.

Larsson, Edvin. *Christus als Vorbild: Eine Untersuchung zu den paulinischen Tauf- und Eikontexten*. ASNU 23. Lund-Uppsala: Gleerup, 1962.

Laurance, John D. "The Eucharist as the Imitation of Christ." *TS* 47 (1986): 286–96.

Lazure, Noël. *Les Valeurs Morales de la Théologie Johannique*. Paris: Gabalda, 1965.

Lee, Jae Hyun. "'Think' and 'Do' Like the Role Models: Paul's Teaching on the Christian Life in Philippians." Pages 625–43 in *The Language and Literature of the New Testament*. Edited by Lois Fuller Dow, Craig A. Evans, and Andrew W. Pitts. BINS 150. Leiden: Brill, 2017.

Légasse, Simon. "Paul et les Juifs d'après 1 Thessaloniciens 2,13–16." *RB* 104 (1997): 572–91.

Léon-Dufour, Xavier. *Lecture de l'Évangile selon Jean*. 3 vols. Paris: Seuil, 1988, 1990, 1993.

Le Roux, Elritia. *Ethics in 1 Peter: The* Imitatio Christi *and the Ethics of Suffering in 1 Peter and the Gospel of Mark—a Comparative Study*. Eugene, OR: Wipf and Stock, 2018.

Lészai, Lehel. *Discipleship in the Synoptics*. Cluj: Presa Universitară Clujeană, 2017.

Leung, Mavis M. "Ethics and *Imitatio Christi* in 1 John: A Jewish Perspective." *TynBul* 69 (2018): 111–31.

Levine, Baruch A. *The JPS Torah Commentary: Leviticus.* Philadelphia: Jewish Publication Society, 1989.

Lévy, Carlos. "Philo's Ethics." Pages 146–71 in *The Cambridge Companion to Philo.* Edited by Adam Kamesar. Cambridge: Cambridge University Press, 2009.

Lieu, Judith M. *I, II & III John: A Commentary.* Louisville: Westminster John Knox, 2008.

Lindars, Barnabas. "Imitation of God and Imitation of Christ." *Theology* 76 (1973): 394–402.

Lindemann, Andreas. *Die Clemensbriefe.* HNT 17. Tübingen: Mohr Siebeck, 1992.

Löhr, Hermut. "The Epistles of Ignatius of Antioch." Pages 91–115 in *The Apostolic Fathers: An Introduction.* Edited by Wilhelm Pratscher. Waco, TX: Baylor University Press, 2010.

Longenecker, Richard N. *The Epistle to the Romans: A Commentary on the Greek Text.* Grand Rapids: Eerdmans, 2016.

Longenecker, Richard N., ed. *Patterns of Discipleship in the New Testament.* Grand Rapids: Eerdmans, 1996.

Lookadoo, Jonathon. "Categories, Relationships and Imitation in the Household Codes of 1 Clement, Ignatius and Polycarp: A Comparison with Household Codes in the Pauline Corpus." *Neot* 53 (2019): 31–52.

Lücking, Stefan. *Mimesis der Verachteten: Eine Studie zur Erzählweise von Mk 14,1–11.* SBS 152. Stuttgart: Katholisches Bibelwerk, 1992.

Lund, Glen. "The Joys and Dangers of Ethics in John's Gospel." Pages 264–89 in *Rethinking the Ethics of John: "Implicit Ethics" in the Johannine Writings.* Edited by Jan G. van der Watt and Ruben Zimmermann. CNNTE 3. WUNT 291. Tübingen: Mohr Siebeck, 2012.

Luz, Ulrich. *Matthew 1–7: A Commentary.* Hermeneia. Minneapolis: Fortress, 2007.

———. *The Theology of the Gospel of Matthew.* Cambridge: Cambridge University Press, 1995.

Macaskill, Grant. *Union with Christ in the New Testament.* Oxford: Oxford University Press, 2013.

MacDonald, Dennis Ronald. "Imitation." Pages 407–10 in *Oxford Encyclopedia of Bible and Ethics.* Edited by Robert L. Brawley. Oxford: Oxford University Press, 2014.

———. "Imitations of Greek Epic in the Gospels." Pages 372–84 in *The Historical Jesus in Context.* Edited by Amy-Jill Levine, Dale C. Allison, and John Dominic Crossan. Princeton: Princeton University Press, 2006.

MacDonald, Dennis Ronald, ed. *Mimesis and Intertextuality in Antiquity and Christianity.* Harrisburg, PA: Trinity Press International, 2001.

Malbon, Elizabeth Struthers. *In the Company of Jesus: Characters in Mark's Gospel.* Louisville: Westminster John Knox, 2000.

Malherbe, Abraham J. *The Cynic Epistles: A Study Edition.* SBLSBS 12. Missoula, MT: Scholars Press, 1977.

———. "Exhortation in First Thessalonians." *NovT* 25 (1983): 238–56.
———. *The Letters to the Thessalonians*. AB 32b. New York: Doubleday, 2000.
———. *Moral Exhortation: A Greco-Roman Sourcebook*. Library of Early Christianity 4. Philadelphia: Westminster, 1986.
Malina, Bruce J. *The New Testament World: Insights from Cultural Anthropology*. 3rd ed. Louisville: Westminster John Knox, 2001.
Malina, Bruce J., and Richard L. Rohrbaugh. *Social-Science Commentary on the Gospel of John*. Minneapolis: Fortress, 1998.
Marcar, Katie. "Following in the Footsteps: Exemplarity, Ethnicity and Ethics in 1 Peter." *NTS* 68 (2022): 253–73.
Marchal, Joseph A. *Hierarchy, Unity, and Imitation: A Feminist Rhetorical Analysis of Power Dynamics in Paul's Letter to the Philippians*. SBLAB 24. Atlanta: Society of Biblical Literature, 2006.
Marcus, Joel. *Mark 1–8*. AB 27. New York: Doubleday, 2000.
———. *Mark 8–16*. AYB 27a. New Haven, CT: Yale University Press, 2009.
Marguarat, Daniel. *Paul in Acts and Paul in His Letters*. WUNT 310. Tübingen: Mohr Siebeck, 2013.
Marmorstein, Arthur. "The Imitation of God (*Imitatio Dei*) in the Haggadah." Pages 106–21 in A. Marmorstein, *Studies in Jewish Theology*. Edited by J. Rabbinowitz and M. S. Lew. New York: Oxford University Press, 1950.
Marshall, Christopher D. *Faith as a Theme in Mark's Narrative*. SNTSMS 64. Cambridge: Cambridge University Press, 1989.
Marshall, I. Howard. *The Epistles of John*. NICNT. Grand Rapids: Eerdmans, 1978.
Martin, Michael. "'Example' and 'Imitation' in the Thessalonians Correspondence." *SwJT* 42 (1999): 39–49.
Martin, Ralph P. *A Hymn of Christ: Philippians 2:5–11 in Recent Interpretation and in the Setting of Early Christian Worship*. 3rd ed. Downers Grove, IL: InterVarsity Press, 1997.
———. *Philippians*. TNTC 11. Leicester: Inter-Varsity Press, 1987.
Martyn, J. Louis. *Galatians*. AB 33a. New York: Doubleday, 1997.
Matera, Frank J. *New Testament Ethics: The Legacies of Jesus and Paul*. Louisville: Westminster John Knox, 1996.
Mathew, Bincy. *The Johannine Footwashing as the Perfect Sign of Love: An Exegetical Study of John 13:1–20*. WUNT 2/464. Tübingen: Mohr Siebeck, 2018.
Mayer, Roland G. "Roman Historical *Exempla* in Seneca." Pages 299–315 in *Seneca: Oxford Readings in Classical Studies*. Edited by John G. Fitch. Oxford: Oxford University Press, 2008.
McAdon, Brad. *Rhetorical Mimesis and the Mitigation of Early Christian Conflicts: Examining the Influence That Greco-Roman Mimesis May Have in the Composition of Matthew, Luke, and Acts*. Eugene, OR: Wipf and Stock, 2018.

McGrath, Alister. "In What Way Can Jesus Be a Moral Example for Christians?" *JETS* 34 (1991): 289–98.

McNeel, Jennifer Houston. *Paul as Infant and Nursing Mother: Metaphor, Rhetoric, and Identity in 1 Thessalonians 2:5–8*. SBLECL 12. Atlanta: SBL Press, 2014.

Meeks, Wayne A. "The Man from Heaven in Paul's Letter to the Philippians." Pages 329–36 in *The Future of Early Christianity: Essays in Honor of Helmut Koester*. Edited by Birger A. Pearson et al. Minneapolis: Fortress, 1991.

———. *The Moral World of the First Christians*. Library of Early Christianity 6. Philadelphia: Westminster, 1986.

Melberg, Arne. *Theories of Mimesis*. Literature, Culture, Theory 12. Cambridge: Cambridge University Press, 1995.

Méndez, Hugo. "Did the Johannine Community Exist?" *JSNT* 42 (2020): 350–74.

Merk, Otto. "Nachahmung Christi: Zu ethischen Perspektiven in der paulinischen Theologie." Pages 302–36 in *Wissenschaftsgeschichte und Exegese: Gesammelte Aufsätze zum 65. Geburtstag*. Edited by Roland Gebauer, Martin Karrer, and Martin Meiser. BZNW 95. Berlin: de Gruyter, 1998.

Merwe, Dirk G. van der. "*Imitatio Christi* in the Fourth Gospel." *Verbum et Ecclesia* 22 (2001): 131–48.

Metzger, Bruce M. *A Textual Commentary on the Greek New Testament*. 2nd ed. Stuttgart: Deutsche Bibelgesellschaft, 1994.

Meyer, Esias E. "The Dark Side of the *Imitatio Dei*: Why Imitating the God of the Holiness Code Is Not Always a Good Thing." *OTE* 22 (2009): 373–83.

Michaelis, Wilhelm. "μιμέομαι, μιμητής, συμμιμητής." *TDNT* 4:659–74.

Michaels, J. Ramsey. *The Gospel of John*. NICNT. Grand Rapids: Eerdmans, 2010.

Middleton, Paul. *Radical Martyrdom and Cosmic Conflict in Early Christianity*. LNTS 307. London: T&T Clark, 2006.

Mielke, Charles Theodore. "Christian Love and the Imitation of Christ in the *Epistle to Diognetus*: A Second-Century Example of Christian Discipleship." D.Ed. diss., Southern Baptist Theological Seminary, 2017.

Milchner, Hans Jürgen. *Nachfolge Jesu und Imitatio Christi: die theologische Entfaltung der Nachfolgethematik seit den Anfängen der Christenheit bis in die Zeit der devotio moderna—unter besonderer Berücksichtigung religionspädagogischer Ansätze*. RKK 11. Münster: LIT, 2004.

Milgrom, Jacob. *Leviticus 17–22*. AB 3a. Garden City, NY: Doubleday, 2000.

Mills, Kathleen Elizabeth. *The Kinship of Jesus: Christology and Discipleship in the Gospel of Mark*. Eugene, OR: Wipf and Stock, 2016.

Mittleman, Alan L. *A Short History of Jewish Ethics: Conduct and Character in the Context of Covenant*. Chichester: Wiley-Blackwell, 2012.

Moessner, David P. "'The Christ Must Suffer': New Light on the Jesus–Peter, Stephen, Paul Parallels in Luke–Acts." *NovT* 28 (1986): 220–56.

Moloney, Francis J. *The Gospel of Mark: A Commentary*. Peabody, MA: Hendrickson, 2002.

———. "A Sacramental Reading of John 13:1–38." *CBQ* 53 (1991): 237–56.

Moo, Douglas J. *The Letters to the Colossians and to Philemon*. Grand Rapids: Eerdmans, 2008.

Morgan, Teresa. *Popular Morality in the Early Roman Empire*. Cambridge: Cambridge University Press, 2007.

Moss, Candida R. *The Myth of Persecution: How Early Christians Invented a Story of Martyrdom*. New York: HarperOne, 2013.

———. *The Other Christs: Imitating Jesus in Ancient Christian Ideologies of Martyrdom*. Oxford: Oxford University Press, 2010.

Mosser, Carl. "Rahab Outside the Camp." Pages 383–404 in *The Epistle to the Hebrews and Christian Theology*. Edited by Richard Bauckham et al. Grand Rapids: Eerdmans, 2009.

Motia, Michael. "Three Ways to Imitate Paul in Late Antiquity: Ekstasis, Ekphrasis, Epektasis." *HTR* 114 (2021): 96–117.

Mounce, William D. *Pastoral Epistles*. WBC 46. Nashville: Nelson, 2000.

Naiweld, Ron. "Mastering the Disciple: Mimesis in the Master–Disciples Relationships of Rabbinic Literature." Pages 257–70 in *Metapher–Narratio–Mimesis–Doxologie: Begründungsformen frühchristlicher und antiker Ethik*. Edited by Ulrich Volp, Friedrich W. Horn, and Ruben Zimmermann. CNNTE 7. WUNT 356. Tübingen: Mohr Siebeck, 2016.

Nelson, Peter K. *Leadership and Discipleship: A Study of Luke 22:24–30*. SBLDS 138. Atlanta: Scholars Press, 1994.

Neyrey, Jerome H. *The Gospel of John*. NCBC. Cambridge: Cambridge University Press, 2007.

Nicolet, Philippe. "Le Concept d'imitation de l'apôtre dans la correspondance paulinienne." Pages 393–415 in *Paul, une théologie en construction*. Edited by Andreas Dettwiler, Jean-Daniel Kaestli, and Daniel Marguerat. Le Monde de la Bible 51. Geneva: Labor et Fides, 2004.

Nielsen, Jesper Tang. "The Narrative Structures of Glory and Glorification in the Fourth Gospel." *NTS* 56 (2010): 343–66.

Niemand, Christoph. *Die Fusswaschungserzählung des Johannesevangeliums: Untersuchungen zu ihrer Entstehung und Überlieferung im Christentum*. SA 114. Rome: Pontificio Ateneo S. Anselmo, 1993.

Nightingale, Andrea Wilson. "Liberal Education in Plato's *Republic* and Aristotle's *Politics*." Pages 133–73 in *Education in Greek and Roman Antiquity*. Edited by Yun Lee Too. Leiden: Brill, 2001.

———. "Mimesis: Ancient Greek Literary Theory." Pages 37–47 in *Literary Theory and*

Criticism: An Oxford Guide. Edited by Patricia Waugh. Oxford: Oxford University Press, 2006.

Nolland, John. *The Gospel of Matthew: A Commentary on the Greek Text*. NIGTC. Grand Rapids: Eerdmans, 2005.

———. *Luke 1–9:20*. WBC 35a. Dallas: Word, 1989.

Nussbaum, Martha C. "Philosophy and Literature." Pages 211–41 in *The Cambridge Companion to Greek and Roman Philosophy*. Edited by David Sedley. Cambridge: Cambridge University Press, 2003.

Nygaard, Mathias. *Prayer in the Gospels: A Theological Exegesis of the Ideal Pray-er*. BINS 114. Leiden: Brill, 2012.

Oakes, Peter. *Philippians: From People to Letter*. SNTSMS 110. Cambridge: Cambridge University Press, 2001.

O'Connor, M. John-Patrick. *The Moral Life according to Mark*. LNTS 667. London: Bloomsbury T&T Clark, 2022.

Oepke, Albrecht. "Nachfolge und Nachahmung Christi im Neuen Testament." *AELKZ* 71 (1938): 853–69.

Olmstead, Wesley G. "Jesus, the Eschatological Perfection of Torah, and the *Imitatio Dei* in Matthew." Pages 43–58 in *Torah Ethics and Early Christian Identity*. Edited by Susan J. Wendel and David M. Miller. Grand Rapids: Eerdmans, 2016.

Ong, Walter J. "Mimesis and the Following of Christ." *Religion and Literature* 26, no. 2 (1994): 73–77.

Orr, Peter. *Christ Absent and Present: A Study in Pauline Christology*. WUNT 2/354. Tübingen: Mohr Siebeck, 2014.

Otto, Eckart. "Forschungsgeschichte der Entwürfe einer Ethik im Alten Testament." *VF* 36 (1991): 3–37.

Parris, David P. "Imitating the Parables: Allegory, Narrative and the Role of Mimesis." *JSNT* 25 (2002): 33–53.

Pattarumadathil, Henry. *Your Father in Heaven: Discipleship in Matthew as a Process of Becoming Children of God*. AnBib 172. Rome: Pontifical Biblical Institute, 2008.

Patte, Daniel. *The Challenge of Discipleship: A Critical Study of the Sermon on the Mount as Scripture*. Harrisburg, PA: Trinity Press International, 1999.

———. *Discipleship according to the Sermon on the Mount: Four Legitimate Readings, Four Plausible Views of Discipleship, and Their Relative Values*. Valley Forge, PA: Trinity Press International, 1996.

Paulsen, Henning. *Die Briefe des Ignatius von Antiochia und der Brief des Polykarp von Smyrna*. HNT 18. Tübingen: Mohr Siebeck, 1985.

Pennington, Jonathan T. *The Sermon on the Mount and Human Flourishing: A Theological Commentary*. Grand Rapids: Baker Academic, 2017.

Petersen, Anders Klostergaard. "Attaining Divine Perfection through Different Forms of Imitation." *Numen* 60 (2013): 7–38.
Petitfils, James. *Mos Christianorum: The Roman Discourse of Exemplarity and the Jewish and Christian Language of Leadership*. STAC 99. Tübingen: Mohr Siebeck, 2016.
Pitta, Antonio. "The Degrees of Human Mimesis in the Letter to the Romans." Pages 221–38 in *Non mi vergogno del Vangelo, potenza di Dio*. Edited by Francesco Bianchini and Stefano Romanello. AnBib 200. Rome: Gregorian and Biblical Press, 2012.
Pitts, Andrew W. "The Origins of Greek Mimesis and the Gospel of Mark: Genre as a Potential Restraint in Assessing Markan Imitation." Pages 107–36 in *Ancient Education and Early Christianity*. Edited by Matthew Ryan Hauge and Andrew W. Pitts. LNTS 533. New York: Bloomsbury T&T Clark, 2016.
Platt, Verity. *Facing the Gods: Epiphany and Representation in Graeco-Roman Art, Literature and Religion*. Cambridge: Cambridge University Press, 2011.
Plummer, Robert L. "Imitation of Paul and the Church's Missionary Role in 1 Corinthians." *JETS* 44 (2001): 219–35.
Porter, Stanley E. *The Apostle Paul: His Life, Thought, and Letters*. Grand Rapids: Eerdmans, 2016.
Potolsky, Matthew. *Mimesis*. New York: Routledge, 2006.
Proudfoot, C. Merrill. "Imitation or Realistic Participation? A Study of Paul's Concept of 'Suffering with Christ.'" *Int* 17 (1963): 140–60.
Putthoff, Tyson L. *Ontological Aspects of Early Jewish Anthropology: The Malleable Self and the Presence of God*. BRLJ 53. Leiden: Brill, 2017.
Quinn, Jerome D. *The Letter to Titus*. AB 35. New York: Doubleday, 1990.
Rabens, Volker. "The Dilemma of Human Agency in John: Ethics and Anthropology in the Fourth Gospel." Pages 257–81 in *Images of the Human Being*. Edited by Cosmin Pricop, Karl-Wilhelm Niebuhr, and Tobias Nicklas. WUNT 521. Tübingen: Mohr Siebeck, 2024.
———. "The Holy Spirit and Deification in Paul: A 'Western' Perspective." Pages 187–220 in *The Holy Spirit and the Church according to the New Testament*. Edited by Predrag Dragutinovic, Karl-Wilhelm Niebuhr, and James Buchanan Wallace. WUNT 354. Tübingen: Mohr Siebeck, 2016.
———. *The Holy Spirit and Ethics in Paul: Transformation and Empowering for Religious-Ethical Life*. 2nd ed. WUNT 2/283. Tübingen: Mohr Siebeck, 2013.
———. "Johannine Perspectives on Ethical Enabling in the Context of Stoic and Philonic Ethics." Pages 114–39 in *Rethinking the Ethics of John: "Implicit Ethics" in the Johannine Writings*. Edited by Jan G. van der Watt and Ruben Zimmermann. CNNTE 3. WUNT 291. Tübingen: Mohr Siebeck, 2012.
———. "Sein und Werden in Beziehungen: Grundzüge relationaler Theologie bei Pau-

lus und Johannes." Pages 91–143 in *Relationale Erkenntnishorizonte in Exegese und Systematischer Theologie*. Edited by Walter Bührer and Raphaela Meyer zu Hörste-Bührer. MThSt 129. Leipzig: Evangelische Verlagsanstalt, 2018.

Rahmsdorf, Olivia L. *Zeit und Ethik im Johannesevangelium: Theoretische, methodische und exegetische Annäherungen an die Gunst der Stunde*. CNNTE 10. WUNT 2/488. Tübingen: Mohr Siebeck, 2019.

Ravasz, Hajnalka. *Aspekte der Seelsorge in den paulinischen Gemeinden: Eine exegetische Untersuchung anhand des 1. Thessalonicherbriefes*. WUNT 2/443. Tübingen: Mohr Siebeck, 2017.

Reece, Steve. *Paul's Large Letters: Paul's Autographic Subscription in the Light of Ancient Epistolary Conventions*. LNTS 561. London: Bloomsbury T&T Clark, 2017.

Reed, Annette Yoshiko. "The Construction and Subversion of Patriarchal Perfection: Abraham and Exemplarity in Philo, Josephus, and the Testament of Abraham." *JSJ* 40 (2009): 185–212.

Reeves, Rodney. *Spirituality according to Paul: Imitating the Apostle of Christ*. Downers Grove, IL: IVP Academic, 2011.

Reinhartz, Adele. "On the Meaning of the Pauline Exhortation: '*Mimētai Mou Ginesthe*—Become Imitators of Me.'" *SR* 16 (1987): 393–403.

Reis, David M. "Following in Paul's Footsteps: *Mimēsis* and Power in Ignatius of Antioch." Pages 287–305 in *Trajectories Through the New Testament and the Apostolic Fathers*. Edited by Andrew F. Gregory and C. M. Tuckett. Oxford: Oxford University Press, 2005.

Rengstorf, Karl H. "μανθάνω, κτλ." *TDNT* 4:390–461.

Reumann, John. *Philippians*. AYB 33b. New Haven, CT: Yale University Press, 2008.

Ricoeur, Paul. *Time and Narrative*. Vol. 1. Chicago: University of Chicago Press, 1984.

Rodd, Cyril S. *Glimpses of a Strange Land: Studies in Old Testament Ethics*. Edinburgh: T&T Clark, 2001.

Roller, Matthew B. *Models from the Past in Roman Culture: A World of Exempla*. Cambridge: Cambridge University Press, 2018.

Romilly, Jacqueline de. *A Short History of Greek Literature*. Chicago: University of Chicago Press, 1985.

Rothschild, Clare K. *New Essays on the Apostolic Fathers*. WUNT 375. Tübingen: Mohr Siebeck, 2017.

Rowe, Christopher. "Plato." Pages 98–124 in *The Cambridge Companion to Greek and Roman Philosophy*. Edited by David Sedley. Cambridge: Cambridge University Press, 2003.

Ruthven, Jon. "The 'Imitation of Christ' in Christian Tradition: Its Missing Charismatic Emphasis." *JPT* 16 (2000): 60–77.

Sanders, Boykin. "Imitating Paul: 1 Cor 4:16." *HTR* 74 (1981): 353–63.

Sandnes, Karl Olav. *Early Christian Discourses on Jesus' Prayer at Gethsemane*. NovTSup 166. Leiden: Brill, 2016.

Schenke, Ludger. *Die Wundererzählungen des Markusevangeliums*. SBB 5. Stuttgart: Katholisches Bibelwerk, 1974.

Schippers, Adriana Maria. "Dionysius and Quintilian: Imitation and Emulation in Greek and Latin Literary Criticism." PhD diss., Leiden University, 2019.

Schlier, Heinrich. "δείχνυμι, κτλ." *TDNT* 2:25–33.

Schliesser, Benjamin. *Abraham's Faith in Romans 4: Paul's Concept of Faith in Light of the History of Reception of Genesis 15:6*. WUNT 2/224. Tübingen: Mohr Siebeck, 2007.

Schnackenburg, Rudolf. *The Johannine Epistles*. Translated by R. and I. Fuller. London: Burns & Oates, 1992.

Schnelle, Udo. *Die Johannesbriefe*. ThHK 17. Leipzig: Evangelische Verlagsanstalt, 2010.

Schoedel, William R. *Ignatius of Antioch: A Commentary on the Letters of Ignatius of Antioch*. Hermeneia. Philadelphia: Fortress, 1985.

Scholtissek, Klaus. "'Ein Beispiel habe ich euch gegeben . . .' (Joh 13,15): Die Diakonie Jesu und die Diakonie der Christen in der johanneischen Fußwaschungserzählung als Konterkarierung römischer Alltagskultur." Pages 303–22 in *Textwelt und Theologie des Johannesevangeliums: Gesammelte Schriften (1996–2020)*. WUNT 452. Tübingen: Mohr Siebeck, 2020.

Schrage, Wolfgang. *The Ethics of the New Testament*. Translated by David E. Green. Edinburgh: T&T Clark, 1988. Translation of *Ethik des Neuen Testaments*. Göttingen: Vandenhoeck & Ruprecht, 1982.

Schulz, Anselm. *Nachfolgen und Nachahmen: Studien über das Verhältnis der neutestamentlichen Jüngerschaft zur urchristlichen Vorbildethik*. SANT 6. Munich: Kösel, 1962.

Seaford, Richard. "Introduction." Pages 1–12 in *Reciprocity in Ancient Greece*. Edited by Christopher Gill, Norman Postlethwaite, and Richard Seaford. Oxford: Oxford University Press, 1998.

Sedley, David. "Becoming Godlike." Pages 319–37 in *The Cambridge Companion to Ancient Ethics*. Edited by Christopher Bobonich. Cambridge: Cambridge University Press, 2017.

Segovia, Fernando F. *The Farewell of the Word: The Johannine Call to Abide*. Minneapolis: Fortress, 1991.

———. "John 13:1–20, the Footwashing in the Johannine Tradition." *ZNW* 73 (1982): 31–51.

———. *Love Relationships in the Johannine Tradition: Agapē/Agapan in 1 John and the Fourth Gospel*. SBLDS 58. Chico, CA: Scholars Press, 1982.

Severino, Sally K., and Nancy K. Morrison. "Three Voices / One Message: The Importance of Mimesis for Human Morality." *Contagion: Journal of Violence, Mimesis, and Culture* 19 (2012): 139–66.

Shin, Sookgoo. *Ethics in the Gospel of John: Discipleship as Moral Progress.* BINS 168. Leiden: Brill, 2019.

Shiner, Whitney Taylor. *Follow Me! Disciples in Markan Rhetoric.* SBLDS 145. Atlanta: Scholars Press, 1995.

Sierksma-Agteres, Suzan J. M. "Imitation in Faith: Enacting Paul's Ambiguous *Pistis Christou* Formulations on a Greco-Roman Stage." *International Journal of Philosophy and Theology* 77 (2016): 119–53.

Small, Brian C. *The Characterization of Jesus in the Book of Hebrews.* BINS 128. Leiden: Brill, 2014.

Smalley, Stephen. "The Imitation of Christ in 1 Peter." *Churchman* 75 (1961): 172–78.

———. "The Imitation of Christ in the New Testament." *Themelios* 3 (1965): 13–22.

Smit, Peter-Ben. *Paradigms of Being in Christ: A Study of the Epistle to the Philippians.* LNTS 476. New York: Bloomsbury T&T Clark, 2013.

Smith, Carl B. "Ministry, Martyrdom, and Other Mysteries: Pauline Influence on Ignatius of Antioch." Pages 37–56 in *Paul and the Second Century.* Edited by Michael F. Bird and Joseph R. Dodson. LNTS 412. London: T&T Clark, 2011.

Smith, Murray J. "The Gospels in Early Christian Literature." Pages 181–208 in *The Content and Setting of the Gospel Tradition.* Edited by Mark Harding and Alanna Nobbs. Grand Rapids: Eerdmans, 2010.

Smith, Tyler. *The Fourth Gospel and the Manufacture of Minds in Ancient Historiography, Biography, Romance, and Drama.* BINS 173. Leiden: Brill, 2019.

Söding, Thomas. "Die Nachfolgeforderung Jesu im Markusevangelium." *TTZ* 94 (1985): 292–310.

Sörbom, Göran. "The Classical Concept of Mimesis." Pages 19–28 in *A Companion to Art Theory.* Edited by Paul Smith and Carolyn Wilde. Oxford: Blackwell, 2002.

Spohn, William C. *Go and Do Likewise: Jesus and Ethics.* New York: Continuum, 2007.

Standhartinger, Angela. "'Join in Imitating Me' (Philippians 3.17): Towards an Interpretation of Philippians 3." *NTS* 54 (2008): 417–35.

———. "Weisheitliche Idealbiografie und Ethik in Phil 3." *NovT* 61 (2019): 156–75.

Stanley, David M. "Become Imitators of Me: The Pauline Conception of Apostolic Tradition." *Bib* 40 (1959): 859–77.

———. "Imitation in Paul's Letters: Its Significance for His Relationship to Jesus and to His Own Christian Foundations." Pages 127–41 in *From Jesus to Paul: Studies in Honour of Francis Wright Beare.* Edited by Peter Richardson and John C. Hurd. Waterloo, ON: Wilfrid Laurier University Press, 1984.

Stefaniw, Blossom. "A Disciplined Mind in an Orderly World: Mimesis in Late Antique Ethical Regimes." Pages 235–55 in *Metapher–Narratio–Mimesis–Doxologie:*

Begründungsformen frühchristlicher und antiker Ethik. Edited by Ulrich Volp, Friedrich W. Horn, and Ruben Zimmermann. CNNTE 7. WUNT 356. Tübingen: Mohr Siebeck, 2016.

Stephenson, Lisa P. "Getting Our Feet Wet: The Politics of Footwashing." *JPT* 23 (2014): 154–70.

Stewart, Eric C. "Social Stratification and Patronage in Ancient Mediterranean Societies." Pages 156–66 in *Understanding the Social World of the New Testament*. Edited by Dietmar Neufeld and Richard E. DeMaris. London: Routledge, 2010.

Steyn, Gert J. "Luke's Use of *ΜΙΜΗΣΙΣ*? Re-opening the Debate." Pages 551–57 in *The Scriptures in the Gospels*. Edited by C. M. Tuckett. BETL 131. Leuven: Peeters, 1997.

Stirling, Greg. "*Mors philosophi*: The Death of Jesus in Luke." *HTR* 94 (2001): 383–402.

Stovell, Beth M. "Love One Another and Love the World: The Love Command and Jewish Ethics in the Johannine Community." Pages 426–58 in *Christian Origins and the Establishment of the Early Jesus Movement*. Edited by Stanley E. Porter and Andrew W. Pitts. TENTS 12. Leiden: Brill, 2018.

Swartley, Willard M. *Covenant of Peace: The Missing Peace in New Testament Theology and Ethics*. Grand Rapids: Eerdmans, 2006.

———. "The Imitatio Christi in the Ignatian Letters." *VC* 27 (1973): 81–103.

Talbert, Charles H. "Discipleship in Luke–Acts." Pages 62–75 in *Discipleship in the New Testament*. Edited by Fernando F. Segovia. Philadelphia: Fortress, 1985.

———. *Reading the Sermon on the Mount: Character Formation and Decision Making in Matthew 5–7*. Grand Rapids: Baker Academic, 2004.

Taveirne, Maarten. "Das Martyrium als *imitatio Christi*: Die literarische Gestaltung der spätantiken Märtyrerakten und -passionen nach der Passion Christi." *ZAC* 18 (2014): 167–203.

Terrill, Robert E. "Reproducing Virtue: Quintilian, Imitation, and Rhetorical Education." *Advances in the History of Rhetoric* 19 (2016): 157–71.

Thiselton, Anthony C. *The First Epistle to the Corinthians*. NIGTC. Grand Rapids: Eerdmans, 2000.

Thomas, John Christopher. *Footwashing in John 13 and the Johannine Community*. JSNTSup 61. Sheffield: JSOT Press, 1991.

Thompson, James W. *Moral Formation according to Paul: The Context and Coherence of Pauline Ethics*. Grand Rapids: Baker Academic, 2011.

Thompson, Michael B. *Clothed with Christ: The Example and Teaching of Jesus in Romans 12.1–15.13*. LNTS 59. Sheffield: Sheffield Academic Press, 1991.

Thompson, W. H. Paul. *Pauline Slave Welfare in Historical Context: An Equality Analysis*. WUNT 2/570. Tübingen: Mohr Siebeck, 2023.

Thyen, Hartwig. *Das Johannesevangelium*. 2nd ed. HKNT 6. Tübingen: Mohr Siebeck, 2015.

Thysman, Raymond. "L'Éthique de l'Imitation du Christ dans le Nouveau Testament: Situation, Notations et Variations du Thème." *ETL* 42 (1966): 138–75.
Tinsley, E. J. *The Imitation of God in Christ: An Essay on the Biblical Basis of Christian Spirituality*. London: SCM, 1960.
Tolmie, D. François. *Jesus' Farewell to the Disciples: John 13:1–17:26 in Narratological Perspective*. BINS 12. Leiden: Brill, 1995.
Tomson, Peter J. "The Lord's Prayer at the Faultline of Judaism and Christianity." Pages 261–77 in *Studies on Jews and Christians in the First and Second Centuries*. WUNT 418. Tübingen: Mohr Siebeck, 2019.
Too, Yun Lee. *The Rhetoric of Identity in Isocrates: Text, Power, Pedagogy*. Cambridge: Cambridge University Press, 1995.
Tooman, William A. "Between Imitation and Interpretation: Reuse of Scripture and Composition in Hodayot (lQHa) 11:6–19." *DSD* 18 (2011): 54–73.
Towner, Philip F. *The Letters to Timothy and Titus*. NICNT. Grand Rapids: Eerdmans, 2006.
Trozzo, Lindsey M. *Exploring Johannine Ethics: A Rhetorical Approach to Moral Efficacy in the Fourth Gospel Narrative*. WUNT 2/449. Tübingen: Mohr Siebeck, 2017.
Turner, David L. *Matthew*. BECNT. Grand Rapids: Baker Academic, 2008.
Turpin, William. "Tacitus, Stoic *Exempla*, and the *praecipuum munus annalium*." *ClAnt* 27 (2008): 359–404.
Vakirtzis, Andreas. "Mimesis, Friendship, and Moral Development in Aristotle's Ethics." *Rhizomata* 3 (2015): 125–42.
Van Seters, John. "Creative Imitation in the Hebrew Bible." *SR* 29 (2000): 395–409.
Vandenberg, Kathleen M. "Revisiting Imitation Pedagogies in Composition Studies from a Girardian Perspective." *Contagion: Journal of Violence, Mimesis, and Culture* 18 (2011): 111–34.
Via, Dan O. *The Ethics of Mark's Gospel—In the Middle of Time*. Philadelphia: Fortress, 1985.
Wanamaker, Charles A. *The Epistles to the Thessalonians: A Commentary on the Greek Text*. NIGTC. Grand Rapids: Eerdmans, 1990.
Ward, Graham. "Mimesis: The Measure of Mark's Christology." *Journal of Literature and Theology* 8 (1994): 1–29.
Watson, Francis. *The Fourfold Gospel: A Theological Reading of the New Testament Portraits of Jesus*. Grand Rapids: Baker Academic, 2016.
Watt, Jan G. van der. "Der Meisterschüler Gottes (von der Lehre des Sohnes)—John 5,19–23." Pages 745–54 in *Kompendium der Gleichnisse Jesu*. Edited by Ruben Zimmermann. Gütersloh: Gütersloher Verlagshaus, 2007.
———. "The Ethos of Being Like Jesus: Imitation in 1 John." Pages 415–40 in *Ethos und Theologie im Neuen Testament: Festschrift für Michael Wolter*. Edited by Jochen Flebbe and Matthias Konradt. Neukirchen-Vluyn: Neukirchener Verlag, 2016.

---. *Family of the King: Dynamics of Metaphor in the Gospel according to John.* BINS 47. Leiden: Brill, 2000.

---. *A Grammar of the Ethics of John: Reading John from an Ethical Perspective.* 2 vols. WUNT 431, 502. Tübingen: Mohr Siebeck, 2019, 2023.

---. "Reciprocity, Mimesis and Ethics in 1 John." Pages 257–76 in *Erzählung und Briefe im johanneischen Kreis*. Edited by Uta Poplutz and Jörg Frey. WUNT 2/420. Tübingen: Mohr Siebeck, 2016.

Watt, Jan G. van der, and Ruben Zimmermann, eds. *Rethinking the Ethics of John: "Implicit Ethics" in the Johannine Writings*. CNNTE 3. WUNT 291. Tübingen: Mohr Siebeck, 2012.

Webster, John B. "The Imitation of Christ." *TynBul* 37 (1986): 95–120.

Weder, Hans. "Das neue Gebot: Eine Überlegung zum Liebesgebot in Johannes 13." Pages 187–205 in *Studien zu Matthäus und Johannes/Études sur Matthieu et Jean*. Edited by Andreas Dettwiler and Uta Poplutz. ATANT 97. Zürich: TVZ, 2009.

Weima, Jeffrey A. D. *1–2 Thessalonians*. BECNT. Grand Rapids: Baker Academic, 2014.

Weiss, Konrad. "πούς." *TDNT* 6:624–31.

Wenham, David. *Paul: Follower of Jesus or Founder of Christianity?* Grand Rapids: Eerdmans, 1995.

---. *Paul and Jesus: The True Story*. London: SPCK, 2002.

Wenham, Gordon J. *The Book of Leviticus*. NICOT 3. Grand Rapids: Eerdmans, 1979.

---. "The Gap between Law and Ethics in the Bible." *JJS* 48 (1997): 17–29.

Wick, Peter. "'Ahmt Jesus Christus mit mir zusammen nach!' (Phil 3, 17): *Imitatio Pauli* und *imitatio Christi* im Philipperbrief." Pages 309–26 in *Der Philipperbrief des Paulus in der hellenistisch-römischen Welt*. Edited by Jörg Frey and Benjamin Schliesser. WUNT 353. Tübingen: Mohr Siebeck, 2015.

Wild, Robert A. "'Be Imitators of God': Discipleship in the Letter to the Ephesians." Pages 127–43 in *Discipleship in the New Testament*. Edited by Fernando F. Segovia. Philadelphia: Fortress, 1985.

Wilhite, Shawn J. "'That We Too Might Be Imitators of Him': The *Martyrdom of Polycarp* as *Imitatio Christi*." *Churchman* 129 (2015): 319–36.

Wilkins, Michael J. *Discipleship in the Ancient World and Matthew's Gospel*. 2nd ed. Grand Rapids: Baker, 1995.

Wilkinson, Sam. *Republicanism during the Early Roman Empire*. London: Continuum, 2012.

Williams, Donald L. "The Israelite Cult and Christian Worship." Pages 110–24 in *The Use of the Old Testament in the New and Other Essays*. Edited by James M. Efird. Durham, NC: Duke University Press, 1972.

Williams, H. H. Drake. "Imitate Me as I Imitate Christ: Considering the Jewish Perspective in Paul's Use of Imitation in 1 Corinthians." Pages 209–24 in *The Crucified*

Apostle: Essays on Peter and Paul. Edited by Todd A. Wilson and Paul R. House. WUNT 2/450. Tübingen: Mohr Siebeck, 2017.

———. "'Imitate Me': Interpreting Imitation in 1 Corinthians in Relation to Ignatius of Antioch." *Perichoresis* 11 (2013): 75–93.

Williams, Joel F. *Other Followers of Jesus: Minor Characters as Major Figures in Mark's Gospel*. JSNTSup 102. Sheffield: JSOT Press, 1994.

Williams, Matthew Nantlais. "'Good News to the Poor'? Socio-Economic Ethics in the Gospel of John." PhD diss., Durham University, 2021.

Witherington, Ben. *1 and 2 Thessalonians: A Socio-Rhetorical Commentary*. Grand Rapids: Eerdmans, 2006.

———. *Grace in Galatia: A Commentary on St. Paul's Letter to the Galatians*. Grand Rapids: Eerdmans, 1998.

———. *Paul's Letter to the Philippians: A Socio-Rhetorical Commentary*. Grand Rapids: Eerdmans, 2011.

Witmer, Stephen E. *Divine Instruction in Early Christianity*. WUNT 2/246. Tübingen: Mohr Siebeck, 2008.

Wolbert, Werner. "Vorbild und paränetische Autorität: Zum Problem der Nachahmung des Paulus." *MTZ* 32 (1981): 249–70.

Wolter, Michael. *Das Lukasevangelium*. HNT 5. Tübingen: Mohr Siebeck, 2008.

———. "Die ethische Identität christlicher Gemeinden in neutestamentlicher Zeit." Pages 61–90 in *Woran Orientiert Sich Ethik?* Edited by Wilfried Härle and Reiner Preul. MJT 13. Marburg: Elwert, 2001.

Woodruff, Paul. *The Necessity of Theatre: The Art of Watching and Being Watched*. Oxford: Oxford University Press, 2008.

Wright, Christopher J. H. *Old Testament Ethics for the People of God*. Leicester: InterVarsity, 2004.

Wulf, Christoph. "Mimetic Learning." *Designs for Learning* 1 (2008): 56–67.

Yarbro Collins, Adela. *Mark*. Hermeneia. Minneapolis: Fortress, 2007.

Yoder, John Howard. *The Politics of Jesus*. 2nd ed. Grand Rapids: Eerdmans, 1994.

Yoder, Keith L. "Mimesis: Foot Washing from Luke to John." *ETL* 92 (2016): 655–70.

Zadorojnyi, Alexei V. "Mimesis and the (Plu)past in Plutarch's Lives." Pages 175–98 in *Time and Narrative in Ancient Historiography: The "Plupast" from Herodotus to Appian*. Edited by Christopher B. Krebs and Jonas Grethlein. Cambridge: Cambridge University Press, 2012.

Zagzebski, Linda Trinkaus. *Exemplarist Moral Theory*. Oxford: Oxford University Press, 2017.

———. "Exemplarist Virtue Theory." *Metaphilosophy* 41 (2010): 41–57.

Zimmermann, Ruben. "Is There Ethics in the Gospel of John? Challenging an Outdated Consensus." Pages 44–80 in *Rethinking the Ethics of John: "Implicit Ethics" in the*

Johannine Writings. Edited by Jan G. van der Watt and Ruben Zimmermann. CNNTE 3. WUNT 291. Tübingen: Mohr Siebeck, 2012.

———. *The Logic of Love: Discovering Paul's "Implicit Ethics" through 1 Corinthians*. Translated by Dieter T. Roth. Lanham, MD: Fortress Academic, 2018. Translation of *Die Logik der Liebe: Die "implizite Ethik" der Paulusbriefe am Beispiel des 1. Korintherbriefs*. BThSt. Neukirchen-Vluyn: Neukirchener Verlag, 2016.

Zistakis, Alexander H. "Mimēsis—Imitation as Representation in Plato and His Modern Successors." Pages 159–71 in *The Many Faces of Mimesis*. Edited by Heather L. Reid and Jeremy C. DeLong. Sioux City, IA: Parnassos, 2018.

Zlatev, Jordan. "Mimesis: The 'Missing Link' between Signals and Symbols in Phylogeny and Ontogeny?" Pages 93–122 in *Mimesis, Sign and Language Evolution*. Edited by Anneli Pajunen. Publications in General Linguistics 3. Turku: University of Turku, 2002.

Zoran, Gabriel. "Between Appropriation and Representation: Aristotle and the Concept of Imitation in Greek Thought." *Philosophy and Literature* 39 (2015): 468–86.

Zumstein, Jean. "Le Lavement des Pieds (Jean 13,1–20): Un Exemple de la Conception Johannique du Puvoir." *RTP* 132 (2000): 345–60.

Index of Authors

Achtemeier, Paul J., 319–20
Adam, A. K. M., 72
Agan, C. D. (Jimmy), 3, 14, 139, 327–28, 339
Allison, Dale C., 125
Annas, Julia, 374
Archee, Ray, 1–2
Arnold, Bradley, 275, 278
Arnold, Clinton E., 287
Attridge, Harold W., 318
Auerbach, Eric, 23
Augenstein, Jörg, 189, 196

Baban, Octavian, 103
Barbarick, Clifford A., 320–21, 324–27
Barclay, John M. G., 247, 251–52
Barrett, C. K., 176
Barth, Markus, 287
Barton, John, 82–84, 352
Barton, Stephen, 103
Bauckham, Richard, 13, 189, 191–92
Beck, Brian E., 146
Becker, Daniel, 1
Becker, Eve-Marie, 270–71, 357
Beers, Holly, 143, 149
Belleville, Linda L., 230, 255–56, 260–61, 265

Bennema, Cornelis, 22, 61, 67, 91, 117–19, 146, 156–58, 161, 168, 175, 181, 183, 186–87, 207, 213, 217, 220, 223–24, 241, 248, 299, 323, 327, 340, 353, 359, 371, 374
Berding, Kenneth, 223, 332, 340
Best, Ernest, 103, 112, 151
Betz, Hans Dieter, 9–12, 32–33, 77, 79, 81, 85, 89, 92, 95, 106–7, 127–31, 141, 229–30, 241, 244, 257, 261, 282, 293, 313
Black, C. Clifton, 112
Blanton, Thomas R., 19, 238, 265, 295, 309, 365
Bock, Darrell L., 141–42, 145–46, 264
Bockmuehl, Markus, 267–68, 270, 273, 275–80, 282–83, 286
Bøe, Sverre, 140
Boer, Willis Peter de, 7–9, 11–12, 29, 32–34, 39, 73, 77, 79, 81, 85, 87, 89, 95, 106–8, 116, 128, 149–50, 162, 185, 195, 219, 229–30, 238, 242–43, 245–48, 250–51, 258–61, 263, 266, 277–79, 282, 285, 287, 290, 293–95, 305, 308, 310, 313, 317–18, 320, 323, 350
Böhl, Felix, 94–95, 98
Bond, Helen, 110, 112–13, 118, 121
Bonhoeffer, Dietrich, 2
Bovon, François, 143

413

INDEX OF AUTHORS

Bowden, Chelsea Mina, 46
Brant, Jo-Ann A., 66, 176, 232, 238–39, 242–44, 246–49, 256, 260, 266, 277–78, 310
Brawley, Robert L., 188
Breytenbach, Cilliers, 326
Brickle, Jeffrey E., 219, 360
Brown, Raymond E., 117, 162, 176, 182
Bruce, F. F., 271, 297
Bryan, Steven M., 176, 202
Bryce, Raymond, 270
Buber, Martin, 2, 75, 78, 82
Bultmann, Rudolf, 182, 199
Buol, Justin, 223, 267, 317, 320, 327, 329–35, 340
Burridge, Richard A., 3, 10, 12, 14, 104, 107, 109, 123–25, 128, 137–38, 144, 146–47, 157, 189, 221, 229, 245, 306–7, 353
Buschmann, Gerd, 335
Byers, Andrew J., 218
Byrskog, Samuel, 123–24, 126

Cable, Paul S., 274, 276–77, 283
Calvin, John, 204
Campbell, Douglas A., 313, 368, 375
Capes, David B., 9–10, 13, 65, 85, 87, 97–98, 104, 110, 113, 125, 219, 245, 262–63, 311, 353, 369
Castelli, Elizabeth A., 33, 85, 230, 233, 248, 256, 258–59, 261, 277, 284, 298, 305, 309, 331
Chapman, Stephen B., 81
Chaze, Micheline, 95
Chilton, Bruce, 145
Clarke, Andrew D., 230, 232–33, 242–44, 250–51, 257, 259–60, 265, 273, 287, 289–91, 293–95, 304–5
Cobb, L. Stephanie, 223, 334, 340
Cockayne, Joshua, 11, 13–14, 224, 369–70

Collins, Raymond F., 289, 292
Collinson, Sylvia Wilkey, 104, 108–9, 123, 138, 143
Coloe, Mary L., 188, 192, 203
Conzelmann, Hans, 289
Copan, Victor A., 9, 20, 33, 65-66, 73, 90, 92–93, 98, 107, 230, 234, 238, 242, 244–45, 256–63, 277–79, 282–83, 305, 311–12, 315
Corbett, Edward P. J., 31
Coulot, Claude, 242
Crouzel, Henri, 10
Culpepper, R. Alan, 189
Culy, Martin M., 21
Czachesz, István, 17, 368

Davies, Eryl W., 82–84
Davis, Philip G., 109–12
Davis, Phillip A., 317–18
Dehandschutter, Boudewijn, 332
Dibelius, Martin, 289
Dodd, Brian J., 233, 238, 241, 255–56, 258–59, 280–82, 293, 295, 298–99, 311–13
Donfried, Karl Paul, 240
Dschulnigg, Peter, 120–21
Duff, Tim, 61, 63
Dunn, James D. G., 293, 296–97
Dupertois, Rubén R., 31, 33, 37, 66–67
Dupont, Jacques, 130
Duyndam, Joachim, 2, 368–69, 374–75
Dyer, Bryan R., 317–18

Eastman, Susan Grove, 235, 238, 266, 272, 284, 292–93, 296, 310, 313, 366
Ehrensperger, Kathy, 76, 230, 256, 258
Ellington, Dustin W., 260
Elliott, John H., 319–21
Ellis, E. Earle, 289
Evans, Craig A., 95
Eve, Eric, 24

Index of Authors

Fantham, Elaine, 32, 48–50, 58–59, 64–65
Fee, Gordon D., 244, 257, 260, 262, 273, 278–79, 282, 284
Feldmeier, Reinhard, 56, 124, 128, 141, 320, 352
Fewster, Gregory P., 268–69
Fiore, Benjamin, 19, 31, 33, 52–53, 73, 231–33, 238–40, 244–45, 249, 252, 256, 260, 265, 273, 277–79, 289–91, 293, 295, 298, 309, 311, 313, 365
Fischer, Annalisa, 1
Fitzmyer, Joseph A., 142, 144, 257, 295
Fletcher, Michelle Linda, 65
Fossheim, Hallvard, 39, 41
Foster, Paul, 240, 298
Foster, Robert J., 315
Fowl, Stephen E., 230, 269, 273, 283
France, R. T., 129, 132, 135
Frey, Jörg, 189, 196
Friis, Martin, 75
Furnish, Victor Paul, 199, 238, 244, 260, 278

Garrels, Scott R., 2
Garrett, Susan R., 118
Gebauer, Gunter, 3–4, 21, 29–30, 36–37, 66, 73, 375
Geoffrion, Timothy C., 267, 278, 280
Gerhardsson, Birger, 15–16, 95–97
Getty, Mary Ann, 254
Gill, Christopher, 34
Gloyn, Liz, 53
Gordon, John-Stewart, 374
Gorman, Michael J., 158–59, 161, 200, 211, 218, 268–70, 290, 300, 302, 321
Green, Joel B., 141, 145
Griffiths, Michael, 10, 12, 76, 78, 95, 105, 111–12, 128, 147–48

Grönum, Nico J., 216, 368
Gundry, Robert H., 119–21

Halliwell, Stephen, 2–3, 20, 24, 29–30, 32, 35–40, 73
Hamerton-Kelly, Robert G., 255
Hariman, Robert, 44–46
Harrison, James R., 31, 47, 73, 236, 238, 245, 251, 259–60, 278, 308–9, 357
Hartin, Patrick J., 79
Hartog, Paul Anthony, 160, 187, 226, 330, 332–35
Hauerwas, Stanley, 367, 374
Hauge, Matthew Ryan, 24
Hawthorne, Gerald F., 107, 268, 270–71, 273, 275–78, 281–83
Hays, Richard B., 235, 237, 259, 268, 293, 313, 315
Heath, Jane M. F., 241, 249–50, 262
Heath, Malcolm, 46
Heil, John Paul, 118
Henderson, Suzanne Watts, 112
Hengel, Martin, 107–8, 112
Herrmann, Arnd, 117
Hill, Charles E., 336
Holmes, Arthur F., 374
Holmes, Michael W., 334, 337
Hood, Jason B., 3, 10–12, 14, 29, 74, 76–78, 84, 105, 107, 110–11, 113, 123–25, 138–39, 142, 147–48, 221, 229, 259, 297, 307, 315, 317, 350
Hooker, Morna D., 116
Hörcher, Ferenc, 34–35, 47
Horn, Friedrich W., 12, 106–7
Horrell, David G., 237–38, 260, 265, 268, 271–73, 293, 306–7, 313
Horst, William, 336–37
Houlden, J. Leslie, 198
Houston, Walter J., 82–84

415

INDEX OF AUTHORS

Hursthouse, Rosalind, 374
Hurtado, Larry W., 109–10
Hwang, Jin Ki, 239, 259, 306

Iverson, Kelly R., 121

Jedan, Christoph, 33
Jefford, Clayton N., 324, 333, 335–38
Jenks, R. Gregory, 270
Jensen, Michael, 1, 13–16, 235–36, 238, 244, 248, 251, 259, 265, 270, 273, 282, 295, 297, 301, 303, 309–11
Johnson, Luke Timothy, 289, 291–92
Joosten, Jan, 79

Kaell, Hillary, 2
Karakolis, Christos, 312
Karrer, Martin, 318
Käsemann, Ernst, 3
Keener, Craig S., 201
Kennedy, George A., 35, 71
Kierkegaard, Søren, 2
Kille, D. Andrew, 10, 13–14, 221, 234, 238, 307, 369
Kim, Seyoon, 261
Kim, Yung Suk, 239, 266, 307
Kistemaker, Simon J., 320
Kittel, Gerhard, 107
Koester, Craig R., 318
Kooten, George H. van, 32–33, 63, 78–79, 91–92, 276, 284, 287–88, 295, 302
Kurz, William S., 68, 71, 85–86, 88, 145–47, 150, 276, 278–79, 283
Kwon, Soon-Gu, 2, 10, 104, 107

Labahn, Michael, 122, 193
La Bua, Giuseppe, 51
Lamb, Gregory E., 319
Lambrecht, Jan, 259
Landolt, Jean-François, 148, 278

Langlands, Rebecca, 16, 19, 47, 49, 64–68, 73, 320, 325
Lappenga, Benjamin J., 266
Larsson, Edvin, 9–10, 107, 313
Laurance, John D., 144–45, 263
Lazure, Noël, 216
Lee, Jae Hyun, 284
Légasse, Simon, 247
Léon-Dufour, Xavier, 195
Le Roux, Elritia, 320
Lészai, Lehel, 87, 96, 104
Leung, Mavis M., 76, 82, 84, 158, 161, 165, 218
Levine, Baruch A., 79
Lévy, Carlos, 90
Lieu, Judith M., 197
Lindars, Barnabas, 9
Lindemann, Andreas, 325
Löhr, Hermut, 223, 332, 340
Longenecker, Richard N., 104, 294
Lookadoo, Jonathon, 329
Lücking, Stefan, 24
Lund, Glen, 224–25
Luz, Ulrich, 123, 129–30

Macaskill, Grant, 15, 317, 320
MacDonald, Dennis Ronald, 21, 24
Malbon, Elizabeth Struthers, 119
Malherbe, Abraham J., 31, 239–40, 245–46, 252–53, 333
Malina, Bruce J., 21
Marcar, Katie, 19, 320, 365–66
Marchal, Joseph A., 230, 277
Marcus, Joel, 117, 119
Marguarat, Daniel, 243
Marmorstein, Arthur, 93, 95
Marshall, Christopher D., 120–21
Marshall, I. Howard, 162
Martin, Michael, 243, 253, 257

Index of Authors

Martin, Ralph P., 268, 270, 274–76, 281, 283
Martyn, J. Louis, 293
Matera, Frank J., 109, 123, 138, 158, 242–43, 251, 267, 305–6
Mathew, Bincy, 191
Mayer, Roland G., 47, 53–54, 66
McAdon, Brad, 24
McGrath, Alister, 3
McNeel, Jennifer Houston, 244
Meeks, Wayne A., 30–31, 33–34, 68, 271, 352
Meiser, Martin, 122
Melberg, Arne, 39, 366
Méndez, Hugo, 156
Merk, Otto, 7, 233, 238, 244, 253, 256, 260–61
Merwe, Dirk G. van der, 157, 186
Metzger, Bruce M., 187
Meyer, Esias E., 82, 84
Michaelis, Wilhelm, 32, 85, 89, 230–31, 298
Michaels, J. Ramsey, 178
Middleton, Paul, 334
Mielke, Charles Theodore, 336–37
Milchner, Hans Jürgen, 9, 107
Milgrom, Jacob, 79–80, 93
Mills, Kathleen Elizabeth, 104
Mittleman, Alan L., 80
Moessner, David P., 149
Moloney, Francis J., 116, 120, 189
Moo, Douglas J., 297
Morgan, Teresa, 33, 46–47
Morrison, Nancy K., 17
Moss, Candida R., 3, 10–11, 14, 107, 112, 148–49, 150, 230, 273, 278, 294, 305, 315–17, 320, 323–25, 329–30, 333–35, 339–41

Mosser, Carl, 318
Motia, Michael, 304
Mounce, William D., 290

Naiweld, Ron, 96
Nelson, Peter K., 143
Neyrey, Jerome H., 179
Nicolet, Philippe, 233–34, 238, 241–42, 244, 253, 260, 278, 293
Nielsen, Jesper Tang, 179
Niemand, Christoph, 188–89, 192
Nightingale, Andrea Wilson, 35, 39, 108
Nolland, John, 129–30, 135, 141
Nussbaum, Martha C., 34, 374
Nygaard, Mathias, 147

Oakes, Peter, 277, 279
O'Connor, M. John-Patrick, 70–71, 88, 90, 122–23
Oepke, Albrecht, 7
Olmstead, Wesley G., 128
Ong, Walter J., 9, 107
Orr, Peter, 245, 361, 376
Otto, Eckart, 82, 84

Parris, David P., 103
Pattarumadathil, Henry, 123
Patte, Daniel, 124, 126, 137
Paulsen, Henning, 330
Pennington, Jonathan T., 129
Petersen, Anders Klostergaard, 340–41, 351
Petitfils, James, 30, 47, 66, 88, 90, 320, 324, 326, 340, 365
Pettigrove, Glen, 374
Pitta, Antonio, 296–97
Pitts, Andrew W., 31, 33–34, 58–59, 68, 72
Platt, Verity, 4
Plummer, Robert L., 266
Porter, Stanley E., 288

INDEX OF AUTHORS

Potolsky, Matthew, 1, 3–4, 29–30, 35, 37–39, 72, 375
Proudfoot, C. Merrill, 7
Putthoff, Tyson L., 75–76, 91

Quinn, Jerome D., 291

Rabens, Volker, 195, 211, 225, 302, 308
Rahmsdorf, Olivia L., 161, 188, 220–21
Ravasz, Hajnalka, 242, 245, 255, 303, 308
Reece, Steve, 240
Reed, Annette Yoshiko, 88, 90, 365
Reeves, Rodney, 230
Reinhartz, Adele, 230, 232, 238–39, 259–61, 277–78
Reis, David M., 328, 331
Rengstorf, Karl H., 107
Reumann, John, 282–83, 285
Ricoeur, Paul, 24, 103
Rodd, Cyril S., 83
Rohrbaugh, Richard L., 21
Roller, Matthew B., 19, 67, 320
Romilly, Jacqueline de, 30
Rothschild, Clare K., 324–25
Rowe, Christopher, 32
Ruthven, Jon, 143, 148

Sanders, Boykin, 258–59
Sandnes, Karl Olav, 117–18, 133, 146, 324, 333–34
Schenke, Ludger, 120–21
Schippers, Adriana Maria, 57, 65, 67–69, 71
Schlier, Heinrich, 144
Schliesser, Benjamin, 294
Schmitz, Yola, 1
Schnackenburg, Rudolf, 162, 199
Schnelle, Udo, 197
Schoedel, William R., 328–29
Scholtissek, Klaus, 193

Schrage, Wolfgang, 199
Schulz, Anselm, 7–9, 11–12, 33, 77, 87, 92, 95, 106–7, 116, 128–29, 133, 141–42, 148, 151, 172, 197, 229, 241, 250, 257, 260, 273, 286–87, 293, 295, 297, 313, 319
Seaford, Richard, 22
Sedley, David, 33
Segovia, Fernando F., 189, 196, 198, 204
Severino, Sally K., 17
Shin, Sookgoo, 59, 63, 159, 200–201, 204, 226
Shiner, Whitney Taylor, 104, 112, 213
Sierksma-Agteres, Suzan J. M., 33, 56, 72, 92, 236–37, 272, 284, 293
Small, Brian C., 317
Smalley, Stephen, 8, 106, 263, 295, 318–19
Smit, Peter-Ben, 47, 267–68, 273, 276, 278–82, 284
Smith, Carl B., 331
Smith, Murray J., 223, 340
Smith, Tyler, 59–60, 353
Söding, Thomas, 113, 116
Sörbom, Göran, 3
Spohn, William C., 138, 144, 192
Standhartinger, Angela, 239, 277, 332
Stanley, David M., 7, 273
Stefaniw, Blossom, 40, 309, 350, 367
Stephenson, Lisa P., 189
Stewart, Eric C., 21
Steyn, Gert J., 24
Stirling, Greg, 150
Stovell, Beth M., 200
Swartley, Willard M., 113, 147, 242, 277, 317, 320, 330–31

Talbert, Charles H., 128, 147
Taveirne, Maarten, 339–40
Terrill, Robert E., 56
Thiselton, Anthony C., 262–63

Index of Authors

Thomas, John Christopher, 188–91, 193
Thompson, James W., 229
Thompson, Michael B., 295–96
Thompson, W. H. Paul, 80, 84, 288, 294, 298
Thyen, Hartwig, 180
Thysman, Raymond, 7, 14, 107
Tinsley, E. J., 3, 7–9, 11–12, 29, 74, 76–78, 84, 104–7, 111, 147–50, 175, 229, 257, 295, 306, 318–19, 350
Tolmie, D. François, 195
Tomson, Peter J., 133
Too, Yun Lee, 43, 45–46, 240
Tooman, William A., 75
Towner, Philip F., 289–91
Trozzo, Lindsey M., 158, 161, 207, 212, 216, 220–21
Turner, David L., 129, 135
Turpin, William, 47, 53–54, 66

Vakirtzis, Andreas, 41, 67
Vandenberg, Kathleen M., 59
Van Seters, John, 75
Via, Dan O., 116

Wanamaker, Charles A., 244, 246
Ward, Graham, 103
Warner, Laceye C., 81
Watson, Francis, 118, 145–46, 340
Watt, Jan G. van der, 22, 108, 156, 158–61, 175, 187–88, 191–92, 196–98, 200–201, 209, 211–13, 216, 219, 221
Webster, John B., 3
Weder, Hans, 195
Weima, Jeffrey A. D., 244, 246, 250
Weiss, Konrad, 191

Wenham, David, 244, 261
Wenham, Gordon J., 82, 84
Wick, Peter, 273
Wild, Robert A., 287
Wilhite, Shawn J., 333–35
Wilkins, Michael J., 104–5, 108
Wilkinson, Sam, 46
Williams, Donald L., 77, 145, 263
Williams, H. H. Drake, 81, 86, 97–98, 255, 330–31
Williams, Joel F., 119, 121
Williams, Matthew Nantlais, 192, 204
Witherington, Ben, 243, 246, 267–68, 270–71, 275–78, 280, 282, 284, 293, 308
Witmer, Stephen E., 108, 143, 178, 183
Wolbert, Werner, 231, 238, 252, 260–61, 287, 298, 318
Wolter, Michael, 141, 199
Woodruff, Paul, 35
Wright, Christopher J. H., 77
Wulf, Christoph, 1, 3–4, 21, 29–30, 36–37, 66, 73, 368, 375

Yarbro Collins, Adela, 118
Yoder, John Howard, 14, 81
Yoder, Keith L., 156

Zadorojnyi, Alexei V., 60, 63–64
Zagzebski, Linda Trinkaus, 14, 17, 19, 67, 368, 374–75
Zimmermann, Ruben, 17, 156, 193, 257, 259–60, 263
Zistakis, Alexander H., 29
Zlatev, Jordan, 368
Zoran, Gabriel, 29, 36
Zumstein, Jean, 189

Index of Subjects

analogy, 13, 16, 18–21, 77, 89, 114–15, 127–28, 134–38, 141–44, 221, 294, 315–16, 324, 327, 346
assimilation, 32–33, 63, 65, 79, 91–92, 214, 272, 284, 287–88, 296–97, 301, 352

behavior. *See* ethics/ethical
biography (Greco-Roman), 10, 47, 59–60, 68, 104, 125, 139, 219, 353n12

chain of mimesis. *See* mimetic chain
chreia, 46, 118n59
Christlike(ness), 15, 17, 23, 159, 234, 257, 278, 283–84, 300–302, 310, 357, 360, 364, 367, 372. *See also* theosis
Christosis, 302, 321. *See also* theosis
civic education, 34–35, 45–47, 64, 346, 374. *See also* education
cloning, 16, 24, 41, 50, 65, 132, 181, 183, 214, 265, 271, 307, 349, 356, 363–67, 373. *See also* replication
consequentialism, 374
contemplation, 33n16, 40, 42, 51, 301–2, 321, 325–26
copy(ing). *See* replication
corporate mimesis, 247–49, 267, 273, 275, 299–301, 304, 306–7, 328, 357, 371
countercultural, 192, 284n270, 308, 356

deification, 17, 218, 302, 341, 369. *See also* theosis
deontological ethics, 84, 373–74
didactic tool or strategy, 24, 64, 95, 123, 173, 183, 278, 284, 308, 346, 348, 351, 355, 367, 373. *See also* education
discernment, 14, 48–49, 51–52, 54, 58, 60–66, 68, 73, 84, 92, 124–25, 214, 220, 283, 301–2, 307, 363, 371. *See also* moral reasoning
divine family. *See* family
divinization, 340–41, 351. *See also* theosis
drama (Athenian/Greek), 34–35, 37, 346
duplication, 160, 188, 225, 368. *See also* replication

education, 24, 29, 31–39, 41, 45–47, 53, 64–66, 73, 90, 92, 97, 107–8, 230, 236, 252, 256, 266, 272, 303, 308, 320, 346–49, 355, 367, 373–74. *See also* didactic tool or strategy
emulation, 17–18n67, 56, 65, 72, 244, 249, 364
ethics/ethical, 1, 13, 15, 17, 23, 30, 33–34, 38–40, 46–47, 67–68, 81–93, 97, 99, 151, 157, 207–12, 226–29, 313–14, 345–52, 355–58, 367, 373–75

420

Index of Subjects

Eucharist, 145, 263, 327. *See also* Lord's Supper
example/exemplar: absent/unseen exemplars, 5, 13, 16, 21, 130, 218–19, 238, 244–46, 254, 272, 283, 285, 300, 310–11, 357, 361–62, 369–71, 373; associating with exemplars, 43, 48, 52–53, 56, 61, 64, 73, 92, 98, 213, 217, 299–300, 356, 364, 366; historical/past examples, 42, 48, 51, 53, 63, 66n110, 70–71, 87, 98–99, 244, 272n209, 280, 318, 321, 325, 365, 369; literary examples, 122, 137, 161, 219, 223, 254, 285–86, 311–12, 315, 355, 359, 361–62, 370, 373; living examples, 50–53, 65, 130, 155, 219, 223–24, 254, 280–81, 285–86, 300, 312, 318, 321, 325, 355, 359–61, 365–66, 370–71; observing exemplars, 20–21, 24, 43–45, 48–53, 56, 59, 61, 65, 70–71, 73, 77, 79–80, 90, 92, 96, 98, 108, 132, 143, 155, 175–76, 180–81, 183, 189, 205–6, 213, 215, 219–20, 227, 243–48, 254, 257, 266, 268, 279, 281–86, 300–301, 311, 318, 325, 327, 333, 346–49, 361–64, 371–73; reconstructing exemplars, 10, 219–20, 223–24, 227, 234, 246, 254, 263, 300, 311–12, 348, 361–62, 373; remembering exemplars, 42, 98–99, 144–45, 155, 219–20, 223, 234, 249, 254, 258, 279, 285, 300–301, 311–12, 361–62, 369; scriptural examples, 85, 87–90, 231, 326–27, 365; selecting exemplars, 36, 41, 44, 48–50, 52–53, 55–56, 64–67, 92, 213, 299, 305, 356, 364–65; surrogate examples, 233, 257, 299–300, 302, 304–5, 311–12, 349, 359, 361–63, 373
exemplification, 19, 34, 118, 121, 138, 152, 175, 244, 252, 257, 275, 284, 308, 311–12, 318, 326, 349, 357, 362, 364–65
existential mimesis, 18, 135, 166, 173–74, 178, 198, 200–204, 206, 217, 225–26, 273–74, 288, 295–97, 309, 328, 358

family, 17, 29, 33, 42, 45, 51, 53, 64–65, 73, 89–90, 97, 320, 346, 351; divine/spiritual family, 24, 130, 134, 175, 182–84, 195–96, 200, 202–6, 209–12, 215–17, 226, 252, 256, 266, 287, 292, 303, 308, 314, 320, 322, 346–49, 351, 355–56, 366–67, 374
fine arts, 8, 29, 32
following Jesus/God, 6, 9, 76–77, 105–9, 111–14, 125–26, 139–40, 185–86, 347, 354–55
footwashing, 5, 138, 187–92, 194–99, 205, 211, 213–16, 328, 355, 357, 372, 376
forgiveness, 80, 82, 133, 135, 137, 154, 286–87, 297–98, 314, 339, 349, 356, 372
formation. *See* transformation

Gethsemane, 116–18, 122, 132–33, 136, 145–47, 155, 347–48

Hellenization, 8, 12, 86, 97, 350
hermeneutics of mimesis, 11, 222–23, 364–72
historical examples. *See* example/exemplar
historical Jesus, 13, 233–34, 244, 306n361, 369–70
Holy Spirit. *See* Spirit (divine/holy)
household. *See* family
humility, 6, 8, 10, 21, 105, 109, 123, 137, 154, 191, 230, 271, 284, 307, 314, 326, 330, 332, 339, 349, 356, 372

identity, 77, 119, 158, 160, 192, 197, 210–13, 206, 209–13, 217, 226, 267, 270–71, 307, 309, 320, 357, 366–67, 374
image of God, 6, 75, 77–79, 82, 91–92, 287, 369
imitatio anxiety, 3, 14

421

INDEX OF SUBJECTS

imitatio Christi, 2–3, 6, 13, 147, 223, 233, 237, 270, 319, 323, 333–35, 339, 371
imitatio Dei, 82, 84, 352
imitation. *See* mimesis
interpretation (of an example/exemplar), 65–68, 191–92, 214–17, 220, 301, 339, 348, 364, 366–68

language of mimesis. *See* mimetic language
literary examples. *See* example/exemplar
living examples. *See* example/exemplar
Lord's Supper, 144–45, 150, 153–55, 263–64, 347–48. *See also* Eucharist
love command, 164, 193–200, 205, 215–16, 351

martyrdom, 3, 6, 13, 110, 150, 223, 276, 323–26, 330, 332–35, 337–41, 349–50, 360
mediated mimesis. *See* modes of mimesis
memory, 50n81, 57, 85, 224, 227, 234, 249, 253, 257, 346, 348, 361–62. *See also* example/exemplar: remembering exemplars
mimesis: as cognitive, 24, 40–41, 44, 55, 63, 65–66, 68, 72, 132, 157, 188, 191–92, 205–6, 214, 217–18, 238, 254, 260, 284, 301–2, 307, 337, 346, 348–49, 356, 363, 366, 368, 371, 373; conceptual domain, 214n134, 370, 372; as creative, 24, 32, 34, 39–41, 44–47, 55, 58, 65, 72, 138, 157, 183, 188–92, 205, 216, 225–27, 254, 284, 301–2, 307, 346, 348–49, 356, 366–69, 373; definition, 3, 17, 345–46; as didactic tool, 24, 64, 173, 183, 278, 284, 308, 346, 348, 351, 355, 367, 373; of God/gods, 7–8, 29, 32, 63, 73, 76–85, 87, 91–95, 97, 128–29, 133, 137, 141–42, 152–54, 165, 173–74, 185, 204, 212, 286–87, 304, 336–37, 339, 347, 350–52, 356; Greco-Roman model of mimesis, 45, 56, 64–68, 98, 155, 213–14, 218, 299–303, 339, 365, 373; historical origins, 11–12, 36, 64, 76, 97–99, 347, 350–51; Johannine model of mimesis, 213–18; as participation, 15, 24, 108, 185, 217–18, 226, 235, 238, 269–70, 272, 302, 310, 346, 356, 366; Pauline model of mimesis, 299–303; place in ethics, 122–23, 137, 150, 207–13, 226, 313–14, 357–58; as representation, 8, 29, 32, 36, 61, 73, 79, 89, 91, 190, 192, 225, 282; semantic domain, 13, 16, 18, 161, 172, 174, 355, 372; traces of, 97, 108–9, 111, 122, 125–26, 137, 139–40, 151–53, 186, 205, 262, 288, 321, 347, 350, 354
mimetic chain, 22, 69, 183–84, 193, 196, 207, 209–10, 212, 226, 241, 249, 254, 260, 266, 291–92, 299–302, 304, 307–8, 331, 335, 349, 357, 359
mimetic characters, 35, 118–22, 136–37, 146–50, 152–53, 155, 161, 220, 227, 315, 347–48, 355, 359, 366
mimetic ethics, 17, 23, 41, 73, 87, 92, 212, 218, 249, 284, 288, 306, 313, 349, 356, 358–60, 366–67, 373–74
mimetic language, 12–13, 16, 18, 23, 25, 84, 87, 89, 92, 114, 116, 126, 133–34, 137, 141, 150, 161, 174, 225, 229, 303–5, 314, 323, 339, 347–48, 353–55, 360, 363, 372–73, 377–79
mimetic strength (as heuristic device), 18, 133, 151–53, 168–72, 174, 208–9, 353
mindset, 14–15, 220, 284, 307, 349, 363, 371
mnemonic mimesis, 73, 98, 155, 227, 249, 254, 257, 285, 311, 314, 362

Index of Subjects

model. *See* example/exemplar
model of mimesis, 29–30, 45, 64–65, 155, 213–15, 218, 299–303, 339, 364–65, 373
modes of mimesis, 73, 155, 227, 311, 314, 362
moral progress, 42, 45, 56, 58, 62, 65, 73, 90, 93, 159, 346, 364
moral reasoning, 66, 215–18, 222, 227, 254, 260, 271, 284, 301, 307, 314, 356, 363, 368, 371–72, 375–76. *See also* discernment
moral transformation. *See* transformation
mos maiorum, 46, 67

observing exemplars. *See* example/exemplar
orator(y). *See* rhetorical education/tradition
other-regard, 237, 307, 314, 349, 356, 372

parent(al), 1, 29, 33–34, 65, 73, 90, 130, 243–44, 252, 256–57, 261, 287, 293, 308, 346, 349, 356, 373, 376
participation. *See* mimesis: as participation
pedagogy. *See* education
performative mimesis, 18, 173–74, 178, 200, 204, 206, 225–26, 274, 309, 358
personal example. *See* example/exemplar
poetry, 32, 34, 36–40, 42, 47, 62
polis, 30, 33–35, 39, 46, 347, 352
politics, 34–35, 39, 46, 51, 267n181, 347, 352, 374

reciprocity, 21–23, 127, 133, 141, 179, 184, 211–12, 235, 272, 324, 337
reconstructing exemplars. *See* example/exemplar
Reformed tradition, 2–3, 14

religion, 29, 32, 73, 97, 340–41, 346, 351, 355, 373
remembering examples. *See* example/exemplar
remembrance. *See* memory
replication, 2, 24, 41, 44, 54–55, 58, 65, 72, 131–32, 145, 181, 189–92, 215–16, 265, 282, 301, 356, 363–64, 366, 370, 373
rhetorical education/tradition, 30–31, 41, 47, 50, 56, 67–68, 239, 326, 346

scriptural examples. *See* example/exemplar
self-denial, 8, 110, 112–13, 121–22, 125–26, 137, 139–40, 152, 154, 230
self-giving, 8, 10, 113, 116, 135, 140, 154, 195–97, 200, 205, 230, 237, 241, 243, 245, 253–54, 259, 265, 271, 286, 293, 306–7, 314, 349, 372
Sermon on the Mount, 123–24, 126–34, 137, 347, 355
servanthood/service, 109–10, 113, 116, 119–20, 122, 135, 137, 142–43, 150, 154, 188–93, 198–200, 211, 214–16, 226, 274, 276, 281, 284, 356–57, 372
Spirit (divine/holy), 19–20, 114, 117–18, 136, 146–49, 180–83, 202, 210, 218, 220, 223–27, 242, 295, 359, 363, 370–72, 376
spiritual(ity), 177, 188, 191, 230, 244, 252, 256–57, 261, 266, 277, 284, 287, 294, 303, 305, 308, 310, 349, 352, 356, 371, 374
studying examples. *See* example/exemplar: observing exemplars

teacher, 1, 5, 45, 50, 65, 73, 90, 95–96, 105, 108, 135, 192n85, 252, 272, 373, 376
theater, 34, 72
theosis, 158–59, 217–18, 227, 302, 310, 321, 336, 341, 367

transformation, 21, 24, 42, 49, 56, 65, 73, 92, 98, 203, 213–15, 217–18, 226–27, 267, 283–84, 301–2, 321, 325, 327, 335, 339, 364–65, 367, 376

unity, 6, 163, 200–202, 205, 255, 271, 326–28, 330–32, 339, 356, 372

utilitarian ethics, 374

virtue/virtuous, 10, 18, 29, 35, 41–44, 47–48, 53, 59–63, 65, 81, 85–86, 88–92, 231, 234, 290, 301, 326, 339, 346, 356, 375

virtue ethics, 47, 373–74

walking in God's ways. *See* following Jesus/God

WWJD movement, 2–3

Index of Scripture and Other Ancient Sources

Old Testament/ Hebrew Bible

Genesis
1:26	6, 77, 91, 98
1:26–27	78–79, 81, 86, 91
1:27	369
2:7	91
3:21	94
5:1	78
5:1–3	79
5:3	78
9:6	78
18:1	94
18:4	191
25:11	94

Exodus
14:31	274
15:2	93
20:8–11	80, 316
25:9	80, 86, 143, 316
25:40	80, 86, 316

Leviticus
11:44–45	79, 129
17–26	83
19:2	7, 78–83, 93, 129–30, 151, 319, 351
19:18	129, 351
19:34	80

Deuteronomy
1:16–17	80
5:15	81, 84
10:17–18	80
10:17–19	80–81, 84
10:18–19	6–7, 81, 351
10:19	80
12:30	81
13:4	93
15:15	81, 84
16:18–20	80
18:13	129
18:15	142
18:18	142
24:17–18	81, 84
34:6	94

1 Samuel
20:14	77
25:41	191

2 Samuel
9:3	77
22:16	130

1 Chronicles
28:11–12	80, 86, 316

Isaiah
6:9–10	148–49
7:14	130
11:2	181
51:1–2	81
54:13	183

Jeremiah
25:4	274

Ezekiel
1:26–28	78

Daniel
3:12	86

Deuterocanonical Books

1 Maccabees
2:23–26	85

INDEX OF SCRIPTURE AND OTHER ANCIENT SOURCES

2:49–70	85	**4 Maccabees**		4.154	88
2:51–61	86	6:18–19	86	5.98	88
		6:29	116	5.129	88
2 Maccabees		9:23	86, 98, 239	5.306	88
4:16	86	13:9	86, 98	7.142–143	88, 99
6:28	86	17:21	116	7.143	98
6:31	86	17:23	86, 98	8–10	88
				8.24	88
Sirach		**Pseudo-Phocylides**		8.193	88
17:1–3	79	77	87	8.196	88
44:1–50:24	86			8.251	88
44:16	86	**Sibylline Oracles**		8.315	88
		1:99	87	9.44	88
Wisdom of Solomon		1:309	87	9.99	88
2:23	79	1:331–333	87	9.173	88
4:2	86	2:146	87	9.243	88
9:8	86, 311	3:27	87	9.282	88
15:9	86	4:35–36	87	10.37	89
		8:269–271	87	10.47	89
PSEUDEPIGRAPHA				10.50	89
		Testament of the Twelve Patriarchs		12.239–241	89
Ahiqar				17.109–110	89
26:15	87	T. Ab. 20:15	87, 98	17.312–313	89
		T. Ash. 4:3	87		
1 Enoch		T. Benj. 3:1	87	**Philo**	
106:5	86–87	T. Benj. 4:1	87, 98		
106:10	86–87	T. Levi 8:14	87	*Abr.* (*On the Life of Abraham*)	
4 Ezra		**ANCIENT JEWISH WRITERS**		60	90
15:48	87			*Congr.* (*On the Preliminary Studies*)	
		Josephus		69–70	90
Joseph and Aseneth					
13:12	191	*Ant.* (*Antiquities*)		*Decal.* (*On the Decalogue*)	
20:3	191	1.19	88	100	92
		1.68	88	120	92
Letter of Aristeas		1.148–256	88		
188	87	1.154–155	88	*Det.* (*That the Worse Attacks the Better*)	
210	87	1.200	88		
280–281	87	3.28	88	83	91

426

Index of Scripture and Other Ancient Sources

Ebr. (On Drunkenness)
90 — 89
95 — 90, 98

Fug. (On Flight and Finding)
63 — 92, 287

Her. (Who Is the Heir?)
55 — 91

Leg. (Allegorical Interpretation)
1.31–33 — 91
1.36–42 — 91
1.42 — 91
1.45 — 91
1.47–48 — 91
1.48–49 — 91
3.96 — 91
3.102 — 89, 316

Migr. (On the Migration of Abraham)
12 — 92
133 — 90
149 — 90, 92

Mos. (On the Life of Moses)
1.302–303 — 85, 90
1.303 — 92
1.325 — 90
1.158 — 92–93
1.158–159 — 90
1.160–161 — 90
2.74 — 89

Opif. (On the Creation of the World)
16–19 — 90
25 — 91
69 — 91
79 — 92
134–135 — 91
135 — 91
139 — 91
144 — 76, 91–92

Post. (On the Posterity of Cain)
104 — 20, 89

Praem. (On Rewards and Punishments)
114 — 93
114–115 — 90, 92
114–116 — 66, 92

QG (Questions and Answers on Genesis)
2.62 — 91

Sacr. (On the Sacrifices of Cain and Abel)
65 — 90, 98
68 — 90, 98

Somn. (On Dreams)
1.206 — 89

Spec. (On the Special Laws)
2.225 — 92
4.73 — 91
4.123 — 91
4.182 — 90, 92, 98
4.188 — 92

Virt. (On the Virtues)
66 — 90
70 — 90
166–168 — 92
168 — 91
205 — 91

NEW TESTAMENT

Matthew
1:18 — 135
1:23 — 130
1:24 — 135
2:5 — 135
3:15 — 135
3:16 — 136
4:19 — 126, 152, 154
4:19–20 — 125
4:20 — 125
4:20–22 — 105
4:21 — 126
4:22 — 125
4:23–24 — 126
4:25 — 105, 125, 127
5–7 — 127, 130, 134, 137
5:1 — 127
5:2–12 — 123
5:5 — 124–25
5:7 — 125
5:8 — 134
5:9 — 134
5:12 — 127
5:14 — 127
5:15–16 — 127
5:16 — 127, 134
5:17 — 124
5:17–48 — 129
5:19 — 127
5:19–20 — 125
5:20 — 128–29
5:21–47 — 128, 142
5:21–48 — 124
5:34 — 134
5:43 — 129
5:43–47 — 128
5:43–48 — 124
5:44 — 128, 194

427

INDEX OF SCRIPTURE AND OTHER ANCIENT SOURCES

5:44–45	128, 141	6:16	127, 130–31, 134–35,	10:24	106
5:45	134, 141		152	10:25	106, 135–37, 143,
5:45b	128	6:16–18	130–31		152, 154
5:48	6, 7, 80, 104–5, 108,	6:18	134	10:37	125–26
	124–25, 127–30,	6:24	134	10:38	105, 125–26, 152,
	134–35, 137, 141–42,	6:26	134		154
	151–52, 154, 351,	6:29	127, 135	10:39	126
	356, 367	6:30	127, 134	11:16	135
6:1	130–32, 134	6:32	134	11:25–27	123
6:1–6	130	6:33	134, 137	11:29	106, 124–25, 136
6:1–18	123, 130–31	7:11	134	12:1–8	128
6:2	127, 130–31, 134,	7:12	127	12:7	128
	137, 152	7:17	127	12:15	125
6:2–4	130–31	7:21	134	12:40	134–35
6:4	134	7:24	127–28, 135	12:46–50	126
6:5	127, 130–32, 134–35,	7:24–27	124	13:24	136
	152	7:26	127–28, 135	13:31	136
6:5–6	130–31	7:28	127	13:33	136
6:6	134	7:29	127, 135	13:40	134
6:7	127, 130–31, 134, 137,	8–11	123	13:40–42	134
	152	8:1	105, 125, 127	13:43	135
6:7–8	132	8:4	125	13:44	136
6:7–15	130–31	8:10	125	13:45	136
6:8	127, 130–31, 134–35,	8:11	145	13:47	136
	152	8:16–17	126	13:47–50	135
6:8–13	133	8:19	105	13:52	106
6:9	127, 131, 133–35, 137,	8:19–20	125	14:13	125
	152	8:21–22	125–26	14:21	136
6:9–13	131, 154	8:23	125	14:23	123
6:9a	131	9:1–13	128	15:7	130
6:10	127, 133, 135	9:9	125–26	15:10–20	137
6:12	124, 127, 131, 133,	9:13	106, 126, 128	16:24	106, 125–26, 152,
	144, 154, 286	9:27	125		154
6:12–13	132	9:36	136	16:24–26	137
6:12–15	298	10:1	126	16:25	126
6:13a	133	10:1–8	154	17:2	135
6:14	134	10:7–8	126	17:12	135
6:14–15	133, 286	10:16	135	17:20	135
6:15	134	10:16–42	137	17:24–27	137

Index of Scripture and Other Ancient Sources

18:1–4	135	23:28	135	1:15	122
18:1–9	137	23:29	130	1:17	109, 111–12, 152, 154
18:3–4	136–37, 152, 154	24:9–14	136	1:17–18	111
18:15–35	138	24:27	134	1:18	105, 111–12
18:17	134	24:32	106	1:20	111–12, 114
18:21–35	298	24:36–25:46	137	1:21	122
18:23	136	24:37	134	1:22	115
18:23–35	124, 133	24:38–39	134	1:29–31	119
18:33	133, 135–36, 151–52, 154, 286	25:1	136	1:31	119
		25:14	134	1:34	6, 111, 114
18:35	133, 135, 286	25:17	136	1:38–39	6, 111, 122
19:1–12	137	25:32	134	1:39	114
19:2	125	26:19	135	2:7	114
19:21	125–26	26:24	136	2:8	114
19:27	105, 125	26:35	136	2:12	114
19:28–29	126	26:36–44	123	2:13	122
20:1	136	26:36–46	136, 152, 154	2:14	111–12
20:5	136	26:39	126, 132–33	2:15	111
20:20–28	137	26:41a	133	2:17	112
20:25–28	143	26:42	132–33	3:7	111
20:26	135–37, 152	26:55	135, 334	3:13–15	111, 154
20:26–28	134, 151, 154	27:26	125	3:13–19	110
20:27–28	108	27:31	126	3:14	111, 113, 119–20
20:28	116, 135, 137, 152	27:35	126	3:14–15	109, 111, 114, 120
20:29	125	27:41	136	3:15	111
20:34	125	27:55	125	3:20–21	113
21:6	136	27:57	106	3:31–35	110, 113
21:30	136	28:3–4	135	3:33–35	123
21:36	136	28:6	136	3:35	105
22:2	136	28:15	135	4:1–34	122
22:18	130	28:18–20	110	4:26	114
22:26	136	28:19	106, 126	4:30	115
22:30	135			4:30–32	19
22:39	136	**Mark**		4:31	115
23:13	130	1:10	114	4:31–32	115
23:15	130	1:12–13	117	4:33	114
23:23	130	1:13	119	5:14–17	120
23:25	130	1:14	111, 113	5:18	119
23:27	130	1:14–15	114	5:19	120

429

INDEX OF SCRIPTURE AND OTHER ANCIENT SOURCES

5:20	120	9:33–37	109, 119	12:13–17	123
5:24	105, 111	9:34	113, 120	12:21	115
6:1	105, 111	9:35	113, 119	12:25	115
6:2	122	9:36–37	109	12:28–34	261
6:3	113	9:42	109	12:31	115, 194
6:6	122	9:42–50	261	12:34	122
6:6b–13	120	10:1	114, 122	12:40	131
6:7–13	6, 111, 114, 154	10:1–12	123	13	117
6:11	109	10:13	116	13–14	146
6:12	120	10:13–16	109	13:9	117
6:12–13	109	10:14	116	13:9–11	110
6:15	115	10:14–15	122	13:9–13	113
6:34	115, 122	10:15	114, 116, 122, 152, 154, 347	13:10	114, 120
7:6	114			13:11	109, 117, 136, 146
7:15	261	10:16	116	13:18	117
7:18	114	10:21	111–12	13:20	117
8:11–12	117	10:23–25	122	13:28	106, 114
8:22–10:52	113, 120	10:28	111–12, 152, 154	13:29	114
8:24	115	10:29–30	110	13:34	115, 117
8:27	111, 113, 120	10:30	111	13:35	117
8:27–29	120	10:32	111, 113, 120–21	13:36	117
8:31	110, 113, 123	10:33	113	13:37	117
8:31–35	121	10:33–34	113, 121	14:16	114
8:33–9:1	104	10:35–45	119, 121	14:21	114
8:34	104–6, 111–13, 121, 152, 154	10:36	120	14:31	115
		10:39	105	14:32–34	117
8:34–37	110	10:41–45	116	14:32–42	117, 152, 154
8:34–38	109	10:42–45	105	14:33–34	117
8:35–37	113	10:43	114, 116, 119, 122, 347	14:33–41	109
9:1	122			14:35	117
9:2	114	10:43–44	113, 116, 119, 135	14:35–36	118
9:3	114	10:43–45	110, 116, 119, 135, 143, 151–52, 154	14:36	112
9:13	114			14:37–38	118
9:21	114	10:45	112–13, 116, 119, 135, 261	14:38	117–18, 146
9:26	115			14:48	115
9:31	113, 123	10:46	120	14:49	122
9:33	113, 120	10:51	120	14:53–65	110
9:33–34	111, 119	10:52	111, 113, 120–21	14:54	111
9:33–35	121	11:6	114	14:59	114

430

14:72	114	5:4	140–41	9:48	143
15:8	114	5:10	140	9:51–19:27	150
15:21	113, 121	5:10–11	152, 154	9:57	140
15:25	112	5:11	105, 139–40	9:58	140
15:31	115	5:14	141	9:59	140
15:39	114	5:17–26	147–48	9:59–62	140
15:40–41	119	5:28	139–40	9:61	140
15:41	111	5:31–32	140	10:3	142
16:7	114	5:33	144	10:9	140, 154
16:8	110	6:12–13	147	10:17	140, 154
16:15	114	6:17–49	140, 150	10:18	142
16:20	114	6:23	139	10:21	142
		6:27–28	128, 141	10:27	142
Luke		6:27–29	149	10:30–35	144
1:2	141	6:27–35	142	10:37	138, 144, 150, 153–54
1:23	142	6:31	141, 144		
1:25	142	6:35	128, 141	11:1	20, 132, 141
1:41	141	6:35b–36	124	11:1–4	131, 138, 146
1:44	141	6:36	6, 7, 80, 94, 104–5, 130, 133, 141–42, 144, 150–51, 153–54, 286, 351, 356, 367	11:2–4	132
1:55	141			11:4	144, 146, 149
1:70	141			11:30	142
2:15	141			11:33–36	138
2:20	141	6:37–42	142	11:36	142
2:21–24	148	6:40	106, 138, 143, 153	11:44	142
2:23	141	6:46	105	12:10	149
2:39	141	6:47–49	144	12:21	142
2:41–42	148	7:9	139	12:27	142
2:48	142	7:31–32	144	12:38	142
3:21–22	147	7:36–50	156	12:43	142
3:22	141	8:2–3	140	12:54	142
3:23	140	8:10	148	13:3	144
4:15	140	8:19–21	140	13:18–21	144
4:16	140	8:28	148	13:28–29	145
4:18–19	140	9:1–2	140, 154	14:12–14	138
4:25	141	9:11	105, 139	14:15–24	142
4:29	140	9:15	142	14:25	140
4:34–35	148	9:23	105, 112, 140, 152, 154	14:26	106, 140
4:41	148			14:27	106, 121, 140, 152, 154
4:35	140	9:23–24	140		

INDEX OF SCRIPTURE AND OTHER ANCIENT SOURCES

14:33	104, 106, 140	22:39	139, 146	1:46	217
15	138	22:39–46	153–54	1:51	180
15:11–32	142	22:40	146	3:2	178
15:19	142	22:41–45	146	3:3	175
16:17	148	22:42	140, 146	3:3–5:1	175
17:6	142	22:43–44	145–46	3:5	175, 182, 201
17:10	108, 142, 150, 153–54	22:46	146	3:8	19
		22:69	148	3:12–13	180
17:24	142	23:11	142	3:13	180
17:26	141–42	23:26	121	3:16	21, 190, 199, 222, 337
17:28	141	23:27	140, 148		
18:11	142, 144	23:33	140	3:17	179
18:15	143	23:34	138, 147–48	3:19–21	160
18:17	143, 150, 153–54	23:34a	148	3:31	180
18:22	105, 140	23:46	140, 148	3:31–32	180
18:28	105, 140	23:49	140	3:34	162, 165, 178, 181
18:30	140	23:50	148	3:34–35	176
18:43	140	24:24	141–42	3:35	167, 179
19:31	142	24:36–38	147	4:7–10	190
19:32	141	24:39	141	4:8	190
21:12–19	146	24:46	142	4:14	209
21:15	148			4:28–30	209
21:35	142	**John**		4:29	217
22:1	147	1	213	4:31–34	190
22:13	141	1–4	173	4:34	177
22:15	144	1–12	159	4:35–38	208
22:19	144, 153–54, 264	1:4	167, 177	4:38	179
22:19–20	264	1:5	210	4:39	209
22:24	143	1:7	210	5	176–77
22:24–27	143	1:12–13	175	5:1–16	176
22:25	143	1:13	201	5:1–18	180
22:25–26a	142, 153	1:14	13, 220	5:11	177
22:25–27	143	1:18	176, 180, 215, 356	5:15	177
22:26	143	1:32	181	5:17	176–77
22:26–27	116, 143, 150, 154	1:35–37	210	5:19	162, 165, 167–68, 173–78, 180, 212, 329
22:26b–27	153	1:37–39	185		
22:27	143, 146	1:37–40	186		
22:29	142, 153	1:38	178, 217	5:19–20	176–77, 180, 183, 187, 207, 215
22:31	142	1:39	213, 217		

Index of Scripture and Other Ancient Sources

5:19–20a	176	7:16–17	178	10:14–15	169, 173, 208, 351, 356
5:19–23	175	7:18	217		
5:19b	180	7:24	222	10:14b–15a	162, 207
5:20	167, 176, 179	7:34	202	10:18	188
5:20a	177	7:36	202	10:30	163, 201, 205, 215
5:20b	177, 180	7:37–38	213	10:32	176
5:21	166–68, 173–74, 177–79, 182, 207, 209, 215	7:38	178	10:38	163
		7:38–39	209	10:41–42	210
		8	186	11:25	178
5:23	20	8:4	178	11:28	178
5:26	166–68, 173–74, 177–79, 209, 215	8:23	180, 201	11:41–42	181
		8:24	187	12:16	166
5:27	177	8:26	162, 167–68, 173, 176, 178, 181, 183, 207, 210, 215	12:25–26	185
5:30	222			12:26	165, 169, 173, 185, 202, 208, 329
5:35	210				
5:36	177	8:28	162, 165, 168, 173, 176, 178, 181, 183, 207, 210, 215	12:26a	186
6:24	217			12:26b	185
6:29	179, 208			12:27–28	181
6:31–32	190	8:30–31	187	12:28	180
6:35–40	213	8:30–47	185	12:32	177
6:37	178	8:31–32	178, 184, 210	12:45	205, 356
6:39	178	8:34–36	203	12:49	178
6:39–40	177	8:37	187	12:49–50	162, 178, 181, 210, 215
6:40	177	8:38	178, 180–81, 187, 215		
6:44	177–78	8:38–39	168, 173	12:50	165, 169, 173, 176, 178, 207
6:45a	183	8:38a	187		
6:46	180	8:38b	187	13	5, 132, 187, 192, 197, 205, 213, 230, 271
6:53	177	8:39–40	160		
6:54	177	8:39–44	187	13–17	159, 173, 194
6:57	163, 168, 173, 177–78, 207–9	8:39–47	187	13:1	194
		8:40	187	13:1–11	188–89
6:60–71	213	8:41	187	13:1–17	156, 213
6:63	178, 182	8:44	186–87	13:2	199
6:65	178	8:44–46	187	13:4	188, 196
6:66	185	8:48	186	13:4–5	189, 214
6:68	178	8:55	187	13:4–12a	213–14
6:70	213	8:59	187	13:4–17	190
6:70–71	199	9:39–41	190	13:6–11	189
7:16	162, 178, 183	10:11	196	13:7	188

433

13:10–11	199	14:6	178, 209, 222	15:13	166, 196, 199, 221–23, 340
13:12	188	14:8–9	176, 205, 215	15:13–14	22
13:12–17	188–89	14:9	356	15:14	208
13:12–20	189	14:10	205	15:15	162, 168, 170, 173, 176, 178, 207, 215
13:12a	189, 214	14:10–11	163		
13:12b	189, 191–92, 214, 216	14:12	165, 169, 173, 179, 207–8	15:16	213
13:13–14	178, 192	14:14	178	15:18–16:4a	195
13:14	165, 169, 173, 190–91, 198, 214	14:15	195	15:26	182
		14:16	168–69, 182	15:26–27	202, 210
13:14–15	189–90, 208, 213–14	14:17	182	15:27	179, 194, 199, 210
		14:17–18	182	16:12–15	210, 220, 222–23, 371
13:14–16	21, 211	14:19	165, 169, 173, 208–9		
13:15	6, 22, 132, 159, 163, 169, 173, 187–88, 190, 194, 208, 212, 214–15, 355, 372	14:20	163	16:13	182–83
		14:21	195	16:13–15	168, 170, 182
		14:23	182, 195, 222, 371	17	200, 204, 328
		14:24	162, 178	17:1	180
13:15b	190	14:26	182, 220, 223, 371	17:2	178
13:16	191–92, 214	14:27	162, 169	17:4	177, 180
13:17	190–91, 214	14:31	179	17:4–5	180
13:17a	191	15:1–7	213	17:6	178
13:20	193, 328	15:1–17	195	17:8	162, 178, 222
13:30	194	15:4	165, 170, 186, 208	17:9	178
13:31–32	180	15:4–10	165	17:11	6, 21, 159, 170, 173, 200–201, 208, 216, 351, 356
13:34	6, 21–22, 124, 159, 163–65, 169, 173, 188, 193, 194, 196, 198, 208, 210–12, 216, 222, 287, 298, 351, 357	15:7	222		
		15:9	22, 163, 170, 173, 179, 193–94, 207, 210–11, 215	17:11b	162
				17:14	6, 159, 170, 173, 178, 201, 205, 208
		15:9–17	195	17:14b	162
13:34–35	194	15:9a	195	17:16	6, 159, 162, 170, 173, 201, 205, 208
13:34a	164, 194, 215, 298	15:9b	195		
13:34b	164, 194, 215, 298	15:10	6, 162, 170, 173, 186, 194, 207–8	17:18	6, 159, 163–64, 170, 173, 179, 199, 201–2, 205, 208, 210, 216
13:35	195, 199, 201, 211, 357				
		15:10a	195		
13:36–38	185	15:10b	196	17:19	222
14:2–3	202–3	15:12	6, 22, 159, 162, 170, 173, 193–94, 196, 208, 210–12	17:20	179, 199, 202, 209–10
14:3	165–66, 169, 173, 202, 208, 329				
				17:20–22	211

Index of Scripture and Other Ancient Sources

17:21	163–64, 171, 173, 200–201, 208, 351, 356	2:1–4	147	16	279
		2:4	141	16–17	241
		2:22	141	16:1–3	281
17:21–22	6, 159, 216	2:39	169	16:3–4	148
17:21–23	163, 202, 205	2:42	143	16:17	148
17:21a	202	3:1–10	147	17	247
17:21b	202	3:4	147	17:14–15	281
17:22	179, 200–201, 208, 210, 215	3:12	142	17:19	143
		3:22	142	18:2	295
17:22a	168, 171, 173, 179, 207	5:12	147	18:5	258
		5:28	143	18:11	258, 301
17:22b	162, 171, 173, 351, 356	5:41	139	18:18	148
		6:8	147	18:21	148
17:23	201	6:10	147	19:11	147
17:24	165–66, 171, 173, 202, 208, 329	6:12–14	148	19:15	148
		7:17	141	20:6	148
18:11	223, 340	7:37	142	20:16	148
18:37	184	7:42	141	20:18	138
19:30	177	7:43	143	20:34	142
19:35	220	7:44	141, 143, 378	20:34–35	150, 153
20	220	7:48	141	20:35	142
20:15	217	7:51	142	21:21–24	148
20:16	178	7:52–53	143	22:3	85, 141
20:17	179, 203	7:55–56	148	23:11	142–43
20:21	6, 159, 163, 171, 173, 179, 199, 202, 207–8, 210, 215–16	7:59	148	23:25	143
		7:60	147–48	28:8	147
		8	148–49	28:26–27	148
20:23	208	8:1–3	85		
20:25	355	8:2	148	**Romans**	
20:31	213	9:1–2	85	1:13	20
21:6–8	208	10:47	142	1:23	296
21:18–19	185	12:3	147	4:1–12	294, 303
21:24	220	12:15–17	147	4:11	294
		13:2–3	147	4:12	294, 297, 304, 306, 354, 360
Acts		13:12	143		
1:10	142	14:3	147	5–6	294
1:14	147	14:9	147	5:6–8	245, 265
1:24–26	147	15:8	20, 141	5:12	294
2	142	15:15	141	5:12–6:23	295

435

INDEX OF SCRIPTURE AND OTHER ANCIENT SOURCES

5:14	296	3:1–4:21	255	9:14–15	237
5:19	294	3:5	258	9:21	237, 293
5:21	294	3:9	258	9:23	260
6:4	294, 296, 304, 306, 360	3:21–4:1	258	9:27	263
		4:1	258	10	259, 262
6:4–5	296–97, 304, 309	4:6	258	10:1	256
6:5	295–96	4:9–13	159, 167, 311	10:1–5	262
6:8	295	4:14	256–58	10:1–13	263, 299
7–8	295	4:14–15	256	10:4	262
7:14–25	295	4:14–16	287, 303	10:5	262
8:3	296–97	4:14–17	256	10:6	262, 303
8:4–5	371	4:14–21	255, 259	10:7	263
8:14	371	4:15	256	10:7–9	262, 304
8:9–17	371	4:16	5, 228, 231–33, 235, 239–40, 255–56, 258–60, 262, 266, 293, 299–301, 303–4, 306, 310, 359	10:7–10	262
8:29	79, 203, 302			10:10	262, 304
12–15	297			10:11	262, 304
12:1–2	297			10:14	263
12:2	287, 302			10:14–22	263
13:14	296–97			10:16	264
15:1	295	4:16–17	266, 300, 311	10:19	263
15:1–3	295–96	4:17	256–57, 299, 304	10:20–21	264
15:1–9	235	5:1	256	10:31–33	260, 266
15:1–13	295	5:3–5	259	10:31–11:1	259
15:3	295	7:14	256	10:32–33	262
15:5–9	295	7:17	255	11	263–64, 266
15:7	295–97, 300, 304, 306, 311, 329, 360	8	259	11:1	5, 228, 231–35, 239–40, 244–45, 255–57, 259–60, 262–63, 266, 279, 283, 293, 299–301, 304, 306, 311–12, 359
		8–10	259–61, 263, 266		
15:23–27	297	8:1	263		
		8:4	263		
1 Corinthians		8:6	201, 256		
1–4	255–56, 266	8:7	263		
1:8	229	8:9	259		
1:10	255–56	8:10	263	11:1–2	306, 311
1:10–17	255	8:10–11	260	11:2	261, 312
1:10–4:5	258	9	237, 259–60	11:16	255
1:10–4:13	255–56	9:1	261	11:23–25	144
1:10–4:21	256, 258	9:1–18	251	11:23–26	263–64, 300, 306, 311
1:13	256	9:6–7	260		
1:18–2:16	255	9:12–13	260	11:24	245, 265

436

Index of Scripture and Other Ancient Sources

11:27–34	264	8:5	265	4:32	286, 288, 297, 304, 306, 360
12:31	266	8:9	261, 265	4:32–5:2	286–88, 313
13:11	256	8:9–15	237	5:1	5, 228, 233, 240, 255, 286–87, 303–4, 351, 356, 367
14:1	266	8:10–11	265		
14:12	266	9:2	265, 267		
14:20	256	10:1	261, 265		
14:33	255	11:2	267		
14:39	266	11:7–9	251	5:1–2	286
15:3	245, 265	11:23–33	267	5:2	245, 265, 287–88, 304
15:15–18	304	13:4	261, 265		
15:24	256			5:8	288
15:49	20	**Galatians**		5:15	288
16	264–65, 266	1:4	245, 265	5:21–33	288, 313
16:1	264, 299–300, 304, 306	1:13–14	85	5:21–6:9	288
		2:1–4:7	294	5:24	288
16:2	264	2:20	245, 265, 293–94	5:25	245, 265, 288, 304, 306, 329, 360
16:21	240	3:6–7	292		
		4:6–7	371	5:28–29	288
2 Corinthians		4:12	228, 231–33, 235, 292–93, 299, 301–4, 306	6:9	288
1:24	265				
3:15–16	302			**Philippians**	
3:18	79, 203, 302	4:12–20	235	1:1	274–75, 281
4:4	304, 309, 356	4:19	293, 303	1:5	281
4:5	256, 265	5:16	371	1:7	271
4:7–12	267	5:18	371	1:10	229
4:10	261, 265	5:25	371	1:12–18	275
4:10–11	262	6:2	237, 293–94, 329	1:19–26	275, 288
4:11	203	6:11	240	1:20	275
5:15	245, 265	6:17	294	1:20–25	275
6:4–10	267			1:21–24	275
7:7	266–67	**Ephesians**		1:21a	275
7:11	267	1:4	229	1:21b	275
8	248, 264–65	4:1	288	1:22	275
8–9	237	4:17	287–88, 304	1:23	275
8:1–4	165	4:17–19	287	1:24	275
8:1–7	248	4:17–24	288, 313	1:25	275
8:1–11	299–300, 304, 306	4:20–24	287	1:27	267, 271
8:1–15	235	4:24	287	1:27–30	267
8:4–5	265	4:25–5:5	288	1:27–2:4	268, 270

437

1:27–2:18	268	2:23	281	4:9	253, 274, 279–80, 300–301, 311
1:29–30	279	2:24	276		
1:30	279	2:25	281, 311	4:10	271
2	237, 260	2:25–30	299	4:10–20	281
2–3	279	2:26–27	281		
2:1–11	235	2:30	281	**Colossians**	
2:2	271	3	278	1:13–14	298
2:3–4	257	3:1–11	276	1:14	297
2:4	260, 275, 281, 333	3:1–21	235	1:15	79, 304, 309, 356
2:4–5	275	3:4–6	85, 276, 280	1:22	229
2:5	268–69, 270–71, 277, 301	3:4–7	276–78	2:9	356
		3:4–11	276	2:13–14	297–98
2:5–8	245	3:4–14	276, 278	3:10	79
2:5–11	237, 260, 268–69, 273, 285, 300–301, 304, 311	3:4–16	276	3:13	235, 286, 297–98, 304, 306, 351, 356, 360, 367
		3:7	276		
		3:8–11	276		
2:6	270	3:10	276, 303	3:13b	297
2:6–7	271, 276	3:10–11	278	3:25–4:1	298
2:6–8	270, 273, 275, 277, 281, 283	3:12	283	4:1b	298
		3:14–15	273	4:14	264
2:6–11	235, 268, 270, 272–74, 276, 280, 300, 307, 359, 361	3:15	271, 277		
		3:15–16	277	**1 Thessalonians**	
		3:17	5, 228, 231–33, 239, 241, 255, 267, 277, 302–4, 306, 357, 359	1–2	248
2:7	270, 272, 274–76, 296–97, 362			1:1	241
				1:2–10	241
2:8	270, 281			1:2–2:16	249
2:9–11	271, 273–74, 309	3:17–18	277, 283	1:4–10	246
2:12	273, 300–301, 307, 357, 371	3:17a	274–80, 282, 299, 371	1:5	242–43, 249, 253, 258
		3:17b	280, 282, 285, 299–300, 304–6, 311, 371	1:5–6	231, 252, 254, 311
2:12–13	272			1:5–8	241
2:12–18	268, 273, 275			1:5a	243
2:13	273			1:5b	243–44
2:15–16	273	3:18–19	283, 302	1:6	5, 228, 231–33, 235, 239, 240–42, 244, 246–50, 253, 255, 261, 283, 299–300, 303–4, 306, 359
2:17	275–76, 362	3:19	271		
2:17–18	279	3:20	267, 271		
2:19	281, 311	3:20–21	276, 278		
2:19–22	257	3:21	203, 273, 276, 303		
2:19–24	299	4:2	271	1:6–8	237, 248, 301, 311
2:20	281	4:8	279, 301	1:6a	242, 244
2:22	258, 281				

1:6b	243–44	3:7	240	1:3–7	290
1:7	240–41, 248, 299, 303–4, 306	3:13	229, 240, 244, 252	1:3–20	232, 289
		4:1	240, 247, 252–53, 257	1:12–17	289
1:7–8	246	4:1–2	252	1:16	231, 289–91
1:7–10	242	4:2	247	2:6	245, 265
1:8	247	4:10	240, 253	3:10–12	290
1:9–10	240	4:11	250	3:14–15	290
2:1	243	4:11–12	250, 252	4:6	190
2:1–2	249	4:12	240	4:6–8a	290
2:1–12	243, 252–54, 311, 361	4:18	240	4:11–16	290
		5:10	245	4:12	257, 281, 290, 299–300, 303, 306, 311
2:2	243, 247, 279	5:11	240		
2:3–6	243	5:12–14	250		
2:4	252	5:14	240, 250	4:13	290
2:5	243, 249	5:23	229, 244, 252	4:13–16	291
2:7	243, 252, 256, 303			5:1–2	289
2:7–9	242	**2 Thessalonians**		5:10	191
2:8	243, 265	1:1	240	6:2	290
2:9	243, 250–52, 254	1:4	243	6:20–21	290
2:9–10	300	2:17	240		
2:10	244, 252	3:6	240, 250–53	**2 Timothy**	
2:11	243, 249, 252, 256, 303	3:6–9	254, 311	1:2	292
		3:6–12	250	1:3	289
2:11–12	243	3:6–13	235, 250, 252, 300	1:3–18	232, 289
2:12	240, 252	3:7	5, 228, 239–40, 255, 283, 299, 303–4, 359	1:5	269
2:13	247			1:13	231, 290–91
2:13–15	235			3:1–4:8	232, 289–90
2:13–16	246–47	3:7–9	142, 231–33, 240, 250–53, 301	3:8	289
2:13a	247			3:10	231, 290, 299–300, 304, 354
2:13b	247	3:7–10	252		
2:14	5, 228, 233, 240–41, 243, 246–50, 253, 255, 265, 299–300, 303–4, 306	3:9	5, 228, 239–40, 254–55, 299, 303–4, 306, 359	3:10–4:8	292
				4:11	264
				4:20	289
		3:11	240, 252		
2:14–16	231, 243, 247, 311	3:11–12	250	**Titus**	
2:14a	247	3:12	240, 250	1:4	292
2:14b	247	3:17	240	1:5	289, 291
2:15–16	248			1:5–16	291
3:1–5	243	**1 Timothy**		2:1–15	291
3:2	240	1:2	292	2:6–8	291

INDEX OF SCRIPTURE AND OTHER ANCIENT SOURCES

2:7	290, 299–300, 303, 306, 311	12:2	317	5:3	319
		12:2–3	317	5:4	319
2:14	245, 265, 291	12:25–26	269		
3:12	289	13:7	5, 318	**2 Peter**	
		13:13	317	1:4	203

Philemon

		James		**1 John**	
8–9	298	2:21	315	1:1–3	13, 220
9	298	2:25	315	1:2	167, 203
12	298	2:26	315	1:3	219, 360
14	289	3:5	315	1:3–7	202
17	289	5:7–8	315	1:5	210
18–19	298	5:10	315	1:5–7	160
19	240	5:11	315	1:6	165, 208, 209
20	289	5:17	315	1:6–7	216
21b	298			1:7	160, 172
22	289	**1 Peter**		2:1	163, 182, 203
24	264	1:14	319	2:6	6, 158, 160, 163–64, 171, 173, 186, 198, 204–5, 207–8, 216, 221–22
		1:15	321		
Hebrews		1:15–16	7, 130, 319, 351		
1:3	356	1:16	78		
2:17	316	2	320	2:8–11	160, 199
3:1–2	317	2:2	319	2:15	194
4:10	316	2:4–8	321	2:15–17	160
4:11	316	2:5	319	2:20	223
4:14–16	317	2:11	319	2:27	223
4:15	317	2:21	294, 319–20, 325, 354	2:28	165, 167, 203
5:4–5	316			2:28–3:3	203
5:7–8	317	2:21–25	319	2:29	160, 163, 208
6:12	5, 318	2:22–25	320	3–4	200
6:12–15	318	2:25	319	3:2	167, 171, 173, 203, 208, 211, 214–15, 217
6:13–15	318	3:5	319		
7:15	317	3:5–6	321	3:2b	167, 203
7:26	317	3:6	319	3:2b–3	163, 203
8:5	316	3:18–22	321	3:3	6, 158, 160, 162, 167, 171, 173, 198, 203–4, 207–8, 222
9:23–24	316	3:18–4:1	319		
10:25	317–18	3:20–21	321	3:4–6	163, 203
11	317–18	4:1	320	3:5	167, 198, 203–4
11–12	317				
11:4–38	318				

440

Index of Scripture and Other Ancient Sources

3:7	6, 160, 162–63, 167, 171, 173, 198, 203–4, 208, 211, 215, 222	4:19	172, 197, 337	**RABBINIC WORKS**	
		4:20	198		
		4:20–21	199	**Mishnah**	
3:8	167, 187, 203	4:21	194, 198	Šabb. (Šabbat)	
3:9	175	5:1	175	6.9	93
3:10–17	199	5:2	208		
3:11	194, 196–97	5:3–4	196	**Tosefta**	
3:11–13	194	5:6	182		
3:11–18	196	5:16	204	Ber. (Berakot)	
3:12	162, 171, 173			1.1	96–97
3:14	211, 215	**2 John**			
3:14–18	215	1	197	Demai	
3:16	158, 165–66, 172–73, 194, 196, 198–99, 204, 208, 211–12, 215, 221–23, 340	4	209, 216	5.24	97
		5	194		
		6	216	**Talmud (Babylonian)**	
		9	222–23, 258	B. Bat. (Baba Batra)	
3:16–17	160	**3 John**		130b	97
3:17	196–97, 215, 222	1	197	B. Qam. (Baba Qamma)	
3:17–18	211	3	209	91b	93
3:18	194, 197	3–4	216		
3:22	208	5–8	211	Ber. (Berakot)	
3:23	194	9–12	162, 219	62a	96
4:7	194	11	5, 87, 156, 161–62, 172–74, 219, 353, 360	ʿErub. (ʿErubin)	
4:7–8	197			62ab	93
4:7–21	194, 197–98, 204			93b–94a	97
4:9–10	179, 197–98, 199	11–12	360	Meg. (Megillah)	
4:9–11	197	12	355	28b	97
4:11	165, 172–73, 193–94, 197, 208, 212, 222, 351, 356, 367	**Jude**		Šabb. (Šabbat)	
		7	316	21a	97
4:12–13	163			133b	93
4:14	179	**Revelation**			
4:15	163	1:5	316	Sanh. (Sanhedrin)	
4:16b	197	2:13	316	52b	93
4:17	158, 165, 172–73, 194, 198, 204, 208, 337, 351, 356, 367	3:14	316	Soṭah	
		3:21	273, 316	14a	93–94
		14:4	315	49a	76
4:17b	163	17:6	316		

INDEX OF SCRIPTURE AND OTHER ANCIENT SOURCES

Yoma
15a   93

Zebah
38a   93

Targums

Tg. Ps.-J. (Targum Pseudo-Jonathan)
Lev 22:28   94, 141
Deut 6:4   201
Deut 34:6   93–94

Other Rabbinic Works

Midr. Tanh. Bechukotai (Midrash Tanhuma Bechukotai)
4   95

Pirqe R. El. (Pirqe Rabbi Eliezer)
16.3   94
17.1   94

Sipra Shemini
12.3   93

EARLY CHRISTIAN WRITINGS

Acts of Peter
3.1–3   289

1 Clement
3:1–4   324
4:1–13   325
5:1   324
5:1–7   325
5:3   325
5:7   289, 324–25, 333
6:1   324
7:1   325
7:4   326
9–11   326
9:2   326
13:2   324–25
16   326
16:3   324
16:6   324
16:6–7   324
16:7   324
16:17   324–26, 333
17:1   5, 323–24, 326
17:1–18:17   326
19:1–3   326
29:3   324
32:2   324
33:8   324–26
46:1   324, 326
46:1–2   327
55:1   324, 326
56:14–15   324
63:1   324, 326

Didache
4:11   337
8:2   133
8:2–3   338
8:3   133
9:4   338
11:1   338
13:2   338

Eusebius
Hist. eccl. (*Historia ecclesiastica*)
2.22.2–8   289
6.12.1–6   240

Ignatius

To the Ephesians
1:1   5, 323, 329
1:3   329
2:1   328
4:1   327
5:1   328
6:1   328
10:1   329
10:1–3   329
10:2   5, 323, 330
10:3   5, 323, 329–30

To the Magnesians
5:2   327, 330
6:2   327
7:1   328
10:1   5, 323, 329

To the Philadelphians
1:2   327
2:1   329
7:2   5, 323, 328–30
10:1   330
11:1   329

To Polycarp
1:2   329
2:3   327
4:1   329
5:1   329

To the Romans
4:2   330
6:1–3   223
6:3   5, 323, 330, 335

To the Smyrnaeans
8:1   328
12:1   5, 323, 328–29

Index of Scripture and Other Ancient Sources

To the Trallians

1:2	5, 323, 329
2:1	327
3:1	327
3:2	328

Irenaeus

Haer. (Adversus haereses)

3.3.4	332
3.12.10	150

Justin Martyr

1 Apol. (Apologia i)

67.3–5	340

Letter of Barnabas

7:3	335
7:7	335
7:10–11	335
8:1–2	335
12:5–6	335

Letter to Diognetus

9:1–2	336
9:6	336
10:1–2	337
10:2	337
10:3	337
10:3–4	337
10:4	336–37
10:4–6	5, 323, 336–37
10:5	336
10:6	336
10:7	336
10:7–8	337

Martyrdom of Polycarp

1:1	333
1:1–2	333
1:2	5, 323, 333, 340
2:2	335
4:1	334
7	334
11:1	335
13:3	335
14:2	223, 340
15:2	335
17:3	5–6, 223, 323, 334
19:1	5–6, 223, 323, 334
20:1	335
22:1	335, 354

Muratorian Fragment

38–39	289

Polycarp

To the Philippians

1:1	5, 323, 332
1:2	333
8–10	333
8:2	5, 270, 323, 325, 333
9:1	333
10:1	270, 333

Shepherd of Hermas

Mandate 1

4:9	338

Mandate 10

1:5	338

Mandate 12

6:2	338

Similitude 2

1:2	338
1:7	338

Similitude 3

1:3	338

Similitude 9

20:3	338

Vision 3

6:6	338
8:7	338
9:7	338
11:3	338

Vision 4

1:1	338
2:5	338
3:4	338
3:6	338

GRECO-ROMAN LITERATURE

Aristotle

Eth. nic. (Ethica nicomachea)

1103a–1104a	41
1103b	41
1124b	40–41
1156b	41
1171b12	41
1172a11–14	41
1176a	41
1177b31–33	32
1178b27	32

Poet. (Poetica)

1448b5–9	1, 39
1448b5–23	40
1448b10–12	40
1449b	35
1449b24–27	35

Pol. (Politica)

1336a–b	39

INDEX OF SCRIPTURE AND OTHER ANCIENT SOURCES

Cicero

Arch. (Pro Archia)

14	51

De or. (De oratore)

1.6–23	48
2.85–98	48
2.89	49–50
2.90	49
2.91	49
2.92	49
2.92–95	48, 50
2.95	50
2.96	49
2.98	49
3.26–37	50

Div. Caec. (Divinatio in Caecilium)

25	50

Mur. (Pro Murena)

66	51

Off. (De officiis)

1.78	48, 59, 73
1.121	48
1.132–134	48
1.140	48
2.46	48
3.6	48

Phil. (Orationes philippicae)

11.23	51

Sen. (De senectute)

77	51

Sest. (Pro Sestio)

47–48	50

65	50
68	50

Verr. (In Verrem)

2.3.41	50

Demosthenes

Fals. leg. (De falsa legatione)

19.268–273	70

Olynth. (Olynthiaca)

3.21	70

Rhod. lib. (De Rhodiorum libertate)

15.35	70

Syntax. (Peri syntaxeōs)

13.26	70

Dionysius of Halicarnassus

Ant. rom. (Antiquitates romanae)

5.75.1	71

Epictetus

Diatr. (Diatribai [Dissertationes])

2.14.11–13	72
3.4.3–5	72
3.15	72
3.22.45–49	72

Ench. (Enchiridion)

29	72

Euripides

Hel. (Helena)

939–943	33

Isocrates

Aerop. (Areopagiticus)

84	42

Against the Sophists

16–18	45

Antid. (Antidosis)

7	240
13	240
28	240
54	240
88	240
141	240
239	240
277	44

Archid. (Archidamus)

82–84	42

Ep. (Epistulae)

8.10	240
9.15	240

Evag. (Evagoras)

1–4	42
3	73
5–11	42
12–72	42
73–75	42
76–77	42–43
80–81	42–43

Nicocles, or the Cyprians

61	42

Index of Scripture and Other Ancient Sources

On the Peace
36–37   42
142   42

Panath. (Panathenaicus)
16   46, 73, 240

To Nicocles
31   43
38   42

To Philip
11–12   46
27   46
113   42

Plato

Apol. (Apologia)
23C   239

Leg. (Leges)
817b   36

Phaedr. (Phaedrus)
248a   32
252c–d   32
253a–b   32

Prot. (Protagoras)
325e–326a   37

Resp. (Respublica)
392d–398b   38

Theaet. (Theaetetus)
176a–b   92, 287
176b   32–33

Tim. (Timaeus)
39d–e   36
44–47   32
293   32

Plutarch

Adol. poet. aud. (Quomodo adolescens poetas audire debeat)
8 (26a–b)   62

Adul. am. (De adulatore et amico)
2 (50a–b)   63
8–9 (53b–c)   63

Arat. (Aratus)
1.2   64

Brut. (Brutus)
2.1   60

Cat. Min. (Cato Minor)
65.4   60

Cim. (Cimon)
14.3   60

Cons. Apoll. (Consolatio ad Apollonium)
33   64

Curios. (De curiositate)
11   63

Dem. (Demosthenes)
9.3   61

Demetr. (Demetrius)
1.6   61

Inim. util. (De capienda ex inimicis utilitate)
11 (92f)   62

Lyc. (Lycurgus)
27.3   60

Mar. (Marius)
35.1   60

Pel. (Pelopidas)
26.5   60

Per. (Pericles)
1.2–3   60
1.4   60–61
2.2–3   60–61

Rect. rat. aud. (De recta ratione audiendi)
6   63

Rom. (Romulus)
29.2   60

Sera (De sera numinis vindicta)
5 (550d)   53

Sol. (Solon)
29.3   60

Thes. (Theseus)
11.1   60

Ti. C. Gracch. (Tiberius et Caius Gracchus)
4.4   61–62

Virt. Prof. (Quomodo quis suos in virtute sentiat profectus)
84b–c   62

Polybius

Hist. (Histories)
1.1.2   70
1.2.8   70–71
10.21.4   71

Pseudo-Crates

Ep. (Epistulae)
20.13	239

Pseudo-Diogenes

Ep. (Epistulae)
14.4	239
38.25–30	240
46.6–11	240

Pseudo-Isocrates

Demon. (Ad Demonicum)
5–12	43–44
51–52	44
52	55

Quintilian

Inst. (Institutio oratoria)
2.2.8	59
10.1.15	57
10.1.19	57
10.1.108	51
10.1.108–109	57
10.1.112	51, 57, 317
10.2.1–2	58
10.2.6–9	58
10.2.14–16	58–59
10.2.19–21	59
10.2.23–26	59
10.2.27–28	59

Seneca (the Younger)

Ep. (Epistulae morales)
6.5–6	52
7.8	52–53
11.8–10	56
31.11	56
33.7–8	73
33.7–11	53–54
52.7–9	53
58.6	51
84.3–4	55
84.5–9	55
98.13	73
98.14	53
100.7	51
104.16–33	53
107.10	51–52

Theon

Exercises
13.105	71

Xenophon

Cyr. (Cyropaedia)
8.1.21	69
8.6.10	69
8.6.13–14	69–70

Mem. (Memorabilia)
1.2.3	70
3.5.14	70
3.10.1–8	70
4.2.40	70